third edition

Human Behavior
and the
Social Environment

*Shifting Paradigms in Essential
Knowledge for Social Work Practice*

Joe M. Schriver
University of Arkansas–Fayetteville

Allyn and Bacon
Boston • London • Toronto • Sydney • Tokyo • Singapore

To two very different women who hold in common the strength, gentleness, and empowering worldview that are the essence of feminism, diversity, humanity—and social work. Their differences and their commonalties have enriched my worldview and my life immensely.

Catharine Owens Schriver
Beverly L. "Bev" Steimla

Editor in Chief, Social Sciences: Karen Hanson
Editorial Assistant: Karen Corday
Marketing Manager: Jacqueline Aaron
Editorial Production Service: Chestnut Hill Enterprises, Inc.
Manufacturing Buyer: Julie McNeill
Cover Administrator: Linda Knowles
Electronic Composition: Omegatype Typography, Inc.

Library of Congress Cataloging-in-Publication Data

Schriver, Joe M.
   Human behavior and the social environment : shifting paradigms in essential knowledge for social work practice / Joe M. Schriver.—3rd ed.
      p.   cm.
   Includes bibliographical references and index.
   ISBN 0-205-32969-1 (alk. paper)
   1. Social psychology.   2. Behavioral assessment.   3. Social interaction.   4. Social systems.   5. Paradigms (Social sciences)   6. Social service.   I. Title.

HM1033 .S37 2000
302—dc21

00-063952

Printed in the United States of America
10 9 8 7 6 5 4   RRD-VA 05 04 03 02

Photo Credits: chaps. 1, 7, 9: Will Hart; chaps. 3, 6 (pp. 353, 362): Robert Harbison; chaps 4, 5, 6 (p. 369), 8: Don House.

Contents

Preface to Third Edition

As with so many things from the trivial to the substantive, the coming of the new millennium influenced my thinking about revisions for this third edition. My thinking about this edition and my research for it focused on answering the question: What do we need to know as social workers to increase and maintain our relevance in a rapidly changing domestic and global social environment? Several key areas emerged as I worked to answer this question. Some of these areas seem to call for a return to social work fundamentals that are a part of our history, and some seem to call for a willingness to engage in a world that is daily coming into existence and is largely yet to come. Some of these areas—reassuringly—also reinforced the usefulness of the traditional/ alternative paradigm conceptual framework offered in this and previous editions. However, I continue to recognize this framework is only one attempt to conceptualize the vast amounts of information needed to understand and respect the lived worlds of the people with whom we work.

New and more explicit attention is given in this edition to the impact of the social environment on human behavior at all levels. To accomplish this the traditional notion of HBSE is deconstructed and presented as SEHB in a number of areas to refocus attention on the social environment and seek parity with the attention traditionally given to human behavior. This deconstruction seems consistent with the historical social reform roots of social work. An attempt to integrate HBSE knowledge with policy/practice concerns is more evident in this edition to highlight the SEHB/HBSE interconnections.

The historic concern of social work for poverty reduction is emphasized throughout much of this edition. We seem too often to lose sight of the pervasive existence and impact of poverty in the lives of the people with whom and for whom we work. We also seem too often to forget that poverty reduction remains central to the purposes of social work. Yet, a review of our literature and the literatures of many other disciplines calls out for recognizing the central role played by poverty in so many social, health, and economic indicators of well-being. As a result, the impact of poverty and the importance of poverty reduction are interwoven through much of this edition. Poverty and poverty reduction are addressed at individual, family, organizational, community, and global levels. In a number of places technological poverty is addressed using the concept of digital divide. In other areas such fundamental poverty concerns as the impact of hunger and malnutrition on human developmental outcomes are addressed.

Technology is addressed more critically and more extensively in this edition. The potential of technology both to exacerbate and to reduce poverty receives attention. For example, the impact of the digital divide and attempts to overcome it at the organizational level in schools are addressed. In addition, the use of new technologies in social work assessment and intervention is discussed. For example, Global Information Systems (GIS) technology is discussed as both an assessment and a policy/practice tool.

Another theme expanded on and consistent with increased attention to social environmental concerns is community level theory and practice. Chapter 9 has been extensively revised and expanded to present some of the exciting new developments in this area of practice. Within the expanded community theme is that of comprehensiveness. Comprehensive community-building and renewal initiatives that synthesize both people- and place-based strategies are presented. In addition, community strategies for poverty reduction using assets/strengths-based theory are addressed. The concept of virtual community also receives additional attention in this edition.

Global concerns also receive additional attention in a number of areas in this edition. Global issues are dealt with in several ways, including: the impact of immigration on individuals and families, global poverty in terms of hunger and malnutrition, and the digital divide.

Diversity and culturally competent social work practice continue to receive significant attention in this edition. Public policy issues relevant to diversity such as multiethnic adoption and foster care, demographic population shifts, and the role of census definitions of diversity on public policy are addressed.

I hope the revisions made for this edition reflect the substantive more than the trivial concerns we will face as social workers in this new century.

EXCERPTS FROM SECOND AND FIRST EDITION PREFACES

Second Edition Excerpt

This edition included increased attention to the complexity and richness of human diversity, especially in the areas of diversity within diversity and multiple diversities. The multiple and complex meanings attached to the concepts of culture, race and ethnicity are explored more extensively. Whiteness and development of white identity received particular attention in this edition. Content on emerging technology and its impact on human behavior and the social environment at multiple levels has been added. This edition, for example, included new content on virtual communities and each chapter includes internet search terms the reader can use to explore the vast information about HBSE available through the world wide web.

First Edition Excerpts

Social workers have too often interpreted integration of knowledge from other disciplines as synonymous with reducing that knowledge to the lowest common denominator. We have also used a limited number of disciplines from which we integrate knowledge for informing our practice and thinking. We have neglected important sources of knowledge and processes for gaining knowledge outside the narrow confines of the social and behavioral sciences. Even in these areas we have limited ourselves to only a few disciplines, primarily sociology and psychology. We have failed to recognize, appreciate, and use the full range of the arts and sciences. In so doing, we have cheated ourselves out of some of the most current, exciting, and challenging streams of thought. What is more problematic, we are denying the people with and for whom we work important new avenues for defining, pursuing, and resolving many of the problems with which we must deal.

Not a small part of this conundrum has been oversimplification, resulting from reliance on only one or a few traditional paradigms from which to pursue understanding and action. This is the case not only in social work; a positivistic, hierarchical, Eurocentric, patriarchal paradigm has dominated and held power over virtually all fields of knowledge, from physics to history to the arts. This unfortunately has led too often to a belief in only one route to only one answer rather than many routes to many answers.

Alternative paradigms for creating knowledge and for perceiving the world around us offer exciting and largely untouched possibilities. Alternative ways of viewing the world such as interpretive, consensual, non-Eurocentric, and feminist perspectives can add much to what we know and what we need to know to *do* social work. They require us, however, to drop some comfortable stances and instead to embrace uncertainty, ambiguity and, yes, even chaos. Such a change requires us to critically examine some long-held and cherished paradigms. While traditional paradigms have offered much guidance and assistance in addressing important issues, they often have been taken as givens, as comprehensive, as timely and timeless ways of knowing the worlds around us. These paradigms have become hegemonic and have largely gone unexamined, uncriticized, unchallenged.

A NOTE ABOUT BIAS AND THE AUTHOR

I should make explicit, though it is no doubt obvious from the above discussion, that I am biased. I recognize the contributions of traditional perspectives and approaches to creating and valuing knowledge, but I believe that we as humans will not realize our collective (and I believe individual) potential for well-being as long as we do not embrace alternative perspectives and worldviews such as those described in this book. Therefore, while traditional perspectives and paradigms are presented in this book, the reader should keep in mind that the author generally finds these perspectives lacking. This author believes that the perspectives used to define and describe "normal" or "optimal" human behavior and experience too often represent the beliefs and realities of only a privileged few. This privileged few too often includes only those who have the power, the good fortune, the gender, the color, the wealth, or the sexual orientation consistent with and reflected in traditional perspectives and worldviews.

The reader should also be aware that, though in many respects this book is a critique of traditional paradigm thinking, this author is a product of the traditional institutions that create and enforce those traditional perspectives and worldviews. This author, too, shares many of the characteristics of the "privileged few." Therefore, writing this book has been an effort to question, to examine and to expand my own worldview.

PLAN OF THE BOOK

Human Behavior and the Social Environment begins with a presentation of the basic purposes and foundations of social work and social work education. Principles, and fundamental concepts necessary for acquiring and organizing knowledge about human behavior and the social environment (HBSE) are also presented. Next, a conceptual framework for thinking about both traditional and alternative ways in which knowledge is created and influenced is outlined. This conceptual framework is accompanied by discussion of some widely used approaches and fundamental themes guiding social workers in the selection, organization, and use of knowledge about human behavior and the social environment. The book then uses the notions of traditional and alternative paradigms to organize and present a variety of models, theories and concepts concerning HBSE.

At least one full chapter (two chapters are included on individual behavior and development) is devoted to content about each of the social system levels required of professional social work education by the Curriculum Policy Statements (CPS) of the Council on Social Work Education. Knowledge for practice with individuals, families, groups, organizations and communities as well as content on the interaction among these systems are presented.

Throughout the book a series of "Illustrative Readings" is provided to give additional depth and perspective in a variety of areas. These readings are also intended to extend content in the text emphasizing the importance of including the widest possible range of different human voices and experiences in our efforts to more fully understand HBSE.

In Chapter 1 broad concepts, core concerns, and basic assumptions addressed in the book are presented. This chapter addresses the place of "Human Behavior and the Social Environment" as one of the essential foundation areas of social work education. It outlines the fundamental assumptions underlying the content of the book. The concept of paradigm is defined along with discussion of its implications for social workers. The core values and purposes of social work outlined in the Curriculum Policy Statements of the Council on Social Work Education are summarized and placed in the context of this book. Guidance is offered in this chapter for analyzing paradigms from the perspective of social work values. The importance of critical thinking and historical perspective when thinking about worldviews and the dynamics of social change is discussed. This chapter emphasizes the importance of understanding the complex and multiple meanings of such fundamental concepts as culture, ethnicity and race. The interconnections of these concepts with those of power and empowerment are also addressed.

Chapter 2 provides a conceptual framework for organizing a wide range of knowledge for social work practice. This framework is built upon the foundations of traditional and alternative paradigms for creating and using knowledge for practice. Traditional and alternative paradigms are outlined according to five basic dimensions of each paradigm. The traditional paradigm is presented through discussion of five processes and products that characterize the "ways of knowing" and major influences determining what is "worth knowing" in traditional paradigm thinking. These five dimensions are: 1) Positivistic, scientific, objective, and quantitative approaches to creating and valuing knowledge; as well as the powerful influences of 2) Masculinity/ Patriarchy; 3) Whiteness; 4) Separateness, impersonal, competitive perspectives; and 5) Privilege. The alternative paradigm is presented using five processes and products that characterize "ways of knowing" and major influences determining what is "worth knowing" in alternative paradigm thinking. These five dimensions are: 1) Interpretive, intuitive, subjective, qualitative approaches to creating and valuing knowledge; as well as the significant influences of 2) Feminism; 3) Diversity; 4) Interrelatedness, personal and integrative perspectives; and 5) Oppressions.

Chapter 3 incorporates content on some of the fundamental issues, concerns and tools important to social workers in efforts to develop and use knowledge for practice. This chapter attempts to integrate some of the themes of alternative paradigm thinking with existing and emerging perspectives and tools in social work. This chapter addresses the importance of metaphor, the appreciation of ambiguity, the significance of language and words, the interrelatedness of personal and political issues, and the importance of inclusiveness in gaining a social work perspective. This chapter emphasizes the importance of assessment in social work as the process of using or applying knowledge of HBSE in social work practice. It outlines a number of traditional, mid-range, and alternative theoretical approaches to understanding HBSE.

Chapters 4 and 5 are devoted to presenting and examining traditional and alternative theories and models of individual development. Chapter 6 presents content on familiness from traditional and alternative perspectives. Chapter 7 is devoted to content on small group systems and functioning from both traditional and alternative standpoints. Chapter 8 focuses on organizational and management theories, both traditional and alternative. Chapter 9 addresses traditional and alternative notions of community. Chapter 10 presents implications for using alternative paradigm thinking as a means of integrating all the foundation areas of social work education—HBSE, Practice, Policy, Research, Field, Social and Economic Justice, Values and Ethics, Diversity and Populations-at-Risk.

The book is intended for use in one or two course HBSE sequences in baccalaureate or graduate social work programs.

ACKNOWLEDGMENTS

Those friends and colleagues I listed in the second edition remain a supportive community for me from around the country. That community is ever expanding and for that I am most grateful. For the third edition, the comments of reviewer Larry Icard, University of Washington, were most helpful and the review by Valerie McFarland, a former student who used the second edition as a text, was much appreciated.

I noted in the first edition that my son, Andrew, then almost two years old, had taught me more about human behavior and the social environment than anyone else. Andrew, now at eight years old you continue to be the best of teachers as you share your curiosity and wonder about humans and our worlds.

My editors, Judy Fifer and Karen Hanson, my production editor, Myrna Breskin, and Alyssa Pratt, who has managed much of the later stage editing and production, have been incredibly understanding, supportive and flexible as usual.

Cathy Owens Schriver, as with the other editions—I could not have done it without you.

JMS

1  Human Behavior and the Social Environment (HBSE) and Paradigms

Topics Addressed in This Chapter:

A NOTE ABOUT USING THE INTERNET WITH THIS BOOK

Central to using new technology is the Internet and its World Wide Web. We hope you are already familiar with and using the World Wide Web to access a wide variety of information. If you are not yet a "Web surfer," we encourage you to learn more about the World Wide Web and to begin to enjoy its benefits. One very helpful resource for social work students and faculty who want to know more about the Web and its potential benefits for social workers is the *Allyn and Bacon Quick Guide to the Internet for Social Work* (2000), published by Allyn and Bacon and written by Joanne Yaffe and Doug Gotthoffer. The computing services department of the college or university you are attending can also be a good source of information on how to connect to and use the Internet.

To assist you in using the Internet to explore topics and issues presented in this book, at the end of each chapter will be an "Internet Search Guide." This guide will list some basic concepts or terms from the chapter that I have found helpful in exploring the Net. In addition, specific World Wide Web sites related to each chapter can be found by going to the Allyn and Bacon Web site at **http://www/abacon.com** and following the links to Schriver or the title of this book: *Human Behavior and the Social Environment: Shifting Paradigms in Essential Knowledge for Social Work Practice.* The Allyn and Bacon Web site contains many other links of interest to social work students and faculty. I hope you find this information useful and enjoy this additional opportunity to expand your understanding of human behavior and the social environment.

*T*he purpose of human behavior and the social environment content within the social work curriculum is to provide us with knowledge for practice. We need to continually look at this content for how to apply what we are learning about human behavior and the social environment to social work practice and to our lives. As we move through the material in this book, we will struggle to integrate what we are learning here with what we have learned and are learning from our own and others' life experiences, from our other social work courses, and from our courses in the liberal arts and sciences. We will try to weave together all these important sources of knowing and understanding into an organic whole that can continue to develop and guide us in our social work practice and in our lives.

PURPOSES, FOUNDATIONS, AND ASSUMPTIONS

We will think of our efforts, explorations, and progress as we move through this book as a journey. Before we begin our journey we will place the content and purposes of this human behavior and the social environment (HBSE) book within the context of the purposes and foundations of social work education as they have been defined by the Council on Social Work Education (CSWE). The **Council on Social Work Education** is the organization responsible for determining and monitoring the standards to which accredited undergraduate and graduate social work education schools and programs in the United States are expected to adhere.

Purposes of Social Work

The purposes of social work will guide us throughout our journey to more completely understand HBSE. These purposes emerge today from the history of the social work profession and its continuing concern for improving the quality of life, especially for vulnerable populations. According to the CSWE, the overall purpose of the profession of social work is "the enhancement of human well-being" and the "alleviation of poverty and oppression" (1992:97, 135). From this overall purpose flow four more specific purposes:

1. *The promotion, restoration, maintenance, and enhancement of the functioning of individuals, families, groups, organizations, and communities by helping them to accomplish tasks, prevent and alleviate distress, and use resources.*

2. *The planning, formulation, and implementation of social policies, services, resources, and programs needed to meet basic human needs and support the development of human capacities.*

3. *The pursuit of policies, services, resources, and programs through organizational or administrative advocacy and social and political action, so as to empower groups at risk and promote social and economic justice.*

4. *The development and testing of professional knowledge and skills related to these purposes.* (CSWE 1992:97, 135)

Foundation Areas

The educational curriculum for preparing professional social work practitioners to fulfill the purposes of social work is designed around and must include nine basic foundation areas. These include:

1. Social work values and ethics
2. Diversity

3. Promotion of social and economic justice
4. Populations at risk
5. Human behavior and the social environment (HBSE)
6. Social welfare policy and services
7. Social work practice
8. Research
9. Field practicum

While human behavior and the social environment is the focus of this book, we also devote significant attention to social work values and ethics, diversity, promotion of social and economic justice, and populations at risk. These areas are described in more detail below. In addition, content in this book includes and helps you integrate a variety of information directly related to social welfare policy and services, social work practice, research, and field practicum. For example, as we noted above, HBSE content is knowledge for use in your social work practice. The other foundation areas are also intricately interwoven within the content of this book. Many of the issues we address have very direct implications for social welfare policy. As we learn about and examine traditional and alternative theories about HBSE, we integrate research content. You need the content of all these foundation areas to successfully complete your field practicum and move into your professional social work career. We return to the importance of integrating all of these areas in Chapter 10. Next we look a bit more closely at what is expected by CSWE and the professional social work community of the HBSE foundation area.

Human Behavior and the Social Environment

[Undergraduate and graduate] programs of social work education must provide content about theories and knowledge of human bio-psycho-social development, including theories and knowledge about the range of social systems in which individuals live (families, groups, organizations, institutions, and communities). The human behavior and the social environment curriculum must provide an understanding of the interactions between and among human biological, social, psychological, and cultural systems as they affect and are affected by human behavior. The impact of social and economic forces on individuals and social systems must be presented. Content must be provided about the ways in which systems promote or deter people in maintaining or achieving optimal health and well-being. Content about the values and ethical issues related to bio-psycho-social theories must be included. Students must be taught to evaluate theory and apply theory to client situations. (CSWE 1992:102, 140–141)

The other social work education foundation areas of central and continuing concern to us as we pursue our journey to more fully understanding HBSE are described below.

Social Work Values and Ethics

Among the values and principles that must be infused throughout every social work curriculum are the following:

1. *Social workers' professional relationships are built on regard for individual worth and dignity and are furthered by mutual participation, acceptance, confidentiality, honesty, and responsible handling of conflict.*

2. *Social workers respect people's right to make independent decisions and to participate actively in the helping process.*

3. *Social workers are committed to assisting client systems to obtain needed resources.*

4. *Social workers strive to make social institutions more humane and responsive to human needs.*

5. *Social workers demonstrate respect for and acceptance of the unique characteristics of diverse populations.*

6. *Social workers are responsible for their own ethical conduct, the quality of their practice, and seeking continuous growth in the knowledge and skills of their profession.* (CSWE 1992:100–101, 139–140)

These values are consistent with those identified in the National Association of Social Workers' *Standards for the Classification of Social Work Practice* (1982).

Diversity

Professional social work education is committed to preparing students to understand and appreciate human diversity. Programs must provide curriculum content about the differences and similarities in the experiences, needs, and beliefs of people. The curriculum must include content about differential assessment and intervention skills that will enable practitioners to serve diverse populations. Each program is required to include content about population groups that are particularly relevant to the program's mission. These include, but are not limited to, groups distinguished by race, ethnicity, culture, class, gender, sexual orientation, religion, physical or mental ability, age, and national origin.

Promotion of Social and Economic Justice

Programs of social work education must provide an understanding of the dynamics and consequences of social and economic injustice, including all forms of human oppression and discrimination. They must provide students with the skills to promote social change and to implement a wide range of interventions that advance the achievement of individual and collective social and economic justice. Theoretical and practice content must be provided about strategies of intervention for achieving social and economic justice and for combatting the causes and effects of institutionalized forms of oppression.

Populations at Risk

> *Programs of social work education must present theoretical and practice content about the patterns, dynamics, and consequences of discrimination, economic deprivation, and oppression. The curriculum must provide content about people of color, women, and gay and lesbian persons. Such content must emphasize the impact of discrimination, economic deprivation, and oppression upon these groups. Each program must include content about populations at risk that are particularly relevant to its mission. In addition to those mandated above, such groups include, but are not limited to, those distinguished by age, ethnicity, culture, class, religion, and physical or mental ability.* (CSWE 1992: 100–102, 139–140)

Assumptions

We begin our journey through this book with several very basic assumptions.

1. We make the assumption that how we view the world and its people directly affects the way we will practice social work.

2. The way we view the world and its people already affects the way we behave in our daily lives.

3. Our work as social workers and our lives are not separate from each other.

4. Our lives are not separate from the lives of the people with whom we work and interact.

5. While our lives are interconnected with the lives of the people with whom we work and interact, we differ from each other in many ways. As social workers we must respect these differences and learn from them. Our differences can be celebrated as rich, positive, and mutual sources of knowledge, growth, and change for all concerned.

6. The assumptions we make about ourselves and others are strongly influenced by our individual and collective histories and cultures.

7. Change is a constant part of our lives and the lives of the people with whom we work.

Such assumptions as these are reflected in what we will come to conceptualize in this book as an alternative paradigm for thinking about social work. Before we discuss alternative paradigms further, we will explore the more general concept of paradigm.

PARADIGMS AND SOCIAL WORK

A **paradigm** "is a world view, a general perspective, a way of breaking down the complexity of the real world" (Lincoln & Guba 1985:15). Paradigms constitute "cultural patterns of group life" (Schutz 1944). More specifically, Kuhn (1970 [1962]:175) defines a paradigm as "the entire constellation of beliefs, values, techniques, and so on shared by the members of a given community." Paradigms shape and are shaped by values, knowledge, and beliefs about the nature of our worlds. The values, knowledge, and beliefs about the world that make up paradigms are often so "taken for granted" that we are virtually unaware of their existence or of the assumptions we make because of them. For social workers the notion of paradigm is particularly important, because if we can become conscious of the elements that result in different world views, this awareness can provide us with tools to use to think about and to understand ourselves, others, and the environments we all inhabit. Notions of paradigm can help us understand more completely the past perspectives, current realities, and future possibilities about what it means to be human. Furthermore, the notion of paradigm can help us understand our own and others' roles in creating and re-creating the very meaning of humanness.

Specifically for our purposes here, thinking in terms of paradigms can provide us with new ways of viewing and grasping humans' behaviors in individual, family, group, organizational, and community contexts. The concept of paradigm can serve us very well to order and to increase our awareness of multiple theories, models, and perspectives about human behavior and the social environment. The notion of paradigm can help us understand the way things are, and, equally important for social workers, it can help us understand the way things *might* be.

Two Types of Paradigms: Traditional and Alternative

In this book we are concerned with exploring two quite different but not mutually exclusive kinds of paradigms. One of these we refer to as traditional or dominant paradigms. The other we will call alternative or possible paradigms. We explore in some detail the characteristics of both of these kinds of paradigms in Chapter 2. For now, when we refer to **traditional or dominant paradigms,** we simply mean the paradigms or world views that have most influenced the environments that make up our worlds. When we refer to **alternative or possible paradigms,** we mean world views that have had less influence and have been less prominent in shaping our own and others' views about humans and their environments. For example, the belief that quantitative and objective approaches provide the most dependable (or the most accurate) avenues to understanding the world around us reflects two core elements of the traditional and dominant paradigm.

An example of quantitative and objective elements of traditional or dominant paradigm thinking related to social work can be illustrated through the following approach to assessing and identifying community needs in order to design and implement services to meet those needs. According to the traditional or dominant approach, we assume that we can best understand the needs of the people in the community through use of a survey. We distribute a questionnaire to a random sample of community residents. We design the questionnaire using a list of specific possible needs from which the community respondents can select. We ask the respondents to make their selections by completing the questionnaire we have designed and returning it to us. Once the questionnaires are returned, we do a statistical analysis of the responses. We use this quantitative analysis based on the frequency of responses to our questions to determine the community's needs. We then set about bringing into the community the resources and people we believe are necessary to design and implement services to meet the needs determined through the survey.

The belief that we can learn as much or more about the world around us from qualitative and subjective, as from quantitative and objective, approaches to understanding reflects an alternative and nondominant view of the world. Using the same social-work-related example as above, let's take an alternative approach to understanding the needs of a particular community in order to design and implement services to meet those needs. Our alternative approach will have us not simply asking community members to answer questions about typical community needs we have previously devised and listed in a questionnaire. We will instead first go into the community and involve as many different people representing as many diverse groups (not a random sample) as possible. We will involve these community members not primarily as respondents to predetermined questions but as partners in determining what the questions should be, how the questions should be asked (individual or group face-to-face meetings, perhaps), and who should do the asking (the community members themselves, rather than outside "experts," for example) (Guba and Lincoln 1989; Reason 1988). We are primarily interested in finding and understanding needs emerging from the real-life experiences of community people. We seek articulation of needs described in the language of the community members themselves. As this process is carried out, we continue to work as partners with community members in gathering resources and connecting people together to address the needs they have articulated. This process focuses on involving the community members directly in creating resources and in delivering services in their community.

The two processes described above represent quite different approaches to doing the same thing. Though the two approaches are not necessarily mutually exclusive, they do operate from very different assumptions about us as social workers, about the appropriate level of involvement of a community's citizens, and about our relationships with one another. Traditional approaches see the two groups of people—those doing the studying and intervening ("us") and those being studied and to whom interventions are directed ("them")—as separate from each other, with very different roles to play. Alternative approaches see the parties involved as interconnected partners in a mutual and emergent process.

Paradigm Analysis, Critical Thinking, and Deconstruction

Paradigm analysis is a helpful process for becoming more aware, constructively critical, and analytical in our interactions inside and outside the formal context of our education—in our work and in our interpersonal relationships. Put simply, **paradigm analysis** is learning to "think paradigm." It is a process of continually asking questions about what the information, both spoken and unspoken, that we send and receive reflects about our own and others' views of the world and its people, especially people different from ourselves. It is a process of continually "thinking about thinking." Paradigm analysis requires us to continually and critically evaluate the many perspectives we explore for their consistency with the core concerns of social work we outlined above. It is important to recognize that such critical thinking as that required of paradigm analysis is a helpful, positive, and constructive process, rather than a negative or destructive one.

The process of critical thinking required to do the paradigm analysis outlined below can be thought of as "deconstructive" rather than as destructive. In carrying out the tasks of paradigm analysis outlined below it is helpful to be aware of the importance and meaning of the concepts of critical thinking and deconstruction.

Critical Thinking

In debating the importance and possibility of teaching critical thinking in social work education, Gibbs argues that it is an essential part of the education process for social workers. A general definition of **critical thinking** is "the careful and deliberate determination of whether to accept, reject, or suspend judgment about a claim" (Moore and Parker in Bloom and Klein 1997:82). How does one engage in the process of critical thinking? Gibbs et al. describe the perspective necessary for critical thinking as well as the processes we use to "do" critical thinking:

1. A predisposition to question conclusions that concern client care and welfare;

2. Asking "does it work?" and "how do you know?" when confronted with claims that a method helps clients, and also questioning generalizations about treatment methods;

3. Weighing evidence for and against assertions in a logical, rational, systematic, data-based way; and

4. Analyzing arguments to see what is being argued, spotting and explaining common fallacies in reasoning, and applying basic methodological principles of scientific reasoning (see Chapter 2 for a description of the steps involved in the scientific method). (Gibbs 1995:196)

Deconstruction

Gaining answers especially to question number 5 below may involve what some scholars currently are referring to as a process of deconstruction. **Deconstruction** is a process of analyzing "texts" or perspectives "that is sensitive . . . to marginalized voices" (Sands and Nuccio 1992:491) and "biased knowledge" (Van Den Bergh 1995:xix). Through deconstruction "biased knowledge can be altered by reconstructing truth through inclusion of the voices of disempowered people. Knowledge that had previously been marginalized can then be centered (Hooks 1984 in Van Den Bergh 1995:xix). Deconstruction requires that we do "not accept the constructs used as given; instead [we look] at them in relation to social, historical, and political contexts. The deconstructionist identifies the biases in the text, views them as problematic, and 'decenters' them. Meanwhile, the perspectives that are treated as marginal are 'centered,'" (Sands and Nuccio 1992:491). Through this process of moving marginal voices to the center, more inclusive understandings and pictures of reality emerge. Missing or marginalized voices begin to be heard and begin to become a significant part of the paradigm creation process.

Paradigm Analysis

Paradigm analysis involves first of all asking a set of very basic questions about each of the perspectives we explore in order to determine its compatibility with the core concerns of social work. These questions are:

1. Does this perspective contribute to preserving and restoring human dignity?

2. Does this perspective recognize the benefits of, and does it celebrate, human diversity?

3. Does this perspective assist us in transforming ourselves and our society so that we welcome the voices, the strengths, the ways of knowing, the energies of us all?

4. Does this perspective help us all (ourselves and the people with whom we work) to reach our fullest human potential?

5. Does the perspective or theory reflect the participation and experiences of males and females; economically well-off and poor; white people and people of color; gay men, lesbians, bisexuals, and heterosexuals; old and young; temporarily able-bodied and people with disabilities?

The answers we find to these questions will tell us generally if the perspective we are exploring is consistent with the core concerns of social work. The answer to the final question will tell us about how the paradigm came to be and who participated in its development or construction.

SEHB or HBSE?: A Critical Thinking Deconstructive Example

A critical thinking and deconstructive approach can and should be applied to our thinking about the subject of this book and the CSWE requirement that content on "human behavior and the social environment" be included as one of the foundations of your social work education. For example, we might question the very name of this foundation area—Human Behavior and the Social Environment. Why is "human behavior" first in the name and "social environment" second? How might the perspectives and content of this book and this course change if the course or the foundation area were referred to as "Social Environment and Human Behavior?" One might argue that if this were the name, a significant shift in both perspective and content would need to take place. The very order of the chapters in this book might need to be reversed. If the social environment is primary and human behavior is secondary in the name, rather than trying to understand individual human behavior (human development) first, we might focus first on the impact of larger systems on the individual human. We might begin by trying to understand the important influences of the larger social environment—the community, for example, or society or culture—on the individual's development. As a result, you might explore Chapter 9—the community chapter—before you read Chapters 4 and 5—the chapters concerned with individual development. There might also be only one chapter focused on individual behavior and development and two chapters devoted to understanding community systems.

To critically think about this question requires us to ask questions about more than this book or this course. It requires us to think about the priorities of social work education and practice. Should social work be primarily about understanding and intervening at the level of the individual, or should our primary focus be understanding and intervening in the larger social environment in order to fulfill the purposes of social work—"the enhancement of human well-being and the alleviation of poverty and oppression?" This is a question members of the profession have struggled with throughout much of our history. It is an issue we will struggle with and will return to as we move through the chapters in this book. One way that we will do so is by including discussion of content from the perspective of the "social environment and human behavior" in a number of the remaining chapters.

Poverty Reduction

If we were to shift our focus to Social Environment and Human Behavior (SEHB), what would this really mean in terms of changes in priorities for social work education and practice? One of the critical shifts would be a return in the profession to a primary focus on **poverty reduction.** If we look at the purposes of social work—"the enhancement of human well-being and the alleviation of poverty and oppression," we see poverty reduction as a prominent component of our purposes. If we look at the required foundation areas for social work education, we see "social and economic justice." Achieving social and economic justice is in large part a function of poverty reduction. As we look at the various system levels of concern to us, we will consistently see that poverty status is closely associated with how well one does on virtually all the social and health indicators. Poverty is directly linked to barriers to attaining a good education, to maintaining health throughout the life span, to family and community well-being, to access to and use of technological resources, to violence and abuse, and to infant mortality and low-birth weight babies. Low birth weight is a predictor of many health and developmental risks in children. Rank and Hirschl argue that "whether the discussion revolves around welfare use, racial inequalities, single-parent families, infant mortality, economic insecurity, or a host of other topics, poverty underlies each and every one of these subjects" (Rank and Hirschl 1999:201).

Poverty and Oppression

Perhaps most important as we proceed on our journey is to attend to the linkages and intertwining of oppression and poverty. We will explore in a number of places in this book the clear linkage between oppression and poverty status. For example, we need to carefully examine why being a member of an oppressed group or population-at-risk—a person of color, a woman, a person with a disability—makes one so much more likely to be poor in U.S. society and globally than a member of the dominant group (white male of European heritage). We begin this exploration of linkages between poverty and social and health status with this chapter's Illustrative Reading 1.1: "Toward Understanding the Association of Socioeconomic Status and Health: A New Challenge for the Biopsychosocial Approach," by Anderson and Armstead. We will explore the notion of the interlocking nature of oppressions, especially race, gender, and class (income), further in Chapter 2 when we examine the place of oppression in alternative paradigm thinking.

SEHB: A Global Context

Perhaps one of the most dramatic examples of the need to consider the social environment at least equally if not first in attempts to understand human behavior is the increasingly global context in which we live. The increasing influence of the global context as a level of the social environment influencing human behavior at all other levels needs to be recognized. As we proceed through the chapters in this book we will regularly explore human behavior from a social environmental perspective. We will look at individual, family, community, social, economic, and policy issues through an increasingly global lens.

Poverty: A Global Context

One of the most fundamental ways of understanding global poverty is by examining hunger and malnutrition. It is difficult for many persons in the United States to appreciate that for many people around the world each day is a struggle for enough food to survive. Hunger and malnutrition both globally and in the United States will be explored in Chapter 5.

Technology: Social Work and HBSE/SEHB

As we will see in the chapters that follow, technology continues to reshape our ability to communicate locally and globally, and it is also a major social and environmental influence on human behavior at individual, family, group, organizational, and community levels. As technology continues to play an increasingly influential role in our lives both at the individual and collective levels, it is essential that we become increasingly better able to assess and understand the impact of technology in multiple areas of human behavior and the social environment. We must learn to use technology as one of the important tools to assist us in achieving the purposes of social work.

However, we must approach technology and the changes it brings from a critical perspective. In order to accomplish this, we must think about both the benefits of technology and its limits. For social workers, it is especially important to recognize the potential of technology to increase rather than decrease the gap between the "haves" and the "have-nots" in the United States and more importantly in a global context. This increasing gap in access to technology and its benefits is referred to as the **digital divide.** As we proceed through coming chapters we will attend to the benefits and limitations of technology for increasing human well-being, alleviating poverty and oppression, and increasing our understanding of human behavior and the social environment at multiple levels. We will also explore policy and practice implications surrounding technology.

Paradigms and History

To help us apply a critical thinking approach to explore either traditional or alternative paradigms, we need to develop some sense of historical perspective about the contexts out of which these world views emerged. Neither the traditional nor their alternative counterparts came about in a historical vacuum. They instead emerged as points along a historical continuum or stream marked by humans' attempts to understand their own behaviors, the behaviors of others, and the environments in which they lived.

Pre-Modern/Pre-Positivism

A historical perspective can help us appreciate that the paradigms we will explore as traditional and currently dominant were considered quite alternative and even radical at the times of their emergence. For example, the emergence of **humanism**—a belief in the power of humans to control their own behaviors and the environments in which they lived—in Europe at the opening of the Renaissance (mid-1400s) and at the ending of the Middle Ages (the early 1400s) was an alternative, and for many a radical, paradigm at that time. Humanism was considered by many, especially those in power, to be not only alternative but also dangerous, wrong, and heretical. Humanism was considered an affront to scholasticism, the traditional paradigm or world view that had been dominant throughout much of Europe in the Middle Ages (approximately A.D. 476–mid-1400s). **Scholasticism** (approximately A.D. 800–mid-1400s) was a world view that saw a Christian god, represented by the Roman Catholic Church, as the sole determiner and judge of human behavior. This Christian god was the controller of the entire natural world or environment in which humans existed. Similarly, **Protestantism,** was a world view placed in motion by Martin Luther during the early 1500s. It questioned the absolute authority of the Roman Catholic Church and the Pope as the sole representative of God, and was seen as another radical alternative affronting the existing world view. The emergence of both humanism and Protestantism were alternative ways of viewing humans and their environments that called into question, and were seen as significant threats to, the then existing dominant and traditional ways of viewing the world (Manchester 1992; Sahakian 1968).

Modernism/Positivism

Another important perspective from which to get a sense of the historical continuum out of which paradigms emerge is that of the birth of world views explaining human behavior and the environments we inhabit through science. The emergence of world views that explained the world through science were in some ways extensions of the humanistic paradigm. Science was a powerful tool through which humans could gain control of their behaviors and of the universe they inhabited. Science allowed humans to understand the world by directly observing it through the senses and careful measurement, experimentation, and analysis of what was observed. The emergence of scientific thinking or positivism during the period called the Enlightenment or the "Age of Reason" in the 17th and 18th centuries, however, was also a significant challenge to humanism and represented an alternative paradigm itself. Scientific thinking questioned humanism's central concern for gaining understanding through such expressions as art, literature, and poetry. A scientific world view saw humanism and its reflection in the humanities as a traditional and insufficient way of viewing the world.

Science sought to extend, if not replace, humanism's ways of knowing and understanding the world with a more reliable and comprehensive perspective that was *cosmos centered* rather than [*hu*]*man centered* (Sahakian 1968:119). The humanities raised questions and sought answers by looking to and rediscovering the great ideas and expressions of humans from the past, such as the classic works of the Romans and Greeks. Science offered keys to unlocking the secrets of the universe and the future through new ways of asking and answering questions. Science promised not only new questions and new ways of posing them but also answers to questions both new and old (Boulding 1964).

The empirical observations of Galileo Galilei in the first half of the 1600s confirming the earlier findings of Copernicus in the early 1500s, for example, literally provided a new view of the world (Manchester 1992:116–117). This new and alternative view moved the earth from the stable and unmoving center of the universe to one in which the earth was but one of many bodies revolving around the sun. The threat posed by such a dramatically different view of the world as that of Copernicus to the traditional Roman Catholic theology-based paradigm is captured eloquently by Manchester in his book *A World Lit Only by Fire:*

> *The Scriptures assumed that everything had been created for the use of man. If the earth were shrunken to a mere speck in the universe, mankind would also be diminished. Heaven was lost when "up" and "down" lost all meaning— when each became the other every twenty-four hours.* (1992:229)

According to Manchester, it was written in 1575 that "No attack on Christianity is more dangerous . . . than the infinite size and depth of the universe" (1992:229).

Much about the traditional paradigms that we explore in the next chapters has its roots in science and scientific ways of thinking that we virtually take for granted today. These approaches to understanding our worlds are centered in empirical observation and rational methods of gaining knowledge. So, science offers us a current example of what was, in a historical sense, an alternative paradigm becoming a traditional paradigm today. As has historically been the case, changes in paradigms currently taking place—what we will call *alternative paradigms*—call into question, challenge, and seek to extend our world views beyond those that have science and a scientific approach as the central tool for understanding human behavior and the social environment.

Postmodernism/Post-Positivism

Berman (1996), for example, notes that the basic methods and assumptions of the traditional scientific paradigm that emerged during the seventeenth-century Enlightenment have not solely resulted in progress for people and the earth. Berman (1996:33) argues that the scientific, also referred to as "the mechanical paradigm sees the earth as inert, as dead, or at best as part of the solar system, which is viewed as a kind of clockwork mechanism . . . and one consequence of [this view] was the opening of the door to the unchecked exploitation of the earth." In addition Berman suggests that science leaves little room for the spiritual and subjective elements of the world and its mechanistic tendencies leave little motivation for seeing the world as a living system. He makes an important observation that: "As a tool, there is nothing wrong with the mechanistic paradigm. But for some reason, we couldn't stop there; we had to equate it with all of reality and so have arrived at a dysfunctional science and society at the end of the twentieth century" (Berman 1996:35). We will explore in more detail both the elements of scientific method and alternatives to the scientific paradigm in the next two chapters.

For now we simply need to recognize that today there is considerable discussion and considerable disagreement as well, about whether we have moved or are moving in history to the point that we live in a post-positivist or postmodern world in which science and scientific reasoning are less likely to be considered the only, the best, or even the most accurate means for understanding the world around us. As noted above, we will explore some of the concepts related to postmodernism and post-positivism in the coming chapters.

Historical Periods in Summary

Before we proceed to look at social work in the context of history it may be helpful for us to try to get a glimpse or an overview (though a very incomplete and over-simplified view) of some of basic periods of history. Below are two different perspectives on the past that can help us do this. One is provided by Lincoln and Guba (1985) and looks at the past and present from the perspective of the role of science, specifically positivism, as central. The other perspective provided by Lather (1991) uses the notion of modernism as central to looking at the past and the present in terms of knowledge production, views of history, and the economy.

Three Historical Eras Suggested by Lincoln and Guba:

1. *The Prepositivist Era:* Aristotelian argument that everything in the world "occurred 'naturally.' Attempts by humans to learn about nature were interventionist and unnatural, and so distorted what was learned." (Wolf 1981, p. 23 in Lincoln and Guba 1985, p. 18).

2. *The Positivist Era:* "Positivism may be defined as 'a family of philosophies characterized by an extremely positive evaluation of science and scientific method'." (Reese 1980; in Lincoln and Guba 1985, p. 19). Early adherents (early nineteenth century) saw this paradigm as "potentially revolutionary in many fields (ethics, religion, and politics) as well as philosophy where it eventually was confined. However, its major impact was in the scientific method for studying and understanding the world." (Lincoln and Guba 1985:19)

3. *The Post-Positivist Era:* "Perhaps the *most* unexpected aspect of postpositivism is that its basic tenets are virtually the reverse of those that characterized positivism. . . . Where positivism sees its central purpose to be prediction, the new paradigm is concerned with understanding. . . . [W]here positivism is deterministic and bent on certainty, the new paradigm is probabilistic and speculative." Most of the distinctions between the positivist paradigm and the new "naturalistic" paradigm originated in the natural or 'hard' sciences. Lincoln and Guba suggest the argument for the new paradigm can be made even more strongly in the study of humans—social and behavioral research (Lincoln and Guba 1985:19, 30).

Three Historical Eras Profiled by Lather:

1. *Premodern:* Centrality of church/sacred basis of determining truth and knowledge; feudal economy; history as divinely ordered

2. *Modern:* Centrality of secular humanism, individual reason, and science in determining truth; the industrial age, capitalism, and bureaucracy as bases of economic life; history as linear in the direction of constant progress driven by human rationality and science. Ideal of ignorance to enlightenment to emancipation of human potential as the "inevitable trajectory of history."

3. *Postmodern:* Existing/traditional knowledge and knowledge creation processes intensely questioned. Emphasis on multiple ways of knowing through processes that are non-hierarchical, feminist influenced, and participatory; economy more and more based on information, technology, and global capitalism; view of history as nonlinear, cyclical, continually rewritten. "Focus on the present as history, the past as a fiction of the present." (Lather 1991:160–161)

Social Work History: Science and Art

That we should find ourselves wondering about alternative approaches to those based solely on a scientific approach to understanding HBSE is significant and timely for us as social workers (and soon-to-be social workers). A scientific approach to doing social work has been a major avenue used by social workers to attempt to understand and intervene in the world during the short history of social work as a field of study and practice. Although we have claimed allegiances to both art and science, we have preferred that science guide our work. This is not surprising, given the power and faith in the scientific approach that has pervaded the modern world of the nineteenth and twentieth centuries. The period of the late nineteenth and twentieth centuries coincides with the birth and development of social work as an organized field of knowledge and practice.

Many of the historical arguments and issues concerning traditional and alternative paradigms—humanism, science, religion—for understanding our worlds and ourselves have parallels in the history of social work. The mission, concerns, and purposes of social work all reflect beliefs about the nature of the world and people. The concern of social work with individuals, families, and communities in interactions and interdependence, as well as its concern for social reform to bring about improvements in individual and collective well-being, reflects important beliefs about the nature of the world and its inhabitants.

Goldstein (1990:33–34) reminds us that social work has followed two quite distinct tracks to put its mission into practice. These two distinct tracks parallel in a number of ways the two quite different world views or paradigms represented by humanistic and scientific perspectives. Goldstein reminds us that, while social work adopted a scientific approach to pursuing its mission, it did not discard completely its humanistic inclinations. These divergent paths have led us to multiple approaches to understanding humans' behaviors and the environments they inhabit and within which they interact. These paths have at times and for some of us led to "Freudian psychology, the empiricism of behavioral psychology, and the objectivity of the scientific methods of the social sciences" (1990:33). At other times we have followed much different paths in "existential, artistic, and value-based" alternatives (1990:35). Goldstein finds social workers today (as he finds the social sciences generally) turning again toward the humanistic, subjective, or interpretive paths. This is a direction quite consistent with the alternative paradigms for understanding human behavior and the social environment that we will explore in the chapters to come. This alternative path allows social workers "to give more serious attention to and have more regard for the subjective domain of our clients' moral, theological, and cultural beliefs, which . . . give meaning to the experiences of individuals and families" (England 1986 in Goldstein 1990:38).

Both/And Not Either/Or

Much of the emphasis in this book is on shifting to alternative paradigms and transcending the limits of traditional and dominant paradigm thinking. It is important to realize, though, that our journey to understanding Human Behavior and the Social Environment (referred to as HBSE throughout this book) is not to *either* one *or* the other worldview. Our journey will take us to *both* traditional *and* alternative destinations along the way. After all, traditional scientific worldviews have revealed much valuable knowledge about ourselves and our worlds.

We will try in this book to learn about alternative paradigms and to challenge and extend ourselves beyond traditional paradigms in which science is the single source of understanding. However, in order to understand alternative paradigms, we need to be cognizant of traditional theories about human behavior and development. We will challenge traditional paradigms as incomplete, as excluding many people, and as reflecting biases due to the value assumptions and historical periods out of which they emerged. These inadequacies, however, render traditional theories nonetheless powerful in the influences they have had in the past, that they currently have, and that they will continue to have on the construction and application of knowledge about human behavior and the social environment. Traditional approaches provide important departure points from which we may embark on our journey toward more complete, more inclusive, and less-biased visions (or at least visions in which bias is recognized and used to facilitate inclusiveness) of HBSE. Many of the alternative paradigms we will visit began as extensions or reconceptualizations of existing traditional worldviews.

There is another very practical reason for learning about theories that emerge from and reflect traditional paradigms. The practice world that social workers inhabit and that you will soon enter (and we hope transform) is a world constructed largely on traditional views of human behavior and the social environment. To survive in that world long enough to change it, we must be conversant in the discourse of that world. We must have sufficient knowledge of traditional and dominant paradigms of human behavior and development to make decisions about what in those worldviews we wish to retain because of its usefulness in attaining the goal of maximizing human potential. Knowledge of traditional and dominant paradigms is also necessary in deciding what to discard or alter to better serve that same core concern of social work.

Understanding the historical flow or continuum out of which differing world views emerged over time is an important means of recognizing the changes in perspectives on the world that at any given moment are likely to seem stable, permanent, and unchangeable. Even the changes occurring over time in the Western worldviews illustrated in the examples above give us a sense that permanency in approaches to understanding our worlds is less reality than perspective at a particular point in time. One way to conceptualize these fundamental changes occurring over time is to think in terms of paradigm shift.

Paradigm Shift

A **paradigm shift** is "a profound change in the thoughts, perceptions, and values that form a particular vision of reality" (Capra 1983:30). To express the fundamental changes required of a paradigm shift, Thomas Kuhn (1970) uses the analogy of travel to another planet. Kuhn tells us that a paradigm shift "is rather as if the professional community had been suddenly transported to another planet where familiar objects are seen in a different light and are joined by unfamiliar ones as well" (p. 111). The elements of this analogy—travel, another planet or world, viewing both familiar and new objects in a different light—are consistent with our efforts in this book to travel on a journey toward a more complete understanding of HBSE. Our journey will take us to other people's worlds and it will call upon us to view new things in those worlds and familiar things in our own worlds in new ways and through others' eyes. As we continue on our journey we should try to appreciate that the process of taking the trip is as important and enlightening as any final destination we might reach.

Paradigms are not mysterious, determined for all time, immovable objects. Paradigms are social constructs created by humans. They can be and, in fact, have been changed and reconstructed by humans throughout our history (Capra 1983:30). Kuhn ([1962] 1970:92), for example, discusses scientific and political revolutions that result in paradigm shifts and changes. Such changes, Kuhn suggests, come about when a segment of a community, often a small segment, has a growing sense that existing institutions are unable to adequately address or solve the problems in the environment—an environment those same institutions helped create. The actions taken by the dissatisfied segment of the community can result in the replacement of all or parts of the older paradigm with a newer one. However, since not all humans have the same amount of influence or power and control over what a paradigm looks like and whose values and beliefs give it form, efforts to change paradigms involve conflict and struggles (Kuhn [1962] 1970:93).

Use of the notion of paradigm shift will enable us to expand our knowledge of human behavior and the social environment and to use this additional knowledge in our practice of social work. It can free us from an overdependence on traditional ways of viewing the world as the only ways of viewing the world. It can allow us to move beyond these views to alternative possibilities for viewing the world, its people, and their behaviors.

The concept of paradigm shift allows us to make the transitions necessary to continue our journey to explore alternative paradigms and paradigmatic elements that represent the many human interests, needs, and perspectives not addressed by or reflected in the traditional and dominant paradigm. The concept of paradigm shift is also helpful in recognizing relationships between traditional and alternative paradigms and for tracing how alternative paradigms often emerge from traditional or dominant ones. As we noted earlier, many alternative paradigms originate as responses to or revisions/expansions of traditional or dominant paradigms. Traditional or dominant paradigms and alternative or possible paradigms for human behavior are often not necessarily mutually exclusive.

As we discussed in our exploration of paradigms and history, different paradigms can be described as different points in a progression of transformations in the way we perceive human behavior and the social environment. The progression from traditional and dominant to alternative and possible that we envision here is one that reflects a continuous movement (we hope) toward views of human behavior more consistent with the core concerns and historical values of social work and away from narrow perspectives that include only a privileged few and exclude the majority of humans. In some cases, this progression will mean returning to previously neglected paradigms. Such a progression, then, does not imply a linear, forward-only movement. It might more readily be conceived as a spiral or winding kind of movement. The world views illustrated in our discussion of history, for example, represented the perspectives almost exclusively of Europeans. Very different world views emerged in other parts of the world. Myers (1985:34), for example, describes an Afrocentric worldview that emerged over 5,000 years ago among Egyptians that posited the real world to be both spiritual and material at once. This holistic perspective found God manifest in everything. The self included "ancestors, the yet unborn, all of nature, and the entire community" (Myers 1985:35). Many scholars suggest that this paradigm continues to influence the world views of many people of African descent today. This Afrocentric paradigm clearly offers an alternative to European humanist or scientific paradigms that emerged during the Renaissance. Such an alternative emphasizing the interrelatedness of individuals and community and their mutual responsibility for one another encompasses much that is valuable and consistent with the core concerns of social work. The notion of a continuum helps us to understand the importance and usefulness of knowing about dominant paradigms at the same time that we attempt to transcend or shift away from the limits of traditional paradigms and move toward ones that are more inclusive and that more fully reflect the core concerns of social work.

Paradigm Shift, Social Work, and Social Change

The concept of paradigm change has significant implications for us as social workers. If you recall from earlier discussion, the basic purposes of social work include social change or social transformation in their call for us to be involved in social and political action to promote *social and economic justice*. Social change is also required in our call to enhance human well-being and to work on behalf of oppressed persons and *populations at risk* denied access to opportunities and resources or power. When we as social workers become a part of the processes of changing paradigms and the institutions that emerge from them, we are, in essence, engaging in fundamental processes of social change and transformation.

We can use the information we now have about paradigms and paradigm analysis to change or replace paradigms that create obstacles to people's meeting their needs and reaching their potentials. Since paradigms are reflected throughout the beliefs, values, institutions, and processes that make up our daily lives, we need not limit our thinking about paradigms only to our immediate concerns here about human behavior and the social environment. We can apply what we know about paradigms and paradigm change throughout our education and practice. For us as students of social work, that means we must become aware of the nature of the paradigms reflected throughout all foundation areas of our studies in social work—HBSE, social work values and ethics, social and economic justice, diversity, populations at risk, research, practice, policy, and field practicum. We certainly also must begin to analyze the nature and assumptions of the paradigms we encounter through our course work in the arts and humanities (music, theater, visual arts, philosophy, literature, English, languages, religious studies), social sciences (economics, political science, psychology, sociology, anthropology, history), and natural sciences (biology, physics, chemistry, geology, geography) as well as through our own personal histories and life experiences.

Socialization is the process of teaching new members the rules by which the larger group or society operates. Socialization involves imparting to new members the knowledge, values, and skills according to which they are expected to operate. For example, the social work education process in which you are currently involved is a process for socializing you to the knowledge, values, and skills expected of professional social workers. (We will explore the concept of socialization further in a later section.)

In a more general sense, we are socialized to and interact with others in the social environment from paradigmatic perspectives. These perspectives are not only imparted to us through formal education in the schools but also through what we are taught and what we learn from our families, religious institutions, and other groups and organizations as well. We are influenced by worldviews and we reflect the worldviews to which we have been socialized. The worldview likely to have influenced us most if we were socialized through the educational system in the United States is the traditional or dominant paradigm. The influence of this paradigm is pervasive, even if the worldviews of our families or cultures are in conflict with parts or all of the traditional or dominant paradigm. Because of the power accorded thinking consistent with the traditional paradigm, it is extremely difficult for alternative paradigms to be accorded legitimacy. It is not, however, impossible. As we shall see, it is quite possible through understanding traditional and alternative paradigms and the dynamics of paradigm change that we can exercise choice in the paradigms or worldviews through which we lead our lives. We suggest here that social changes resulting from shifts in worldviews inherently and inextricably flow from changes in the way we as individuals view our worlds. This position is consistent with the suggestion of much alternative paradigm thinking, in particular that of feminism, that *the personal is political.*

In order to use our understanding of paradigms to support processes of social change/transformation we must first engage in the process of paradigm analysis we described earlier. Paradigm analysis, you might recall, requires us to ask a set of questions that can guide us, in our education and practice, toward adopting and adapting approaches to understanding human behavior and the social environment that incorporate perspectives consistent with the core concerns of social work.

As we suggested earlier, a significant responsibility for us as social workers is assisting people whose needs are not met and whose problems are not solved by the institutions and processes in the social environment that emerge from and reflect the dominant/traditional paradigms. Much of what social work is about involves recognizing, analyzing, challenging, and changing existing paradigms. An essential step in fulfilling this important responsibility is learning to listen to, respect, and effectively respond to the voices and visions that the people with whom we work have to contribute to their own well-being and to the common good. In this way paradigms that too often have been considered permanent and unchangeable can be questioned, challenged, altered, and replaced. More important, they can be changed to more completely include the worldviews of persons previously denied participation in paradigm-building processes.

Such a perspective on knowledge for practice allows us to operate in partnership with the people with whom we work. It allows us to incorporate their strengths, and it provides us an opportunity to use social work knowledge, skills, and values in concert with those strengths in our practice interactions.

The possible or alternative paradigms of human behavior with which we will be concerned are those that enrich, alter, or replace existing paradigms by including the voices and visions—values, beliefs, ways of doing and knowing—of persons who have usually been left out of the paradigm building that has previously taken place. It is interesting, but not coincidental, that the persons who have usually been left out of paradigm-building processes are often the same persons with whom social workers have traditionally worked and toward whom the concerns of social workers have historically been directed.

Much of our work as we proceed through the remaining chapters of this book will involve understanding, critiquing, and analyzing traditional or dominant paradigms as well as alternative, more inclusive paradigms. We will engage in these processes as we explore theories and information about individual human behavior in the contexts of families, groups, organizations, and communities. Central to understanding, critiquing, and analyzing paradigms is consideration of the concepts of culture, ethnicity, and race in relation to paradigms.

PARADIGMS, CULTURE, ETHNICITY, AND RACE

A paradigm, as the concept is used here, encompasses a number of different but interrelated concepts. Among the concepts that can help us understand the complexities and variations of world views or paradigms held by different people are culture, ethnicity, and race. Even though, as Helms (1994:292) notes these terms "are often used interchangeably . . . neither culture nor ethnicity necessarily has anything to do with race, as the term is typically used in U.S. society." Each of these terms include a variety of meanings and are used in different ways depending on the context of their use and the worldview held by their users. For example, each of these concepts, in the hands of their users, can either be a very strong and positive force for unity and cooperation or an equally strong and negative force for divisiveness and domination. We will examine some of the interrelated meanings of these concepts next.

Culture and Society: Multiple Meanings

A very basic and traditional definition of **culture** is that it is the "accumulation of customs, values, and artifacts shared by a people" (Persell 1987:47–48). Even more basic is the definition offered by Herskovits that culture is "the human-made part of the environment" (Lonner 1994:231). **Society** can be defined as a "group of people who share a heritage or history" (Persell 1987:47–48). Lonner (1994:231) suggests that culture is "the mass of behavior that human beings in any society learn from their elders and pass on to the younger generation." This definition links the concepts culture and society as converging on or uniting with one another and adds the suggestion that culture is learned from others in the society. The transmission of culture can happen in two ways. It can occur through **socialization,** which is the teaching of

How might the people in this photo and their activity reflect the concepts of culture, ethnicity, and race discussed on the following pages? How might the meanings differ depending on whether the people in the photo or others (you, for example) provide the definitions?

culture by an elder generation to a younger one very explicitly through formal instruction and rules. This transmission process can also occur through **enculturation** by "implicitly or subtly" teaching the culture to the younger generation "in the course of everyday life" (Lonner 1994:234).

These definitions reflect the sense that culture is constructed by groups of people (societies), is made up of beliefs, practices, and products (artifacts), and is passed from one generation to another. However, many people would argue that culture is considerably more complex and varied than is implied by the definitions above.

Helms (1994) suggests, for example, that culture might be thought of as at least two very different entities or types: "a macroculture (symbolized here as CULTURE) and a variety of subsidiary cultures identified with particular collective identity groups (symbolized here as 'culture')." Helms' definition of *culture* as "the customs, values, traditions, products, and sociopolitical histories of the social groups" seems quite similar to the traditional definitions given above, however, her reference to these cultures as "subsidiary" and existing "within a CULTURE, where CULTURE refers to the dominant society or group's [belief system] or worldview" (1994:292) provides a significantly alternative perspective. Helms has added the dimension of dominance and power to the concept of culture. As we will see later the notion of power differences is an important element necessary for understanding differences between traditional or dominant and alternative paradigms.

The definitions above all emphasize similarities and commonalties among the people who make up cultures and societies. It is very important for us as social workers to be careful not to overgeneralize about these similarities. We need to recognize that "culture does not simply make people uniform or homogenize them: 'It rather sets trends from which in some cases it allows, and in other case even encourages, deviation: be it by attributing differentiating roles, or simply by encouraging individual differences in fashion, imagination, or style. In other words, a culture seems to need both uniformity and individuality" (Boesch 1991 in Lonner 1994:233).

Ethnicity

Ethnicity is "socially defined on the basis of cultural criteria. . . . Thus, customs, traditions, and values rather than physical appearance per se define ethnicity" (Van Den Berghe in Helms 1994:293). Helms (1994:293) suggests that ethnicity might "be defined as a social identity based on the culture of one's ancestors' national or tribal groups as modified by the demands of the CULTURE in which one group currently resides." As with her definitions of culture, Helms includes the impact of dominant or more powerful groups on other groups in her definition of ethnicity. She notes that the social identity that is ethnicity may be adapted or altered by groups as a result of demands of dominant or more powerful groups. However, she is careful to note the limits of a more powerful group in determining ethnicity for another group. She does this by differentiating between ethnic classification and ethnic identity. **Ethnic classification** is defined "from the outside in" and it "may be inferred from external criteria such as physical characteristics or symbolic behaviors (for example, ethnic dress)." **Ethnic identity,** on the other hand is "defined from the inside (of the person) out (to the world)" and is "self-defined and maintained because it 'feels good' rather than because it is necessarily imposed by powerful others" (Helms 1994: 293–294).

Multiple Meanings of Race

The word **race** has historically had a variety of meanings. These meanings have varied over time. Consistently, though, the very term *race* in U.S. society is highly charged emotionally and has different meanings and very different consequences for different people. We will explore race here as a multifaceted concept and as a concept that must be considered contextually. We will also find that the meaning of race is consistently used in U.S. society as an arena for power struggle. Racial distinctions are often used as a means of attaining and holding power by dominant group members over less powerful groups. At this point, we address the concept of race in terms of its cultural and social meanings and we give some attention to misconceptions that race is primarily a biological rather than primarily a social construction with biological elements only secondary. We briefly explore the uses of racial designations for oppression and for solidarity and liberation. Chapter 2 addresses the dimensions of traditional and alternative paradigms dealing with whiteness, diversities, and oppressions.

Race: Biology, Culture, or Both

There has been ongoing argument in this society over what we mean by "races." Spickard (1992:13–14) suggests that "the most common view has been to see races as distinct types. That is, there were supposed to have been at some time in the past four or five utterly distinct and pure races, with physical features, gene pools, and the character qualities that diverged entirely one from another." The biological terms related to this purist view of races as types are **genotype** which means genetic structure or foundation and **phenotype** which means physical characteristics and appearance.

Spickard (1992:15) also stresses that

> *in the twentieth century, an increasing number of scientists have taken exception to the notion of races as types. James C. King (1981), perhaps the foremost American geneticist on racial matters, denounces the typological view as "make-believe" (p. 112). Biologists and physical anthropologists are more likely to see races as* subspecies. *That is, they recognize the essential commonality of all humans, and see races as geographically and biologically diverging populations. . . . They see all human populations, in all times and places, as mixed populations. There never were any 'pure' races.*

Most scientists today have concluded, "that race is primarily about culture and social structure, not biology . . . [and that] while it has some relationship to biology . . . [it] is primarily a sociopolitical construct. The sorting of people into this race or that in the modern era has generally been done by powerful groups for the purposes of maintaining and extending their own power." (Spickard 1992:13–14)

Race and Power

Spickard (1992:19) argues that "from the point of view of the dominant group, racial distinctions are a necessary tool of dominance. They serve to separate the subordinate people as "Other." Putting simple, neat racial labels on dominated peoples—and creating negative myths about the moral qualities of those peoples—makes it easier for the dominators to ignore the individual humanity of their victims. It eases the guilt of oppression." For example, in U.S. society "the typological view of races developed by Europeans arranged the peoples of the world hierarchically, with Caucasians at the top, Asians next, then Native Americans, and African at the bottom—in terms of both physical abilities and moral qualities" (Spickard 1992:14).

While race is often used as a tool of domination it

> *is by no means only negative, however. From the point of view of subordinate peoples, race can be a positive tool, a source of belonging, mutual help, and self-esteem. Racial categories . . . identify a set of people with whom to share sense of identity and common experience. . . . It is to share a sense of peoplehood that helps locate individuals psychologically, and also provides the basis for common political action. Race, this socially constructed identity, can be a powerful tool, either for oppression or for group self-actualization.* (Spickard 1992:19)

Race: Biology, Culture, Power

As we noted earlier the concepts of culture, society, ethnicity, and race are closely intertwined. Helms and Gotunda (in Helms 1994) argue that race as it is used in the United States has three types of definitions that reflect this intertwining of multiple concepts:

1. Quasi-biological race: *based on visible aspects of a person that are assumed to be racial in nature, such as skin color, hair texture, or physiognomy [facial features]. "Group-defining racial characteristics generally*

are selected by the dominant or sociopolitically powerful group. . . . Thus, in the United States, White people specify the relevant racial traits and use themselves as the standard or comparison group." For example, "Native Americans are considered 'red' as compared to Whites; Blacks are black in contrast to Whites."

2. Sociopolitical race: *efforts to differentiate groups by means of mutually exclusive racial categories also imply a [hierarchy] with respect to psychological characteristics, such as intelligence and morality, with gradations in skin color or other relevant racial-group markers determining the group's location along the hierarchy. On virtually every socially desirable dimension, the descending order of superiority has been Whites, Asians, Native American, and Africans."*

3. Cultural race: *the customs, traditions, products, and values of (in this instance) a racial group.* (Helms 1994:297–299)

Social Work and Cultural Competence

It is not enough for social workers to simply understand the abstract complexities that make up definitions of culture, society, ethnicity, or race. Because respect for diversity is so central to social work values and practice and because culture is such an important tool for understanding human diversity, social workers are beginning to make considerations about culture and cultural differences central to what we consider to be competent social work practice. The notion of culturally competent social work practice and what it involves has been described for multiple levels and areas of practice including individual practitioners and clients, families and agencies.

Cultural Competence is defined as "a set of congruent behaviors, attitudes, and policies that come together in a system, agency, or among professionals and enable that system, agency, or those professionals to work effectively in cross-cultural situations" (Cross in Rounds et al. 1994:5). In addition, cultural competence is reflected in "a program's ability to honor and respect those beliefs, interpersonal styles, attitudes and behaviors both of families who are clients and the multicultural staff who are providing services. In so doing, it incorporates these values at the levels of policy, administration and practice (Roberts 1990)" (Rounds et al. 1994:5–6).

Cross et al. (1989 in Rounds et al. 1994:6–7) outline five essential elements of culturally competent practice:

1. *Acknowledging and valuing diversity:* "recognition that cultural differences exist and that they play a major role in individual, family, and community development and functioning"

2. *Conducting a cultural assessment:* Awareness "of one's own culture and how it shapes beliefs and behavior, both personal and professional" and at the agency level, assessment of "how cultural beliefs are reflected in their staffing patterns and hiring practices, relationships with communities that they serve, and in agency policies and procedures."

3. *Recognizing and understanding the dynamics of difference:* awareness of "how differences in race and culture between clients and practitioners influence interactions"

and awareness of "the ways in which racism and the current status and long history of race relations affect the interaction and establishment of rapport between racially and ethnically different clients and practitioners."

4. *Acquiring cultural knowledge:* "Practitioners need to have an in-depth understanding of the cultural background of their clients."

5. *Adapting to diversity:* "The culturally competent social worker is able to adapt social work skills to the needs and styles of the client's culture."

Culturally competent social work practice—its meaning and its application—is emerging as one of the most critical aspects of social work practice. It is especially important as the diversity of the U.S. population continues to increase. Culturally competent practice is also increasingly important as we become more and more interrelated with other people in the world as a result of the rapid shifts toward ever more global economics, communication, and transportation. Culturally competent social work practice is addressed in more detail in Chapter 3 as one of the "Tools for Social Work Practice" and is the focus of Illustrative Reading 3.1.

Paradigms, Culture, and Society

Paradigms or world views simultaneously shape and reflect the institutions and processes shared by people in a society. However, there is a great deal of variation in the specific paradigmatic elements—the parts that constitute a paradigm—and the degree to which these parts are shared by different persons in the same society. This is especially true in the United States, although it is often unrecognized. Paradigmatic elements include the processes, beliefs, values, and products that make up cultures and give multiple meanings to such concepts as ethnicity and race. They include and are reflected in such varied expressions of cultures as art, music, science, philosophy, religion, politics, economics, leisure, work, and education. As Logan (1990:25) suggests, "culture must be viewed in the sense of the spiritual life of a people as well as material and behavioral aspects." As in the case of the concept of society, there is tremendous variation in the nature of the paradigmatic elements that constitute different cultures and the degree to which these elements are shared by the peoples of the United States. It is contended here that this variation, this diversity, is a rich and essential, although underutilized, resource for understanding human behavior and the social environment.

Social Work and the Liberal Arts

In order to help prepare us for culturally competent social work practice, in this book we will search for ways to become aware of the many paradigmatic elements that influence our day-to-day lives and the ways we experience our worlds. Because paradigmatic elements are so interwoven with the many expressions of cultures and societies, it is essential for social workers to have as wide a range of opportunities as possible to learn and to think about these important elements and expressions. One way this is accomplished is through requirements that all social work education be based on a foundation of studies in a wide range of multidisciplinary liberal arts and sciences courses. Our studies in these courses can provide us new avenues to understand our own cultures and the cultures of others.

Social workers have recognized these valuable avenues to understanding human behavior and the social environment for a long time. They are considered so important in the overall education of social workers that content in the liberal arts and sciences disciplines is a requirement for the accreditation of social work programs by the Council on Social Work Education. In undergraduate social work education this liberal arts and sciences foundation must be integrated along with the required social work courses (CSWE 1992). In graduate social work study students are expected to bring from their undergraduate experiences a background that includes study in liberal arts and sciences (CSWE 1992). The CSWE defines a liberal arts perspective in the following way:

> *A liberal arts perspective provides an understanding of one's cultural heritage in the context of other cultures; the methods and limitations of various systems of inquiry; and the knowledge, attitudes, ways of thinking, and means of communication that are characteristic of a broadly educated person. Students must be capable of thinking critically about society, about people and their problems, and about such expressions of culture as art, literature, science, history, and philosophy. Students must have direct knowledge of social, psychological, and biological determinants of human behavior and of diverse cultures, social conditions, and social problems.* (CSWE 1992:99–100, 138)

As we proceed we will try, through this book, to connect what we are thinking and learning about human behavior and the social environment with the experiences and knowledge we have (we all have a great deal!) and are continually gaining through the liberal arts and sciences.

Lather suggests a helpful way of thinking about the liberal arts and sciences as "human sciences" which encompass social, psychological, and biological sciences as they relate to humans. The definition of "human science" she puts forth suggests a broader, more inclusive approach to understanding human behavior through the liberal arts and sciences. **Human science** "is more inclusive, using multiple systems of inquiry, 'a science which approaches questions about the human realm with an openness to its special characteristics and a willingness to let the questions inform which methods are appropriate'" (Polkinghome quoted in Lather 1991:166). This more inclusive and open approach to achieving understanding is consistent with the perspective or stance we take in this book toward alternative paradigms for understanding HBSE.

Howard Goldstein (1990), a social worker, offers us a very useful perspective on how knowledge from the liberal arts (the humanities) can help us do better social work. He suggests that much understanding about the continuously unfolding and complex nature of the lives of the people with whom we work (and of our own lives) can be achieved through study in the liberal arts. Goldstein reminds us that study in the liberal arts can help us learn what questions are important to ask. In other words, the liberal arts can help us learn to *think*—about ourselves and about others. Goldstein (1990) suggests that for social workers

> *the kinds of creative, imaginative, and reflective thought that are required to grasp the world as it is interpreted by the client can be stirred by the humanities. In art, literature, drama, philosophy, religion, and history, we discover that our own and our clients' triumphs and struggles have been played*

out in a multitude of ways in an effort to make sense of living and find meaning within it. The humanities do not profess to offer answers; rather, they encourage the kind of disciplined questioning and reflection that are fundamental to what effective practice may be (p. 41).

Creative thinking that helps us ask questions that lead us toward understanding the experiences and the worlds of the people with whom we work, as well as our own, is central to what social work practice is all about.

Paradigms, Power, and Empowerment

Examination of the paradigms that simultaneously shape and are reflected in cultures and societies such as those in the United States can tell us much about power relations and the differential distribution of resources. Concerns about power, inequality, and resource distribution are, we must remember, core concerns for social workers. Our study of paradigms can help us understand a number of things about inequality and differences in power and resources.

Power: Social and Economic Justice

Of major concern to social workers are power and resource differences (social and economic justice) that result from one's gender, color, sexual orientation, religion, age, ability, culture, income, and class (membership in populations at risk). These differences have resulted in the exclusion of many persons from having a place or a voice in dominant or traditional paradigms that guide decision making in this society. Differences such as those listed above have resulted in the worldviews of some individuals and groups having much more influence than others on the institutions and processes through which human needs must be met and human potential reached. It is the contention in this book that when some of us are denied opportunities to influence decision-making processes that affect our lives we are all hurt. We all lose when the voices and visions of some of us are excluded from paradigms and paradigm-building processes. By listening to the voices and seeing the world through the eyes of those who differ from us in gender, color, sexual orientation, religion, age, ability, culture, income, and class we can learn much about new paradigms or worldviews that can enrich all our lives. Close attention to, and inclusion of the voices and visions of, persons different from us can greatly expand, with exciting new possibilities, our understanding of human behavior and the social environment—and our understanding of what it means to be human.

Empowerment

Empowerment is a concept helpful to us as we think about the importance of power for understanding paradigms and its role in achieving the basic purposes of social work. **Empowerment** involves redistributing resources so that the voices and visions of persons previously excluded from paradigms and paradigm-building processes are included. Specifically, empowerment is the process through which people gain the power and resources necessary to shape our worlds and reach our full human potential. Empowerment suggests an alternative definition of power itself. A very useful alternative definition of power has been suggested by African American feminists. This definition rejects the traditional notion of power as a commodity used by one person or group to dominate another. It instead embraces "an alternative vision of power based on a humanist vision of self-actualization, self-definition, and self-determination" (Lorde 1984; Steady 1987; Davis 1989; Hooks 1989 cited in Collins 1990:224). This alternate vision seems much more consistent with the purposes and foundations of social work than traditional conceptualizations of power that define power as "power over" someone else for our own benefit.

As social workers we are especially concerned, in our explorations of alternative visions of power, with the empowerment of those persons who differ from the people whose voices and visions are represented disproportionately in the traditional and dominant paradigms. The persons most disproportionately represented in traditional paradigms are "male, white, heterosexual, Christian, temporarily able-bodied, youthful with access to wealth and resources" (Pharr 1988:53). Our alternative vision seeks the empowerment of women, people of color, gay men and lesbians, non-Christians, nonyoung, persons with disabilities, non-European descended, low-income, and non-middle- or non-upper-socioeconomic-class persons.

The purpose of **empowerment is in essence the purpose of social work:** *to preserve and restore human dignity, to benefit from and celebrate the diversities of humans, and to transform ourselves and our society into one that welcomes and supports the voices, the potential, the ways of knowing, the energies of us all.* "Empowerment practice in social work emerged from efforts to develop more effective and responsive services for women and people of color (Gutierrez et al. 1995:534)" Empowerment focuses on changing the distribution of power. It "depicts power as originating from various sources and as infinite because it can be generated in the process of social interaction" (Gutierrez et al. 1995:535). As we proceed through this book and consider a variety of perspectives on individuals, families, groups, organizations, and communities, we need to keep in mind their potential for empowering all persons and for facilitating social change or social transformation. As we proceed we will continually weigh what we discover about any of the paradigms and perspectives we explore against the historic mission and core concerns of social work—"the enhancement of human well-being" and the "alleviation of poverty and oppression" (CSWE 1992:97, 135). The tasks we set for ourselves as we continue our journey toward more complete understanding of HBSE are certainly challenging ones. However, like the assumptions of interconnectedness and interdependence we made at the beginning of this chapter about social work, ourselves, and the people with whom we work, the topics and tasks we take on as we proceed through this book are interconnected and interdependent.

SUMMARY/TRANSITION

This chapter has presented you with information and perspectives in a number of areas. It has introduced you to the place and importance of human behavior and the social environment content in the social work curriculum. It has described HBSE content as required content for all accredited social work education programs that, in concert with a wide range of content from the liberal arts and sciences, builds a foundation of knowledge upon which to base social work practice. The chapter has presented a number of guiding assumptions about the interrelationships among ourselves, others, and social work practice.

Definitions of the concept of paradigm or world view have been presented, along with discussions of the related notions of paradigm analysis and paradigm shift and their significance for social workers and social change. This chapter has introduced the notions of traditional or dominant paradigms and alternative or possible paradigms. These concepts have been placed in context through discussion of their emergence and change over time within a historical continuum. Attention has been given in this chapter to the purposes and foundations of social work that form its historic mission to enhance human well-being and alleviate poverty and oppression. Issues of power and empowerment as they relate both to understanding paradigms and to the core concerns of social work have been discussed. The exclusion of many diverse persons from traditional and dominant paradigms has been introduced. In addition the complexities and multiple definitions of culture, ethnicity and race were introduced. The concepts and issues in this chapter present the foundation themes that will guide us throughout our journey to understanding human behavior and the social environment in the chapters that comprise this book. The concepts and issues presented in this chapter are intended to provide a base from which to explore in more detail dimensions of traditional and alternative paradigms in the next chapter.

Internet Search Guide

If you want to learn more about some of the topics discussed in this chapter by exploring the Internet, you can search the Net for the terms listed below. Remember that as you are "surfing" the Net, any of the search terms listed below can take you in many different directions.

1. culture and paradigms
2. National Association of Social Workers
3. paradigm shift
4. socialization
5. empowerment
6. CSWE
7. poverty
8. global economy
9. technology and human services
10. technology and society

If you would like to visit specific Web sites related to this chapter, go to the Allyn and Bacon Web site at **http://www.abacon.com** and follow the links to Schriver or *Human Behavior and the Social Environment: Shifting Paradigms in Essential Knowledge for Social Work Practice*. There you will find a selection of sites related to content in this chapter.

REFERENCES

Berman, M. (Winter 1996). "The shadow side of systems theory." *Journal of Humanistic Psychology, 36*(1).

Bloom, M., and Klein, W. (Eds.). (1997). *Controversial issues in human behavior in the social environment*. Boston: Allyn and Bacon.

Boulding, Kenneth E. (1964). *The meaning of the 20th century: The great transition.* New York: Harper-Colophon.

Capra, Fritjof. (1983). *The turning point: Science, society, and the rising culture.* Toronto: Bantam Books.

Collins, Patricia Hill. (1990). *Black feminist thought: Knowledge, consciousness, and the politics of empowerment.* Boston: Unwin Hyman, Inc.

Council on Social Work Education (CSWE). (1992). *Handbook of accreditation standards and procedures* (4th ed.). Alexandria, VA: Author.

Gambrill, E., and Gibbs, L. (1996). *Critical thinking for social workers: A workbook.* Thousand Oaks, CA: Pine Forge Press.

Gibbs, L. G., Blakemore, J., Begun, A., Keniston, A., Preden, B., and Lefcowitz, J. (1995). "A measure of critical thinking about practice." *Research on Social Work Practice, 5*(2): 193–204.

Goldstein, Howard. (1990). "The knowledge base of social work practice: Theory, wisdom, analogue or art?" *Families in Society, 71*(1): 32–43.

Guba, Egon G., and Lincoln, Yvonna S. (1989). *Fourth generation evaluation.* Newbury Park, CA: SAGE Publications.

Gutierrez, L., Delois, K., and Linnea, G. (November 1995). "Understanding empowerment practice: Building on practioner-based knowledge." *Families in Society: The Journal of Contemporary Human Services.*

Helms, J. E. (1994). "The conceptualization of racial identity and other 'racial' constructs." In Trickett, E. J., Watts, R. J., and Birman D. (Eds.). (1994). *Human diversity: Perspectives on people in context.* San Francisco: Jossey-Bass.

Kuhn, Thomas S. ([1962] 1970). *The structure of scientific revolutions* (2nd ed.). Chicago: The University of Chicago.

Lather, P. (1991). *Getting smart: Feminist research and pedagogy with/in the postmodern.* New York: Routledge.

Lincoln, Y. S., and Guba, E. G. (1985). *Naturalistic inquiry.* Beverly Hills: Sage.

Logan, Sadye. (1990). "Black families: Race, ethnicity, culture, social class, and gender issues." In Logan, S., Freeman, E., and McRoy, R. *Social Work Practice With Black Families.* New York: Longman.

Lonner, W. J. "Culture and human diversity." In Trickett, E. J., Watts, R. J., and Birman D. (Eds.). (1994). *Human diversity: Perspectives on people in context.* San Francisco: Jossey-Bass.

Manchester, William. (1992). *A world lit only by fire: The medieval mind and the renaissance: Portrait of an age.* Boston: Little, Brown and Company.

Myers, Linda J. (1985). "Transpersonal psychology: The role of the afrocentric paradigm." *Journal of Black Psychology, 12*(1): 31–42.

National Association of Social Workers (NASW). (1982). *Standards for the classification of social work practice.* Silver Spring, MD: NASW.

Persell, Caroline Hodges. (1987). *Understanding society: An introduction to sociology.* New York: Harper and Row.

Pharr, Suzanne. (1988). *Homophobia: A Weapon of Sexism.* Inverness, CA: Chardon, Press.

Rank, M., and Hirschl, T. (1999). "The likelihood of poverty across the American adult life span." *Social Work, 44*(3): 201–216.

Reason, Peter, (Ed.) (1988). *Human inquiry in action: Developments in new paradigm research.* London: SAGE Publications.

Root, Maria P. P. (Ed.). (1992). *Racially mixed people in America.* Newbury Park, CA: Sage.

Rounds, K. A., Weil, M., and Bishop, K. K. (January 1994). "Practice with culturally diverse families of young children with disabilities." *Families in Society: The Journal of Contemporary Human Services.*

Sahakian, William S. (1968). *History of philosophy.* New York: Barnes and Noble Books.

Sands, R., and Nuccio, K. (1992). "Postmodern feminist theory in social work." *Social Work, 37:* 489–494.

Schutz, Alfred. (1944). "The stranger: an essay in social psychology." *American Journal of Sociology, 49:*499–507.

Spickard, P. R. "The illogic of American racial categories." In Root, Maria P. P. (Ed.). (1992). *Racially mixed people in America*. Newbury Park, CA: Sage.

Trickett, E. J., Watts, R. J. and Birman, D. (Eds.). (1994). *Human diversity: Perspectives on people in context*. San Francisco: Jossey-Bass.

Van Den Bergh, N. (Ed.). (1995). *Feminist practice in the 21st century*. Washington, DC: NASW Press.

ILLUSTRATIVE READING 1.1

The following illustrative reading by Anderson and Armstead both illustrates and helps us understand the complex interplay of a variety of forces influencing human behavior and the social environment that have been of concern to us in Chapter 1. The reading focuses on the interrelatedness of health and socioeconomic status and a variety of other factors. The areas addressed in the reading are directly relevant to the concerns and values of social work. A central purpose of social work, we have said, is the promotion of health and well-being. We have also noted that one of the foundation areas of social work is social and economic justice, along with the accompanying concern for alleviating poverty and oppression. Other foundation areas we have discovered include human diversity and populations at risk. We have also stressed in this chapter that a key perspective for helping us understand human behavior and the social environment is a bio-psycho-socio-cultural approach. The authors of this reading, though it is from the medical literature, bring together a number of these important concerns for social workers and demonstrate the very real consequences in terms of **morbidity** (illness or disease rates) and **mortality** (death rates) on life chances and quality of life for diverse persons. They illustrate the linkages among such basic issues as gender, age, environmental conditions, ethnicity, income level, health status, and even the geographic locales in which we carry out our day-to-day lives.

Toward Understanding the Association of Socioeconomic Status and Health: A New Challenge for the Biopsychosocial Approach

Norman B. Anderson, PhD, and Cheryl A. Armstead, PhD

The association of socioeconomic status (SES) with morbidity and mortality is a ubiquitous finding in the health literature. One of the principal challenges for biobehavioral researchers is understanding the mechanisms that link SES with health outcomes. This article highlights

Departments of Psychiatry and Psychology, Social and Health Sciences, Duke University, and The Geriatric Research Education and Clinical Center, Durham Veterans Affairs Medical Center, Durham, North Carolina (N.B.A.) and Department of Psychology, University of North Carolina, Columbia, South Carolina (C.A.A.). N. Anderson and C. Armstead. "Toward Understanding the Association of Socioeconomic Status and Health: A New Challenge for the Biopsychosocial Approach." *Psychosomatic Medicine,* v. 57, 1995, pp. 213–225. Reprinted by permission of Lippincott Williams & Wilkins.

possible pathways by which SES may influence health. It also provides a discussion of socio-demographic and geographical modifiers of the SES-health relationship and offers several potentially fruitful directions for future research.

Key words: SES, health, ethnicity, gender, age, mechanisms.

INTRODUCTION

It is appropriate that the first article in this special issue on shared determinants of health outcomes focuses on social class, because understanding the relationship between social class and health requires addressing each of the other topics that constitute this volume. In the health literature, the terms social class and socioeconomic status (SES) are often used interchangeably. However, in some disciplines, such as sociology, these terms often have different meanings. As many authors have noted (1–4), there are explicit theories of social class and specific social class categories, as developed by Marx (4, 5), Dahrendorf (3, 6), Weber (7), and others, that have not heretofore been used to examine health outcomes. For this article, we use the expression SES as a synonym for education, income, or occupation. These are the principal ways by which SES has been operationalized in the literature.

This article addresses the following topics. First, it provides a brief overview of the relationship between SES and health outcomes. Second, it highlights possible mechanisms whereby SES may influence health. Our purpose is not to provide an exhaustive summary of this vast literature because there are a number of publications that adequately serve this purpose. Our goal is to provide a relatively brief introduction to this field. Next, we provide a more detailed discussion of sociodemographic and geographical modifiers of the SES-health relationship, given the lack of emphasis on these areas in most previous reviews. Finally, we outline one approach for future research on SES and health.

SES AND HEALTH

A relationship between SES and health has apparently existed for some time. Davey Smith et al. (8) examined the height of graveyard obelisks in the Victorian burial grounds of Glasgow, Scotland. Among individuals who died between 1800 and 1920, the age at death was significantly older for individuals with taller grave markers, whose families were presumably wealthier and could afford the taller obelisks. In 1924, researchers in Providence, Rhode Island analyzed United States Bureau of the Census data from 1865 and found that mortality rates were higher among nontaxpayers compared with taxpayers in that city. Nontaxpayers were lower income people who were exempted from income tax obligations (9).

More recent studies have also shown a consistent inverse relationship between SES and morbidity and mortality rates. Figure 1.1 provides a representation of the association between SES and health in developed countries. As one moves up the SES ladder, morbidity and mortality rates generally decrease. This inverse relationship is observed whether SES is measured using education, income, or occupational status and does not appear to be an artifact of the more physically ill individuals drifting down the SES hierarchy (10, 11). The SES-health gradient extends to a wide array of health problems,

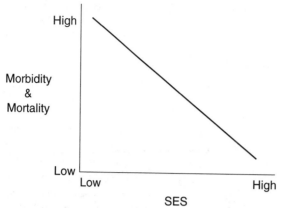

FIGURE 1.1   Representation of the relationship
between SES and health outcomes

including heart disease, cancer, stroke, diabetes, hypertension, infant mortality, arthritis, back ailments, mental illness, kidney diseases, and many others (12) and may predict prognosis after illness is present (13, 14). For more detailed information on specific studies on SES and health, there are several excellent reviews available (1, 11, 15–18).

What Accounts for the Linkage?

Perhaps *the* most pressing question for health researchers is how SES influences health outcomes or how it "gets under the skin." Figure 1.2 shows six categories of variables that might participate in the linkage between SES and health. These include sociodemographic; economic; social, environmental, and medical; behavioral and psychological; physiological, and health outcome variables. Although this diagram is a convenient method of illustrating many of the factors that may be involved in the SES-health linkage, it does not truly capture the numerous and complex interactions that may occur both within and across categories. However, using the SES literature, we hope to provide illustrative examples of some of these interactions.

SES and Access to Health Care

It is frequently assumed that SES differences in access to health care (Figure 1.2, Category 3) can account for SES differences in health outcomes. Indeed, this is one of the strongest arguments for universal health care coverage in the United States. However, although universal health care coverage is critically important, its initiation will probably *not* level out the SES-health gradient.

According to Adler et al. (15), there are at least three reasons why this is true. First, countries that have universal health insurance show approximately the same SES-health gradient as that found in the United States where such insurance is not provided. Second, SES differences can be found at the upper range of the SES hierarchy in which health insurance coverage is likely to be more universal. Third, SES

FIGURE 1.2   Possible factors linking SES and health

1 Socio-demographic	2 Socioeconomic Status	3 Social, Environ., Medical	4 Psychological & Behavioral	5 Physiological	6 Outcomes
Age Ethnicity Gender Location	Education Income Occupation Family Wealth Perceived SES Economic Mobility Childhood SES Material Possessions Trading/ Bartering Practices National Income Distribution	Residential Characteristics Occupational Environment Social Support Social/ Professional Hierarchy Access to Health Care	Psychological Distress Personality Factors Health-Promoting Behaviors Health-Damaging Behaviors	Cardiovascular Immune Muscular Endocrine Height Weight	**Health and Illness**

differences appear in diseases that are amenable to treatment and those that are not (e.g., different types of cancers). Thus, even after the implementation of much needed health care reform in the United States, the SES-health gradient will more than likely persist.

SES and Residential Characteristics

In recent years, researchers have become increasingly aware of the potential importance of residential environment (Figure 1.2, Category 3) as a mediator of the SES-health relationship. As one moves down the SES ladder, residential choices become more limited. In fact, many of the environments in which individuals lower on the SES hierarchy live are associated with mortality rates independent of individual SES. Haan et al. (11) provide one of the most complete reviews of this literature. They state that many studies that examine community environment and SES show clear associations between SES and related environmental exposures and health outcomes. Most studies used both ecological measures of the environment and ecological measures of health, such as death rates in a geographical area (11). Few studies have linked ecological measures of the residential or physical environment with *individual*-level health status or health behaviors (19, 20).

One study that did link ecological measures of SES with individual outcomes was conducted by Haan et al. (19), who examined 9-year mortality rates as a function of poverty area in a random sample of residents aged 35 and older in Oakland, California. The United States Bureau of the Census defines poverty areas as those with a high percentage of families with low income, substandard housing, and lower than average educational attainment. After the multivariate adjustment for 15 potential confounders, including age, race, sex, initial health status, and individual SES, poverty area was associated with all-cause mortality rates after 9 years. Thus, the Haan et al. data suggest that poverty area may represent a new independent risk factor for individually assessed adverse health outcomes but one that is certainly correlated with individual SES.

SES and Psychological and Behavioral Factors

SES may influence health outcomes through its association with behavioral and psychological risk factors (Figure 1.2, Category 4). For example, it has been known for at least two decades that persons lower in SES experience more stressful life events and more subjective distress than their higher SES counterparts (21–24). Despite this, research has generally failed to support the hypothesis that their subjective burden is *due to* greater stress exposure (21, 22, 25). Instead, empirical research shows that the emotional *impact* of stressful life events is greater in individuals lower in SES compared with those higher in SES (21, 22, 24), suggesting that the former may have greater vulnerability to stress. In addition to subjective distress, other psychological characteristics such as depression (26, 27), hostility (28, 29), and locus of control (30–32) have also shown a consistent relationship with SES. Higher levels of SES have been associated with lower levels of depression and hostility and with an internal locus of control. Other psychological and personality constructs either remain relatively unexplored with respect to SES or the results thus far have been equivocal. These include anger, anxiety, Type A behavior, optimism, hardiness, subjective well-being, and neuroticism.

It is also possible that SES may exert its effects on health through the performance or lack of performance of health-promoting or health-damaging behavior. For example, with decreasing SES, research has clearly documented an increase in smoking prevalence (16, 33–35), a decrease in physical activity (36–37), an increased consumption of high-fat diets (38), and decreased knowledge about health (33).

SES and Physiological Processes

If SES is linked to health outcomes in a causative way, we should expect that it is also linked to physiological systems relevant to specific disorders (Figure 1.2, Category 5). Unfortunately, little research has examined this issue. Most large epidemiological data sets that contain good measures of SES do not have detailed physiological data. At the same time, most laboratory studies with sophisticated physiological assessments fail to assess SES thoroughly. The possible exception to this is studies examining blood pressure where higher SES is related to lower blood pressure levels and a lower prevalence of hypertension (39–43). Hypertension, of course, is a risk factor for stroke, heart disease, and renal disease. Matthews et al. (44) recently examined the association of educational attainment with biological risk factors for heart disease in middle-aged women. They found that, with lower levels of education, the subjects' risk factor profiles were more atherogenic. Women with low SES had higher systolic blood pressure; low-density lipoprotein (LDL) cholesterol, apolipoprotein B, and triglyceride levels; fasting and 2-hour glucose values; 2-hour insulin values; and body mass indices and lower high-density lipoprotein (HDL) cholesterol levels and HDL/LDL ratio. Recently, Wilson et al. (45) found an inverse association between plasma fibrinogen concentration and three measures of SES (income, education, and lifetime occupation) after controlling for several covariants. In a comprehensive review of the literature on SES and obesity, Sobal and Stunkard (46) reported that, in developed countries, there was a strong inverse relationship between SES and obesity among women, with mixed results in men and children. Conversely, in developing countries, there was a *positive* association between SES and obesity among men, women, and children (46).

SOCIODEMOGRAPHIC FACTORS AND SES

Although the SES-health gradient is seen in every demographic group in the United States in which it has been examined, certain sociodemographic factors may influence the level of SES and the magnitude and nature of the SES association with health. These sociodemographic factors include age, ethnicity, gender, and location (Figure 1.2, Category 1).

Ethnicity, SES, and Health

The moderating effects of sociodemographic variables are perhaps most clearly seen with ethnicity, especially regarding differences between blacks and whites. It is well known that ethnicity influences SES in the United States. For example, African-Americans have a significantly lower SES than whites by every measure (47, 48). What is not often recognized, however, is that at most levels of SES, morbidity and mortality rates are higher for blacks than for whites. Using data from the 1986 National Health Interview Survey, Pappas et al. (49) reported that, even given the same educational attainment, mortality rates are higher among black men and women compared with their white counterparts (Figures 1.3 and 1.4). The black-white disparity is especially striking at the low end of the SES hierarchy. These data are particularly relevant given that black-white differences in health are often attributed to group differences in SES. That is, if blacks and whites were "matched" on SES, the group differences in health would be eliminated or at least substantially reduced. Indeed, some research indicates that ethnic group differences in SES can account for group differences in some health outcomes (11, 42). Yet, the Pappas et al. (49) data suggest that the issue may be more complex than is generally acknowledged. More importantly, however, is the possibility that there may be ethnic group differences in the nature and experience of SES. If this were so, research designed to understand the processes responsible for the SES-health gradient should be ethnic group specific and should not stop at the level of explaining group differences. This issue is addressed in the following section.

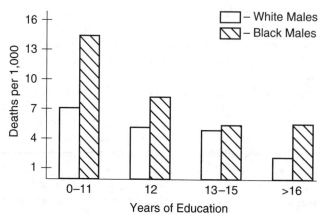

FIGURE 1.3 Mortality rate in males by ethnicity and education (From Pappas et al. (49), with permission.)

Ethnicity, SES, and Environmental Exposures

Clear relationships have been found between ethnicity, SES, and residential, social, and occupational environments (Figure 1.2, Category 3). Demographic research has shown that blacks in the largest United States metropolitan areas experience a phenomenon called "hypersegregation" or an extreme level of residential isolation from other groups and an associated "isolation from the amenities, opportunities, and resources that affect social and economic well-being" (50). This hypersegregation is the result of a number of factors, but most notable is the severe and pervasive housing discrimination against blacks at every level of SES, especially at the low end (51). This

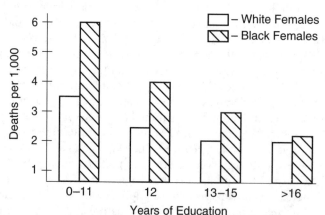

FIGURE 1.4 Mortality rate in females by ethnicity and education (From Pappas et al. (49), with permission.)

residential discrimination and resulting hypersegregation has social, economic, and ultimately health consequences.

William Wilson (52) showed that poverty is associated with different residential environments for blacks than for whites. Among residents of the five largest cities in the United States, Wilson found that in 1980, 68% of all poor whites lived in census-defined *non*poverty areas, whereas only 15% of poor blacks and 20% of poor Hispanics lived in nonpoverty areas. Furthermore, whereas only 7% of whites lived in extreme poverty areas, 39% of all poor blacks and 32% of all poor Hispanics lived in extreme poverty areas. Given the data presented earlier on the effects of living in impoverished environments on health (19), it is possible that residential environments partially explain the disparity in health outcomes between poor blacks and poor whites.

Furthermore, potentially health protective social relationships may occur less often in high-poverty environments. African-Americans residing in high-poverty areas have a higher percentage of individuals reporting being unmarried, having no current partner, and having no best friend compared with those living in nonpoverty areas. These findings on the relative lack of potentially supportive social relationships have also been observed in whites (53, 54). Finally, African-Americans in general, but especially low-income blacks, are disproportionately exposed to hazardous waste facilities and uncontrolled toxic waste sites (55).

Given these substantial differences in residential environments, researchers should be cautious in comparing poor blacks with poor whites on variables related to SES. As quoted in Wilson (52), "simple comparisons between poor whites and poor blacks would be confounded with the fact that poor whites reside in areas which are ecologically and economically different from poor blacks. Any observed relationships involving race would reflect, to some unknown degree, the relatively superior ecological niche many poor whites occupy with respect to jobs, marriage opportunities, and exposure to conventional role models" (56). Thus, even when statistical controls for SES "explain" ethnic group differences in health, researchers should be cognizant of the fact that the processes by which SES influences health may not be uniform across groups based on differences in residential environments.

Ethnicity, SES, and Psychological and Behavioral Factors

Relatively little research has examined interactions of ethnicity, SES, and psychological and behavioral factors related to health. Literature on ethnic differences in health behavior frequently statistically control for SES rather than examining its interaction with ethnicity. Of the studies that have looked at these interactions, findings suggest that blacks with lower SES have a higher risk profile than other groups, which could possibly account for their higher mortality rate.

John Barefoot et al. (28), using a national sample, showed that Cook/Medley hostility scores were higher for nonwhites (who were predominantly black) compared with whites at most levels of SES, but especially at the low end of SES. Because the Cook/Medley scale taps into feelings of cynicism, perceived threat, and mistrust, one could interpret these findings as evidence of *adaptive* coping responses by poorer blacks to the more threatening environments in which many reside. However, although such responses are potentially adaptive on one hand, they may increase the risk for heart disease (57). Kessler and Neighbors (58) found that blacks with low SES reported more stress in their lives than did whites with low SES and upper income blacks. Finally, some epidemiological studies have documented a higher prevalence of smoking among blacks, especially among low-income blacks, who are at the greatest risk for lung cancer and heart disease (59)

Ethnicity, SES, and Physiological Processes

Although black-white differences have been observed on a number of physiological variables, few studies have examined the interaction of SES and ethnicity. The one exception is in the area of obesity where black women have been shown to have a higher prevalence during their adult years compared with black men, white women, and white men. Compared with white women, the prevalence of obesity in black women is higher at every level of SES, but especially among persons with lower SES (60, 61). Finally, although black-white differences have been observed in studies of cardiovascular reactivity (62) few analyses have examined the interactions of ethnicity with SES. A recent study by Armstead et al. (63) found SES to be inversely associated with reactivity to a stressful interview among black women but not among white women.

In conclusion, given the differences in the nature and experience of SES in blacks and whites, we suggest future research focus more carefully on how SES might be influencing health outcomes differently in the two groups. We further suggest that the effects of SES on behavioral and psychosocial functioning be explored in other cultural groups including Asian-Americans, Latinos, and Native Americans.

SES AND OTHER SOCIODEMOGRAPHICS: AGE, GENDER AND LOCATION

Relative to ethnicity, there has been relatively less research on the interactions of SES with age, gender, or location as they relate to health outcomes. However, there is sufficient evidence to warrant a closer examination of how SES interacts with these sociodemographic variables.

Age

The relationship between SES and health begins at the earliest stages of life. For example, according to *Healthy People 2000*, approximately three-fourths of the deaths in the 1st month of life and 60% of all infant deaths occurred among low birth weight infants. Low and very low birth weight births are associated with lower SES.

Among children aged 1 to 14 years, the leading cause of death is unintentional injuries, which account for nearly one-half of all childhood deaths. The rate of unintentional injuries is especially high among Native American children (67), although no clear SES gradient has been reported. According to a review of the SES and child health literature (68), an SES-health linkage has been found with the following health problems: lead poisoning, vision problems, otitis media and hearing loss, cytomegalic inclusion disease, and iron deficiency anemia. In addition, mental retardation, learning disorders, and emotional and behavioral problems also occur at greater frequency among children with lower SES (65).

Among adolescents and young adults (ages 15–24 years), unintentional injuries associated with motor vehicle accidents, homicide, and suicide are the leading cause of death. Of these, SES is mostly clearly associated with homicide, especially for young black men (67).

There have been a handful of reports examining the relationship between age, SES, and health in the adult population. Studies have reported that the SES differential is most apparent during the middle years (69–71) but may be apparent even among the very old (72).

To address the question of the interaction of age and SES on health, House et al. (73) examined data from both the Americans' Changing Lives (ACL) Survey and the 1985 National Health Interview Survey (NHIS). Using a composite measure of SES from the ACL that combined income and occupation to create four SES categories (lower, lower-middle, upper-middle, and upper), House et al. found that, for the youngest cohort (persons 25–34 years of age), there was virtually no effect for SES on the number of chronic health conditions, functional status, and limitations of daily activities. Of individuals in the lowest SES category, the prevalence of chronic conditions peaked between ages 55 and 64 years; in the two highest SES categories, this peak did not occur until after age 75. The same general pattern was true for functional status and limitation of daily activities, i.e., practically no differences related to SES among persons 25 to 34 years of age, striking differences between ages 55 and 64, and a convergence of SES groups for persons older than age 75. These findings were generally replicated in the NHIS data. Interestingly, in the House et al. study, younger persons of lower SES experienced a degree of health impairment similar to that of *older* persons of higher SES. Thus, the House et al. findings suggest that "upper socioeconomic groups substantially postpone functional limitations into the later years of life, but the lower socioeconomic groups experience significant functional limitations quite early."

Gender

In the United States, there are striking gender differences in SES. In families that consist of a married couple with children younger than 18 years of age, the median annual income is approximately $41,000. If the wife is absent from these families (male householder/wife absent), this figure drops to $31,000. With the husband absent from these families (female householder/husband absent), the median income is only approximately $18,000 (74). In other words, female householder families earn only 57% of male householder families. Similarly, the median income for single females without children is only 62% of that of single males without children. In addition, investment in education does not bring comparable income returns for men and women. Female college graduates earn only 65% of the income of male college graduates: female high school graduates earn only 68% of the income [of] male high school graduates. Even more striking is the gender difference in the percentage of low-income households. For married couples, only 10% make less than $15,000/year; for families in which the female is absent (male householder), the rate is 18%. However, this rate jumps to 42% for households in which the husband is absent (female householder). In nonfamily households that make less than $15,000/year, the rate is 32% for males and 51% for females.

The SES-health link has been confirmed for men and women. However, some gender differences have been observed in the impact of SES over time. Feldman et al. (75) examined SES-related mortality rates for middle-aged and older white men and women using 1960 data from the Matched Record Survey and 1971 to 1984 data from the first National Health and Nutrition Examination Survey. Although death rates declined between 1960 and 1971 to 1984 for men and women, the decline was more rapid for the more educated men compared with those who were less educated. This led to a stronger relationship between SES and mortality rates among men in 1971 to 1984. In contrast, the decline in death rates for women was about the same in 1960 and 1971 to 1984 regardless of educational attainment. Thus, the effects of education on mortality rate became stronger over time among men but remained unchanged over time in women. These gender differences were largely due to greater SES effects on cardiovascular disease mortality rates in men than in women. Similarly, Pappas et al. (49) showed that, between 1960 and 1986, the association of educational attainment and mortality rate increased by 20% in black and white women, but by more than 100% in men, which suggests that the SES-related disparity in mortality rate increased over time to a greater degree for men than for women.

Beyond the aforementioned trends in SES-health relationships over time, there are clearly other issues pertaining to SES and gender that require further examination. Obesity is a case in point. According to Sobal (76), the strongest inverse relationship between obesity and SES in developed countries is for adult women, with a more mixed pattern for other age-sex groups. In a study of black women, Croft et al. (77) found an inverse relationship of SES to age-adjusted body mass index in women but not in men. Other studies suggest complex interactions between gender, ethnicity, and SES with respect to body weight. Some evidence indicates that, although there may be a strictly inverse relationship between body mass and educational attainment among white women, there may be an inverted-U association among black women and among both black and white men, with body mass reaching a maximum around 8 to 12 years of education for black women and around 12 to 15 years of education for black and white men (78).

The SES and gender interactions on body mass may be associated with variations in physical activity level. In a study of physical activity in men and women with lower and higher SES, Ford et al. (36) found that women with lower SES reported the least amount of physical activity, with the highest amount being reported by the women with higher SES. Men with higher and lower SES reported activity levels that fell between these two female groups.

There are a number of other issues relating to gender, SES, and health that warrant further investigation. These include SES interactions with women's multiple home and work roles (79), the greater exposure to hazardous occupations in low-income men (80), experience of gender discrimination by SES status (81, 82), the potential differential impact of husbands' versus wives' SES on family SES and health outcomes (83), and the influence of SES on maternal and reproductive health (20). The association of SES with pregnancy outcomes is especially critical given the high rates of infant mortality and low birth weight infants among women with low SES. Even among those low birth weight infants who survive, they may be at higher risk for adult health problems (84, 85).

Location

Although SES and health have shown an inverse relationship in practically all developed countries, recent studies suggest that a *positive* correlation may be observed in some developing countries for certain health problems. Bunker et al. (86) found that higher occupational status among male civil servants in Nigeria was related to higher blood pressure levels. This affect was not explained by body mass index, alcohol intake, or years in the urban environment. In a separate study of Nigerian factory workers, education was found to have a significant positive association with blood pressure that was independent of age, body mass index, pulse, and alcohol consumption (87). These recent findings are provocative and suggest that we cannot always assume that the inverse SES-health gradient is universal in the developing world.

Even in developed countries, differences in income distribution may be predictive of national health outcomes. Studies by Wilkinson (88) suggest that, in Western industrialized countries where income distribution is more equitable (defined as the percentage of gross national income received by the least well-off families), there is an overall longer average life expectancy. Moreover, Wilkinson found a striking inverse relationship ($r = -.73$) between annual changes in the percent of the population in relative poverty and the annual changes in life expectancy. That is, those countries that evidenced the largest annual decrease in the national poverty rate also experienced the greatest annual increase in life expectancy.

FUTURE RESEARCH DIRECTIONS

In an area of research as complex and encompassing as SES and health, there is an almost infinite array of potential research directions and unanswered questions. However, we would like to focus on three areas that represent a good portion of the deficits in our knowledge of SES-health affects: measurement of SES, mechanisms linking SES and health, and SES interventions.

Measurement

Without question, education, income, and occupation as measures of SES have been extraordinarily useful for health researchers, despite some methodological challenges they present (83). As useful as these three measures have been, there may be measures of SES that are of equal or greater predictive value in some populations. Some of these alternative measures of SES are listed in Figure 1.2 (Category 2) and include indices of family wealth: perceived SES; economic mobility across generations; community-level measures of SES; SES during childhood; the use of trading or bartering for goods or services; material possessions such as cattle, land, and housing structures in some countries; and, for cross-national studies, national income distribution. With respect to family wealth (defined as liquid assets), ethnic group differences have been found, even with the same level of family income. The median family wealth for whites in the United States is $17,500, but only approximately $300 for blacks and $32 for Hispanics (89, 90). This may be at least one explanation for the black-white differences in health status at similar levels of educational attainment (49). Also, it is unclear how health is related to intergenerational mobility, that is, moving up or down the income or occupational hierarchy or up the educational ladder relative to one's parents (91, 92). It would also be interesting to know whether exposure to poverty during childhood has an impact on adult health (92, 93), and if so, are there critical periods during childhood when economic deprivation is most detrimental (85). In addition, in some rural areas of developing countries, the measure of SES by material possessions such as land, the nature of housing structures, or cattle might be useful predictors of health status (94). Finally, some groups in the United States, particularly in some ethnic minority populations, may rely more on trading, exchange, or bartering for goods and services in addition to the cash economy. Here, caution must be taken then in comparing these groups with those who depend solely on a cash economy to purchase services, food, or health care (95).

Mechanisms and Interventions

Beyond these measurement issues, a good deal of the needed research on SES and health could be organized using the 2 × 2 matrix shown in Figure 1.5. The matrix identifies two principle research areas: a) mechanisms and b) interventions that might reduce the impact of SES. It also identifies two groups of potential modifiers of SES mechanisms and interventions: sociodemographic factors and the SES gradient.

Mechanisms. First, we need a more complete understanding of the mechanisms linking SES and health. Research in this area is uneven in that we know a great deal about the influence of SES on health-damaging behaviors such as smoking and lack of exercise but practically nothing about how SES affects physiological processes. We also need to be cognizant of the potential modifying effects of sociodemographic factors (discussed earlier) and the SES gradient. The SES gradient presents special conceptual challenges (16). To illustrate this point, Figure 1.6 shows different points of comparison along the SES gradient. It would be important to determine whether the mechanisms that account for the health differences between say, Groups A and B

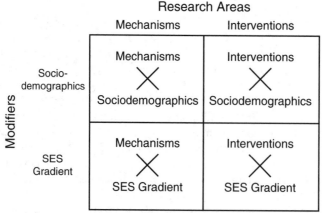

FIGURE 1.5   Areas in which research on SES and health is needed

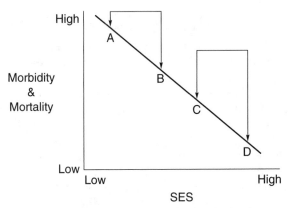

FIGURE 1.6   Possible comparisons along the SES gradient

along this gradient, are similar or different from those that explain the differences between Groups C and D. At the present time, it is unclear whether the mechanisms that mediate the health differences between people in poverty compared with the middle class are the same as those that are responsible for health differences between the middle class and the affluent.

One possibility in this regard is that, as one moves up the SES ladder, the nature of residential environments may change from those with largely health-damaging effects (poverty areas) to those with a relative lack of such deleterious effects, or what could be called low-risk areas (middle-class suburbs). However, the residential environments of the affluent may even be health *enhancing* when one considers the potential positive affect elicited either by living in a beautiful wooded area or next to a lake, by owning a swimming pool or an alarm system, or even by simply living in a quiet area. There may also be SES gradient differences in daily hassles, optimism, or perceived control over life circumstances, especially in the presence of higher demands in persons with lower SES. Any of these processes could have short-term physiological effects and long-term health consequences and should be examined as a function of age, gender, and ethnicity.

Interventions. Finally, given the SES association with health, the question becomes what do we do about it. In other words, do we have effective interventions for countering the untoward effects of low SES? Certainly, we have effective interventions for say, reducing smoking regardless of SES, but one must ask whether it is more difficult for people struggling with chronic economic difficulties to adopt and maintain healthful lifestyles compared with the more affluent (1, 18, 96, 97). If it is more difficult, we need to develop innovative strategies targeted specifically toward persons with lower SES. For example, are there coping strategies or skills that could be taught to assist low-income persons with life circumstances that may be characterized by high demand and low control?

In addition, we have to ask ourselves this question: what is the role of health researchers in exploring interventions to *improve* SES (i.e., increasing educational attainment or income)? If we assume that SES is causally related to adverse health outcomes, should not we, as health professionals, also be concerned with exploring ways to improve SES, especially with approaches that facilitate the movement of people out of poverty? This could have the biggest payoff in terms of influencing the mechanisms that link SES and health. If we begin to think this way, it raises some intriguing research questions that have not heretofore been in the domain of "health" research. For example, what are effective methods for reducing the high school dropout rate? How do we increase participation in literacy programs? What is the socioeconomic impact of job training programs? What are effective strategies for reducing housing discrimination that affects low and high SES African-Americans? What is the economic impact of free, state-supported higher education? Finally, are there specific *skills* that will enable individuals to improve their SES? For instance, what skills are required to achieve a higher-paying or higher-status job, move out of a high-risk residential environment, or improve educational attainment through adult education? Can these skills be taught and used effectively to improve SES? And if so, is the risk for illness reduced?

In conclusion, SES is indeed a ubiquitous aspect of health functioning. As such, it touches on the research and clinical interests of practically everyone interested in the biopsychosocial approach to health. Our challenge, then, is to use the unique advantages of the multidisciplinary approach to address this critical public health concern.

REFERENCES

1. Williams DR: Socioeconomic differentials in health: A review and redirection. Soc Psychol Q 32:81–99, 1990
2. House J: Social structure and personality. In Rosenberg M, Turner R (eds): Social Psychology: Sociological Perspectives. New York, Basic Books, 1981, 525–561
3. Robinson R, Kelly J: Class as conceived by Marx and Dahrendorf: Effects on income inequality and politics in the United States and Great Britain. Am Sociological Rev 44: 38–58, 1979
4. Wright EO, Perrone L: Marxist class categories and income inequity. Am Sociological Rev 42:32–55, 1977
5. Marx K: Wage-Labor and Capital. New York, International Publishers, 1849
6. Dahrendorf R: Class and Class conflict in Industrial Society. Stanford, CA, Stanford University Press, 1959
7. Weber M: Economy and Society. New York, Bedminister, 1968
8. Davey Smith G, Carroll D, Rankin S, et al: Socioeconomic differentials in mortality: Evidence from Glasgow graveyards. BMJ 306:1554–1557, 1992
9. Chapin S, Fello A: Deaths among taxpayers and non-taxpayers: Income tax. Providence 1865. Am J Public Health 14:647–651, 1924
10. Fox AJ, Goldblatt P, Jones D: Social class mortality differentials: Artefact, selection or life circumstance. J Epidemiol Community Health 39:1–8, 1985
11. Haan MN, Kaplan GA, Syme SL: Socioeconomic status and health: Old observations and new thoughts. In Bunker J. Gomby D, Kehrer B (eds): Pathways to Health: The Role of Social Factors. Menlo Park, CA, Henry H. Kaiser Family Foundation, 1989, 76–135
12. Pincus T, Kallahan L, Burkhauser R: Most chronic diseases are reported more frequently by individuals with fewer than 12 years of formal education in the ages 18–64 in the United States population. J Chronic Dis 40:865–874, 1987
13. Williams RB, Barefoot JC, Kaliff RM, et al: Prognostic significance of social and economic resources among medically treated patients with angiographically documented coronary artery disease. JAMA 267:520–524, 1992
14. Ruberman W, Weinblatt E, Goldberg JD, et al: Psychosocial influences on mortality after myocardial infarction. N Engl J Med 11:552–559, 1984

15. Adler N, Boyce T, Chesney M, et al: Socioeconomic inequities in health: No easy solution. JAMA 269:3140–3145, 1993
16. Adler N, Boyce T, Chesney M, et al: Socioeconomic status and health: The challenge of the gradient. Am Psychol 49:15–24, 1994
17. Marmot MG, Kogevinas M, Elston MA: Social/economic status and disease. Annu Rev Public Health 8:111–135, 1987
18. Carroll D, Bennett P, Davey Smith G: Socio-economic health inequities: Their origins and implications. Psychol Health 8:295–316, 1993
19. Haan MN, Kaplan GA, Camacho T: Poverty and health: Prospective evidence from the Alameda County study. Am J Epidemiol 125:989–998, 1987
20. Krieger N: Women and social class: A methodological study comparing individual, household and census measures as predictors of black/white differences in reproductive history. J Epidemiol Community Health 45:35–42, 1991
21. McLeod JD, Kessler RC: Socioeconomic status differences in vulnerability to undesirable life events. J Health Soc Behav 31:162–172, 1990
22. Dohrenwend BS: Social class and stressful life events. In Hare E and Wing J (eds): Psychiatric Epidemiology. London, Oxford University Press, 1970, 313–319
23. Dohrenwend B: Social status and stressful life events. J Pers Soc Psychol 28:225–235, 1973
24. Kessler RC: Stress, social status and psychological distress. J Health Soc Behav 20:259–273, 1979
25. Kessler RC: A disaggregation of the relationship between socioeconomic and psychological distress. Am Sociological Rev 47:752–764, 1982
26. Murphy JM, Oliveri D, Monson R, et al: Depression and anxiety in relation to social status. Arch Gen Psychiatry 48:223–229, 1991
27. Kaplan G, Roberts R, Camacho T, et al: Psychosocial predictors of depression: Prospective evidence from the Human Population Laboratory Studies. Am J Epidemiol 125:206–220, 1987
28. Barefoot J, Peterson B, Dahlstrom W, et al: Hostility patterns and health implications: Correlates of Cook-Medley Hostility Scale scores in a national survey. Health Psychol 10:18–24, 1991
29. Scherwitz, Perkins L, Chesney M, et al: Cook-Medley Hostility Scale and subsets: Relation to demographic and psychosocial characteristics in young adults in the CARDIA study, Psychosom Med 53:36–49, 1991
30. Phares E: Locus of control. In London H. Exner E (eds): Dimensions of Personality. New York, Wiley, 1976 263–314
31. Steele R: The relationship of race, sex, social class and social mobility to depression in normal adults. J Soc Psychol 104:37–47, 1978
32. Battle E, Rotter J: Children's feelings of personal control as related to social class and ethnic group. J Pers 31:482–490, 1963
33. Winkleby M, Fortmann S, Barrett D: Social class disparities in risk factors for disease: Eight-year prevalence patterns by level of education. Prev Med 19:1–12, 1990
34. Marmot M, Smith GD, Stansfield S, et al: Health inequities among British civil servants: The Whitehall II study. Lancet 337:1387–1393, 1991
35. Escobedo L, Anda R, Smith P, et al: Sociodemographic characteristics of cigarette smoking initiation in the United States. JAMA 264:1550–1555, 1990
36. Ford E, Merritt R, Heath G, et al: Physical activity behaviors in lower and higher socioeconomic status populations. Am J Epidemiol 133:1246–1256, 1991
37. Cauley JA, Donfield S, Laport R, et al: Physical activity by socioeconomic status in two population based cohorts. Med Sci Sports Exerc 23:343–352, 1991
38. Jeffrey R, French S, Foster J, et al: Socioeconomic status differences in health behaviors related to obesity: the healthy worker project. Int J Obes Relat Metab Disord 15:689–696, 1991
39. Dyer R, Stamler J, Shekelle R, et al: The relationship of education to blood pressure: Findings on 40,000 employed Chicagoans. Circulation 54:987–992, 1976

40. Hypertension Detection and Follow-Up Program Cooperative Group: Race, education, and prevalence of hypertension. Am J Epidemiol 106:351–361, 1977

41. Syme SL, Oakse T, Friedman G, et al: Social class and racial differences in blood pressure. Am J Public Health 64:619–620, 1974

42. Keil J, Tyroler H, Sandifer S, et al: Hypertension: The effects of social class and racial admixture: The results of a cohort study in the black population of Charleston, South Carolina. Am J Public Health 67:634–639, 1977

43. James SA: Psychosocial and environmental factors in black hypertension. In Hall W, Saunders E, Shulman N (eds): Hypertension in Blacks: Epidemiology, Pathophysiology, and Treatment. Chicago, Yearbook Medical Publishers, 1985, 132–143

44. Matthews K, Kelsey S, Mellahn E, et al: Educational attainment and behavioral and biologic risk factors for coronary heart disease in middle-aged women. Am J Epidemiol 129:1132–1144, 1989

45. Wilson T, Kaplan GA, Kauhanen J, et al: Association between plasma fibrinogen concentration in five socioeconomic indices in the Kuopio Ischemic Heart Disease Risk Factor Study. Am J Epidemiol 137:292–300, 1993

46. Sobal J, Stunkard AJ: Socioeconomic status and obesity: A review of the literature. Psychol Bull 105:260–275, 1989

47. Farley R, Allen W: The Color Line and the Quality of Life in America. New York, Oxford University Press, 1987

48. Jaynes G, Williams R, Jr: A Common Destiny: Blacks and American Society. Washington, DC, National Academy Press, 1989

49. Pappas G, Queen S, Hadden W, et al: The increasing disparity and mortality between socioeconomic groups in the United States, 1960 and 1986. N Engl J Med 329:103–109, 1993

50. Massey DS, Denton NA: Hypersegregation in U.S. metropolitan areas: Black and Hispanic segregation among five dimensions. Demography 26:373, 1989

51. Massey DS, Denton NA: American Apartheid: Segregation and the Making of the Underclass. Cambridge, MA, Harvard University Press, 1993.

52. Wilson WJ: The Truly Disadvantaged: The Inner City, the Underclass, and Public Policy. Chicago, University of Chicago Press, 1987

53. Belle D: The impact of poverty on social networks and supports. Marriage Fam Rev 5:89–103, 1982

54. Berkman L, Breslow L: Health and Ways of Living. New York, Oxford University Press, 1983

55. Bullard RD: Dumping in Dixie: Race, Class, and Environmental Quality. Boulder, CO, Westview Press, 1994

56. Testa, M. Personal communication to William Wilson, cited in reference 52.

57. Barefoot JC, Dahlstrom W, Williams RB: Hostility, CHD incidence and total mortality: A 25-year follow-up study of 255 physicians. Psychosom Med 45:59–63, 1983

58. Kessler R, Neighbors H: A new perspective on the relationship among race, social class and psychological distress. J Health Soc Behav 27:107–115, 1986

59. Novotny T, Warner K, Kendrick J, et al: Smoking by blacks and whites: Socioeconomic and demographic differences. Am J Public Health 78:1187–1189, 1987

60. Gillum RF: Overweight and obesity in black women: A review of published data from the National Center for Health Statistics. J Nat Med Assoc 79:865, 1987

61. Kumanyika S: Obesity in black women. Epidemiol Rev 9:31, 1987

62. Anderson NB, McNeilly M, Myers H: Autonomic reactivity and hypertension in blacks: A review and proposed model. Ethn Dis 1:154–170, 1991

63. Armstead CA, Anderson NB, Lawler KA: The Interaction of Socioeconomic Status, Ethnicity and Cardiovascular Reactivity Among Women. Presented at the annual meeting of the American Psychosomatic Society, Boston, 1994

64. Centers for Disease Control: National Vital Statistics. Heightsville, MD, Department of Health and Human Services,

65. President's Commission on Mental Retardation: Preventing the New Morbidity: A Guide for State Planning for the Prevention of Mental Retardation and Related Disabilities As-

sociated with Socioeconomic Conditions. Washington, DC, Department of Health and Human Services, 1988

66. Secretary's Task Force on Black and Minority Health: Report of the Secretary's Task Force on Black and Minority Health. Washington, DC, Department of Health and Human Services, 1985
67. Public Health Service: Healthy People 2000: National Health Promotion and Disease Prevention Objectives. Washington, DC, Department of Health and Human Services, 1990
68. Starfield EL: Child health and social status. Pediatrics 69:550–557, 1982
69. National Center for Health Statistics: Health Characteristics According to Family and Personal Income. Series 10, 137. Heightsville, MD, Department of Health and Human Services, 1985
70. Antonovsky A: Social class, life expectancy and overall mortality. Milbank 45:37–73, 1967
71. Katagawa E, Hauser P: Differential Mortality in the United States: A Study in Socioeconomic Epidemiology. Cambridge, MA, Harvard University Press, 1973
72. National Center for Health Statistics: Health Statistics on Older Persons: United States, 1986—Vital and Health Statistics. Series 3, No. 25. (Publication No. PHS 37-1409). Heightsville, MD, Department of Health and Human Services 1987
73. House JS, Kessler RC, Herzog A, et al: Age, socioeconomic status and health. Milbank Q 68:383–411, 1990
74. United States Bureau of the Census: Statistical abstract of the United States, 1993 113th Edition. Washington, DC, United States Bureau of the Census, 1993
75. Feldman J, Makuc D, Kleinman J, et al: National trends in educational differentials in mortality. Am J Epidemiol 129:919–933, 1989
76. Sobal J: Obesity and socioeconomic status: A framework for examining relationships between physical and social variables. Med Anthropol 13:231–247, 1991
77. Croft J, Strogatz D, James S, et al: Socioeconomic and behavioral correlates of body mass index in black adults: The Pitt County Study. Am J Public Health 82:785–787, 1992
78. Leigh J, Fries J, Hubert H: Gender and race differences in the correlation between body mass and education in 1971–1975 NHANES I. J Epidemiol Community Health 46:191–196, 1992
79. Wortman C, Biernat M, Lang E: Coping with role overload. In Frankenhaeuser M, Lundberg U, Chesney M, et al (eds): Women, Work and Health: Stress and Opportunities. New York, Plenum Press, 1991, 85–110
80. Waldron I: Effects of labor force participation on sex differences in mortality and morbidity. In Frankenhaeuser M, Lundberg U, Chesney M, et al (eds): Women, Work and Health: Stress and Opportunities. New York, Plenum Press, 1991, 17–38
81. Krieger N: Racial and gender discrimination: Risk factors for high blood pressure? Soc Sci Med 7:1273–1281, 1990
82. LaDou J: Women workers: International issues. Occup Med 8:673–683, 1993
83. Liberatos P, Link B, Kelsey J: The measurement of social class in epidemiology. Epidemiol Rev 10:87–121, 1988
84. Barker DJP: Fetal and Infant Origins of Adult Disease. London, British Medical Journal, 1992
85. Ben-Shlomo Y, Davey Smith G: Deprivation in infancy or in adult life: Which is more important for mortality risk? Lancet 1:532–534, 1991
86. Bunker C, Ukoli F, Nwankwo M, et al: Factors associated with hypertension in Nigerian civil servants. Prev Med 21:710–722, 1992
87. Ogunlisi A, Osotimehin B, Abbiyessuku F, et al: Blood pressure and educational level among factory workers in Ibadan, Nigeria. J Hum Hypertens 5:375–380, 1991
88. Wilkinson RG: Income distribution and life expectancy. BMJ 305:165–168, 1992
89. Kaplan G: Research directions in health policy implications. Presented at the joint symposium of the American Psychosomatic Society and Society of Behavioral Medicine "Super-highways for Disease: Shared Determinants of Health Outcomes," Boston, 1994
90. Smith JP: Racial and ethnic differences in wealth using the HRC. Unpublished report. University of Michigan, Ann Arbor 1993

91. Stern J: Social mobility and the interpretation of social class mortality differentials. J Soc Policy 12:27–49, 1983
92. Nystrom Peck AM: Childhood environment, intergenerational mobility, and adult health—evidence from Swedish data. J Epidemiol Community Health 46:71–74, 1992
93. Lynch JW, Kaplan G, Cohen R, et al: Childhood and adult socioeconomic status as predictors of mortality in Finland. Lancet 343:524–527, 1994
94. Bourdillon M: The Shona Peoples. Gweru, Zimbabwe, Mambo Press, 1987
95. Anderson NB, Task Group Members: Summary of Task Group Recommendations from the National Conference on Sociocultural & Behavioral Perspectives on Ethnicity & Health. *Health Psychol,* in press, 1995
96. Pugh, Power C, Goldblatt T, et al: Women's lung cancer mortality, socio-economic status and changing smoking patterns. Soc Sci Med 32:1105–1110, 1991
97. Kario J. Koskenvuo M: A prospective study of psychological and socioeconomic characteristics, health behavior and morbidity in cigarette smokers prior to quitting compared to persistent smokers and non-smokers. J Clin Epidemiol 41:139–150, 1988

ILLUSTRATIVE READING 1.2

The illustrative reading by Ewalt and Mokuau critically and from a culturally sensitive perspective examines the fundamental social work value of self-determination. These authors give us an illustration of the importance of respecting and understanding differences in worldview (paradigms) even with such a basic, almost taken-for-granted, value of social work as self-determination. They stress the difference in a eurocentric/ dominant paradigm view of self-determination as highly individualistic decision making rights and a Pacific worldview that stresses self-determination as decision making that is intricately interwoven with group and collective rights and responsibilities. Ewalt and Mokuau suggest that even among some Western persons (persons of lower socioeconomic status and women) a "collectivist or group centered" view of self-determination may be much more genuine, meaningful and appropriate than the traditional "individualistic" perspective on self-determination. This reading helps us to begin to critically examine in culturally appropriate and sensitive ways, traditional assumptions about the meaning of even such a basic social work value as self-determination.

Self-Determination from a Pacific Perspective

Patricia L. Ewalt and Noreen Mokuau[*]

Self-determination is viewed as a fundamental principle of social work. Indeed, Levy (1983) observed a "reflection in the social work literature of a preoccupation, if not an obsession, with the concept and ramifications of client self-determination" (p. 904). An examination of such a fundamental principle provides an opportunity to assess its relevance and applicability for multicultural populations.

It has been proposed that the principle of self-determination is universal. However, in its current use, the term "self-determination" is overly reliant on Northern European–American individualistic values; therefore, the practice implications for social work are substantial. Practice that urges individuals toward self-realization without consideration of group-oriented values is discordant with non-Western orientations (Budman, Lipson, & Meleis, 1992; Inclan & Hernandez, 1992; Pedersen, Fukuyama, & Heath, 1989; Tung, 1991) and may be inappropriate for many Western people as well (Papajohn & Spiegel, 1975).

This article examines prevailing interpretations of self-determination as suggested in the literature and also presents the high valuation on group preferences among Pacific peoples using case examples. The article suggests how social work practice can be improved through a reinterpretation of the meaning of self-determination.

INTERPRETATIONS OF SELF-DETERMINATION

Separation from the Group

Weick and Pope (1988) summarized *self-determination* as "clients' right to make their own decisions, their right to actively participate in the helping process, and their right to lead a life of their own choosing" (p. 10). Freedberg (1989) provided a similar definition: "self-determination, that condition in which personal behavior emanates from a person's own wishes, choices, and decisions" (p. 33). In composing this definition, Freedberg relied on an essay by Berlin (1975), "Two Concepts of Liberty," in which the author discussed the freedom or liberty to do or be what one wants to do or be without interference by other people and the idea that humans are capable of rationally determining their own actions.

Thus, self-determination is clearly linked with the literature from which the prevailing middle-class American ethic of individualism is drawn:

> *The feeling of being in control is especially important to people whose parents and grandparents lived lives so dominated by insecurity that control—and self-reliance—became the prerequisites for nearly everything else. Greater control spells more security, and with sufficient security people can start to loosen unwanted social ties and to make more of their own choices about their lives.* (Gans, 1988, p. 2)

Rooted in individualism, self-determination is discussed in terms of freedom of the individual to exercise self-direction and choice (Hollis, 1966) and of full development of the personality and an inner capacity for knowing what is best (Weick & Pope, 1988). Indeed, as Gans (1988) delineated, freedom from group expectations is regarded as self-reliance, a sign of strength. Separation from the group, as contrasted with belonging to the group, is viewed as providing the security that people desire (Schwartz, 1989).

Equivalence to Maturity

Separation from external influences on one's decision making is so highly valued in the United States that autonomy is considered to be a benchmark of one's maturity. Personal control is viewed as fundamental to one's self-development (Gans, 1988), and the assumption exists that the more a person feels and acts autonomous of the group, the more healthy and mature the person.

In the individualistic view, external forces are enemies of self-determination. External forces of society are seen as constant threats to the individual's freedom to choose (Lemmon, 1983; Levy, 1983). Rarely is contributing to the group's well-being considered integral to self-determination, and rarely is placing the group's well-being first seen as signifying maturity.

GROUP WELL-BEING AS A COMPONENT OF SELF-DETERMINATION

A more complex understanding of self-determination, extending beyond identity solely with individualism, is provided by cultures other than those descended from Northern Europe. Inherent in many cultures are values that emphasize the collective over the individual as a perspective on self-determination. In addition, populations of color have experienced histories of oppression that have further affected their ideas of autonomy and maturity.

Oppression and Self-Determination

Dana (1981) emphasized the contrast between the views of middle-class, white Americans and people of color about self-determination:

> *The core belief of middle-class, white America in autonomy, or immanent self-sufficiency, has never been a major component of the heritage of minority groups [American Indians, African Americans, Hispanic Americans, and Asian Americans].*
>
> *All four of these minority groups differ from most white, middle-class people in their world view. They typically experience less personal power, feel less control over their own lives, and they may also feel that they should not be directly responsible for themselves or experience greater control over their own lives. Such world view differences suggest that many current mental health and rehabilitation practices requiring responsibility, initiative, and personal involvement for their success simply will not make sense to many minority persons. (p. 354)*

Pinderhughes (1983) provided insight into the relative meaninglessness of self-determination when people, their families, and their social groups are powerless: "The existence or non-existence of power on one level of human functioning . . . affects and is affected by its existence or nonexistence on other levels of functioning—for example, intrapsychic, familial, community–ethnic–cultural, and societal" (p. 332). Gutierrez (1990) explicated "the effect that [group] powerlessness has on reducing the ability to exercise personal control" (p. 149). Whereas white, middle-class people may desire self-reliance, people of color may "go it alone" out of despair. When the stresses become extreme and families are totally overwhelmed, they learn to function in an autonomous fashion and to value going it alone. This comes not from a goal of self-actualization and realization but from feeling a sense of being alone and without any help (Pinderhughes, 1983).

Yet this very separation from the group causes the family to become vulnerable through isolation. Enhancement of connection to and strengthening of the group is indicated as contrasting with strengthening of autonomy (Pinderhughes, 1983). Through considering the condition of oppression, one can appreciate that discerning appraisal is required to comprehend how the concept of self-determination may apply to each person. Self-expression is an insufficient criterion. Individual achievement, attained competitively and through deciding what is best for one's self or immediate family, may in fact be devalued both by the person and the group. As paradoxical as it may seem from an individualistic perspective, self-directedness may require a strengthening rather than a dissolution of the person's connection with and commitment to the group.

A PACIFIC PERSPECTIVE

Self-determination for the cultures of the Pacific region is defined by values of collective affiliation rather than by individualism. Pacific cultures are scattered across 64 million square miles of Pacific Ocean (Quigg, 1987) in the geographic areas of Melanesia, Micronesia, and Polynesia. There is a rich diversity among Pacific island cultures in historical origins, languages, social organization, levels of political integration, and lifestyle practices (Linnekin & Poyer, 1990; Oliver, 1988). Diversity also exists in acculturation and the degree to which Pacific peoples adopt the worldviews and values of American culture. However, within this diversity, there is a common emphasis on group affiliation that is the basis for a unique perspective on self-determination.

An essential element of Pacific island cultures is the affiliative nature of relationships: "The person is not an individual in our Western sense of the term. The person is instead a locus of shared biographies: personal histories of people's relationships with other people and with other things. The relationship defines the person, not vice-versa" (Lieber, 1990, p. 72). An individual is characterized by social relationships and a shared identity that comes from "sharing food, water, land, spirits, knowledge, work and social activities" (Linnekin & Poyer, 1990, p. 8). Illustrations of the importance of Pacific Islander group identity and cohesiveness are plentiful. For example, Micronesians such as the Trukese have traditionally relied on the matrilineage as a source of identity (Hezel, 1989). Polynesians such as the Maoris talk about "group rhythm" (Kanahele, 1986) and the importance of the gathering and uniting of people (Stirling & Salmond, 1985). The Chamorros of Guam in Polynesia emphasize traditional values of role interdependence and reciprocity (Untalan, 1991) in identity formation. The identities of the Solomon Islanders in Melanesia originate in strong attachments to the land and the interrelationships of the family system (Gegeo & Watson-Gegeo, 1985).

The pronounced value of group identity and cohesiveness among the diverse cultures of the Pacific region undergirds other major values and permeates lifestyle practices. The following sections examine the dominant position of values and practices of group affiliation among the two largest Pacific Islander populations in the United States—Hawaiian and Samoan.

Hawaiian Culture

In Hawaiian culture, the individual is viewed in the context of relationships. A person is defined by others and defines himself or herself by the quality of his or her relationships with family members, the community, the land, and the spiritual world

(Ito, 1987; Mokuau & Tauili'ili, 1992). According to Handy and Pukui (1977), the Hawaiian concept of the individual is most clearly depicted in the matrix of the *'ohana* (family). The family, which consists of relatives by blood, marriage, and adoption, extends on a genealogical continuum binding people from the past, present, and future. Emphasis is consistently placed on the needs of the family unit rather than on the needs of any individual member.

Three values that reflect the strong emphasis on relationships in the Hawaiian family and group are *laulima* (cooperation), *kokua* (helpfulness), and *lokahi* (unity). Kanahele (1986) described the integral nature of these values in Hawaiian culture:

> *The term laulima means many hands, and it expresses perfectly the Hawaiian sense of all persons in the family working together for a common purpose. Once established in the behavior of the basic 'ohana unit, cooperation was easily transferred to working with other 'ohana in a communal setting. . . . Inseparably linked with cooperation is the value of kokua . . . a willingness of individuals to work voluntarily with each other. (p. 347)*

Each member of a family or group has a defined assignment, and members "collaborate in unity (lokahi), subordinating personal glory to reaching the goals of the whole group" (pp. 347–348). Contributions to unity and harmony are more valued in Hawaiian culture than are competitive success or self-satisfaction (Howard, 1974).

Lifestyle practices that support the value of group affiliation are numerous and include honoring commitments to family and friends, providing aid to people in need, and engaging in situations of cooperative fellowship, even when these situations incur material deprivation for oneself (Howard, 1974).

Vignette 1. Leialoha, a Hawaiian man, is a skilled automobile mechanic who is consistently called on by family and friends to repair their personal cars. He is not known for turning people down and has willingly serviced relatives' and friends' cars at the end of his workday and often on weekends. He refuses monetary compensation, even though he still struggles with his own financial worries, and is most appreciative of the companionship and food that are shared with him once cars are repaired. Sometimes his generosity has extended to giving away special and costly automobile tools that family members or friends have admired. The frequent requests by family and friends are testimony to people's confidence in Leialoha's skills and their recognition of his inclination to help others.

Vignette 2. Debra, a Hawaiian woman, was interested in practicing medicine in the community in which she had recently completed her medical education. Here she was offered a physician's position with a reputable family clinic and a good salary. Combined with her comfortable living quarters and her network of friends, remaining in this community was an attractive option for Debra. However, her family, and in particular her parents, wished for Debra to establish her practice in the community in which she was raised. To do so would require her to move from the city back to her native community. Although there were a few moments of hesitation, Debra quickly adjusted and aligned her values with those of her family. She reasoned that by returning to her native community she would be reunited with her family and be available to provide medical care to members of her family and a community with severe health problems.

Samoan Culture

Samoan culture places a strong emphasis on relationships. "Dominant values . . . in Samoan culture focus on the family, communal relationships and the church" (Mokuau & Chang, 1991, p. 159). The family is viewed as the most important agency of human interactions (Territory of American Samoa, Office of the Governor, 1990).

Life is organized around the *aiga* (family) or the *aiga potopoto* (extended family), which are hierarchical systems with clearly defined roles. The highly structured organization of the family defines an individual's roles and responsibilities and guides the individual in interactions with others. In Samoan culture, older people have status over young people, titled people such as *matais* (chiefs) have status over untitled people, men have status over women, and men and women have status over children (Brigham Young University, Language and Intercultural Research Center, 1977).

One Samoan proverb captures the importance of the family: "*Sei fono le pa'a ma ona vae*" (Let the crab meet with his legs). According to Fuhrel (1980), the crab is the family and the legs are the different members of the family. The proverb means that when there is a gathering of families and a decision is not made, a chief may indicate that he has to consult with his family before he can decide his answer.

Each family member works for the well-being of the entire extended family, which sometimes may be as large as an entire village (Mokuau & Tauili'ili, 1992). The church assumes a pivotal role in reinforcing the closely structured social order and harmonious functioning of the family. In turn, families support the activities and practices of the church through attending regularly and donating financial contributions and volunteer time. The values that support this group orientation include reciprocity (the mutual exchange of services, goods, and privileges), interdependence, and cooperation (Mokuau & Tauili'ili, 1992).

Several lifestyle practices reflect and reinforce the importance of relationships in Samoan culture. One of the best known ritualized practices of Samoan culture is sometimes referred to as "trouble" (*fa'alavelave*) (Calkins, 1962), the practice of mutual support during lifecycle events such as weddings, christenings, and funerals. It is referred to as "trouble" because of the constant depletion of resources to support the collective.

Sharing is also an inherent part of Samoan culture. Attached to sharing, however, is a cultural expectation that the person who receives a gift will reciprocate the act at some later time: "Families share with their neighbors and friends. . . . We give or share something with someone and they give something in return" (Tusa, 1982, p. 17).

Vignette 1. Pita, a Samoan man, moved to the western United States about six years ago with his wife and two children. When members of his extended family travel to the United States, they often stay with Pita and rely on his household for shelter, food, and other assistance. Last year, Pita's household of four expanded to include one uncle, two cousins, and four nieces and nephews. In addition to assisting and caring for extended family members when they visit, Pita also sends money back to his family in American Samoa for special events. Several *fa'alavelave* occurred last year, including the birth of a first son to his sister, the marriage of another sister, and the death of an elder, and each time Pita sent money home.

Vignette 2. Susan brings to her new home in the United States a sense of sharing and relationship that draws from her Samoan heritage. Examples relate to her generosity with Samoan products such as tapa (cloth), coconut soap, and fine mat that she has brought from Samoa to her new home. When a non-Samoan friend visited Susan's home and admired a *tapa* wall hanging that covered a large portion of the hallway wall, Susan went into her bedroom and came back with another large *tapa* product and offered it to her friend. The friend, very surprised and a little embarrassed, finally accepted the gift and desired to reciprocate Susan's gracious gesture.

CONTEXT OF OPPRESSION

As populations of color, Hawaiian, Samoan, and other Pacific Islander groups have historically experienced oppression from colonizing nations that have undermined the efforts of Pacific nations at self-government (Trask, 1989). The sovereign nation movement of Hawaiians in the 1990s is an example of a people collectively asserting their rights for self-governance (Mokuau, in press). Hawaiians are recognizing that political, economic, educational, and health benefits and privileges cannot occur as long as the entire population is disenfranchised. Self-determination for Hawaiians and other Pacific Islanders has greater meaning in the sense of the entire population's empowerment. As social work pioneer Bertha Capen Reynolds suggested, the self-directing potential of individuals cannot be increased without considering economic and political realities (cited in Freedberg, 1989).

IMPLICATIONS FOR SOCIAL WORK

Definition of Self-Determination

Self-determination has two definitions. One is concerned with self-direction—that "only the individual knows or can come to know what he or she needs in order to live and to grow fully" (Weick & Pope, 1988, p. 13). In this connotation, the client's self-direction for what to do and be is held preeminent over decisions that the professional authority might prefer. The burden of proof for a departure from this rule rests with the professional person.

The second definition is that one should be free to do or be what one wants without group restraints (Berlin, 1975; Freedberg, 1989; Gans, 1988). However, reference to one's own wishes separate from one's social ties is not necessarily appropriate. Decision making is more complex than separating into exclusive categories what is in other people's interest and what is in one's own interest. It is necessary to appreciate how contributions to group interest may ultimately strengthen the person as well.

In addition to non-Western peoples, reference to group rather than individual interests may be a dominant feature with Western people of lower socioeconomic class and women. For example, according to Schneider and Smith (1987), "whereas the middle class lays strong emphasis upon the self-sufficiency and solidarity of the nuclear family against all other kinship ties and groupings, [in] the lower class . . . the emphasis is upon keeping open the options—upon maximizing the number of relationships which involve diffuse solidarity" (p. 221). Similarly, women are more inclined toward a more collectivist orientation than are men (Benhabib, 1987; Gilligan, 1987; Kaplan, 1984; Leventhal-Belfer, Cowan, & Cowan, 1992). In this respect, there may be a convergence of feminine values with non-European values (Harding, 1987). The situation, however, is not so clear-cut as to support the notion that women necessarily desire to be collectivist in orientation. Indeed, in some definitions of feminism, it is deemed that "women should become more competitive, assertive, individualistic, and self-directed" (Nes & Iadicola, 1989). Costin (1992) attributed a decline in interest in the problem of cruelty to children to a diminishing connection between women's and children's issues within feminism, seemingly indicating an increase in individualism and a lessening of relational qualities within at least some forms of feminism. Variations related to gender nevertheless re-emphasize the importance of careful identification of the pathway each person desires to take toward self-determination. For some this may be a renewal, not a shunning, of obligations to others.

Assessment, Goal Setting, and Intervention

The principle of self-determination, in the sense of freedom from imposition of the social worker's goals, continues to apply from the earliest moments of contact with individuals, families, and groups. As Pinderhughes (1989) commented, traditional approaches have tended to emphasize diagnosis and cure as "fixed entities not dependent on the individual's perception of what is wrong and what needs fixing" (pp. 13–14). Hence, the assessment may tend to be based on what the professional thinks clients ought to view, rather than what clients do view, as wrong.

Self-determination, however, may include fulfilling group obligations, not necessarily ridding oneself of them. Part of the assessment entails assessing the extent of clients' identity with their cultural group of origin and whether they wish to strengthen this identity (Pinderhughes, 1989). Goal setting may include strengthening ties with extended family and community as ends in themselves and also as a support for achieving other desired goals.

Methods of choice in working with clients toward their goals are also an aspect of self-determination. As described by Dana (1981), actions in conjunction with and under the influence of the extended family may be most desired. Therefore, observance of self-determination should be enhanced in all aspects of practice. The principle should, however, be separated from any inherent connection with self-directedness apart from group relationships.

Practice Theory

It appears that the fundamentally valid principle of self-determination has acquired, through use in a particular context, a culturally biased interpretation. Independence was prized over interdependence, individual status over group achievement. Instead, the values of interdependence should be given equal weight with independence as people define their problems and goals. Independence from group goals is not necessarily a measure of health or maturity.

Furthermore, each fundamental principle of social work should be subjected to scrutiny to assess cultural bias. Gould (1988) suggested a "recognition of ideological value imperatives and prescriptions underlying practice models" (p. 145). A systematic reanalysis is required of universal practice principles to determine if they are fundamentally flawed or culturally biased.

REFERENCES

Benhabib, S. (1987). The generalized and the concrete other: The Kohlberg–Gilligan controversy and moral theory. In E. F. Kittay & D. T. Meyers (Eds.), *Women and moral theory* (pp. 154–177). Totowa, NJ: Rowman & Littlefield.

Berlin, S. I. (1975). Two concepts of liberty. In F. E. McDermott (Ed.), *Self-determination in social work* (pp. 141–153). Boston: Routledge & Kegan Paul.

Brigham Young University, Language and Intercultural Research Center. (1977). *People of Samoa.* Provo, UT: Author.

Budman, C. L., Lipson, J. G., & Meleis, A. I. (1992). The cultural consultant in mental health care: The case of an Arab adolescent. *American Journal of Orthopsychiatry, 62,* 359–370.

Calkins, F. (1962). *My Samoan chief.* Honolulu: University of Hawaii Press.

Costin, L. B. (1992). Cruelty to children: A dormant issue and its rediscovery, 1920–1960. *Social Service Review, 66,* 183–184.

Dana, R. H. (1981). Epilogue. In R. H. Dana (Ed.), *Human services for cultural minorities* (pp. 353–355). Baltimore: University Park Press.

Freedberg, S. (1989). Self-determination: Historical perspectives and effects on current practice. *Social Work, 34,* 33–38.

Fuhrel, F. (1980). Proverbs: Let the crab meet with his legs. In M. Luaiufi, E. Fa'afeu, & F. Fuhrel (Eds.), *Fa'a Samoa Pea* (p. 66–68). Pago Pago: American Samoa Community College.

Gans, H. J. (1988). *Middle American individualism.* New York: Free Press.

Gegeo, D., & Watson-Gegeo, K. A. (1985). Patterns of suicide in West Kwara'ae, Malaita, Solomon Islands. In F. X. Hezel, D. H. Rubinstein, & G. M. White (Eds.), *Culture, youth and suicide in the Pacific: Papers from an East–West Center Conference* (pp. 182–197). Honolulu: University of Hawaii, Pacific Islands Studies Program.

Gilligan, C. (1987). Moral orientation and moral development. In E. F. Kittay & D. T. Meyers (Eds.), *Women and moral theory* (pp. 19–33). Totowa, NJ: Rowman & Littlefield.

Gould, K. H. (1988). Asian and Pacific Islanders: Myth and reality. *Social Work, 33,* 142–147.

Gutierrez, L. M. (1990). Working with women of color: An empowerment perspective. *Social Work, 35,* 149–153.

Handy, E. S. C., & Pukui, M. K. (1977). *The Polynesian family system in Kau, Hawaii.* Rutland, VT: Charles E. Tuttle.

Harding, S. (1987). The curious coincidence of feminine and African moralities: Challenge for feminist theory. In E. F. Kittay & D. T Meyers (Eds.), *Women and moral theory* (pp. 296–315). Totowa, NJ: Rowman & Littlefield.

Hezel, F. X. (1989). Suicide and the Micronesian family. *Contemporary Pacific, 1*(1 & 2), 43–74.

Hollis, F. (1966). *Casework: A psychosocial therapy.* New York: Random House.

Howard, A. (1974). *Ain't no big thing: Coping strategies in a Hawaiian-American community.* Honolulu: University Press of Hawaii, East–West Center Books.

Inclan, J., & Hernandez, M. (1992). Cross-cultural perspectives and codependence: The case of poor Hispanics. *American Journal of Orthopsychiatry, 62,* 245–247.

Ito, K. L. (1987). Emotions, proper behavior (hana pono), and Hawaiian concepts of self, person, and individual. In A. B. Robillard & A. J. Marsella (Eds.), *Contemporary issues in mental health research in the Pacific Islands* (pp. 45–71). Honolulu: University of Hawaii, Social Science Research Institute.

Kanahele, G. H. S. (1986). *Ku kanaka, stand tall.* Honolulu: University of Hawaii Press and Waiaha Foundation.

Kaplan, A. G. (1984). *The "self in relation": Implications for depression in women.* (Work in Progress, Working Paper No. 14.) Wellesley, MA: Wellesley College, Stone Center for Developmental Services and Studies.

Lemmon, J. A. (1983). Values, ethics, and legal issues. In A. Rosenblatt & D. Waldfogel (Eds.), *Handbook of clinical social work* (pp. 845–852). San Francisco: Jossey-Bass.

Leventhal-Belfer, L., Cowan, P. A., & Cowan, C. P. (1992). Satisfaction with child care arrangements: Effects on adaptation to parenthood. *American Journal of Orthopsychiatry, 62,* 165–177.

Levy, C. S. (1983). Client self-determination. In A. Rosenblatt & D. Waldfogel (Eds.), *Handbook of clinical social work* (pp. 904–919). San Francisco: Jossey-Bass.

Lieber, M. D. (1990). Lamarckian definitions of identity on Kapingamarangi and Pohnpei. In J. Linnekin & L. Poyer (Eds.), *Cultural identity and ethnicity in the Pacific* (pp. 71–101). Honolulu: University of Hawaii Press.

Linnekin, J., & Poyer, L. (1990). Introduction. In J. Linnekin & L. Poyer (Eds.), *Cultural identify and ethnicity in the Pacific* (pp. 1–15). Honolulu: University of Hawaii Press.

Mokuau, N., & Chang, N. (1991). Samoans. In N. Mokuau (Ed.), *Handbook of social services for Asian and Pacific Islanders* (pp. 155–169). Westport, CT: Greenwood Press.

Mokuau, N., & Matsuoka, J. (in press). Turbulence among a native people: Social work practice with Hawaiians. *Social Work.*

Mokuau, N., & Tauili'ili, P. (1992). Families with Native Hawaiian and Pacific Island roots. In E. W. Lynch & M. J. Hanson (Eds.), *Developing cross-cultural competence* (pp. 301–318). Baltimore: Paul H. Brookes.

Nes, J. A., & Iadicola, P. (1989). Toward a definition of feminist social work: A comparison of liberal, radical, and socialist models. *Social Work, 34,* 12–21.

Oliver, D. L. (1988). *The Pacific Islands.* Honolulu: University of Hawaii Press.

Papajohn, J., & Spiegel, J. (1975). *Transactions in families.* San Francisco: Jossey-Bass.

Pedersen, P. P., Fukuyama, M., & Heath, A. (1989). Client, counselor, and contextual variables in multicultural counseling. In P. P. Pedersen, J. G. Draguns, W. J. Lonner, & J. E. Trimble (Eds.), *Counseling across cultures* (3rd ed., pp. 23–52). Honolulu: University of Hawaii Press.

Pinderhughes, E. B. (1983). Empowerment for our clients and for ourselves. *Social Casework, 64,* 331–338.

Pinderhughes, E. B. (1989). *Understanding race, ethnicity, and power.* New York: Macmillan.

Quigg, A. (1987). *History of the Pacific Islands Studies Program at the University of Hawaii: 1950–1986.* Honolulu: University of Hawaii, Pacific Island Studies Program.

Schneider, D. M., & Smith, R. T. (1987). Class differences and sex roles in American kinship and family structure. In R. N. Bellah, R. Madsen, W. M. Sullivan, A. Swidler, & S. M. Tipton (Eds.), *Individualism and commitment in American life: Readings on the themes of habits of the heart* (pp. 211–223). New York: Harper & Row.

Schwartz, E. E. (1989). Social work and individualism: A comparative review. *Social Work, 34,* 167–170.

Stirling, E., & Salmond, A. (1985). *Eruera: The teachings of a Maori elder.* Auckland, New Zealand: Oxford University Press.

Territory of American Samoa, Office of the Governor. (1990). *Mental health plan 1989–1991.* Pago Pago: Author.

Trask, H.-K. (1989). Empowerment of Pacific people. In D. S. Sanders & J. K. Matsuoka (Eds.), *Peace and development: An interdisciplinary perspective* (pp. 133–139). Honolulu: University of Hawaii, School of Social Work.

Tung, M. (1991). Insight-oriented psychotherapy and the Chinese patient. *American Journal of Orthopsychiatry, 61,* 186–194.

Tusa, S. A. (1982). Proverbs: We give the lo and get the lo in return. In M. Tu'ufuli, S. A. Tusa, & Timoteo (Eds.), *Fa'a Samoa Pea* (pp. 16–23). Pago Pago: American Samoa Community College.

Untalan, F. F. (1991). Chamorros. In N. Mokuau (Ed.), *Handbook of social services for Asian and Pacific Islanders* (pp. 171–182). Westport, CT: Greenwood Press.

Weick, A., & Pope, L. (1988). Knowing what's best: A new look at self-determination. *Social Casework, 69,* 10–16.

2  *Traditional and Alternative Paradigms*

Topics Addressed in This Chapter:

➤ **DIMENSIONS OF TRADITIONAL AND DOMINANT PARADIGM**
Positivistic/Scientific/Objective/Quantitative: Ways of Knowing
    Positivistic
    Scientific
    Objective
    Quantitative
Masculinity/Patriarchy
    Patriarchy
    Masculinity
    Women and Patriarchy
Whiteness
    Whiteness, Power, and Social Institutions
    Whiteness and Ethnocentrism
    Racisms and Power
    Three Types of Racism
Separate/Impersonal/Competitive
    Separateness and Impersonality
    Competitiveness: Binaries and Hierarchies
Privilege
    Norm of Rightness
    White Privilege

➤ **DIMENSIONS OF ALTERNATIVE/POSSIBLE PARADIGMS**
Interpretive/Intuitive/Subjective/Qualitative: Ways of Knowing
    Interpretive Knowledge
    Intuitive Knowledge
    Subjective Understanding
        Spirituality
        Religion and Spirituality
    Qualitative Approaches
    Alternative Approaches to Knowing: Heuristic, Naturalistic, and Postmodern
        Heuristic Research
        Naturalistic Inquiry
        Naturalistic Research and Rigor: Trustworthiness Criteria
        Postmodern Ways of Knowing

*T*his chapter outlines the conceptual framework we will use throughout this book. Traditional and alternative paradigms for gathering and organizing knowledge for social work practice are described, compared, and contrasted in this chapter. Five dimensions of traditional and alternative paradigms are outlined. These five dimensions offer some basic perspectives social workers can use to organize a wide range of information about human behavior and the social environment from a number of different disciplines. This framework provides the basic vehicles we will use on our journey to more comprehensive and critical understanding of human behavior and the social environment.

DIMENSIONS OF TRADITIONAL AND DOMINANT PARADIGM

Like paradigms or worldviews in general, the traditional and dominant paradigm is viewed here as a set of interrelated and interlocking dimensions through which what and how we know about the world around us is created, communicated, and controlled. These dimensions include methods (processes), attributes, perspectives, standards, and ways of relating. When these dimensions come together to form the traditional and dominant paradigm, they represent in large part what we are taught to believe in the United States to be right and true.

The traditional and dominant paradigm gains its specific identity in the following ways. It gives primacy to the use of **positivistic, scientific, objective, and quantitative methods (processes)** for creating knowledge upon which to base actions and beliefs. The dominant paradigm places primary value on and reflects **masculine attributes and patriarchal perspectives.** The dominant paradigm evaluates persons' worth and importance according to standards of **whiteness.** Relations with others are constructed with concern for maintaining high degrees of **separateness and impersonality.** Within the dominant paradigm concepts and people tend to be placed in

oppositional or competitive positions in relation to each other. **Privileged status** is awarded according to the degree to which one displays and adheres to the methods (processes), attributes, perspectives, standards, and ways of relating to others that characterize the traditional and dominant paradigm. We will explore in more depth these dimensions of the traditional and dominant paradigm in the sections that follow.

Positivistic/Scientific/Objective/Quantitative: Ways of Knowing

An important means of understanding the traditional and dominant paradigm is the examination of methods or processes through which knowledge or information is gained and evaluated. These methods or processes are in themselves important components of the traditional and dominant paradigm at the same time that they are mechanisms for creating that worldview. They represent both "ways of knowing" and what is considered "worth knowing." They are central "processes" and essential qualities of "products" in the traditional paradigm. In other words, they are in many respects both *how* and *what* we need to know according to the traditional and dominant paradigm.

Characteristics of this dimension of the traditional and dominant paradigm are: **positivistic, scientific, objective, and quantitative.** These dual purpose characteristics are presented here as an interrelated group. These characteristics are considered together because they are so often applied almost interchangeably in references to the "ways of knowing" and to what is accorded "worth knowing" (or valid knowledge) according to the traditional paradigm. However, separate descriptions and discussions of these process/product characteristics are presented below for clarity. While we discuss each of these interrelated characteristics separately, we must keep in mind that these characteristics combine to form a single perspective or standpoint from which the world is viewed and evaluated.

Positivistic

The first of these characteristics is a positivistic approach or positivism. Positivism is also often referred to as **empiricism** (Imre 1984:41; Bottomore 1984:22–23). The words **positivism** and **empiricism** refer to *the belief that knowledge is gained through objective observations of the world around us.* Conclusions drawn about that world must be based only on those objective observations (Manheim 1977:12–14; Dawson et al. 1991:247–8, 432). The positivist or empiricist standpoint suggests that *we can know the world with certainty only if we can observe it through our senses.* This perspective carries the assumption that any capable person observing the same event, experience, or object will see, feel, taste, smell, or hear that event, experience or object in exactly the same way. "Truth" or "knowledge" is in fact verified in this way and only in this way (Manheim 1977:12, Dawson et al. 1991:19–20). While many researchers consider positivism and empiricism synonymous, other scholars differentiate the terms. They suggest that *positivism* is a more narrow concept, always based on use of the scientific method (see the next page) to determine what is knowledge. *Empiricism* is sometimes considered a broader or more inclusive concept that may be applied to ways of gaining knowledge other than through scientific method, such as through qualitative approaches (Heineman Pieper 1995:xxiii; Tyson 1995:9).

Scientific

The second characteristic necessary for knowing and evaluating the world according to the traditional and dominant paradigm is science or the scientific approach. Like the positivistic or empiricist standpoint, a scientific approach requires observation of experiences, events, or objects through our senses. In addition, the **scientific approach** requires *"systematic, controlled, empirical, and critical investigation of hypothetical propositions about the presumed relations among natural phenomena"* (Kerlinger 1973:11). It is through this kind of investigation of the relationship among observable phenomena that we come to know the world and its occupants according to the scientific approach. It is difficult to understate the power accorded the scientific approach to determining what we know and what is worth knowing in dominant U.S. society. In the box below is a summary of the scientific method.

THE SCIENTIFIC METHOD

"Scientific Method consists of a series of steps for conducting research and a set of prescriptions about how scientific knowledge should be created and judged"

Steps in Scientific Method

1. Choosing research topics
2. Constructing hypotheses
3. Selecting methods
4. Collecting data
5. Analyzing data
6. Interpreting findings and drawing conclusions. (Alix 1995:41)

Objective

Central to the scientific approach is the third characteristic necessary for knowing and evaluating the world according to the traditional and dominant paradigm—objectivity. An **objective approach** *places a premium on being "unbiased, unprejudiced, detached, impersonal."* **Objectivity** is *"the characteristic of viewing things as they 'really' are"* (Manheim 1977:10). Objectivity requires that the values of the studier be kept completely separate from any event, experience, or object being studied. The person with a scientific perspective "believes . . . that there is some ultimate link between logical thinking and empirical facts . . . that objective reality not only exists, but is essentially in one piece, so that there should be no disparity between what is logical and what is empirical" (Dawson et al. 1991:20).

Quantitative

It is not surprising that a paradigm such as the traditional and dominant paradigm—with so much emphasis on gathering and validating knowledge through systematic, objective observations, using our human senses and the senses of others for verifying that knowledge—places great importance on keeping a record of the nature and number of the events, experiences, or objects observed. Thus, the fourth ingredient necessary for knowing and evaluating the world according to the traditional and dominant paradigm is quantitative. A **quantitative approach** *assumes that "all materials are potentially quantifiable" (Kerlinger 1973:529). This approach seeks answers to questions by making generalizations about people and things "based on precisely measured quantities"* (Dawson et al. 1991:436). Value, veracity, importance, and power are determined by how often and how much or how many of a given commodity has been observed or accumulated.

As we continue our exploration of other dimensions of the traditional and dominant paradigm, we need to keep in mind their interrelatedness with this powerful and fundamental group of interlocking characteristics. It is through struggling with the complexities of the interwoven nature of the dimensions of the traditional and dominant paradigm that we can come to appreciate the power of this paradigm in our own and others' lives. Just as these four characteristics—positivistic, scientific, objective, and quantitative—depend upon and reinforce each other throughout this "way of knowing" and this means of judging what is "worth knowing," we must recognize the interdependence of this group of process/products with other dimensions of the traditional and dominant world view.

Masculinity/Patriarchy

The traditional and dominant paradigm places great value on, and reflects attributes that have come to be associated with, maleness or masculinity. This emphasis on valuing masculine attributes has resulted in a system or set of perspectives and institutions referred to as a patriarchy. Interestingly, we will see in our exploration of the masculinity/patriarchy dimension of the traditional and dominant paradigm that a number of the processes/products discussed above—positivistic, scientific, objective, quantitative—have come to be associated closely with maleness or masculinity. These processes/products are also important elements of patriarchal perspectives and institutions.

Patriarchy

Literally, **patriarchy** means *"the rule of the fathers."* In the social sciences, the meaning of patriarchy is very close to this literal definition. "A **patriarchy** *is a society in which formal power over public decision and policy making is held by adult men"* (Ruth 1990:45). This is a helpful definition for us to use in our exploration of the traditional and dominant paradigm. It implies that the nature of the society and institutions in which we live, their values and priorities, are determined almost exclusively through patriarchy, which is the "embodiment of masculine ideals and practices" (Ruth 1990: 45). It is the contention in this book that the United States is a patriarchy in that public (and many private) decisions and policies are in fact made almost entirely by men. We need only think about the gender composition of such public-policy and decision-making arenas as state legislatures and the U.S. Congress and Supreme Court to verify this assertion (although challenges to exclusive patriarchy are reflected in the candidacies and election of women).

We can find evidence and examples of patriarchy and its influence in realms of our lives other than politics. Belenky et al. (1986:5–6), for example, remind us "that conceptions of knowledge and truth that are accepted and articulated today have been shaped throughout history by the male-dominated culture." They assert that men have drawn on their own perspectives and visions to construct prevailing theories, to write history, and to set values "that have become the guiding principles for men and women alike." Belenky et al. focus their analysis primarily on the patriarchal domination of our educational institutions. Educational institutions, we must remember, are fundamental shapers and socializers of the members, male and female, of society. If you are reading this book as part of a course in a school or program of social work, you are being socialized within the context of an educational institution.

Masculinity

If patriarchy is the embodiment of control over decision and policy making by men, what are some of the attributes of maleness or masculinity that are reflected in patriarchal decisions and policies? Different observers differ somewhat about the specific attributes of masculinity. Ruth provides one useful list of attributes that are representative of what she calls the **"patriarchal ideal of masculinity."** These attributes include: "aggressiveness, courage, physical strength and health, self-control and emotional reserve, perseverance and endurance, competence and rationality, independence, self-reliance, autonomy, individuality, sexual potency" (Ruth 1990:47).

Easlea (in Ruth 1990:61) provides an illustration of how some of these masculine attributes are reflected in and influence processes and products in the natural sciences, specifically physics. He illustrates how two different dimensions of the traditional and dominant paradigm—masculinity and science—are intertwined. Easlea concurs with the anthropologist Traweek that "those most prestigious of physicists—the members of the high-energy physics 'community'—display the highly masculine behavioral traits of 'aggressive individualism, haughty self-confidence, and a sharp competitive edge' " (Easlea in Ruth 1990:61). This mirroring of masculine traits within physics should come as no surprise when one considers the extent of overrepresentation of men in the field. In the early 1980s "women made up only 2 percent of the faculty of the 171 doctorate-awarding physics departments" in the United States (n. 3, Easlea in Ruth 1990:61).

As long ago as 1913, Bertrand Russell offered an interesting description of the "scientific attitude of mind." His description is strikingly consistent with the attributes of masculinity, the perspectives of patriarchy, and the other characteristics (positivist, objective, scientific, quantitative) of the traditional and dominant paradigm we examined earlier. Russell suggested that "the scientific attitude of mind . . . involves a sweeping away of all other desires in the interests of the desire to know—it involves the suppression of hopes and fears, loves and hates, and the whole subjective emotional life, until we become subdued to the material, able to see it frankly, without preconceptions, without biases, without any wish except to see it as it is" (Easlea in Ruth 1990:63).

Women and Patriarchy

If such fundamental social institutions as politics, education, and the sciences reflect overwhelmingly male attributes and patriarchal perspectives, what are the consequences for women? Westkott (1979:424) offers an observation important for us as students of human behavior about the consequences for women of a traditional and dominant worldview that is so heavily influenced and controlled by masculinity and patriarchy. She observes that "the male character structure and patriarchal culture mutually reflect and support one another through social, political, and economic institutions." The result, she believes, is that "women and other deviants must either become invisible or their estrangement from, or failure in, such a society must be explained in terms of their 'natural' inferiority. . . . These social contexts . . . are patriarchal: through the organization of social relations women are controlled by men and are culturally devalued" (Westkott 1979:424).

The powerful interlocking nature of the positivistic, scientific, objective, and quantitative dimension of the traditional/dominant paradigm, along with that of masculinity/patriarchy can hardly be understated. We will continue to explore the consequences and implications for women and for others of the traditional and dominant paradigm as we proceed through this book. Next, however, we will explore how, from the standpoint of the traditional and dominant paradigm, people are viewed and evaluated according to standards of whiteness.

Whiteness

The traditional and dominant paradigm is inordinately influenced by, and its content controlled by, white persons of European descent. What this has come to mean is that all persons, both white and nonwhite, have come to be judged or evaluated in virtually all areas of life according to standards that reflect the values, attitudes, experiences, and historical perspectives of white persons, specifically white persons of European descent. This perspective is so influential that the traditional and dominant world view is increasingly referred to as Eurocentric.

Whiteness, Power, and Social Institutions

The dimension of whiteness, as in the cases of the masculinity/patriarchy and positivistic/scientific/objective/quantitative dimensions, permeates processes and products that make up our worlds and that shape and are shaped by the traditional and dominant worldview. For examples of the predominance of whites in positions of power in this society, one need only look again to the public decision- and policy-making arenas as we suggested in our exploration of masculinity/patriarchy. Pharr (1988) suggests that we also examine through a lens of color the leadership of other social institutions, such as finance and banking, churches and synagogues, and the military. Such an examination will reveal that not only does whiteness predominate in the leadership of social institutions, but it permeates the very nature of what is communicated through those social institutions as well. Pharr reminds us that "in our schools, the primary literature and history taught are about the exploits of white men, shown through the white man's eyes. Black history, for instance, is still relegated to one month, whereas 'American history' is taught all year round" (Pharr 1988:54).

Collins (1989:752) reminds us that when one group, white males, for example, controls fundamental social processes such as the "knowledge-validation" or education/research process, other voices and ways of knowing are suppressed. She notes that

◢
EXPLORING WHITENESS

To more directly explore the dimension of whiteness and to bring this exploration a little closer to home, you might ask the following questions. How many courses focusing on African Americans, Asian Americans, Latinos, or Native Americans are taught in your college or university? Are they required or elective? How many courses focusing on people of color have you taken? How many white students enroll in these courses? How many courses focusing on the experiences of white, Eurocentric people must people of color take in order to meet the graduation requirements in your college or university—history, philosophy, art, music, drama, literature? How many non-Western (non-Eurocentric) civilization courses are required? What was the extent of resistance to the introduction of courses focusing on the history, experiences, and cultural expressions of people of color, if such courses exist at all? These same questions could be asked also about courses reflecting the history and experiences of women in relation to the dimension of masculinity/patriarchy.

"since the general culture shaping the taken-for-granted knowledge of the community of experts is one permeated by widespread notions of Black and female inferiority, new knowledge claims that seem to violate these fundamental assumptions are likely to be viewed as anomalies." In fact, questions about such notions are unlikely even to be raised "from within a white-male-controlled academic community" (Collins 1989:752).

Whiteness and Ethnocentrism

Leigh (1989:6–7) notes that the existing dominant paradigm is highly ethnocentric in its white European bias. This bias has resulted in the oppression of other races and cultures by design. **Ethnocentrism** is the tendency to see one's own group as more important, more valuable than others. We will return to this concept later, but suffice it to say here that white Eurocentric ethnocentrism is a powerful influence in the traditional dominant paradigm. Leigh believes that the negative worldview of African Americans by a dominant white society is a barometer for how all people of color are viewed. He concludes that social institutions, including social work, have historically failed and continue to fail to recognize minority experiences and wrongfully use white majority experiences as the model experience (Leigh 1989:9). In other words the white bias of the traditional/dominant paradigm excludes as lacking any significant value the experiences of people of color.

Again, we notice that fundamental elements of the traditional and dominant paradigm are interwoven. The processes for creating knowledge, masculine and patriarchal attributes and perspectives, and standards of whiteness all interconnect in the traditional and dominant worldview. These interconnecting elements create the conditions for excluding those persons who do not behave in accordance with, or reflect these fundamental dimensions of, the dominant paradigm.

Racisms and Power

One way that whiteness finds negative expression in this society is through racism. Jones in Carter and Jones (1996) provides a definition of racism emphasizing the ability of a more powerful group to subordinate a less powerful group:

> *Racism results from the transformation of race prejudice and/or ethnocentrism through the exercise of power against a racial group defined as inferior, by individuals and institutions with the intentional or unintentional support of the entire (race or) culture.*

Based on the general definition of racism above, Jones in Carter and Jones demonstrate that it is possible to further define and identity the operation of racism at individual, institutional, and cultural levels.

Three Types of Racism

1. *Individual Racism:* "One considers that Black people (or people of color) as a group are inferior to Whites because of physical (genotypical and phenotypical) traits. [She or] he further believes that these physical traits are determinants of (inferior) social behavior and moral or intellectual qualities, and ultimately presumes that this inferiority is a legitimate basis for inferior social treatment of Black people (or people of color) in American society."

2. *Institutional Racism:* "those established laws, customs, and practices which systematically reflect and produce racial inequalities in American society . . . whether or not the individuals maintaining those practices have racist intentions" (Jones 1972). "The clearest indication of institutional racism is disparity in the circumstances of Whites and people of color, which continues from the past into the present."

3. *Cultural Racism:* "the belief in the inferiority of the implements, handicrafts, agriculture, economics, music, art, religious beliefs, traditions, language and story of African (Hispanic, Asian and Indian) peoples; . . . [and the belief that] Black (and other non-White) Americans *have no* distinctive implements, handicrafts, agriculture, economics, music, art, religious beliefs, traditions, languages or story apart from those of mainstream white America" (Carter and Jones 1996:2–3).

Separate/Impersonal/Competitive

The traditional and dominant paradigm places primacy in relations and relationships on separation, impersonality, and on viewing the world in oppositional or competitive ways. Often this has meant the world has been viewed in what has been referred to as binary or competing and oppositional terms such as "either/or" and "we/they" rather than in cooperative and inclusive terms such as "both/and" and "us" (Derrida in Scott 1988:7).

Separateness and Impersonality

In Western philosophy this focus on separateness is seen in the traditional concern for separation of mind (thought) from body (physical). In the natural and the social sciences emphasis is placed, as we saw earlier in our discussions of the scientific approach generally and in physics specifically, on separating personal values from the empirical process of knowledge building. The scientific process, in fact, has long considered any integration of subjective and objective elements as contaminating the process of knowledge building. Science, in order to be scientific, must be conducted impersonally. The education of natural scientists continually stresses the importance of being value free, of being objective, of separating studier from studied (subject from object). The social sciences and many in social work have modeled their approaches to knowledge building on the impersonal and value-free tenets of the natural sciences.

Impersonality and separateness are also associated closely with such valued masculine attributes as independence, autonomy, and individuality. These, you will recall, are elements of the "patriarchal ideal of masculinity." The value placed on these attributes in combination with the importance placed on separateness and impersonal approaches has heavily influenced the nature and focus of research on human development and behavior. Belenky et al., for example, remind us that "the Western tradition of dividing human nature into dual . . . streams" has resulted in our learning "a great deal about the development of autonomy and independence . . . while we have not learned as much about the development of interdependence, intimacy, nurturance, and contextual thought" (Belenky et al. 1986:6–7).

We will look in some detail at issues of autonomy and interdependence in Chapters 4 and 5 when we explore traditional and alternative approaches to understanding individual behavior and development. Belenky et al. also point out that "the mental processes that are involved in considering the abstract and the impersonal have been labeled 'thinking' and are attributed primarily to men, while those that deal with the personal and interpersonal fall under the rubric of 'emotions' and are largely relegated to women" (1986:7). Again, the interweaving of the dimensions of the traditional and dominant paradigm are obvious.

Competitiveness: Binaries and Hierarchies

When ideas or characteristics are divided into **dichotomies or binary oppositions**—as French philosopher/linguist Jacques Derrida refers to this tendency to separate into opposite and competing forces—the opposing sides tend to be hierarchical, with one term dominant or prior, the opposite term subordinate and secondary (Scott 1988:7). Collins also stresses the tendency of such dichotomous thinking to carry strong implications of systemic inequality. She stresses that "dichotomous oppositional differences invariably imply relationships of superiority and inferiority, hierarchical relationships that mesh with political economies of domination and subordination" (Collins 1986:20).

The Western philosophical tradition, Derrida argues, rests on these binary oppositions or dichotomies in many other areas such as unity/diversity, identity/difference, presence/absence (Scott 1988). Collins addresses the meaning of dichotomous thinking from an African American feminist perspective in the context of human oppression. In doing so she demonstrates the interlocking and interdependent nature of the several dimensions of the traditional/dominant paradigm. "Either/or dualistic thinking, or . . . the construct of dichotomous oppositional difference, may be a philosophical linchpin in systems of race, class, and gender oppression," she believes. "One fundamental characteristic of this construct is the categorization of people, things, and ideas in terms of their difference [separateness] from one another." The examples of dichotomies she provides—black/white, male/female, reason/emotion, fact/ opinion, and subject/object (Collins 1986:20)—speak loudly of the dichotomies implicit in the traditional and dominant paradigm.

Social work also has a history of struggling with dichotomies or dualities. Berlin points out that social work "is built on a foundation of dualities." She notes our contrasting commitments to "individual adaptation and social change" or "to humanistic values and scientific knowledge development." Social work continues to struggle over which side of these dualities to align itself with. Over our history we have moved from side to side at different points—sometimes moving toward a focus on individual change, sometimes toward social change; sometimes emphasizing our humanistic values as primary, sometimes emphasizing scientific aspects of social work. Many would argue that our alignments have more often gone with individual adaptation and science than with social change and humanistic values. That the struggle and tension continue to involve both sides of these dichotomies rather than shifting entirely to one side and remaining there can be considered a strength of the field (Berlin 1990:55).

Privilege

The impact of the traditional and dominant paradigm in all its varied manifestations is hardly neutral or value free. The paradigmatic elements that we have explored so far all carry with them differential meanings and very different results for different people. Those who benefit are those who define, fit, and enforce the processes, attributes, perspectives, standards, and ways of relating that characterize the traditional and dominant paradigm. The set or system of benefits that accrue to these persons is referred to as **privilege.** We end our examination of the elements of the traditional and dominant paradigm with a brief exploration of privilege. The concept of privilege will be a continuing concern for us as we move on in our journey toward greater understanding of human behavior and the social environment.

Norm of Rightness

Privilege is used synonymously here with what Pharr (1988:53) refers to in discussing the common elements of oppressions as a **"defined norm, a standard of rightness and often righteousness."** This norm is used to judge all other persons. It is backed up by institutional and economic power; by institutional and individual violence. In the United States, Pharr characterizes the determiner and enforcer of this norm as "male, white, heterosexual, Christian, temporarily able-bodied, youthful with access to wealth and resources." She makes an important observation about this "defined norm" that is essential to our understanding of privilege. She urges us to remember "that an established norm does not necessarily represent a majority in terms of numbers; it represents those who have the ability to exert power and control over others" (Pharr 1988:53).

White Privilege

In U.S. society, the ability to exert power and control over others is often associated with whiteness, what one might refer to as *white privilege.* However white people are often unaware or unwilling to recognize how closely whiteness is associated with privilege in the U.S. Helms (1994:305) suggests that the reality, existence, and persistence of white privilege is often denied by white people. This denial may even take the form of denying that an identifiable privileged white racial group exists. She argues that "Dis-avowal of the existence of White privilege takes the form of denying that a White *racial* group exists that benefits from White privilege." We will further explore issues and mod-els related to white racial identity and identity development in Chapter 5.

Privilege is that powerful but often unspoken and taken-for-granted sense that one fits, that one is an active and powerful participant and partner in defining and making decisions about one's world. It is that sense that one's worldview is in fact dominant. Privilege is the sum total of the benefits one accrues as a result of that dom-inance. Unfortunately, such a definition of privilege is accompanied by the reality that this privilege is gained and maintained at the expense of others: It is exclusive.

Peggy McIntosh, a feminist scholar, offers dramatic, real-life examples of the benefits that accrue to those of us who reflect characteristics of the "norm of right-ness" and who "fit" the dimensions of the traditional and dominant paradigm. McIn-tosh specifically addresses what she refers to as "skin-color privilege," or what we have referred to here as "whiteness." However, implications for the meaning of privilege flowing from other attributes of the "norm of rightness" can be deduced from her examples as well. The following are some particularly illuminating and concrete ex-amples of what it means on a day-to-day basis to have white privilege. These exam-ples can help bring to a conscious level many of the "taken-for-granted" aspects of both whiteness and other elements of privilege.

As a white person, McIntosh, points out that:

- *I can turn on the television or open to the front page of the paper and see people of my race widely and positively represented.*
- *I can be sure that my children will be given curricular materials that testify to the existence of their race.*
- *I can be reasonably sure that if I ask to talk to "the person in charge," I will be facing a person of my race.*
- *I can easily buy posters, postcards, picture books, greeting cards, dolls, toys, and children's magazines featuring people of my race.*
- *I can be late to a meeting without having the lateness reflect on my race.*
- *I can choose blemish cover or bandages in "flesh" color and have them more or less match my skin.* (McIntosh 1992:73–75)

McIntosh offers many more examples illustrating the privileges that accrue to white people by virtue of their color. (The reader is encouraged to read McIntosh's article, "White Privilege and Male Privilege," cited at the end of this chapter.)

DIMENSIONS OF ALTERNATIVE POSSIBLE PARADIGMS

As is the case with paradigms in general, alternative paradigms are sets of interrelated and interlocking dimensions through which what and how we know about the world around us is created, communicated, and controlled. Like all paradigms, alternative paradigms include methods (processes), attributes, perspectives, standards, and ways of relating.

The alternative paradigms we explore here incorporate **interpretive, intuitive, subjective, and qualitative** products and processes for creating knowledge upon which to base actions and beliefs. Alternative paradigms do not necessarily exclude the processes and products (positivistic, scientific, objective, quantitative) of the traditional/ dominant paradigm. They do not, however, recognize those processes and products as the only or necessarily the most appropriate avenues to understanding and action. The alternative paradigms we consider value and reflect **feminine attributes and feminist perspectives.** They do not give primacy to masculine attributes or patriarchal perspectives. The alternative paradigms we explore evaluate persons' worth and importance according to standards of the inherent worth and dignity of all humans, and they especially recognize the benefits of **human diversity.** Persons are not evaluated according to standards of whiteness. The alternative paradigms we will explore structure relations with others around recognition of the **interconnected and personal** nature of our relationships with other persons and with the elements of the worlds around us. Separateness and impersonality are seen as obstacles to constructing effective relationships. The alternative paradigms with which we are concerned do not assume a competitive stance in which people or ideas are in opposition to one another. They instead focus on the **integrative and complementary** nature of differences among people and ideas. The alternative paradigms through which we will attempt to view our worlds seek recognition of oppressions and the elimination of conditions and relations that allow some persons and groups privilege at the expense of others. These are the critical dimensions of alternative paradigms through which we will attempt to find and create new ways to view our worlds. These interrelated dimensions are explored in more detail in the following sections.

Interpretive/Intuitive/Subjective/Qualitative: Ways of Knowing

In our discussion of the traditional and dominant paradigm, we noted that examination of the methods and processes through which knowledge or information is gained and evaluated is essential for understanding that paradigm. The methods and processes for gaining and evaluating information and knowledge are essential components of and avenues for creating alternative worldviews as well. Our alternative paradigms are characterized by an emphasis on "ways of knowing" that are more interpretive, intuitive, subjective, and qualitative than those of the dominant paradigm we explored earlier in this chapter. These characteristics also represent alternative types of knowledge "worth knowing." Although these alternative ways of knowing and of evaluating what is worth knowing often have not been valued within the purview of the traditional and dominant paradigm, they offer essential avenues for social workers to gain a more complete understanding of humans, our behaviors, and the social environments we construct and inhabit.

The interpretive, intuitive, subjective, and qualitative dimension of alternative paradigms for understanding human behavior is discussed in some detail next. Although we discuss the characteristics—interpretive, intuitive, subjective, and qualitative—of this dimension separately, it is important to keep in mind that all these characteristics are interrelated and combine to form the process/products of the alternative worldviews we are seeking to understand.

Interpretive Knowledge

The first characteristic of alternative paradigm knowledge building and validating processes we will consider is the interpretive aspect. While they are often controversial, shifts toward more interpretive approaches to understanding humans and their behaviors have been under way for some time. (In Chapter 1, you might recall, we explored in some detail the concept and consequences of "shifts" in paradigms.) Edmund Sherman (1991:69) discusses shifts occurring in the ways we think about and gather information in the social sciences. He notes that many people in these fields "are questioning just how scientific the social sciences can and should be." Rather than using the "science" dimension (positivistic, scientific, objective, quantitative) of the traditional/dominant paradigm as the sole methodology for understanding our worlds, some social scientists are shifting to methods more characteristic of those used in the liberal arts, specifically, the humanities.

Sherman suggests that representative of this shift are changes in the language used to describe knowledge-gathering methods or processes in the social sciences. He notes that many social scientists are using words such as " 'interpretation,' 'hermeneutics,' and 'rhetoric' in calling for a new mode of inquiry that draws as much from the humanities as from the natural sciences, if not more" (Winkler 1985 in Sherman 1991:69). These descriptors—interpretation, hermeneutics, rhetoric—are much more consistent with knowledge-gathering processes in the liberal arts and humanities than those in the natural sciences. It should come as no surprise that those of us who depend on knowledge of human behavior to do our work would look to the "humanities"—"the branches of learning having primarily a cultural character" (Webster 1983)—for help in understanding the human condition.

A term often used as a synonym for these **interpretive approaches** to gaining understanding is **hermeneutics.** According to Webster, "Hermeneutics can be most simply defined as 'the science of interpretation' " (1983:851). Perhaps a good way to expand our understanding of interpretive or hermeneutic approaches to knowledge building is to visit some of the humanities from which the concept is taken—philosophy and history. Philosopher and historian Wilhelm Dilthey used the term **hermeneutics** to denote ". . . the discipline concerned with the investigation and interpretation of human behavior, speech, institutions, etc., as essentially intentional" (Dilthey in Sherman 1991:71). Dilthey's hermeneutic approach to understanding history "emphasized the 'reliving' or entering into the subjective, experiential worlds of those who lived and originally wrote about the historical events under study" (Sherman 1991:71). This meaning sounds a lot like what we are seeking to learn to do as we study HBSE, does it not?

This interpretive, hermeneutic approach is quite similar to what social workers mean when we talk about such basic concepts as **"empathy"** and **"beginning where the client is."** These interpretive approaches to knowing are concerned in large part with understanding the meaning of human experiences. These attempts to understand the meaning of human experiences take us well beyond the realm of traditional scientific approaches to knowledge building. They take us out of the laboratory and into the everyday worlds in which we and the people with whom we work actually live our lives.

This search involves going from the detached observation characteristic of science to the kind of expressive involvement more often associated with the arts. Reason and Hawkins (in Reason 1988:80) suggest that the meaning of experience "needs to be discovered, created or made manifest, and communicated." This is accomplished "when we tell stories, write and act in plays, write poems, meditate, create pictures, enter psychotherapy, etc. When we partake of life we create meaning; the purpose of life is making meaning." These diverse methods/processes for expanding our understanding of human behavior and experience hold rich and varied potential (some already in use, such as art therapy, others virtually unexplored) for use by social workers. These approaches or "ways of knowing" are unavailable through the knowledge-building processes of the traditional/dominant paradigm.

Another important benefit of a hermeneutic or interpretive approach to understanding is its emphasis on encouraging "observers to understand their own preconceptions and take into account their own values." (Dean and Fenby 1989:48) This is another core concern for the practice of professional social work. As social workers we must develop **self-awareness**—an awareness of the influence of our personal world view on our own behaviors and on our perceptions of the behavior of others.

Intuitive Knowledge

A second characteristic of alternative routes to knowing and understanding is **intuition** or **intuitive knowledge.** Fritjof Capra (1983), a physicist who has written about the implications of changes or shifts (see discussion of paradigm shifts in Chapter 1) in the natural sciences for rethinking our ways of learning and knowing in the social sciences, explains that "**intuitive knowledge** . . . is based on a direct, nonintellectual experience of reality arising in an expanded state of awareness. It tends to be synthesizing, holistic, and nonlinear." Reason (1981) offers a similar description in the profile proposed by Jung to describe persons who use intuition as a way of knowing. These persons "take in information through their imagination, and are interested in the whole, in the gestalt; they are idealists, interested in hypothetical possibilities, in what might be, in the creation of novel, innovative viewpoints" (Reason 1981:44). This kind of holistic thinking, the ability to see the "big picture," is essential to social work knowledge and practice. It is especially necessary if we are to appreciate the complexity of human behavior and the social environment.

The intuitive element of our alternative paradigm is often difficult to grasp, especially for those of us (and that is virtually all of us) who have been educated almost exclusively to think according to the dominant paradigm. Zukav (1980:40) suggests one way to become conscious of intuitive ways of knowing: "The next time you are awed by something, let the feeling flow freely through you and do not try to 'understand' it. You will find that you *do* understand, but in a way that you will not be able to put into words. You are perceiving intuitively." Abraham Maslow (1962) referred to such intuitive knowledge as "peak experience." More commonly, we talk about "the light bulb going on" in our heads when we suddenly attain new understanding, but we are not sure precisely how we attained that understanding. Esterson (in Reason and Rowan 1981:169) describes the combination of interpretation and intuition as part of the process in new paradigm research leading to the emergence of a hypothesis about or "some interpretation of the events being considered—some guess as to what's going on . . . this often appears as an intuitive flash, emerging between a period of active reflection and a period of rest."

Some scholars suggest that intuition plays a part in knowledge-building processes of all kinds, even those in the natural sciences. Polanyi (1964 in Moustakas 1981:209) suggests that "some intuitive conception of the general nature of things" is involved in "every interpretation of nature, whether scientific, non-scientific or anti-scientific." Some social workers historically have referred to this more intuitive/interpretive aspect of knowledge building as the art of social work.

Subjective Understanding

A third element valued in alternative approaches to gaining knowledge and closely related to intuitive ways of knowing is **subjective understanding.** Subjective knowledge, like intuitive ways of knowing, respects the personal experience as an important/valuable/valued influence on what is known and how we view the world. James Hillman (1975 in Reason 1988:80) describes the powerful personal and experiential aspects of subjective understanding: "My soul is not the result of objective facts that require explanation; rather it reflects subjective experiences that require understanding." Belenky et al. also describe subjective knowledge as "a perspective from which truth and knowledge are conceived of as personal, private, and subjectively known or intuited" (1986:15).

Subjective knowledge calls into question the exclusive focus on objectivity as *the* most valuable path to knowing that is characteristic of the dominant paradigm. Belenky et al. remind us of the Eurocentric bias at work in thinking of objectively derived knowledge as the only real or legitimate knowledge. Such a perspective is not universal: "In many non-Western and non-technological societies, subjective knowledge and intuitive processes hold a more esteemed place in the culture" (Belenky et al. 1986:55). To accept as valuable knowledge that which comes about through personal, subjective experience is an example of respecting and learning through diverse non-Western, alternative paradigms.

A **subjective perspective** on knowledge building assumes that "realities are not objectively 'out there' but are constructed by people, often under the influence of a variety of social and cultural factors that lead to shared constructions" (Guba and Lincoln 1989). Knowledge building or the development of understanding from this perspective "involves a state of awareness which integrates our subjective experience with our critical faculties so that we can develop a perspective on our discoveries and learning" (Reason 1988:230). This kind of knowledge building begins with and values personal experiences and perspectives, but it is also influenced by and develops collective meanings through rigorous processes of exchanging criticism and sharing of personal/subjective experiences with others in the social and cultural environment. Thus, personal or subjective approaches to knowledge building require rigorous processes of validation and testing in social and environmental contexts (Reason and Rowan 1981:xii–xiv).

In a study of the ways women derive and validate knowledge, Belenky et al. identified "subjective knowers." Their description of subjective knowers suggests how neglected and unrecognized intuitive or subjective sources of understanding remain. One of the women in their study eloquently described the intuitive/subjective dimensions of these avenues to knowing about and understanding the world around her: "There's a part of me that I didn't even realize I had until recently—instinct, intuition, whatever. It helps me and protects me. It's perceptive and astute. I just listen to the inside of me and I know what to do" (Belenky et al. 1986:69). This woman articulates not only the personal and powerful nature of this way of knowing, but she also reminds us that we are often unaware of this important and personally affirming dimension of knowing. Social workers who recognize, respect, and trust this way of knowing open up important pathways to insight into human behavior at the same time that we facilitate the active, personal involvement in the knowledge-building process of those persons with whom we work.

Spirituality. An often neglected area of subjective approaches to understanding is that of spirituality. Cowley and Derezotes suggest that social workers must "begin to look at the spiritual dimension—along with other dimensions such as physical, emotional, cognitive, cultural, organizational, or socio-political—in the client systems, organizations, and communities that they serve" (1994:33). Sermabeikian points out that "Our professional knowledge and understanding of spirituality can be enhanced by an examination of traditional and nontraditional religions and of nonreligious humanistic and existential philosophies" (1994:182).

Cowley and Derezotes note that spirituality is considered by many to be a "universal aspect of human culture." However, they are also careful to point out (and as we differentiate below) "spirituality is not considered as equivalent with *religion, religiosity, or theology.* . . . The use of the word 'spiritual,' then is neither a statement of belief per se nor a measure of church attendance; indeed an atheist can have a profound spiritual life." They do point out clearly, however, their conclusion of the importance of spirituality as a part of our subjective understanding and experience of ourselves and the world around us. They assert that "spirituality is an essential aspect of being that is existentially subjective, transrational, nonlocal, and nontemporal" (Cowley and Derezotes 1994:33).

Sermabeikian points out the alternative paradigm thinking necessary to incorporate understanding of spirituality. She suggests that "To understand the spiritual perspective, we must be willing to reverse our usual way of thinking and looking, which is linear and externally focused. We must look beyond what is easily counted and accounted for and examine what does not fit into our categories and conceptions of the world. There can be no preconceived notions about what may be helpful. The spiritual perspective requires that we look at the meaning of life, that we look beyond the fears and limitations of the immediate problem with the goal of discovering something inspirational and meaningful rather than focusing on the past and on pathology" (1994:179). To express the fundamental nature of spirituality for humans Sermabeikian uses Siporin's description of the transcendent and multisystem nature of spirituality. Siporin suggests that "It is in terms of a spiritual dimension that a person strives for transcendental values, meaning, experience and development; for knowledge of an ultimate reality; for belonging and relatedness with the moral universe and community; and for union with the immanent, supernatural powers that guide people and the universe for good and evil" (1994:180). Elkins et al. (in Sermabeikian 1994:180–181) also provide a helpful listing of dimensions and concepts they believe are intertwined with the notion of spirituality.

Religion and Spirituality. While spirituality is not the equivalent of religion or religiosity, as we noted above, the two concepts are often related in many ways. Canda

NINE DIMENSIONS OF SPIRITUALITY:

1. Transcendent dimensions
2. Meaning and purpose in life
3. Mission in life
4. Sacredness of life
5. Material values
6. Altruism
7. Ideals
8. Awareness of the tragic
9. Fruits of spirituality

(1989:39) differentiates between religion and spirituality. **Spirituality** is "the general human experience of developing a sense of meaning, purpose, and morality." **Religion,** on the other hand is the "formal institutional contexts of spiritual beliefs and practices" (Canda 1989:39).

Canda recommends a comparative approach to incorporating religious content into social work and offers a set of guidelines for approaching issues related to religion and spirituality in practice. The guidelines suggest the social worker:

1. *Examines religion and spirituality as general aspects of human culture and experience*
2. *Compares and contrasts diverse religious behaviors and beliefs*
3. *Avoids both sectarian and anti-religious biases*
4. *Encourages dialogue that is explicit about value issues and respects value differences*
5. *Examines the potential benefit or harm of religious beliefs and practices*
6. *Emphasizes the relevance of the social worker's understanding of religion to providing effective service to clients.* (1989:38–39)

Canda also presents Wilber's description of several common ways of defining religion in sociological and psychological thinking:

- *An engagement of non-rational, intuitive, and symbolic mental activity*
- *An existential process of developing personal and collective understandings of life's meaning, purpose, and the integration of self and world*
- *A psychosocial attempt to defend against anxiety aroused by crisis, suffering, and the inexplicable*
- *A personal and collective process of developing greater depth of communion between the human and the divine or transcendent*
- *A fantasy produced as the result of developmental fixation or regression*

- *An esoteric aspect of behavior involving participation in institutions of religion and codifications of belief*
- *An esoteric aspect of human experience involving mystical awareness and expanded states of consciousness.*   (1989:39)

It is important to develop an open and critical approach to understanding spirituality and religion and the roles they play in our personal, community, and social lives. For example, Sermabeikian notes the potential of spirituality and religion to be both helpful and harmful depending on the nature of their expression. She notes specifically that

As a human need, spirituality is multidimensional, and as such it can be manifested in healthy and unhealthy ways. Bergin (1990) noted that "spiritual phenomena have equal potential for destructiveness, as in the fundamentalist hate groups" (p. 401). Religious pathology, rigid ideologies, religious fervor associated with mental illness, cult involvement, and the non-constructive consequences of certain beliefs and practices present additional challenges to professionals.   (1994:181–182)

Sermabekian suggests there is a spiritual component in social work: "Our professional spirituality could be defined as the collective inspiration derived from the ideal of human compassion or well-being that drives us to advance our cause" (1994:182).

Qualitative Approaches

A fourth avenue to knowing valued in alternative paradigms is **qualitative information and approaches.** Capra suggests that "a true science of consciousness will deal with qualities rather than quantities, and will be based on shared experience rather than verifiable measurements. The patterns of experience constituting the data of such a science cannot be quantified into fundamental elements, and they will always be subjective to varying degrees" (Capra 1982:376). Our alternative paradigm for gathering and creating social work knowledge respects and values qualitative ways of knowing. This area of knowledge seeking and understanding is especially fitting for studying HBSE because of its consistency with social work values, practices, and goals. The qualitative characteristic is interwoven with the other characteristics—interpretive, subjective, intuitive—of this dimension of alternative-paradigm thinking we have discussed here.

Dawson et al. point out some of the challenges of **qualitative research.** This demanding approach to research "seeks to discover what kinds of things people are doing, what kinds of processes are at work, what kinds of meaning are being constructed, what kinds of purposes and goals inform the participants' acts, and what kinds of problems, constraints, and contingencies they see in the worlds they occupy" (Dawson et al. 1991:244). This description of qualitative ways of knowing is strikingly consistent with the concerns, practices and values of social work. A qualitative approach focuses on "people's own written or spoken words and observations" and "directs itself at settings and the individuals within those settings holistically" (Bogdan and Taylor in Dawson et al. 1991:244). Qualitative ways of knowing respect the importance of "subjective meanings of events to individuals and groups" (Epstein in Dawson et al. 1991:244). This approach also "allows the acceptance of multiple rationales, conflicting value systems, and separate realities" (Rodwell in Dawson et al.

1991:244). In this way it shares with social work an appreciation of diversity and of the importance of participation and partnership by all persons involved.

Westkott (1979:19) reminds us that an "emphasis upon the idea that subject and object are humanly linked converges with the interpretive tradition in the social sciences." To her, this interpretive tradition offers an important challenge to "the mainstream positivist emphasis upon objectivity." Westkott refers to this interconnectedness of subject and object as intersubjectivity. She stresses that intersubjectivity does not mean that the two parties to the research process—"the studied and the studier," for example—have the same understandings. But quite to the contrary, meaning or understanding emerges out of a dialogue between the two parties. Through this dialogue new knowledge and understanding emerge quite unpredictably (Westkott 1979:426). Westkott's description aptly communicates the reciprocal, process-focused, creative, and rather ambiguous nature of our behaviors as humans and of our efforts to find solutions to human problems.

Rowan and Reason (1981:113) argue similarly that "a true human inquiry needs to be based firmly in the experience of those it purports to understand, to involve a collaboration between 'research[er]' and 'subjects' so that they may work together as co-researchers, and to be intimately involved in the lives and praxis [actions] of these co-researchers." They do point out, though, that such a partnership approach is not easy and requires fundamental changes in our consciousness (our overall perspective), especially given the predominance of the traditional paradigm's focus on objectivity and separateness.

Alternative Approaches to Knowing: Heuristic, Naturalistic, and Postmodern

Two interrelated alternative approaches to traditional positivistic, scientific, objective, and quantitative approaches to creating knowledge and understanding are heuristic and naturalistic research approaches or paradigms. These approaches include viewing the creation and communication of knowledge in ways much more consistent with alternative interpretive, intuitive, subjective, and qualitative ways of knowing. It is important to note that rather than simply being the opposite of traditional ways of knowing (scientific, positivistic, etc.) heuristic approaches encompass many aspects of traditional scientific approaches. Heuristic researchers simply do not consider traditional scientific approaches to be the only or necessarily the best approaches to knowledge building. Note in the discussion below that heuristic research is referred to as scientific, though, the meaning of "science" is very different from traditional positivistic, quantitative, objective views of science. Many supporters of heuristic approaches suggest these approaches are especially applicable to the human-focused concerns of social workers. We will examine both heuristic and naturalistic modes of inquiry or research next. One way to begin to think about these alternative approaches is to think of them as closely related and to some extent containing each other. Heuristic approaches, however, seem to be more general ways of thinking about doing research and naturalistic approaches as described here are more specifically focused on the methods and "how-tos" of conducting research using a naturalistic paradigm.

Heuristic Research. Heineman Pieper, one of social work's leading proponents of this approach, defines **heuristic** very broadly to mean "any problem-solving strategy that appears likely to lead to relevant, reliable, and useful information." She adds that "a 'heuristic' is a problem-solving strategy whose goal is utility rather than certainty" (1995:207). The heuristic researcher takes the realistic view that real-life problems are too complex, interactive, and perceiver-dependent to lend themselves to comprehensive analysis and exact solutions" (Heineman Pieper 1995:209). Tyson offers perhaps the most inclusive description of heuristic research in her statement that "One of the central ideas in the heuristic approach to scientific research . . . is that all ways of knowing are heuristics, and that not one way of knowing is inherently superior to any other for generating scientific knowledge" (1995:xiv).

While both Tyson and Heineman Pieper refer to the heuristic paradigm as scientific, Heineman Pieper is careful to distinguish between traditional and alternative meanings of science and to argue that the heuristic approach is more appropriate for social work research, especially in the context of practice: "Unlike the logical positivist paradigm, the heuristic paradigm welcomes the complex, ill-structured, substantively important problems that have been social work's abiding focus" (1995:207). In addition, she argues that heuristic approaches can produce information more directly meaningful to both social work practitioners and the consumers of our services. "In contrast to the logical positivist assumption that the five senses give us direct reports of reality, reality is actually constructed through the interpretation of sensory experience within a preexisting framework of meanings. In other words, knowledge is to some extent perceiver dependent. . . . [T]he heuristic researcher selects types of data and methods of data gathering for their appropriateness both to the theory chosen to guide the research and also to the problem under study. . . . The heuristic paradigm suggests that practitioners' and clients' judgments should be evaluated by the same rules as any other data, namely, by whether they lead to useful knowledge and more effective service" (Heineman Pieper 1995:211–212). However, heuristic research proponents acknowledge a number of misunderstandings about this approach.

Heuristic and naturalistic research advocates hope that increasing attention to research done consistent with this alternative paradigm will be not only more meaningful for practitioners and consumers of research, but will actually re-engage practitioners in doing research, because this approach to research does not alter their practice and does respect their abilities and judgments as appropriate and important in the research process. This alternative has the potential for removing the false separation, proponents believe, that has existed between research and practice and between researchers and practitioners, because they are one and the same. They point out that

> *Practitioners, who for the last forty years have unjustly been made to feel that their experienced and educated judgments are unscientific and, therefore, unimportant, can join the effort to devise creative and productive ways to study and shed light on the complex, multifactorial, overdetermined problems that plague us all.* (Heineman Pieper 1995:xxvi)

Naturalistic Inquiry. A more specifically delineated approach to naturalistic research has been described by Lincoln and Guba. They offer the following definition of naturalistic inquiry and then describe fourteen "interdependent characteristics" of naturalistic inquiry. **Naturalistic inquiry** is devoted to understanding *actualities, social realities, and human perceptions that exist untainted by the obtrusiveness of formal measurement or preconceived questions. It is a process geared to the uncovering of many idiosyncratic but nonetheless important stories told by real people, about real events, in real and natural ways. . . . Naturalistic inquiry attempts to present 'slice-of-life' episodes documented through natural language and representing as closely as possible how people feel, what they know, and what their concerns, beliefs, perceptions, and understanding are.* (Wolf and Tymitz in Guba and Lincoln 1981:78)

FOURTEEN INTERDEPENDENT CHARACTERISTICS OF NATURALISTIC INQUIRY (RESEARCH)*

1. *Natural setting:* Researcher carries out research in the natural setting or context of the entity for which study is proposed because "realities are wholes that cannot be understood in isolation from their contexts, nor can they be fragmented for separate study of the parts."

2. *Human instrument:* Researcher uses "him- or herself as well as other humans as the primary data-gathering instruments (as opposed to paper-and-pencil . . . instruments) because it would be virtually impossible to devise . . . [prior to entering the research environment] a non-human instrument with sufficient adaptability to encompass and adjust to the variety of realities that will be encountered."

3. *Utilization of tacit knowledge:* Research argues for valuing "tacit (intuitive, felt) knowledge in addition to propositional knowledge (knowledge expressible in language form) because often the nuances of the multiple realities can be appreciated only in this way."

4. *Qualitative methods:* Researcher uses "qualitative methods over quantitative (although not exclusively) because they are more adaptable to dealing with multiple [and less quantifiable] . . . realities."

5. *Purposive sampling:* Researcher is likely to forego "random or representative sampling in favor of purposive or theoretical sampling because he or she thereby increases the scope or range of data exposed (random or representative sampling is likely to suppress more deviant cases) as well as the likelihood that the full array of multiple realities will be uncovered."

6. *Inductive data analysis:* Researcher "prefers inductive (to deductive) [see below for definitions of inductive and deductive] data analysis because that process is more likely to identify the multiple realities to be found in those data."

Continued

FOURTEEN INTERDEPENDENT CHARACTERISTICS OF NATURALISTIC INQUIRY (RESEARCH) *Continued*

7. *Grounded theory:* Researcher "prefers to have the guiding substantive theory emerge from (be grounded in) the data because *no* [pre-existing] . . . theory could possibly encompass the multiple realities that are likely to be encountered.

8. *Emergent design:* Researcher "elects to allow the research design to emerge (. . . unfold) rather than to construct it preordinately (a priori) because it is inconceivable that enough could be known ahead of time about the many multiple realities to devise the design adequately."

9. *Negotiate Outcomes:* Researcher "prefers to negotiate meanings and interpretations with the human sources from which the data have chiefly been drawn because it is their constructions of reality that the inquirer seeks to reconstruct."

10. *Case study reporting mode:* Researcher "is likely to prefer the case study reporting mode (over the scientific or technical report) because it is more adapted to a description of the multiple realities encountered at any given site."

11. *Idiographic interpretation:* Researcher "is inclined to interpret data including the drawing of conclusions **idiographically** (in terms of the particulars of the case) rather than **nomothetically** (in terms of lawlike generalizations) because different interpretations are likely to be meaningful for different realties."

12. *Tentative application:* Researcher "is likely to be tentative (hesitant) about making broad application of the findings because realities are multiple and different."

13. *Focus-determined boundaries:* Researcher "is likely to set boundaries to the inquiry on the basis of the emergent focus (problem for research, evaluands, for evaluation, and policy option for policy analysis) because that permits the multiple realties to define the focus (rather than inquirer preconceptions)."

14. *Special criteria of trustworthiness:* Researcher "is likely to find the conventional trustworthiness criteria insufficient (validity, reliability, and objectivity) for naturalistic inquiry. Will probably need to define substitute criteria . . . in place of positivist trustworthiness criteria" [(Lincoln and Guba 1985:39–43) [See below for alternative examples of "trustworthiness criteria".]

The concepts, inductive and deductive reasoning, can help differentiate knowledge creation using traditional positivistic approaches and those using alternative approaches such as naturalistic inquiry. **Inductive reasoning** is reasoning "from particular instances to general principles. . . . In induction one starts from observed data and develops a generalization which explains the relationships between the objects observed." **Deductive reasoning** is reasoning "from the general to the particular, applying a theory to a particular case . . . in deductive reasoning one starts from some general law and applies it to a particular instance" (Rubin and Babbie 1997:48).

Naturalistic Research and Rigor: Trustworthiness Criteria. Rigor for both traditional scientific inquiry and naturalistic inquiry involves four concerns. These concerns are listed below along with examples of mechanisms that can be used in naturalistic research contexts to test for these measures of rigor. [Note: Postivitistic scientific terms comparable to the naturalistic terms are listed in parentheses.]

1. *Truth Value/Credibility (Internal Validity):* How do you know the findings are true? Corroborate findings with multiple audiences and groups; recontact and recheck findings consistently over time; establish standards for adequacy against which to check credibility with various audiences; use "triangulation" (use multiple measurement processes for the subject under study).

2. *Applicability/Fittingness (External Validity):* How do you know if the findings from this research are applicable to other people and contexts? How can you answer the question of "fittingness"? Ask the potential audience to which the information may be applied if it is applicable in their situation as it was found to be in the original research context. Think of generalizations as "working hypotheses" subject to change depending on changes in situations or contexts or times. The notion of "thick description," is useful: "literal description of the entity being evaluated, the circumstances under which it is used, the characteristics of the people involved in it, the nature of the community in which it is located, etc."

3. *Consistency/Auditability (Reliability):* How do you know if the same results would occur if research was replicated? Naturalistic inquiry, given its "context-based" nature, is rarely replicated. However, researcher must still answer questions about the consistency with which the research was carried out. Suggestions for addressing consistency include internal reliability check with different members of a research team cross-checking each other's work as it progresses; external reliability checks by bringing in outside evaluators or "judges" to "audit" the work as it progresses.

4. *Neutrality/Confirmability (Objectivity):* How do you know the effects of your research result from the subjects and materials you are studying or from your own biases, interests, perspectives as the researcher? Data must be factual and confirmable; recognize that values of the researcher do in fact enter into the research; try for objectivity of facts over the false notion of objectivity of researcher. (Guba and Lincoln 1981:103–127)

Postmodern Ways of Knowing. As we saw in Chapter 1, many scholars today are beginning to think of the current period in which we live as one of paradigm shift from modernism and an almost complete allegiance to traditional ways of knowing (positivistic, scientific, objective, quantitative) to a postmodern period in which traditional ways of knowing are increasingly questioned at many levels. This shift toward postmodern thinking is increasingly influencing the way many social workers approach both education and practice. Ann Hartman (1995:xix), in her introduction to Tyson's book, *New Foundations for Scientific and Behavioral Research: The Heuristic Paradigm,* conveys her sense of the rise and subsequent questioning of traditional ways of knowing that is so much a part of postmodernism. Hartman speaks of this reaction to the privileging of traditional scientific and university-based ways of knowing as

> *the complex social and political processes that gradually concentrated knowl-edge-power in the hands of primarily university-based researchers, and how as positivist discourse about the nature of 'truth' became increasingly privi-leged, other knowledge, other ways of knowing were discredited or subju-gated.... [T]he privileging of the methods of science has led to the subjugation of both previously established erudite [scholarly] knowledge and local popular or indigenous knowledge, located on the margins, 'exiled from the legitimate domains of the formal knowledge.'* (White & Epson 1990, p. 26 in Hartman 1995)

Given this time of turbulence about the very bases of how and what we know as fact or truth, it is important for us to examine a bit more closely what we mean by postmodernism and concepts related to postmodernism. Lather describes her vision of the postmodern world in an interesting way that captures much of what is central to postmodern thinking. Lather's description also reflects much about the various di-mensions of alternative paradigm thinking we explore in this book. Lather quotes a statement by Riley that "we live in both/and worlds full of paradox and uncertainty where close inspection turns unities into multiplicities, clarities into ambiguities, uni-vocal simplicities into polyvocal complexities" (Riley 1988 in Lather 1991:xvi). Van Den Bergh, a social worker, describes the postmodern perspective as one questioning the "taken for granted" or "grand" theories we take almost as givens in social work. She also sees postmodernism as indicative of the coming of significant change in the "taken for granted" assumptions we make (1995:xii–xiv). Van Den Bergh gives as examples of "grand theory" used in social work (often borrowed from other social sci-ences), systems and ecological theories, ego psychology, cognitive or behavioral theo-ries, psychological and moral development paradigms, and political or economic models of societal relations such as Marxism. In the chapters that follow in this book we will examine many of these theories as they apply to our work as social workers. Postmod-ernists would suggest, however, that we critically examine these theories each time we attempt to apply them in our work, so that we do not overgeneralize and assume they apply to every person, family, group, organization, or community with which we work.

Sands and Nuccio (1992) suggest a number of implications of postmodern and theory for social work education and practice. In addition, they define and differen-tiate a number of terms helpful in understanding postmodernism. Postmodern schol-ars often use the terms *structuralism* and *poststructuralism* in their work. Lather describes how she differentiates the two related terms, postmodern and poststruc-tural: "I sometimes use *postmodern* to mean the larger cultural shifts of a post-industrial, post-colonial era and *poststructural* to mean the working out of those shifts within the arenas of academic theory" (1991:4). So, for Lather, postmodernism indicates the paradigm shift she sees taking place in the larger culture and society. Poststructural-ism reflects the theory and theory-building taking place to attempt to explain this par-adigm shift. Sands and Nuccio (1992:490–491) compare their meanings of the terms "structuralism" and "poststructuralism." **Poststructuralism** "both incorporates and transforms structuralism. Whereas **structuralists** view meaning that is produced within language as fixed, **poststructuralists** see meaning as multiple, unstable, and open to interpretation (Weedon 1987). . . . **Poststructuralists** look at meaning in relation to the particular social, political, and historical contexts in which language is spoken or written. They view discourses (bodies of language or *texts* [this concept of "text" is described in more detail in Chapter 3]) and readers as situated, rather than neutral. Accordingly, poststructuralists move away from 'grand theory,' which purports to assert universal truth" (emphasis added).

Through the use of such concepts as poststructuralism, Sands and Nuccio reinforce the stance that "Postmodernists devalue the search for universal laws and theories and focus on local meanings that are socially constructed. . . . Postmodern philosophers object to binary categories and emphasize diversity, multiplicity, and pluralism. They view categories such as gender, race, and class as too reductive (1992:492). The concept of deconstruction we described in Chapter 1 is a tool postmodernists use to consider the voices and perspectives excluded in the search for universal laws and theories.

Comparison of Traditional and Alternative Ways of Knowing

It may be helpful at this point to compare some of the basic differences between traditional and alternative paradigms in terms of the "ways of knowing" or building knowledge. In comparing the paradigms along this dimension, the reader is encouraged to consider the implications of the other paradigmatic dimensions with which we have been concerned in this chapter: masculinity/patriarchy; whiteness; separateness/impersonality/competitiveness; privilege and feminisms; diversities; interrelatedness/personal/integrativeness; oppressions. Which of the paradigms for research compared below seem most consistent with which of the other elements of the traditional and alternative paradigms we have examined?

TABLE 2.1 Contrasting Positivist and Naturalist Axioms

Axioms About	Positivist Paradigm	Naturalist Paradigm
The nature of reality	Reality is single, tangible, and fragmentable.	Realities are multiple, constructed, and holistic.
The relationship of knower to the known	Knower and known are independent, a dualism.	Knower and known are interactive, inseparable.
The possibility of generalizations	Time- and context-free generalizations (nomothetic statements) are possible.	One time- and context-bound working hypotheses (idiographic statements) are possible.
The possibility of causal linkages	There are real causes, temporally precedent to or simultaneous with their effects.	All entities are in a state of mutual simultaneous shaping, so that it is impossible to distinguish causes from effects.
The role of values	Inquiry is value-free.	Inquiry is value-bound.

Lincoln, Y. S. and Guba, E. G. *Naturalistic Inquiry,* p. 37. Copyright © 1985 by Sage Publications, Inc. Reprinted with permission.

Lincoln and Guba also differentiate positivistic and naturalistic research in the following ways:

- *Positivism emphasizes* **exogenous** *research:* "research in which all aspects of the research, from problem definition through instrumentation, data collection and analysis, and use of findings, have been researcher-determined—to the virtual exclusion of **endogenous research**—that is, research in which the respondents have equal rights to determination."
- *Positivism emphasizes* **etic** *research*—"that is, research carried out with an outside (objective) perspective—to the virtual exclusion of **emic research**—that is, research carried out with an inside perspective (subjective)." (Lincoln and Guba 1985:27)

Demo and Allen note that Lather includes postmodern approaches in her adaptation of Habermas' notion of multiple approaches to knowledge-building based on the type of outcomes sought:

1. *Traditional approaches to science are rooted in positivism, in which the goal is to* **predict**
2. *Hermeneutic, naturalistic and interpretive approaches to science are rooted in phenomenology, in which the goal is to* **understand**
3. *Critical approaches to science, which overlap with neo-Marxist and feminist perspectives, are praxis-oriented, in which the goal is to* **emancipate**
4. *Poststructural or postmodern approaches, in which the goal is to* **deconstruct** (1996:429).

The interpretive/intuitive/subjective/qualitative dimension of the alternative paradigm, and the related alternative "ways of knowing" described above along with the other dimensions of alternative paradigms we will explore next, offer a more holistic approach to understanding—to finding meaning. Feminism, the dimension of the alternative paradigm we will explore next, integrates the elements of the interpretive/intuitive/subjective/qualitative dimension. It moves us still closer to a holistic approach to understanding HBSE—to finding meaning.

Feminisms

Feminism offers a significant and far-reaching approach to developing alternative paradigms for understanding human behavior and the social environment. Feminism or feminist thinking is both an essential dimension of the alternative paradigm we wish to develop and explore and an alternative paradigm or worldview in itself. Feminism is multidimensional and has many meanings to different people. It is perhaps really more accurate to think in terms of feminisms than in terms of feminism. Ruth (1990:3) suggests the comprehensive, multidimensional nature of feminism. She presents feminism as "a perspective, a worldview, a political theory, a spiritual focus, or a kind of activism." Ruth (1990:3) also demonstrates the complexity of and varied perspectives about what feminism is. She offers several useful definitions of feminism excerpted from Cheris Kramarae and Paula A. Treichler's *Feminist Dictionary*. These definitions offered by leading feminist scholars and activists provide important glimpses of feminism as a worldview, as political theory and action, and, perhaps most important, as an alternative to many of the limiting dimensions that constitute the dominant paradigm.

> *[Feminism] is an entire world view or gestalt, not just a laundry list of "women's issues." Feminist theory provides a basis for understanding every area of our lives, and a feminist perspective can affect the world politically, culturally, economically, and spiritually.* (Charlotte Bunch, *Learning Our Way*, 1983)

> *Feminism means finally that we renounce our obedience to the fathers and recognize that the world they have described is not the whole world. . . . Feminism implies that we recognize fully the inadequacy for us, the distortion, of male-created ideologies, and that we proceed to think, and act, out of that recognition.* (Adrienne Rich, *Of Woman Born*, 1976)

> *Feminism is the political theory and practice to free all women; women of color, working-class women, poor women, physically challenged women, lesbians, old women, as well as white economically privileged heterosexual women. Anything less than this is not feminism . . .* (Barbara Smith in Cherrie Moraga and Gloria Anzaldua, *This Bridge Called My Back*, 1981)

> *It is a commitment to eradicating the ideology of domination that permeates Western Culture on various levels—sex, race, and class, to name a few—and a commitment to reorganizing U.S. society, so that the self-development of people can take precedence over imperialism, economic expansion, and material desires.* (bell hooks, *Ain't I a Woman*, 1981)

These definitions underscore the importance of social workers' incorporating feminist thinking into our efforts to understand HBSE and in our practice of social work. These definitions are linked quite directly to the core concerns of social work we explored earlier in Chapter 1. Feminism and social work share many of these core concerns.

Van Den Bergh and Cooper, social workers, offer a definition of feminism that reflects the consistency between this conceptual framework and the purposes and values of social work. They say "*feminism* is a conceptual framework and mode of analysis that has analyzed the status of women (and other disempowered groups), cross-culturally and historically to explain dynamics and conditions undergirding disparities in sociocultural status and power between majority and minority populations (in Van Den Bergh 1995, p. xii).

Fritjof Capra (1983:415) finds feminism consistent with and encompassing other alternative paradigms such as ecological and holistic worldviews. Ecological and holistic approaches also offer important perspectives for expanding our understanding of HBSE. He suggests, for example, that the "spiritual essence of the ecological vision seems to find its ideal expression in the feminist spirituality advocated by the women's movement." Capra reminds us that "feminist spirituality is based on awareness of the

SHARED CHARACTERISTICS BETWEEN SOCIAL WORK AND FEMINIST WORLDVIEWS

- The development of all human beings through service
- The intrinsic worth and dignity of all human beings
- The intrinsic importance of active participation in society
- The necessity for removing obstacles to self-realization
- The prevention and elimination of discrimination in services, work, employment, and common human needs.

Source: Swigonski 1994:389

oneness of all living forms and of their cyclical rhythms of birth and death, thus reflecting an attitude toward life that is profoundly ecological."

In the box, Wetzel (in Swigonski 1994: 389) offers a helpful comparison of feminist and social work worldviews.

Capra offers a vision of a world emerging from feminist ideals. It is a vision, important for men to realize, in which both men and women are more free to reach their full human potential. Capra offers this glimpse and prediction:

> *Thus the feminist movement will continue to assert itself as one of the strongest cultural currents of our time. Its ultimate aim is nothing less than a thorough redefinition of human nature, which will have the most profound effect on the further evolution of our culture.* (1983:416)

To accomplish such re-visioning of the world, feminism requires recognition of current inequality. Donadello (1980:214–215) suggests that central to the definition of feminism "is the conscious explicit awareness that women in our culture and in society are systematically denied equal rights, opportunities, and access to the services and goods available in the society." Out of the recognition of current inequalities can come change. Such change must include exchanging "a patriarchal system for a healthier commitment to an equalitarian system providing the potential and opportunity for self-actualization for everyone." This humanistic worldview will emphasize the value of "every individual and offer each a maximum of human freedom and dignity." This perspective not only unites the core concerns of social work with feminism, but it clearly distinguishes feminist perspectives from a traditional/dominant perspective.

Bricker-Jenkins and Hooyman (1986:8) further unite social work and feminism in their description of feminism from a social work perspective. They assert that "feminism insists on removing any sanction from choices that are judged to be inimical to human development, freedom, and health. . . . [A]n underlying consensus exists: that barriers to the realization of the full and unique human potential of women can and must be challenged and changed."

These descriptions of the goals and ideology of feminism are not only consistent with the values and philosophy of social work but are also consistent with the alternative worldview we seek to articulate here.

Feminism, Social Work and Postmodernism

There are many commonalties between feminist and postmodern perspectives which in turn share commonalties with a social work worldview. However, there have also been some significant difficulties reconciling purist postmodernism and social work and feminist perspectives. Postmodernism in its purist form claims to be apolitical and everything is subject to deconstruction. Feminism and social work are clearly "political." Postmodernism also is suspicious of categories and general versus local knowledge, while social work focuses on such "categories" as gender, race, class, and sexual orientation as central to its very purposes as a profession (Van Den Bergh 1995:xxv–xxvi).

Feminist Standpoint Theory. One attempt at reconciling this tension is suggested by Van Den Bergh, using Swigonski's and other writers' perspectives on standpoint theory. She suggests that (1995:xxvii) "**Standpoints** are truths or knowledge created through awareness of reality gleaned from particular social locations. The concept of standpoint assumes that all people see the world from the place in which they are situated socioculturally. What is considered to be real depends on one's standpoint and is grounded in experiences related to one's position within the sociocultural topography."

Van Den Bergh points out that "Where this perspective differs from earlier feminist analysis is in the standpoint emphasis on multiplicity and diversity within women's experiences. As opposed to proposing a unilateral feminist standpoint, there are multiplicities (that is, African American women's standpoints, lesbian standpoints, Latina standpoints, and older women's standpoints" (1995:xxvii). This allows a degree of respect for the particular or local experience of specific women within the larger universe of "women." It also reflects the need to think about feminist perspectives and feminisms as plural rather than singular.

Diversities

A key to conceptualizing an alternative paradigm for understanding human behavior and the social environment is recognition of the centrality of **diversity and difference.** The importance of human diversity is interwoven with all the other dimensions of our alternative paradigm. Diversity is central to alternative routes to knowledge building, to feminism, to interrelatedness, and to understanding and eliminating oppressions. Our alternative paradigm for more comprehensively understanding HBSE recognizes human diversity as a source of strength, creativity, wonder, and health. This alternative paradigm is one in which processes of discovery are central. It is one in which there is not one answer but many answers; not one question but many questions. Only by recognizing both our differences and our similarities as humans can we proceed toward reaching our full potential. The search for an alternative paradigm is at its core a search for diversity. It is a search for new ways to answer age-old questions. It is a process of attempting to allow voices, long silenced, to be heard. Our alternative paradigm is one in which the complex questions of human behavior welcome and respect multiple answers suited to the multiple needs and views of the humans with whom social workers interact.

The human diversities with which we are concerned include those resulting from gender, color, sexual orientation, religion, age, disabling condition, culture, income, and class. Acquainting ourselves with the voices and visions of these different individuals and groups will provide us with important, useful, and creative alternative ways of thinking about such basic concerns of social work and HBSE as individuals, families, groups, organizations, and communities. Next, we will explore some examples of how the worldviews of diverse people and groups can provide social workers with new ways to think about HBSE.

Diversities and Worldviews: What Can We Learn from Others?

One example of diverse avenues to understanding human experience more completely can be found in elements of a worldview based on the experiences and history of many persons of African descent. Collins summarizes the origins and elements of an Afrocentric worldview. These views, she says, "reflect elements of a core African values system that existed prior to and independently of racial oppression." In addition,

> *Black people share a common experience of oppression. These two factors foster shared Afrocentric values that permeate the family structure, religious institutions, culture, and community life of Blacks in varying parts of Africa, the Caribbean, South America, and North America. . . . This Afrocentric consciousness permeates the shared history of people of African descent through the framework of a distinctive Afrocentric epistemology.* (Collins 1990:206)

These experiences translate into values and perspectives that shape a worldview quite different from those that emerge from dominant paradigms. "The African world view begins with a holistic conception of the human condition" (White in Everett et al. 1991:46). It places emphasis on such values as the importance of "collectivity, sharing, affiliation, obedience to authority, belief in spirituality, and respect for the elderly and the past." These historical values exist alongside values that emerged over time as a response to oppression. Pinderhughes refers to this set of oppression-influenced values as "victim values." This set of values includes an emphasis on "cooperation to combat powerlessness; strict obedience to authority in the context of felt oppression; strength; toughness of character; present-time orientation (since the past is painful and there is no future); suppression and channeling of feelings into music, art, and other creative activities; and belief in luck, magic and spirituality" (Pinderhughes 1982: 109–110). These two sets of values converge in many different combinations and result in the vast differences in individual perspectives and family forms that exist among African Americans. Respect for and understanding of this complex set of values is essential to expanding our understanding of HBSE.

The experiences and perspectives of lesbians and gay men also have rich potential for providing new insight into questions of human behavior. These experiences and perspectives have much to offer, not only in terms of understanding the complexities of sexual orientation—lesbian/gay, bisexual and heterosexual—but also in providing new perspectives on such wide-ranging but essential concerns as human diversity itself, innovative alternative structures for family, and strengths-based perspectives on help seeking.

We can learn about what it means to be bicultural through the experiences of lesbians and gay men who must function simultaneously in both the heterosexual and gay/lesbian worlds. We will discuss **biculturality** or the ability to function in two cultures simultaneously in more detail in later chapters. At this point we simply need to be aware that members of diverse groups such as lesbians and gay men and people of color are expected to be able to function effectively according to the expectation of both the dominant paradigm and their own alternative worldviews. This ability to be bicultural, however, is usually not expected of members of the dominant group. Models for becoming bicultural are important for us as social workers, since we will frequently be called upon to work with persons from many different cultural backgrounds.

Alternative perspectives of some Native American cultures offer helpful models for seeing strength in diversity. These cultures offer models not of merely accepting such differences as those between gay and nongay persons, but of finding respected roles and responsibilities for these special members of the community. Brown (1989:450) discusses the findings of research with some Native American communities in which gay and lesbian members are "perceived as seers, shamans, capable of greater wisdom than their clearly heterosexually defined peers." These cultures perceive of their gay and lesbian members as transcending limits imposed by roles traditionally assigned to people based on gender.

Brown suggests also that gay men and lesbians may be redefining what it means to seek help from professional mental health care givers. She suggests that for many gay men and lesbians seeking help may be seen as a sign of strength rather than as a sign of weakness. She suggests that gay men and lesbians may have redefined help seeking to be indicative of health and health-seeking behaviors very appropriate for "sanely managing to live in the ambiguity, which . . . is the situation for most late 20th century Americans." Brown suggests that such a perspective might well be appropriate for many people other than those who are gay and lesbian (1989:456). Such a perspective indicates an important shift toward a strengths-based approach to seeking assistance. We will discuss strengths-based approaches in Chapter 3.

Many other similarly significant alternatives to traditional paradigm thinking can be found by exploring diversity. Belief systems about the appropriate relationship of humans to the natural environment of many Native American, Asian American, and African American people also offer much that might well be essential to our very survival on this planet. These diverse groups have shared a historic sense that humans must exist in harmony with all the elements of the natural world—human, animal, or inanimate. Such belief systems result in a deep respect and concern for preserving the natural world. This sense of interconnectedness and mutual responsibility is quite consistent with core concerns of social work as well as alternative paradigm dimensions. This perspective is quite different from dominant perspectives based on the belief that the natural world is to be controlled and harnessed in service to humans. The dominant perspective has resulted too often in the abuse and destruction of the natural environment in order to control and exploit it for the immediate benefit of humans.

Learning about diversity can expand our understanding of still another area of concern to social workers. We can find helpful alternative perspectives on the roles of elders and their contributions to the common good. Many Native American, African American, and Asian American families and communities reserve positions of great respect and importance for their elder members. Many families and communities of African heritage, for example, see elders as holding the wisdom of the culture, and they entrust them to impart their wisdom and the history of the people to younger members through oral tradition. Other meaningful roles for elders, especially for grandparents, are found in actively participating in child rearing and in assuming foster and adoptive parent roles for the family's children when necessary. In many African American families and communities, responsibilities for child rearing may be shared among parents and grandparents as well as other adult and elderly members of the community who function as grandparents and care givers outside the traditional blood-related or legally sanctioned family network. Such inclusiveness not only finds more opportunities for meaningful roles for elders, it also affords a larger system of care givers for the community's children. Through such extended systems as these there is the opportunity for mutual benefits and obligations across generations and traditional family boundaries (Beaver 1990:224; Turner in Everett et al. 1991:50–51).

Diversity within Diversity: Beyond Binaries

The traditional paradigm tendency to view the world in binary terms of either/or greatly oversimplifies the richness and multiple realities of many persons. The historic tendency of the dominant group (whites) literally to see the world in "black and white" reflects this binary tendency.

Historically, "U.S. society was widely spoken of as consisting of two races, one white and one black. The white-Caucasian-European race was deemed biologically pure. People with any known African ancestry ('one drop of black blood') [This was the so-called: "one-drop" rule or "the rule of hypodescent" (Daniel 1992:336)] were put in the black-Negro-African American category. Other people—those who were neither white nor black—were seldom noted or were placed on the margins" (Spickard et al. 1996:14).

The Census. This binary tendency to deny multiple racial realities was perhaps most clearly reflected in past U.S. Census Bureau policy. However, this is changing. According to the AmeriStat Population Reference Bureau and Social Science Data Analysis Network, "the shifting labels and definitions used in the U.S. census reflect the growing diversity of the population and changing political and social climate." According to AmeriStat:

> *The first population census in 1790 asked enumerators to classify free residents as white or "other." Slaves were counted separately. By 1860, the census requested that residents be classified as white, black, or mulatto [see Table 2.2]. American Indian and Chinese were added as separate categories in 1870. In the 1890 census, census-takers were instructed to distinguish the color of household members as white, black, octoroon (one-eighth black), quadroon (one-quarter black), mulatto (one-half black), or as Chinese, Japanese, or American Indian.* (AmeriStat 2000)

Fortunately, over time racial categories have dramatically increased until in the 1980 and 1990 censuses "there were 43 racial categories and subcategories on the 1990 census forms, including white, black; American Indian, Eskimo, or Aleut; Asian or Pacific Islander, with 11 Asian subcategories and four Pacific Islander subcategories; other race; and Hispanic origin grid with 15 subcategories that included

TABLE 2.2   Race/Ethnicity Categories in the Census 1860–2000

Census	1860	1890[1]	1900	1970	2000[2]
Race	White	White	White	White	White
	Black	Black	Black (of Negro descent)	Negro or Black	Black, African American, or Negro
	Mulatto	Mulatto			
		Chinese	Chinese	Chinese	Chinese
		Indian	Indian	Indian (Amer.)	American Indian or Alaska Native
		Quadroon			
		Octoroon			
		Japanese	Japanese	Japanese	Japanese
				Filipino	Filipino
					Asian Indian
				Korean	Korean
				Hawaiian	Native Hawaiian
					Vietnamese
					Guamanian or Chamorro
					Samoan
					Other Asian
					Other Pacific Islander
				Other	Some other race
Hispanic ethnicity				Mexican	Mexican, Mexican Amer., Chicano
				Puerto Rican	Puerto Rican
				Central/So. American	
				Cuban	Cuban
				Other Spanish	Other Spanish/Hispanic/ Latino
				(None of these)	Not Spanish/Hispanic/ Latino

Source: 200 Years of U.S. Census Taking: Population and Housing Questions 1790–1990. U.S. Department of Commerce. U.S. Bureau of the Census. Available: http://www.ameristat.org/racethnic/census.htm. Reprinted with permission. Population Reference Bureau, www.ameristat.org

[1]In 1890, mulatto was defined as a person who was three-eights to five-eights black. A quadroon was one-quarter black and an octoroon one-eighth black.

[2]Categories printed in the 2000 Census Dress Rehearsal questionnaire.

Note: Prior to the 1970 census, enumerators wrote in the race of individuals using the designated categories. In subsequent censuses, respondents or enumerators filled in circles next to the categories with which the respondent identified. Also beginning with the 1970 census, persons choosing American Indian, other Asian, other race, or (for the Hispanic question) other Hispanic categories, were asked to write in a specific tribe or group. Hispanic ethnicity was asked of a sample of Americans in 1970 and of all Americans beginning with the 1980 census.

Mexican, Puerto Rican, Cuban, and other Hispanic (U.S. Bureau of the Census 1992)" (Spickard et al. 1996:15).

For the first time, the year 2000 census allowed respondents to mark multiple categories. With this change as many as 63 racial combinations were possible. The year 2000 census was also more responsive to persons of Hispanic heritage. The Census Bureau coding (including the option of writing in specific group of origin, such as Salvadoran, Nicaraguan, Argentinean, etc.) allowed over 30 Hispanic or Latino(a) groups to be specified. This is a significant change, allowing multiracial people to more accurately report their multiracial identities (Armas 2000; Bureau of the Census 2000).

Multiple Diversities. In addition to multiple diversity in terms of race, culture, and ethnicity, there is growing recognition that individuals may identify with other multiple diversities. It is extremely important to recognize that diversity is not a unitary status, though it is often considered to be so. There is considerable variability among the members of any one diverse group. In addition, individuals may simultaneously have membership in multiple diverse groups. For example, an individual may identify as a gay male, person of color, with a physical disability. All of these identifications have significance for how people see themselves and how others view them. These multiple identities interact in complex ways as a person grows and develops and interacts in different social environments. Spickard points out that "Genetic variability within populations is greater than the variability between them" (1992:16). This variability is true in terms of gendered categories as well. Demo and Allen, in their discussion of gender and sexual orientation, note that "It is important to recognize that there is greater variability within gendered categories than between males and females as gender groups" (1996:418).

Fong et al. stress that "Social workers have a responsibility to consciously reverse the historic binary system, enforced more strongly against African Americans than people of any other race or ethnicity, by seeking to understand the full background of clients and clients' perceptions of their identities, rather than allocating them into preconceived categories" (1996:21). Parks et al. expressed similar concerns about the counseling and development field in their statement that "Another weakness in many recent theories and treatment approaches is that they assume that racial and gender groups are essentially monolithic. Little attention is paid to the question of the various types of identification an individual might have with his or her race and gender and, in turn, the effect that these attitudes might have on functioning. Many theorists instead present a psychology of women or a Black psychology that is meant to apply to all women or to all Blacks" (1996:624). Root stresses that "The recent consideration of multidimensional models has allowed the possibility that an individual can have simultaneous membership and multiple, fluid identities with different groups. . . . These models abolish either/or classifications systems that create marginality" (1992:6). When we explore identity development more completely in Chapters 4 and 5 we will return to issues of multiple diversity.

The above examples demonstrate that, like feminism, diversity is much more than a single dimension of an alternative paradigm for thinking about HBSE. The notion of diversity opens doors to a multitude of alternative paradigms. Through the door of diversity we can enter worlds offering vastly differing and rich ways of thinking about the world and the individuals, families, groups, organizations, and communities that make it up. Diversity, then, is not a single dimension of a single alternative paradigm; it offers both a cornerstone and an organizing framework for our attempts to think more broadly, more progressively, more creatively, more humanely about HBSE in every chapter at every point throughout this book.

Interrelatedness/Personal/Integrative

The alternative paradigms with which we are concerned are characterized by a recognition of the **interrelatedness and interconnectedness** of all humans. Many alternative paradigm thinkers go beyond recognition of the interrelatedness of all humans with each other to suggest "the intrinsic and ineluctable interconnectedness of all phenomena, human or otherwise" (Guba and Lincoln 1989:66). Many Afrocentric, Native American, and Asian influenced worldviews share this sense of the interrelatedness of humans with all elements of the environment in which we exist. Such a holistic perspective is useful and appropriate for social work with its concern for human behavior in the context of the larger environment. Alternative paradigm thinking challenges us to take the broadest most inclusive approach possible to what constitutes context or environment.

Capra suggests that from new perspectives in physics emerges a picture of the physical world characterized by an extremely high degree of interrelatedness. He suggests that the new perspectives in physics have significant implications for and connections with the "human sciences." The new perspectives in physics are based on "the harmonious interrelatedness" of the components of the natural world. Capra finds this view of the world inconsistent with dominant paradigm perspectives that see society made up of unconnected and competing forces. To bring social and economic theory in line with newer perspectives in the natural sciences, Capra believes that "a radically different social and economic structure will be needed: a cultural revolution in the true sense of the word" (1983:17–18). Such a statement from the perspective of a physicist about social change has striking and interesting links to core social work values and philosophy.

Ann Weick, a social worker, also suggests that we look to emerging alternatives to the traditional paradigm in the natural sciences to inform our thinking about society. She, like Capra, suggests that new perspectives in physics (quantum theory) illustrate the centrality of interrelatedness. Using the findings in physics as a metaphor, she believes, we can recognize "that human behavior is set within a web of relationships where dynamic interaction is a key feature. It is not possible to isolate one element in the web without disrupting the pattern or patterns in which it exists." (Weick 1991:21).

Jean Baker Miller, a researcher who has extensively studied and developed alternative perspectives on women's development, finds the importance of connection and interrelatedness with others central to the individual development of women. Miller stresses that "women stay with, build on, and develop in a context of connections with others. Indeed, women's sense of self becomes very much organized around being able to make and then to maintain affiliations and relationships." Miller's findings are quite contrary to dominant paradigm perspectives on individual development that stress the importance of separation, individuation, and autonomy in the development of both men and women. Miller posits "that for everyone—men as well as women—individual development proceeds *only* by means of connection. At the present time, men are not as prepared to *know* this" (1986:83). We will return to the importance of connection and relationship in human development in Chapter 5 (see also Illustrative Reading 5.1 by Miller).

An important aspect of interrelatedness especially significant to social workers is that of mutuality or partnership between the actors involved in human interactions. This mutuality is central to the approaches we take to understanding HBSE in this book. We learn about ourselves through our attempts to understand the behaviors of others and we learn about others through our attempts to understand our own behaviors. Such a perspective emphasizes that as social workers we are not separate from the persons with whom we interact and work. We are, instead, partners in a mutual process of seeking meaning and understanding. Out of this mutual meaning and understanding can come action to help ourselves and the people with whom we work to reach our fullest potential as humans. One form of this relationship-based action to accomplish personal and collective goals is referred to as **social capital.** We will examine this concept in more detail in later chapters.

Alternative paradigms of concern to us also recognize the importance and power of personal experience and action to understand and transform the elements of our worlds. This standpoint emphasizes that our personal day-to-day experiences, challenges, accomplishments, and struggles have meaning and importance. For it is through our personal day-to-day experiences that we come to know our worlds. It is through sharing our personal experiences with those around us that we recognize similarities and differences between our experiences of the world and those of others.

The process of sharing personal experiences and analyses of those experiences results not only in more fully understanding the world around us, but it can result in joining with others around us to transform that world to allow ourselves and others more opportunity to reach our human potential. This process is perhaps most effectively and completely developed in the women's movement and in liberation movements in some third world countries through what is known as consciousness-raising or CR. This approach assumes not only that the personal is important, but that it is political. Joining together to share personal experiences not only validates those experiences, but it can also empower us to take action. As Longres and McLeod point out in their discussion of the place of consciousness-raising in social work practice, CR "enables people to become involved in overcoming ways by which societal conditions negatively affect their lives. . . . [It can] enable people to make connections between adverse conditions in the fabric of society and the problems experienced by them in everyday life, and, through action, to overcome those conditions" (1980:268).

The personal characteristic of an alternative paradigm requires a rethinking of traditional approaches in many areas. Alternative approaches, unlike traditional approaches to the study of history, for example, see history not simply as a story of "great" people and "great" events, it is the stories of all of us and of *all* of the events that shape *all* our lives. Respecting and valuing our personal experiences and perspectives can be an important source of empowerment, especially for persons whose experiences and lives are not reflected in histories and institutions that emerge from the dominant/traditional paradigm. Collins (1986:16) suggests that recognizing and valuing the importance of our own personal experiences in the face of oppressive forces that seek to devalue those personal experiences are an important part of overcoming oppression.

Oppressions

Collins (1990) finds oppositional or binary thinking that places differences (among people, beliefs, etc.) in direct opposition to or competition with one another to be an important part of dominant paradigm approaches for ordering and valuing people and information. In this respect, she finds binary thinking a major component linking oppressions. If this is the case, then more integrative and cooperative processes are likely to offer means for reducing interlocking oppressions. Integrative approaches call for us to think in terms of both/and rather than in dichotomous either/or terms. Such an integrative perspective also allows us to take seriously such diverse approaches as Eastern philosophical notions of balance, and quantum notions of interrelatedness of observer and observed.

Interlocking Oppressions

In our explorations we will seek recognition and awareness of what Collins (1990: 222ff.) refers to as **"interlocking systems of oppression."** We will focus our concern on oppressions as they manifest themselves throughout the institutions and systems that constitute U.S. society. This alternative approach recognizes the interrelatedness of oppressions and the interconnections between oppressions and the other dimensions of both traditional/dominant and alternate paradigms. We will recognize that oppression in any institution directed toward any individual or group is connected with and results in oppression in other institutions and of many other individuals and groups. This interrelated or interlocking quality gives oppression its systemic nature.

Such a multifaceted and interconnected conceptualization of oppression requires a significant change in thinking for many of us. Collins suggests that we must move away from simple additive approaches that may recognize oppression in multiple institutions or directed toward multiple persons or groups, but do not recognize the interplay of these oppressions among different systems. Collins illustrates the interlocking nature of oppressions from the perspective of the multiple and interlocking oppressions experienced by African American women. She suggests that black feminist thought offers an alternative paradigm for understanding oppressions by calling for "a fundamental paradigmatic shift that rejects additive approaches to oppression. Instead of starting with gender and then adding in other variables such as age, sexual orientation, race, social class, and religion, Black feminist thought sees these distinctive systems of oppression as being part of one overarching structure of domination" (Collins 1990:222). This paradigm assumes "that each system needs the others in order to function" (Collins 1990:222).

"Attention to the interlocking nature of race, gender, and class oppression is a . . . recurring theme in the works of Black feminists" (Collins 1986:19) and recognition of these complex and mutually reinforcing dynamics is essential for social workers. The implications of this alternative perspective on oppression are multiple for social workers. As Collins points out, "this viewpoint shifts the entire focus of investigation from one aimed at explicating elements of race or gender or class oppression to one whose goal is to determine what the links are among these systems" rather than prioritizing one form of oppression as being primary (Collins 1986:20).

A somewhat similar point about the interconnectedness of oppressions is made by Pharr (1988:53). She says, "It is virtually impossible to view one oppression, such as sexism or homophobia, in isolation because they are all connected: sexism, racism, homophobia, classism, ablement, anti-Semitism, ageism. They are linked by a common origin—economic power and control—and by common methods of limiting, controlling and destroying lives." As students of social work and of HBSE, we must critically examine each theory, perspective, or paradigm that we explore, whether traditional or alternative, for its implications for recognizing and challenging existing interlocking systems of oppression.

Oppressions and Oppressors

Paulo Freire (1992) looked at the mutual impact of oppression on both the oppressed and the oppressor: "Once a situation of violence and oppression has been established, it engenders an entire way of life and behavior for those caught up in it—oppressors and oppressed alike. Both are submerged in this situation, and both bear the marks of oppression" (Freire in Myers and Speight 1994:108). Freire refers to this as dehumanization and emphasizes that "those whose humanity was stolen and those who stole it are both dehumanized." An oppressor's belief system, according to Freire, perceives everything as an object of domination, resulting in a materialistic concept of existence. The oppressed often cannot perceive the oppressive system and instead end up identifying with their oppressor. They may internalize the opinion the oppressor holds of them" (Myers and Speight 1994:108). "Devaluation of self results from a self-negation fostered by the internalization of experiences of discrepancy, ambiguity, and rejection—what has come to be called 'internalization of racism' and 'internalized oppression'" (Kich 1992:307–308).

Oppressions and Social and Economic Justice

For social workers, awareness of the multiple dynamics and impacts of oppressions is only the first step. Awareness must lead to action which in turn can lead to change resulting in social and economic justice. Watts provides a helpful sketch showing how awareness of oppression and injustice can evolve into action to end oppression and injustice (Figure 2.1). This sketch demonstrates the important relationship of theory to practice and the interrelatedness of personal and political perspectives. It also reflects the need for multisystem analysis and action (individual, group, organizational, community, society (1994:67–68).

SUMMARY/TRANSITION

In this chapter we have outlined a conceptual framework for approaching human behavior and the social environment content. The conceptual framework is built around the notions of traditional and alternative paradigms. A traditional paradigm was explored through five interrelated dimensions. The dimensions included the following: (1) positivistic/scientific/objective/quantitative; (2) masculinity/patriarchy; (3) whiteness; (4) separateness/impersonalness/competitiveness; and

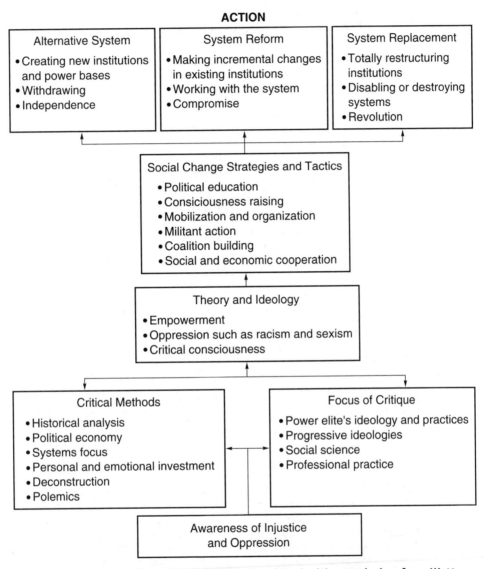

ACTION

Alternative System	System Reform	System Replacement
• Creating new institutions and power bases • Withdrawing • Independence	• Making incremental changes in existing institutions • Working with the system • Compromise	• Totally restructuring institutions • Disabling or destroying systems • Revolution

Social Change Strategies and Tactics
- Political education
- Consciousness raising
- Mobilization and organization
- Militant action
- Coalition building
- Social and economic cooperation

Theory and Ideology
- Empowerment
- Oppression such as racism and sexism
- Critical consciousness

Critical Methods	Focus of Critique
• Historical analysis • Political economy • Systems focus • Personal and emotional investment • Deconstruction • Polemics	• Power elite's ideology and practices • Progressive ideologies • Social science • Professional practice

Awareness of Injustice and Oppression

FIGURE 2.1 Sociopolitical Perspectives. Reprinted with permission from Watts, R. J. "Paradigms of diversity." In E. Trickett, R. Watts, and D. Berman (Eds.), *Human diversity: Perspectives on people in context*, pp. 66–67 (Fig. 3.3). Copyright © 1994. Reprinted by permission of John Wiley & Sons, Inc.

(5) privilege. An alternative paradigm was explored also through five interrelated dimensions. The dimensions included the following: (1) interpretive/intuitive/subjective/qualitative; (2) feminism; (3) diversity; (4) interrelatedness/personal/integrative; and (5) oppressions.

The implications of traditional and alternative paradigms for understanding HBSE will be our primary concern in the next chapter. In Chapter 3 we will explore ways of using our new understandings of dominant and alternative paradigms for gathering knowledge for use in social work practice. We will also explore some of the tools available to social workers to do our work.

Internet Search Guide

If you want to learn more about some of the topics discussed in this chapter by exploring the Internet, you can search the Net for the terms listed below. Remember that as you are "surfing" the Net, any of the search terms listed below can take you in many different directions. If you would like to visit specific Web sites related to this chapter, go to the Allyn and Bacon Web site at **http://www.abacon.com** and follow the links to Schriver or *Human Behavior and the Social Environment: Shifting Paradigms in Essential Knowledge for Social Work Practice.* There you will find a selection of sites related to content in this chapter.

1. positivism
2. patriarchy
3. whiteness
4. feminism
5. diversity
6. racism
7. Postmodernism

REFERENCES

Alix, E. K. (1995). *Sociology: An everyday life approach.* Minneapolis: West.

AmeriStat. (2000). *Race and ethnicity in the census: 1860–2000,* [Web site]. AmeriStat Population Reference Bureau and Social Science Analysis Network. Available: http://www.ameristat.org/racethnic/census.htm [2000, 4/4/00].

Armas, G. (2000, March 13, 2000). Administration puts out new guidelines for multiracial categories. *Northwest Arkansas Times.*

Beaver, Marion. (1990). "The older person in the black family." In *Social work practice with black families.* Logan, Sadye, Freeman, Edith, and McRoy, Ruth (Eds.). New York: Longman.

Belenky, Mary F., Clinchy, Blythe M., Goldberger, Nancy R., and Tarule, Jill M. (1986). *Women's ways of knowing: The development of self, voice, and mind.* New York: Basic Books, Inc.

Berlin, Sharon B. (1990). "Dichotomous and complex thinking." *Social Service Review, 64*(1): 46–59.

Bottomore, Tom. (1984). *The Frankfurt school and critical theory.* London: Tavistock Publications.

Bowser, B. P., and Hunt, R. G. (Eds.). (1996). *Impacts of racism on white Americans* (2nd ed.). Thousand Oaks, CA: Sage.

Bricker-Jenkins, Mary, and Hooyman, Nancy R. (Eds.). (1983). *Not for women only: Social work practice for a feminist future.* Silver Spring, MD: NASW, Inc.

Brown, L. (1989). "New voices, new visions: Toward a lesbian/gay paradigm for psychology." *Psychology of Women Quarterly* 13: 445–458.

Bureau of the Census. (2000). *Census 2000, Frequently asked questions.* U.S. Bureau of the Census. Available: http://www.census.gov/dmd/www/genfaq.htm

Canda, E. R. (1989). "Religious content in social work education: A comparative approach." *Journal of Social Work Education, 25*(1): 36–45.

Capra, Fritjof. (1983). *The turning point: Science, society, and the rising culture.* Toronto: Bantam Books.

Carter, R. T., and Jones, J. M. (1996). "Racism and white racial identity merging realities." In Bowser, B. P. and Hunt, R. G. (Eds.) *Impacts of racism on white Americans.* (2nd ed.). Thousand Oaks, CA: Sage.

Collins, Patricia Hill. (1986). "Learning from the outsider within: The sociological significance of black feminist thought." *Social Problems, 33*(6): 14–32.

Collins, Patricia Hill. (1989). "The social construction of black feminist thought." *Signs, 14*(4): 745–773.

Collins, Patricia Hill. (1990). *Black feminist thought: Knowledge, consciousness, and the politics of empowerment.* Boston: Unwin Hyman, Inc.

Cowley, A. S., and Derezotes, D. (1994). "Transpersonal psychology and social work education." *Journal of Social Work Education, 30*(1): 32–41.

Dawson, Betty G., Klass, Morris D., Guy, Rebecca F., and Edgley, Charles K. (1991). *Understanding social work research.* Boston: Allyn & Bacon.

Daniel, G. R. (1992). Beyond Black and White: the new multiracial consciousness. In Root, M. P. P. (Ed.). *Racially mixed people in America.* Newberry Park, CA: Sage Publications.

Dean, Ruth G., and Fenby, Barbara L. (1989). "Exploring epistemologies: Social work action as a reflection of philosophical assumptions." *Journal of Social Work Education, 25*(1): 46–54.

Demo, D. H., and Allen, K. R. (1996). "Diversity within lesbian and gay families: Challenges and implications for family theory and research." *Journal of Social and Personal Relationships, 13*(3): 415–434.

Donadello, Gloria. (1980). "Women and the mental health system." In Norman, Elaine and Mancuso, Arlene (Eds.). *Women's issues and social work practice.* Itasca, IL: F. E. Peacock Publishers, Inc.

Easlea, Brian. (1990). "Patriarchy, scientists, and nuclear warriors." In Sheila Ruth (Ed.). *Issues in feminism.* Mountain View, CA: Mayfield.

Everett, Joyce, Chipungu, Sandra, and Leashore, Bogart. (1991) (Eds.). *Child welfare: An Africentric perspective.* New Brunswick: Rutgers University Press.

Ewalt, P. L., Freeman, E. M., Kirk, S. A., and Poole, D. L. (1996). *Multicultural issues in social work.* Washington, DC: NASW Press.

Fong, R., Spickard, P. R., and Ewalt, P. L. (1996) "A multiracial reality: Issues for social work." In Ewalt, P. L., Freeman, E. M., Kirk, S. A., and Poole, D. L. (Eds.). *Multicultural issue in social work.* Washington, DC: NASW Press.

Guba, E. G., and Lincoln, Y. S. (1981). *Effective evaluation.* San Francisco: Jossey-Bass.

Guba, Egon G., and Lincoln, Yvonna S. (1989). *Fourth generation evaluation.* Newbury Park, CA: SAGE Publications.

Hartman, A. (1995). Introduction. In Tyson, K. (Ed.). *New foundations for scientific social and behavioral research: The heuristic paradigm.* Boston: Allyn and Bacon.

Heineman Pieper, M. (1995). Preface. In Tyson, K. (Ed.). *New foundations for scientific social and behavioral research: The heuristic paradigm.* Boston: Allyn and Bacon.

Heineman Pieper, M. (1995). "The heuristic paradigm: A unifying and comprehensive approach to social work research." Tyson, K. (Ed.). *New foundations for scientific social and behavioral research: The heuristic paradigm.* Boston: Allyn and Bacon.

Helms, J. E. (1994). "The conceptualization of racial identity and other 'racial' constructs." In Trickett, E. J., Watts, R. J., and Birman D. (Eds.). (1994). *Human diversity: Perspectives on people in context*. San Francisco: Jossey-Bass.

Hillman, James. (1988). In Peter Reason (Ed.). *Human inquiry in action: Developments in new paradigm research*. London: SAGE Publications.

Imre, Roberta Wells. (1984). "The nature of knowledge in social work." *Social Work, 29*(1): 41–45.

Kerlinger, Fred N. (1973). *Foundations of behavioral research*. New York: Holt, Rinehart and Winston, Inc.

Kich, George K. (1992). "The Developmental Process of Asserting a Biracial, Bicultural Identity." In Root, M. P. P. (Ed.). *Racially mixed people in America*. Newberry Park, CA: Sage Publications.

Lather, P. (1991). *Getting smart: Feminist research and pedagogy with/in the postmodern*. New York: Routledge.

Leigh, James. (1989). "Black Americans: Emerging identity issues and social policy." *The Annual Ellen Winston Lecture*. Raleigh: North Carolina State University.

Lincoln, Y. S., and Guba, E. G. (1985). *Naturalistic inquiry*. Beverly Hills: Sage.

Longres, J., and McLeod, E. (May 1980). "Consciousness raising and social work practice." *Social Casework, 61*: 267–276.

Manheim, Henry L. (1977). *Sociological research: Philosophy and methods*. Homewood, IL.: The Dorsey Press.

Maslow, Abraham H. (1962). *Toward a psychology of being*. Princeton: Van Nostrand.

McIntosh, Peggy. (1992). "White privilege and male privilege. A personal account of coming to see correspondences through work in Women's Studies." In Margaret Anderson and Patricia Hill Collins (Eds.). *Race class and gender: An anthology*. Belmont, CA: Wadsworth Publishing Co.

Miller, Jean Baker. (1986) *Toward a new psychology of women*. (2nd ed.). Boston: Beacon.

Moustakas, Clark. (1981). "Heuristic research." In Peter Reason and John Rowan (Eds.). *Human inquiry: A sourcebook of new paradigm research*. New York: Wiley and Sons.

Myers, L. J., and Speight, S. L. (1994). "Opimtal theory and the psychology of human diversity." In Trickett, E. J., Watts, R. J. and Birman D. (Eds.). (1994). *Human diversity: Perspectives on people in context*. San Francisco: Jossey-Bass.

Parks, E. E., Carter, R. T., and Gushue, G. V. (1996, July/August). "At the crossroads: Racial and womanist identity development in black and white women." *Journal of Counseling and Development, 74*: 624–631.

Pharr, Susanne. (1988). *Homophobia: A weapon of sexism*. Inverness, CA: Chardon.

Pinderhughes, Elaine. (1982). "Afro-American Families and the Victim System." In McGoldrick, M., Pearce, J., and Giordano, J. *Ethnicity and family therapy*. New York: Guilford.

Reason, Peter (1988). "Reflections." In Peter Reason. (Ed.). *Human inquiry in action: Developments in new paradigm research*. London: SAGE Publications.

Reason, Peter. (1981). "Methodological approaches to social science by Ian Mitroff and Ralph Kilmann: An appreciation." In Peter Reason and John Rowan. (Eds.). *Human inquiry: A sourcebook of new paradigm research*. New York: John Wiley and Sons.

Reason, Peter, and Hawkins, Peter. (1988). "Storytelling as inquiry." In Peter Reason (Ed.). *Human inquiry in action: Developments in new paradigm research*. London: SAGE Publications.

Reason, Peter, and John Rowan. (Eds.). (1981). *Human inquiry: A sourcebook of new paradigm research*. New York: John Wiley and Sons.

Root, M. P. P. "Within, between, and beyond race." In Root, Maria P. P. (Ed.). (1992). *Racially mixed people in America*. Newbury Park, CA: Sage.

Rubin, A., and Babbie, E. (1997). *Research methods for social work*. (3rd ed.). Pacific Grove, CA: Brooks/Cole.

Ruth, Sheila. (1990). *Issues in feminism*. Mountain View, CA: Mayfield Publishing Co.

Sands, R., and Nuccio, K. (1992). "Postmodern feminist theory in social work." *Social Work* 37: 489–494.

Scott, Joan W. (1988). *Gender and the politics of history.* New York: Columbia University Press.

Sermabeikian, P. (1994). "Our clients, ourselves: The spiritual perspective and social work practice." *Social Work, 39*(2): 178–183.

Sherman, Edmund. (1991). "Interpretive methods for social work practice and research." *Journal of Sociology and Social Welfare, 18*(4): 69–81.

Spickard, P. R. (1996). "The Illogic of American Racial Categories." In Root, M. P. P. (Ed.). *Racially mixed people in America.* Newberry Park, CA: Sage Publications.

Spickard, P. R., Fong, R., Ewalt, P. L., Freeman, E. M., Kirk, S. A., and Poole, D. L. (Eds.). *Multicultural Issues in Social Work.* Washington, DC: NASW Press.

Swigonski, M. E. (July 1994). "The logic of feminist standpoint theory for social work research." *Social Work, 39*(4): 387–393.

Trickett, E. J., Watt, R. J., and Birman D. (Eds.). (1994). *Human diversity: Perspectives on people in context.* San Francisco: Jossey-Bass.

Turner, Robert J. (1991). "Affirming consciousness: The Africentric perspective." In Joyce, E., Chipungu, S., and Leashore, B. (Eds.). *Child welfare: An Africentric perspective.* New Brunswick, NJ: Rutgers University Press.

Tyson, K. (1995). "Editor's Introduction" *Heuristic research. New foundations for scientific social and behavioral research: The heuristic paradigm.* Boston: Allyn and Bacon.

Tyson, K. (Ed.) (1995). *New foundations for scientific, social and behavioral research: The heuristic paradigm.* Boston: Allyn and Bacon.

Van Den Bergh, N. (Ed.). (1995). *Feminist practice in the 21st century.* Washington, DC: NASW Press.

Watts, R. J. (1994). "Paradigms of diversity." In Trickett, E. J., Watts, R. J., and Birman, D. (Eds.). *Human diversity: Perspectives on people in context.* San Francisco: Jossey-Bass.

Webster's New Universal Unabridged Dictionary (2nd ed.) (1983). In Edmund Sherman, "Interpretive methods for social work practice and research." *Journal of Sociology and Social Welfare, 18*(4): 69–81.

Weick, Ann. (1991). "The place of science in social work." *Journal of Sociology and Social Welfare, 18*(4): 13–34.

Westkott, Marcia. (1979). "Feminist criticism of the social sciences." *Harvard Educational Review, 49*(4): 424–430.

Zukav, Gary. (1980). *The dancing wu li masters: An overview of the new physics.* Toronto: Bantam Books.

ILLUSTRATIVE READING 2.1

The following illustrative reading by Castex examines, from a variety of perspectives, the concept of "diversity within diversity" as it relates to Hispanic/Latino (a) persons. This reading illustrates clearly the dangers of over-generalizing about any single person or group of people. Castex, however, also illustrates a number of common concerns and patterns reflected within Hispanic/Latino (a) populations such as poverty and income status, family composition and household size, and demographics related to age. Another extremely important issue the author addresses is that of externally imposed designations and definitions of diverse ethnic groups that are damaging to members of the group because of their overgeneralizations about all members of a group and the resulting denial of individual and intragroup diversity. She especially notes traditional approaches to defining culture as a group of traits held equally by all members sharing a similar cultural heritage are overly simplistic and closer in reality to stereotyping than to realistically describing culture. Some of the areas of diversity within diversity to look for (and look for their possible implications for social work practice) in this reading include: national origin, language, family names, racial ascription, religion, and immigration and citizenship status.

Providing Services to Hispanic/Latino Populations: Profiles in Diversity*

Graciela M. Castex

Social workers in many settings find themselves providing services to clients characterized as Hispanics or Latinos, a group with which they may have had little experience. Although the literature makes frequent reference to Hispanics as a very diverse group, there has been little discussion of the socially important differences and similarities among Hispanics and how these differences and similarities may affect the provision of services. Instead, discussions about the provision of social services to Hispanic people often quickly focus on cultural attributes taken as common among subgroups, primarily Mexican Americans (or Chicanos), Puerto Ricans, and Cubans. Questions that may arise in the mind of the practitioner are, What is the Hispanic population? If subgroups are diverse, in what ways are they diverse, and in what ways are they similar? What does it mean for culturally and racially diverse peoples to be perceived as members of a single ethnic group, and what are the implications of a client's ascription to this diverse group for practice?

Hispanic clients pose increasing challenges for social workers. This already large group is growing rapidly, and indicators such as age distribution and low median income levels indicate a rapidly increasing need for social services. The high numbers of recent immigrants, who often have limited English (Moore & Pachon, 1985) and experience a host of cultural factors that differentiate them from others in the population, add to the complexity of the challenge.

This chapter profiles the Hispanic/Latino population in the United States. It very briefly places the interactions of this group in the context of contemporary theories of ethnicity and discusses the diversity and similarities among members of the Hispanic/Latino group by examining key social features. The common experience of ascription to an ethnic minority in the United States has served as a primary unifying force that gave impetus—in a bidirectional process with state institutions—to the creation and maintenance of the Hispanic/Latino group.

HISPANICS: A STATISTICAL PROFILE

In April 1990, according to the U.S. Bureau of the Census, there were approximately 22 million people of Hispanic origin (referred to as Hispanics in the census literature) living in the United States out of a total population of 248.7 million. Hispanics, with 9.0 percent of the population, constituted the second largest minority group in the country after black Americans, with 12.1 percent. Because some census respondents identified themselves as both black and Hispanic, however, non-Hispanic blacks are only 11.8 percent of the nation's population. Furthermore, although census estimates are not available, the general assumption is that Hispanics are more likely to be undercounted than non-Hispanics (U.S. Bureau of the Census, 1991b, 1991c, 1991d).

The social needs of Hispanics are underlined by their standing in four social indexes:

1. poverty: In 1992, 26.2 percent of Hispanic families had incomes below the poverty level, compared with 10.3 percent of non-Hispanic families. Twelve percent of the children in the United States were Hispanic in 1992, but 21 percent of the children living in poverty were Hispanic; of all Hispanic children, 39.9 percent lived in poverty in 1992 (U.S. Bureau of the Census, 1993a).

2. income: The 1992 median income of non-Hispanic white households ($33,388) was 46.1 percent higher than that of Hispanic households ($22,848) (U.S. Bureau of the Census, 1993b).

3. family composition: Hispanics had a higher ratio of single-parent families (30 percent) than non-Hispanics (20 percent), and the ratio rose to 43 percent for the Puerto Rican–origin Hispanic subgroup (U.S. Bureau of the Census, 1991a).

4. demographics: The Hispanic population is young compared with non-Hispanics, with median ages in 1990 of 26.0 and 33.5 years, respectively; 30 percent of Hispanics and 21 percent of non-Hispanics are less than 15 years of age. Although accurate long-range demographic forecasts are difficult (one census projection predicts a Hispanic population of 128.3 million by 2050), short-range phenomena such as a high proportion of group members at or near childbearing age, a relatively high fertility rate, and high documented and undocumented net immigration rates guarantee a continued rapid growth of the Hispanic population during the next generation (U.S. Bureau of the Census, 1993c, 1993d).

ETHNIC GROUP CONCEPT

The Hispanic/Latino group, created by a federal order in the late 1970s, constitutes a valid social category that can be called an ethnic group and is increasingly regarded as such by those so ascribed. However, this usage may be counterintuitive for those trained to equate a list of cultural traits—a "culture"—with the ascription of ethnic status. But the U.S. government defined and formally created the Hispanic ethnic group on May 4, 1978. According to the Office of Management and Budget (1978), a Hispanic is "a person of Mexican, Puerto Rican, Cuban, Central or South American or other Spanish culture or origin, regardless of race" (p. 19269).

This definition largely focuses on the countries of origin and assumes that people in those countries have a common "Spanish culture," which is also shared by some people living in the United States. Although "Hispanic" was chosen by the federal government as the name of the group, many people so ascribed preferred to call themselves by another name, such as Latino or Latina. The formation of the Hispanic group should not be seen as unique; Native Americans and African Americans are two other examples, and similar phenomena are common in other countries.

The creation of an ethnic group in a dialectic with the state is a common social process. For the Hispanics in the United States, the process was bidirectional, involving state institutions and those so ascribed, to identify, control, and provide needed services to members of the new group (Castex, 1990; Enloe, 1981; Hayes-Bautista & Chapa, 1987; Nelson & Tienda, 1985).

If ethnic groups are regarded primarily as bearers of cultural traits, the bulk of which are passed from generation to generation, practitioners might assume that the federal government characterized Hispanics as belonging to a single group because they shared many significant cultural traits. Because this population is culturally diverse, from this culture-based perspective (which current anthropological and sociological ethnicity theory largely rejects) the designation "Hispanic" might be regarded as confusing at best.

The standard perspective among social theorists regarding the nature and functioning of ethnic groups—which began to be rigorously established in the late 1960s and early 1970s by Barth (1969), Cohen (1974), and Vincent (1974), among others—considers ethnicity to arise from groups interacting with other groups and social structures. In this perspective no ethnic group can exist without other groups to interact with: An ethnic group cannot exist in isolation. Ethnic identity is always expressed in dynamic processes of interaction with others. Barth (1969) pointed out that although particular cultural traits (for example, language or religion) may be important in the formation of a group and in the maintenance of group boundaries, no one can predict which traits will prove important in advance or which will continue to be ethnically significant in the future. Others have expanded Barth's arguments, elucidating the ways in which the state and other social structures affect ethnic group mobilization, maintenance, demobilization, and the joining together or splitting apart of groups to form new groups (Enloe, 1981; Horowitz, 1985; Wolf, 1982).

This perspective has directly or indirectly begun influencing discussions of ethnicity and cultural awareness in social work (Green, 1982; Pinderhughes, 1988, 1989). An understanding of Hispanic, or any other, ethnicity is impossible in the older paradigm; members of ethnic groups were presumed to "carry" a whole list of cultural traits, which sound suspiciously like stereotypes. The alternative viewpoint, however, emphasizes the need not only to value but also to expect diversity in a group. This view encourages development of strategies that avoid stereotypes when addressing the needs of the client.

HISPANIC ETHNICITY IN PRACTICE

Social workers need to keep in mind many features and issues deriving from the Hispanic client's ethnic status, in addition to the client's individual needs. Practitioners should prepare intellectually, emotionally, and clinically in anticipation of serving the Hispanic client. Prime features often regarded as ethnically significant and certainly important when interacting with clients include (but are not limited to) national origin, language, family names, religion, racial ascription, and immigration or citizenship status.

National Origin

Hispanics come from 26 nations according to the federal definition. There are significant differences among these nationalities; the languages, economic resources, educational systems, status structures, and customs vary dramatically from country to country. In addition, individual countries are often very ethnically diverse. The countries included by the Census Bureau are in North America (United States, Mexico), Central America (Guatemala, Honduras, El Salvador, Belize, Nicaragua, Costa Rica, Panama), the Caribbean (Cuba, Puerto Rico, Dominican Republic), South America (Venezuela, Colombia, Ecuador, Peru, Bolivia, Chile, Paraguay, Argentina, Uruguay, Brazil, French Guiana, Suriname, and Guyana; the last three, lacking Spanish origin, are sometimes referred to as non-Hispanic South America, and the state language of Brazil is Portuguese), and Europe (Spain).

A social worker probably encounters clients coming from fewer countries, however. Persons describing themselves as of Mexican origin on the 1990 census constituted 60.4 percent of the Hispanic total, Puerto Ricans were 12.2 percent, and Cubans were 4.7 percent of the total. The catchall "other Hispanic" category covered 22.8 percent of Hispanics and included persons from all the other defined countries as well as some very old Hispanic communities in the United States (U.S. Bureau of the Census, 1991b).

The historical experiences of each country with the United States and the European colonialists are very different and can affect the ethnic self-identification of clients. Immigrants' attitudes toward the United States especially may be conditioned by these histories; long-time Dominican residents in New York, for example, sometimes express reluctance to become U.S. citizens; they still associate the United States with the suppression of the popular revolt in the Dominican Republic in 1965 and the subsequent military occupation by U.S. forces (personal communication with A. Goris, Hunter College instructor, Department of Puerto Rican Studies, March 17, 1992). Similarly complex feelings may be described by Mexicans, Nicaraguans, Salvadorans, Chileans, and Cubans. The feelings may not always be negative, but the actions of the state may evoke reactions dating from before the client's emigration or may even have contributed to the emigration. National background also affects the ease of obtaining legal residence status or, at times, refugee status. Practitioners working with Hispanic clients need to do the following:

- Ask where the client is from. What is the client's nationality?
- Ask if the client is a member of an ethnic group within that nationality.
- Become familiar with the group history and the history of the group's migration.

- Identify formal or informal providers of services directed toward members of this national group, such as religious and civic organizations, sports clubs, political organizations, and political officeholders.

Language

Many non-Hispanics assume that most Hispanics speak the same language—Spanish—or that their near forebears spoke it. This assumption follows the 19th-century tendency to equate language, nationality, and ethnic status, even though the relationship of language and ethnicity has always been complex in the United States (Smith, 1989; Worsley, 1984). In fact, the home language of 3.05 million of the 14.61 million Hispanics counted in the 1980 census was not Spanish (Moore & Pachon, 1985).

Hispanics in the United States and residents of the 25 other countries of origin speak five major European languages (Spanish, Portuguese, French, Dutch, and English). They also speak such major Native American languages (each with millions of speakers) as Quechua, Mayan (a family of languages), Aymara, and Guarani, as well as many other Native American languages and creole dialects. Such language diversity is not a trivial point: Spanish may be a second language for many Spanish-speaking Hispanic immigrants. Immigrants from highland Guatemala (Mayan), highland Peru and Bolivia (Quechua and Aymara), and coastal Honduras (Garifuna, a creole language; Castex, in press) are common in the United States.

The assumption that Hispanics are normally fluent and literate in Spanish sometimes has damaging practical consequences for individual Hispanics, particularly in work-related situations. For example, a monolingual Spanish caseload should not be assigned to students or workers whose facility with the language is limited to discussions of the weather.

Similarly, not all Hispanic clients are fluent in Spanish. The situation may be even more complex, however. An agency sensitive to the needs of its clients, for example, may have materials and forms printed in Spanish, and the social worker may presume that all clients can read them. But some clients may not be literate in Spanish. Or some may speak both English and Spanish but may only be able to read English, making discussions of forms and legal documents very complex.

In addition, Hispanic clients speak a number of regional Spanish dialects. Speech in any language can serve as a social marker, however. The social worker should be sensitive, therefore, to situations in which the speech of the interviewer may indicate a status that differs from the client's. The interviewer's social status as indicated by Spanish usage may be higher or lower than that indicated by his or her English usage (Green, 1982; Kadushin, 1983).

The social worker attempting to communicate with Hispanic clients will find it helpful to

- find out what language the client communicates best in
- be sensitive to the possibility that people who are in crisis or who are experiencing powerful emotions may have additional difficulties communicating in a second or third language

- use trained people as interpreters or translators if such action seems appropriate and review literature on interviewing techniques when using interpreters.

Family Names

Many Hispanics have surnames that differ from those traditionally regarded as Spanish. While "Juan Garcia" is used colloquially as the Spanish equivalent of "John Smith," some Hispanics really are named Smith. And some Garcias in the United States are not Hispanic. The founding father of Chile was named O'Higgins, and the names of the current presidents of Peru, Argentina, and Chile—Fujimori, Menem, and Aylwin—are Japanese, Syrian, and Welsh in origin, respectively. Especially since 1800 there have been waves of migration to Latin America and the Caribbean from all over the world, particularly from Italy, France, Germany, and the Middle East but also from East Asia, Eastern Europe, and sub-Saharan Africa.

Regarding a surname as an indicator of ethnic status reached the height of absurdity when the Census Bureau tried to develop statistics on Hispanics on the basis of Spanish surnames. In preparing for the 1970 census, Spanish surnames were defined as any surname listed more than 25 times in the 1962 Havana, Cuba, telephone directory, thus excluding Cubans named Johnson or Lipshitz. The Havana list supplemented a 1950 list derived from the Mexico City and San Juan, Puerto Rico, directories. Had Eamon de Valera's mother not returned to Ireland from Brooklyn when he was a child, the first president of the Irish Republic would have been counted as Hispanic because his name began with "de." The "Martin" problem signaled the surname system's collapse, as thousands of people of British ancestry became "hispanized" because their last name appeared more than 25 times in a telephone directory (U.S. Bureau of the Census, 1975).

An additional source of confusion for practitioners may result from the Spanish language naming system, which differs from traditional English practice. Patrilineal descent is traced in naming through the second to the last name. The mother's maiden name (her father's) becomes a child's last name. In other words, Juan Garcia Jones's father's name is Garcia and his mother's name is Jones. Juan will pass on the Garcia name to his children as their second to last name, and so on.

Under Spanish common law, women do not acquire their husband's name on marriage. Garcia's mother, Señora Jones, is legally a Jones, not a Garcia. Forms including a husband's name—Señora Jones de Garcia—rarely have other than honorific status. Passports, airline tickets, and such are often issued in maiden names, which some countries require women to use when signing official documents. Therefore, social workers can make no assumptions about marital status or feminist attitudes because a couple uses different surnames.

Social workers will find it useful to

- make no firm assumptions about language use, ethnic status, or recent heritage based on a name
- ask a client how to pronounce or spell a name

- remember that persons in the same household may have different surnames (married names may have no legal standing, and the extended family may include aunts, uncles, cousins, grandparents, grandchildren, even godchildren and godparents, living together)
- keep in mind that some people may not use their legal names because they fear attention from immigration authorities.

Racial Ascription

Racial ascription is generally regarded as cultural rather than biological among social theorists. The particular biological traits that significantly determine racial ascription vary from society to society. Skin color, hair texture, class status, and other traits may all interact differentially to determine racial ascription; therefore, ascription is primarily a cultural phenomenon. A white Dominican, for example, may be *trigueño* (mixed, literally "wheat-colored") in Puerto Rico and black in Georgia (Harris, 1964; Mintz, 1971; Stephens, 1989).

Hispanics are racially diverse by any system of definition. Individual Hispanics might be characterized in the United States as white or European American, Native American, African American, East Asian, South Asian, and perhaps other racial types. In many countries, discrimination based on ascription as an *indio* (Native American) may be the most socially significant racial designation. But even then, to live like a *blanco* (white or European) is often to become one (Comitas, 1967; Harris, 1964).

The U.S. census of 1990 identifies Hispanics as a category separate from race. When asked to identify race in a separate question, Hispanic respondents identified themselves as follows: white, 11.5 million; black, 770,000; American Indian, 165,000; Asian, 305,000; other race, 9.5 million. These figures communicate a significant message: Whereas 51.7 percent of the Hispanic population identified itself as white, 42.7 percent of the Hispanics self-identified as another race. Hispanics constitute 97.5 percent of the other race category for the nation as a whole. Most of these self-identified racially as Hispanic, Latino, Chicano, La Raza, mestizo, or some other term that referred to Hispanic origin (U.S. Bureau of the Census, 1991d).

Clients who may have become classified as African American only after their arrival in the United States may be experiencing serious racial discrimination for the first time. As a result, the practitioner must keep in mind the need to consult with the client regarding his or her racial status and to be sensitive to the possibility that he or she may have experienced a dramatic change in social status because of the U.S. system of racial ascription. Such a change can affect self-esteem, relations with others, and real opportunities.

Religion

Perhaps the majority of Hispanics are Roman Catholics, but there are very large (and growing) Protestant Hispanic populations both in the United States and in the countries of origin, as well as significant populations of other faiths. In addition, the beliefs and practices of many Hispanics have been influenced by or derive directly from

African and Native American belief systems that may be syncretized with Christian or Catholic beliefs in forms such as santeria. For example, the botanicas (stores that sell herbal medicines and religious images) are communal centers in the expression of the spiritist beliefs that inform santeria (Borello & Mathias, 1977).

The cultural component and practices of Hispanic believers may differ quite extensively from the practices of non-Hispanic coreligionists in the United States (McCready, 1985). Hispanics and the once largely Irish hierarchy of the Catholic Church in the United States, for example, have had a long and complex struggle to achieve mutual understanding (to put the matter politely). Although differences between Hispanic Methodists and non-Hispanic Methodists may exist, most Protestant denominations are relatively less hierarchical and therefore in practice more open to different styles of observance (Weyr, 1988).

The Catholic Church and other denominations have developed many programs to address the social needs of Hispanics. These vary locally and run the gamut from soup kitchens to legal assistance for immigrants. Umbrella organizations encompassing other faiths have also been active, especially in working with immigrants and refugees. When making referrals, religious institutions may be important resources. It is important to keep in mind that

- religious institutions involving a variety of faiths may provide organizational support for and leadership to Hispanic communities.
- if it appears relevant, social workers should determine clients' religious affiliations, if any.
- social workers should make no assumptions about clients' experiences in their native country. For example, some Hispanics have experienced severe religious discrimination in their country of origin.

Ascription by Self or Others

Most Hispanics, when asked to describe their cultural heritage or ethnic identity, will first respond with a reference to their nationality (such as Mexican, Puerto Rican, Peruvian), even in the second or third immigrant generation. If one were to ask them about any broader self-identification, the term Hispanic would until recently rarely be heard; Latino or Latina is more common (Hayes-Bautista & Chapa, 1987).

When determining ethnic status, however, it is useful to look at the social context in which it is expressed. A single person can have many ethnicities, including a national ethnicity and a supraethnicity, when dealing with large-scale social institutions such as national or international systems or encompassing state structures. (Changes in state structures almost invariably radically affect ethnic expression. Contemporary Yugoslavia and the former Soviet Union, British India in 1947, and Austria–Hungary in 1918 are striking examples.)

Hispanics are a composite group with enough feelings of similarity to aid coalition forming when confronting large-scale structures, which in turn may find it convenient to regard Hispanics as a single group (Greeley, 1977; Royce, 1982). In other situations this large-scale sense of selfhood need not be called into play—in a neigh-

borhood of Hispanics nationality might be the identifying factor; in a neighborhood
of Mexican Americans, other local or ancestral criteria might come into play.

The state and the larger society, the "others," have named the Hispanic. In
many respects, naming is the result of and a response to oppression and exploitation:
One might speak of "greaser" or "wetback" ethnicity. By a purification of terms, such
terms have come to refer to the more acceptable Hispanic or Latino ethnicity.

There are problems with the term "Hispanic." It reminds many persons so ascribed of the colonial exploitation of the Spanish state; many Hispanics have no ancestors from the Iberian Peninsula. The term "Latino," however, also excludes the
Native American, African, Asian, or non-Latin European backgrounds of many Hispanics. But ethnicity may transcend terminology in the search for symbolic effectiveness. In situations in which ethnic identification may be important, the social worker
might find it helpful to let people identify themselves, to remember that ascriptions
may vary by social context, and to remember that individuals may not see themselves
as members of the group they have been placed in.

Immigration or Citizenship Status

One great division in the Hispanic community is between those who have the legal
right to both live and remain in the United States ("documented") and those who
do not ("undocumented"). In addition, there are numerous classifications of documented status (such as refugee status) that affect access to public services. Legal status affects mobility, employment availability, the ability to assert rights, and even the
ability to plan for the future on more than a day-to-day basis.

The date of entry into the United States is a key piece of information for those
providing services to almost any immigrant. A verifiable entry date may render the
undocumented client eligible for a regularization of status under various laws that
offer protection and amnesties. For all immigrants, date of entrance communicates
information about the opportunities in the United States at the time of migration and
conditions in the country of origin at that time.

All noncitizens, even undocumented noncitizens, have rights, however. These
include a child's right to schooling, the right to basic medical care, and the right to
due process. Immigrants' rights group are sources of materials setting forth the rights
of noncitizens and the policies of local governments and agencies in defense of those
rights (National Center for Immigrant Students, 1991; New York Department of City
Planning, 1990).

No matter how the client looks, sounds (even if there is no trace of a Spanish
accent), or behaves, a social worker should consider whether or not documentation
status is affecting the issues a client brings to the relationship. Social workers will find
it useful to

- become acquainted with the services available to aid documented and undocumented people with various statuses.
- be sensitive to the possibility that clients who appear evasive or resistant to
suggestions may be frightened about revealing undocumented status. Social

workers can emphasize the degree of confidentiality that they can offer clients and include some legal advice about agency, local, and federal policies.

- keep abreast of current immigration regulations.

CONCLUSION

During the 19th century and early in the 20th century, Hispanics were legally discriminated against in the United States; they have always suffered from oppression, violence, and disrespect (Moore & Pachon, 1985). This suppression of group members, sanctioned by the state at various levels as well as by other social institutions and combined with the mounting rate of post–World War II immigration, led to the creation of the population we now call Hispanic or Latino. The population began to form a group as part of multidirectional interactions among component groups as well as interactions among the new group, federal and state authorities, and other institutions that were attempting to address perceived needs and pressures in an administratively convenient manner (Enloe, 1981; Moore & Pachon, 1985; Weyr, 1988). This process has led to an increasing group consciousness both organizationally and symbolically, as indicated by the ethnic self-identification in the 1990 census.

Yankauer (1987), reviewing a series of articles on terminology, commented that "whatever cohesion exists within the diverse groups covered by the term 'Hispanic,' it is the product of prejudice and discrimination directed against them" (p. 15). When confronted with the special needs and challenges of a large and growing population, the government began labeling, and the component groups tended to band together to more effectively confront the state and other discriminatory groups or institutions. Individuals tend to identify themselves as Hispanic or not depending on the level of interactions with other systems. Large systems tend to elicit responses of the amalgamated group; interactions at the neighborhood and more personal levels are likely to elicit more restricted identifications. Peeling the onion of Hispanic ethnicity may well lead to additional ethnicities, depending on the group or institution with which it is interacting.

REFERENCES

Barth, F. (1969). Introduction. In F. Barth (Ed.), *Ethnic groups and boundaries* (pp. 3–38). Boston: Little, Brown.

Borello, M. A., & Mathias, E. (1977, August–September). Botanicas: Puerto Rican folk pharmacies. *Natural History*, pp. 65–73.

Castex, G. M. (1990). An analysis and synthesis of current theories of ethnicity and ethnic group processes using the creation of the Hispanic group as a case example. *Dissertation Abstracts International, 51,* 07A (University Microfilms No. 90-33820).

Castex, G. M. (in press). Hondurans. In K. T. Jackson (Ed.), *Encyclopedia of New York City.* New Haven, CT: New York Historical Society and Yale University.

Cohen, A. (1974). Introduction: The lesson of ethnicity. In A. Cohen (Ed.), *Urban ethnicity* (pp. ix–xxiv). London: Tavistock.

Comitas, L. (1967). Education and social stratification in Bolivia. *Transactions of the New York Academy of Sciences, 9* (7, Series 2), 935–948.

Enloe, C. H. (1981). The growth of the state and ethnic mobilization: The American experience. *Ethnic and Racial Studies, 4,* 123–136.

Greeley, A. (1977). Minorities: White ethnics. In J. B. Turner (Ed.-in-Chief), *Encyclopedia of social work* (17th ed., Vol. 2, pp. 979–984). Washington, DC: National Association of Social Workers.

Green, J. W. (1982). *Cultural awareness in the human services.* Englewood Cliffs, NJ: Prentice Hall.

Harris, M. (1964). *Patterns of race in the Americas.* New York: W. W. Norton.

Hayes-Bautista, D. E., & Chapa, J. (1987). Latino terminology: Conceptual bases for standardized terminology. *American Journal of Public Health, 77,* 61–68.

Horowitz, D. L. (1985). *Ethnic groups in conflict.* Los Angeles: University of California Press.

Kadushin, A. (1983). *The social work interview.* New York: Columbia University Press.

McCready, W. C. (1985). Culture and religion. In P. S. J. Cafferty & W. C. McCready (Eds.), *Hispanics in the United States: A new social agenda* (pp. 49–61). New Brunswick, NJ: Transaction Books.

Mintz, S. (1971). Groups, group boundaries and the perception of race. *Comparative Studies in Society and History, 13,* 437–450.

Moore, J., & Pachon, H. (1985). *Hispanics in the United States.* Englewood Cliffs, NJ: Prentice Hall.

National Center for Immigrant Students. (1991). Immigrant students' right of access. *New Voices, 1*(1), 4.

Nelson, C., & Tienda, M. (1985). The structuring of Hispanic ethnicity: Historical and contemporary perspectives. *Ethnic and Racial Studies, 8,* 49–74.

New York Department of City Planning, Office of Immigrant Affairs. (1990). *Immigrant entitlements made (relatively) simple* (DCP No. 90-14). New York: Author.

Office of Management and Budget. (1978, May 4). Directive 15: Race and ethnic standards for federal statistics and administrative reporting. *Federal Register, 43,* 19269.

Pinderhughes, E. (1988). Significance of culture and power in the human behavior curriculum. In C. Jacobs & D. D. Bowles (Eds.), *Ethnicity & race: Critical concepts in social work* (pp. 152–166). Silver Spring, MD: National Association of Social Workers.

Pinderhughes, E. (1989). *Understanding race, ethnicity, and power.* New York: Free Press.

Royce, A. P. (1982). *Ethnic identity.* Bloomington: Indiana University Press.

Smith, A. (1989). The origins of nations. *Ethnic and Racial Studies, 12,* 340–367.

Stephens, T. M. (1989). The language of ethnicity and self-identity in American Spanish and Brazilian Portuguese. *Ethnic and Racial Studies, 12,* 138–145.

U.S. Bureau of the Census. (1975). *Comparison of persons of Spanish surname and persons of Spanish origin in the United States* (Technical Paper 38). Washington, DC: U.S. Government Printing Office.

U.S. Bureau of the Census. (1991a). The Hispanic population in the United States: March 1990 (Current Population Reports, Series P-20, No. 449). Washington, DC: U.S. Government Printing Office.

U.S. Bureau of the Census. (1991b). *Resident population distribution for the United States, regions, and states, by race and Hispanic origin: 1990* (Press Release CB91-100). Washington, DC: Author.

U.S. Bureau of the Census. (1991c). *Census Bureau releases counts on specific racial groups* (Press Release CB91-215). Washington, DC: Author.

U.S. Bureau of the Census. (1991d). *Census Bureau releases 1990 Census counts on Hispanic population groups* (Press Release CB91-216). Washington, DC: Author.

U.S. Bureau of the Census. (1993a), *Poverty in the United States: 1992* (Current Population Reports, Series P-60, No. 185). Washington, DC: U.S. Government Printing Office.

U.S. Bureau of the Census. (1993b). *Money income of households, families, and persons in the United States: 1992* (Current Population Reports, Series P-60, No. 184). Washington, DC: U.S. Government Printing Office.

U.S. Bureau of the Census. (1993c). *Population projections of the United States, by age, sex, race, and Hispanic origin* (Current Population Reports, Series PS-25, No. 1104). Washington, DC: U.S. Government Printing Office.

U.S. Bureau of the Census. (1993d). *Hispanic Americans today* (Current Population Reports, Population Characteristics, Series P-23, No. 183). Washington, DC: U.S. Government Printing Office.

Vincent, J. (1974). The structuring of ethnicity. *Human Organization, 33,* 375–378.

Weyr, T. (1988). *Hispanic U.S.A.: Breaking the melting pot.* New York: Harper & Row.

Wolf, E. (1982). *Europe and the people without history.* Berkeley: University of California Press.

Worsley, P. (1984). *The three worlds: Culture and world development.* Chicago: University of Chicago Press.

Yankauer, A. (1987). Hispanic/Latino—What's in a name? *American Journal of Public Health, 77,* 15–17.

3  Paradigm Thinking and Social Work Knowledge for Practice

Topics Addressed in This Chapter:

*T*his chapter presents some tools for us to use in our efforts to understand traditional and alternative paradigms and to gain what we need to do social work practice. These tools include frameworks, concepts, models, and theories. We will use these tools as we would use maps or directions when trying to find our way to a destination we have not visited before. These maps and directions can help guide us on our journey through traditional and alternative paradigms in our search for more complete understandings of human behavior and the social environment.

In addition to frameworks, concepts, models, and theories, we will use a number of other tools to help us "think about thinking" including: metaphor, appreciation for ambiguity, the intersection of personal and political issues (or individual and social change), the importance of language and words, and social work assessment.

We will use all these different forms of guidance to help us make connections between traditional and alternative paradigms and issues important to us as social workers. The tools, directions and maps we explore in this chapter are intended to be of assistance to us in traveling on all the journeys we shall take in this book. They can help us gain more complete understanding of humans' individual, family, group, organizational, and community behaviors and of the social environments that influence and form the contexts in which human behavior takes place. Equally important, these tools can help us do our work as social workers.

TOOLS AND TERMS FOR THINKING ABOUT THINKING

Before we explore some specific tools for practice, we will explore some tools for thinking about thinking. These tools are intended to help us understand the processes involved in creating and organizing knowledge.

We previously defined paradigm as the "entire constellation of beliefs, values, techniques, and so on shared by the members of a given community." Others (Dawson et al. 1991:16; Brown 1981:36) add that research paradigms incorporate theories, models, concepts, categories, assumptions, and approaches to help clarify and formulate research. All these notions are central to the approach taken in this book, but what do we really mean when we use such terms? There is a good deal of overlap among and ambiguity about the meanings of these terms. However, they also have some commonly accepted meanings that we might agree upon for use in this book.

Ontology and Epistemology

Two important terms for helping understand the creation and organization of knowledge are *ontology* and *epistemology*. Stanley and Wise (in Van Den Berg 1995) suggest that **ontology** is a "theory about what is real." (We address the meaning of "theory" later in this section.) Van Den Bergh suggests on a larger scale that social work's **ontological** perspective about clients and their problems (we might add their strengths as well) "is that they are contextually based in the client's history or 'life space' " [or environment]. **Epistemology** can be defined as "the study of knowledge and knowledge-generating processes" (1995:xii). An **epistemology** is a "theory about how to know" what is reality (Tyson 1995:10). It is the study of how knowledge is created. Harding defines epistemology as "a theory of knowledge, which includes such questions as 'Who can be a knower?' and 'what test must beliefs pass in order to be legitimated as knowledge?' " (in Trickett et al. 1994:16) The discussions in Chapter 2 about how knowledge is created according to traditional and alternative paradigms, then, can be referred to as discussions and comparisons of two very different approaches to the study of knowledge and knowledge-creation processes (epistemologies) and two approaches to determining the nature of reality (ontology).

Concepts are "general words, terms, or phrases that represent a class of events or phenomena in the observable world. . . . Concepts direct our attention, shape our perceptions, and help us make sense of experience" (Martin and O'Connor 1989:39). We will consider many different concepts as we proceed on our journey. "A **conceptual framework** (also known as a school of thought, a substantive theory, or a conceptual scheme) is defined as a set of interrelated concepts that attempt to account for some topic or process. Conceptual frameworks are less developed than theories but are called theory anyway" (Martin and O'Connor 1989:39). The meaning we give to **conceptual framework** in this book is that of a conceptual scheme consisting of a set of interrelated concepts that can help explain human behavior in the context of environment. Our "conceptual scheme" consists of the two kinds of paradigms—traditional and alternative—that we outlined in the previous chapter. Each of these paradigms was divided into five dimensions. The dimensions include theories, feminist theory for example, and concepts such as diversity or oppression.

Mullen (in Grinnell 1981:606) uses Siporin's definition of a **model** as "a symbolic, pictorial structure of concepts, in terms of metaphors and propositions concerning a specific problem, or a piece of reality, and of how it works . . . a problem-solving device." We will discuss several models for helping us expand our understanding of human behavior and the social environment later in this chapter. The models we will explore include social systems, life span, and ecological models. We will also describe a strengths-based model for selecting knowledge upon which to base our social work practice.

Dawson et al. (1991:438) describe **theory** as "a reasoned set of propositions, derived from and supported by established evidence, which serves to explain a group of phenomena." Martin and O'Connor (1989:39) suggest that theory "most often indicates a conceptual framework that accounts for a topic or process in the observable world." Shafritz and Ott (1987:1) say that "by **theory** we mean a proposition or set of propositions that seeks to explain or predict something." These definitions of theory are helpful because they suggest that theories function to give us directions or they act as guides that suggest some explanation about why something happens as it does. It is important to recognize that theories are only guesses based on observations about how and why things happen as they do. Theories do not offer absolute answers.

The theories with which we are concerned in this book are those that seek to explain a variety of aspects of human behavior. We are concerned here with the traditional theories we have relied most heavily on for explaining our behaviors, their environmental contexts, and the possible interplay of person and environment. We are also interested here in alternative theories that offer other possible explanations in addition to traditional and dominant theories of human behaviors, their environmental contexts, and the possible interaction of person and environment.

What do we mean when we refer to environment? When we refer to **environment** we mean the social and physical context or the surroundings in which human behavior occurs. In addition to the social and physical context, we concur with Germain (1986:623) that environment also includes such elements as time and space. These unseen but influential aspects of environment are especially important to social workers when working across cultures. Different cultures emphasize very different perspectives on such unseen elements as time and space. For example, members of one culture may arrange their activities and environments according to very precise time schedules (as is the case with most members of urban, dominant, white society in the United States). Members of other cultures may arrange their activities in an environment divided by much more natural and less specific divisions of time such as morning, afternoon, and evening or according to seasonal changes (as is the case with many Native American cultures and with many traditional rural and agrarian people). If we are not aware of alternative perspectives on these unseen but critical environmental characteristics, we risk insult and misunderstanding in our interactions with others.

The Meaning of Metaphor

Another tool for helping us to expand our understanding of HBSE is metaphor. Much thinking in social work directed toward understanding HBSE is done with the assistance of metaphors. Social work is not alone in this respect, for much social science thinking is carried out with the assistance of metaphors. Certainly metaphors are used often to communicate ideas about ourselves and the world around us. Aristotle defined **metaphor** as "giving a thing a name that belongs to something else" (Aristotle quoted in Szasz 1987:137). Much of our ability to understand the world and the behaviors of humans comes from our ability to use metaphor. We attempt to explain something we do not yet understand by comparing it to or describing it in terms of something we do understand.

In the introduction to this chapter, we employed metaphors to describe the things we are going to try to achieve in this chapter. We used the concepts of tools, maps, and the process of receiving directions to a new destination as metaphors for what we are attempting to do in this chapter. The comparison of our efforts in this book to develop understanding of HBSE to the processes and tasks involved in traveling on a journey is also a metaphor. We must recognize the limits of metaphors at the same time that we appreciate their helpfulness. When we say something is comparable or similar to something else, we are not saying the two things are exactly the same. Social systems thinking is similar to a map, for example, but it is not in fact a map as maps are traditionally defined. As with all tools for improving our understanding of HBSE, we must use metaphors critically. We must appreciate what they are as well as what they are not. These cautions about the use of metaphors to help us understand and explain phenomena suggest a need to be conscious of ambiguity.

The Necessity of Appreciating Ambiguity

To be ambiguous or to exhibit ambiguity is often considered a negative attribute. This is especially true when our thinking is confined to traditional "either/or" approaches to understanding the world around us. Such approaches leave no room for the vagaries or subtleties that alternative approaches incorporate as essential elements for understanding the complexity and richness of human experience and behavior.

In our travels we will try to make room for and appreciate the usefulness of ambiguity. We will try to suspend our dependence on the need for certainty. We will attempt to recognize that from appreciating ambiguity can come more complete understanding. **Ambiguity** is a healthy sense of "maybe" or "could sometimes be" rather than a need to always be able to answer a question "definitely" or "must always be." Let's explore the implications for social workers of the concept of ambiguity.

Ann Weick (1991:19) aptly describes the need to incorporate ambiguity into social workers' thinking and theorizing about human behavior and the social environment. She suggests appreciating ambiguity as one way to correct for the limits of metaphorical thinking. She reminds us that "the basic problem with any theory or map is that it becomes reified [considered real in some absolute sense]; by using the map, we come to believe that it presents the world the way it really is." She suggests that "it takes discipline and confidence to treat theory the way it must be treated: as a provisional, imperfect and occasionally useful way to package and repackage the continual blur of images and ideas that bombard us." Her words paint a helpful picture of the benefits and limits of incorporating ambiguity into our thinking processes.

Weick (1991:23) suggests the importance of appreciating ambiguity for social workers by using as a metaphor the appreciation of uncertainty and unpredictability within quantum theory in the natural sciences. Quantum theorists posit that uncertainty and unpredictability are as characteristic of behavior in the physical world as traditional Newtonian assertions that certainty and predictability characterize reality in the physical world. If we think for a moment about human behavior from the perspective of quantum theorists, Weick suggests, we will find ourselves including ambiguity as a necessary element for achieving understanding. This alternative way of thinking, however, requires us to shift from the traditional natural science paradigm that suggests that certainty and predictability are the keys to understanding to alternative paradigms flexible enough to allow room for ambiguity. Such alternative perspectives recognize that humans are at least as likely to behave unpredictably as they are to behave in completely predictable ways. We will explore some extensions of other theories from the natural sciences that might help us appreciate ambiguity later in this chapter (see discussion of chaos and complexity).

Using this metaphor can help us recognize that "the nature of [human] relationships is not governed by determinism. Human behavior is acausal, in the sense that human action, except in the most narrow sense, cannot be predicted from prior behavior" (Weick 1991:21). Prediction is really only possible when based on the aggregate behavior of large groups. One cannot accurately or consistently predict the behavior of any single individual within the group. As social workers we need to recognize this as an important limitation of statistics that present aggregate data. Such data is helpful in pointing out patterns or trends, but it is much less useful as a tool for predicting the behavior of any one individual. For example, aggregate data may help us recognize a dramatic increase in the number of teenage pregnancies over time. However, it does not tell us with any certainty about the specific factors leading to the pregnancy of the teenage client sitting at our desk.

The Personal as Political: Individual and Social Change

Feminist theory incorporates not only the fundamental spirit of social work but many of the dimensions of alternative paradigm thinking we have been exploring in this book. It incorporates the power of people's personal stories and experiences as avenues to understanding human behavior and for bringing about social change. It, in essence, unites the personal and the political through its focus on "consciousness raising that occurs when people explore their own stories or the stories of others in troubling circumstances" (Goldstein 1990:40–41).

Bricker-Jenkins (1991:279), in her overview of dimensions of feminist social work practice, provides an important summary of the meaning and implications of seeing individual and social change as closely interconnected—of the unity of the personal and the political. She asserts that "individual and collective pain and problems of living always have a political and/or cultural dimension." Bricker-Jenkins and Hooyman (1986:14) remind us that "our feelings about ourselves and our conditions— our consciousness—are shaped by political forces." They also remind us that the "sum of our individual actions create the social order, [and] we are thereby responsible to each other for our actions" (1986:14). These assertions about feminism and feminist social work practice both inform and reinforce the importance of recognizing that what we do (or do not do) as individuals influences the social and political environment as well. Likewise, what happens at the sociopolitical level has an impact on our individual lives. Bricker-Jenkins and Hooyman explain this interdependent dynamic in terms of social work practice: "In the process of taking collective action to change the historical, material and cultural conditions reflected in clients' shattered images and personalized in their psychic pains, we expect to change our *selves* as much as anything else" (1986:14).

Human Behavior and the Social Environment (HBSE) and Social Environment and Human Behavior (SEHB)

We raised the question in Chapter 1 about the implications of the name "human behavior and the social environment," and questioned how our focus might shift if we referred instead to "social environment and human behavior." Some social work scholars suggest a similar consideration in discussing traditional perspectives on the relationship of the individual and social change missions of social work.

Traditional perspectives on social work have often included debates about whether social workers should focus their energies and attention on the individual or on the social aspects of our worlds. The perspective suggested here is that we can and must focus our energies and attention on both the individual and the social simultaneously. As in the feminist perspective described above, it is not a question of either/or, but both/and. As Bricker-Jenkins and Hooyman (1986:13) put it, "we change our world by changing ourselves as we change our world." Put another way, one might say that in order for me to be better off, you must be better off—we must be better off.

Our discussion of HBSE versus SEHB reminds us that the way we arrange words can carry a suggestion of the priority or importance given to those words. Next we discuss the significance of words themselves as carriers of meaning and power.

The Substantive Nature of Language and Words

It is vitally important that social workers recognize and continually reflect on the content and messages conveyed by the language and words we and others use. Language and words are primary means through which we communicate the nature of the paradigms we use to understand human behavior and the social environment. Language and words also play an important part in shaping our own and others' views of the world. The implications of language and words for us as social workers include but go well beyond the narrow and traditional meanings of these words. They are themselves important vehicles for assisting us in our journey toward fuller understanding of HBSE.

Language, Texts, and Discourse

Joan Scott (1988:34) describes an expanded view of language that reflects its substantive nature as a vehicle for increasing our understanding of our worlds. Scott's description offers us a means to better appreciate the central place of language and words in understanding HBSE. She describes **language** as "not simply words or even a vocabulary and set of grammatical rules but, rather, a meaning-constituting system: that is, any system—strictly verbal or other—through which meaning is constructed and cultural practices organized and by which, accordingly, people represent and understand their world, including who they are and how they relate to others."

Scott (1988) suggests that we be carefully analytical of the language of the specific "texts" we use to construct, describe, and understand our worlds. "**Texts**," she says, are not only books and documents (like this book, for example) but also "utterances of any kind and in any medium, including cultural practices" (institutionalized cultural rituals, such as those surrounding marriage in many cultures, for example). In addition to these expanded notions of language and text, Scott offers the helpful concept of discourse. She uses Michel Foucault's conceptualization of **discourse** as neither a language nor a text "but a historically, socially, and institutionally specific structure of statements, terms, categories, and beliefs" through which meaning is constructed, conveyed, and enforced. This notion of discourse certainly includes the languages and texts we create and use to describe and define our worlds, but it goes beyond this to include organizations and institutions that make up our worlds. This notion of discourse also incorporates the important concepts of conflict and power through which meanings are contested, controlled, or changed.

This expanded vision of language and discourse offers a helpful way for social workers to build and practice our analytical skills as we seek to examine alternative and traditional paradigms for their consistency with the core concerns of social work. In fact such a vision allows us to incorporate in our analyses such elements of core concerns as power, empowerment, and conflict.

As social workers, we need to continually "read" or "deconstruct" the world around us for the meanings it conveys about the core concerns of social work. This is especially important for us to do as we examine theories and models for understanding HBSE, for it is through these theories and models that we construct the meanings we use and convey in our social work practice. This perspective on language and words also underscores the importance of such basic social work skills as listening, clarifying, and restating. (If you have not already explored and/or practiced these skills, you will in all likelihood get the opportunity to do so before you complete your social work education.)

This notion of our worlds as made up of fields of discourse through which meanings are created and conveyed suggests that the meanings created can and do change over time according to the historical, political, and social contexts of the times. These meanings, created by humans, can therefore be changed by human efforts. The process of changing meanings and the organizations and institutions through which those meanings are constructed and communicated reflects the essence of the process of social change or social transformation. Thus, once again, we see the interconnectedness of the concepts with which we are concerned as we proceed through this chapter and the remainder of the book on our journey to understand traditional and alternative paradigms (for HBSE).

Language: Exclusiveness versus Inclusiveness

Several of the perspectives we have discussed come together around issues of inclusiveness versus exclusiveness in our efforts to understand HBSE and to practice social work. Concern for the emergent and process nature of knowledge and knowledge building, concern for the unity of personal and political dimensions, and concerns about the power of words and language all can be thought of in relation to the issue of inclusiveness or exclusiveness.

An important example of the complex interplay of the personal and political implications of language and words as we construct knowledge about others is reflected in the words used to name the diverse peoples of the United States. The process of naming or labeling has important implications for social work and for thinking about issues of inclusiveness and exclusiveness.

Language: Labels and People of Color. Asamoah et al. point out that the **labels** applied to racial/ethnic groups are of major significance. They are "structural perceptions with implications for access to power, distribution of resources, and for social policy and practice." In addition, labels "can be inclusive or exclusive, can promote unity or divisiveness, can blur or highlight the distinctions between cultural, political and national identity, and can positively or negatively affect daily social interaction among and between groups" (1991:9).

Central to both the personal identity implications and the political meanings of labels of diverse peoples is the issue of who controls the naming or labeling. In reference to African Americans, Harding (in Asamoah et al. 1991:10) "suggested that self-identification is the foundation on which a sense of peoplehood develops and provides the rootage necessary to effectively meet mainstream challenges." So, in accordance with this suggestion and with social workers' concern for self-determination, we should find out from and respect the names preferred by the persons with whom we work rather than assume that the name with which we may be most familiar and comfortable is appropriate. This is especially the case with persons who have historically been oppressed and denied access to power. It is also important to recognize that even self-determined labels can change over time in accordance with the changing perspectives and experiences of individuals and groups. It is the responsibility of the social worker to remain current with the descriptive labels preferred by the range of diverse persons with whom we work.

The Meanings of "Minority." Another issue related to specific labels for diverse peoples is the more general descriptive word minority. Asamoah et al. suggest that the term **minority** "obliterates the uniqueness of groups and implies that those subsumed under the term share certain characteristics, which may not be the case" (1991:10). This kind of overgeneralization robs persons of their individuality and uniqueness. This certainly is an important consideration given our earlier discussion of Diversity within Diversity (see Chapter 2) The National Association of Black Social Workers has campaigned to abolish the term minority because of its negative political connotations. "Once the impression is formed that an individual belongs to a devalued group . . . then every event and every encounter gets processed through this lens" (Asamoah et al. 1991:20).

The term **minority** is also inaccurate in reference to many groups, such as women, who are a numerical majority. It is also inaccurate in this sense for many persons of color who are part of numerical majority groups in many cities and regions of the United States. It is important to recognize, though, that there is not universal agreement on whether the term "people of color" is always more descriptive or appropriate than the term "minority." Some people argue that "minority" is an appropriate term when referring to oppressed people if we are referring to the rights, resources, and opportunities available to or held by members of different groups. For example, black South African people, a vast numerical majority, were in fact a minority when comparing their access to rights, power, and resources with that held by whites who were clearly a numerical minority. The recent advances in dismantling apartheid in the struggles of black South Africans for rights, power, and resources more in keeping with their numerical majority signifies that minority status defined in terms of rights, power, and resources can in fact change over time as a result of demands and actions on the part of the oppressed "minority" population.

A key to the personal and political implications of labeling is the issue of whether the label is determined by members inside the group or by persons external to the group. Whenever the label is imposed externally by persons other than members of the group being named, the members of the group end up being evaluated "in terms of how or whether they measure up to some external standard, the parameters of which may not even be totally known to them" (Asamoah et al. 1991:20). A large body of sociological theory referred to as labeling theory focuses on this aspect of labeling. **Labeling theory** "describes the ability of some groups to impose a label of 'deviant' on certain other members of society" (Persell 1987:163).

A consequence, then, for members of oppressed groups of naming themselves is empowerment. As Asamoah et al. (1991:20) remind us, "Once we define ourselves, it no longer matters what 'they' call us. What matters is what 'we' answer." Clearly, again, the interplay of the various vehicles for achieving understanding of HBSE is apparent when we think about the importance of words and naming for their ability to determine who is included and who is excluded in the worldviews we create.

Language: Inclusiveness and Persons with Disabilities.   Patterson et al. stress that it is important to remember that a "disability represents only one facet of any person" (1995:76). They also note that in 1990 there were 43 million people with disabilities in the United States and that people with disabilities constitute the largest "minority" in the United States. Language is a significant element of both defining and reflecting a paradigm that is inclusive and respectful of persons with disabilities. Patterson et al. suggest that **inappropriate language is language that:**

1.   *reinforces myths [and] stereotypes about people with disabilities:*
     - *'wheelchair bound,' 'confined to a wheelchair,' 'afflicted,' 'suffers from' vs. 'uses a wheelchair'*
     - *'you do that just like a normal person' implies the person with a disability is abnormal versus 'able-bodied'*
     - *disability, sickness and disease are not synonyms*
2.   *equates the person with the disability by using the disability as a noun*
     - *'the disabled', 'the handicapped,' 'the blind': "they equate people with their disability . . . the disability is . . . only one characteristic of a unique and complex person."*
3.   *uses demeaning and outdated words and phrases when referring to people with disabilities.*
     - *terms that no longer have scientific meaning: 'crippled,' 'idiot,' 'handicapped.'*   (1995:77–78)

Patterson et al. stress that **disability** is the preferred term, and refers to "a physical, mental, emotional or sensory condition that limits a person in any major life area, such as self-care, transportation, communication, mobility, activities of daily living, and work" (1995:78).

Language and Sexual Orientation: No Words. In addition to inappropriate language or labels for members of diverse groups, an important issue for lesbian and gay family members is the lack of words, labels, guidelines, and norms for the relationships in which gay and lesbian family members are involved. For example, Demo and Allen raise a number of questions/issues about the lack of language or words to convey relationships, roles and meanings for lesbian and gay persons and their families:

1. *How does an adolescent refer to her biological mother's lifelong partner?*
2. *How should family members and others refer to the abiding family friend whose frequent and nurturing involvement with the family resembles a loving uncle or brother?*
3. *What if he is also the daughter's biological father through donor inseminations?*
4. *What terms and norms govern how lesbian or gay partners refer to and interact with their affinal kin, such as their partner's parents or siblings?* (1996:426)

Technology

As we noted in Chapter 1 new technologies are increasingly providing new tools for social work education and practice. Distance learning technologies such as Web-based supplements to traditional courses as well as complete courses offered on line in addition to such technologies as compressed interactive video (CIV) are expanding the tools available for social work education. These new tools offer exciting possibilities for improving the access to social work education and for providing more individualized education for many students. Gardner describes the changes that technology can bring to education:

> In the future, however, education will be organized largely around the computer. Computers will permit a degree of individualization—personalized coaching or tutoring—which in the past was available only to the rich. All students may receive a curriculum tailored to their needs, learning style, pace, and profile of mastery, and record of success with earlier materials and lessons. Indeed, computer technology permits us to realize, for the first time, progressive educational ideas of "personalization" and "active, hands-on learning" for students all over the world. (Gardner 2000)

However, new technological tools are also sometimes criticized for their lack of personal face-to-face exchanges among students and teachers. It is important to recognize these new technologies as tools for enhancing opportunities for education, rather than as mechanisms for replacing traditional approaches to education.

It is also important to recognize that new skills are necessary to both teach and learn using these technologies. A most basic skill set necessary is referred to as digital literacy. According to Gilster, "Digital literacy is the ability to understand information and—more important—to evaluate and integrate information in multiple formats that the computer can deliver. Being able to evaluate and interpret information is critical." Digital literacy also requires the use of critical thinking skills. Gilster emphases that "you can't understand information you find on the Internet without evaluating its sources and placing it in context" (in Pool 1997).

Technology is also providing a range of new tools for assisting social workers in practice with individuals, groups, organizations, and communities. In addition to e-mail and conferencing technologies (such as listserves) that allow professionals new means of communicating with each other and with consumers of their services, there are interesting technologies emerging for use at the community and policy levels. Among these are geographic information systems (GIS). GIS are "computer systems for capturing, storing, manipulating, analyzing, displaying, and integrating spatial (that is, geographical or locational) and nonspatial (that is, statistical or attribution) information" (Queralt and Witte 1998). GIS technology combines satellite global positioning and mapping systems with data such as census data and agency data on client demographics to generate reports and maps that can show both patterns and trends of service use and service needs. According to Queralt and Witte, some of the uses of GIS technology include:

- To assess the sociodemographic characteristics of the neighborhoods served by the agency
- To assess whether the supply of services in a given community is adequate and appropriate for the target population in order to determine which areas may be in special need of outreach initiatives, such as activities to encourage the development of services in neighborhoods where the supply appears deficient
- To help determine the locations of new branch offices, client groups to be targeted, and services to be offered
- To delineate catchment areas for various facilities (for example, special schools, transitional aid offices, specialized health services, outpatient psychiatric services), taking into consideration maximum distances and travel times appropriate to the life situations of potential clients
- To map the flow of clients to and from various community services; for example, to compute travel times and distance from areas with large concentrations of elderly people to the closest geriatric hospital or from home to work for those transitioning from welfare to work
- To plan routes; for example, in community policing, to develop daily police patrol routes that cover the areas where crimes are most frequently reported (1998)

GIS is just one example of new technologies that can be important tools in understanding human behavior and the social environment.

Social Work and Assessment

Much of the purpose of HBSE is gaining sufficient information and perspectives to be able to effectively assess the social contexts in which you are working and the people with whom you are working in order to determine how to appropriately interact and intervene in those contexts and with the persons with whom you work. Norman and Wheeler suggest a three-dimensional model of social work assessment. They assert that "practitioners must keep in mind that each individual is unique, with unique experiences, perceptions, feelings, and behaviors, and yet has much in common with other human beings." They offer a model that recognizes that any individual is:

1. like no other *human being: "The fact that a client is a woman does not mean that she shares the views and experiences of other women."*

2. like some others *(other females or other males): "all humans are identified as belonging to subgroups or categories. Gender is one of those categories and should be considered in assessments or interventions."*

3. like all others *in the human community (female and male): "humans share common needs." Jung (1964) "proposed a 'collective unconscious,' a storehouse of latent memory traces inherited from humanity's ancestral past." "To fully understand a single human being, we must first comprehend all human beings, that is, the commonalties that connect us all."* (1996:208–210)

While references in this model are to individuals, the authors suggest such a schema can assist in assessment with clients systems of varying sizes. Try substituting family, group, organization, or community in each of the three dimensions above. At each system level we must recognize uniqueness, similarities with others in similar categories, and universal human commonalties.

Social Work Assessment and Other Disciplines

Bergen (1994) offers a helpful continuum of assessment processes carried out with differing degrees of interaction with and across disciplines. Much of your work as a social worker will be carried out through interaction with other helping professionals from a variety of disciplines. Bergen's continuum suggests that there are a variety of degrees of cross-disciplinary interaction possible depending to a great extent on the context in which assessment occurs. Bergen uses the example of assessment of young children to describe three quite different approaches to cross-disciplinary work. Her model is described below:

Defining a Transdisciplinary Perspective

1. Multidisciplinary Assessment: *involves having each professional conduct a separate evaluation, using the major instruments or procedures common in that discipline. The results are then reported in writing to an individual who is central to the process (e.g., a director of a medical or clinical team). In this model, the professionals who do the assessment are often not involved in developing the intervention plan . . . Parents are*

> *involved primarily in making sure their children get to the various pro-fessional offices where the assessments will be made and in hearing the re-sults of the assessment from each professional's perspective.*

2. Interdisciplinary Assessment: *the assessments are still conducted inde-pendently by the professionals, using their discipline-specific instruments. However, there are usually communication and results-sharing among the assessors, often through a meeting with the parent and at least some of the team members. Typically, at the group meeting each professional takes a turn in telling the parent the results and giving recommenda-tions for intervention. . . . and although the parent is asked to question or comment, the assessment profile and the decisions regarding appro-priate intervention are usually made by each professional prior to the meeting and are not often changed as a result of the team meeting.*

3. Transdisciplinary Assessment: *differs both in the procedures for assess-ment and in the determination of actions based on the assessment. At least in its ideal form, parents are involved even before the actual assess-ment procedures begin; they are asked to give their own assessment of the child and to identify areas of concern that the parents feel are particu-larly important to assess and remediate. The parents also have the op-portunity to identify needs of the family that relate to their child, and to affirm the strengths they can bring to that child's care and education. Then the team as a whole decides on the appropriate methods for assess-ing each child and conducts an integrated assessment, using the methods from all disciplines that appear to be appropriate.* (Bergen 1994:6)

Bergen's cross-disciplinary approach to assessment seems especially well-suited to more holistic approaches consistent with alternative paradigm thinking. A combi-nation of Norman and Wheeler's social work assessment model and Bergen's model, particularly transdisciplinary assessment, may be an especially beneficial approach to thinking about assessment in your work. We explore some specific traditional assess-ment tools in Chapter 4, and we explore strengths-based approaches to assessment later in this chapter.

TOOLS FOR SOCIAL WORKERS: THEORIES FOR PRACTICE

Traditional Theoretical Approaches

There are a number of traditional theories about humans' behavior and their inter-actions in the social environment that originate in the social and behavioral sciences. For example, if you have completed introductory level psychology, sociology, an-thropology, or political sciences courses prior to taking this HBSE course, a number of the theories described in the following sections may be familiar to you. As we pro-ceed through the other chapters in this book it may be helpful to refer back to the theories described here to help you connect the social work emphases on individuals, families, groups, organizations, and communities to these traditional approaches to understanding human behavior in a variety of contexts.

Functional Theory

According to Alix, "The functionalist perspective favors a consensus view of social order. It sees human beings as naturally caring and cooperative but also as rather undisciplined. They need some regulation to keep them from pursuing goals that are beyond their means. This control is exercised through consensus—agreement among most of a society's members" (1995:27). Henslin describes the central idea of **functional theory** as the belief "that society is a whole unit, made of interrelated parts that work together" (1996:11). Alix notes, however, that "critics . . . claim that the perspective's view that everything in society (including such negative arrangements as racial/ethnic and gender discrimination) somehow contributes to the functioning of society as a whole renders the perspective inherently conservative" (1995:29).

Conflict Theory

Conflict theory offers a dramatic contrast to functional theory. "Unlike the functionalist who views society as a harmonious whole, with its parts working together, **conflict theorists** see society as composed of groups fiercely competing for scarce resources. Although alliances or cooperation may prevail on the surface, beneath that surface is a struggle for power" (Henslin 1996:13). Karl Marx, the founder of conflict theory, believed "the key to all human history is class struggle. In each society, some small group controls the means of production and exploits those who do not" (Henslin 1996:13). Basically, "**the conflict perspective** favors a coercion view of the social order." In this view, human beings are self-interested and competitive, but not necessarily as the result of human nature. . . . We are forced into conflict with one another over such scarce resources as wealth and power. The **conflict perspective** sees as the basis of social order the coercion of less powerful groups and classes by more powerful groups and classes" (Alix 1995:29).

Interactionist Theory

This area of theory differs from either conflict or functional theory and focuses on the nature and meaning of the interactions between and among humans. There are several theoretical variations of interactionist theory. Interactionist theory takes a more micro (individuals or small groups) than macro (societal) approach to attempting to explain human behavior. It is also a bit less traditional in that it focuses on subjective meanings of behavior. From the **interactionist perspective** behavior is "much less scripted. Instead, it appears more fluid, more tentative, even negotiable. In other words, although people may have been given parts to play in society, they have a good deal of freedom in how they are going to play the parts—for example, with or without enthusiasm" (Alix 1995:31). Alix describes three variations on interactionist theory.

Exchange Theory: *proposes that human interaction involves rational calculations. People calculate how much pleasure and pain they are likely to experience in current social situations based on their experience in past situations. . . . They seek to repeat pleasurable situations and to avoid painful ones.* (1995:33)

Symbolic Interaction Theory: *proposes that, in addition to any objective assessment of the costs and benefits of interacting with other people, you also are involved in a subjective, symbolic process . . . symbolic interaction theory proposes that, before interacting, human beings size up one another in terms of these symbolic meanings. Ex. woman, instructor, student. . . .* (1995:33–34)

Dramaturgical Theory: *Goffman's (1922–1882 [sic]) more theatrical (and more cynical) view of human society . . . portrays people as actors in the literal sense. We act out our everyday lives on a succession of stages (social situations). We script scenes (interaction episodes) to serve our interests We dress ourselves in the costumes of the characters we play.* (1995:35)

Role Theory

Role theory is one influential area of theory about human behavior. **Role theory** seeks to explain behavior as action taken in accordance with agreed-upon rules of behavior for persons occupying given positions. For example, we might behave in accordance with our roles as parent, sibling, worker, student, teacher, and so forth. We will explore roles people play as members of groups, in Chapter 7, and we will explore gender roles in the context of family, in Chapter 6.

Psychoanalytic Theory

Psychoanalytic theory is one of the most influential theories for explaining human behavior. We will explore psychoanalytic theory, in Chapter 4, as a traditional theory of individual development focusing on internal and often unconscious origins of human behavior.

Behavioral/Learning Theory

Behavioral theory or **learning theory,** in contrast to psychoanalytic theory, sees human behavior as almost entirely determined through learning that takes place as a result of reinforcement of our behaviors by others or as a result of our observation of behaviors modeled by others. The reinforcement or modeling necessary for learning behaviors comes almost exclusively from the environment. In Chapter 5 we will explore alternative theories of individual development, such as theories of women's development, the development of ethnic identity, and gay and lesbian identity development. Many of these alternative theories see human development as a result of the interactions of multiple factors, some of which come from within us and some of which come from the social environment.

Mid-Range Theoretical Approaches

There are several theoretical approaches that we can consider mid-range theories that can help us understand HBSE. These are theories that go beyond traditional theories and emphasize the importance of the social environment as a critical factor in human behavior. These middle-range theories also incorporate notions of change over time more than the traditional theories we explored above. However, these theories nevertheless flow from traditional paradigm thinking and tend not to emphasize dimensions of alternative paradigm thinking such as interpretive and intuitive ways of knowing, feminist approaches, diverse worldviews, and issues of power and oppression. The middle-range theories or perspectives we will consider here are human development, life span, life course, and social systems or ecological frameworks.

Human Development

Theories of human development have been extremely important in social work approaches to understanding and assessing human behavior and the social environment. Bergen defines **human development** as

1. Changes *in the structure, function, or behavior of the human organism*
2. *that occur* over some period of time *(which may be of long or brief duration)*
3. *and are* due to an interactive combination *of maturation and learning (heredity/environment interaction)* (1994:13)

Life Span Perspective

Another common framework used by social workers for organizing knowledge about human behavior is referred to as the life span perspective. This perspective is most often used in discussing human behavior at the individual level. However, life span perspectives can be applied also to families, groups, organizations, and even communities.

A life span perspective is sometimes used almost interchangeably with life cycle or stage theories about human behavior. The perspective on life span taken here is one that is broader and less linear than traditional life-cycle or stage-based theories. Newman and Newman (1991) outline a set of underlying assumptions about a life span perspective on individual development that is compatible with the broader, less linear approach taken here.

The Newmans' approach to life span development of the individual is organized around four major assumptions. While they make these assumptions specifically about individual life span, with some adaptation these assumptions can provide helpful guidance to us as we explore human behavior at a variety of levels in a variety of contexts. Their assumptions follow:

1. *Growth occurs at every period of life, from conception through old age.*
2. *Individual lives show continuity and change as they progress through time. An awareness of processes that contribute to both continuity and change is central to an understanding of human development.*
3. *We need to understand the whole person, because we function in an integrated manner on a day-to-day basis. To achieve such an understanding we need to study the major internal developments that involve physical, social, emotional, and thinking capacities and their interrelationship.*
4. *Every person's behavior must be analyzed in the context of relevant settings and personal relationships. Human beings are highly skilled at*

> *adapting to their environment. The meaning of a given behavior pattern*
> *or change must be interpreted in light of the significant physical and so-*
> *cial environments in which it occurs.* (Newman and Newman 1991:4)

These assumptions allow somewhat more emergent, holistic, and contextual alternatives to traditional ways of thinking about how individuals (and other social system levels) develop and change over time.

Life Course Theory

Life course theory expands the notion of life span approaches. It is especially helpful as a tool for understanding better the complexities of family as the context or environment of the individuals developing within it. Demo and Allen (1996:426) see **life course theory** as helpful because it looks at families with greater attention to the complexity and variability that are a part of people's lives. According to Demo and Allen "this framework focuses on the multiple trajectories and social contexts (e.g. family, employment and community) shaping individual lives and the unique and overlapping pathways and trajectories within families." They note that "by examining social age, developmental age and historical age, researchers can identify cohorts who experience similar slices of history from different developmental vantage points, thereby illuminating the intersections of biography and history" (Demo and Allen 1996:426–27). **Life course theory** is a contextual, processual, and dynamic approach. It looks at change in individual lives and in family units over time by tracing individual developmental *trajectories* or paths in the context of the development of family units over time. It also addresses multiple system levels along the continuum of micro or small systems to macro or large systems by attending to individual, family, and community intersections during the life course. Life course is concerned with the interconnections between personal biographies or life stories and social-historical time (Bengston and Allen 1993:469–499).

While life course theory is more inclusive of context, it nevertheless can be considered relatively traditional in that it "does not challenge the status quo, does not explain the marginalization of certain family types and does not recognize the influence of intersecting power hierarchies (e.g. race, gender and sexual orientation)" (Demo and Allen 1996:427). We examine life course theory in more detail in Chapter 6. We consider it here as somewhat alternative or middle-range theory because it is more inclusive of a number of contexts, processes, and potentials consistent with a number of elements or themes of alternative paradigm thinking including as Kain notes historical and social contexts, process and change dynamic and diversity (1993:499).

Social Systems/Ecological Perspectives

Social systems perspectives (Anderson and Carter 1990; Martin and O'Connor 1989) and ecological perspectives (Germain 1991) have for some time been important frameworks for organizing social work knowledge and for conceptualizing approaches to using that knowledge in practice. There is some disagreement about the similarities and differences between social systems and ecological approaches. It is clear that general systems theory, because its application includes the entire physical world as well as the human world, differs from both social systems and ecological perspectives that concern themselves primarily with humans and their interactions with each other and the world around them. The ecological perspective, however, explicitly defines the environment as including physical (nonhuman) elements. Social systems perspectives are less explicit about the place and role of nonhuman elements in the environment. Some would also argue that social systems and ecological approaches differ in their conceptualizations of boundaries and exchange across boundaries that occur in human interactions. Recognizing these areas of disagreement, we will consider these two perspectives similar enough to be treated together here.

Social systems or ecological perspectives can help us bridge the gap between traditional and alternative paradigms. Central to these approaches, for example, are notions of the interrelatedness or interconnectedness of the various components constituting individual behavior and the parts of the social environments in which individuals interact with each other. These approaches also tend to recognize that we must grasp both process and change if we are to understand HBSE. These notions are consistent with some of the dimensions of alternative paradigms we have explored.

While they recognize their importance for social workers, social systems and ecological perspectives, however, tend to be less focused on and offer less direction regarding fundamental social transformation or social change and the unity of personal and political issues than is the emphasis in much alternative paradigm thinking, such as that found in feminist or empowerment perspectives. Social systems perspectives recognize that systems are constantly changing or "in process," but they tend to emphasize these change processes as functional and self-righting much more than they emphasize the possibility of these processes to reinforce existing exclusion and oppression within systems. (See Social Systems critiques below.)

Both social systems and ecological perspectives do recognize that adaptation sometimes involves altering the environment. Anderson and Carter (1990:39), for example, "reject the view that the adjustment must be made only by the system and not by the suprasystem or environment." Germain (1979:8), in her discussion of the ecological perspective, stresses that "living organisms adapt to their environments by actively changing their environment so that it meets their needs." She uses the examples of nest building by birds and tilling the land by humans. It is important to recognize that the level and intensity of alteration of the environment suggested by both social systems and ecological theorists is more incremental (adaptive) than the more fundamental structural or institutional changes called for by some alternative paradigm theorists. For example, feminists call for fundamental changes in the distribution of personal and political power and in the ways people relate to each other in the environment in order to bring an end to oppression of women and other groups denied equal power by the dominant group. Social systems and ecological perspectives nevertheless are helpful vehicles to use in our journey.

Capra (1983) finds a place for ecological and social systems approaches in his alternative approaches emerging from new thinking in the natural sciences. He suggests that these approaches to understanding the social world are closely connected to alternative ways of viewing the physical world. He suggests, for example, that

> *Deep ecology is supported by modern science . . . but is rooted in a perception of reality that goes beyond the scientific framework to an intuitive awareness of the oneness of all life, the interdependence of its multiple manifestations*

and its cycles of change and transformation. When the concept of the human spirit is understood in this sense, as the mode of consciousness in which the individual feels connected to the cosmos as a whole, it becomes clear that ecological awareness is truly spiritual. (Capra 1983:412)

Capra also connects systems and ecological thinking to feminist and spiritual perspectives, other important elements of our alternative paradigm framework. He asserts that "the spiritual essence of the ecological vision seems to find its ideal expression in the feminist spirituality advocated by the women's movement, as would be expected from the natural kinship between feminism and ecology, rooted in the age-old identification of woman and nature" (1983:415). "Feminist spirituality is based on awareness of the oneness of all living forms and of their cyclical rhythms of birth and death, thus reflecting an attitude toward life that is profoundly ecological" (Capra 1982:415). Again we find the various directions and maps for pursuing alternative views of HBSE, in this case social systems and ecological perspectives, intersecting and interconnecting with other dimensions of new paradigm thinking such as feminist perspectives, although as we noted earlier, they also represent very different approaches.

Because systems models have been applied at so many levels of human behavior, as we continue our journey in this book, we will find systems perspectives among vehicles for explaining individual human behavior as well as human behavior in the context of families, groups, organizations, and communities. Sometimes systems models will represent traditional thinking and sometimes they will represent alternative approaches in this book.

Social Systems Terms. The themes or assumptions of the various systems perspectives presented will be quite similar to those discussed above. However, there will be considerable variation in the specific terms used to describe social systems' structures and dynamics. Anderson and Carter's (1990) treatment of social systems, perhaps the most widely used set of terminology for discussing social systems in HBSE courses in the United States, is summarized here to provide us a social systems map for HBSE. There are others, such as the "open systems applications" model of Martin and O'Connor (1989), that offer rather comprehensive social systems frameworks as well. The approach taken by Anderson and Carter is for the most part compatible with the systems perspectives you will find in the chapters that follow, although the specific terms used may vary.

Anderson and Carter (1990:266–267) define a **system** as "an organized whole made up of components that interact in a way distinct from their interaction with other entities and which endures over some period of time." They offer a number of basic systems concepts that communicate the ideas essential to a social systems perspective. They suggest that all social systems, large or small, are simultaneously part of other systems and a whole in themselves. This they refer to as **holon.** They suggest it is essential, in order to use social systems thinking, that we set a perspective that allows us to focus by declaring a **focal system,** the system of primary concern. Only after a focal system has been declared can we begin to distinguish the parts or **subsystems** of which the focal system is composed from the parts and other entire social systems constituting the environment or **suprasystem** surrounding and influencing the focal system.

In addition to these basic perspective-setting concepts, Anderson and Carter suggest other fundamental aspects of social systems. Among these are the concept of

energy, or the "capacity for action," "action," or the "power to effect change" (1990:11). Energy is a rather inclusive aspect of systems and suggests their dynamic or "process" nature. Energy is what allows systems to move, regardless of the direction in which they move. Energy is necessary for a social system to remain alive, it is the "stuff" that makes a system go. A healthy system can be characterized by **synergy** or the ability to use energy to create new energy. A system that is losing energy faster than it is creating or importing it is characterized by **entropy.** It is "running down"; it is in a state of decline (1990:13). Another fundamental aspect of social systems, according to Anderson and Carter, is organization. **Organization** is the "grouping and arranging of parts to form a whole, to put a system into working order" (1990:20). Organization provides structure for a system, just as energy provides or drives process. These concepts suggest that the system must be able to sufficiently organize or arrange its components to accomplish its goals or get its work done. Important concepts related to structure or organization of social systems include **boundary,** the means by which the parts of a system can be differentiated from the environment in which the system exists. Anderson and Carter offer an interactional definition of boundary as the location "where the intensity of energy interchange is greater on one side of a certain point than it is on the other, or greater among certain units than among others." They stress that boundary does not mean barrier, because systems must exchange energy with other systems across their boundaries in order to survive and thrive. This process of energy exchange is accomplished through **linkage.** A social system can be relatively **open** or relatively **closed** to energy exchange across its boundaries (Anderson and Carter 1990:29–31).

Additional systems characteristics discussed by Anderson and Carter (and others) include **hierarchy,** the particular order in which system parts are arranged; **differentiation,** a division of labor among system parts, and **specialization,** a division of labor in which only certain parts can perform certain functions; **socialization,** imparting to system parts the rules for behavior, and **social control,** the pressure (persuasive or coercive) put on deviant system parts to return to behavior in accord with the rules of the system; **communication,** the transfer of energy to accomplish system goals, and **feedback,** the information received by systems about the progress toward goals and the system's response to that information (1990:31–38). The concept of **adaptation** was described earlier in this section as the system's ability to change itself or adjust to the environment in order to respond to new conditions.

Together these basic concepts create a "language" of social systems that we will find useful at various points along our journey to understand HBSE. These concepts are often used in discussions of both traditional and alternative perspectives on HBSE. In this respect they tend to seem fairly neutral. Their real power flows from the context in which they are used and the purposes for which they are used. These basic concepts can be used to defend and maintain the status quo or they can be used to indicate the need for change. The perspective of the user of these concepts is essential to their meaning in any particular context.

Social Systems Critiques.   Given the potential for social systems thinking to be both a mechanism for maintaining the status quo and for indicating the need for change, we will explore some recent critiques of social systems thinking. In addition, we explore some more alternative views on systems thinking. These more recent alternatives will include chaos and complexity theory as well as the Gaia hypothesis. We should note that

Berman's (1996) critique of system thinking includes traditional social systems notions as well as the more recent alternatives of chaos/complexity and the Gaia hypothesis.

A number of the criticisms are summarized below. As you read this criticism, consider whether you find the criticisms justified, whether some are justified and some are not, and what you might do as a social worker to minimize the weaknesses suggested by this criticism. Finally, ask yourself whether systems thinking is, in fact, an appropriate approach to organizing social work knowledge for practice.

CRITICISMS OF SYSTEMS THEORY

1. *Systems thinking consists of confusing generality and ambiguity* which make it difficult to operationalize through empirical research. *It helps conceptualize/ organize phenomena, but it does not explain anything* (Whitechurch and Constantine 1993:346).

2. *Every part of the system has equal weight,* thus elements of little importance have same weight as elements with major importance (Whitechurch and Constantine 1993:346).

3. *It is potentially coercive in nature.* Potential for megamachine version of "holistic" society, totalitarian in nature, managed by social engineers (Berman 1996:39).

4. *View of reality as a system of information exchange omits the social contexts.* It omits power differences and assumes equality. "It presupposes a society of equals in which all conflicts can be resolved by means of improved communication." However, "the truth is that the relationship of oppressor to oppressed is not one of semantics, and this sort of misguided emphasis can serve to reinforce political inequality by assuming it does not exist" (Berman 1996:39).

5. *Question of whether the cybernetic model is really very different from mechanistic thinking.* Is a computer not simply a very sophisticated clock? If everything is a functional system of interconnected feedback loops it can easily be argued "that victims (e.g., battered wives) are co-creating the violence being done to them." Rather than regarding power as an "epistemological error", in "reality it is fundamental to human relations" (Berman 1996: 39–41).

6. *It is anti-individual:* The systems "emphasis on wholes, as opposed to parts" suggests that systems thinking "tends not to allow a place for individual differences or for individuals apart from the whole" (Berman 1996:41).

7. *The metaphors from science to human behavior stretch too far.* "the gap that exists between the laboratory research and the philosophical extensions that the authors wish to draw form this" (Berman 1996:42).

Continued

CRITICISMS OF SYSTEMS THEORY   *Continued*

8. *Argument that worldviews are shaped by vested interests: systems approach serves very well the current global economic sector.* "It did not arise in a so-cioeconomic vacuum. Its concepts and conclusions are conditioned by the social and economic processes of the late 20th century." "I know of no way that one could prove, for example, that the earth is dead *or* alive. All one can say is that it displays both mechanical and organic aspects, and probably a few others as well" (Berman 1996:44).

9. *Social systems is very conservative.* Notion that overall, everything is in har-mony. "The evolutionary-systemic vision comes down on the side of the status quo" or a "tyranny of harmony"; "much of the systems orienta-tion is consistent with the propositions of structural-functionalism with its notorious justification of inequality and caste in complex society" (Berman 1996:39–45).

In addition to the general criticism of systems thinking above, feminist scholars have criticized social systems approaches for their neglect of biases against women built into social systems. This has been especially true of criticisms directed to social systems approaches in family therapy. For example, feminist scholars point out that resources and power in society are "so unequally distributed to favor men over women and chil-dren" that it is impossible to be unbiased or rational in application of systems theories. Critics also point out that systems thinking suggests "that all parts of the system con-tribute *equally* to dysfunction" and as a result such interpersonal problems as violence and incest are minimized (Whitechurch and Constantine 1993:325).

Alternative Theoretical Approaches

Some emerging alternative theoretical approaches for understanding human behavior and the social environment call into question many of the taken-for-granted assump-tions of traditional paradigm thinking. These theories provide social workers with al-ternative tools to use for understanding HBSE and for using that understanding in practice. These alternative approaches emphasize such dimensions of the alternative paradigm as subjective, interpretive, intuitive, qualitative thinking, interrelatedness, positive elements of human diversity, feminist thinking, and commitment to action to end oppression. The alternative approaches we explore next include: strengths-based, wellness, empowerment, cultural competence, assets, standpoint, and transpersonal spiritual. We will also explore alternative extensions of social systems thinking in-cluding chaos, complexity, and gala theories.

Strengths-Based Perspective

De Jong and Miller (1995) and Saleebey (1992, 1996) remind us that adopting a strengths perspective as individuals and as a profession requires a significant paradigm shift away from traditional approaches to practice. De Jong and Miller find that strengths "assumptions are grounded in the poststructural notion that social workers must increasingly respect and engage clients' ways of viewing themselves and their worlds in the helping process. Or, to put it differently, the strengths perspective asserts that the client's 'meaning' must count for more in the helping process, and scientific labels and theories must count for less" (1995:729).

In his description of the elements of the strengths perspective, Saleebey also notes the fundamental change required of us in adopting this perspective:

> *The strengths perspective demands a different way of looking at individuals, families, and communities. All must be seen in the light of their capacities, talents, competencies, possibilities, visions, values, and hopes, however dashed and distorted these may have become through circumstance, oppression, and trauma. The strengths approach requires an accounting of what people know and what they can do. . . . It requires composing a roster of resources existing within and around the individual, family, or community. . . . Pursuing a practice based on the ideas of resilience, rebound, possibility, and transformation is difficult because, oddly enough, it is not natural to the world of helping and service. . . . Such a 're-vision' demands that [social workers] suspend initial disbelief in clients.* (1996:297–298)

Strengths: Related Concepts and Sources. There are a number of important concepts related to a strengths-based approach including the concepts of empowerment, resilience, membership, dialogue and collaboration, and suspension of belief. We explored empowerment in Chapter 1. Here we can see how the definition of this concept is applied from a strengths perspective: **empowerment:** "means assisting individuals, families, and communities in discovering and using the resources and tools within areas around them" (Saleebey 1996:298). We will examine further an empowerment perspective on practice in a later section. Another important concept related to a strengths perspective is resilience. **Resilience:** "means the skills, abilities, knowledge, and insight that accumulate over time as people struggle to surmount adversity and meet challenges" (Saleebey 1996:298). Scannapieco and Jackson expand the concept of resilience to go well beyond traditional notions of individual resilience. They suggest that while resilience "has been most often defined as an individual's ability to overcome adversities and adapt successfully to varying situations. . . . Recently, the concept of resilience has been used to describe families and schools and communities" (1996:190). Another key concept for understanding the strengths perspective is membership. According to Saleebey **membership** "means that people need to be citizens—responsible and valued members in a viable group or community. To be without membership is to be alienated, and to be at risk of marginalization and oppression" (1996:298–299). Membership suggests that "as people begin to realize and use their assets and abilities, collectively and individually, as they begin to discover the pride in having survived and overcome their difficulties, more and more of their capacities come into the work and play of daily life" (Saleebey 1996:299).

Saleebey illustrates that a "strengths based approach is an alternative to traditional pathology based approaches which underly much of social work knowledge and

COMPARISON OF PATHOLOGY AND STRENGTHS

Pathology	Strengths
Person is defined as a 'case'; symptoms add up to a diagnosis.	Person is defined as unique; traits, talents, resources add up to strengths.
Therapy is problem focused.	Therapy is possibility focused.
Personal accounts aid in the evocation of a diagnosis through reinterpretation by an expert.	Personal accounts are the essential route to knowing and appreciating the person.
Practitioner is skeptical of personal stories, rationalizations.	Practitioner knows the person from the inside out.
Childhood trauma is the precursor or predictor of adult pathology.	Childhood trauma is not predictive; it may weaken or strengthen the individual.
Centerpiece of the therapeutic work is the treatment plan devised by practitioner.	Centerpiece of work is the aspirations of family, individual or community.
Practitioner is the expert on clients' lives.	Individuals, family, or community are the experts.
Possibilities for choice, control, commitment, and personal development are limited by pathology.	Possibilities for choice, control, commitment, and personal development are open.
Resources for work are the knowledge and skills of the professional.	Resources for work are the strengths, capacities, and adaptive skills of the individual, family, or community.
Help is centered on reducing the effects of symptoms and the negative personal and social consequences of actions, emotions, thoughts, or relationships.	Help is centered on getting on with one's life, affirming and developing values and commitments, and making and finding membership in or as a community.

From Saleebey (1996:298). Copyright 1996, National Association of Social Workers, Inc., *Social Work*. Reprinted with permission.

practice theory" (1996:298). Saleebey's comparison of the two approaches is provided in the box, "Comparison of Pathology and Strengths."

Strengths-Based Assessment. Earlier in this chapter we explored the importance of assessment as an essential part of both understanding HBSE and applying that understanding in practice. Assessment is an especially essential part of and is central to the strengths perspective. Cowger reminds us that "If assessment focuses on deficits, it is likely that deficits will remain the focus of both the worker and the client during remaining contacts [and that].... Assessment is a process as well as a product" (1994:264–265). In the box, "Guidelines for Strengths Assessment," (pp. 141-2)

GUIDELINES FOR STRENGTHS ASSESSMENT

1. *Give preeminence to the client's understanding of the facts.* "The client's view of the situation, the meaning the client ascribes to the situation, and the client's feelings or emotions related to that situation are the central focus for assessment."

2. *Believe the client.* "Central to a strengths perspective is a deeply held belief that clients ultimately are trustworthy. . . . clients' understandings of reality are no less real than the social constructions of reality of the professionals assisting them."

3. *Discover what the client wants.* "What does the client want and expect from service? . . . What does the client want to happen in relation to his or her current situation?"

4. *Move the assessment toward personal and environmental strengths.* Must recognize there are obstacles, but "if one believes that solutions to difficult situations lie in strengths, dwelling on obstacles ultimately has little payoff."

5. *Make assessment of strengths multidimensional.* Strengths and resources are both internal and external (environmental), "the client's interpersonal skills, motivation, emotional strengths, and ability to think clearly." The client's "family network, significant others, voluntary organizations, community groups, and public institutions." Multidimensional assessment "also includes an examination of power and power relationships in transactions between the client and the environment."

6. *Use the assessment to discover uniqueness.* "Assessment that focuses on client strengths must be individualized to understand the unique situation the client is experiencing."

7. *Use language the client can understand.* Professional jargon does not help establish "mutual participation of the worker and the client." Assessment products "should be written in simple English and in such a way as to be self-explanatory."

8. *Make assessment a joint activity between worker and client.* This can help minimize the power imbalance between worker and client. "The client must feel ownership of the process and the product and can do so only if assessment is open and shared."

9. *Reach a mutual agreement on the assessment.* There should be no secret assessments. "All assessments in written form should be shared with clients."

10. *Avoid blame and blaming.* "Blame is the first cousin of deficit models of practice."

11. *Avoid cause-and-effect thinking.* "Causal thinking represents only one of many possible perspectives of the problem situation and can lead to blaming.

Continued

> ## GUIDELINES FOR STRENGTHS ASSESSMENT *Continued*
>
> Client problem situations are usually multidimensional, have energy, rep-
> resent multidirectional actions, and reflect dynamics that are not well-
> suited to simple causal explanations."
>
> **12.** *Assess; do not diagnose.* "Diagnosis is understood in the context of pathol-
> ogy, deviance, and deficits. . . . diagnosis is associated with a medical model
> of labeling that assumes unpopular and unacceptable behavior as a symp-
> tom of an underlying pathological condition." (Cowger 1994:265–267)

Cowger (1994) provides some helpful guidelines for conducting strengths-based assessments that appreciate that different persons' views of reality regarding any situation
(including those held by workers and clients about the same situation) vary widely
and "are interactive, multicausal, and ever-changing."

A strengths-based approach requires **dialogue and collaboration** with the people with whom we work. This requires the formation of a genuine relationship between the social worker and the person with whom she or he is working marked by
empathy, inclusiveness, and equality. Perhaps most important, it requires the social
worker to listen, really listen, to what the other person has to say and to value the
client's voice as essential to understanding and action. Collaboration requires the social worker to exchange the expert role for a role as partner with the client in completing a "mutually crafted" product. Finally, Saleebey calls for the strengths-based
worker to **suspend disbelief**—in other words, we must not only listen to and really
hear what the client has to say, the worker must believe the client and not assume the
client has "faulty recall, distorted perceptions, and limited self-awareness" that render what the client says as somehow suspect or only partially true (Saleebey,
1997:10–11).

Criticisms of Strengths Perspective. Many social workers are finding the strengths
perspective to be an alternative to more traditional approaches to practice. However,
the perspective has been questioned by some social workers in terms of whether it really is an alternative and whether it is a helpful alternative perspective. Saleebey outlines some of these criticisms and offers a response from his perspective as an advocate
for the strengths approach.

1. *It's just "positive thinking" in disguise:* **Response:** Strengths is more than
uplifting words and sayings about everything being ok. For people to reach the point
of really seeing themselves as strong, worthy, competent is extremely hard work both
for the social worker and the person or communities involved.

2. *Reframing misery:* Notion that strengths approach simply reframes reality
in such a way that conditions don't change and transformation does not take place,
but instead clients are taught to "reconceptualize their difficulties so that they are san-
itized and less threatening to self and others." **Response:** "The strengths perspective
does not deny reality; it demands some reframing, however, to develop an attitude

and language about the nature of possibility and opportunity and the nature of the individual beneath the diagnostic label."

3. *Pollyannaism:* Strengths perspective "ignores how manipulative and dangerous or destructive clients and client groups can be. The argument is, apparently, that some people are simply beyond redemption." **Response:** Strengths approach does not deny that some people engage in behavior and hurtfulness to themselves and others beyond our ability to understand. However, strengths approach demands that we "ask what useful qualities and skills or even motivation and aspirations these clients have. . . . Social workers cannot automatically discount people. There may be genuinely evil people, beyond grace or hope, but it is best not to make that assumption first."

4. *Ignoring reality:* Downplays real problems. **Response:** "does not discount the problems of clients. . . . All helpers should assess and evaluate the sources and remnants of client troubles, difficulties, pains, and disorders." However, they must also "calculate how clients have managed to survive thus far and what they have drawn on in the face of misfortune." (Saleebey 1996:302–303)

Wellness

Closely associated with the strengths perspective is wellness theory. Jones and Kilpatrick assert the premise of wellness theory to be that "the thoughts and feelings we experience directly affect our physical functioning and well-being, just as our physical functioning directly affects our emotional states and thought processes" (1996:262). The **wellness** perspective recognizes the extremely strong and important relationship between "body, mind and environment and health and wellness." (Saleebey 1996:300) and that "the unit of attention is the physical, mental, spiritual, and social well-being of the individual, family, and/or specific population involved in the intervention process" (Jones and Kilpatric 1996:263). Jones and Kilpatrick believe the complex interplay of these areas has significant influence in "keeping people well, assisting individuals in regenerating after trauma, and helping individuals and communities survive the impact and aftermath of calamity and ordeal" (Saleebey 1996:300). "Wellness theory recognizes that the development of the wellness state is an ongoing, life-long process. Quality of life, rather than length of life, is of primary concern" (Jones and Kilpatrick 1996:264).

Jones and Kilpatrick define **wellness** as "a state of harmony, energy, positive productivity, and well-being in an individual's mind, body, emotions, and spirit. The state of wellness also extends to the relationships between the individual and his or her family and other interpersonal connections as well as the relationships between, the person and his or her physical environment, community, and larger society" (1996:259). Saleebey suggests that "positive beliefs about one's self and condition play a significant role in health maintenance and regeneration . . . [and] emotions, too, have a profound effect on wellness and health. They may act as signals for the body's immune and recuperative responses" (1996:301).

Philosophical, Biological and Social Components of Wellness. Illustrations of philosophical, biological, and social theories that inform wellness theory and emphasize the interplay of multiple aspects of our lives in the creation and maintenance of wellness include constructivism, psychoneuroimmunology, and social development theory.

Constructivism is the theory that "for any single event or situation" there are multiple perceptions of reality all of which have validity. People in the helping relationship work to respect and understand the narratives that constitute reality for the persons involved. . . . "In wellness theory the client's role is as important as the practitioner's role" (Jones and Kilpatrick 1996:263). Practitioners must be honest about what they do not know and respect that the client is the expert on his/her situation (Jones and Kilpatrick 1996:260, 264–265). Practitioners must be as informed as possible about what helps people stay well. **Psychoneuroimmunology** is a biological perspective that informs wellness theory and focuses on "the reciprocal relationship between mind and body" (Jones and Kilpatrick 1996:261). It assumes "the mind and body are inseparable and that continuous reciprocal communication occurs between the mind and the various organ systems of the body via the brain's chemistry" (Jones and Kilpatrick 1996:261). Social development theory is a social or macro perspective on how the larger society either helps or hinders in the creation and maintenance of wellness. **Social development theory** "recognizes the societal and political aspects of human functioning and attempts to address inequities caused by oppression or discrimination targeted toward certain subgroups of society" (Jones and Kilpatrick 1996:261). We explore social development theory in more detail in Chapter 9 in our discussion of communities.

Wellness and Social Change. It is important to realize and reinforce that wellness theory is a theory for both individual and social change. Jones and Kilpatrick remind us that "*Wellness theory can be used to empower oppressed groups such as the aging poor, the homeless, and people with disabilities, targeting enhanced quality of life as its primary goal*" (1996:260). The box on "Wellness and Disabilities" can help us recognize this.

Empowerment

We explored the basic concept of empowerment in Chapter 1 and we noted it as a central component of a strengths-based perspective above. Now we will explore empowerment as a combination of theory and practice and as a process of change as well.

Gutierrez et al. suggest that "empowerment practice in social work emerged from efforts to develop more effective and responsive services for women and people of color" (1995:534). **Empowerment** "focuses on changing the distribution of power" and it "depicts power as originating from various sources and as infinite because it can be generated in the process of social interaction (Gutierrez et al. 1995:535). For Gutierrez et al., empowerment has multiple characteristics and can occur at multiple levels including individual, group and community. Empowerment is:

1. Both a *theory and practice* that deal with issues of power, powerlessness, and oppression and how they contribute to individual, family, or community problems and affect helping relationships.

2. A perspective whose *goal* is to increase personal, interpersonal, or political power so that individuals, families, or communities can take action to improve their situations.

WELLNESS AND DISABILITIES: ILLUSTRATIONS OF THE APPLICATION OF WELLNESS THEORY

An interesting application of wellness theory to working with persons with disabilities is offered by Jones and Kilpatrick. They stress that *"Wellness does not preclude having a disability or experiencing positive stress"* (1996:259).

1. A wellness perspective applied to working with persons with disabilities first and foremost requires that everyone "involved in the goal-identification and problem-solving process [must] separate the individual from the disability because these two entities are not interchangeable" (Jones and Kilpatrick, 1996:264).

2. "If society, the helping professions, and the general public were to truly embrace the idea that it is acceptable to be disabled, then people might concentrate on reducing the barriers to life with disability" (Asch and Mudrick in Jones and Kilpatrick 1996:261). For example: "In Martha's Vineyard during the nineteenth century, the majority of the families inhabiting that area had relatives who were deaf. To facilitate communication in the community, virtually everyone learned American Sign Language. Within a brief period, signing became so common that hearing people often used it to communicate among themselves. Individuals signed to one another across the water while fishing when voicing was not effective. For a time, language barriers dissolved and deafness did not imply disability" (Shapiro in Jones and Kilpatrick 1996:261).

3. "In macro social work practice, disability activists have reauthored their stories in an effort to change society's perceptions and attitudes toward disability and people who have disabilities. . . . They have redefined disability as a challenge that can be met through assistive technology and personal-care assistance that allow the person with a disability to work and live independently at the same level as people without disabilities" (Jones and Kilpatrick 1996:263). We explore the independent living movement in more detail in Chapter 9.

From Jones and Kilpatrick (1996). Wellness theory: A discussion and application to clients with disabilities, Families in Society. Reprinted with permission of Manticare Publishers.

3. A *process* that can take place on the individual, interpersonal, and community levels of intervention. It consists of the following subprocesses:

- development of group consciousness
- reduction of self-blame
- assumption of personal responsibility for change
- enhancement of self-efficacy (1995:535).

In what ways do the people in this photo communicate wellness and empowerment perspectives concerning persons with disabilities?

According to Gutierrez et al., empowerment occurs through *intervention methods* that include:

- Basing the helping relationship on collaboration, trust, and shared power
- Utilizing small groups
- Accepting the client's definition of the problem
- Identifying and building upon the client's strengths
- Raising the client's consciousness of issues of class and power
- Actively involving the client in the change process
- Teaching specific skills
- Using mutual-aid, self-help and support groups
- Experiencing a sense of personal power within the helping relationship
- Mobilizing resources or advocating for clients (1995:535).

Gutierrez contrasts empowerment and traditional coping approaches. She notes that "The coping perspective has most typically looked at how the person/environmental fit can be improved upon by making changes on the individual or psychological level . . . [while] the empowerment perspective focuses almost exclusively on how environments can be modified to improve the person/environment fit" (1995:208–209).

Cultural Competence

A **cultural competence** approach to thinking about and doing social work is emerging as one of the most essential perspectives for social work as it struggles to maintain its effectiveness and relevance in a twenty-first century marked by an increasingly diverse U.S. population. In addition, global economic, political, and technological realities make interacting with persons different from ourselves an almost daily occurrence. This trend toward more diversity and globalization can be expected to increasingly influence not only our personal life experiences but our professional work as social workers as well. A number of scholars have worked to define what we mean by culturally competent social work practice (Green 1999; Leigh 1998; Lum 1999; Weaver 1999). Although a good deal of progress has been made toward a definition, we will likely continue to see the concept evolve in the future. Cultural competence is often described as a continual process of striving and learning rather than a clear end product. Diller, for example, describes cultural competence as "a developmental process that depends on the continual acquisition of knowledge, the development of new and more advanced skills, and an ongoing self-evaluation of progress" (Diller 1999:10). Lum defines **cultural competency** as "the experiential awareness of the worker about culture, ethnicity, and racism; knowledge about historical oppression and related multicultural concepts; development of skills to deal effectively with the needs of the culturally diverse clients;" and the process of continuous learning to incorporate new multicultural knowledge (Lum 1999:174).

Weaver summarizes three major principles of **cultural competence:**

- *The human services provider must be knowledgeable about the group in question;*
- *The human services provider must be able to be self-reflective and to recognize biases in himself or herself and within the profession;*
- *The human services provider must be able to integrate this knowledge and reflection with practice skills.* (Weaver 1998:204)

These definitions and principles reflect the critical need for a culturally competent social worker to have knowledge about the members of the different cultures with which we work; self-awareness of our own culture, biases, and racism; a willingness to continually learn both about others and ourselves as cultural beings; and a willingness to incorporate our knowledge into practice skills. It is important to recognize that cultural competent practice is essential, whether working with individuals, families, groups, organizations, or communities.

Tools for Social Workers from an SEHB Perspective—Poverty Reduction and Assets Development

Theoretical tools are also needed to address the fundamental concern for poverty reduction. Some exciting approaches and tools are emerging in social work and other fields to address this issue. Many of these tools and approaches share a focus on strengths-based thinking, but differ in their concern for addressing poverty in more comprehensive ways at the macro or community level. These tools include assets-development approaches that shift the focus of poverty policies and programs from an income support (or traditional welfare check to meet subsistence requirements) to an assets approach to allow people and communities to move permanently out of poverty. Rather than simply supporting persons' and communities' continuing subsistence at poverty or below-poverty levels, these approaches foster the development of individual and collective reserves of resources to invest in home ownership, education, or business enterprises that can result in moving out of poverty. These newer, more comprehensive, community-based approaches focus on developing reserves of individual, family, and community human, financial, and social capital rather than simply supporting existence within an environment of permanent poverty. These tools include community-building initiatives, community renewal, assets development, and social capital. We will examine these tools and concepts related to poverty reduction in more detail in Chapter 9.

Standpoint Theory

In Chapter 2, standpoint theory was described as an approach to research and practice perspectives that combined a postmodern concern for recognizing political, personal, and social contexts as an integral part of the research and practice environment with the historical concerns of feminism for political action to end oppression. Swigonski defines a **standpoint** as

> *a social position from which certain features of reality come into prominence and other aspects of reality are obscured. From a particular social standpoint, one can see some things more clearly than others. Standpoints involve a level of conscious awareness about two things: A person's location in the social structure and that location's relationship to the person's lived experience (Hartsock 1987). One's standpoint emerges from one's social position with regard to gender, culture, color, ethnicity, class, and sexual orientation and how these factors interact and affect one's everyday world.* (1993:172)

Standpoint theory emphasizes the strengths and potential contributions of marginalized groups because of their lived experiences. Swigonski calls upon researchers to identify areas of study out of the life experiences of marginalized groups and "to take these groups . . . out of the margins and place their day-to-day reality in the center of research" (1993:173). According to Swigonski, "Standpoint theory builds on the assertion that the less powerful members of society experience a different reality as a consequence of their oppression." As a result of this different reality, "to survive, they must have knowledge, awareness, and sensitivity of both the dominant group's view of society and their own—the potential for 'double vision' or consciousness—and thus the potential for a more complete view of social reality" (Swigonski 1993:173).

Transpersonal/Spiritual Approaches

As we noted in the discussion of spirituality in Chapter 2, this is an area many social work educators and practitioners believe has been neglected in both the contexts of social work education and of practice. We explore some current thinking here about transpersonal and humanistic psychology and their potential adaptability to social work education and practice. Clearly the areas of transpersonal and humanistic psychology and their applications to social work are currently considered alternative approaches.

Cowley and Derezotes call for a paradigm shift toward "incorporating the phenomenological aspects of transpersonal theory that come from Eastern contemplative practice"—to help incorporate spiritual aspects of being into social work education and practice (1994:32). They suggest that "Transpersonal means going beyond the personal level . . . to include the spiritual or higher states of consciousness" (1994:33). They place transpersonal psychology among the basic theoretical paradigms of the discipline. They note that transpersonal psychology was referred to by Maslow as the Fourth Force in psychology:

- *First Force: Dynamic (psychoanalytic)*
- *Second Force: Behavioral*
- *Third Force: Experiential, humanistic, existential*
- *Fourth Force: Transpersonal*   (Cowley and Derezotes 1994:34)

Transpersonal psychology was an alternative theory that challenged the notion of such psychologists as Maslow that self-actualization was the highest level of human development. You might recall our discussion of Maslow's notion of peak or "aha" experience as an example of intuitive understanding in Chapter 2. Transpersonal psychology is a synthesis of Eastern and Western psychologies that "offers an expanded notion of human possibilities that goes beyond self-actualization and beyond ego . . . and beyond the limitations of time and/or space" (Cowley and Derezotes 1994:33).

Social workers operating from transpersonal theory "would consider human potential as inherently able to evolve beyond self-actualization toward states of exceptional well-being and self-transcendence" (Cowley and Deregotes 1994:34). Such social workers believe "the needs for meaning, for higher values, for a spiritual life, are as real as biological or social need" (Keen in Cowley and Derezotes 1994:34).

Sermabeikian (1994:179) points out that the psychologist, Carl Jung, "sought to prove that the spiritual dimension is the essence of human nature." Two important concepts for Jung were the notions of "**collective unconscious** and the **archetypes of the psyche,** thought to contain the inherited and accumulated experiences of the human and prehuman species evidenced by the symbols, myths, rituals, and cultures of all times" (emphasis added). Walsh and Vaughan (1994:10) stress a similar conceptualization but one differentiated by levels of consciousness by Ken Wilber a leading transpersonal psychologist. Wilber hypothesizes two distinct lines of evolution:

1. The average or collective consciousness
2. The pioneers who preceed and inspire the collective (shaman, yogi, saint, sage) (Walsh and Vaughn 1994:10).

Wilber argues that we need to use multiple paradigm approaches to help us understand the complexity of human behavior and the social environment. He suggests that there are three epistemological modes or ways of knowing:

1. The sensory: scientific approaches to knowing.
2. The intellectual or symbolic: hermeneutic or interpretive approaches.
3. The contemplative: intersubjective testing by masters/teachers in this realm (Walsh and Vaughn 1994:11–14).

Wilber argues that "reality is multilayered and that the levels of existence form an ontological hierarchy, or *holoarchy* as he prefers to call it, that includes matter, body, mind, and spirit" (Walsh and Vaughn 1994:16–17). Wilber suggests that "we first identify with the body, then with the ego-mind, and perhaps thereafter, as a result of contemplative practices, with more subtle mental realms and eventually pure consciousness itself"(Walsh and Vaughn 1994:17). Wilber also notes that the concept of ontological hierarchy has historically been used to dominate and devalue the lower end of the spectrum, e.g. the body, emotions, sexuality, and the earth" (Walsh and Vaughn 1994:17).

While perhaps controversial, these notions of transpersonal realities that transcend those we experience through our senses everyday, may be valuable to us as we attempt to more fully understand the behaviors and worldviews of ourselves and those with whom we work.

Alternative Extensions of Systems Approaches

Since social systems thinking has been and continues to be such an important force in conceptualizing and organizing the way social workers think about humans and their interactions with the social environment, we will now return to systems approaches and explore some more recent extensions of this approach. Recently systems thinking has been extended beyond using it to understand the basic order of systems to include disorder or chaos and other types of complexity within both human and other physical systems. Another interesting extension of systems thinking is the Gaia hypotheses which has called into question some of our basic thinking about human evolution and about the relationship of humans to the inanimate world.

Chaos/Complexity

Krippner provides a definition of chaos theory that comes from the dynamical systems theory of mathematics. He explains that "**chaos theory** *is the branch of mathematics for the study of processes that seem so complex that at first they do not appear to be governed by any known laws or principles, but which actually have an underlying order. . . .* Examples of chaotic processes include a stream of rising smoke that breaks down and becomes turbulent, water flowing in a stream or crashing at the bottom of a waterfall, electroencephalographic activity of the brain, changes in animal populations, fluctuation on the stock exchange, and the weather. All of these phenomena involve the interaction of several elements and the pattern of their changes over time as they interact . . ." (emphasis added). Krippner explains that "Chaos theorists . . . look for patterns in nature that, while very complex, nonetheless contain a great degree of eloquent and beautiful order, and chaos theory attempts to direct investigators to a cosmic principle that can both simplify and deepen their understanding of nature" (1994:49).

James Gleick, in one of the first books published for readers outside of mathematics and the natural sciences, described the intense paradigm shift within the natural sciences that chaos theory was causing. Gleick posited that

> *Where chaos begins, classical science stops. For as long as the world has had physicists inquiring into the laws of nature, it has suffered a special ignorance about disorder in the atmosphere, in the turbulent sea, in the fluctuations of wildlife populations, in the oscillations of the heart and the brain. The irregular side of nature, the discontinuous and erratic side—these have been puzzles to science, or worse, monstrosities.* (1987:3)

Gleick believes that chaos cuts across the many different scientific disciplines and "poses problems that defy accepted ways of working in science. It makes strong claims about the universal behavior of complexity" (1987:5). Gleick believes this shift will help return the natural sciences to considering questions of more direct and immediate meaning to humans. For example, he points out that

> *Physicists are beginning to return to serious consideration of phenomena on a human scale as opposed to either the cosmos or the tiniest of particles. And in this turn they are finding equal wonder at the complexity and unpredictability of these everyday phenomena. . . . They study not just galaxies but clouds. . . . The simplest systems are now seen to create extraordinarily difficult problems of predictability. Yet order arises spontaneously in those systems—chaos and order together.* (Gleick 1987:6–8)

Gleick stresses that chaos and complexity theorists believe they have discovered that contrary to traditional scientific thinking "tiny differences in input could quickly become overwhelming differences in output—a phenomenon given the name '**sensitive dependence on initial conditions.**' In weather, for example, this translates into what is only half-jokingly known as the **Butterfly Effect**—the notion that a butterfly stirring the air today in Peking [sic] can transform storm systems next month in New York" (1987:18).

Order in Disorder. According to Gleick: "Those studying chaotic dynamics discovered that the disorderly behavior of simple systems acted as a *creative* process. It generated **complexity:** richly organized patterns, sometimes stable and sometimes unstable, sometimes finite and sometimes infinite, but always with the fascination of living things" (1987:43). A related concept for describing this notion of order within disorder is that of fractal. **Fractals** are "geometric patterns with repetitive self-similar features have been called 'fractal' . . . because of their fractional dimensions." Mandelbrot, a scientist who studied "irregular patterns in natural processes" found "a quality of self-similarity. . . . **Self-similarity** is symmetry across scale. It implies recursion, pattern inside of pattern. . . . Self-similarity is an easily recognizable quality. Its images are everywhere in the culture: in the infinitely deep reflection of a person standing between two mirrors, or in the cartoon notion of a fish eating a smaller fish eating a smaller fish eating a smaller fish" (Gleick 1987:103).

Gleick and others suggest that chaos and complexity theory reflect a paradigm shift of major proportions within science. Think about our discussion in Chapter 1 of history and how what were once alternative paradigms, became traditional and dominant wordviews held universally by large groups of people. If traditional approaches to science are replaced by or even begin to substantively include notions of chaos and complexity, how might our definitions of both physical and social realities change? To many people today, this is not a question to consider in the future, it is a part of present discourse about the nature and behavior of reality.

While chaos theory has typically been considered within the realm of mathematics and the natural sciences, interest in this phenomenon is rapidly spreading to the social sciences and to other areas of the natural sciences such as health care and medicine.

Chaos, Biology, and Health. Krippner points out that, for example,

> *Chaos theory has also been used to construct models of illness and health that take exception to certain aspects of medical models. For example, the standard medical model holds that a healthy body has rather simple rhythms. . . . An unhealthy body, therefore, would have a more complex, less controlled tempo. Contrary to this notion*
>
> 1. *In leukemia, the number of white blood cells changes dramatically from week to week but is more predictable than that of healthy people who have chaotic fluctuations in their levels of white blood cells.*
>
> 2. *Congestive heart failure is typically preceded by a stable, periodic quickening and slowing of respiration.*
>
> 3. *The brain 'has to be highly irregular; if not you have epilepsy.'*
>
> 4. *Brains of schizophrenics . . . suggest that 'the schizophrenia victim is suffering from too much order—trapped order.'* (Briggs and Peat 1989 in Krippner 1994:54–55).

Chaos and Creativity. Others have applied the notions of complexity and chaos to psychology and creativity. Rossi suggests that "human creativity may have an underlying chaotic process that selectively amplifies small fluctuations and molds them into coherent mental states experienced as thought and imagination" (in Richards 1996:53–54). Richards also argues that "chaotic models seem particularly appropriate for humanistic psychology—they are open, complex, evolving, and unpredictable—by contrast with the linear, bounded, cause-and-effect models of a more constrained science of human behavior. They also, to reemphasize, seem to provide the ultimate in uniqueness along with the ultimate in interconnectedness" (1996:57).

Gaia

Perhaps the most controversial alternative extension of systems thinking flowing from chaos and complexity theory is known as the **Gaia Hypothesis.** This is a perspective on systems thinking that goes well beyond the traditional notions of thinking in terms of specific systems, for example, social systems or human systems, to viewing the entire earth as a whole system. James Lovelock and Lynn Margulis are usually credited with formulating and putting forward the Gaia hypothesis. Lovelock and Margulis's **Gaia theory** includes two fundamental components:

1. *The planet is . . . a "super organismic system."*
2. *Evolution is the result of cooperative not competitive processes.* (Stanley 1996:www)

Lovelock describes the "Earth as living organism" component of the Gaia hypothesis in the following excerpts:

> *The entire range of living matter on Earth from whales to viruses and from oaks to algae could be regarded as constituting a single living entity capable of maintaining the Earth's atmosphere to suit its overall needs and endowed with faculties and powers far beyond those of its constituent parts . . . [**Gaia** can be defined] as a complex entity involving the Earth's biosphere, atmosphere, oceans, and soil; the totality constituting a feedback of cybernetic systems which seeks an optimal physical and chemical environment for life on this planet.* (Stanley:www)

Stanley (1996:www) describes the Gaia hypothesis as follows

> *Just as human physiology can be viewed as a system of interacting components (nervous, pulmonary, circulatory, endocrine systems, etc.), so too can the Earth be understood as a system of four principal components (atmosphere, biosphere, geosphere, and hydrosphere).*

The Gaia Hypothesis calls into question some of the basic Darwinian notions about survival of the fittest as the central component of evolution. Stanley (1996:www) uses Capra's description of Margulis' theory about evolution as cooperation-based rather than competition-based to describe how it contrasts with Darwinian evolutionary theory:

> *In classical science nature was seen as a mechanical system composed of basic building blocks. In accordance with this view, Darwin proposed a theory of evolution in which the unit of survival was the species, the subspecies, or some other building block of the biological world. But a century later it has become quite clear that the unit of survival is not any of these entities. What survives is the organism-in-its-environment.*
>
> *An organism that thinks only in themes of its own survival will invariably destroy its environment and, as we are learning from bitter experience, will thus destroy itself.*
>
> *From the system point of view the unit of survival is not [an] entity at all, but rather a pattern of organization adopted by an organism in its interactions with its environment.* (Stanley 1996:www)

Margulis has said Darwin's theory was not incorrect, but merely incomplete. She contended that her research on the evolution of certain organisms (referred to as endosymbiosis) revealed that a symbiotic, or mutually beneficial, relationship was central to their ongoing evolution. She contended that "symbiosis, not chance mutation [as Darwin had theorized], was the driving force behind evolution and that the cooperation between organisms and the environment are the chief agents of natural selection—not competition among individuals" (Stanley 1996:www).

Lovelock argued for this extended notion of symbiotic and system-like functioning as an enlargement of ecological theory:

> *By taking the species and their physical environment together as a single system, we can, for the first time, build ecological models that are mathematically stable and yet include large numbers of competing species. In these models increased diversity among the species leads to better regulation.* (Stanley 1996:www)

When the activity of an organism favors the environment as well as the organism itself, then its spread will be assisted; eventually the organism and the environmental change associated with it will become global in extent. The reverse is also true, and any species that adversely affects the environment is doomed; but life goes on (Stanley 1996:www).

SUMMARY/TRANSITION

In this chapter we have explored some additional tools that can help organize and guide our thinking as we proceed to examine alternative and traditional perspectives on human behavior at a variety of levels—individual, family, group, organization, and community. We have explored the use of metaphors, the need to appreciate ambiguity, the unity of personal or individual and political or social change, the power of language and words, and the need to consider inclusiveness and exclusiveness as we continue our journey. We summarized a number of traditional, middle-range, and alternative theories used by social workers to think about HBSE. Along with our knowledge of the dimensions of traditional and alternative paradigm thinking, we will now use this collection of tools to continue our journey toward more complete understanding of human behavior and the social environment.

Internet Search Guide

If you want to learn more about some of the topics discussed in this chapter by exploring the Internet, you can search the Net for the terms listed below. Remember that as you are "surfing" the Net, any of the search terms listed below can take you in many different directions. If you would like to visit specific Web sites related to this chapter, go to the Allyn and Bacon Web site at **http://www.abacon.com** and follow the links to Schriver or *Human Behavior and the Social Environment: Shifting Paradigms in Essential Knowledge for Social Work Practice*. There you will find a selection of sites related to content in this chapter.

1. epistemology
2. role theory
3. psychoanalytic theory
4. behavioral theory
5. learning theory
6. exclusiveness
7. inclusiveness
8. strengths perspective
9. social systems
10. ecological perspective
11. ontology
12. functional theory
13. conflict theory
14. symbolic interaction theory
15. disability
16. spirituality
17. chaos theory
18. complexity theory
19. Gaia
20. wellness
21. human development theory
22. Global Information Systems (GIS)
23. Assets Development

REFERENCES

Alix, E. K. (1995). *Sociology: An everyday life approach.* Minneapolis: West Publishing.

Anderson, Ralph, and Carter, Irl. (1990). *Human behavior in the social environment: A social systems approach* (4th ed.). New York: Aldine de Gruyter.

Asamoah, Yvonne, Garcia, Alejandro, Hendricks, Carmen Ortiz, and Walker, Joel. (1991). "What we call ourselves: Implications for resources, policy, and practice." *Journal of Multicultural Social Work,* 1(1): 7–22.

Bengston, V. L., and Allen, K. R. (1993). "The life course perspective applied to families over time." In Boss, P. G., et al. (Eds.). *Sourcebook of family theories and methods: A contextual approach.* New York: Plenum Press.

Bergen, D. (1994). *Assessment methods for infants and toddlers: Transdisciplinary team approaches.* New York: Teachers College Press, Columbia University.

Berman, M. (Winter 1996). "The shadow side of systems theory." *Journal of Humanistic Psychology,* 36(1): 28–54.

Boss, P. G., Dogherty, W. J., LaRossa, R., Schumm, W. R., and Steinmetz, S. K. (Eds.). (1993). *Sourcebook of family theories and methods: A contextual approach.* New York: Plenum Press.

Bricker-Jenkins, Mary, and Hooyman, Nancy, (Eds.). (1986). *Not for women only: Social work practice for a feminist future.* Silver Spring, MD: National Association of Social Workers, Inc.

Bricker-Jenkins, Mary, Hooyman, Nancy, and Gottlieb, Naomi (Eds.). (1991). *Feminist social work practice in clinical settings.* Newbury Park, CA: SAGE Publications.

Bricker-Jenkins, Mary. (1992). "Building a strengths model of practice in the public social services." In Dennis Saleebey (Ed.). *The strengths perspective in social work practice.* White Plains, NY: Longman, Inc.

Brown, Edwin G. (1981). "Selection and formulation of a research problem." In Richard M. Grinnell, Jr, *Social work research and evaluation.* Itasca, IL.: F. E. Peacock Publishers, Inc.

Capra, Fritjof. (1983). *The turning point: Science, society, and the rising culture.* Toronto: Bantam Books.

Cowger, C. D. (1994). "Assessing client strengths: Clinical assessment for client empowerment." *Social Work, 39*(3): 262–268.

Cowley, A. S., and Derezotes, D. (1994). "Transpersonal psychology and social work education." *Journal of Social Work Education, 30*(1): 32–41.

Dawson, Betty, Klass, Morris D., Guy, Rebecca F., and Edgley, Charles K. (1991). *Understanding social work research.* Boston: Allyn and Bacon.

DeJong, P., and Miller, S. D. (November 1995). "How to interview for client strengths." *Social Work, 40*(6): 729–736.

Demo, D. H., and Allen, K. R. (1996). "Diversity within lesbian and gay families: Challenges and implications for family theory and research." *Journal of Social and Personal Relationships, 13*(3): 415–434.

Diller, J. (1999). *Cultural diversity: A primer for the human services.* Belmont: Brooks/Cole Wadsworth.

Gardner, H. (2000). "Technology remakes the schools." *The Futurist, 34*(2): 30–32.

Germain, Carel. (1979). *Social work practice: people and environments, an ecological perspective.* New York: Columbia University.

Germain, Carel. (1986). "The life model approach to social work practice revisited." In Francis Turner (Ed.). (3rd ed.). *Social work treatment.* New York: Free Press.

Germain, Carel. (1991). *Human behavior in the social environment: An ecological view.* New York: Columbia University Press.

Gleick, J. (1987). *Chaos: The making of a new science.* New York: Penguin Books.

Goldstein, Howard. (1990). "The knowledge base of social work practice: Theory, wisdom, analogue, or art?" *Families in Society, 71*(1), 32–43.

Green, J. (1999). *Cultural awareness in the human services: A multi-ethnic approach.* (3rd ed.). Boston: Allyn and Bacon.

Gutierrez, L. M. (Sept. 1994) "Beyond coping: An empowerment perspective on stressful life events." *The Journal of Sociology and Social Welfare, 21*(3): 201–214.

Gutierraz, L. M., DeLois K. A., and Glen Maye, L. (1995). "Understanding empowerment practice: Building on practitioner-based knowledge." *Families in Society: The Journal of Contemporary Human Services,* 534–543.

Henslin, J. M. (1996). *Essentials of sociology: A down-to-earth approach.* Boston: Allyn and Bacon.

Jones, G. C., and Kilpatrick, A. C. (May 1996). "Wellness theory: A discussion and application to clients with disabilities." *Families in Society: The Journal of Contemporary Human Service, 77*(5): 259–267.

Kain, E. L. (1993). "Application: Family change and the life course." In Boss, P. G., et al. (Eds.). *Sourcebook of family theories and methods: A contextual approach.* New York: Plenum Press.

Krippner, S. (Summer 1994). "Humanistic psychology and chaos theory: The third revolution and the third force." *Journal of Humanistic Psychology, 34*(3): 48–61.

Lather, P. (1991). *Getting smart: Feminist research and pedagogy with/in the postmodern.* New York: Routledge.

Leigh, L. (1998). *Communicating for cultural competence.* Boston: Allyn and Bacon.

Lum, D. (1999). *Culturally competent practice: A framework for growth and action.* Pacific Grove: Brooks/Cole.

Martin, Patricia Yancey, and O'Connor, Gerald G. (1989). *The social environment: Open systems applications.* White Plains, NY: Longman, Inc.

Mullen, Edward J. (1981). "Development of personal intervention models." In Richard M. Grinnell, Jr. *Social work research and evaluation*. Itasca, IL: F. E. Peacock Publishers, Inc.

Newman, Barbara, and Newman, Philip. (1991). *Development through life: A psychosocial approach* (5th ed.). Pacific Grove, CA: Brooks/Cole Publishing Company.

Norman, J., and Wheeler, B. (1996). "Gender-sensitive social work practice: A model for education." *Journal of Social Work Education, 32*(2): 203–213.

Patterson, J. B., McKenzie, B., and Jenkins, J. (1995). "Creating accessible groups for individuals with disabilities." *The Journal of Specialists in Group Work, 20*(2): 76–82.

Persell, Carolyn. (1987). *Understanding society* (2nd ed.). New York: Harper and Row.

Pool, C. (1997). "A new digital literacy: a conversation with Paul Gilster." *Educational Leadership, 55*: 6–11.

Queralt, M., and Witte, A. (1998). "A map for you? Geographic information systems in the social services." *Social Work, 43*(5): 455–469.

Richards, R. (Spring 1996). "Does the lone genius ride again? Chaos, creativity, and community." *Journal of Humanistic Psychology, 36*(2): 44–60.

Saleebey, D. (1997). "Introduction: Power in the people." In D. Saleebey (Ed.). *The strengths perspective in social work practice* (2nd ed., pp. 3–19). New York: Longman.

Saleeby, D. (May 1996). "The strengths perspective in social work practice: Extensions and cautions." *Social Work, 41*(3): 296–305.

Saleebey, Dennis. (1992). *The strengths perspective in social work practice*. White Plains, NY: Longman, Inc.

Scannapieco, M., and Jackson, S. (1996). "Kinship care: The African American response to family preservation." *Social Work, 41*(2): 190–196.

Scott, Joan W. (1988). "Deconstructing equality-versus-difference: Or, the uses of poststructuralist theory for feminism." *Feminist Studies, 14*(1): 33–50.

Sermabeikian, P. (1994). "Our clients, ourselves: The spiritual perspective and social work practice." *Social Work, 39*(2): 178–183.

Shafritz, Jay M., and Ott, J. Steven. (1987). *Classics of organization theory*. Chicago: The Dorsey Press.

Stanley, D. (1996). *The Giants of Gaia*. Web Publication by Mountain Man Graphics: Australia. http://magna.com.au/~prfbrown/gaia_jim.html

Swigonski, M. E. (Summer 1993). "Feminist standpoint theory and the questions of social work research." *Affilia, 8*(2): 171–183.

Szasz, Thomas Stephen. (1987). *Insanity: The idea and its consequences*. New York: John Wiley and Sons, Inc.

Trickett, E. J., Watts, R. J., and Birman, D. "Toward an overarching framework for diversity." In Trickett, E. J., Watts, R. J., and Birman, D. (Eds.). (1994). *Human diversity: Perspectives on people in context*. San Francisco: Jossey-Bass.

Tyson, K. (1995). *New foundations for scientific and behavioral research: The heuristic paradigm*. Boston: Allyn and Bacon.

Van Den Berg, N. (Ed.). (1995). *Feminist practice in the 21st century*. Washington, DC: NASW.

Walsh, R., and Vaughan, F. (1994). "The worldview of Ken Wilber." *Journal of Humanistic Psychology, 34*(2): 6–21.

Weaver, H. (1998). "Indigenous people in a multicultural society: Unique issues for human services." *Social Work, 43*(3): 203–211.

Weaver, H. N. (1999). "Indigenous people and the social work profession: Defining culturally competent services." *Social Work, 44*(3): 217.

Weick, Ann. (1991). "The place of science in social work." *Journal of Sociology and Social Welfare, 18*(4): 13–34.

Weick, Ann. (1992). "Building a strengths perspective for social work." In Dennis Saleebey, (Ed.). *The strengths perspective in social work practice*. White Plains, NY: Longman, Inc.

Whitechurch, Gail G., and Constantine, Larry L. (1993). "Systems Theory." In Boss, P. G., et al. (Eds.). *Sourcebook of family theories and methods: A contextual approach*. New York: Plenum Press.

ILLUSTRATIVE READING 3.1

The illustrative reading by Weaver is intended to help us focus on the importance and complexity of culturally competent social work practice. This reading illustrates the importance of blending and adapting general social work knowledge, values, and skills with the needs, experiences, and worldviews of the diverse persons, groups, and communities with whom we work. For example, the containment skills described by Weaver offer an important divergence from some of the traditional intervention approaches commonly used by many mainstream social workers. In addition, the reading reinforces the importance of understanding our own values and biases while being willing to continuously learn about the cultures, histories, realities, and diversity within diversity of those with whom we work. This reading also demonstrates the importance of an equal focus on social environmental realities—poverty and oppression-related realities—to that on human behavior at the individual level. Finally, and perhaps most important, this reading illustrates that achieving cultural competence is a continuous learning process for both individual social workers and the profession as a whole. Cultural competence is not an endpoint but a continuous series of journeys to many, many worlds different from one's own.

Indigenous People and the Social Work Profession: Defining Culturally Competent Services

Hilary N. Weaver

During the past decade much has been said about the need to include cultural issues as a factor in the helping process. The discussion in social work literature has moved from cultural sensitivity to cultural competence, the ability to integrate cultural knowledge and sensitivity with skills for a more effective and culturally appropriate helping process. This article reports the results of a study of culturally competent helping practices with Native Americans. Sixty-two Native American social workers and social work students completed a survey on knowledge, skills, and values necessary for culturally competent service provision to Native American clients. As both Native Americans and helping professionals, the survey respondents are in an ideal position to articulate how best to serve the Native American population. This article fills a gap in the literature by providing empirical information on culturally competent social work with Native Americans.

Key words: *American Indian; cultural competence; indigenous peoples; Native Americans*

Striving for cultural competence comes from a recognition that U.S. society is rapidly becoming more diverse, and along with this growing diversity come divergent beliefs, norms, and value systems (Manoleas, 1994; Mason, Benjamin, & Lewis, 1996; Matthews, 1996; McPhatter, 1997; Ronnau, 1994; Sowers-Hoag & Sandau-Beckler, 1996). As recently stated by the Associate Commissioner of the Children's Bureau, U.S. Department of Health and Human Services, "If we care about families and chil-

Hilary N. Weaver, DSW, is assistant professor, School of Social Work, State University of New York, Buffalo, 311 Baldy Hall, Buffalo, NY 14260-1050; e-mail: hweaver@acsu.buffalo.edu. Copyright 1999, National Association of Social Workers, Inc., Social Work.

dren, we have an ethical imperative to make culture and cultural competence central to everything we do" (Williams, 1997, p. 14).

In part, striving for cultural competence is a recognition of the profession's ethnocentric foundation. Social work has historical roots in England, and this cultural legacy may lead social workers to operate from a professional belief system antithetical to cultural values, norms, and beliefs of some clients (Weaver, 1998). "The acknowledgement that Eurocentric values have dominated the sciences and have been propagated as cultural universals . . . begins to set in motion the inevitable clash between dominant and nondominant cultural behaviors. This distinction often represents a point of friction between systems (and the professionals therein) and consumers" (Mason et al., 1996, p. 168). In the past social workers and welfare systems have imposed American middle-class norms as rigid standards for clients (Pinderhughes, 1997).

The current *NASW Code of Ethics* (1996) is evidence of social workers' increasing recognition of the importance of cultural competence. In earlier versions, issues of culture and race were listed or implied in various subsections. Now, the code is not only explicit but dedicates a full section (section 1.05) to cultural competence.

Most models of cultural competence consist of qualities that fall under the general components of knowledge, skills, and values (Matthews, 1996; McPhatter, 1997). Knowledge about various cultural groups is essential for cultural competence (Dana, Behn, & Gonwa, 1992; Manoleas, 1994; Mason et al., 1996; Matthews, 1996; Pierce & Pierce, 1996; Ronnau, 1994; Sowers-Hoag & Sandau-Beckler, 1996). It is important to know that diversity exists within ethnic or cultural groups (Mason et al., 1996). Social workers must recognize that relationships between helping professionals and clients may be strained because of historical or contemporary distrust between various groups, in particular, but not limited to, relationships between groups of color and the dominant society (Mason et al., 1996). The legacies of devastating colonial histories are a constant part of the contemporary reality of groups of color (Manoleas, 1994). "The significance of difference in the helping encounter is compounded by the dynamics of power, for the power inherent in the practitioner role is compounded by the status assignment (power) associated with the cultural/social group identity of both client and practitioner" (Pinderhughes, 1997, p. 22).

Awareness of the professional's own values, biases, and beliefs is important for cultural competence (Mason et al., 1996; Ronnau, 1994; Sowers-Hoag & Sandau-Beckler, 1996). A culturally competent helping professional must value diversity and understand the dynamics of difference (Manoleas, 1994; Mason et al., 1996; Ronnau, 1994; Sowers-Hoag & Sandau-Beckler, 1996). Culturally competent practitioners go through a developmental process of shifting from using their own culture as a benchmark for measuring all behavior (Krajewski-Jaime, Brown, Ziefert, & Kaufman, 1996).

Knowledge and values must be integrated with social work skills for culturally competent practice (Manoleas, 1994; Sowers-Hoag & Sandau-Beckler, 1996; Weaver, 1997). Skills must be adapted to meet the needs of diverse clients (Ronnau, 1994). The three components of cultural competence are interactive, and none is sufficient in and of itself to bring about appropriate practice. Striving for cultural competence is a long-term, on-going process of development (McPhatter, 1997).

In addition to material that discusses general components of cultural competence, an increasing amount of literature focuses on cultural competence with African Americans and Latinos. Several current articles cover culturally competent services with various ethnic populations, including Green (1999) and Iglehart and Becerra (1995). Articles that focus on culturally competent social work with African Americans include Gray and Nybell (1990), Jagers and Mock (1993), Randolph and Banks (1993), Schiele (1996), Stevenson and Renard (1993), and Williams (1992). Readers seeking to increase their cultural competence with Latinos may consult Castex (1994), Gutierrez and Ortega (1991), Simoni and Perez (1995), Mason, Marks, Simoni, Ruiz, and Richardson (1995), and Zuniga (1992).

The literature on cultural competence is primarily theoretical and conceptual. Often models are based on practice experience but have not been evaluated in a systematic way. Among the few empirical works are Dana et al. (1992), and Krajewski-Jaime et al. (1996). Dana and colleagues used a content analysis of the literature to develop a checklist of characteristics of culturally competent agencies. Krajewski-Jaime and colleagues applied a cultural competence scale to students in an international setting. I have not been able to identify any empirical work on cultural competence with Native Americans; however, this article begins to address that gap in the literature.

There are roughly 2 million Native Americans in the United States (U.S. Bureau of the Census, 1993). Although their survival in the face of decimating diseases and destructive U.S. policies speaks to the resilience of indigenous cultures and peoples, they are greatly overrepresented in the child welfare system (Hogan & Siu, 1988; MacEachron, Gustavsson, Cross, & Lewis, 1996; Mannes, 1995; Wares, Wedel, Rosenthal, & Dobrec, 1994; Weaver & White, in press), suffer disproportionately from a variety of health problems (May, 1988; Parker, 1994; Stillman, 1992; Wuest, 1991), and are among the poorest people in the United States (Little Eagle, 1993; Stillman, 1992; U.S. Bureau of the Census, 1993). Practice with Native Americans clearly falls within the social work mandate to serve vulnerable and oppressed clients. Although it is not possible to pinpoint the exact number of native people receiving assistance from social workers and other helping professionals, indigenous people are present in many helping systems. Likewise, it is difficult to estimate the number of Native American social workers. With the exception of the American Indian Social Work Educators' Association (active membership approximately 30), there is no functioning national association of Native American social workers. Although it is critical to train indigenous social workers to provide care in their home communities, all social workers must be accountable for providing culturally competent services.

METHOD

I used a survey to gather information from Native American social workers and social work students on their beliefs about culturally competent services with Native American clients. The cultural competence portion of the survey consisted of three questions: (1) What knowledge should a helping professional bring to working with Native American clients or groups in a culturally competent manner? Explain; (2) What skills should a helping professional bring to working with Native American clients in a culturally competent manner? Explain; and (3) What attitudes or values should a helping professional bring to working with Native American clients in a culturally competent manner? Explain.

The study replicates a project that my colleagues and I conducted with Maori helping professionals in New Zealand. We developed the survey instrument, then a

Native American doctoral student and I modified the instrument to fit the Native American cultural context. A later publication will examine similarities and differences in these indigenous populations. The areas of cultural competence examined in this survey reflect areas of cultural competence consistently identified in the human services literature. Another phase of the project will gather data from Native American clients on their beliefs concerning culturally competent helping.

Using data from the Council on Social Work Education (CSWE), I identified eight schools of social work with the highest number of Native American students. Surveys were distributed in seven of the eight schools, and two schools provided lists of graduates to whom surveys were mailed. In addition, surveys were sent to the membership of the American Indian Social Work Educators' Association, and snowball sampling techniques were used to identify other Native American social workers. An instructional cover letter that introduced the project was attached to each survey. Batches of surveys were sent to schools because exact numbers of Native American students often were unknown, or contacts anticipated distributing additional surveys in the community (that is, 25 surveys may have been sent to a contact at a particular school, but fewer probably were distributed). Although the exact number of surveys that reached potential respondents is unknown, 240 were sent. Eleven surveys were returned by the post office, five were returned with incomplete data or blank, and 62 completed surveys were returned. In all, 78 of the 240 were accounted for, leading to an approximate response rate of 33 percent. It is difficult to say if those who did not respond differed from their counterparts who completed the survey; however, respondents came from a variety of tribal backgrounds representative of the population of Native Americans.

I reviewed the data and categorized it according to themes. Initially, I reviewed the data in groups on the basis of education level (BSW student, MSW student, post-MSW, post-PhD) and gender. No differences were identified in statements made by people with different levels of education or based on gender, so I merged and reviewed all data together. It is possible that cultural competence did not vary by education level, because CSWE requirements for cultural content do not vary between the BSW and MSW level, and no accrediting body monitors or requires cultural content in doctoral education. As I reviewed the data, it became clear that many people had similar responses. Such responses were then grouped together. For example, many respondents indicated that knowledge of history was imperative. Each response that discussed history was then sorted into a group that became the history theme described in the next section. A second Native American researcher was involved in the initial stages of the project but withdrew for health reasons before the data were analyzed. Although the withdrawal of the researcher presented challenges for reliability and validity, my extensive immersion in the data and reviewing of the data over an extended period helped to ensure the quality of the analysis. The work in progress was presented to a group of qualitative researchers and modified with their input.

FINDINGS

Demographics

Respondents were mostly female, roughly half were students, and most practitioners and all teachers had at least an MSW (see Table 1). Nineteen people identified with

TABLE 1 Education Level

	Student		Practioner/Administrator			Teacher	
	BSW	MSW	BSW	MSW	PhD	MSW	PhD
Male	0	7	0	3	2	2	4
Female	7	21	1	9	0	2	4

more than one tribe or nation, with one person listing six nations. (Those who listed more than one nation in a confederacy, such as Colville Confederated Tribes, were counted as one nation.) Many people who identify with more than one nation are descended from different Native American groups or have strong nonbiological ties such as marrying into another nation. Thirty-six nations were represented in the survey with 18 represented by two or more people. The nations with five or more respondents—Lakota, 14; Chippewa, 7; Navajo, 7; Iroquois, 7; Cherokee, 5; Blackfeet, 5—roughly correspond to the Native nations with populations over 100,000 (Cherokee, Navajo, Chippewa, and Lakota/Sioux) (U.S. Bureau of the Census, 1993).

The themes that emerged from the data were classified into the three categories commonly identified in the literature as necessary for culturally competent social work practice: (1) knowledge, (2) skills, and (3) values. All subsequent quotations are the words of the respondents.

Knowledge

Four important areas of knowledge were identified: (1) diversity, (2) history, (3) culture, and (4) contemporary realities. The diversity theme is important in and of itself and provides a context for other themes. Social workers must recognize that variation exists among Native nations in factors such as beliefs, customs, and spirituality. One respondent stated, "American Indians are not alike, [do not] speak the same language, [n]or have the same tribal system. Each tribe is different." It is also important to recognize that diversity exists among people within nations. Each client is an individual who may or may not have a strong cultural connection or may experience that cultural connection differently than another native person.

Another theme was the importance of history. Historical knowledge includes understanding treaties, the sovereign status of Native American nations, and federal Indian policy. Social workers also must be familiar with history and laws related to social services with Native Americans, including how the federal government and its policies have fostered dependence. Respondents said that social workers must understand the "effects of oppression, colonialism, [and] racism, [they must know the] history of U.S. extermination and 'assimilation' policies. [they must have] knowledge of the history of government relations and the creation of dependency, [they must also have] knowledge of the amount of loss on all levels that Indian people have experienced." Social workers must understand the atrocities of the indigenous holocaust in this country and the unresolved pain associated with it.

A third theme was cultural knowledge, which includes a knowledge of communication patterns, worldviews, belief systems, and values. A native person's identity often is grounded in a sense of community or being a member of a group rather than based on a sense of individuality. Although diversity among Native American groups exists, common core cultural values were mentioned, such as the importance of family and extended family, respect for elders, matriarchal structures, spirituality, importance of tradition, and issues of death and mourning. "When individuals have no knowledge base then it seems that it is easier for both service providers and clients to get offended. Actions, words, etc., go misunderstood, unnoticed, misinterpreted. It's very hard to teach, help within a culture if you have no understanding of the people, culture, rituals, traditions, etc."

Contemporary realities was the final knowledge theme. Social workers must understand tribal politics, indigenous organizations, the structure of reservations, and urban Native American communities. Social workers also must become familiar with the federal trust responsibility, federal agencies such as the Indian Health Service and the Bureau of Indian Affairs, and federal laws such as the Indian Child Welfare Act and how these relate to the concept of tribal sovereignty. Social workers must understand contemporary roles of native peoples, families, and communities. They must understand issues of loss and posttraumatic stress disorder while also recognizing strengths in contemporary Native American communities.

Skills

Skills for culturally competent social work with Native Americans are not radically different from those generally required for practice. Some skills, however, do have particular importance or relevance given cultural considerations with this population. The skills identified can be grouped into two major themes: (1) general skills and (2) containment skills.

Among general skills, communication and problem solving were frequently mentioned as important. One respondent commented, "The biggest (most important) skill I can think of is the ability to interact and engage Indian people (collectively and individually) in a problem-solving process that's based on the definition of the problem and arrival of the solution from an Indian perspective." A strengths perspective and the ability truly to empathize with Native American clients are important skills.

In addition to general skills, many respondents emphasized the need for social workers to have containment skills, involving patience, the ability to tolerate silence, and listening—all skills that require social workers to be less verbally active than they might be with clients from other cultures. Containment skills require social workers to refrain from speaking, as opposed to the skills listed earlier that require more verbal activity (Shulman, 1992). As one respondent observed, competent social work with Native American clients requires "patience, tolerance, to actively listen, to avoid 'jumping' in to say what is on one's mind. To be humorous and to accept being the target of the humor." As another respondent put it, patience is required because "generations of oppression . . . takes time to change" (ellipses in original). Social workers must respect silences and be willing to sit quietly to listen and learn. They must resist impulses to talk to fill silences.

Values

Four major value themes emerged: (1) helper wellness and self-awareness, (2) humility and willingness to learn, (3) respect, open-mindedness, and a nonjudgmental attitude, and (4) social justice. The theme of helper wellness and self-awareness is based on the belief that without balance in their own lives, helpers are not able to provide competent services. Social workers should be grounded in their own cultures and spirituality. As one respondent described it: "The professional should have their own set of values taught by their role models. These positive values and a sense of positive self-respect and things around them will enable continued positive helping." In addition, social workers must be aware of their own biases, beliefs, and stereotypes and keep these out of the helping relationship.

Another theme was the importance of humility and a willingness to learn. As one respondent stated, "An attitude of 'I will continually be educated by others *including* my clients' is utmost. If one is based in academic arrogance, then they are useless to Native Americans."

Respect, open-mindedness, and the ability to be nonjudgmental were other themes: "I think it's more important for a service provider to be more accepting, appreciative, respectful of other's values; appreciate the differences, not define people by them, not judge people or cultures, but learn from, respect, appreciate, and help." A social worker must "set aside prejudices regarding race, religion, socioeconomic class, etc. [One must have an] ability to grasp [a] different worldview [and an] ability to appreciate different value systems even when it clashes with one's own."

In a theme that goes beyond respect and withholding judgment, many respondents called for social justice, which includes decolonization, and an active acknowledgment of oppression and the unique status of Native Americans. Decolonization involves recognizing, then shedding, the mindset associated with colonial processes by which one culture subjugates another and defines it as inferior. Respondents stated that social workers must acknowledge and support the fact that "special rights of American Indians [are] not based on race but on laws and special legislation. Services provided to American Indians [should] not [be] viewed as [a] handout or moral obligation—but as payment for land and rights given up by American Indians." Social workers should be dedicated to the concept of tribal sovereignty and carry through with a commitment to individual and tribal self-determination. Many respondents called for advocacy for Native American rights and cultural empowerment. Social workers must recognize the power and control aspects found in many human relationships and not replicate these within the social work context. They must demonstrate a value for change by "recognizing [their] own class bias and colonial presence; . . . [they must show] unconditional acknowledgment."

DISCUSSION

The data provide answers to the following questions: What knowledge is necessary? What skills are needed? and, What values are associated with culturally competent services for Native Americans? It is noteworthy that there are no major contradictions in the data. Although respondents did not give identical answers, strong agreement and consistency among responses led to emergence of clear themes.

The findings confirm and expand the literature on culturally competent social work with Native Americans. Theoretical and conceptual writings in this area generally focus on culturally specific knowledge and skills tailored for this population. With the exception of self-awareness, less has been written about value stances associated with culturally competent social work with this population. In particular, the emphasis on social justice in this study adds another dimension to the literature.

It is not possible for social workers to know all aspects of all cultures, but it is important for them to understand that diversity exists within and among Native Americans and to have a general sense of history, culture, and contemporary realities of clients. Skills for work with Native American clients reflect those necessary for competent helping with any population, yet some skills are particularly important. Social workers assisting indigenous clients should pay particular attention to containment skills—patience, listening, and allowing productive silences.

The respondents identified certain value stances necessary for culturally competent helping. In particular, social workers must be aware of their own stereotypes and focus on their own wellness as helpers and human beings. They must display humility and willingness to learn, rather than arrogance and professional superiority. They must show respect and be open-minded and nonjudgmental. Last, these values must be mobilized into an active stance of social justice. The helper must recognize and combat oppression while supporting rights derived from the inherent sovereignty of indigenous peoples.

This study was conducted with a national sample, which helps the reader generalize the findings to many Native American populations. Caution must be used, however, in rigidly applying any concepts to a particular Native American client without a comprehensive assessment of that person as a cultural being. As the findings indicate, diversity exists among native peoples. These findings serve as general guidelines for all social workers interested in increasing their cultural competence with Native American clients. Beyond the general guidelines, the client is the practitioner's best source of assistance in developing cultural competence.

It is difficult to speculate whether people who did not return surveys differ from those who did. It is clear, however, that surveys were returned from all regions of the country and were representative of the most populous Native American nations. making it reasonable to speculate that the findings are representative of the general population of Native American social workers.

CONCLUSION

The data have clear implications for practice. To provide culturally competent social work to Native clients, a social worker must

- understand and appreciate diversity among and within Native American populations
- know the history, culture, and contemporary realities of specific Native American clients
- have good general social work skills and strong skills in patience, listening, and tolerance of silence

- be aware of his or her own biases and need for wellness
- display humility and a willingness to learn
- be respectful, nonjudgmental, and open-minded
- value social justice and decolonize his or her own thought processes.

This study builds on theoretical work on cultural competence. Researchers must find ways to measure cultural competence empirically. This study examined the beliefs of indigenous social workers. Studies that examine the beliefs of indigenous clients and evaluate the actions of social workers will be important steps in building this knowledge base. This study currently is being replicated with other Native American helping professionals and other indigenous populations. Research also should be conducted with other cultural groups. With these studies we can develop an empirically based picture of cultural competence and better serve clients from a variety of backgrounds.

REFERENCES

Castex, G. M. (1994). Providing services to Hispanic/Latino populations: Profiles in diversity. *Social Work, 39,* 288–296.

Dana, R. H., Behn, J. D., & Gonwa, T. (1992). A checklist for the examination of cultural competence on social service agencies. *Research on Social Work Practice, 2,* 220–233.

Gray, S. S., & Nybell, L. M. (1990). Issues in African-American family preservation. *Child Welfare, 69,* 513–523.

Green, J. W. (1999). *Cultural awareness in the human services.* Needham Heights, MA: Allyn & Bacon.

Gutierrez, L. M., & Ortega, R. (1991). Developing methods to empower Latinos: The importance of groups. *Social Work with Groups, 1*(2), 23–43.

Hogan, P. T., & Siu, S. (1988). Minority children and the child welfare system. *Social Work, 33,* 493–498.

Iglehart, A. P., & Becerra, R. M. (1995). *Social services in the ethnic community.* Needham Heights, MA: Allyn & Bacon.

Jagers, R. J., & Mock, L.O. (1993). Culture and social outcomes among inner-city African American children: An Afrographic exploration. *Journal of Black Psychology, 19,* 391–405.

Krajewski-Jaime, E. R., Brown, K. S., Ziefert, M., & Kaufman, E. (1996). Utilizing international clinical practice to build inter-cultural sensitivity in social work students. *Journal of Multicultural Social Work, 4*(2), 15–29.

Little Eagle, A. (1993, February 11). Ten years later: Shannon still poorest county in the nation. *Indian Country Today,* p. A5.

MacEachron, A. E., Gustavsson, N. S., Cross, S., & Lewis, A. (1996). The effectiveness of the Indian Child Welfare Act of 1978. *Social Service Review, 70,* 451–463.

Mannes, M. (1995). Factors and events leading to the passage of the Indian Child Welfare Act. *Child Welfare, 74,* 264–282.

Manoleas, P. (1994). An outcome approach to assessing the cultural competence of MSW students. *Journal of Multicultural Social Work, 3*(1), 43–57.

Mason, H. R. C., Marks, G., Simoni, J. M., Ruiz, M. S., & Richardson, J. L. (1995). Culturally sanctioned secrets? Latino men's nondisclosure of HIV infection to family, friends, and lovers. *Health Psychology, 14*(1), 6–12.

Mason, J. L., Benjamin, M. P., & Lewis, S. (1996). The cultural competence model: Implications for child and family mental health services. In C. A. Heflinger & C. T. Nixon

(Eds.), *Families and the mental health system for children and adolescents* (pp. 165–190). Thousand Oaks, CA: Sage Publications.

Matthews. L. (1996). Culturally competent models in human service organizations. *Journal of Multicultural Social Work. 4*(4), 131–135.

May, P. A. (1988). The health status of Indian children: Problems and prevention in early life. In S. P. Manson & N. G. Dinges (Eds.), Behavioral health issues among American Indians and Alaska Natives: Explorations on the frontiers of the biobehavioral sciences. *Journal of the National Center Monograph Series, 1*(1), 244–289.

McPhatter, A. R. (1997). Cultural competence in child welfare: What is it? How do we achieve it? What happens without it? *Child Welfare, 76,* 255–278.

National Association of Social Workers. (1996). *Code of ethics.* Washington, DC: Author.

Parker, J. G. (1994). The lived experience of Native Americans with diabetes within a transcultural nursing perspective. *Journal of Transcultural Nursing, 6*(1), 5–11.

Pierce, R. L., & Pierce, L. H. (1996). Moving toward cultural competence in the child welfare system. *Children and Youth Services Review, 18,* 713–731.

Pinderhughes, E. (1997). Developing diversity competence in child welfare and permanency planning. *Journal of Multicultural Social Work, 5*(1/2), 19–38.

Randolph, S. M., & Banks, H. D. (1993). Making a way out of no way: The promise of Africentric approaches to HIV prevention. *Journal of Black Psychology, 19,* 204–214.

Ronnau, J. P. (1994). Teaching cultural competence: Practical ideas for social work educators. *Journal of Multicultural Social Work, 3*(1), 29–42.

Schiele, J. H. (1996). Afrocentricity: An emerging paradigm in social work practice. *Social Work, 41,* 284–294.

Shulman, L. (1992). *The skills of helping: Individuals, families, and groups.* Itasca, IL: F. E. Peacock.

Simoni, J. M., & Perez, L. (1995). Latinos and mutual support groups: A case for considering culture. *American Journal of Orthopsychiatry, 65,* 440–445.

Sowers-Hoag, K. M., & Sandau-Beckler, P. (1996). Educating for cultural competence in the generalist curriculum. *Journal of Multicultural Social Work, 4*(3), 37–56.

Stevenson, H. C., & Renard, G. (1993). Trusting ole' wise owls: Therapeutic use of cultural strengths in African-American families. *Professional Psychology: Research and Practice, 24,* 433–442.

Stillman, P. (1992, September 23). Racism, poverty contribute to high cancer death rates. *Lakota Times.*

U.S. Bureau of the Census. (1993). *We the . . . first Americans.* Washington DC: U.S. Government Printing Office.

Wares, D. M., Wedel, K. R., Rosenthal, J. A., & Dobrec, A. (1994). Indian child welfare: A multicultural challenge. *Journal of Multicultural Social Work, 3*(3), 1–15.

Weaver, H. N. (1997). Training culturally competent social workers: What students should know about Native people. *Journal of Teaching in Social Work, 15* (1/2), 97–112.

Weaver, H. N. (1998). Indigenous people in a multicultural society: Unique issues for human services. *Social Work, 43,* 203–211.

Weaver, H. N., & White, B. J. (in press). Protecting the future of indigenous children and nations: An examination of the Indian Child Welfare Act. *Journal of Health and Social Policy.*

Williams, C. (1997). Personal reflections on permanency planning and cultural competency. *Journal of Multicultural Social Work, 5*(1/2), 9–18.

Williams, O. J. (1992). Ethnically sensitive practice to enhance treatment participation of African American men who batter. *Families in Society, 73,* 588–595.

Wuest, J. (1991). Harmonizing: A North American Indian approach to management of middle ear disease with transcultural nursing implications. *Journal of Transcultural Nursing, 3*(1), 5–14.

Zuniga, M. E. (1992). Using metaphors in therapy: Dichos and Latino clients. *Social Work, 37,* 55–60.

4 ✦ *Traditional/Dominant Perspectives on Individuals*

Topics Addressed in This Chapter:

*A*s we proceed we need to continually weigh what we discover about any of the paradigms and perspectives we explore against the historic mission and core concerns of social work—"the enhancement of human well-being" and the "alleviation of poverty and oppression" (CSWE 1992).

As we consider different perspectives (traditional in this chapter and alternative in the following chapter) on individuals, we need to keep in mind their potential roles in facilitating or hindering social change/transformation.

The tasks we set for ourselves as we continue our journey toward more complete understanding of HBSE are certainly challenging ones. However, like the assumptions of interconnectedness and interdependence we made in Chapter 1 about social work, ourselves, and the people with whom we work, all the chapters of this book are interconnected and interdependent. For example, in this chapter and the next one we focus on individuals, but we will not leave the things we learn and the questions we raise about individual development and behavior when we reach the end of the next two chapters. After we complete our exploration of traditional and alternative perspectives on the individual, in this chapter and the next one, the chapters that follow these— on familiness, groups, organizations, and community(ies)—will continue to be heavily concerned with individual development. Families, groups, organizations, and communities are, in fact, fundamental contexts within which our own and others' individual development takes place. These contexts affect our development as, simultaneously, we affect the nature of these contexts.

A CRITICAL PERSPECTIVE ON DEVELOPMENTAL JOURNEYS: LADDERS TO CLIMB?

Perhaps the most traditional and widely used models of individual behavior and development are linear approaches focusing on a chronological series of age-related developmental stages and tasks. These models or frameworks present the tasks and expectations of human development as though we each must "climb a developmental ladder." We step onto the first rung at conception or birth (depending on the particular model or theorist) and we step off the last rung at death.

These linear approaches are attractive because they offer an optimistic view of development as continuous growth and progress. They also lend simplicity, predictability, and order to the apparent chaos of human change (Steenbarger 1991:288). However, these approaches tend to leave us with the impression that the "developmental ladder" is virtually the same for everyone and that the ladder is equally accessible to everyone. They oversimplify the complexities, diversities, and ambiguities that characterize human development.

Critiques of Traditional Stage-Based Theories of Individual Development

A number of scholars have described a variety of criticisms of traditional theories of human development, especially strict adherence to linear stage theories of development. In order to maintain a critical approach to using traditional theories of development in our work as social workers, we should be aware of these critiques. The critiques below center around overemphasis on individual or internal influences and minimizing the impact of environmental influences on development; the inadequacy of chronological age as the determiner of transition from one stage to the next; overemphasis on development as achievement rather than simply change; and inadequacy for explaining or incorporating human diversity. (We examine stage theory from the perspective of understanding small group development and family development in Chapters 7 and 8.)

The Social Environment and Traditional Theories of Individual Development: Too Little "SE" and Too Much "HB"

This critique of traditional theories of individual development is consistent with our concern for considering HBSE from an SEHB perspective. What were some of the consequences, if traditional theories of individual development had their primary emphases on internal processes of development to the exclusion of social environmental influences? One critical consequence of the omission of concern for social environmental processes was failure to consider the impact of poverty and oppressions on development. Traditional perspectives failed to question how individual developmental experiences and outcomes might be very different for persons living in poverty and/or faced with oppression from the larger environment because of gender, race/ethnicity, sexual orientation, or disability, than for financially well-off persons not faced with oppression.

Global Perspective and Traditional Theories of Individual Development. Another area related to concern about the underemphasis of social environmental issues in traditional thinking about individual development is that of a global or international perspective. Chatterjee and Hokenstad argue that

> *Full appreciation and understanding of human behavior in the context of the social environment requires inclusion of an international and comparative dimension. . . . The globalization of contemporary society influences all*

aspects of human life. A world economy increasingly impacts on the social and psychological well-being of individuals in every country. Worldwide problems such as environmental pollution and global warming affect everyone's biological well-being. Mass migration of people coupled with increasingly unequal distribution of wealth among nations have a direct impact on the quality of life for most if not all Americans. (Chatterjee and Hokenstad 1997:186)

In addition, the lack of international perspectives in traditional theories of individual human behavior causes omission of a comparative approach and risks assumptions that human behavior can be measured everywhere with the same "yardstick." Chatterjee and Hokenstad argue that "only a comparative mode of analysis can provide full understanding of how people function in different social environments" (1997:186). For example, "cross-national . . . research helps students identify culturally specific behaviors" such as "what certain groups take to be the 'right' way for performing basic human tasks such as disciplining children or toilet training. . . . or how different cultures construct their views of the sacred" (Chatterjee and Hokenstad 1997:186–7).

Environmental, Internal, Chronological Issues

Criticisms of stage-based theories include **failure to consider environmental influences sufficiently.** Miller notes that "Bronfenbrenner (1977) describes the greatest limitation of the study of human development as the failure to go beyond the focus on the individual; he suggests that a full understanding of individual development requires an examination of the larger social ecology" (1992:34). Another criticism of stage theories is their **overemphasis on internal processes.** D'Augelli "suggests that many current models of lesbian and gay male identity formation suffer from an excessive emphasis on the internal processes of personal development, usually conceived of in stage-model terms" (1994:324–328). A third criticism of stage theories stresses the **limits of chronological age.** Jendrek and other critics of age-stage based approaches suggest that connections between chronological age and life periods (traditional role sets such as grandparenthood) have become blurred. They suggest instead the notion of "fluid-cycle" patterns. "This model also contains patterns and expectations, but they are *less* likely to be geared to age" (1994:207).

These increasing variations lead "proponents of the fluid-cycle model [to] argue, therefore, that it becomes difficult to distinguish major life events in terms of age. Despite the theme of orderliness in the life-course literature, research suggests "that 'disorder' may be more 'normal' than 'order' " (Jendrek 1994:207). This is consistent with notions of chaos and complexity and with other alternative paradigm approaches that question both "grand narratives or theories" such as 'life course' and orderly stage-based approaches to human development.

Developmental Change as Achievement

Bergen reminds us that the achievement orientation prevalent in dominant U.S. society has resulted in seeing " 'development as achievement.' Thus, American parents and teachers see young children's developmental changes as the attainment of milestones or stages that mark progress." Bergen (quoting Feinman and Bruner) "questions our view that development is progress rather than just change" and urges us to remember that "human beings, whatever their age, are completed forms of what they are" (1994:13). This definition of "development as achievement" leads to such concepts as " 'developmental delay,' which implies that, for some young children, developmental achievements have not occurred in a timely, sequential fashion." Bergen reminds us that "the sequences, milestones, and stages outlined by numerous researchers and theorists describe normative developmental features, usually called *universals* of development. However, these professionals, like most parents, have also found that wide *individual variations* occur within the universal developmental patterns. The individual variations form a range within typical development that has been called the 'range of normality.' Extreme variations that go beyond the borders of these ranges have traditionally been categorized as atypical developmental patterns or disabilities" (1994:13).

Summary of Critiques

Steenbarger (1991:288–289) summarizes "three particularly troublesome shortcomings" for which these models have been criticized.

1. "In their emphasis on linearity, stage-based models cannot account for the complexity of human development."

2. "In their emphasis on invariant sequences of structural unfolding, stage-based models cannot account for important situational influences in the developmental process."

3. "In an attempt to reduce development to uniform sequences, stage-based theories embody troublesome value premises."

By emphasizing uniformity these theories "implicitly negate the values of pluralism and diversity."

Stage Theories and Diversity

To explore these criticisms further, let us return to our "developmental ladder" analogy. Not only do traditional linear developmental approaches assume that for everyone the ladder is the same type or design, but they also assume that everyone's ladder has the same number of rungs (steps), the same distance between rungs (steps), the same total height, and the same width between the sides. Traditional developmental theories also too often assume that the context or environment in which the developmental ladder exists is virtually identical or at least equally benign for everyone. This assumption leads us to believe that for everyone the ladder is leaning at the same incline, against the same surface, and that each person climbing the ladder steps onto the first rung from the same surface at the bottom and steps off the last rung onto the same surface at the ladder's top.

We know, though, that the characteristics of ladders and the conditions or contexts in which they are used vary tremendously. (See Figure 4.1.) If all ladders were the same regardless of environmental conditions, they would be of extremely limited use.

How can one use a five-foot stepladder to change the light bulb in a twenty-foot-high street light? A ladder's effectiveness depends a great deal on the task to be accomplished, the type of ladder available, the conditions in which it is used, and, perhaps most important, its effectiveness is determined by the skill and ability of the person using it. Effective approaches to human development must incorporate similarly diverse characteristics and conditions as well. Effective approaches to understanding human development must recognize that developmental ladders vary tremendously according to the needs, resources, and environments of individuals.

In addition to the tremendous variation in the characteristics of ladders and the conditions in which they are used, we also recognize that sometimes a ladder of any type is not the most appropriate or useful tool to get from one place to another. (And even if it is, we may not have a ladder available to us.) A ladder is of limited use, for example, if we need to get from Arkansas to Washington.

Sometimes a level sidewalk, a bridge, an inclined plane, a circular stairs, an elevator, an automobile, a jet, a space shuttle, or even a "transporter" from the fictional *USS Enterprise* of Star Trek might be more appropriate and useful in moving us along. Lacking any of these alternatives, sometimes we might be forced simply to try to jump from one point to the next. Sometimes, depending on needs, conditions, final destinations, or available resources, a combination of or even *all* these tools for getting from one place to another might be useful. Ladders are but one tool for getting us from one place to another. Linear developmental ladder or stage models of human development are but one tool for understanding our developmental journeys.

FIGURE 4.1 **In the first illustration the person is unable to change the bulb in the streetlight because the ladder is not tall enough. In the second illustration the ladder is tall enough to reach the bulb but is inaccessible to the person in the wheelchair.**

Developmental Perspectives: Commonality and Diversity

Recognizing, incorporating, and respecting developmental diversity does not require that we deny the many developmental tasks and needs shared by all humans. Certainly we have many developmental tasks and needs in common. These commonalities are a vital source of the bonds that serve to unify all people. These commonalities remind us that we are all linked in basic ways that define our common humanity and reflect common rights and responsibilities. However, it is the contention here that these commonalities should not overshadow or be valued any more than our rich diversities.

There are many common developmental tasks and needs, but all people do not develop at the same pace, in the same environments/conditions, or with the same resources or hindrances (obstacles). Unidimensional or linear approaches to individual behavior and development might result in ineffective social work practice and may be contrary to social work values. Such approaches deny the uniqueness of individuals and deprive many persons of the opportunity to celebrate their developmental uniqueness.

For example, a traditional developmental perspective is to assume that the task of walking unaided is a universal developmental task. However, development of the ability to walk unaided by other persons or devices is not a developmental task shared by all persons (or even by most persons). Consider, for a moment, realities such as developmental differences at birth, accidents, and physical changes as a result of aging or disease. Expanding the task of walking unaided to that of achieving sufficient mobility to negotiate one's environment and to allow one to maximize her/his human potential is inclusive of many more of us, at many more points in the life course.

To illustrate both commonality and diversity in development we will examine next the developmental universal, play, and then we will explore developmental risks and conditions that result in very different developmental experiences and results for different persons. We will also explore some common assessment tools used to assess developmental commonality and diversity.

Play: A Universal of Human Development

Play is an example of a developmental universal, shared by all developing humans, but unique to each developing human in the specific activities and contexts in which it takes place. Play is also a significant assessment context for social workers to understand individual and group human behavior and development. What follows is an examination of this developmental universal in terms of definition, learning, characteristics, and functions of play.

Definition of Play

1. Play is the way children learn what none can teach them. It is the way they explore and orient themselves to the actual world of space and time, of things, animals, structures, and people.

2. To move and function freely within prescribed limits.

3. Play is children's work.

What Children Learn through Play

1. They are helped to develop social relationships and skills.
2. They learn to use play materials and equipment with others.
3. They learn to take turns.
4. They learn how to ask for what they want or need.
5. They understand the role of others (mother, baby, father, doctor, etc.).
6. They master skills.

Characteristics of Play

1. Play is pleasurable (even when there are no signs of enjoyment, it is still gratifying to the players).
2. Play serves no particular purpose (it does not mean that play is unproductive).
3. Play is spontaneous and voluntary rather than obligatory.
4. Play actively involves the player.

Functions of Play

1. Play may serve as a means of helping the child solve a problem.
2. Play serves as a means of self-assertion through which a child can declare his or her needs.
3. In play, contact with other children and the need to communicate with them help stimulate language growth.

Learning is a continuous process. Young children are learning to manage impulsive behavior, to gain skill in living, and to work with others (adapted from University of Arkansas Nursery School 1996).

Developmental Risk Assessment

Bergen (1994) provides a helpful approach to thinking about several types of vulnerabilities or developmental risks that may challenge the developmental processes of humans and result in diverse developmental experiences and outcomes. These vulnerabilities are often considered in assessment approaches and tools used by a variety of disciplines. We will examine several of these assessment tools in the following section. When you examine the assessment tools, see if you can connect the tool to the three arenas of risk—established, biological, and environmental—Bergen describes.

1. *Established Risk:* These "conditions include neurological, genetic, orthopedic, cognitive, or sensory impairments or other physical or medical syndromes that have been strongly linked to developmental problems. . . . Established risks are often called disabilities. They include diagnoses such as Down's syndrome, spina bifida, cerebral palsy, blindness, limb loss or deformity, and other such genetic, motor, sensory, and cognitive impairments."

2. *Biological Risk:* "conditions are physical or medical trauma experiences that occur in the prenatal period, during the birth process, or in the neonatal period

that have a high probability of resulting in developmental delay but that do not always cause delay. . . . For example, extremely low birth weight is often related to developmental delay; however, some children who are of low birth weight are able to overcome this condition and do not experience permanent delays in development."

3. *Environmental Risk:* "conditions are those factors in the physical setting (e.g., substandard housing, exposure to lead paint) or in the family or other social institutions (e.g., parent caregiving capabilities, low socioeconomic level, cultural values that preclude medical care) that have the potential to influence negatively young children's developmental progress. Negative environmental conditions internal to the family (e.g., family violence, parental drug abuse) and external to the family (e.g., unemployment, lack of access to health care) have an impact both on the development of all family members and on the capacity of these families to provide appropriate environments for their young at-risk children" (Bergen 1994:4–5).

Traditional Developmental Assessment Tools. We outlined some different types of cross-disciplinary approaches in Chapter 3. We also mentioned that social workers are often members of multidisciplinary assessment teams. One of the clearest ways to gain an understanding of traditional perspectives on determining individual developmental vulnerabilities is to examine the assessment principles, language, and tools used by various professions. Figure 4.2 provides an overview of traditional developmental principles, typical examples of developmental principles, and relation to risk conditions for each developmental principle.

Kalmanson notes that in assessing developmental vulnerabilities "patterns of behavior are more important to identify because they may be likely to indicate intervention is needed, while 'singular behaviors are likely to indicate individual differences within the normal range of development' " (in Bergen 1994:36). Figure 4.3 presents an overview Kalmanson's indicators of developmental vulnerabilities in infants and toddlers.

For newborns and very young infants the Apgar and Brazelton Neonatal Assessment scales are commonly used. The Apgar Score (Figure 4.4) is used at one and five minute intervals after birth to assess five characteristics of newborns indicative of overall health. An overall Apgar score of 10 indicates the best condition possible. The Brazelton Scale (Figure 4.5) assesses behavioral and neural functioning and is considered a "better predictor of later developmental outcomes than the Apgar Score" (Bergen 1994:42).

Figure 4.6 provides a summary of common medical diagnostic tests and procedures. Any one or combination of these tests and procedures may be used depending on concerns of medical staff. Figure 4.7 provides an overview of the elements of a physician's psychosocial assessment form.

Figure 4.8 provides a helpful overview of assessment terms commonly used by psychologists. These terms reflect a number of elements of traditional paradigm approaches to measuring and understanding human behavior.

Figures 4.9, 4.10, and 4.11 provide examples of assessment concepts and terms used by speech and hearing professionals. The information in these figures help give a sense of degrees of hearing loss as well as comparative sound levels and definitions of basic speech concepts.

FIGURE 4.2   Developmental Principles, Typical Examples, and Relation to Risk Conditions

Principles	Typical Examples	Risk Conditions
1. Human beings are active in the process of their own development.	Infants actively seek stimulation by visual search and by grasping or moving toward novel phenomena.	Children who are at risk actively select and attend to environmental stimuli and attempt to act on these stimuli; if disabilities hamper self-efficacy, adaptive devices and social stimulation must be enablers of action.
2. Development change can occur at any point in the life span.	Adolescent parents and middle adult parents experience developmental change when they have a child.	Those at risk may not reach some developmental milestones until they are older, but they will continue to make progress; education continues to make a difference throughout the life span.
3. The process is not a smooth, additive one; it involves transitions and cycles, which include chaotic and disorganized as well as integrated and coordinated periods.	In the "terrible twos" the child strives for autonomy while still being dependent and so behavior fluctuates between seeking nurturing and gaining control of self and others.	Those at risk also experience setbacks, plateaus, disorganized periods, and new beginnings; these cycles may not be evidence of pathology but of developmental transition periods similar to those of typical children.
4. Biological maturation and hereditary factors provide the parameters within which development occurs.	A child's physique (e.g., wiry or solidly built) may affect timing of walking.	Biological and hereditary factors affect the levels of progress and the end points of development in areas of risk.
5. Environments can limit or expand developmental possibilities.	A child with poor nutrition or who is confined to a crib may walk later than is typical.	Certain types of delay (e.g., language, social) are very much influenced by home, school, and community environments.
6. There are both continuity and discontinuity (i.e., gradual, stable growth, and abrupt changes) in development.	The temperament of a child (e.g., slow-to-warm-up) may be evident throughout life; thinking patterns will differ qualitatively from infancy to adolescence.	Continuity of development may be less easily recognized and discontinuities may be more noticeable or attributed to non-developmental causes in those at risk.
7. Many developmental patterns and processes are universal (i.e, they follow similar time intervals, durations, and sequences of change in most individuals, no matter what their cultural group).	Children in all cultures use a type of "baby" grammar when they first learn to talk.	Children at risk will also show these patterns, although they may be distorted or delayed due to disabilities.

(continued)

FIGURE 4.2 *Continued*

Principles	Typical Examples	Risk Conditions
8. There are unique individual biological characteristics as well as culturally and environmentally contingent qualities that influence timing, duration, sequence, and specificity of developmental change.	Most girls talk earlier than boys, but in cultures where mothers talk more to boys, they talk early; girls in some cultures are permitted to be active and in those cultures they show higher activity levels.	Children at risk are more likely to have unique characteristics and experiences that influence how universals of development are manifested.
9. Developmental changes may be positive or negative, as they are affected by health and other factors.	A chronic illness may affect a child's progress and cause some regression to "baby" behavior.	Children with severe or progressive syndromes may show deteriorating development; a balance between maintenance of positive developmental signs and control of negative indicators may be required.
10. Developmental change intervals tend to be of shorter time spans for younger than older individuals.	Infants' motor skills are very different at 6 months and at 1 year, but there is not much change in motor skills between ages 15 and 17.	Time intervals of change are often long with children with disabilities, but developmental progress will usually occur more quickly at younger rather than older ages, making early intervention important.

Reprinted by permission of the publisher. From: Bergen, D. (1994). *Assessment Methods for Infants and Toddlers*. New York: Teachers' College Press, Columbia University. All rights reserved.

Normal and Abnormal: Traditional and Alternative Perspectives

If we are concerned with traditional and alternative perspectives on individual behavior and development, we must question the very concepts of **normal** and **abnormal** as they are traditionally presented to us. To discuss human behavior in narrow terms of aggregates or so-called norms or average behaviors is consistent with dominant/traditional paradigm thinking. Others have gone even farther to suggest "that a statistical concept of 'normal' can be pathological since it reflects only false consciousness. . . . [A] false consciousness of ideologies and norms imposed from outside the individual and resulting in social and organizational behaviors that are characteristically pathological and neurotic" (Fromm in Gemmill and Oakley 1992:116).

When we recognize that social workers work with persons, groups, families, organizations, and communities with endless combinations of individual needs, histories, cultures, experiences, and orientations, the concept of "normal" must be questioned. We must seek some more holistic alternative for achieving understanding. Normal for whom?; in whose eyes?; according to whose values?; during what time period?; in what context?; under what conditions? we must ask.

FIGURE 4.3 Developmental Vulnerabilities in Infants and Toddlers

	Infancy	Toddlerhood
Self-Organization	Difficulty with regulation of states, irritability, crying, trouble falling asleep Attention seems random, not focused or responsive to adult interaction	Little organized attention to people or objects Difficulty falling asleep, wakes up irritable Irregular food intake
Social-Emotional	Unresponsive Lack of reciprocal gaze Absence of anticipatory response to being held Seems to prefer being alone Fails to form strong personal attachments	Little or no reciprocal interaction/play Little attachment to primary caregivers Indifference or extreme prolonged distress at comings or goings of primary caregivers Absence of imitative play
Motor	Lack of motor response to voice Arches back when held Doesn't mold to parent's body, limp	Disorganized, random movement Impulsive racing and falling Apathetic, little interest in movement
Sensory Integration	Easily upset by extraneous sounds/sights, startles easily Trouble coordinating input from parents (can't look at mother while being held and talked to)	Easily startled Doesn't localize sound Overwhelmed by moderate stimulation and withdraws Engages in self-stimulation
Language	Absence of cooing in response to parents' vocalizations Lack of attention to parent's voice	Absence of communication/gestures Little imitation of words No words for important people/objects Lack of intentionality in communication

Reprinted by permission of the publisher. From: Bergen, D. (1994). *Assessment Methods for Infants and Toddlers.* New York: Teachers' College Press, Columbia University. All rights reserved.

FIGURE 4.4 Immediate Evaluation of the Newborn: The Apgar Score

Sign	0	1	2
1. Heart rate	Absent	Below 100	Over 100
2. Respiratory effort	Absent	Slow, irregular	Good, crying
3. Muscle tone	Limp	Some flexion of extremities	Active, motion
4. Response to catheter in nostril (tested after oropharynx is clear)	No response	Grimace	Cough or sneeze
5. Color	Blue, pale	Body pink, extremities blue	Completely pink

Reprinted with permission from Apgar (1953). "A proposal for a new method of evaluation of a newborn infant, Anesthesia and Analgesia." Reprinted by permission of Lippincott Williams & Wilkins. From: Bergen, D. (1994). *Assessment Methods for Infants and Toddlers.* New York: Teachers' College Press, Columbia University. All rights reserved.

FIGURE 4.5   Infant Neurodevelopmental Assessment: Brazelton Neonatal Behavioral Assessment Scale (BNBAS)

A 7 cluster scoring scheme summarizes the Brazelton Scale Scores:

1. Habituation:
   Habituation to a bright light, a rattle, a bell, a pinprick

2. Orientation:
   Attention to visual and auditory stimuli

3. Motor processes:
   Quality of movement and tone

4. Range of state:
   Peak of excitement
   Rapidity of buildup
   Irritability
   Lability of state

5. Regulation of state:
   Cuddliness
   Consolability
   Self-quieting
   Hand-to-mouth activity

6. Autonomic stability:
   Tremors
   Startles
   Reactive skin color changes

7. Reflexes:
   Number of abnormal reflexes

We will try here to learn to think about multiple ranges and ways of ordering and understanding what is "normal" human behavior and development. In the next chapter, we will explore more holistic approaches in recognition of the diverse characteristics, needs, histories, and environments of the persons with whom we interact. We can best accomplish this by seeking out developmental approaches/perspectives/models that emerge from the persons who live and represent those experiences, conditions, and histories.

Traditional perspectives on what is "normal" human behavior leave much unanswered and much to be desired if we are searching for ways to make maximum use of the strengths of people and if we are attempting to respect people's differences as sources of strengths. Weick (1992:22) reminds us that traditional notions of "normal" flow from efforts to view human behavior only from a scientific or positivistic perspective. Such a perspective "searches for law-like occurrences in the natural world" or "norms." Weick argues for different approaches that help us build less rigid or limiting theories of human growth and development; that are "unhinged from the lockstep view of what is considered 'normal' development" (Weick 1992:23). These alternative approaches should be "fluid models built on assumptions that recognize the creative and powerful energy underlying all human growth" (Weick 1992:23).

"Normal" is assumed here to be extremely relative—to individual, environment, culture, gender, history, race, class, age, ability, and sexual orientation—and to the complex interplay of these diversities. To be "abnormal" is, in fact, "normal" for most of us, if we focus on our rich diversity. This contradictory-sounding assertion requires

FIGURE 4.6   Common Diagnostic Tests and Procedures

Ultrasound scan	Uses sound waves to look inside different parts of the body. The image on the screen is transferred to a regular X-ray film for the doctor to interpret.
Electrocardiogram (EKG)	A recording of the child's heartbeats. The EKG detects changes or alterations in heart rate and rhythm, in heart ventricular size and heart strain (e.g., coronary artery occlusion).
Computer tomography (CT)	A type of X-ray that takes pictures of the child's brain and abdomen. At certain times medication is given intravenously. This medicine circulates in the blood and causes parts of the brain or abdomen to show up more clearly on the pictures.
Spinal tap	Measures the amount of pressure in the spinal canal; removes a small amount of fluid for examination. After the lower part of the spine has been anesthetized, a needle is inserted in the spinal canal and fluid is withdrawn.
Electroencephalogram (EEG)	A recording of the electrical activity generated by the brain that represents the summed results of excitatory and inhibitory postsynaptic potentials.
Magnetic resonance (MRI)	A noninvasive imaging method of examining the brain and other internal organs of the body. This test uses magnetic fields instead of X-ray to produce images on film by computer analysis. The MRI provides excellent detail of anatomic structures.
Event related potential (ERP)	Assesses a transient electrical signal following stimulation of a peripheral sensory modality (e.g., ear-brainstem evoked response; eye-visual evoked response; peripheral nerve-somatosensory evoked response). The signal is recorded over the appropriate area of the scalp with EEG electrodes. The small signal needs to be averaged to be detectable and differentiated from ongoing EEG activity.
Extracorporeal membrane oxygenation (ECMO)	Machine acts as an artificial heart and lung membrane adding oxygen for a baby whose own heart or lungs cannot get enough oxygen into the blood to circulate through the body. The goal of ECMO is to let the heart and lungs recover while the baby is supported by the ECMO.
Ventricular shunt	A small tube that has been placed in the child's head to reduce hydrocephalus. The shunt carries extra fluid from the head to the blood stream (ventriculo-jugular [VJ] shunt) or to the abdomen (ventriculo-peritoneal [VP] shunt) where it is absorbed.
Shunt-o-gram	Used to determine why a child's ventricular shunt is not working properly. A small needle is put into the valve of the shunt. Fluid is drawn out of the valve and sent to the laboratory for testing. A dye that shows up on X-rays is put into the valve and X-rays are taken. After pumping the shunt, X-rays are again taken to watch the dye pass through the shunt tube.

FIGURE 4.7   Contents of the Physician Psychosocial Assessment Form

Category	Specific Problems
Physical growth	Slow weight gain, non-organic failure and development to thrive, obesity
Sleep	Trouble sleeping, sleepwalking, night terrors
Motor	Hyperactivity, overactivity; gross motor delay, fine motor delay
Cognitive–language	Mental retardation, learning disabilities, language delay, attention problems, speech problems
School	School failure, school refusal, absenteeism or truancy
Behavior	Enuresis, temper tantrums, fire setting, stealing, tics, encopresis, excessive masturbation
Psycho-physiological	Recurring stomach pain, headaches, recurring knee or leg pain
Feelings	Anxiety or nervousness, feelings of depression, low self-esteem, excessive anger or irritability
Thought	Delusions, hallucinations, incoherence
Peer activity	No confidence, social isolation, fighting and bullying
Parent-child	Problems separating, physical abuse, psychological abuse, sexual abuse, physical neglect
Social	Lack of housing, frequent moves, financial problems, sexual abuse (other than parent)
Family	Divorce or separation, physical or mental illness of parent, drug or alcohol abusing parent, parental discord, spouse abuse, few social ties, problems with siblings, death of parent

Reprinted with permission from Horwitz, McLeaf, Leventhal, Forsyth, & Speechly (1992). Reprinted by permission of the American Academy of Pediatrics. From: Bergen, D. (1994). *Assessment Methods for Infants and Toddlers.* New York: Teachers' College Press, Columbia University. All rights reserved.

FIGURE 4.8   Assessment Terms Used by Psychologists

Achievement	the amount of success children exhibit at a given task
Average	the most representative measurement or score (expressed as mean, median, or mode)
Developmental norm	age at which 50% of tested group successfully completes the task
Normative	measurement results within the average or typical range
Norms	typical scores on standardized measures representative of certain groups (e.g., age, ethnic, or local)
Psychometrics	measurement of human cognitive, motor, or affective behavior using a standard of performance
Reliability	the extent to which a test or observation shows consistent results
Standard scores	scores that are mathematically transformed so that results from different tests can be compared
Standardized tests	testing processes that use consistent methods, materials, and scoring procedures
Validity	the extent to which a test or observation measures what it is intended to measure

Reprinted by permission of the publisher. From: Bergen, D. (1994). *Assessment Methods for Infants and Toddlers.* New York: Teachers' College Press, Columbia University. All rights reserved.

FIGURE 4.9   Categories of Sound Loss and Effects on Language and Cognition

Mild Hearing Loss (15–30 dB HTL)

- Vowel sounds are clear, except for voiceless consonants such as "s" (*lost* may be heard as *loss*).
- Hearing of short unstressed words and less intense speech sounds are inconsistently perceived.

Moderate Hearing Loss (30–50 dB HTL)

- Most speech sounds at conversational levels are lost, but with amplification can be heard.
- Sounds of low energy and high frequency, such as fricatives (see Figure 4.11), may be distorted or missing (*stroke* may be heard as *soak*).
- Short unstressed words are not heard.
- Difficulty learning abstract concepts, multiple word meanings, and development of object classes.

Severe Hearing Loss (55–70 dB HTL)

- Only loud environmental sounds and intense speech at close range can be heard.
- Language does not develop without amplification.
- Vowel sounds and consonant group differences can be heard with amplification.
- Development of grammar rules and abstract meanings is delayed or missing.

Profound Hearing Loss (75–90 dB HTL)

- Not even intense speech sound can be heard without amplification.
- Hearing does not have a major role in language acquisition, without amplification.

Note: dB = decibel; HTL = hearing threshold level

Reprinted by permission of the publisher. From: Bergen, D. (1994). *Assessment Methods for Infants and Toddlers.* New York: Teachers' College Press, Columbia University. All rights reserved.

FIGURE 4.10   Examples of Different Sound Pressure Levels

Decibel	Stimulus
20	Forest
30	Whisper
60	Conversation
80	Average street traffic

Reprinted by permission of the publisher. From: Bergen, D. (1994). *Assessment Methods for Infants and Toddlers.* New York: Teachers' College Press, Columbia University. All rights reserved.

us to recognize that by "abnormal" we mean a wide range of differences, some of which fit traditional definitions of pathology such as schizophrenia or criminality, but most of which simply mean different from or alternative to the norms established according to traditional/dominant paradigms, theories, and assumptions about human behavior and development.

Our wide-ranging differences result in wide ranges of what can be considered normal. However, all of us as humans also share developmental "milestones" or

FIGURE 4.11   Definitions of Speech Elements

Voiced sounds	Produced by flow of air from the lungs causing the vocal chords to vibrate ("u" as in cup). All vowels are voiced sounds.
Voiceless sounds	Produced by flow of air without vibration of the vocal chords ("p" as in pit; "f" as in fun).
Fricatives	Consonants produced by rapid changes in pressure constricted through air passage cavities. They come in voiced or unvoiced pairs ("z," "s").
Plosives	Consonants produced by brief obstructing of vocal track so sound comes in quick bursts. They are also paired ("p," "b").
Nasals	Voiced consonants in which sound passes through the nose (*man*).

Reprinted by permission of the publisher. From: Bergen, D. (1994). *Assessment Methods for Infants and Toddlers*. New York: Teachers' College Press, Columbia University. All rights reserved.

expectations in the sense that if the milestone is not reached, or is not reached within some appropriate range of time, some adjustment will be required by the person or by others in the environment to allow the individual to continue on his/her developmental journey toward reaching her/his fullest human potential.

To accommodate both the realities of diversity and the commonalities in human behavior, development approaches to gathering knowledge for practice that equally respect common developmental milestones and differences are required. Understanding both traditional and alternative approaches to individual development will help us achieve this balance.

Richards points out the costs of confusing diversity with abnormality and notes "How tragic if we mindlessly equate the abnormal with the pathological and demean the very diversity that can be enhancing and life-giving. To function fully as human beings, we need to broaden and redefine our acceptable 'limits of normality' " (1996:50).

Traditional Definition of Intelligence: IQ

An example of one of the most influential traditional mechanisms for determining what is normal is that of traditional **Intelligence Quotient** or **IQ.** Traditional views of intelligence refer to a general level of intelligence that is most often referred to as "g" or general intelligence. **General intelligence** is defined "operationally as the ability to answer items on tests of intelligence." The test scores then infer underlying intelligence, called **IQ** or an **intelligence quotient** through the use of "statistical techniques that compare responses of subjects at different ages." The fact that these scores are correlated "across ages and across different tests" is used to support the notion that intelligence does not change much with age or training or experience (Gardner 1993:15).

The cultural bias of IQ tests has been a controversial issue in the use of IQ tests to determine access to and positions within various social institutions like schools, the military and the workplace. **Cultural bias** refers to the perceived advantage gained by persons taking intelligence tests who are members of the same dominant culture as the persons creating the test. In addition, this bias works to the disadvantage of persons not from the dominant culture who take the test. For example, Stephen Jay

Gould in his book, *The Mismeasure of Man,* argued that IQ tests served to continue and to exacerbate the historic exclusion of many lower SES [Social-Economic Status] persons, especially many African Americans (in Herrnstein and Murray 1994:11–12).

A current traditional approach to IQ is that put forth by Herrnstein and Murray in the book, *The Bell Curve.* They support the notion of "g" or general intelligence. In addition they argue that IQ tests do not necessarily reflect cultural bias. They argue that when "properly administered, IQ tests are not demonstrably biased against social, economic, ethnic, or racial subgroups" (1994:23). In Chapter 5 we will further explore the notion of intelligence as a factor in individual development and we will examine an alternative perspective on intelligence offered by Gardner and referred to as multiple intelligence that challenges the traditional notion of IQ.

Developmental Paradigms and Social Work

Like the need for variety in models for moving from one place to another, knowledge of a wide range of different developmental theories and perspectives is essential for effective social work practice. Knowledge of diverse theories can provide us with multiple tools for multiple applications. This is especially true given the rich and varied range of people and experiences with which social workers deal. The worldviews or paradigms from which our perspectives on human behavior and development emerge must adequately recognize the dramatic developmental variations among individuals. These variations may include the very nature of the specific tasks to be accomplished, the timing of those tasks, the means used to accomplish tasks, and the historical and current patterns of resource availability or denial available for use in accomplishing tasks. In other words, we must recognize that such differences as race, class, sexual orientation, and gender have significant impact on the nature of our developmental experiences.

If these variations are not recognized or if differences are only narrowly recognized, the theories and approaches we use to guide our social work practice will offer helpful guidance for only some persons and will be confusing, frustrating, and even damaging to others. Theories or perspectives that neglect to take into account variations in individuals' characteristics, histories, and environments render those individuals at variance as developmentally inadequate (abnormal) or entirely invisible. If traditional developmental theories or perspectives reflect only the developmental experiences of white, middle-class, heterosexual, males, for example, it is extremely likely that people of color, low-income persons, gay men or lesbians, and women will either be ignored completely by the theories or perspectives or they will be found to be inadequate or abnormal according to the criteria of the traditional theories.

The Traditional and the Possible (Alternatives)

Chapter 5 will focus on exploration of alternative approaches to understanding human behavior and development. However, in order to understand these alternative approaches, we need to be cognizant of the more traditional theories about human behavior and development. Traditional theories are incomplete, they exclude many people, and they reflect biases due to the value assumptions and historical periods out of which they emerged. However, these inadequacies do not decrease the powerful influences these traditional theories have had in the past, currently have, and will continue to have on the construction and application of knowledge about human behavior and development. Traditional approaches also provide a departure point from which we may embark on our journey, in Chapter 5, toward more complete, more inclusive, and less biased visions (or visions in which bias is recognized and used to facilitate inclusiveness) of development to improve all our efforts to reach our fullest potential. Many of the alternative models of development we will explore began as extensions or reconceptualizations of traditional theories.

There is another very practical reason for learning about traditional theories of human behavior and development. The practice world that social workers inhabit and that you will soon enter (and we hope transform) is a world constructed largely on traditional views of human behavior and development. To survive in that world long enough to change it we must be conversant in the discourse of that world. We must have sufficient knowledge of traditional and dominant paradigms of human behavior and development to make decisions about what in those worldviews we wish to retain because of its usefulness in attaining the goal of maximizing human potential, and what we must discard or alter to better serve that same core concern of social work.

Reductionism and Determinism

In order to make appropriate decisions about the traditional approaches we explore we must recognize their limits. The developmental models we have historically used are not representative of even most people when we compare the race, gender, and class diversity of the people with whom social workers work and the race, class, and gender reflected in traditional models. This is to say nothing of differences in sexual orientation, age, and disabling conditions completely ignored or specified as abnormal in many traditional models. Traditional developmental models emphasize almost exclusively the experiences of white, young, middle-class, heterosexual men who have no disabling conditions.

Many traditional theories of human development are also limited because they present people as if they can be reduced simply to the specific elements focused on by the theory. This reductionism, for example, is evident in Erikson's much-used theory of the life cycle. Erikson's theory of development is often presented as if the human is composed entirely of, and behaves and develops solely as a result of, ego dynamics put into place or determined as a result of life experiences occurring during infancy and very early childhood. The same reductionist and deterministic tendencies can be found in the focus on infantile sexuality of Freudian developmental theory, on cognition and young children in Piaget's theory, and on the development of moral judgment in the theory of Kohlberg.

Erikson was aware of these tendencies in his own and in Freud's approaches and cautioned against them: "When men concentrate on an uncharted area of human existence, they aggrandize this area to become the universe, and they reify its center as the prime reality" (Erikson 1963:414–15). When we do this we are left with tremendous voids in our knowledge about human development upon which to base our practice. We will attempt to be aware of this tendency as we explore traditional and dominant perspectives in this chapter. We will also try to guard against this tendency as we explore alternative perspectives in the next chapter.

The reader should be alert to the exclusive use of male pronouns and exclusive references to males in direct quotations of traditional developmental theorists used in this book. This reflects the writing style of the time when the work was done. References to males were considered universal and inclusive of females. An exclusive reference to males also reflects actual populations on which traditional models were based. These models were in fact much more about men's developmental experiences than they were about those of women. They, in effect, rendered women invisible both figuratively and literally.

TRADITIONAL AND DOMINANT DEVELOPMENTAL THEORIES

The following sections offer summaries of several of the most prominent and influential traditional/dominant theories or models for understanding or explaining individual human behavior and development. The approaches presented have been chosen for several reasons. These models represent not the totality of traditional approaches to understanding individual behavior and development, but they are models that have had powerful influences on social work education and practice related to individuals. They have been extremely influential determiners and reflectors of traditional and dominant paradigm thinking in social work and in many other disciplines. Considered together they offer perspectives that address human behavior through the life span. In sum, they also articulate many of the most basic, almost universally used concepts for attempting to understand individual behavior and development. Finally, they are presented here because they have been influential departure points for a number of the alternative approaches to understanding individual behavior and development that we will explore in the next chapter.

The traditional models we will explore are those put forward by Freud, Erikson, Piaget, Kohlberg, and Levinson. While certainly not the only traditional perspectives on individual development, these theories represent some of the most influential thinking about individual human behavior and development during the twentieth century. As we review the fundamentals of these traditional approaches, we will continually evaluate them in terms of their consistency with the dimensions of the traditional and dominant paradigm.

Freud

Historical Perspective

Freud was born in Moravia (a part of what was, prior to the redivision of the Soviet Union and Eastern Europe, Czechoslovakia) in 1856. He attended medical school in Vienna, a place of prominence in medical science at the time. He was trained according to the traditional/dominant paradigm as a medical scientist. His initial scientific research was focused on the physiology and neurology of fish. Freud maintained a scientific perspective in his research later on. His research approach focused on observation rather than experimentation and was reflected later in his development and practice of psychoanalysis. Freud was also influenced by what in his time was called psychic healing, a much more intuitive, less traditional approach to understanding and intervening in human behavior, from which emerged hypnotism (Loevinger 1987: 14–19; Green 1989:33–35). Freud's research and practice in psychoanalysis led him to conclude that the causes of his patients' symptoms could always be found in early childhood traumas and parental relationships (Loevinger 1987:15–16; Green 1989: 36–37).

Freud developed techniques of free association and dream interpretation to trace and intervene in the early traumas and parental relationships that he believed were the source of his patients' distress. Free association is a process in which the patient is encouraged to relax and report any ideas that come to mind. The notion is that all ideas are important and if sufficiently studied and pursued can be connected back to the unconscious and early sources of their symptoms. Dream interpretation consists of studying the content of patients' dreams in order to detect symbolic and hidden meanings that are then used to interpret and help the patient to work through the troubling early experiences in order to resolve their presenting symptoms. (Green 1989; Loevinger 1987).

The Model

Freud's conclusions about often unconscious (unremembered) early experiences as a primary cause of later life troubles and his pursuit of psychoanalysis as a means of intervention in those troubles led him to construct a system through which he explained individual human behavior and development. In 1930 Healy, Bronner, and Bowers presented a summary of many of the basic concepts, processes, and structures that constituted Freud's system. Their work is helpful from a historical perspective because it was written contemporary with much of Freud's actual work and writing. Their approach is also helpful because rather than interpret Freud's work from their own perspectives, they relied heavily on Freud's words and works. This is important because so many different people have interpreted and reinterpreted Freud's work over time, it is often difficult to discern what is really Freud's perspective and what is the adaptation of his ideas by others. Such varied interpretations are understandable given the influence and revolutionary nature of his paradigm at the time, but it is important to have some sense of his original constructs and ideas. Freud's work is also an example of how a paradigm now considered traditional and limited in many ways was at the time of its development and introduction considered quite alternative, even radical.

Healy, Bronner, and Bowers presented Freud's psychoanalysis as a structure that was a synthesis of psychology and biology. They referred to it as a "structure erected within the field of psychobiologic science" (1930:xviii). They summarized this synthesis of biology and psychology:

a. *Biological and psychological development are inseparably interrelated.*

b. *The essential nature of the individual consists in strivings and urges, innate or unlearned, which originally are quite independent of environment.*

c. *Whatever the individual is or does at any given moment is very largely predetermined by his earlier experiences and his reactions to them.*

d. *The earliest years of life represent the period when biological and mental experiences most profoundly influence the individual because he is then less pre-formed or conditioned.*

e. *Existing actively in the mental life of the individual there is a vast amount of which he is unaware.*

f. *The biological and consequently the psychological constitution varies in different individuals.* (1930:xx)

Healy, Bronner, and Bowers suggest that to understand Freud's psychoanalytic paradigm we must first understand what they referred to as the "cardinal formulations" upon which it is based. Their cardinal formulations serve as a useful summary of the basic concepts of this paradigm. **Libido** is "that force by which the sexual instinct is represented in the mind." Libido or eros is "the energy . . . of those instincts which have to do with all that may be comprised under the word 'love.'" The suggestion here is that the concept of libido has a much wider meaning than simply "sex drive." It also incorporates love of self, of others, friendships, and love for humanity in general (1930:2–4).

Green provides a more recent but similar interpretation of this cornerstone of psychoanalytic thought, calling it instinctual or psychic energy (also referred to as nervous energy, drive energy, libido, or tension). Each person is born with a fixed amount of instinctual energy of two types. Eros, the "positive energy of life, activity, hope, and sexual desire," and thanatos, the "negative energy of death, destruction, despair, and aggression" (1989:36, 38–39).

Cathexis "is the accumulation or concentration of psychic energy in a particular place or channel, libidinal or non-libidinal" (Healy et al. 1930:8). This notion of cathexis is somewhat similar to the notion of energy we explored earlier in our discussion of social systems thinking (see Chapter 3). **Polarities** represent aspects of mental life that operate in opposition to one another. This principle of opposites emphasized the polarities of activity-passivity, self-outer world (subject-object), pleasure-pain, life-death, love-hate, and masculine-feminine (Healy et al. 1930:18). Thinking in terms of such polarities as these has much in common with our earlier discussion of the binary or competitive nature of much dominant or traditional paradigm thinking from Chapter 2. **Ambivalence** is the "contradictory emotional attitudes toward the same object" (Healy et al. 1930:20). *Ambivalence* represents an unhealthy or problematic tendency, according to Freudian theory. However, it has some similarity with the concept of ambiguity we discussed in Chapter 3 as a reality of human behavior that social workers must appreciate. *Ambivalence* suggests a negative condition; *ambiguity* suggests an alternative real and necessary aspect of human behavior.

Among the most important cardinal formulations of psychoanalysis is what Healy, Bronner, and Bowers (1930:22) refer to as the "divisional constitution of mental life." Mental life is made up of the conscious, the preconscious, and the unconscious. These notions are indeed essential to understanding Freud's approach. The **unconscious** element of our mental lives is much more powerful than the conscious as an influence on our behavior, according to psychoanalytic thinking. This is a very active part of our being and has much influence on our conscious thought and behavior. The unconscious may either have never been at a conscious level or it may contain once-conscious thought that has become repressed or submerged in the unconscious (Healy et al. 1930:24–28). The **preconscious** "is that part of mental life which in appropriate circumstances, either through an effort of the will or stimulated by an associated idea, can be brought up into consciousness." The preconscious has more in common with the conscious part of our mental selves but can at times function to bring memories from the unconscious to a conscious level. The **conscious** level is the smallest of the three levels and contains thought and ideas of which we are "aware at any given time." The content of the conscious mind is extremely transitory and is constantly changing (Healy et al. 1930:30–32).

Freud found the division of our mental life into *conscious, preconscious,* and *unconscious* helpful but insufficient for explaining human behavior. To more fully explain human behavior he later developed another three-part construct for conceptualizing our mental selves. This construct consisted of id, ego, and superego. He believed that this structure complemented his earlier construct of conscious, preconscious, and unconscious, rather than replacing it (Healy et al. 1930:34). The **id** is the source of instinctive energy. It contains libido drives and is unconscious. It seeks to maximize pleasure, is amoral, and has no unity of purpose (Healy et al. 1930:36). The **ego** represents that part of our mental life that results when id impulses are modified by the expectations and requirements of the external world. Ego emerges out of the id and represents what is commonly thought of as "reason and sanity." Ego strives to be moral and represses tendencies that might give free reign to our unmoral id impulses. The ego is in constant struggle with three influences upon it: "the external world, the libido of the id, and the severity of the super-ego" (Healy et al. 1930:38). The **superego** grows out of the ego and has the capacity to rule it. It is mostly unconscious and represents what we commonly think of as conscience. It is heavily influenced by our parents. It can evoke guilt and "exercise the censorship of morals" (Healy et al. 1930:44–46).

Green's (1989) summary of Freud's conceptualization of psychosexual stages through which humans develop is somewhat consistent with the historical summary of Healy, Bronner, and Bower (1930:80ff). Green suggests five discrete stages, however, while Healy et al. refer to three basic stages, of which the first, infancy, contains three substages (oral, anal, and genital). For clarity here we use Green's model. However, it is helpful to understand that Healy et al. reflect the dominant emphasis in traditional Freudian thinking placed on infancy and infantile sexuality by subsuming several substages under infancy.

Freud's developmental stages focus on critical developmental periods and on the role of sexuality in development from infancy on. Much traditional developmental thinking has its source in this linear, deterministic, and reductionist stage-based model. The first stage is the **oral stage** (birth to about age one). Its focus is on the mouth as a conflicting source of both pleasure (as in taking in nourishment) and pain (denial of nourishment on demand) and on parents as pivotal actors in gratification or denial of oral needs. The second stage is the **anal stage** (about age one to three). The focus of psychic energy shifts at this stage from the mouth to the anus and to control of the elimination of waste and is associated with sexual pleasure, personal power, and control. Conflict over the child's struggle for power and control during the anal stage is most often depicted in toilet training conflicts. These conflicts center on issues of independence and self-control, Freud believed. The third stage, the **phallic stage** (about three to six), is critical in development of sexual identity and sex roles. Instinctual energy is focused on the genitals in this stage and its conflict is around love/hate relationships with parents. Young boys compete for the affection of their mothers with their fathers in the **oedipal complex** that moves the boy through fear of castration by the father in retribution for the boy's desire for the mother, to a compromise in which the boy identifies with the more powerful father and accepts his values, attitudes, behaviors, and habits, resulting in the birth of the superego.

Freud describes a similar, though much less clearly articulated, process for girls that has come to be referred to as the **Electra complex** that takes the girl through penis envy symbolic of the power of the father and males, blaming the mother for depriving her of a penis, to recognition of the impossibility of attaining a penis and a resulting identification with the mother. According to Freud, out of this identification emerges a girl socialized to female sex roles. At this point she has a superego, albeit a weaker superego than that of males, because her lack of a penis prevents castration anxiety and the concomitant psychic strength (superego) that comes from the more intense repression struggles on the part of boys. Regarding women and the development of the superego or conscience, "their Super-ego is never so inexorable, so impersonal, so independent of its emotional origins, as we require it to be in men" (Freud in Healy et al. 1930:51). Healy et al. (1930:51) note that other psychoanalysts of Freud's day agreed "on the more infantile character of the Super-ego in the woman."

Agreement was not universal, however. Healy et al. reported, in their 1930 work on Freud, the important contention of Karen Horney (a female psychoanalyst, we might emphasize) "that the belief in 'penis envy' has evolved as the result of a too exclusively masculine orientation." Horney countered that "the girl has in the capacity for motherhood 'a quite indisputable and by no means negligible physiological superiority.' " She further claimed that there was sufficient data "for believing that 'the unconscious of the male psyche clearly reflects intense envy of motherhood, pregnancy, childhood' " (1930:161). According to Horney, "the whole matter has been approached too much from the male point of view" (1930:163). We shall see in the following chapter that many alternative-paradigm thinkers have taken these observations seriously and seek to redefine human behavior and development in ways that more appropriately and adequately incorporate the realities of girls' and women's developmental experiences.

The fourth stage is **latency** (about five or six to puberty). This stage includes the child's movement out of the family to influences of the larger society, primarily in the company of same-sex peers. Sexual instincts and energy are channeled to sports, school, and social play. Freud gave little attention to this stage because of lack of intense sexual conflict characteristic of the previous and following stages. The fifth stage is the **genital stage** (puberty to adulthood). The focal conflict of this stage is the establishment of mature heterosexual behavior patterns through which to obtain sexual pleasure and love (Green 1989:42–49).

Another influential component in traditional Freudian developmental thinking was that of defense mechanisms. **Defense mechanisms** are automatic patterns of thinking aimed at reducing anxiety (Green 1989:49). Healy et al. (1930:198) refer to defense mechanisms as "dynamisms" that are "very specific processes by which the unconscious Ego attempts to take care of, or to defend itself against, Id urges, desires, wishes." Thinking of these mechanisms as dynamisms or dynamic forces helps communicate their process or active nature. Some major defense mechanisms include

repression, the submergence of memories and thoughts that produce anxiety; **regression,** reversion to an earlier, less anxiety-provoking stage of development; **projection,** attributing one's anxiety-provoking thoughts or feelings to someone else; **reaction formation,** behaving in a way that is the extreme opposite of the anxiety-producing behavior; **displacement,** unconsciously shifting anxiety-producing feelings away from threatening objects or persons (Green 1989:49–51).

Conclusion

The picture of individual development that emerges from Freud's influential model is one consistent in many ways with traditional paradigm thinking. It is linear and stage-based. Although it has been applied and interpreted very broadly, its focus is relatively narrow in its predominant concern for intrapsychic structures and processes. It is constructed on a scientific, positivistic foundation. It is based on masculinist and patriarchal perspectives that assume male experience as central. Gilligan provides evidence that the tendency to use male life as the norm for human development has a long history that goes at least back to Freud (Gilligan 1982:6). Female developmental experiences are described only in terms of their difference from normal or modal male experience. The standards of white Eurocentric culture from which the model emerged are considered universal. It reflects the white European experiences of its founder and of the patients upon which Freud's findings were based. The model reflects an individualistic bias that places primacy on separateness and autonomy as necessary end points for mature development. It is binary, with its emphasis on polarities. Implicit also in the model is the dimension of privilege. This dimension incorporates some of the other dimensions of the traditional/dominant paradigm, and from this synthesis emerges the profile of privilege that characterizes a person who is young, white, heterosexual, Judeo-Christian, male, able-bodied, with sufficient resources and power (Pharr 1988).

SEHB and Freud: A Paradigm Shift from the Social Environment to Individual Behavior

Freud's model has had, as noted earlier, significant influences on social work. Ann Weick (1981:140) refers to psychoanalytic theory, for example, as perhaps "the most important development in shaping the evolution of social work." A fundamental element in this evolution was the shifting of focus in social work's approach to addressing problems toward individual functioning and internal or "intrapsychic phenomena . . . as the critical variables." Such a fundamental shift toward the individual was accompanied by a shift away from environmental concerns as foremost in understanding and addressing issues of well-being. A result of this shift was a medical or pathology (illness) perspective on people's problems rather than a social change or strengths perspective.

A medical or pathology perspective also was historically significant in that it redefined human behavior as predictable according to determinable laws consistent with traditional paradigm thinking, rather than as unpredictable and contextually emergent, which would have been more consistent with alternative paradigm perspectives. Thomas Szasz, in his book *The Myth of Mental Illness,* argues that this trend in psychiatry had significant political meaning. It attempted to obscure the relationship between personal troubles and political issues. It suggested that an individual's problems were solely a result of "genetic-psychological" factors (Szasz 1961:5). On the other hand, Szasz argues, more consistent with alternative paradigm thinking (and more consistent with core concerns of social work), that "psychological laws are relativistic with respect to social conditions. In other words, *the laws of psychology cannot be formulated independently of the laws of sociology*" (1961:7). We cannot understand human behavior unless we simultaneously attend to and seek understanding of the social environment.

To suggest that we consider, in our choices about perspectives for understanding HBSE, these criticisms of Freud's model of individual development and behavior is not to suggest that we discard it wholesale. Much about Freud's approach offered new insight into the complexities of human behavior. Its suggestion that our later mental lives are influenced by the experiences of our earlier lives alone was extremely important, even revolutionary. We must, however, recognize the contradictions between Freud's approach and our attempt to develop holistic, inclusive perspectives consistent with the core concerns of social work. Thus, the recommendation here, as with all models whether traditional or alternative, is to approach this model critically, cautiously, and analytically. It is also important to note that traditional psychoanalytic theory is being questioned and revised in light of concerns about its exclusion of the experiences of many people, especially those of women. Miller (1986:28) notes, for example, that the emphasis of traditional psychoanalytic theory on autonomy and independence as central to healthy growth and development is being challenged by some theorists who say that the ability to form and maintain interdependent relationship with others is of equal importance in healthy growth and development. Miller suggests that the new call to place equal emphasis on relationship and interdependence is emerging from efforts to look at human development from the perspective of women rather than solely from the perspective of men (1986). We will explore this new emphasis more in Chapter 5.

Piaget

Historical Perspective

Piaget, like Freud, began his study and research from a traditional scientific approach. Piaget focused on biology before turning to psychology and human behavior. He became interested in the study of snails and at age twelve he published his first of some twenty papers on snails. Piaget's first work in psychology was in the laboratory begun by Binet, originator of the intelligence test (IQ test) for quantitatively measuring intelligence. Piaget's interest was, however, qualitative rather than quantitative in that he was interested in why the children gave the answers they did to questions rather than in the quantity of their correct answers. His studies were carried out using complex qualitative interviews with young children, including his own three children. His research resulted in a hierarchical stage model of the development of thinking in children that has, like Freud, had a far-reaching impact on traditional thinking about how humans develop (Loevinger 1987:177–182).

The Model

Piaget's developmental model includes four major developmental periods of thinking—sensorimotor, preoperational, concrete operational, and formal operational thought. The **sensorimotor period** is made up of six different stages that constitute "the precursors and first rudimentary stage of intelligence." First, are *impulsive and reflex actions* unconnected with "each other and for their own sake" (sucking). Second, *circular or repetitive actions* (kicking, grasping a blanket) that are gradually combined into two or more schemes (grasping and looking at a blanket simultaneously). To Piaget, a **scheme** (the term scheme is often translated as *schema*) is a pattern of stimuli and movements that together form a unity and result in sensorimotor coordination. Third, *practicing circular or repetitive actions for their consequences* (kicking to shake the crib). The beginning of concentration. Fourth, the baby *"coordinates schemes and applies them to new situations."* This represents the beginning of intentionality or experimentation in using one scheme to accomplish another (pulling a handkerchief to reach a toy underneath). This stage occurs near the end of the first year. The fifth stage *continues experimentation but with more novelty and variation of patterns.* The sixth sensorimotor stage *allows the baby to invent new means of doing things by thinking* rather than only by groping. At this point the baby also learns **object permanence,** which refers to understanding that when an object is out of sight it does not cease to exist (Loevinger 1987:182–183).

The next three periods involve the development of **operational thought (preoperational, concrete operations, formal operations).** In **preoperational thought** the child learns to use signs and symbols to think about and do things with objects and events that are absent. This period begins with the acquisition of language at about 18 months to two years and continues to ages six or seven. Preoperational thought is focused on concrete, external features of an object or situation and centers on the child (is egocentric) (Loevinger 1987:183).

The next period is **concrete operational thought** (about seven to fourteen, but may last through adulthood (Green 1989:178)). The child reasons correctly about concrete things and events and can do so within "a coherent and integrated cognitive system" for organizing and manipulating the world (Falvell in Loevinger 1987:183). The child also begins the development of the ability to perceive what Piaget called conservation. **Conservation** refers to the ability to understand that objects can change in some respect but remain the same object. Conservation of volume refers to the ability to understand that the quantity of liquid remains the same even when it is poured from one container of a given shape into a container of a different shape. For example, pouring a cup of water from a tall slender glass into a short wide glass. The sophistication of the child's understanding of conservation to this point occurs late in this period. The final period is that of **formal operations** (fourteen through adulthood). During this stage the person reasons relatively correctly about hypothetical situations. Important for Piaget was the realization that as the child develops, thinking is not simply a collection of unconnected pieces of information, it is a system of construction. New learning is fitted into what is already known. Piaget referred to this ability as equilibration.

Conclusion

Piaget's model is less traditional in its more qualitative emphasis, but it reflects a developmental world very consistent with traditional paradigm thinking. It is positivistic or empiricist in its focus on knowledge based on direct observation as "real" knowledge. It is linear in its accent on specific progression of stages. It does not recognize differences in developmental experiences emerging from differing experiences resulting from gender. Piaget's model reflects no differentiation in developmental experiences based on race and class. It generally gives no recognition to social or environmental conditions that may impinge on individual development. Thus, it offers little guidance for connecting the personal and the political or on the interrelationships between individual and social change.

As with Freud's model, it is important to recognize that a critical approach such as that taken here is not a suggestion that we completely discard this model. It is to suggest, however, that we examine the model with a critical eye for its consistency with social work concerns. Piaget's work has been extremely influential and helpful in increasing our understanding of how some children learn to think and to think about their experiences of their worlds. His focus on understanding *how* children learn what they learn offers an important alternative to emphasizing only *how much* they learn based on quantifying *how many* correct answers they get on objective tests. To recognize these strengths we need not deny the limitations of this model and of the research upon which it is based.

Kohlberg

Introduction

Kohlberg's research focuses on the development of moral judgment and is in part an outgrowth of Piaget's work. Kohlberg's method involved presenting subjects with a series of moral dilemmas to which they were asked to respond. Piaget's study of moral judgment included only children under twelve or thirteen years of age. Kohlberg extended the ages of his subjects beyond those studied by Piaget by interviewing a large number of adolescent boys (Loevinger 1987:193ff).

The Model

Based on his research, Kohlberg found moral judgment to exist on **"three general levels—preconventional,** characterized by a concrete individual perspective; the **conventional,** characterized by a member-of-society perspective; and the **postconventional,** or principled, characterized by a prior-to society perspective" (Kohlberg in Loevinger 1987:194). Within each of the three general levels are two stages. Thus, Kohlberg's model consists of six distinct stages distributed across three more general levels of judgment.

"Stage 1 is characterized by a punishment-and-obedience orientation." Stage 2 is characterized by hedonism. Stage 3 is focused on "maintaining good relations and the approval of others." Stage 4 is focused on conformity to social norms. Stage 5 is characterized by "a sense of shared rights and duties as grounded in an implied social contract." At stage 6 "what is morally right is defined by self-chosen principles of conscience." (Loevinger 1987:194–195)

Conclusion

Kohlberg's model reflects consistency with the dimensions of the traditional/dominant paradigm. It is based on scientific, positivistic, objectivistic assumptions. The research upon which the model was based included exclusively male subjects. It reflects no recognition for differing developmental experiences based on color or class. It places a premium on development of autonomy, separateness, or individuality. It, like the other models we have explored thus far, portrays development from the perspective of privilege—the assumption of sufficient resources and power to fulfill developmental imperatives.

Analysis/Criticism: "Women's Place" in Freud, Piaget, Kohlberg

Carol Gilligan (1982) examines the developmental theories of both Jean Piaget and Lawrence Kohlberg for their inclusion and treatment of the developmental experiences of women. These theories have much to say, you may recall from the summaries given earlier in this chapter, about the development of moral judgment and a sense of justice. Gilligan also discusses the treatment women received in Freud's theories in relation to these two fundamental developmental tasks. She notes that Freud found women's sense of justice "compromised in its refusal of blind impartiality" (1982:18).

According to Gilligan, in "Piaget's account (1932) of the moral judgment of the child, girls are an aside, a curiosity to whom he devotes four brief entries in an index that omits 'boys' altogether because 'the child' is assumed to be male." Kohlberg's research does not include females at all. His six stages "are based empirically on a study of eighty-four boys whose development Kohlberg has followed for over twenty years." Kohlberg claims that his model fits humans universally, but Gilligan points out, "those groups not included in his original sample rarely reach his higher stages." Women's judgment, for example, rarely goes beyond stage 3 on this six-stage scale. At stage 3 morality is seen in interpersonal terms; goodness is equivalent to helping and pleasing others. Kohlberg implies that only by entering the typically male arenas will women develop to higher stages where relationships are subordinated to rules (stage 4) and rules to universal principles of justice (stages 5 and 6). The paradox presented in Kohlberg's model is that characteristics that traditionally define "goodness" in women—care for and sensitivity to others—are also those that mark them as deficient in moral development. The problem in this paradox of positive qualities perceived as developmental deficiencies, Gilligan suggests, is that the model emerged from the study of men's lives (Gilligan 1982:18). Karen Horney made a very similar assessment many years ago, we might recall from our earlier discussion of Freudian theory and Horney's criticism of its treatment of women.

Erikson

Introduction

The stage-based model derived by Erik Erikson may be the model most often used to teach individual development in HBSE courses in social work curricula and in developmental psychology courses. It is difficult to understate the influence that Erikson's eight-stage model has had on the way individual development through the life span is perceived in this society.

Concepts associated with Erikson's model are used almost universally in the language of traditional human development approaches. Erikson's model is also often the departure point or base from which alternative models and theories of development emerge. Such basic concepts as developmental stage, psychosocial or developmental crisis, and the epigenetic principle all emerge from, and are central in Erikson's approach to individual development. These concepts are often used to describe central developmental processes from alternative paradigm perspectives as well. These concepts have become so central to developmental thinking that we will briefly describe them here. However, as you read the excerpts from Erikson later in this chapter, you are encouraged to take note of his discussion and use of these central developmental concepts as he summarizes his eight-stage model.

For Erikson, human development takes place according to a series of predetermined steps through which the person proceeds as he or she becomes psychologically, biologically, and socially ready. The unfolding of these steps allows the individual to participate in social life in increasingly wide-ranging and sophisticated ways. The model assumes that the environment in which development takes place provides the necessary resources and presents the necessary challenges at the proper times for the individual to move through each step. This process of orderly development through a series of steps is guided by what Erikson refers to as the epigenetic principle. The **epigenetic principle** holds that each step takes place as part of an overall plan made up of all the necessary steps or parts. Each particular developmental step emerges out of the context of the overall plan and each step comes about when the internal and external conditions exist to make the individual especially ready to do what is necessary to take the step. This time of readiness is referred to by Erikson as **ascendancy** (Erikson 1968:92–93). The necessary steps are referred to as developmental stages. A **developmental stage** is a critical period during which an individual struggles to address and resolve a developmental crisis. Resolution of each crisis enables the individual to proceed to the next stage. This process continues until the individual has progressed through all eight developmental stages. For Erikson, **developmental crisis** did not mean an impending catastrophe as much as it meant "a turning point, a crucial period of increased vulnerability and heightened potential" (Erikson 1968 in Bloom 1985:36). See Table 4.1 for an overview of Erikson's eight developmental stages and related ego strengths, crises and explanations.

Erikson's Model: In His Own Words

Erikson's model is so fundamental to traditional paradigm thinking about individual development that it seems appropriate to include in his own words a summary of the model and descriptions of its basic concepts. This illustrative reading "Eight Ages of Man," published by Erikson in 1950, is excerpted from a chapter in the first edition of his widely read and highly influential book, *Childhood and Society*. It provides a summary of his eight stages of the life cycle as he described them at this point in his career. In addition to giving an overview and a "flavor" for Erikson's thinking and writing, this selection reflects the significant influence of Freud and psychoanalytic thought on that of Erikson. The reader is also encouraged to consider critically, gender- and sexual orientation-related references, examples, and assumptions in this excerpt.

TABLE 4.1   Erikson's Psychosocial Stages of Development

No.	Stage Name/Age	Ego Strength	Comment
1	Trust vs. mistrust (0–1 year)	Hope	Trust is developed on the basis of physical comfort and a minimizing of fear. The quality of the care experienced by the infant is the central mechanism for developing trust (e.g., smiles, tenderness). **Crisis is in establishing trust.**
2	Autonomy vs. shame (1–3 years)	Will	With the emergence of locomotion, the infant exercises autonomy. **Crisis = parental restrictions vs. autonomy.** Parents who can support the child in autonomy enable the development of self-reliance in later life.
3	Initiative vs. guilt (3–6 years)	Purpose	The emerging sense of taking initiatives is central. The taking of actions builds up the child's sense of pleasure in competence. If the parents respond punitively, then guilt can become predominant. **Crisis is in taking initiative without experiencing guilt.** Parents can encourage the development of initiative by encouraging actions, answering questions, and supporting hobbies.
4	Industry vs. inferiority (6–12 years)	Competence	Seek identity by inclusion with school-age peers. This leads to intense social striving for competence in the eyes of peers and others so as to avoid feeling interior. **Crisis is in striving for competence.**
5	Identity vs. role confusion (12–17 years)	Fidelity	Cross-roads from childhood to adulthood. Massive physiological changes (e.g., voice, size, coordination reduces, sex characteristics lead to a period of great adjustment). Western society grants a moratorium (i.e., not yet expected to be an adult but no longer seen as a child). **Identity crisis = uncertainty about the future and the child's role in it.** Adolescents often experience the pressure to prematurely adopt an identity, which prevents the resolution of the crisis.
6	Intimacy vs. isolation (young adulthood)	Love	Focus is on the search for a meaningful relationship to which one can be committed. **Crisis is focused on the ability to lose oneself in a committed relationship.** Intimacy crisis is the risking of the consequences of a relationship gone wrong. Isolation is the way of avoiding intimacy.

TABLE 4.1 *Continued*

No.	Stage Name/Age	Ego Strength	Comment
7	Generativity vs. stagnation (middle adulthood)	Care	**Generativity crisis is risking personal investment in people beyond the immediate family.** Self-absorption = stagnation.
8	Ego integrity vs. despair (older adulthood)	Confidence	Satisfied with accomplishments, death is seen as the inevitable end to life. **Crisis is in facing one's end with integrity.** Despair is produced when death is seen as the lost opportunity to achieve something in life.

Wastell (1996) *Journal of Counseling & Development 74*, July/August 1996. pg. 577. © ACA. Reprinted with permission.

EIGHT STAGES OF MAN by Erik Erikson

1. Trust vs. Basic Mistrust

The first demonstration of social trust in the baby is the ease of his feeding, the depth of his sleep, the relaxation of his bowels. The experience of a mutual regulation of his increasingly receptive capacities with the maternal techniques of provision gradually helps him to balance the discomfort caused by the immaturity . . . with which he was born. . . . The infant's first social achievement, then, is his willingness to let the mother out of sight without undue anxiety or rage, because she has become an inner certainty as well as an outer predictability.

. . . If I prefer the word "trust," it is because there is more naivete and more mutuality in it: an infant can be said to be trusting where it would go too far to say that he has confidence. The general state of trust, furthermore, implies not only that one has learned to rely on the sameness and continuity of the outer providers, but also that one may trust oneself and the capacity of one's own organs to cope with urges; and that one is able to consider oneself trustworthy enough so that the providers will not need to be on guard lest they be nipped.

The firm establishment of enduring patterns for the solutions of the nuclear conflict of basic trust versus basic mistrust in mere existence is the first task of the ego, and thus first of all a task for maternal care. But let it be said here that the amount of trust derived from earliest infantile experience does not seem to depend on absolute quantities of food or demonstrations of love, but rather on the quality of the maternal relationship.

2. Autonomy vs. Shame and Doubt

Anal-muscular maturation sets the stage for experimentation with two simultaneous sets of social modalities: holding on and letting go. . . . Outer control at this stage, therefore, must be firmly reassuring. The infant must come to feel

Continued

EIGHT AGES OF MAN   *Continued*

that the basic faith in existence, which is the lasting treasure saved from the rages of the oral stage, will not be jeopardized by this about-face of his, this sudden violent wish to have a choice, to appropriate demandingly, and to eliminate stubbornly. Firmness must protect him against the potential anarchy of his as yet untrained sense of discrimination, his inability to hold on and to let go with discretion. As his environment encourages him to "stand on his own feet," it must protect him against meaningless and arbitrary experiences of shame and of early doubt. . . . Shame supposes that one is completely exposed and conscious of being looked at: in one word, self-conscious. One is visible and not ready to be visible; . . . Shame is early expressed in an impulse to bury one's face, or to sink, right then and there, into the ground. . . .

Doubt is the brother of shame. Where shame is dependent on the consciousness of being upright and exposed, doubt, so clinical observation leads me to believe, has much to do with a consciousness of having a front and a back—and especially a "behind". . . .

3. Initiative vs. Guilt

The ambulatory stage and that of infantile genitality add to the inventory of basic social modalities that of "making," first in the sense of "being on the make." There is no simpler, stronger word to match the social modalities previously enumerated. The word suggests pleasure in attack and conquest. In the boy, the emphasis remains on phallic-intrusive modes; in the girl it turns to modes of "catching" in more aggressive forms of snatching and "bitchy" possessiveness, or in the milder form of making oneself attractive and endearing. . . .

Infantile sexuality and incest taboo, castration complex and superego all unite here to bring about that specifically human crisis during which the child must turn from an exclusive, pregenital attachment to his parents to the slow process of becoming a parent, a carrier of tradition. . . .

The problem, again, is one of mutual regulation. Where the child, now so ready to overmanipulate himself, can gradually develop a sense of paternal responsibility, where he can gain some insight into the institutions, functions, and roles which will permit his responsible participation, he will find pleasurable accomplishment in wielding tools and weapons, in manipulating meaningful toys—and in caring for younger children. . . .

4. Industry vs. Inferiority

Before the child, psychologically already a rudimentary parent, can become a biological parent, he must begin to be a worker and potential provider. With the oncoming latency period, the normally advanced child forgets, or rather sublimates, the necessity to "make" people by direct attack or to become papa and mama in a hurry: he now learns to win recognition by producing things. He has mastered the ambulatory field and the organ modes. He has experi-

Continued

EIGHT AGES OF MAN *Continued*

enced a sense of finality regarding the fact that there is no workable future within the womb of his family, and thus becomes ready to apply himself to given skills and tasks, which go far beyond the mere playful expression of his organ modes or the pleasure in the function of his limbs. He develops industry—i.e., he adjusts himself to the inorganic laws of the tool world. He can become an eager and absorbed unit of a productive situation. To bring a productive situation to completion is an aim which gradually supersedes the whims and wishes of his autonomous organism. His ego boundaries include his tools and skills: the work principle . . . teaches him the pleasure of work completion by steady attention and persevering diligence. . . .

5. Identity vs. Role Diffusion

With the establishment of a good relationship to the world of skills and tools, and with the advent of sexual maturity, childhood proper comes to an end. Youth begins. But in puberty and adolescence all samenesses and continuities relied on earlier are questioned again, because of a rapidity of body growth which equals that of early childhood and because of the entirely new addition of physical genital maturity. The growing and developing youths, faced with this physiological revolution within them are now primarily concerned with what they appear to be in the eyes of others as compared with what they feel they are, and with the question of how to connect the roles and skills cultivated earlier with the occupational prototypes of the day. In their search for a new sense of continuity and sameness, adolescents have to refight many of the battles of earlier years, even though to do so they must artificially appoint perfectly well-meaning people to play the roles of enemies; and they are ever ready to install lasting idols and ideals as guardians of a final identity: here puberty rites "confirm" the inner design for life.

The integration now taking place in the form of ego identity is more than the sum of the childhood identifications. It is the accrued experience of the ego's ability to integrate these identifications with the vicissitudes of the libido, with the aptitudes developed out of endowment, and with the opportunities offered in social roles. The sense of ego identity, then, is the accrued confidence that the inner sameness and continuity are matched by the sameness and continuity of one's meaning for others, as evidenced in the tangible promise of a "career". . . .

6. Intimacy vs. Isolation

It is only as young people emerge from their identity struggles that their egos can master the sixth stage, that of intimacy. What we have said about genitality now gradually comes into play. Body and ego must now be masters of the organ modes and of the nuclear conflicts, in order to be able to face the fear of ego loss in situations which call for self-abandon: in orgasms and sexual unions, in close friendships and in physical combat, in experiences of inspiration by teachers and of intuition from the recesses of the self. The avoidance of such experiences

Continued

EIGHT AGES OF MAN   *Continued*

because of a fear of ego loss may lead to a deep sense of isolation and conse-
quent self-absorption. . . .

While psychoanalysis has on occasion gone too far in its emphasis on genitality as a universal cure for society and has thus provided a new addiction and
a new commodity for many who wished to so interpret its teachings, it has not
always indicated all the goals that genitality actually should and must imply. In
order to be of lasting social significance, the utopia of genitality should include:

1. mutuality of orgasm
2. with a loved partner
3. of the other sex
4. with whom one is able and willing to share a mutual trust
5. and with whom one is able and willing to regulate the cycles of
    a. work
    b. procreation
    c. recreation
6. so as to secure to the offspring, too, a satisfactory development.

It is apparent that such utopian accomplishment on a large scale cannot be an individual or, indeed, a therapeutic task. Nor is it a purely sexual matter by any means.

7. Generativity vs. Stagnation

. . . Generativity is primarily the interest in establishing and guiding the next
generation or whatever in a given case may become the absorbing object of a
parental kind of responsibility. Where this enrichment fails, a regression from
generativity to an obsessive need for pseudo intimacy, punctuated by moments
of mutual repulsion, takes place, often with a pervading sense (and objective
evidence) of individual stagnation and interpersonal impoverishment.

8. Ego Integrity vs. Despair

Only he who in some way has taken care of things and people and has adapted
himself to the triumphs and disappointments adherent to being, by necessity, the
originator of others and the generator of things and ideas—only he may gradually grow the fruit of these seven stages. I know no better word for it than ego
integrity. . . . It is the acceptance of one's one and only life cycle as something
that had to be and that, by necessity, permitted of no substitutions: it thus means
a new, a different love of one's parents. It is a comradeship with the ordering
ways of distant times and different pursuits, as expressed in the simple products
and sayings of such times and pursuits. . . . For he knows that an individual life
is the accidental coincidence of but one life cycle with but one segment of history; and that for him all human integrity stands or falls with the one style of integrity of which he partakes. The style of integrity developed by his culture or

Continued

EIGHT AGES OF MAN   *Continued*

civilization thus becomes the "patrimony of his soul," the seal of his moral paternity of himself. . . . Before this final solution, death loses its sting.

The lack or loss of this accrued ego integration is signified by fear of death: the one and only life cycle is not accepted as the ultimate of life. Despair expresses the feeling that the time is short, too short for the attempt to start another life and to try out alternate roads to integrity. Disgust hides despair. . . .

Trust (the first of our ego values) is here defined as "the assured reliance on another's integrity," the last of our values. . . . And it seems possible to further paraphrase the relation of adult integrity and infantile trust by saying that healthy children will not fear life if their parents have integrity enough not to fear death. . . .

Analysis/Criticism: "Women's Place" in Erikson

Erik Erikson's influential theory of eight developmental stages portrays male development and experience as the norm. Gilligan and others (Berzoff 1989; Miller 1991) analyze and provide critiques of Erikson's theory specifically in terms of the developmental theme of relationship and connectedness and generally in terms of its treatment or representation of women.

Gilligan finds Erikson, when outlining the developmental journey from child to adult, to be talking about the male child. Much of Erikson's model focuses on the development of identity, a sense of who we are. For Erikson the normal steps to development of identity are steps requiring specifically an identity marked by primacy of separateness and autonomy. Gilligan points out, for example, that after the initial stage of establishment of a sense of trust which requires the establishment of a bond, a relationship initially with the infant's care giver (usually mother), the focus of development shifts to individuation.

The stages of autonomy versus shame and doubt, initiative versus guilt, industry versus inferiority, and identity versus identity diffusion all call for resolutions weighted toward separateness, individual drive and competence, and identity as a separate self in adolescence. The individual, then, in Erikson's male model, arrives at the adulthood crisis of intimacy versus isolation having spent all the previous years, with the exception of the establishment of trust in infancy, honing developmental skills that place a premium on separateness. But what is not indicated is that such a model is most likely to result in men who are poorly prepared for incorporating and appreciating the intimacy required of adults.

Erikson does recognize differences in the developmental experiences of women to some extent, but he describes these differences in his work virtually as afterthoughts or asides from the normal male model he presents. In his book *Identity: Youth and Crisis* (1968), for example, he addresses women's different developmental issues and experiences in the second-to-last chapter, "Womanhood and the Inner Space." The last chapter addresses, interestingly, "Race and Wider Identity." Neither of these chapters, based on lectures and papers written in 1964 and 1966 long after his original outline of the eight stages in 1950, resulted in changes or revision in the model. In his 1950 work, *Childhood and Society* (see Illustrative Reading 4.1), he mentions that, in the initiative versus guilt stage, boys' forms of initiative development activities focus on "phallic-intrusive modes" while girls focus on "modes of 'catching' in more aggressive forms of snatching or in the milder form of making oneself attractive and endearing" (Erikson 1950). In his 1968 work, Gilligan notes, Erikson finds identity development in adolescence for girls different from that in boys. However, these differences did not result in changes in his original outline of life cycle stages (Gilligan 1982:12).

Levinson: Adult Development

Introduction

Daniel Levinson recognized that most developmental research began with and focused on the developmental experiences and tasks of very early life. Most traditional models would then apply the concepts and patterns observed or emerging from studies of children to later points in the life cycle. The target of his research, unlike that of the others we have explored thus far, was the developmental experiences and stages of adulthood, primarily what he defined as middle adulthood. Like the other traditional models we have explored, Levinson's model, described in his book, *The Seasons of a Man's Life* (1978), talks about development only in terms of the experiences of men.

The Model

Levinson and his colleagues (1978:18) concluded that generally the life cycle moves through a series of four partially overlapping eras, each of which lasts approximately twenty-two years. Their research also concluded that the cycle can be further broken down into developmental periods that "give a finer picture of the dramatic events and the details of living" (1978:19). Levinson claims a fairly high degree of specificity regarding the ages at which each era begins and ends. The range of variation is, he believes, "probably not more than five or six years." A central concept in Levinson's model is that of transition between eras. Transitions between eras last four or five years and require "a basic change in the fabric of one's life" (1978:19). The eras and transition periods are listed below:

Era 1. [Preadulthood] Childhood and Adolescence: 0–22 years
Early Childhood Transition: 0–3
Early Adult Transition: 17–22

Era 2. Early Adulthood: 17–45
Early Adult Transition: 17–22
Mid-life Transition: 40–45

Era 3. Middle Adulthood: 40–65
Mid-life Transition: 40–45
Late Adult Transition: 60–65

Era 4. Late Adulthood: 60–?
Late Adult Transition: 60–65 (Levinson 1978:20)

In Preadulthood (Era 1) the social environment includes family, school, peer group, and neighborhood. Developmental tasks include becoming disciplined, industrious, and skilled. Puberty occurs at approximately twelve or thirteen and acts as a transition to adolescence, "the culmination of the pre-adult era." The Early Adult Transition (approximately age seventeen to twenty-two) acts as a bridge from adolescence to early adulthood. Levinson says, "during this period the growing male is a boy-man" and experiences extraordinary growth but remains immature and vulnerable as he enters the adult world (1978:21).

Early Adulthood (Era 2) "may be the most dramatic of all eras" with mental and biological characteristics reaching their peaks. This era includes formation of preliminary adult identity and first choices "such as marriage, occupation, residence and style of living." The man during this era typically begets and raises children, contributes his labor to the economy, and moves from a "novice adult" to a "senior position in work, family and community" (1978:22). This is a demanding and rewarding time filled with stress, challenges, and accomplishments according to Levinson.

Middle Adulthood (Era 3), with its Mid-life Transition from about forty to forty-five, Levinson refers to as "among the most controversial of our work" (1978:23). The controversy around discovery of this transition involves its lack of any clear cut universal event such as puberty in marking the transition from childhood to adolescence and early adulthood. This transition period includes more subtle, evolutionary, and thematic changes in biological and psychological functioning, the sequence of generations, and the evolution of careers and enterprises (1978:24).

This era is marked by some decline in "instinctual energies" and biological functions such as sexual capacity. Levinson describes this not necessarily as a deficit, since "the quality of his love relationships may well improve as he develops a greater capacity for intimacy and integrates more fully the tender, 'feminine' aspects of his self. He has the possibility of becoming a more responsive friend to men as well as women" (1978:25). Levinson notes differences in intensity of changes and in individual men's responses to them during this time. "The Mid-life Transition may be rather mild. When it involves considerable turmoil and disruption, we speak of a mid-life crisis." This transition involves a recognition of one's mortality and loss of youth for most men that is not completed here but continues for the remainder of life (Levinson 1978:26).

A key concept in Levinson's model is that of generation. He describes a generation in this way: "Members of a given generation are at the same age level in contrast to younger and older generations. With the passing years, a young adult has the sense of moving from one generation to the next and of forming new relationships with the other generation in his world." A generation "covers a span of some 12–15 years" (1978:27). Levinson uses Jose Ortega Y Gasset's conception of generations as a guide:

1. *Childhood: 0–15;*
2. *Youth: 15–30;*
3. *Initiation: 30–45;*
4. *Dominance: 45–60;*
5. *Old age: 60+.* (1978:28)

Levinson's notion of evolving career and enterprises calls on "every man in the early forties . . . to sort things out, come to terms with the limitations and consider the next step in the journey." Men around forty often experience some culminating event representing a significant success or failure in terms of movement along the life path. Levinson also describes this time of life as a period of "individuation," "a developmental process through which a person becomes more uniquely individual. Acquiring a clearer and fuller identity of his own, he becomes better able to utilize his inner resources and pursue his own aims. He generates new levels of awareness, meaning and understanding" (1978:31–33).

Late Adulthood (Era 4) is not the focus of Levinson's work, but he does give some attention to describing its tasks. He believes this era lasts from sixty to eighty-five. The developmental tasks include balancing the "splitting of youth and age" in order to sustain his youthfulness in a new form appropriate to late adulthood, terminating and modifying earlier life structure, moving off "center stage of his world," finding "a new balance of involvement with society and with the self," to gain a sense of integrity of his life, finding meaning in his life in order to come to terms with death, and making peace with enemies inside the self and in the world—not to stop fighting for his convictions but "to fight with less rancor, with fewer illusions and with broader perspective" (1978:36–38).

Levinson very briefly describes an additional era of Late Adulthood beginning at around eighty. Development at this point in life, while virtually unexplored (in 1978 when Levinson's work was first published), involved, he believed, such fundamental developmental tasks as "coming to terms with the process of dying and preparing for his own death," preparing himself for afterlife if he believes in immortality of the soul or, if not, concern for the fate of humanity and his own part in human evolution, and gaining meaning from life and death generally and his own specifically. "He must come finally to terms with the self—knowing it and loving it reasonably well, and being ready to give it up" (1978:38–39).

After publication of *The Season's of a Man's Life*, Levinson continued to explore adult development. In some of his later work, he stressed the need to develop models that appreciate and incorporate multiple and complex influences on the lives of humans. He emphasized the need to maintain an emphasis on the mutual influences of the individual and the social environment as development unfolds (Levinson 1986). Levinson also extended his theoretical position to include the developmental experiences of women. This extension to include women was based on a study of adult women and development he conducted subsequent to the original work that focused solely on the adult development of men. He concluded that the original model, with very little adaptation, fits equally the experiences of men and women. According to Levinson, "women and men go through the same sequence of periods in adult life structure development, and at the same ages" (Levinson and Levinson 1996:413). However, Levinson found that women's experiences, as they go through the same sequences of periods in adult development, differ from those of men. The major concept used to describe these differential experiences was that of gender splitting. **Gender splitting** is "a rigid division between female and male, feminine and masculine, in all aspects of life" (Levinson and Levinson 1996:414). Levinson found gender splitting to be especially apparent in the male and female experiences of public occupational and domestic spheres of life—"women's work and men's work, feminine and masculine within the self." Levinson posited that gender splitting "is encouraged by the existence of a patriarchal society in which women are generally subordinate to men, and the splitting helps maintain that society" (Levinson and Levinson 1996:414). However, as women increasingly enter the public sphere of work outside the home, Levinson concluded the "lives and personalities of women and men are becoming more similar" (Levinson and Levinson 1996:414). Levinson's perspective on the inclusion of the developmental experiences of both males and females in his model is quite different from that offered by Gilligan (1982) in her critique of Levinson's theory. Berzoff (1989) also questioned the ability to make generalizations about the patterns of adult development for men and women. (See "Analysis/Criticism" sections below.)

Disengagement Theory of Aging

Another traditional approach to understanding adult development, especially later adulthood, is **disengagement theory**. Achenbaum and Bengtson claim that "disengagement theory . . . represents the first truly explicit, truly multidisciplinary, and truly influential theory advanced by social science researchers in gerontology" (1994:756). The "disengagement theory of aging" was originally conceptualized by Cumming and Henry (1961) in their book, *Growing Old*. The central argument of the theory was that "**Disengagement** is an inevitable process of aging whereby many relationships between the individual and society are altered and eventually severed. . . . [It] could be seen in both psychological (ego mechanism) and sociological (role and normative) changes. It was also manifest in loss of morale" (Achenbaum and Bengston 1994:758).

Challenges to Disengagement

Disengagement theory was challenged by researchers who suggested very different and much more varied views of the experiences of persons as they aged. According to Achenbaum and Bengston, Havighurst, in 1957, in putting forth his theory of "the social competence of middle-aged people . . . emphasized that most people ably adjusted their social roles well into their late sixties. Furthermore, he suggested that life satisfaction depended, indirectly at least, on social activity" (1994:759). They also note that in 1968 Smith "challenged both the universality and the functionality in assumptions about 'disengagement' by failing to confirm their propositions in surveys of African Americans, the chronically ill, and poor people." Tallmer and Kutner in 1969 suggested "it is not age which produces disengagement . . . but the impact of physical and social stress which may be expected to increase with age" (in Achenbaum and Bengtson 1994:760). Bengtson reported in 1969 that there appeared to be "more *variation* than *uniformity* in retirement roles and activities across occupational and national groups. . . . there was little evidence for the 'universality' of disengagement" (Achenbaum and Bengston 1994:760). In a similar manner in 1968 and 1969 Neugarten "stressed *diversity* in patterns of aging, and the *variations* in the aged's personalities" (Achenbaum and Bengtson 1994:759).

Does this photo communicate an image consistent with or inconsistent with Disengagement Theory of Aging? In what ways is the image consistent or inconsistent with this theory?

Analysis/Criticism: "Women's Place" in Adult Development

Neugarten, in her research on the process of aging, argued for looking at adult development and aging from multiple perspectives in order to appreciate the diversity in the experience of aging for different people. For example, she noted that in her research she found that individual's experiences of that aging process varied considerably according to both gender and social class. Neugarten was basically arguing against the notion of "biology as destiny" that had been put forth by traditional researchers in the area of adulthood and aging (Achenbaum and Bengtson 1994:759–60).

Achenbaum and Bengtson (1994:759) note that "Neugarten established her eminence in several domains of aging research. First, she stressed the importance of sex- and gender-based differences in biological and social time clocks." Second, she urged that researchers "look at the entire life course in addressing processes of aging, she never assumed invariant continuities in behavioral patterns." Bernice Neugarten laid the foundation for much on the later feminist and alternative approaches to considering diversity, gender, and class in research on adulthood rather than assuming only biological determinants of the aging process.

Carol Gilligan's (1982) research on women also informs adult developmental perspectives. She addresses specifically the exclusively male-based adult developmental model depicted by Levinson and the stages of adult development outlined in Erikson's male-focused model. Gilligan finds that the exclusion of the developmental experiences of women from these models results in incomplete portrayals of human development. The portrayals of the men emerging from these models lack what she considers to be some essential capacities. In existing traditional models of adult development, Gilligan finds "that among those men whose lives have served as the model for adult development, the capacity for relationships is in some sense diminished and the men are constricted in their emotional expression" (1982:154). Existing models display "a failure to describe the progression of relationships toward a maturity of interdependence [and] . . . the reality of continuing connection is lost or relegated to the background where the figures of women appear" (Gilligan 1982:155).

In adolescence and young adulthood, male and female voices reflect quite different central developmental experiences. For men "the role of separation as it defines and empowers the self" seems central. For women, "the ongoing process of attachment that creates and sustains the human community" is focal (Gilligan 1982:156). Gilligan notes that by listening to the previously unheard voices of women in thinking about adult development, one is pressed to reenvision notions of adult development. This new or extended vision is in line with Miller's description of "a psychology of adulthood which recognizes that development does not displace the values of ongoing attachment and the continuing importance of care in relationships" (Gilligan 1982:170). "By changing the lens of developmental observation from individual achievement to relationships of care, women depict ongoing attachment as the path that leads to maturity" (Gilligan 1982: 170).

Gilligan's and others' (Miller 1991 and Berzoff 1989) criticism of the traditional and dominant models of individual development for their male-focused treatment, if not their complete neglect of women, is but one example of limits of traditional developmental thinking. Perhaps as important as the implications of the treatment or neglect of women in traditional developmental thinking that Gilligan speaks of is the need for adult developmental perspectives that allow women to speak and to be heard in order to begin to develop true models of *human development*. As Gilligan points out, "Among the most pressing items on the agenda for research on adult development is the need to delineate *in women's own terms* the experience of their adult life." To listen to and learn from the developmental experiences of women is to include over one half of humanity in models of human development that has traditionally been neglected. It is also essential to realize, as Gilligan suggests above, that to listen to the voices of women is to learn a great deal about what is necessary for more completely understanding the meaning of individual development for both women and men.

Analysis/Criticism: Traditional Developmental Approaches and People of Color

Race in Developmental Research/Erikson

According to Erikson successful human development depends on resolution of intrapsychic conflict about membership in the following groups:

1. gender
2. religion
3. age
4. occupation
5. political ideology
6. sexual orientation (Helms 1992:287)

Consideration of race or ethnicity is conspicuously absent from the list above. Helms notes that Erikson saw "racial-group membership as a significant aspect of negative identity development in African Americans, he had no notion of racial-group membership as a significant aspect of White people's identities. Nor did he have a postulate by which identification with one's racial group could have positive implications for personality adjustment for members of any racial group. . . . Yet in the United States, of the many collective identity groups to which a person might belong, race is the most salient, enduring, recognizable, and inflammatory" (1994:287).

Parks et al. point out the neglect of diversity and the resulting image of diversity as abnormal in much of the individual development literature. They note that "until fairly recently, the literature was essentially comparative and was critical of those who differed from the White male 'norm.' Theories of normal psychological functioning and development in a wide range of areas were developed by studying groups of White men . . . and women and Blacks were seen as deficient when differences between their experiences and those of White men emerged . . . the general image of psychological health was developed from an essentially racist, sexist, and heterosexist frame of reference" (1996:624).

Traditional Developmental Theories and Multiracial People

Traditional theories of human development also do not reflect the complexities of multiracial/ethnic developmental experiences. Miller asserts that "Largely ahistorical and acontextual, developmental models minimize the social-ecological aspect of racial and ethnic classification" (1992:33). Miller describes several limitations of traditional developmental theory related to its neglect of diversities. Compare Miller's limitations described below with the critiques of traditional stage-based developmental theories examined earlier in this chapter.

> *Universality:* "Eriksonian-based models of ethnic identity development assume that the developmental process is universal (i.e., that the content of identity development is immaterial for understanding the psychological process of coming to feel that one is a member of a social group). Similarly, social psychological theories of group affiliation assume that the process itself is always the same, regardless of the specific self-to-other comparisons one makes." *Linearity:* "Particularly for the multiracial individual, the identification process may be far from linear. . . . The multiracial person may select behavior, labels, and perspective based on their immediate utility in a given context. The identity process is linear only to the extent that multiculturalism itself is an end state. . . . the multiracial person may shift in self-perception in appropriate contexts." *Ascription and Duality:* "Eriksonian and social theories assume that the ascribed racial or ethnic identity and heritage of an individual match. . . . These assumptions also often lead to the belief that multiracially identified people are 'mixed up' or maladjusted. . . . Eriksonian and social identity theories suggest that an individual cannot view him- or herself concurrently as a member of two groups." (Miller 1992:33–34)

These limitations reflect the binary or "either/or" nature of traditional paradigm thinking. Clearly this type of thinking does not allow room for inclusion of the richness and complexity of the experiences of persons of color and especially of bi- and multiracial people.

Themes Regarding People of Color in Traditional Developmental Approaches

Spencer (1990:267–269) summarizes some of the themes in traditional approaches to the study of development and people of color. She outlines several characteristics of traditional or dominant approaches that have resulted in inadequate and inaccurate portrayals of the developmental experiences of people of color. She argues that these portrayals have been detrimental to the African American, Asian American, Hispanic American, and Native American people they exclude or inaccurately and incompletely depict. These traditional themes include the following:

1. Traditional-paradigm researchers have often been trained to view race and socioeconomic status as "nuisance" variables to be controlled for.

2. Study of minorities has too often been conducted from the approach of considering minorities as "deviant" from majority-based norms. The "deviance" approach neglected the often creative adaptation of people of color to the developmental barriers placed before them by hostile environments.

3. "Normative" development has too often been defined according to Eurocentric standards, excluding from the norm all but the most assimilated minorities. Cultural differences and structural explanations that recognize inequality and discrimination have often been largely ignored.

4. "The color-blind view of 'people as people' runs counter to unique cultural values, hypothesized cultural learning styles, and associated untoward social experiences. For example, the Western values of individualism and competition are in direct conflict with cooperation and collaboration, values of some minority cultures, notably American Indians, Asian Americans, and African Americans."

5. Treatment of minority group members as if they are invisible, portraying them only in a negative light (e.g., crime suspects) or providing only stereotyped, narrow portrayals (e.g., sports figures) result in a very limited and very limiting set of role models for minority children.

6. Many traditional portrayals reflect a "melting pot" perspective that was suggested over 20 years ago and that did not exist then, does not exist now, will not likely come about in the future, and is not desirable.

7. Such exclusionary and inaccurate portrayals are disadvantageous to the broader culture. Their neglect of minority experiences and problem-solving patterns deny the broader culture the opportunity to "be enriched by the talents, creativity, and intelligence of minority youngsters who have been provided an opportunity to reach their potentials" (1990:267–269).

These themes reflect many of the dimensions of traditional and dominant paradigm thinking. They clearly reflect the need for the creation and application of perspectives on the development of people of color based on the dimensions of alternative paradigms. As is the case with understanding traditional paradigm thinking generally, recognizing the weaknesses of traditional approaches to the study of the development of people of color is important for us as social workers if we are going to be advocates for more inclusive, strengths-based perspectives. The alternative perspectives on development and people of color described in the following chapter offer a number of other perspectives to help increase our understanding of HBSE and upon which to base our practice.

SUMMARY/TRANSITION

This chapter introduced a critical perspective from which to view traditional thinking about individual human development. It described the importance for social workers of applying this critical perspective to traditional thinking about individual development in order to recognize its limitations. It also explored the necessity of appreciating the importance, power, and usefulness of traditional paradigm thinking about individual development for effective social work practice.

This chapter then presented several of the most prominent traditional models of individual development. The models explored included the psychoanalytic approach of Freud; the cognitive developmental approach of Piaget; Kohlberg's extension of Piaget's work to the development of moral judgment; the developmental stage-based model of Erikson so often used to guide social workers; the adult development model of Levinson; and the disengagement theory of aging. Each of these models was subjected to analysis and criticism from the perspective of women's developmental experiences to illustrate their neglect and misrepresentation of women. In addition, a number of limitations of the approaches of traditional paradigms to the treatment of people of color were presented.

In the next chapter we continue our analytic/critical approach to thinking about individual development. In addition, we explore a number of alternative perspectives, some of which emerge as extensions of the traditional models explored in this chapter. These alternative perspectives allow us to think about the developmental experiences of the many individuals (women, people of color, persons with disabilities, gay men and lesbians) neglected or omitted entirely from traditional paradigmatic thinking about individual human development. While the models we explored in this chapter are likely to have been familiar to many of us from other courses, our travels in the next chapter are likely to take many of us to destinations quite new to us.

Internet Search Guide

If you want to learn more about some of the topics discussed in this chapter by exploring the Internet, you can search the Net for the terms listed below. Remember that, as you are "surfing" the Net, any of the search terms listed below can take you in many different directions. If you would like to visit specific Web sites related to this chapter, go to the Allyn and Bacon Web site at **http://www.abacon.com** and follow the links to Schriver or *Human Behavior and the Social Environment: Shifting Paradigms in Essential Knowledge for Social Work Practice*. There you will find a selection of sites related to content in this chapter.

1. reductionism
2. determinism
3. Freud
4. Piaget
5. Kohlberg
6. Erikson
7. Daniel Levinson
8. intelligence (IQ)

REFERENCES

Achenbaum, W. A., and Bengtson, V. L. (1994). "Re-engaging the disengagement theory of aging: On the history and assessment of theory development in gerontology." *The Gerontologist, 34*(6): 756–763.

Bergen, D. (1994). *Assessment methods for infants and toddlers: Transdisciplinary team approaches*. New York: Teachers College Press, Columbia University.

Berzoff, Joan. (1989). "From separation to connection: Shifts in understanding." *Affilia, 4*(1): 45–58.

Bloom, Martin. (Ed.). (1985). *Life span development* (2nd ed.). New York: MacMillan.

Chatterjee, P., and Hokenstad, T. (1997). "Should the HBSE Core Curriculum Include International Theories, Research, and Practice?" In M. K. Bloom, W. (Ed.). *Controversial issues in human behavior in the social environment*. Boston: Allyn and Bacon.

Council on Social Work Education (CSWE). (1992). *Handbook of accreditation standards and procedures*. (4th ed.). Alexandria, VA: CSWE. Author.

Cumming, E., and Henry, W. (1961). *Growing old*. New York: Basic Books.

D'Augelli, A. R. (1994). "Identity development and sexual orientation: Toward a model of lesbian, gay, and bisexual development." In Trickett, E. J., Watts, R. J., and Birman, D. (Eds.). *Human diversity: Perspectives on people in context*. San Francisco: Jossey-Bass.

Erikson, Erik H. (1950) *Childhood and society*. New York: W. W. Norton and Company, Inc.

Erikson, Erik H. (1963). *Childhood and society*. (2nd ed.). New York: W. W. Norton and Company, Inc.

Erikson, Erik H. (1968) *Identity: Youth and crisis*. New York: W. W. Norton and Company, Inc.

Gardner, H. (1993). *Multiple intelligences: The theory in practice*. New York: Basic Books.

Gemmill, G., and Oakely, Judith. (1992). "Leadership an alienating social myth?" *Human Relations* 45(2):113–139.

Gilligan, Carol. (1982). *In a different voice: Psychological theory and women's development*. Cambridge: Harvard University Press.

Green, Michael. (1989). *Theories of human development: A comparative approach*. Englewood Cliffs, NJ: Prentice Hall.

Healy, William, Bonner, Augusta, and Bowers, Anna Mae. (1930). *The structure and meaning of psychoanalysis as related to personality and behavior*. New York: Alfred A. Knopf.

Helms, J. E. (1994). "The conceptualization of racial identity and other 'racial' constructs." In Trickett, E. J., Watts, R. J., and Birman, D. (Eds.). *Human diversity: Perspectives on people in context*. San Francisco: Jossey-Bass.

Herrnstein, R. J., and Murray, C. (1994). *The Bell Curve: Intelligence and class structure in American life*. New York: Free Press.

Jendrek, M. P. (1994). "Grandparents who parent their grandchildren: Circumstances and decisions." *The Gerontologist, 34*(2): 206–216.

Levinson, D., and Levinson, J. (1996). *The seasons of a woman's life*. New York: Knopf.

Levinson, Daniel. (1986) "A conception of adult development." *American Psychologist, 41*(1): 3–13.

Levinson, Daniel J., Darrow, Charlotte N., Klein, Edward B., Levinson, Maria H., and McKee, Braxton. (1978). *The seasons of a man's life*. New York: Alfred A. Knopf.

Loevinger, Jane. (1987). *Paradigms of personality*. New York: W. H. Freeman and Company.

Miller, Jean Baker. (1986). *Toward a new psychology of women*. Boston: Beacon.

Miller, Jean Baker. (1991). "The development of women's sense of self." In Jordan, J., Kaplan, A.., Miller, J.B., Stiver, I., and Surrey, J. *Women's growth in connection: Writings from the Stone Center*. New York: Guilford Press.

Miller, R. L. (1992). "The human ecology of multiracial identity." In Root, Maria P. P. (Ed.). *Racially mixed people in America*. Newbury Park, CA: Sage.

Parks, E., Carter, R., and Gushue, G. (July/August 1996). "At the crossroads: Racial and womanist identity development in Black and White women." *Journal of Counseling and Development, 74*: 624–631.

Pharr, Suzanne. (1988). *Homophobia: A weapon of sexism*. Inverness, CA: Chardon Press.

Richards, R. (Spring 1996). "Does the lone genius ride again? Chaos, creativity, and community." *Journal of Humanistic Psychology, 36*(2): 44–60.

Spencer, Margaret Beale. (1990). "Development of minority children: An introduction." *Child Development, 61*:267–269.

Spencer, Margaret B., and Markstrom-Adams, Carol. (1990). "Identity processes among racial and ethnic minority children in America." *Child Development, 61*: 290–310.

Steenbarger, Brett. (1991). "All the world is not a stage: Emerging contextualist themes in counseling and development." *Journal of Counseling and Development, 70*:288.

Szasz, Thomas Stephen. (1961). *The myth of mental illness: Foundations of a theory of personal conduct*. New York: Harper and Row Publishers, Inc.

University of Arkansas Nursery School. (September 1996). *Play*. Typescript. Fayetteville, AR: Author.

Wastell, Colin A. (1996). "Feminist Developmental Theory: Implications for Counseling" *Journal of Counseling and Development 74*:575–581.

Weick, Ann. (1981). "Reframing the person-in-environment perspective." *Social Work, 26*(2): 140.

ILLUSTRATIVE READING 4.1

This reading includes a discussion of the impact of traditional deviance- and deficit-focused conceptual frameworks on African American children. It assesses and analyzes Erikson's stages of childhood and adolescence and Piaget's stages of cognitive development in relation to the developmental experiences of African American children. It includes a helpful discussion of development from the perspective of African American children and adolescents. This is an important expansion of traditional developmental thinking because as Spencer and Markstrom-Adams (1990:304) point out, traditional models of development ignore many of the essential realities of the developmental experiences of minority youth. **Illustrative Reading 4.1** provides an example of how useful alternative perspectives are sometimes possible by extending traditional perspectives to make them more inclusive of the experiences of members of diverse groups. This reading also incorporates information on the important roles of African American families and communities as well as the impact of educational institutions on the development of their children.

Negotiating the World: The Developmental Journey of African American Children*

Paula G. Gomes and C. Aldrena Mabry

Childhood remembrances are always a drag.
> —*N. GIOVANNI,*
> *"Black Judgments"*

The African American child makes a unique journey to both master normal developmental tasks and meet the environmental challenges of racism, discrimination, oppression, and poverty. Despite these barriers, many children of African American families manage to reach high levels of achievement and excellence. Retaining their African heritage has been a past and continuous struggle for African Americans in a society with Eurocentric values and traditions that are psychologically and culturally incompatible. A review of developmental tasks in the context of Africentric perspective provides one structural framework for examining the complexities faced by the the African American child.

The Africentric paradigm rejects the historical notion that African Americans were stripped of their African heritage through the institution of slavery. It proposes that commonalities in language, dialect, spirituality, religion, and philosophical orientation exist between African Americans and their African ancestors. Africentrism rejects the deficit model of child development, which bases normalcy on white, middle-class behavior patterns. The Africentric paradigm supports competence-based, theoretical models of normal child development, which address the values, customs, attitudes, societal goals, and behavioral orientations of African people. As an underlying conceptual framework, this perspective can stimulate new ways of thinking about, understanding, and investigating African American child development.

This chapter reviews theoretical and research approaches to child development, provides an overview of child development, analyzes the socialization role of the African American family, examines the impact of education during the developmental process, and suggests intervention strategies to enhance the maturational processes of the African American child. The goal is to provide information to and enhance the awareness of those dedicated to fostering the optimal growth and development of African American children.

THEORETICAL APPROACHES AND RESEARCH CHALLENGES

Ways of studying child development have been examined, challenged, and reformulated during the past two centuries. The theoretical and research approaches that emerged in response to the growth and development of African American family patterns during and subsequent to slavery were descriptive. By examining slave narratives written during the late 1800s, these studies provided information about child-rearing and socialization practices of early African American families (Du Bois 1908; Herskovitz [1941] 1958; Woodson 1936).

This descriptive approach to examining African American family patterns was replaced by deficit-oriented research models. Deficit-oriented approaches have been used by social and behavioral scientists to determine the innate or constitutional factors that contribute to the discrepancy between the functioning of African American and white children. The underlying premise of the deficit approach is that the behaviors and skills of white middle-class children represent normal patterns of development, while variations observed among children of color are abberations that produce deficits. The biogenetic-hereditarian model proposes that the genetic inferiority of African Americans has contributed to differences in overall functioning between the races. Emerging in the 1930s, the cultural-deprivation model paralleled the biogenetic-hereditarian model, offering an alternative explanation of differences in racial and cultural life-styles. Most researchers focused on what was described as social pathology and inadequate life experiences in the African American community (Baratz and Baratz 1970). African Americans were depicted as pathological and deviant; and the differences observed between them and white Americans were attributed to the inadequacies of African American families and children.

This emphasis on the deficits of African American culture developed because traditional theories of personality and human development fail to provide a comprehensive understanding of African Americans. Therefore, most of the research and theory used to assess African American children's levels of cognitive, emotional, and physiological development and their models of communication, level of play, relationships with parents, and family functioning is based on a Eurocentric paradigm. Theories and research, formulated with insufficient information, result in a focus on the deficiencies rather than the strengths of African American culture.

To change the direction of research and theories, ecological approaches have been applied to the study of African American child development. Ecologically oriented research provides a framework that promotes a sociological and psychological understanding of relationships within and outside the family system (Billingsley, 1968). As summarized by Peters (1981:216): "Ecological research examines Black families and parent-child interaction from a culture-specific or functional perspective, and the Black family's socialization of its children [is] considered in terms of the values and realities of its Afro-American culture."

Ecological models incorporate competence-based approaches to the study of African American children, which expand the understanding of family practices (parent/child interactions, child rearing, socialization). Competence-based models acknowledge the unique coping and cognitive problem-solving skills that African American children must incorporate into their behavioral repertoire in order to survive the effects of racism and discrimination. The cultural-difference, comparative-relevant, and Africentric models are ecological approaches that have been applied to the study of African Americans.

The cultural-difference and comparative-relevant models promote cultural pluralism and the exploration of social, linguistic, familial, and behavioral practices of culturally different people (Allen 1978; Baratz and Baratz 1970; Labov 1970). Most of the published research focuses primarily on low-income African American children, consists of comparative and interracial studies, and omits race-homogeneous studies (L. Grant 1988; McLloyd and Randolph 1984). According to McLloyd and Randolph (1984), these works impede the development of a rich knowledge base about African American children and limit the understanding of intragroup variability and functioning. The Africentric model, in contrast, promotes the examination of family structure and life-style, cultural practices and adaptations, intragroup differences, interdependent relationships to other racial and ethnic groups, and the biculturation process.

Examination of the theoretical and research approaches used to investigate the process of African American child development points to the conceptual gaps and failures of traditional Eurocentric models. The significant decrease in research articles published by mainstream journals about African American children has generated great concern (L. Grant 1988; McLloyd and Randolph 1984). Rogoff and Morelli (1989) report that researchers are beginning to respond to this concern. They indicate that "pioneering researchers of minorities are beginning to look at the contexts in which children from different cultures develop; and these efforts provide a basis for greater understanding of how culture channels development. Some of the most interesting efforts involve combining approaches from anthropology and education with those of psychology" (p. 347). Research conducted from a multicultural, multidisciplinary perspective is deemed necessary to generate reliable information about cultural differences and human functioning. The challenges for researchers in the social sciences studying African American children and culture are to synthesize observational data gathered in qualitative research studies; to develop theoretical constructs, propositions, and hypotheses; and to proceed with quantitative research. Acquisition and reliable data is crucial for validating theories about the growth and development of African American children.

MATURATIONAL PROCESSES AND SOCIALIZATION

As with other children, the African American child's introduction to the world is through the eyes of parents and family members. Family beliefs and experiences determine, for example, the racial views and perspectives the family presents to the child. Family beliefs, attitudes, and behavior contribute to the child's political and spiritual beliefs and the child's attitude toward race. Socioeconomic status, race, religion, and geographic location are variables that influence the family's socialization practices. This socialization process dictates the child's initial response to education and school, which is the second major socialization experience for children. Educational settings also affect the maturational process of the child by promoting cognitive, affective, and social development. School experiences may support or challenge the lessons learned in the home. The integration of these experiences contributes to the child's self-esteem, achievement, motivation, and sense of identity, and determines how the child interacts, adapts, and attains personal goals in the environment.

This section provides an overview of the socialization experiences of African American children in nuclear and extended families, school, and the community. The roles of race, gender, and class in these various settings are examined, and peer relations and identity issues are explored to determine how they influence the African American child's ability to negotiate and function in the American environment.

Prenatal Period

Healthy child development involves the interaction of genetic and environmental factors (Hetherington and Parke 1975). The biological process begins with conception and progresses as the zygote subdivides into millions of other cells by the process of mitosis (Bichler 1976). This tiny cell subdivision begins the process of development of the organs, systems, and functions of the human body. Within two to eight weeks, the zygote becomes an embryo, which is about one inch in length. Although development is primitive at this level, all major organs and body systems are developing. Development follows the orthogenetic principle of progression through stages, from undifferentiated to differentiated to integrated. For example, during the fetal period, although there is rapid muscular development, the nervous system is also becoming mature, and differentiation leads to the emergence of a system with increasingly refined and circumscribed reflexes, responses, and movements (Hetherington and Parke 1975). Massive gross development occurs prior to fine, integrated functioning.

As the human fetus emerges during the developmental process, expectant mothers report that by the end of the fourth or fifth month the fetus at least occasionally moves, kicks, and hiccups. By the sixth month, the eyes of the human fetus have developed, and the opening and closing of the eyes may occur. By twenty-eight weeks, the fetus enters the age of viability, where the physical systems are sufficiently advanced so that if birth occurs, the infant may survive outside the womb (Hetherington and Parke 1975). Although normal development occurs in a fixed, invariable sequence, with body parts and systems developing at approximately the same time in all fetuses, females have been found to be more developmentally advanced at birth than males. The exact cause of this gender difference is unknown.

The human fetus is most susceptible to extraneous stimuli during the first trimester of the prenatal period. Pregnancy risk factors, which include the mother's dietary habits, preexisting health conditions, as well as the ingestion of nicotine, alcohol, drugs, and other nonnutritive substances, have been found to significantly threaten or alter normal health and development of the fetus (Bichler 1976).

Sickle cell anemia is a hereditary birth defect that seems to be carried through the genetic structure of about 8 percent of African Americans. In most, the tendency of the blood to sickle is not associated with deleterious symptoms. About one in forty, however, is afflicted with the severe, chronic, and sometimes fatal form of sickle cell anemia (Hetherington and Parke 1975). Adverse symptoms tend to occur most often either when both parents of the child are carriers of the sickling gene or at very high altitudes, where oxygen deprivation causes the blood vessels to clog, causing severe pain, tissue damage, and death when critical vessels are blocked in the brain and lungs.

Infancy

The normal human baby emerges from the warm, secure environment of the mother's womb after approximately forty weeks. At birth, the infant's behavior is innate and instinctual. Sucking, grasping, crying, and rooting reflexes are present. The newborn infant is motivated primarily toward pleasure and survival. In the early months, infants sleep, eat, and visually explore bright colors, patterns, and light in their environment. The human face, particularly that of the mother or primary caretaker, is also a major orienting visual stimulus (Hetherington and Parke 1975). The infant quickly learns that the caretaker's presence signals the beginning of feeding, touching, and other caretaking activities. The special relationship or bonding between infant and caretaker that occurs during the early phase of life determines how the child explores and responds to the environment. The nature of this relationship affects later psychomotor, cognitive, and psychological development (Bettelheim, 1967; Bowlby 1958; Ribble 1944).

Erik Erikson (1963) postulated that each individual goes through eight stages or crises in order to achieve mastery of the environment. How successfully the child negotiates each of these stages or crises determines, according to Erikson, his or her subsequent ability to cope with each of the succeeding crises in child development. Erikson's first stage—basic trust versus mistrust—corresponds to birth through the first year of life. The development of trust depends on the parents' success in meeting the child's needs during the first year. For Erikson, when the child can confidently expect need reduction and love, this expectation is generalized to the world at large. However, when care and need reduction are inconsistent, inadequate, and filled with continual rejection, the child's world view becomes one of suspicion and mistrust (Elkind 1970).

Studies of effective child-rearing techniques during infancy demonstrate that good mothers or good caretakers use physical contact and soothe their children with contact, have a heightened sensitivity to the infant's signals of discomfort and insecurities, establish feelings of mutual delight between themselves and their children, and encourage the children to feel that they have the capabilities to affect and change their environment (Biehler 1976).

During the first two years of life, the human infant experiences rapid growth and adjustment to the new environment. The innate, instinctual orienting reflexes progress into large, complex movements that are coordinated and voluntary. Psychomotor development in childhood has been studied over the years to examine the specific ages at which children achieve certain milestones. Bayley (1965) examined the development of African American children and found a general trend toward psychomotor superiority in development, which he suggested was genetically determined. In addition, Smart and Smart (1972) reported that African American children's teeth erupt early and permanent teeth are more mature and larger in size than those of white American children.

Although the sequence of psychomotor development is the same among children, the exact ages of skill acquisition vary within a wide range. The average child, for example, starts walking at twelve to thirteen months of age, although others may start at nine months and for some children walking may be delayed until eighteen months. The current child-development literature deemphasizes exact timetables for various psychomotor stages and, instead, encourages appreciation of individual differences. When overall development is delayed, physicians and other professionals recommend various tests to assess the child's development.

Cognitive development is the process whereby the infant organizes, stores, and memorizes information, and otherwise makes intellectual sense of the environment. The infant is born with some cognitive processes, while others evolve from interactions with and experiences in the environment. Jean Piaget's (1926) theory of cognitive development has been widely accepted as universal. According to this theory the infant and child actively explore and manipulate the environment in order to understand, and, therefore, adapt to it. For Piaget, the process of adaptation begins at birth with universal, innate reflexes and continues into various other stages as the infant discovers increasingly sophisticated modes of operation. The infant is born with a schema, a basic pattern of organized behavior. Adaptation includes two processes: assimilation and accommodation. In assimilation the infant utilizes and interprets new information and incorporates it into the already existing schema. In accommodation the infant changes responses to environmental demands. When the new experiences do not fit into the existing schema, the infant changes to accommodate the new information.

Piaget identified four crucial stages of cognitive development: sensorimotor, preoperational, concrete operations, and formal operations. Although it is widely accepted that all children pass through the stages in the same order, Piaget (1970) also posited that all children go through the stages at about the same ages. The stages build on each other, and the attainments in later stages depend on the mastery of developmental tasks in previous stages. The sensorimotor stage exists from birth to about two years of age. It is categorized by progress in the development of reflexes and habits, and by the imitation and initiation of language. Object permanence is established, whereby the child is able to understand that objects in the environment are permanent and exist in cognitive awareness even when out of visual sight. The child's attention is oriented primarily toward things that move in the environment.

Language development in children appears to be a universal phenomenon; all children, regardless of race, are born with a genetic endowment to learn the complex system of rules needed for communications with a society (Hetherington and Parke 1975). During the first few weeks of life, the infant learns to distinguish the human voice from nonhuman sounds. The mother or primary caretaker's voice is distinguishable from that of other humans. The infant is also capable within the first few weeks of modulating cooing and babbling in response to other sounds. Papolia and Olds (1925) reported that all children, regardless of culture or background, make the same initial sounds (phonemes) and follow the same basic rate, sequence, and rules in language acquisition. All children are believed to acquire language through the processes of imitation, repetition, and reinforcement (Piaget 1926). First words are usually spoken near the end of the first year. One- and two-word phrases occur on the average between eighteen and twenty-four months of age. Language at this stage reflects the child's incomplete cognitive organization. For example, "car" may be used to refer to trucks, cars, and other types of transportation. Although the child may understand that a truck and a car are different, "car" is the only word the child has for vehicles at this stage.

Lenneberg (1967) found that human language-learning capacity is a correlate or result of the maturational process. Houston (1970) postulated that the development of language may be innate or biologically determined. Chomsky (1968) found that children learn language as a result of being placed in an environment where language is spoken. Osser (1970) agreed that the child learns the unique structural rules and linguistic codes of the language within a specific environment. Language development thus appears to be the natural result of the child's innate ability, the child's readiness to learn as a result of maturational and growth processes, and the impact of the spoken language in the particular cultural environment.

Early Childhood

Early childhood refers to ages two to six. Piaget's preoperational stage (two to seven years) corresponds to this stage of development, which is characterized by language acquisition (discussed later in this section). Symbolic and fantasy play activities are also present. The preoperational child is egocentric and unable to take another person's point of view. The child cannot fully comprehend the nature of relationships or the idea of reciprocity. Although capable of understanding that he or she has a brother, the child is unable to comprehend that the brother has a sister. The child centers on one unique feature of an object (for example, color or shape) and is unable to integrate other features.

Erikson's second stage—autonomy versus shame and doubt—occurs in the second year of life, and the third stage—initiative versus guilt—occurs from the third through fifth year; combined, these stages correspond to early childhood. Erikson (1963) argued that in the second stage, the child begins to demonstrate new motor and mental abilities, and is proud of the initiation and development of these skills. According to Erikson, if the child's ability to manipulate is not supported and encouraged, or if the parents or caretakers do for the child what he or she is capable of doing for himself or herself, feelings of shame and doubt are reinforced. These feelings will later interfere with autonomy strivings in adolescence (Elkind 1970). In the third stage—initiative versus guilt—parents and caretakers must give children the freedom to initiate their own motor responses and not restrict their self-motivated behaviors, play, or questions.

Play is a universal activity among children; it contributes to and influences the developmental process. Many psychologists and researchers in child development (Comer and Poussaint 1976; Erikson 1963; Piaget and Inhelder 1969; Wilson 1978) view play as crucial "child's work," necessary for healthy cognitive, social, and emotional growth. The type of play varies according to the age of the developing child. The child begins by engaging in solitary play. Parallel play, or playing alongside another child, is later established. Cooperative play, where the child is able to interact with another in play (for example, by throwing a ball), is achieved during the first and second years.

Through play, the child expresses and develops an understanding of the world by mastering and manipulating the environment through fantasy and imagination. Children imitate and practice what they see, hear, and experience in the environment. Piaget (1926) indicated that play facilitates cognitive development. Themes in play can represent perceptions of the social and emotional experiences in children's lives. Toys serve as their bridge to reality. When toys are specific replicas of objects in the environment, children can use them to understand the adult world.

Applying Erikson's theory to the African American child, DiAngi (1976) suggests that cultural factors, child-rearing practices, and racial and skin-color prejudices within the family and society may help or hinder the progression of the child through these stages. For example, if parents favor one child over another because of skin color or discourage the child's autonomy and initiative because of racism in the society, the child does not develop a positive self-image or world view because natural strivings for trust, autonomy, and initiative are frustrated. Subsequently, the child develops a negative self-image, becomes distrustful of others, and feels guilty about suppressing the drive to achieve and master the environment.

Most researchers have found that ethnoracial awareness starts in early childhood, between the ages of three and five (Clark and Clark 1939; McAdoo 1985; Powell-Hopson and Hopson 1988; Semaj 1980). According to Semaj (1980:77–78):

> By age 4 or 5, children understand that people are categorized into various ethno-racial groups and have some understanding of the group to which they belong, but do not understand the permanence of this classification. Between the ages of 6 and 9, the child's cognitive abilities mature resulting in the acquisition of conversation abilities and the development of racial constancy. By the ages of 8 [to] 11, impersonal and social cognitive development increases, revealing qualitative and quantitative changes in social affect to race.

Semaj stresses that in response to increased experiences with prejudice, the child may lose some of the positive identification with being African American that had been achieved at an early age. He suggests that "Black children in America do not hate themselves, but many do achieve what can be considered a bicultural identity by age 11" (p. 77). This process requires balancing two cultures, which results in the loss or devaluation of personal and cultural perspectives in order to integrate the views of the majority culture.

Language and acquisition takes place at a rapid pace between the ages of twenty and thirty-six months. The child's vocabulary expands greatly to incorporate reality. Some stuttering and disfluencies in the child's speech are common during this period but usually disappear by the age of four. By then, most children comprehend basic rules of grammar and syntax. They can make meaningful sentences within their limited linguistic repertoire.

Hunt (1969) found that until the age of two, the cognitive developmental processes of the African American child do not differ significantly from those of children in other cultures. After the age of two, however, when children learn to label the events and objects around them with language, the labels used by the African American child and the linguistic models by which the African American child communicates are different because the environment is culturally different although the process of labeling is not different. The African American child is not deficient in communication skills but merely uses different labels to define the experiential and environmental milieu.

Although there are commonalities in the language of African Americans and white Americans because of interaction and imitation between the cultures, Wilson (1978) reports that 80 percent of African Americans speak a "radical, nonstandard" English called "Black English." Black English reflects history, a vast cultural background, and the blending of the diverse languages of different African tribes with the language of the Europeans.

Late Childhood

Late childhood, ages six to twelve, corresponds to Piaget's stage of concrete operations (ages seven to eleven). It is characterized by the child's awareness of immediate reality, or the "here and now." The child has an organized system by which objects are manipulated in the environment. Although less egocentric, the child has difficulty understanding the hypothetical and is unable to go far beyond concrete experience. Erikson's fourth stage—industry versus inferiority—occurs in late childhood, from the age of six to the onset of puberty. According to Erikson, the child in this stage develops a sense of "industry" and starts to receive some systematic instruction in school. The role and influence of parents, teachers, and peers are important to help the child master industry. Parents and teachers must encourage the child to ask questions, to make things, and to finish incomplete projects. If the efforts of the child are ridiculed instead of rewarded, the child develops feelings of inferiority and may not try to perform at his or her best. Once feelings of inferiority exist, the child's desire for work may diminish (Elkind 1970).

DiAngi (1976) notes that to negotiate this stage successfully an African American child must be placed in an environment where he or she is continually challenged, stimulated, and encouraged to learn and achieve. If the child is in an atmosphere that is not conducive to learning, frustration may lead to the internalization of negative feelings. The African American child may then develop a negative attitude toward the academic experience and may seek success among peers who share these frustrations.

During Piaget's concrete-and-formal-operations stage, age seven and above, the child is capable of daydreaming and fantasy, which are forms of mental play. Role playing and imitation of adults (mother, father, teacher) are other aspects of this type of play; with them the child learns to experience another's point of reference. McLloyd (1985) described this type of play as pretend play and views it as valuable in cognitive development. Shade and Edwards (1987), observing African American children at play, posit that pretend play is oriented toward the mimicry of people and situations observed within the African American community. Pelligrini (1980) found a strong positive correlation between high frequency of sociodrama and pretend play and skills in reading, spoken language, and writing.

Huizinga (1950) examines play as a social and cultural construction and suggests that it involves the various archetypal activities of different cultures. White (1980) suggests that most African American children are likely to be involved in creative play in which they use castoff furniture and other objects found in their environment. Individual play—where the children interact with toys and objects such as crayons, paper, pencils, and blocks—occurs less often. As the maturational process proceeds in late childhood, play becomes increasingly social. Through sports and games the child explores relationships, rules, roles, and expectations, and learns as well how to get along with others in an adaptive fashion. The child learns to cope with losing and fighting, and how to manage conflicts during cooperative play. Through reading, storytelling, listening to the radio, and watching television, the developing child attempts to understand and conceptualize further.

Shade and Edwards (1987) present the possibility that the kind of play encouraged in the African American family reinforces the values and goals of the culture. It provides the children with the opportunity to negotiate hierarchical relationships, accurately perceive emotions, and empathize with others, all of which are important traits of children with high social intelligence.

Gender-role identification also occurs in late childhood. The socialization experiences of the child in the home, school, and community significantly influence this developmental process. When children are exposed to traditional and non-traditional role models and experiences, they may develop a broad repertoire of gender-role behaviors. The presence of parents, teachers, and other role models has a significant effect on the identity of boys and girls. For African American boys, in particular, a positive relationship with a consistent male role model enhances gender-role development. In the absence of this relationship, other males, including peers, may become the primary socializing agents and have a strong influence on a boy's self-discipline, sex-role development, morality, academic achievement, and interpersonal relationships (Hare 1987; Kunjufu 1984, 1986a, 1986b; Wilson 1978).

Preadolescence and Adolescence

Preadolescence lasts from twelve to fourteen. According to Piaget, from the age of twelve the child is in the stage of formal operations. With abstract reasoning skills established, the child can now engage in higher-level thought processes. The child is capable of problem solving and deductive reasoning. The child also becomes interested in and preoccupied with rules. People who disobey rules, as perceived by the formal-operations child, should be severely punished.

Erikson's fifth stage—identity versus role confusion—is one of the most critical, occurring during the period of adolescence. Adolescents seek some semblance of harmony and order within themselves and the world. If this harmony is not achieved, the result is role confusion. During adolescence peer relations are a major influence in psychological functioning. The youth peer group has been identified as an established entity in the African American community; in it adolescents seek approval, esteem, opportunities for achievement, and positive recognition (Hare 1987; Kunjufu 1984). For many African American youth, these peer experiences are critical because they encourage the achievement of competence, personal growth, and independence by creating a sense of belonging and connectedness for the adolescent.

As African American children enter late adolescence, they begin to solidify their racial identity. Researchers have developed various models to illustrate the stages of race consciousness and identity development that move African Americans from feelings of pain to a sense of pride (Cross 1971; Milliones 1980; Jackson 1976; Thomas 1971). Successful acquisition of a positive African American identity requires synthesis of internal and external experiences. This process is influenced by cultural, familial, societal, and historical factors. African American families and communities can assist adolescents in developing a positive racial identity by celebrating the unique aspects of African American culture.

Grier and Cobbs (1968) maintain that if the African American adolescent fails to establish a place in the societal group, a negative individual or group identity may develop. For economically and emotionally deprived African American youth, severe frustration and negative self-images may cause identification with peers who reject societal norms. Juvenile delinquency, criminal and violent activity, gang membership, and other acts of rebellion may result. Increases in economic distress, single parenting, and negative views about education have left many adolescents vulnerable to the short-term gratification of delinquent activities.

Sexual-identity development is influenced by physical and emotional maturation during preadolescence and adolescence. This period of sexual exploration is marked by confusion because of physiological changes, social pressures, and awareness of moral issues, and identification of sexual feelings and preferences. Adolescent sexual behavior is a major concern because of high rates of teen pregnancy, early sexual experimentation, sexually transmitted diseases, and the acquired-immune-deficiency (AIDS) epidemic. Despite sex education, media campaigns, AIDS-prevention efforts, and high mortality rates, adolescents continue to engage in unprotected sexual activity (Brooks-Gunn, Boyer, and Hern 1988; Brooks-Gunn and Furstenburg 1989; Jenkins 1988). For many adolescents, engaging in risky sexual activities is the result of a combination of factors. Mastery of the developmental task of long-term planning and anticipation of consequences is achieved during this stage of maturation. Therefore, an adolescent's failure to employ mature decision-making and reasoning skills regarding sexual activities may be due to developmental immaturity.

According to Erikson, if the tasks of this stage are not successfully completed, the adolescent is not adequately prepared for adulthood and the later stages of development, which are characterized by intimacy, generativity, integrity. Therefore, an environment that provides support and creative solutions is needed to assist adolescents through this confusing and challenging developmental stage.

FAMILIES: SOURCES OF HOPE, STRENGTH, AND SURVIVAL SKILLS

The African American family plays an important and crucial role in the developmental process of the child by creating the surroundings for the initial socialization experiences. The family meets the basic physical and emotional needs of the child, supplies guidance in the mastery of intrapsychic and developmental tasks, and prepares the child to survive and cope in an oppressive society. The goal for many parents is to assist the child with the development of survival skills that will aid in the attainment of self-actualization. African American nuclear and extended families meet these various challenges during the developmental years through cultural, traditional, and historical channels.

The African American family has been described in various ways. Billingsley (1968) sees it as a unit embedded in a network of interdependent relationships within the African American community and the wider (white) society. Shimkin and Uchendu (1978) highlight the unique cultural resources within families. Nobles (1981) describes the African American family as emphasizing strong family ties, unconditional love, and respect for self and others. The family facilitates acceptance, validation, and the transmission of knowledge and information critical to the survival of the members. Besides these qualities, Hill (1972) delineates five strengths of African American families: a strong work orientation; extended family bonds; egalitarian role functioning; strong religious orientation; and educational aspirations.

Recent economic changes in the United States have effected African American families by increasing the rates of unemployment, poverty, and crime. Wilson (1989: 381) reports that "most Black families are not poor, however, 31% in recent decades lived in poverty and 52% of Black one-parent families were classified as poor." African American children are more likely than white American children to be raised in a poor, single-parent household and to be more confronted with the stressors of lack of time, money, and energy that contribute to emotional distress and frustration (Hare 1987; Kunjufu 1984). These children are usually more vulnerable than others to child abuse, inadequate nutrition and health care, suicide, crime, and emotional deprivation.

Demographic shifts, changes in family structure, and the movement from overt to subtle forms of racism in the United States pose further difficult challenges for

African American children today. In most two-parent families, both parents are working, and they are living away from extended-family members. The number of single-parent families has risen as a result of increases in the divorce rate, increases in teenage motherhood, and the personal choices of women and men. These societal changes have led to increased demands for day care and after-school activities and have decreased the time parents have available for their children.

Nevertheless, the extended family continues to be a major source of support for single- and two-parent families. In the African American community, this family pattern provides direct and indirect support for children and others (Tatum, 1987; Wilson 1989). Wilson (1989:380) indicates that "the extended family's central feature, the familial support network," is manifested in the family members' "propinquity, communications, and cooperation."

African American parents in predominantly white communities face the challenge of providing cultural and community activities that promote children's exposure to and familiarity with African American culture. Tatum (1987) studied middle-class African American families residing in predominantly white communities and their process of survival. She highlighted the complexities of biculturation and specific strategies to manage the social difficulties their children faced. She found that the retention of traditional African American values—promotion of education, religious affiliation and involvement, mutual support and cooperation of family members, and close relationships with extended family—contributed to the survival and success of these families. Parents can also use the resources of the African American community, through religious and volunteer groups, social and public-service organizations, athletic and educational networks, and mental health and prevention services to meet the needs of their children.

The African American child must integrate African American and Euro-American cultural values in order to achieve and to succeed in school, employment, and social interactions. This socialization process may create feelings of ambivalence and frustration because of the inherent racism that exists in American society. For example, when African American children enter school they are often expected to communicate, interact, and learn according to styles that are distinctly different from their styles at home (Ogbu 1985; Vogt, Jordan, and Thorp 1987). The preferred or accepted styles of communication are based on Euro-American norms and must be utilized or adhered to in school and work settings. The implicit message is that African American styles of talking, walking, dressing, thinking, and interacting are not acceptable (Ogbu 1985). African American families, therefore, must counteract these messages by providing educational experiences that are rich in culture and tradition.

THE IMPACT OF EDUCATION

Children spend most of their time once they are school age in educational settings. They move from the major influence of family members to that of teachers, curriculum, and classmates. Schooling fosters "cognitive, affective and social development; and influences the development of a stable self image, acquisition of interaction skills with classmates and peers, learning of social customs and mores, coming to like or dislike school and many other things" (Entwisle and Alexander 1988:450).

The child's initial response to school and the academic process is greatly influenced by parental views on education. Family and community perspectives may vary from identifying education as the primary strategy for surviving, or "making it," in an oppressive society, to viewing it as a major contributor to oppression.

In the classroom, the teacher's responses, comfort level with students of color, views, and expectations influence the child's academic success. Many teachers are confused about how to treat and instruct students of color in their classes. Teaching approaches vary from ignoring to becoming too involved in the student's life. C. Grant (1988) indicates that some teachers take the color-blind approach; some involve students of color when a yearly cultural event happens; and some become "missionaries" in order to help the student. Grant stresses that these efforts usually result in negative responses to education and the academic experience.

Holliday (1985) reports that African American children are socialized to employ a persistent, assertive problem-solving style. However, teachers often reject these traits and label them as inappropriate, which contributes to the child's sense of helplessness. Kunjufu (1984) identifies the fourth grade as a pivotal year for African American boys in academic and personal achievement. Kunjufu attributes the decline in their performance during this year to "less-than-deserved teacher competency in the primary grades, few male teachers, parental apathy, increased peer pressure, and greater emphasis on mass media" (p. 15). These stressors influence the process of adjustment and future academic success of the African American child.

For some minority children, adjustment difficulties in the classroom have been attributed to their cultural backgrounds and exposure to interactional learning styles that are different from those of the mainstream public school (Ogbu 1987). As we have seen, African American children in predominantly white schools are required to master white learning styles and behavior patterns, to cope with being different and the external responses to those differences, and to manage resistance to their presence by finding ways to integrate into the environment. Predominantly African American schools may foster a cultural milieu that conflicts with the larger society's beliefs and expectations of the educational process. Therefore, in many of these academic institutions, traditional Euro-American values are incorporated into the curriculum to instruct students about these differences. The Eurocentric focus of the American educational system has denied all students the opportunity to learn about the racially diverse Americans of the United States. Requirements for school systems include the integration of a multicultural educational model, modifications in curricula and textbooks, attention to diverse learning styles, the use of teaching styles that empower all students, and the promotion of social change (C. Grant 1988; Royal 1988).

Ogbu (1987) observes that beyond cultural differences in the learning process, academic adjustment problems, especially for African American children, are related to distrust of educational institutions because of perceptions of past and current maltreatment and discrimination. If children see individuals in their community who have been given an inadequate education, who have been discriminated against in finding jobs, and who have otherwise been the victims of institutionalized racism, their motivation to achieve academically is diminished. Many African American communities have established programs and cultural experiences for children to compensate for the educational and socialization gaps that exist in most school systems and in some African American family networks.

Many researchers have attempted to identify the factors contributing to the poor school achievement of low-income African American children, the disproportionate number of minority children in educable mentally retarded classes, and motivation difficulties of African American children. Many studies in this area have focused on intelligence testing. The I.Q.-testing debate has primarily highlighted the consistent fifteen-point difference in scores between African Americans and white Americans. Some researchers have attributed the discrepancies in functioning between African American and white children to cultural deprivation, low self-esteem, and genetic inferiority of African American children (Eysenck 1971; Jensen 1969; Shockley 1972). Educators, researchers, and other professionals have challenged these claims and proposed that the cultural bias of assessment techniques, examiner and teacher variables, and substandard educational opportunities are responsible for difficulties faced by African American children on I.Q. tests (Kaufman 1979; Kunjufu 1984; *Larry P. v. Wilson Riles;* C-71-2270 (N.D. Cal.) 1979; Manni, Winikur, and Keller 1984; Mercer and Ysseldyke 1979). Factors affecting I.Q.-test performance continue to be a prominent focus also in the psychological literature.

Moore (1987) found that significant differences between African American and white children occur because of the cultural milieus in which they are socialized. Parental education, income, and child-rearing practices were also found to be major factors that influenced ethnic-group differences in children's skill and performance levels (Moore 1985, 1987). Unfortunately, many studies have focused on the deficits of African American children instead of examining the limitations of the educational environment, the curriculum, assessment techniques, and the intelligence paradigm.

Limited attention has been given to the study of learning potential and learning styles. Learning potential, according to Feurstein (1979), is the individual's ability to become "modified" by a learning experience. "Modifiability" is an individual's capacity for "acting on and responding to sources of information" (Manni, Winikur, and Keller 1984:104). In their use of assessment techniques, many examiners fail to assess what children can learn and focus primarily on what they have already learned. Learning style has been defined by certain cognitive, affective, and psychological behaviors that serve as relatively stable indicators of how learners perceive, interact with, and respond to the learning environment. Emichovich and Miller (1988) reviewed studies on the matching of teaching and learning styles and found significant increases in academic achievement and positive attitudes toward learning when students were taught according to their learning style. Many African American children employ a relational learning style (Akbar 1981; Hale 1982; Kunjufu 1984), which is characterized as one that emphasizes the unique and specific qualities of a phenomenon, notions of difference rather than variations or commonalities of things, fluent spoken language, and affective responses. Further research is needed to investigate teaching and learning styles in order to enhance the educational process for African American children.

Curriculum development and educational reform continue to be a major focus of early childhood education research. C. Grant (1988) proposed the implementation of an education program based on an integrated analysis of class, race, and gender. The goal is for students to understand the effects of power, economics, and culture in society so that they become able to serve the interests of all citizens, especially people of color, the poor, women, and individuals with handicapping conditions. In other words, changes in programming, curriculum, and teaching styles must parallel actual changes in the educational and employment opportunities available to African Americans and others. Teachers and other professionals have an ultimate responsibility to provide quality education for all students. An important feature of education should be to empower students to achieve, and to confront social and cultural barriers to success.

ENHANCING DEVELOPMENTAL EXPERIENCES

The many factors that contribute to the developmental experiences of African American children continue to be explored, challenged, and investigated by social scientists. The conceptual gaps of traditional theoretical and research models are illustrated by the omission of race-homogeneous studies in the literature, which can provide valuable insights about the diversity of African Americans. Research conducted from a multicultural, multidisciplinary perspective is necessary for the acquisition of reliable information pertaining to cultural differences and human functioning. The challenge for researchers interested in the development of African American children is to determine how culture influences the development process. Synthesis of observational data gathered in qualitative research studies that examine all aspects (familial, social, educational, cultural) of the African American child's life is critical.

The African American family assumes an important role in the developmental process by molding and shaping the infant's experiences with the environment. Parents or caretakers should provide consistent physical contact and stimulation for the infant. In early childhood, caretakers should encourage the inherent drive for mastery and support strivings for independence demonstrated by the toddler. During the stages of early childhood, late childhood, and adolescence, children should be exposed to traditional and nontraditional gender-role models and experiences, and to the rich traditions and practices of African American culture. These experiences foster positive racial and gender-role identity and increase self-esteem. Nuclear and extended families can assist the African American child to develop survival skills that promote self-actualization. Families can provide a secure environment of support, acceptance, and validation in which the child can experiment and can practice skills necessary for achievement. The family, through the transmission of knowledge, information, and past experiences of family members, can help the child understand the biculturation process and internalize the valuable lessons needed to overcome societal barriers to success.

Because children spend most of their time in educational settings, school systems must examine the impact of the educational process on all children. Most studies that investigate education and African American children focus on the deficiencies of the children instead of the limitations of the educational programming, assessment techniques, and classroom structure. School systems must integrate a multicultural educational model, modify curricula and textbooks, acknowledge diversity in learning styles, and utilize teaching styles that empower all students.

The African American community has a strong tradition of emphasizing the importance of history, education, and achievement. This community must continue to provide complementary educational opportunities that focus on cultural awareness, social advancement, and historical events to enhance the racial and ethnic pride of African American children. In order to respond to the increased and growing national crises of poverty, crime, drugs, homelessness, teen pregnancy, AIDS, homicide, and suicide, the African American community must generate the strength and energy to combat these social tragedies. Religious and volunteer groups (African American churches and Big Brothers and Big Sisters of America), social and public-service organizations (fraternities, sororities, civil rights organizations, leadership-skills groups), athletic and educational networks (mentor and tutorial programs), and mental health and prevention services (Head Start, teen support groups) must respond to the special needs of children in the African American community. African American families must utilize community mental health services that provide comprehensive support to children, adults, couples, families, and special groups facing stressful life circumstances. Family and community networking is needed to give African American children the necessary problem-solving, mediation, and negotiation skills for surviving the challenges of their developmental journey.

REFERENCES

Akbar, N. 1981. "Cultural Expressions of the African American Child." *Black Child Journal* 2:10.

Allen, W. R. 1978. "The Search for Applicable Theories in Black Family Life." *Journal of Marriage and the Family* 40:117–129.

Baratz, S., and J. Baratz. 1970. "Early Childhood Interventions: The Social Science Base for Institutional Racism." *Harvard Educational Review* 40(1):29–47.

Bayley, N. 1965. "Comparison of Mental and Motor Test Scores for Age 1–15 Months by Sex, Birth Order, Race, Geographic Location and Parents." *Child Development* 36:379–412.

Biehler, R. F. 1976. *Child Development: An Introduction.* Boston: Houghton Mifflin.

Bettelheim, B. 1967. "Where Self Begins." *New York Times Magazine,* February 12.

Billingsley, A., 1968. *Black Families in White America.* Englewood Cliffs, N.J.: Prentice-Hall.

Bowlby, J. 1958. "The Nature of the Child's Tie to His Mother." *International Journal of Psychoanalysis* 39:35.

Brooks-Gunn, J., C. Boyer, and K. Hern. 1988. "Preventing HIV Infection and AIDS in Children and Adolescents." *American Psychologist* 43(11): 958–964.

Brooks-Gunn, J., and F. Furstenburg. 1989. "Adolescent Sexual Behavior." *American Psychologist* 44(2):249–257.

Chomsky, N. 1968. *Syntactic Structures.* The Hague: Mouton.

Clark, K. B., and M. P. Clark, 1939. "The Development of Consciousness of Self and the Emergence of Racial Identification in Negro Preschool Children." *Journal of Social Psychology* 10:591–599.

Comer, J. P., and A. F. Poussaint. 1976. *Black Child Care.* New York: Simon & Schuster.

Cross, W. E. 1971. "Negro-to-Black Conversion Experience: Toward a Psychology of Black Liberation." *Black World* 29(9):13–27.

DiAngi, P. 1976. "Erikson's Theory of Personality Development as Applied to the Black Child." *Perspectives in Psychiatric Care* 14(4):184–185.

Du Bois, W. E. B. 1908. *The Negro American Family.* Atlanta: Atlanta University Press.

Elkind, D. 1970. "Erik Erikson's Eight Stages of Man." *New York Times Magazine* April 5.

Emichovich, C., and G. E. Miller. 1988. "Effects of Logo and Cai on Black First Graders' Achievement, Reflectivity and Self Esteem." *Elementary School Journal* 88(5):473–487.

Entwisle, D. R., and K. L. Alexander. 1988. "Factors Affecting Achievement Test Scores and Marks of Black and White First Graders." *Elementary School Journal* 88(5):449–471.

Erikson, E. 1963. *Childhood and Society.* New York: Norton.

Eysenck, H. J. 1971. *The IQ Argument.* New York: Library Press.

Feurstein, R. 1979. *The Dynamic Assessment of Retarded Performers: The Learning Potential Assessment Device, Theory, Instruments and Techniques.* Baltimore: University Park Press.

Grant, C. 1988. "The Persistent Significance of Race in Schooling." *Elementary School Journal* 88(5):561–569.

Grant, L. 1988. "Introduction: Regenerating and Refocusing Research on Minorities and Education." *Elementary School Journal* 88(5):441–448.

Grier, W. H., and P. M. Cobbs, 1968. *Black Rage*. New York: Basic Books.

Hale, J. E. 1982. *Black Children: Their Roots, Cultures, and Learning Styles*. Provo, Utah: Brigham Young University Press.

Hare, B. R. 1987. "Structural Inequality and the Endangered Status of Black Youth." *Journal of Negro Education* 56(1):100–121.

Herskovits, M. J. [1941] 1958. *The Myth of the Negro Past*. Boston: Beacon Press.

Hetherington, E. M., and R. D. Parke. 1975. *Child Psychology: A Contemporary View*. New York: McGraw-Hill.

Hill, R. B. 1972. *The Strengths of Black Families*. New York: Emerson Hall.

Holliday, B. 1985. "Towards a Model of Teacher-Child Transactional Process Affecting Black Children's Academic Achievement." In *Beginnings: The Social and Affective Development of Black Children*, edited by M. Spencer, G. Brookins, and W. Allen, 117–130. Hillsdale, N.J.: Erlbaum.

Houston, S. H. 1970. "A Reexamination of Some Assumptions about the Language of the Disadvantaged Child." *Child Development* 41(4):947–963.

Huizinga, H. 1950. *Homo Ludens: A Study of the Play Element in Cultures*. Boston: Beacon Press.

Hunt, J. M. 1969. *The Challenge of Incompetence and Poverty*. Urbana: University of Illinois Press.

Jackson, B. 1976. "The Function of a Black Identity Development Theory in Achieving Relevance in Education of Black Students" (Doctoral dissertation, University of Massachusetts, 1976). *Dissertation Abstracts International* 37:5667A.

Jenkins, R. 1988. "Adolescent Sexuality." In *Black Families in Crisis: The Middle Class*, edited by A. F. Coner-Edwards and J. Spurlock, 90–98. New York: Brunner/Mazel.

Jensen, A. R. 1969. "How Much Can We Boost IQ and Scholastic Achievement?" *Harvard Educational Review* 39(1):1–123.

Kaufman, A. 1979. *Intelligence Testing with the WISC-R*. New York: Wiley.

Kunjufu, J. 1984. *Developing Positive Self Images and Discipline in Black Children*. Chicago: African American Images.

_____. 1986a. *Countering the Conspiracy to Destroy Black Boys*. Vol. 2. Chicago: African American Images.

_____. 1986b. *Motivating and Preparing Black Youth to Work*. Chicago: African American Images.

Labov, W. 1970. "The Logic of Nonstandard English." In *Language and Poverty*, edited by F. Williams, 153–189. Chicago: Rand McNally.

Lenneberg, E. H. 1967. *Biological Foundations of Language*. New York: Wiley.

McAdoo, H. P. 1985. "Racial Attitude and Self-Concept of Young Black Children over Time." In *Black Children*, edited by H. P. McAdoo and J. L. McAdoo, 213–242. Beverly Hills, Calif: Sage.

McLloyd, V. C. 1985. "Are Toys Just Toys? Exploring Their Effect on Pretend Play of Low-Income Preschoolers." In *Beginnings: The Social and Affective Development of Black Children*, edited by M. Spencer, G. Brookins, and W. Allen, 81–100. Hillsdale, N.J.:Erlbaum.

McLloyd, V. C., and S. M. Randolph. 1984. "The Conduct and Publication of Research on Afro-American Children: A Content Analysis." *Human Development* 27:65–75.

Manni, J. L., D. Winikur, and M. R. Keller. 1984. *Intelligence, Mental Retardation and the Culturally Different Child: A Practitioner's Guide*. Springfield, Ill.: Charles C Thomas.

Mercer, J. R., and Ysseldyke. 1977. "Designing Diagnostic-Intervention Programs." In *Psychological and Educational Assessment of Minority Children*, edited by T. Oakland, 70–90. New York: Brunner/Mazel.

Milliones, J. 1980. "Construction of a Black Consciousness Measure: Psychotherapeutic Implications." *Psychotherapy: Theory, Research, and Practice* 17(2):458–462.

Moore, E. G. J. 1985. "Ethnicity as a Variable in Child Development." In *Beginnings: The Social and Affective Development of Black Children*, edited by M. Spencer, G. Brookins, and W. Allen, 101–115. Hillsdale, N. J.: Erlbaum.

_____. 1987. "Ethnic Social Milieu and Black Children's Intelligence Test Achievement." *Journal of Negro Education* 56(1):44–52.

_____. 1981. "African-American Family Life: An Instrument of Culture." In *Black Families,* edited by H. P. McAdoo, 77–85. Beverly Hills, Calif.: Sage.

Ogbu, J. U. 1985. "Research Currents: Cultural-Ecological Influences on Minority School Learning." *Language Arts* 62(8):860–869.

_____. 1987. "Variability in Minority School Performance: A Problem in Search of an Explanation." *Anthropology and Education Quarterly* 18(4):312–332.

Osser, H. 1970. "Biological and Social Factors in Language Development." In *Language and Poverty,* edited by F. Williams, 248–264. Chicago: Markham.

Papolia, E., and S. Olds. 1925. *A Child's World: Infancy through Adolescence.* New York: McGraw-Hill.

Pelligrini, A. 1980. "Relationship between Kindergarten Play and Achievement in Reading, Language and Writing." *Psychology in the Schools* 17:530–535.

Peters, M. F. 1981. "Parenting in Black Families with Young Children: A Historical Perspective." In *Black Families,* edited by H. P. McAdoo, 211–224. Beverly Hills, Calif.: Sage.

Piaget, J. 1926. *The Language and Thought of the Child.* New York: Harcourt Brace.

_____. 1970. "Piaget's Theory." In *Carmichael's Manual of Child Psychology,* vol. 1, edited by P. H. Mussen, 703–732. New York: Wiley.

Piaget, J., and B. Inhelder. 1969. *The Psychology of the Child.* New York: Basic Books.

Powell-Hopson, D., and D. S. Hopson, 1988. "Implications of Doll Preferences among Black Children and White Preschool Children." *Journal of Black Psychology* 14(2):57–63.

Ribble, M. 1944. "Infantile Experience in Relation to Personality Development." In *Personality and the Behavior Disorders,* vol. 2, edited by J. Hunt, 621–651. New York: Ronald Press.

Rogoff, B., and G. Morelli, 1989. "Perspectives on Children's Development from Cultural Psychology." *American Psychologist* 40(2):343–348.

Royal, C. L. 1988. "Support Systems for Students of Color in Independent Schools." In *Visible Now: Blacks in Private Schools,* edited by D. T. Slaughter and D. J. Johnson, 55–69. New York: Greenwood Press.

Semaj, L. 1980. "The Development of Racial Evaluation and Preference: A Cognitive Approach." *Journal of Black Psychology* 6(2):59–79.

Shade, B. J., and P. A. Edwards. 1987. "Ecological Correlates of the Educative Style of Afro-American Children." *Journal of Negro Education* 56(1):81–99.

Shimkin, D. B., and V. Uchendu. 1978. "Persistence, Borrowing, and Adaptive Changes in Black Kinship Systems: Some Issues and Their Significance." In *The Extended Family in Black Societies,* edited by D. B. Shimkin, E. M. Shimkin, and D. A. Frate, 391–406. The Hague: Mouton.

Shockley, W. 1972. "Dysgenics, Geneticity, Raciology: A Challenge to the Intellectual Responsibility of Educators." *Phi Delta Kappan* 53:297–307.

Smart, M., and R. Smart. 1972. *Readings in Child Development and Relationship.* 2d ed. New York: Macmillan.

Tatum, B. D. 1987. *Assimilation Blues: Black Families in a White Community.* New York: Greenwood Press.

Thomas, C. 1971. *Boys No More.* Beverly Hills, Calif.: Glencoe Press.

Vogt, L. A., C. Jordan, and R. Tharp. 1987. "Explaining School Failure, Producing School Success: Two Cases." *Anthropology and Education Quarterly* 18(4):276–286.

White, J. L. 1980. "Toward a Black Psychology." In *Black Psychology,* 2d ed., edited by R. L. Jones, 5–12. New York: Harper & Row.

Wilson, A. 1978. *The Developmental Psychology of the Black Child.* New York: Africana Research Publications.

Wilson, M. N. 1989. "Child Development in the Context of the Black Extended Family." *American Psychologist* 44(2):380–385.

Woodson, C. G. 1936. *The African Background Outlined.* New York: Negro Universities Press.

5  Alternative/Possible Perspectives on Individuals

➤ **FOCUS: MEN**
  Men, Masculinity, and Identity
    Masculinities
  NOMAS: An Alternative Vision of Maleness
  Men and Violence
    Violence against Women
    Violence and Perpetrators

➤ **SUMMARY/COMMONALITIES**
  Optimal Theory and Developmental Phases

In this chapter we focus on extending and deepening our understanding of individuals' developmental experiences and the social environments in which these experiences take place. We want to learn to integrate the strengths inherent, but often unrecognized, in the diverse developmental realities, experiences, and strategies of different individuals so we can do better social work.

This chapter incorporates some of the themes presented in Chapter 3 as well. Specifically, this Chapter incorporates the following concepts/themes/perspectives from Chapter 3:

- Accepting and welcoming the ambiguity inherent in human behavior, development, and experience;

- Recognition that the individual and the personal elements of human experiences are intertwined with public and political issues;

- Recognition that the knowledge we explore about how individual humans develop is not a definitive or completed product but is part of ongoing, changing, and emergent processes;

- A commitment and an eagerness to see the strengths reflected in different developmental experiences and struggles;

- Application of the insights and concepts offered by social systems/ecological perspectives;

- Recognition that the language and words we use to explore and explain individual human behavior and development represent very real power relations;

- Continuous assessment of the perspectives we explore for their inclusiveness or their exclusiveness of diverse persons in the approaches they present to explain individual behavior and development; and

- Recognition of the significant role of the social environment (SE) in human behavior (HB).

Destinations

The destination of our journey in this chapter is not some static and final point at which we arrive upon a complete or absolute understanding of "proper individual behavior and development." In fact, our goal in this chapter is not any one destination at all. Our paramount concern is that during the journey we learn about multiple models to use as resources—tools, information, awarenesses, ways of thinking about developmental issues—to help us recognize the developmental commonalities shared by us all as humans and to recognize and respect how different humans develop differently. If there were a single destination it would be that place at which we attain sufficient knowledge upon which to base action to remove barriers to achieving the full human potential of any person with whom we work.

Themes receiving special emphasis in this chapter include diversity, diversity within diversity, multiple diversities, and multiple perspectives on understanding differences. We explored the notion of developmental universals or commonalities in Chapter 4. In this chapter we will be much more concerned with developmental variation as not only acceptable, but as necessary for healthy individual human development and essential for a healthy society as well.

ALTERNATIVE AND POSSIBLE DEVELOPMENTAL THEORIES

The alternative/possible models we will explore focus on developmental approaches that include persons and conditions left out of or only peripherally addressed by traditional models. These approaches also reflect in varying degrees the dimensions of the alternative paradigms for understanding HBSE we outlined in Chapter 2.

We must recognize that no one alternative approach offers a model incorporating all the dimensions of the alternative paradigm. Each, however, provides an alternative to traditional models along at least one, if not several, of the alternative paradigmatic dimensions. This diversity of focuses is in keeping with our search for multiple models and approaches that reflect the differing developmental experiences of diverse persons. Rather than any one alternative's offering some complete and final answer, the alternatives we will explore reflect a variety of attempts to develop multiple answers to the developmental questions emerging from different persons, experiences, and conditions of concern to social workers.

Although the alternatives discussed differ from one another in many ways, they share some important dimensions and themes. They offer voices and visions that are important in responding to the exclusion of many persons from traditional paradigms. They address historical conditions of oppression. Other themes that emerge from some of the alternative perspectives we will explore include:

1. differences in experiences in carrying out the common developmental process of identity formation.

2. a lack of developmental mentors or role models for oppressed and excluded persons.

3. impact on an individual's development of deficit or abnormal status accorded excluded or oppressed persons by traditional models or by dominant society.

4. explicit attention to social environmental (SE) influences on individual development.

Another important structural characteristic of many of the alternative approaches is their **nonlinear, contextual quality.** This characteristic is most obvious in the non-stage-based nature of some of the alternatives we are about to explore. Even the models that emerge from or are adaptations of traditional stage-based models tend to be contextual and nonchronological in the adaptations they make to the traditional models from which they emerge. The approaches and models that follow attempt to include and reflect the dimensions (to varying degrees) of alternative paradigm thinking. They have also been chosen to address alternative perspectives on individual development throughout the life span. The alternative approaches that we explore, you will notice, often have their roots in traditional or dominant models, but they seek to transcend the limits of the traditional models in order to embrace diversity.

The following sections dealing with alternative perspectives on individual development and behavior are organized according to several "focuses"—people of color, women, sexual orientation, people with disabilities, and men. These focuses are intended to highlight developmental issues and tasks faced by different groups but that are not focused on in traditional paradigm research. The concepts and issues dealt with within the specific "focus" sections, however, are not intended to apply exclusively to the persons or groups discussed in a specific section. As we have stressed, there is much overlap, interrelatedness, and similarity among developmental issues, conditions, and experiences of the groups discussed. We must also be extremely aware of the "diversity within diversity." There are wide ranges of variability among members of specific groups. Unless we are aware of diversity within diversity, we risk denying the uniqueness of individuals. It is very important also to recognize the special developmental complexities faced by persons who are simultaneously members of more than one diverse group.

SEHB and Individual Development

One of the themes especially significant in considering alternative perspectives on development is the role played by the larger social environment. As we noted in Chapter 4, few traditional theories of individual development attend to the influence of social environmental factors on development, yet the nature of interaction with the larger environment (for example, experiences of racism, homophobia, or sexism) has a significant influence on development throughout the life course. In addition, the availability of needed resources from the larger social environment for optimum development is a critical factor in developmental outcomes (nutrition, health care, housing, education, etc.).

Andrews and Ben-Arieh describe the critical importance of both positive interaction in and the availability of necessary material resources from the larger environment for optimal development. They point out that "material resources such as food, safe water, clothing, and housing are necessary but insufficient for holistic development. Stable, nurturing social relationships and safe, stimulating environments are essential" (Andrews and Ben-Arieh, 1999:110). There are a number of critical environmental factors associated with positive child development that have emerged from studies of U.S. children:

TABLE 5.1 Variables Associated with Positive Child Development

- Adequate nourishment
- Good health and access to health services when needed
- Dependable attachments to parents or other adult caregivers
- More than one consistently involved adult who provides economic resources, interaction, support, regulation, and positive role modeling to the child
- Firm, consistent, flexible discipline strategies
- Social support and guidance when faced with adversity
- Protection from physcial and psychological harm
- Cognitively stimulating physical and social environments
- Play activities and opportunities to explore
- Meaningful participation in community life appropriate for age and ability
- Access to resources for special needs

Copyright 1999, National Association of Social Workers, Inc., Social Work.

Poverty: *The Social Environment and the Life Span*

Poverty, especially as it affects children and women of childbearing years, often has a profound impact on individual development. Poverty results in a reduction of the resources available in the child's and the mother's environment necessary to provide for positive child development. **Poverty** is, of course, determined by income and "includes money income before taxes." The **poverty threshold** is a concept used by the U.S. Census Bureau "to determine who is poor. Poverty thresholds vary by family size and are updated annually for inflation using the Consumer Price Index" (AmeriStat 2000b). For example, "in 1998 the Census Bureau defined the poverty thresholds as $16,660 for a family of four and $13,003 for a family of three" (AmeriStat 2000a). The Joint Center for Poverty Research reported the following information related to poverty in the United States during 1997:

- 13.3 percent of people in the United States, or 35.6 million people, were poor.
- Almost 20 percent (19.9 percent) of all children under the age of 18 lived below the poverty level; children account for 40 percent of all poor people.
- 24 percent of all women in the United States were poor.
- 31.6 percent of white families, 39.8 percent of African American families, and 47.6 percent of Hispanic families in poverty were headed by women.
- 10.5 percent, or 3.4 million, elderly persons (65+) were poor.
- 27.1 percent, or 3.4 million, persons of Hispanic origin were poor.
- 26.5 percent, or 9.1 million, African Americans were poor.

(Joint Center for Poverty Research 2000)

Poverty in Adulthood. While the information above may be alarming, it is only a part of the picture of poverty in relation to our development through the life course.

By studying patterns of income and participation in service programs using data from what are referred to as "panel studies" or long-term studies (up to 13 years' duration) of income patterns and program participation, new understanding about the likelihood of experiencing poverty in the United States is emerging. Using these data, researchers have discovered how likely it is that any one of us will experience poverty, the degree of the poverty, the length of time we are likely to be poor at any one time, and the differences in likelihood of experiencing poverty depending on whether we are white or African American.

Analyses of these long-term data reveal that poverty is not usually a continuous state for most people. For most people "spells of poverty are fairly brief." However, for those households only slightly above poverty, a fall back into poverty can happen quickly with the loss of a job or the exit of one of the breadwinners from the family. As a result many families will move in and out of poverty over time. Studies of these data also reveal significant differences between African Americans and white Americans. African Americans "were more likely to be touched by poverty and more likely to be exposed to poverty for substantially longer periods" than whites (Rank and Hirschl 1999:202).

Analysis of panel-study data by Rank and Hirschl revealed some startling findings about poverty during the adult years. For example, they found that "60 percent of 20-year-olds in America will experience poverty" for at least a year at some point during their adult lifetime (Rank and Hirschl 1999:205). In other words, rather than poverty being an experience that only happens to others, "a clear majority of Americans" will experience poverty during their adult lifetime.

Of African American adults who reach the age of 75, 91 percent will have spent some time below the poverty line. Of white adults who reach the age of 75, 52.6 percent will have spent time below poverty level. A 1 in 2 chance of experiencing poverty seems large in a society with the affluence of U.S. society; a 9 in 10 chance seems intolerable. The duration of an episode of poverty is also dramatically different for African Americans than for whites. Rank and Hirschl define **dire poverty** as the "equivalent of spending a year below one-half of the official poverty line" (Rank and Hirschl 1999:208–9). For example, if poverty level is $16,000 for a family of four, members of that family would spend at least one year with an income of no more than $8,000. One third of all adult Americans will experience dire poverty. Sixty-eight percent of adult African Americans will experience dire poverty (Rank and Hirschl 1999:211–12).

Rank and Hirschl argue that since most of us will experience poverty during adulthood (to say nothing of the likelihood of childhood poverty) and since poverty underlies so many of the problems confronted by social workers, we should all take a very keen interest in reducing poverty. For as Rank and Hirschl point out, "for the majority of Americans, it is in their direct self-interest to have programs and policies that alleviate . . . the ravages of poverty." They point out that "for the majority of American adults, the question is not if they will experience poverty, but when" (Rank and Hirschl 1999:231–14).

A Global Perspective on Poverty: Hunger

Among the most basic effects of poverty are hunger and malnutrition. Hunger and malnutrition play multiple and complex roles in human developmental outcomes.

Adequate nutrition is necessary for a healthy and productive life. According to the United Nations Food and Agricultural Organization,

> *taking age, gender, height, and weight into account, an adult needs about 1,300 to 1,700 calories per day just to maintain the basal metabolic rate (breathing, pumping blood, and so forth). To perform light activities a person needs about 1,720 to 1,960 calories. A person needs at least 2,100 calories to perform moderate levels of work.* (Seipel 1999:417)

Chronic undernutrition results when the intake of calories is less than 1,900 per day (Seipel 1999:417). Malnutrition and hunger are widespread across the globe, including many persons in the United States. According to the Food Research and Action Center (FRAC), a national organization doing research and policy advocacy to reduce hunger in the United States, "approximately four million American children under age 12 go hungry and about 9.6 million more are at risk of hunger." Twenty-nine percent of these children "live in families that must cope with hunger or the risk of hunger during some part of one or more months of the previous year" (Food Research and Action Council 2000). A total of almost 20 million people in the United States experienced hunger during the 1980s (Seipel 1999:419).

Globally, hunger is pervasive and deadly. The World Health Organization (WHO) estimated that in 1998 "malnutrition was a causative factor in nearly half of the 10.4 million deaths among children under age five in developing countries." Hunger is also a major factor in disease and illness. WHO suggests that "30 percent to 40 percent of the 10 million incidents of cancer that occurred in 1996 could have been prevented by appropriate diets, along with other preventive measures" (Seipel 1999).

This situation is actually a significant improvement from the 1960s, when about 75 percent of people (about 1.6 billion people) "had a food supply that amounted to less than 2,100 calories per person per day." By the 1990s the percentage had dropped to about 10 percent. However, that number still amounted to a staggering 405 million people (Seipel 1999:416).

Seipel stresses that "malnutrition is not a simple problem with a simple solution. It results from the complex interplay of social and biomedical factors" (1999:418). **Food insufficiency** refers to inadequate food supplies or the inability of countries to produce enough food to meet the needs of their population. Approximately 800 million people still face this type of food insecurity or insufficiency. Poverty, of course, plays a significant role in hunger and malnutrition. Seipel also suggests that in many parts of the world gender inequality results in more hunger and malnutrition for women and girls than for men and boys "because of a cultural preference for men over women" (Seipel 1999:419).

These interconnected causes of poverty result in multiple consequences for human development. Malnutrition results in the inability of the body's immune system to fight infection. Malnutrition can result in growth faltering, or stunting and wasting—a failure to grow. Growth faltering is associated with impaired intellectual development and decreased learning opportunities. Also of major and long-term concern are the negative consequences of malnutrition for maternal and child health. Pregnant women who are malnourished are at significantly higher risks for "miscarriage, abortion, and stillbirth." Malnutrition and the associated lack of vitamin and mineral supplements can result in impaired health for both babies and their mothers. One of the most common results of malnutrition for infants is low birth weight. "Low birth-weight babies often do not survive, but if they do survive, their impaired immune systems make them more vulnerable to infection and disease" (Seipel 1999:420–1).

For social workers, a critical question is "what can be done to reduce hunger and malnutrition?" Seipel suggests a number of responses. At the macro and policy levels, one response is efforts to support nations in achieving food security or food sufficiency by either assisting in increasing production of sufficient food within the country or helping insure that nations have the economic capacity to import additional food. Helping to assure that available food supplies are distributed to those families most in need is another response. Of particular importance is creating support systems for women, including increasing educational opportunities, creating a women's support movement to enhance the rights of women, improving technology to reduce women's domestic workload, and promoting political participation by women. As social workers we can also use our skills to build awareness of hunger as a national and international concern and to promote the United Nations principles of human rights including the right of all persons to adequate nutrition (Seipel 1999:420–4).

Identity Development

Spencer and Markstrom-Adams (1990) remind us that according to Erikson, **identity development** is a major developmental task for which the stage is set during childhood and then played out during adolescence. Spencer and Markstrom-Adams (1990:290) suggest that the complexity of identity development increases "as a function of color, behavioral distinctions, language differences, physical features, and long-standing, although frequently not addressed social stereotypes." Stereotypes are generalizations about people based on such characteristics as those listed above. A negative stereotype is similar in many respects to stigma in that both terms refer to negative generalizations about people. In this case stereotypes are based on characteristics of members of minority groups considered negative by members of dominant groups.

In order to acknowledge this complexity, they believe that "new conceptual frameworks shaped by models of normal developmental processes are needed (i.e., as opposed to deviance- and deficit-dependent formulations)." New conceptual paradigms are necessary because "racial and ethnic groups have heretofore been examined through pathology-driven models" (Spencer and Markstrom-Adams 1990:304). See Illustrative Reading 4.1 "Negotiating the World: The Developmental Journey of African American Children," by Gomes and Mabry in Chapter 4.

Traditional developmental theories often ignore the interplay of external societal factors with internal cognitive factors. For example, traditional developmental approaches often assume that experiments showing African American children's preference for white dolls when shown black and white dolls reflect low self-esteem or a negative individual identity rather than a society-wide bias toward whiteness.

Such interpretations ignore contradictory findings from experiments that show African American children having extremely high self-esteem. Spencer and Markstrom-Adams suggest that both responses may be correct and may reflect the developmental complexity of high self-esteem in a world that favors whiteness. This explanation respects that social and internal processes intertwine in issues of race in the United States. They do so in more complex, less linear ways than are often assumed. For example, internalization of white biases in society does not necessarily result in a child of color's loss of or lowered self-esteem (1990:295–310).

Diversity within Diversity

Traditional developmental models assume homogeneity among group members. They assume that all members of a particular group share all characteristics such as family form, socioeconomic status, values, even color. Variations are often as extensive among group members as between one group and another. This diversity in diversity must be recognized in attempts to understand the development of members of minority groups (Spencer and Markstrom-Adams 1990:290–310). For example, we must recognize that there is wide variation among African American families from single parent, female-headed to traditional nuclear, two parent to large extended, multigenerational, and from low-income to middle-income to high-income families. Similarly, it is important to recognize the wide cultural and language variations among Native Americans. This group includes "all North American native people, including Indians, Alaska Natives, Aleuts, Eskimos, and Metis, or mixed bloods" (LaFromboise and Low in Spencer and Markstrom-Adams 1990:294). Among American Indians alone there are over 200 different languages. Likewise, one must recognize that there are significant differences in perspective among Japanese Americans of different generations in the United States. The "immigrant 'Issei,' the American born 'Nisei,' and the second generation of American-born Japanese called 'Sansei' " are seen by each other and themselves as very different (Nagata in Spencer and Markstrom-Adams 1990:294). In addition, there are wide variations among persons of Asian descent based on country or region of origin (Chinese, Korean, Vietnamese, Cambodian, among others). (See Chapter 2 for additional discussions of diversity within diversity.)

A Call for Alternative Models

Traditional perspectives overlook patterns of coping and adaptation by focusing on deficits; strengths and abilities used to survive, cope, and excel in the face of major sociopolitical barriers are ignored. Orthodox perspectives fail to link unique ecosystem or multilevel environmental experiences with life-course models (which integrate historical, sociocultural, biological, and psychological components with behavior response patterns). (See discussion of life course in Chapter 3 and Chapter 6.) The standard or traditional models ignore the opportunity for furthering or broadening our understanding of resilience and risk for youth whose normative experiences require ongoing adaptive coping strategies as a function of race, ethnicity, and/or color (Gibbs and Huang 1989; Spencer and Markstrom-Adams 1990:290–310). (See Chapter 9 for a discussion of resilience and risk.)

Spencer and Markstrom-Adams suggest that to improve our understanding of minority children's development we need alternatives to traditional developmental models that reflect the minority child's developmental processes (identity formation) and that attend to specific needs emerging from the child's developmental context. They suggest that alternative models must:

1. incorporate and explain consequences of status characteristics of race/ethnicity, color, sex, and economic status;

2. address subjective experiences of stress and probable responses;

3. explore intermediate developmental processes to help better understand perception and cognition (ex. doll preference reinterpretation);

4. account for problem-solving patterns or coping strategies given the developmental context; and

5. link minority status, stress, and coping strategies with actual behavioral outcomes (1990:304).

Sexuality

A core element of our identity as human beings is sexuality. Traditional notions of sexuality tend to be binary in that they present sexuality only as either completely heterosexual or completely homosexual. Traditional notions also tend to see sexuality as synonymous with sexual behavior. In addition, traditional paradigm thinking makes the assumption that one's sexuality and the nature of its expression remain constant throughout an individual's life span. Many researchers in the area of sexuality have found significant evidence of a much greater variability among humans in terms of sexuality than indicated by traditional paradigm thinking in this area. Researchers have discovered wide ranges of sexual behaviors, sexuality expressed in many ways in addition to sexual behaviors or activities, and variations in sexual orientation at different points in the life span of many people. For example, Rothblum asks the questions: "Who is bisexual? Does sexual orientation fall on a continuum and, if so, which continuum: sexual feelings, sexual activity, self-identity?" (1994:631). Rothblum notes that "Golden (1987) presented a model of sexual orientation that is multidimensional" (1994:631). The dimensions are sexual identity, sexual behavior, and community participation. Golden suggested that at any point in time a person's sexual identity, behavior, and community participation may be congruent or incongruent with one another (Rothblum 1994:631).

Demo and Allen argue that "Gender and sexual orientation, though often paired, e.g., 'gay man,' are not essential, fixed categories but are emergent, fluid, changing and contested" (1996:416). Klein (in Demo & Allen 1996) reflects the complexity of the concept of sexuality by incorporating seven variables in the concept of sexual orientation and its possible variations:

1. *sexual attraction,*

2. *sexual behavior,*

3. *sexual fantasies,*
4. *emotional preferences,*
5. *social preferences,*
6. *self-identification, and*
7. *lifestyle.* (Demo & Allen 1996:417)

Other factors in understanding sexuality in more complex and alternative ways include not only the issue of a person's sexual behavior versus one's sexual identity but also the issue of "researcher-imposed definitions (which are often based on available and somewhat arbitrary classification schemes)" and may be considerably more narrow than an individual's self definition of his or her sexuality which often reflects much broader variation (Demo & Allen 1996:417).

Alfred Kinsey (Harley 1996:www) categorized the wide variations in terms of sexual orientation as a continuum from exclusive interest in same-sex relationships to exclusive interest in opposite-sex relationships. Kinsey created a scale, graduated between heterosexuality and homosexuality, to rate individuals on actual experiences and psychological reactions. The ratings are as follows:

0–Entirely heterosexual.

1–Predominantly heterosexual, only incidentally homosexual.

2–Predominantly heterosexual, but with a distinct homosexual history.

3–Equally heterosexual and homosexual.

4–Predominantly homosexual, but with a distinct heterosexual history.

5–Predominantly homosexual, only incidentally heterosexual.

6–Entirely homosexual.

Multiple Intelligences

Like sexuality, the concept of intelligence is also a significant influence on individual identity development and plays a significant role in the way others define us. We explored traditional notions of intelligence in Chapter 4. Now we will turn to an alternative perspective on intelligence put forth by Gardner (1988; 1993). Gardner's theory of intelligences has important implications not only for understanding variation in individual development but for analyzing schools and other socializing institutions through which people learn. Gardner suggests that, rather than unitary IQ tests, we should "look instead at more naturalistic sources of information about how peoples around the world develop skills important to their way of life" (1993:7).

Gardner's Alternative Definition of Intelligence

Gardner alternatively defines intelligence as "the ability to solve problems, or to fashion products, that are valued in one or more cultural or community settings" (1993:15). Gardner and his colleagues believe that "human cognitive competence is better described in terms of a set of abilities, talents, or skills . . . call[ed] 'intelligences.' All normal individuals possess each of these skills to some extent; individuals differ in the degree of skill and in the nature of their combination" (1993:15).

Gardner's approach is consistent with alternative paradigm thinking and some postmodern approaches in that rather than focusing only on the "norm" or "center," it focuses on people at the margins in an effort to develop new ways to understand the concept of intelligence and it emphasizes the notion of appreciating local or culture-based knowledge. Gardner notes that in his research he looks at special populations such as "prodigies, idiot savants, autistic children, children with learning disabilities, all of whom exhibit very jagged cognitive profiles—profiles that are extremely difficult to explain in terms of a unitary view of intelligence" (1993:8).

As a result of his research Gardner has posited a set of seven intelligences or "multiple intelligences." He suggests there may be more than seven and that the seven he has discovered are of equal value and not rank ordered in terms of importance (1993:8–9). The seven are:

1. *Linguistic Intelligence:* ability to use language as a form of expression and communication (for example, poets).

2. *Logical-mathematical Intelligence:* This is logical and mathematical ability as well as scientific ability. Much of the current IQ testing is based on skills in the areas of linguistic and logical-mathematical intelligence through its testing of verbal and mathematical skills.

3. *Spatial Intelligence:* the ability to form a mental model of a spatial world and to be able to maneuver and operate using that model (for example, sailors, engineers, surgeons, sculptors, and painters, he suggests have high spatial intelligence).

4. *Musical Intelligence:* the ability to appreciate and use music as a form of expression (for example, singers, composers, musicians).

5. *Bodily-kinesthetic Intelligence:* the ability to solve problems or to fashion products using one's whole body, or parts of the body (for example, dancers, athletes, surgeons, craftspeople).

6. *Interpersonal Intelligence:* the ability to understand other people: what motivates them, how they work, how to work cooperatively with them (for example, successful salespeople, politicians, teachers, clinicians, religious leaders. We might add social workers to this list as well.).

7. *Intrapersonal Intelligence:* a capacity to form an accurate, veridical [truthful] model of oneself and to be able to use that model to operate effectively in life (Gardner 1983:8–9).

Multiple Intelligences and Schools

According to Gardner and others who advocate this alternative definition of intelligence as multiple, "the purpose of school should be to develop intelligences and to help people reach vocational and avocational goals that are appropriate to their particular spectrum of intelligences." This notion of the purpose of schools runs quite contrary to what Gardner refers to as the uniform view of education. The uniform view of education is that "there is a core curriculum, a set of facts that everybody should know, and very few electives." Gardner argues instead for what he calls the individual-centered school.

The **individual-centered school** takes a pluralistic view of education and recognizes "many different and discrete facets of cognition, acknowledging that people have different cognitive strengths and contrasting cognitive styles" (1993:6).

Creativity

Much of the alternative thinking about multiple intelligences is related to the notion of creativity. **Creativity** can be defined as the ability to solve problems in innovative ways. However, creativity is a multifaceted concept involving much more than simply problem solving. Gundry et al. (1994:23–24) look at creativity from four perspectives. These notions of creativity reflect a number of the dimensions of alternative paradigm thinking including interrelatedness, intuitiveness, heuristic approaches, and multiple ways of knowing. These multiple perspectives can help us appreciate the multidimensional nature of creativity. Through this appreciation we can increase our ability to recognize and nurture creativity in ourselves and in the people with whom we work.

Four Theories of Creativity

1. *The Attribute Theory:* "Most creative people have common attributes, such as openness, independence, autonomy, intuitiveness, and spontaneity."

2. *The Conceptual-Skills Theory:* Creative thought involves "solving problems through unconventional modes of thinking, as well as visualizing thoughts or whole models and then modifying them."

3. *The Behavioral Theory:* "A product or outcome is creative to the extent that it signifies a novel and useful behavioral response to a problem or situation. . . . Creative tasks are heuristic in nature, rather than algorithmic, meaning that there is typically no clear way to solve the given problem, so the problem-solver must learn a new path that will lead to a solution." (Note: Remember our exploration of heuristic thinking in Chapter 2.)

4. *The Process Theory:* "Creativity is a highly complex, multifaceted phenomenon that relies on individual talents, skills, and actions, as well as organizational conditions. . . . Creativity is a result of the interplay among the person, the task, and the organizational context" (Gundry et al. 1994:23–24).

The division into "focus" sections that follow is simply intended to assist us in organizing the materials. It cannot be overstated, though, that we must not allow this organizational convenience to hide the interconnections among the individuals, groups, and experiences we explore. We do not want to obscure or oversimplify the reality that issues related to color, gender, sexual orientation, class, age, disabling conditions, and religion interact in powerful ways that influence the developmental experiences of different individuals in countless complex and different ways.

FOCUS: PEOPLE OF COLOR

Introduction

In this chapter (and later chapters, as well) the work of a number of scholars from a variety of disciplines and perspectives who are people of color is presented to delineate in their own terms their developmental experiences. In some cases these perspectives give an alternative voice to existing and traditional developmental models, and in some cases entirely alternative perspectives on development are suggested.

Often alternative perspectives on existing models and completely alternative models offered by these scholars are marked most notably by differences in themes running throughout and transcending developmental stages, phases, periods, or eras. The differences in theme seem to indicate the complex nature of differential life experiences of people of color and whites in U.S. society. Equally important, perhaps, are the similarities marked by shared conceptions of the developmental needs and milestones so fundamentally a part of the developmental journeys of all who are members of the human community. Once again we experience commonality and difference as simultaneous and inseparable elements of humans' developmental experiences. Before we look at specific alternatives, it may be helpful to consider some basic information about people of color in the United States.

Who Are People of Color: Demographic Status

Harrison and colleagues provide a helpful summary and demographic overview of the sizes and preferred names of a number of minority groups in the United States (1990:349). African Americans are the largest ethnic minority group in the United States. Almost all African Americans (96 percent) are the descendants of slaves. The term *African American* as opposed to the term *black* is now preferred by many, but not all, Americans of African descent. American Indians, the smallest minority group in numbers, represent over 500 tribes or nations in the United States and typically prefer their tribal designation to the term *American Indian*. Asian Pacific Americans are the fastest-growing group in the United States, owing in part to the continuing in-migration of members of this group as immigrants and refugees. Members of this group prefer to be identified by their country of origin. The Hispanic group consists primarily of *"mestizo"* peoples born of the Spanish conquest of the Americas who intermixed with populations indigenous to the geographic areas. Persons in this group also prefer ethnic terms that identify their country of origin, and when it is necessary to refer to themselves collectively, many prefer the terms *Latino* [or *Latina*,] or *"la Raza"* (Harrison 1990: 349).

Who Are People of Color: Population and Population Change

The composition of the population of the United States is changing and will continue to undergo dramatic shifts in the proportions of white, non-Hispanic heritage persons and persons of color. Current U.S. Census Bureau projections suggest that by the year 2050 the white, non-Hispanic population will decrease from its current approximately 72 percent of the total population to only a little more than 50 percent.

This dramatic shift will be accompanied by increases in the percentage of persons of color in the population. The most dramatic increase in population will be among persons of Hispanic origin. This group is projected to increase from its current 11.3 percent to 22.5 percent during the period between 2000 and 2050. However, other groups of persons of color will experience population increases as well. Figure 5.1 summarizes these population trends and projections (Bureau of the Census 1995).

Poverty, Health, Education, and People of Color

Poverty disproportionately affects people of color in the United States. For example, in 1997, while 13.3 percent of people in the United States were poor, 26.5 percent of all African Americans were poor and 27.1 percent of all persons of Hispanic origin were poor. Almost twice the percentage of poor people were people of color rather than whites (Joint Center for Poverty Research 2000). Higher rates of poverty among people of color translate into serious differentials in the availability of health care, in educational attainment, and most important, in mortality or death rates. Data from 1997 compiled by AmeriStat (2000d) indicate that of four major causes of death—accidents, suicide, homicide, and HIV—only in the case of suicide were white death rates higher than those for African American or Hispanic heritage persons (see Figure 5.2). AmeriStat suggests that "higher death rates among minorities, particularly those infected with HIV, stem in part from their limited access to health insurance, and consequently, to medical care" (AmeriStat 2000d).

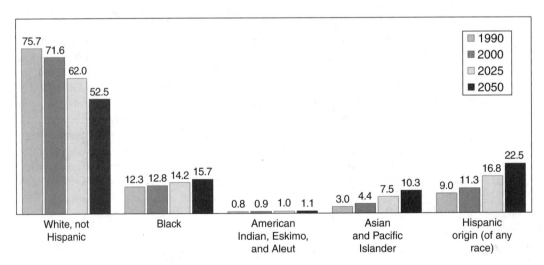

FIGURE 5.1   Percent of the Population, by Race and Hispanic Origin: 1990, 2000, 2025, and 2050 (Middle-series projections)

Source: Current Population Reports, Series P25–1104, *Population Projections of the United States, by Age, Sex, Race, and Hispanic Origin: 1993 to 2050.*

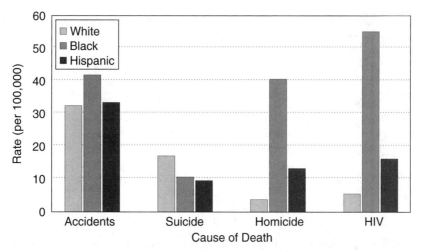

FIGURE 5.2 **Death Rates for Select Causes Among Persons Ages 25–44, by Race/Ethnicity, 1997**

Source: AmeriStat Population Reference Bureau and Social Science Data Analysis Bureau; National Center for Health Statistics. www.ameristat.org. Reprinted by permission.

Educational attainment is another critical area in which people of color are disadvantaged. This is particularly important given that education is a critical element in moving out of poverty. Today's information and technological society makes education even more critical, perhaps, than it has been in the past. Figure 5.3 illustrates how even though the number of persons who did not graduate from high school has dropped dramatically since 1975, the completion rates for African American and Hispanic heritage students was still far lower than for whites.

Policy and People of Color

Poverty reduction is a critical policy issue for social workers, for the nation, and for the globe. Innovative and effective policies and programs to reduce poverty among populations of color are urgently needed. One of the key mechanisms for policy change is through the election of persons to represent us in local, state, and national offices. The number of national legislators who are African American or Hispanic has increased from zero in 1925 to almost 60 in 1999 (see Figure 5.4). However, even with this increase, Congress is still almost 90 percent white, while whites account for only 72 percent of the U.S. population. By 2050 whites, as indicated above, will account for only slightly more than 50 percent of the population (see Figure 5.1) (AmeriStat 2000c).

Developmental Perspectives and People of Color: Emphasis on Children and Youth

There are a variety of general frameworks or models for understanding HBSE (several of which we explored in some detail in Chapter 3) that are particularly helpful in

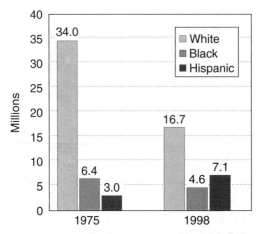

FIGURE 5.3   Percent of Persons Ages 25 and Over Who Did Not Graduate from High School, by Race/Ethnicity, 1975 and 1998

Source: Population Reference Bureau http://www.ameristat.org/edu/5bg.gif. Reprinted by permission.

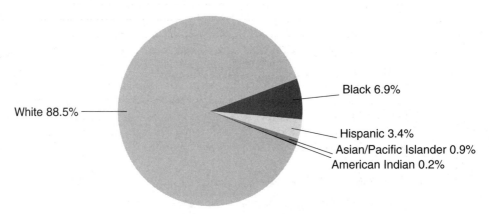

FIGURE 5.4   Voting Members of 106th Congress by Race/Ethnicity

Source: Population Reference Bureau http://www.ameristat.org/racethnic/2bg.gif

grasping the complexities of development for people of color. Gibbs and Huang (1989),* Spencer and Markstrom-Adams (1990), and others describe a number of frameworks for developing this understanding. Many of the applications of these frame-

---

*The discussion of developmental perspectives and people of color, pgs. 250–257, is adapted with permission of the authors and publisher from the book, *Children of Color: Psychological Interventions with Minority Youth,* by Jewelle Taylor Gibbs and Nahme Larke Huang and collaborators, pp. 4–12. Copyright 1989 by Jossey-Bass, Inc., a subsidiary of John Wiley & Sons, Inc.

works are discussed here in the specific context of development of children of color. It is important to recognize, though, that many of these frameworks can be applied to developmental issues faced in adolescence and adulthood and in the contexts of families, groups, organizations, and communities as well. First we will explore a variety of perspectives and their implications for understanding the development of people of color. We will then explore the "Interactive Model" proposed by Gibbs and Huang and collaborators in *Children of Color: Psychological Intervention with Minority Youth* as an example of a model that integrates many of the key components of the several perspectives that follow.

Developmental Perspective

Erikson's model of human development as a progression of developmental stages and crises is described in detail in Chapter 4 (see Box by Erikson in Chapter 4). A strength of Erikson's model, according to Gibbs and Huang (1989:5), is its assistance in helping to identify such important characteristics of the developing person as independence, competence, interpersonal skills, and a sense of identity.

Erikson's focus on the development of a sense of identity, for example, is a central concern of many developmental approaches, both traditional and alternative. Erikson's emphasis on identity formation reminds us how central our sense of "who we are" is to our development throughout life. This may be especially significant if we are attempting to develop a positive sense of who we are in the context of a hostile environment. Such a hostile environment exists for many members of the diverse groups with which we are concerned as social workers.

Another strength of Erikson's developmental perspective, according to Gibbs and Huang (1989:5), is its attention to the connections between the child's relationships to significant individuals in her/his life (parents, teachers, peers) and adjustment to the larger social environment (home, school, and community). Erikson's approach offers some assistance in appreciating the interconnectedness of the child, significant other individuals, and social institutions. Erikson's model does not, however, address the core social work concerns for social or environmental change and for the achievement of social and economic justice to remove barriers preventing individuals from reaching their fullest human potential.

Erikson's perspective also has significant shortcomings, according to Gibbs and Huang (1989:5–6), that render it less than appropriate as a comprehensive approach to understanding the complexities of the development of children of color (and women, poor persons, gay, lesbian, and bisexual persons, and persons with disabilities, we might add). It is biased toward children reared in nuclear families in highly industrialized societies. It is less applicable to children from extended families in nonindustrialized societies where different sets of psychosocial outcomes might be valued. This limit is especially important to recognize when thinking about recent immigrants or children reared on reservations or in "other homogeneous environments."

Another weakness in Erikson's approach is its assumption that self-concept and self-esteem of minority children are significantly affected by the stigma of membership in a devalued ethnic group. Gibbs and Huang remind us that there is considerable evidence that self-esteem and self-concept, essential ingredients in identity development, in children come more substantially and directly from families, close relatives, and friends than from broader society during childhood. Only later when the adolescent expands her/his radius of interaction beyond family and ethnic community does society seem to play a major role in self-esteem and self-concept, they argue. There is much recent research that finds self-esteem and self-concept of minority children and adolescents as high or higher than for their white counterparts. (Powell 1985; Rosenberg and Simmon 1971; Taylor 1976, in Gibbs and Huang 1989:5).

Ecological Perspective

The ecological perspective was discussed in conjunction with social systems thinking in Chapter 3 when we explored some of the tools used by social workers for approaching traditional and alternative perspectives about HBSE. Gibbs and Huang (1989:6–7) describe the ecological perspective as one in which the child and the adolescent are viewed as active agents in "interlocking systems" from family and school to government as it is reflected in social and economic policies. Each of the systems along this continuum from small to large presents risks and opportunities for individuals at each stage of their development.

This perspective is of value because it allows the incorporation of the multiple impacts of poverty, discrimination, immigration, and social isolation on the development of minority children and youth. For example, consistent with ecological thinking is the recognition that poverty has a negative impact on children's lives in multiple ways—in nutrition, housing, education, health, and recreation. The ecological model can also accommodate the accumulative impact of multiple characteristics and conditions on development. Although, as we noted in Chapter 3, ecological and social systems perspectives are less about social and political transformation of environmental systems than about describing and recognizing the interrelatedness of environmental and individual issues. When children are both poor and minority group members, the negative and long-term impact of poverty increases significantly. Recognition of the complex and damaging impacts of multiple stressors such as poverty, minority status, immigrant status, language problems, unemployment, and negative attitudes toward affirmative action efforts combine to significantly add to the challenges faced by low-income minority families in their efforts to provide a stable and nurturing environment for their children's development (Gibbs and Huang 1989:6–7). Gibbs and Huang (1989:7) stress, though, that despite these multiple and intractable ecological stressors, these families show tremendous strengths in their "remarkable resilience, creativity, and competence in meeting tasks of socializing their children in an often hostile and alien environment." We discussed the strengths perspective at some length in Chapter 3.

The ecological perspective also helps us understand the place of family, school, peer group, and community in minority child development and socialization. This perspective, for example, is helpful in understanding the kinds and intensity of conflict that can arise in families of recently arrived immigrants between values and norms in the home and those in the school and community. The impact of such conflicts can be very real and very damaging and may include physical health problems, behavior disorders, school adjustment problems, delinquency, depression, or suicide (Gibbs and Huang 1989:6–7).

Cross-Cultural Perspective

Gibbs and Huang (1989:7–8) find the cross-cultural perspective derived from anthropology helpful in providing a comparative framework for thinking about all human societies. This comparative approach can help us link the impact of large societal systems to individual human behavior. It assumes that all behavior has meaning and serves adaptive functions and that all behavior is governed by sets of rules and norms that promote stability and harmony in the society. It assumes also that behavior contrary to rules and norms disrupts social harmony and that the society will seek to control or regulate such behavior through such institutional mechanisms as shamans, spiritualists, faith healers, or mental health practitioners. We should recognize here that social workers are often key among the mental health practitioners and among other human service workers whom dominant society gives the responsibility for exercising this social control.

A Human Development Alternative Approach to Identity Development

D'Augelli argues that in contrast to linear and more internally-focused approaches to identity development, "from a human development perspective, identity is conceived of as the dynamic process by which an individual emerges from many social exchanges experienced in different contexts over an extended historical period—the years of his or her life" (1994:324).

Miller points out that "racial and ethnic identity are fundamental parts of the psychological profile of any individual who is a member of a racially or ethnically heterogeneous society. . . . Understanding the process by which individuals develop racial and ethnic identities is therefore an important part of understanding the total person" (1992:25). Racial and ethnic identity development take place in the context of intergroup relationships and social interactions within the larger environment. To fully understand racial and ethnic identity development we must consider these as critical elements or influencers of the overall identity development process. Some of the contexts of these intergroup relations are described below:

INTERGROUP RELATIONS IN SEVERAL AREAS NEED TO BE TAKEN INTO ACCOUNT:

Economics "Whether or not groups are economic competitors and economically interdependent, dependent, or independent affects the degree to which group relations are adversarial or cooperative. When one group controls the economic well-being of another, it is likely that the dependent group will be stigmatized."

Continued

INTERGROUP RELATIONS IN SEVERAL AREAS NEED TO BE TAKEN INTO ACCOUNT: *Continued*

Population Ratios "The frequency and probability of interracial contact will influence how often society will confront multiracial issues and how many multiracial people society will have to accommodate."

Societal Images "A group's status in society is reflected in popular images. The balance or imbalance of positive images of groups in society, a by-product of group relationships, affects multiracial or multiethnic experiences by communicating a sense of the value of the groups and by providing (or failing to provide) access to role models."

Socialization by the Collective "A theory of multiethnic or multiracial identification would need to account for the behavior of the collectives representing the multiethnic or multiracial individual in fostering group membership. The extent to which one group might actively socialize individuals into the collective and pass on the values and culture of the group while another group might be passive, disinterested, or even rejective will influence the individual's process of identification."

Historical Legacies "Individuals and groups live their lives in historical space. Both historical relations and alterations in present relations will be important aspects of understanding multiracial identity."

Rules for Intergroup Boundaries "A theory of ethnic identity development that could accommodate multiethnic or multiracial people would need to incorporate rules governing the rigidity or fluidity of boundaries surrounding social groups, principles for accommodating structural change, and rules to describe situational views of self. Identities may not be invariant properties, but may instead alter according to the social context."

Adapted from Miller, R. L. (1992). "The human ecology of multiracial identity." In Root, Maria P. P. (Ed.). *Racially mixed people in America*. Newbury Park, CA: Sage, 24–30.

An Interactive Model

Gibbs and Huang (1989:1–12) provide an analysis of some of the strengths and weaknesses of the approaches to human development described above. They then blend the results of this analysis into their "Interactive Model." They focus their analysis on race and ethnicity, with their attendant implications for social class, as the focal concerns when thinking about development of children of color. Specifically, they offer a synthesis of developmental perspectives, ecological perspectives, and cross-cultural perspectives that highlight and make central race and ethnicity rather than submerging these central elements as peripheral concerns in developmental thinking.

Gibbs and Huang (1989:11–12) propose an alternative, more holistic model they call **"interactive"** that both *incorporates and expands developmental, ecological, human development and cross-cultural perspectives as interacting dimensions of children's developmental life experiences.* They offer this model as a more appropriate and integrative approach to thinking about the development of people of color, specifically children and adolescents. The reader will note this model is characterized by concepts used to describe ongoing realities faced by children of color as they develop. These concepts become threads woven throughout the developmental fabric of these children's lives (and woven throughout their life span). This is an example of the non-stage-based nature of this alternative model.

Ethnicity

In the Gibbs and Huang alternative model, ethnicity is the overarching dimension of child development. It is a thread sewn throughout both internal and environmental experiences. Ethnicity provides a framework for perceiving and responding to the world. It shapes identity, both personal and social. It establishes values, norms, and expectations for appropriate behaviors. It defines parameters for choices and opportunities—social, educational, and occupational. Ethnicity provides the structures and contexts in which developmental tasks are approached. It also has significant impact on the way the external world of school, peers, and community perceive and treat the child (1989:8–12). These alternative developmental perspectives offer helpful definitions, clarifications, and comparisons of a number of concepts essential for social workers if we are to comprehend and respect the complexities of human behavior and development of diverse persons in a variety of social environments.

They offer the definition of ethnicity as "membership in a group of people who share a unique social and cultural heritage that is passed on from generation to generation. . . . Members of an ethnic group believe themselves to be distinctive from others in a significant way" (Gibbs and Huang 1989:9). Ethnic group membership provides "cultural identity and a set of prescribed values, norms and social behaviors"; a framework for forming a child's view of "self, the world and future opportunities"; "it gives meaning to the child's subjective experiences"; it structures interpersonal relationships; and gives "form to behaviors and activities." Ethnicity may determine the kind of family, language, neighborhood, church, school, and role models around which the child's development takes place (Gibbs and Huang 1989:9–10). (See discussion of ethnicity in Chapter 1.)

Biculturality

Ethnicity for children and families of color also results in requirements for dual socialization to both their ethnic world and the dominant white world in which they must interact and survive. The result of the dual socialization process is a person who is bicultural. Bicultural socialization is a process through which parents teach their children to function in two sociocultural environments. This process is influenced by a number of factors. These factors include the degree to which the two cultures share norms, values, perceptions, and beliefs; the availability of cultural translators, mediators, or models; the amount and kind of corrective feedback coming from each culture about one's behavior in that culture; the fit of conceptual and problem-solving style of persons of color with that of the dominant culture; the individual's degree of bilingualism; and the degree of similarity in physical appearance to that of the members of the dominant culture (Gibbs and Huang 1989:11–12).

The combination of race and ethnicity often results in dual developmental challenges due to the combination of differences in culture and visibility (physical or linguistic). The product of this is membership in a minority group. We explored this term in Chapter 3. Minority group membership is distinctive from, but often intertwined with, membership in ethnic or racial groups. Minority groups are "those groups that have unequal access to power, that are considered in some way unworthy of sharing power equally, and that are stigmatized in terms of assumed inferior traits or characteristics" (Gibbs and Huang 1989:10). One should note that this definition of minority group focuses on "power and privilege," not on numbers. Thus, women, a numerical majority, are members of a minority group in terms of their unequal access to power.

Social Class and Caste

The interactive model suggested by Gibbs and Huang includes the element of social class as an important developmental factor. Social class ascribes "a particular position and value to [the child's] family's socioeconomic status (SES)" (Gibbs and Huang 1989:10). Socioeconomic status, like ethnic, racial, or minority group status, is a major determinant of developmental environments and experiences. To a great extent it determines the developmental boundaries for the child's experiences and opportunities in social environment, life-style, level of education, and occupation. Some scholars suggest that the related concept *caste* or *castelike* status is a more accurate descriptor of the social standing and relationship to dominant groups for some members of minority groups in the United States. Ogbu (1978:23) suggests that African Americans have castelike status in the United States. **Caste minorities** are usually regarded by the dominant group as "inherently inferior in all respects. . . . In general, caste minorities are not allowed to compete for the most desirable roles on the basis of their individual training and abilities. The less desirable roles they are forced to play are generally used to demonstrate that they are naturally suited for their low position in society. Thus their political subordination is reinforced by economic subordination" (Ogbu 1978:23).

For many children of color in the United States, the combination of such characteristics as race, ethnicity, social class (or caste), [and gender] result in triple or even quadruple stigmatization. This is the case, for example, for a child who is nonwhite, non-Anglo-Saxon, non-middle-class, and female. This complex stigmatization, or negative labeling owing to such characteristics as race, ethnicity, class, and gender, presents enormous developmental barriers and challenges to be overcome (Gibbs and Huang 1989:10–11). Multiple stigmas can have significant impact on the experiences of the child throughout his or her developmental journey. (See discussion of multiple diversities in Chapter 2.)

Life Span and Adult Developmental Models and People of Color

Cross's Model of African American Identity Development

Cross's original model "emphasized that African Americans differ in their degree of identification with African American culture" (Parks et al. 1996:624). This differential identification was tied to stages of identity development.

Several scholars (Atkinson, Morten and Sue; Sue and Sue in Parks et al. 1996: 624–625) have suggested the catalyst propelling individuals through the stages was societal oppression. Helms noted the "crucial role that the experience of the difference in 'social power' plays in the process of racial identity development" (in Parks et al. 1996:625). The above authors suggest that given the central place of oppression by the dominant group of nondominant group members, the model can be applied to other non-dominant groups. Recent revisions of the model "have shifted from stage-oppression focused development to sequential ego identity statuses and personality integration. Thus, stages have been replaced by statuses, and oppression as the essential feature has been replaced by ego differentiation and personality development" (Parks et al. 1996:625). The Cross model is summarized below:

BLACK RACIAL IDENTITY DEVELOPMENT

Ego-Status	Characterized By
Pre-encounter	Idealization of Whites and Whiteness. Denigration of Blacks and Black culture.
Encounter	Rejection of White culture. Beginning of search for Black identity. Confusion and intense affect mark this transitional stage.
Immersion-Emersion	Withdrawal into Black world. Idealization of Blackness. Embracing of stereotypical image of Blackness. Denigration of Whiteness.
Internalization	Internally defined positive Black identity. Transcendence of racism. Acceptance of positive aspects of White culture.

Adapted from Parks, Carter, and Gushue 1996: *Journal of Counseling and Development*, v. 74, 625. Copyright American Counseling Association. Reprinted with permission.

An Extension of "The Cross Model of Black Identity Development"

Parham (1989:187–226) presents a model of African American identity development that incorporates and expands upon "The Cross Model of Black Identity Development." Parham's extensions integrate Cross's stages of Black identity development with three chronological phases or periods: adolescence/young adulthood, middle adulthood, and later adulthood and they emphasize the high degree of variability among individuals as they struggle with Black identity development. Parham summarizes Cross's four-stage model in which an African American has a "conversion experience" that he refers to as a transformation from "Negro-to-Black." Cross's four stages are Pre-encounter, Encounter, Immersion-Emersion, and Internalization.

1. Pre-encounter.   The individual views the "world from a White frame of reference" and devalues or denies her/his Blackness in thinking, actions, and behaviors. The person's frame of reference is referred to as "deracinated" and is characterized by a white normative standard in which attitudes are "pro-White and anti-Black."

2. Encounter.   The individual experiences significant events or situations, such as housing discrimination because of skin color, that dramatically call into question previous attitudes and frames of reference. This stage involves the realization that his or her previous frame of reference is inappropriate and results in the decision to "develop a Black identity."

3. Immersion-Emersion.   This involves a transition to a new Black identity in which the old frame of reference is discarded. This stage involves immersion in "Blackness" through intense attachment to elements of black culture and withdrawal from interactions with other ethnic groups. The tendency here is to glorify African American people and to denigrate white people.

4. Internalization.   The person at this stage achieves a "sense of inner security and self-confidence with his or her Blackness." At this point there is a general decline of strong anti-white feelings, although African American is the primary reference group. "This person moves toward a more pluralistic, nonracist perspective" (Parham 1989:189–190; Cross 1971).

Patterns of Identity Development Processes

Parham expands on Cross's stages by adding the dimension of life-cycle stages and their impact on the nature of movement through the Cross stages of Afrocentricity. In addition to identity development being a lifelong process, an individual may experience at least three different patterns for dealing with his or her racial identity as he or she moves along the life course (1989:211). These three alternative patterns of addressing issues of racial identity include the following:

1. Stagnation.   According to this alternative, an individual maintains "one type of race-related attitude throughout most of [his or her] lifetime." That is, one could reach and maintain any of Cross's four stages—pre-encounter, encounter, immersion-emersion, or internalization—and remain in that stage for the remainder of his or her lifetime. For the most part, Parham considers this a liability for the individual since it results in a resistance to new experiences or ideas and it makes adjusting to change quite difficult. An exception to stagnation as a developmental liability would be the person who has reached "internalization" and remains at this level.

2. Stagewise Linear Progression (SLP).   According to this alternative, a person moves from one stage to another—pre-encounter through internalization—in linear fashion. This is the developmental pattern most commonly suggested by Black identity development models. This pattern suggests a functional, continuing, and progressive movement toward growth and development. However, its linear nature somewhat oversimplifies the complexity of identity development for many individuals.

3. Recycling. This alternative involves "the reinitiation of the racial identity struggle and resolution process after having gone through the identity development process at an earlier stage in one's life." Parham suggests that recycling completely back to pre-encounter is unlikely, however. A more common pattern might be a person moving from "internalized attitudes into another encounter experience" (Parham 1989:213).

Racial Identity Development through the Life Span

In addition to the above three alternative patterns for addressing African American identity development during one's life, Parham suggests that Cross's four stages—pre-encounter, encounter, immersion-emersion, and internalization—may occur at a number of different phases or stages of the life cycle beginning as early as late adolescence/early adulthood. He suggests that African American identity earlier on in life is largely a reflection of parental attitudes toward societal stereotypes. However, he suggests that home and social environments can influence the particular stage at which the adolescent begins the identity development process.

An individual may also experience any or all of Cross's four phases of Black identity development during middle or later adulthood, according to Parham (1989: 197–209). During these periods, racial identity development struggles are complicated by the more traditional concerns of these development stages. He suggests, for example, that middle adulthood "may be the most difficult time to struggle with racial identity because of one's increased responsibilities and increased potential for opportunities" (1989:202). During late adulthood, traditional tasks include dealing with such social institutions as "social security and retirement, nursing homes, and community resources and recreation facilities." Parham stresses that "undoubtedly, the ways in which late-adulthood Black people interact with these institutions will be influenced by their racial identity attitudes" (1989:207).

Parham's perspective is strengths-based in that it suggests that while oppression is certainly an influence on the process, his model "assumes that Black/African self-identity is an entity independent of socially oppressive phenomena: Black/African identity is actualized through personal thoughts, feelings, and behaviors that are rooted in the values and fabric of Black/African culture itself" (1989:195). Parham's extensions are also consistent with our own social system's perspective and overall emphasis on human behavior and the social environment because they focus on identity development as an interactional process involving *both* internal (individual) and external (environmental) factors.

Parham's extensions help to articulate the complex and continuous nature of racial identity development processes. His extensions also stress the importance of recognizing the highly individualized nature of racial identity development. He emphasizes that

> *recognizing that within-group variability is an important element in understanding Black people cannot be overstated. Tendencies to make between-group comparisons (Black vs. White) and/or to overgeneralize (all Blacks are alike) provides little, if any, conceptual clarity and should be avoided, or at least used with caution.* (1989:223)

The Adult Development of African American Men: An Extension of Levinson's Model of Adult Development

Herbert (1990) argues that theories of human development, in this case theories of adult development, must reflect people of color and the experiences of people of color. He suggests that this is necessary not only to acknowledge the existence of people other than whites, but also to acknowledge the impact of such issues as race and racism on the developmental experiences of people of color and whites alike. Herbert focuses on Levinson's study of the adult development of men. Levinson's model of adult development is described in Chapter 4. Herbert points out that, even though Levinson included five African American participants in his study, he did not examine racial development, and differences between the black and white groups were not systematically studied. Had these issues been explored, he argues, we could have learned important things about the influence of race and racism on blacks and whites alike. As Herbert reminds us, "racial identity is part of everyone's psychosocial development and is fundamental to how a person views self, others, environment, and the relationship of self to the environment" (1990:435).

Herbert's research was similar methodologically to that of Levinson with some important differences. Herbert's research used an all-black sample, was conducted by an African American researcher, and explicitly acknowledged race as an integral part of interviews and analyses. Herbert's results had a number of similarities to those of Levinson but included significant differences as well (1990:435–436).

African American Men's Development and Racism

Developmental periods were experienced in similar chronological ranges for the African American men in Herbert's study and the respondents of Levinson. However, for Herbert's sample, race was an important factor for each individual from childhood through adulthood. For the men studied by Herbert, forming an adult identity was a complex task involving both conscious and "unconscious integration of race into their adult identity and the formation of a racial identity. They had to work at confronting race, racial discrimination, racial prejudice, and racism" (1990:437) as a significant part of their overall developmental experience.

Herbert documented, through the experiences of the men he studied, specific examples of the dynamics of race, discrimination, and racism across social system levels from individuals to social institutions (1990:436). These experiences included "Being denied a bank loan or promotion out of racial considerations; confronting racism in the military establishment, while serving one's country." Herbert also discovered that, unlike the men studied by Levinson, "the formation of *mentor* relationships was not significant for these men" (1990:438). A mentor is a more senior colleague who makes him- or herself available to junior colleagues for advice and guidance. A mentor offers his or her experiences for the benefit of the junior colleague.

In spite of the obstacles faced, the black entrepreneurs studied were successful in their enterprises; an accomplishment "truly remarkable when one considers that only four to six percent [of black-owned firms] survive to the second generation (Dewart 1988 in Herbert 1990), whereas the survival rate for white-owned firms has been estimated to be around 35 percent" (Backhard and Dyer in Herbert 1990:440).

Herbert dramatically illustrates that, while proceeding through similar processes of adult development outlined by Levinson, black men face greater stresses due to societal obstacles and diffuse contradictions and inconsistencies. He stresses that comparisons around the developmental similarities (similar sequences of age-specific periods, for example) between black and white men are greatly complicated when factors of race and racism are introduced, because there is no data on the effects of race and racism on the psychosocial development of white men. We must, Herbert concludes, begin to recognize the effects of race and racism on both white and black men (1990:441).

Herbert summarizes the importance for whites as well as for blacks of replacing traditional developmental theories with alternatives that include issues of racial discrimination, prejudice, and racism. He stresses that

> *Modifying adult psychosocial developmental theory to account for the despicable forces and consequences of racial discrimination, racial prejudice, and racism should not be* solely *a black issue or agenda. White Americans are beneficiaries of the repugnant consequences of the these forces. . . . White people must begin to examine critically their own racial attitudes and behaviors to determine how they are shaped by and how they contribute to the forces of race and racism. . . . Any meaningful discussion about the continued expansion and development of adult psychosocial developmental theory must include consideration of the impact and consequences of racial dynamics, racial discrimination, racial prejudice, and racism on black people and on white people.* (1990:441–442)

New Developmental Tasks. To incorporate the powerful elements of race and racism into developmental theory for both blacks and whites, Herbert proposes two new developmental tasks. First, *"the formation of an explicit individual racial identity that both acknowledges and frees the individual of racism and prejudice."* Second, *"the formation of an individual self-concept dedicated to the eradication and abolition of racial discrimination, racial prejudice, and racism from our society"* (1990:442). These are tasks that need to be addressed at every developmental period throughout the life span. We will explore white racial identity development and the impact of racism below.

Herbert's work declares that the most urgent need of African American men in this society is to incorporate into developmental theory the "recognition, reversal, and abolition of racial discrimination and racism in this white-controlled society." His work also dramatically illustrates the developmental strength of African American men for whom "this most urgent need" is not being met. As he points out, the results of his study of the "total lives of black entrepreneurs" rather than of some more specific, traditional studies with limited and narrow concerns, "such as unemployment, drug abuse and dropout rates," illustrated the strengths of the black entrepreneurs he studied. His study participants "demonstrated an amazing ability not only to survive racial discrimination and racism, but to aspire and achieve under conditions of very few opportunities" (1990:442).

Multiracial Identities

The reality that U.S. society is becoming more and more diverse is reflected in the increasing attention to the experiences, strengths, and challenges of biracial and multiracial people. Kich stresses that "for biracial people, positive identification of themselves as being of dual or multiple racial and ethnic heritages has not been accepted or recognized in a consistent manner over the last several centuries" (1992:304). Yet Spickard argues that "people with more than one racial ancestry do not necessarily have a problem" (1992:13). However, they are faced with challenges both in developing a positive identity as multiracial individuals and in finding acceptance in the wider communities and cultures in which they live. These challenges are often filled with ambiguity and a sense of differentness on the part of the person and the larger community. For example, Kich points out that "The single most commonly asked question of biracial people—What are you?—continually underscores the experience of differentness" (1992:306).

Fong et al. stress the significant benefits and strengths that can accrue from positive identity as a multiracial person. They note that "At the individual level, psychological benefits may accrue to a multiracial individual from opportunities to adopt a multiracial consciousness. For individuals of mixed parentage, it is generally healthful and empowering to embrace both, or all, parts of themselves" (1996:24). The potential benefits at the individual level of identifying oneself as a multiracial person are not always shared by other members of communities of color.

Competing Individual and Community Values

Fong et al. note the complex and often conflicting concerns about multiracial identity for communities of color. They note that

> *Some African American civic leaders, for example, worry that if "biracial"*
> *and mixed become accepted ethnic identities, individuals with dual heritages*
> *will cease to identity as African American and that their numbers and tal-*
> *ents will become unavailable to the African American community. Mass*
> *(1992) echoed this concern, reporting that there is fear in the Japanese Amer-*
> *ican Community that it may "disappear" because mixed people may "hasten*
> *assimilation into mainstream culture."* (Fong et al. 1996:24)

The concerns above have significant implications for census taking and the categories used for counting people. We should note the policy implications especially, since census data form the basis of much policy and decision making about resource distribution in this society. How one and one's group defines membership in that group can have significant consequences for communities of color as Fong et al. point out below:

> *According to Wright (1994), 75 percent to 90 percent of people who identify*
> *themselves in the census as black could alternatively classify themselves as mul-*
> *tiracial. If even a small proportion did so, civil rights programs, including*
> *those related to housing, employment, and education, would be severely af-*
> *fected. Yet recognition of multiraciality need not necessarily decrease the com-*
> *munity of color. Among Native Americans, a high rate of interracial*
> *marriage over the past half-century has resulted in increasing numbers.*

> *There is continued need for policy discussion on these issues with concern for both individual and group well-being.* (1996:25)

Biracial and Multiracial Identity Development

Given the complexities, ambiguities, and competing concerns about biracial and multiracial identify at the community level, it is nevertheless important to explore the processes and struggles individuals must contend with in the development of positive multiracial identity. We will first explore a model for understanding the processes of multiracial identity development across the lifespan. Then we will look at some processes and issues of specific concern for biracial and multiracial children and their parents.

Biracial and Bicultural Identity Development across the Life Span

Kich (1992:305) presents a stage-based model that addresses the challenges of biracial, bicultural identity development throughout the life span.

STAGES OF BIRACIAL, BICULTURAL IDENTITY DEVELOPMENT

1. *An initial awareness of differentness and dissonance* between self-perceptions and others' perceptions of them (initially, 3 through 10 years of age)

2. *A struggle for acceptance from other* (initially, age 8 through late adolescence and young adulthood)

3. *Acceptance of themselves as people with a biracial and bicultural identity* (late adolescence throughout adulthood)

Kich believes "These three stages describe a biracial person's transitions from a questionable, sometimes devalued sense of self to one where an interracial self-conception is highly valued and secure" (1992:305). The stages are described in more detail below.

Stage 1: Awareness of differentness and dissonance
While Kich believes this awareness of differentness and dissonance is first confronted between 3 and 10 years of age, he also believes there is "Cyclic reenactment of these stages . . . during later development, often with greater intensity and awareness"(1992:306). Kich describes dissonance as "an uncomfortable and negative experience of conflict [that] implies a negative judgment about the difference, where the comparison process results in an experience of devaluation and discrepancy. Biracial people describe being seen as 'different' as generally involving an experience of dissonance" (1992:306).

Stage 2: Struggle for acceptance by others
This struggle often is played out in the context of school or community settings. Kich says that "In reaching out of the parental and extended family orbit,

children become more aware of how others see them and their families" (1992: 309). Kich believes that biracial children during this stage often attempt to separate "home, the source of differentness, and school . . . [however,] this separation cannot last." Kich points out that "For many during this stage, an ambivalent relationship is formed with the parent who most personifies the person's experience of differentness and an overidentification occurs with the other parent" (1992:311). Kich also suggests that attempts at **passing** often occur during this period of search for acceptance by others outside the family (1992:309–312). (Passing is also discussed in Chapter 10.)

Stage 3: Self-acceptance and assertion of an interracial identity
The process of positive identity development is both ongoing and uncertain in its resolution:

> *Self-acceptance, substantially different from, yet influenced by, the quest for other-acceptance, may never be fully achieved by anyone. However, the biracial person's ability to create congruent self-definitions rather than be determined by other's definitions and stereotypes may be said to be the major achievement of a biracial and bicultural identity. . . . The stable self-acceptance of biracial and bicultural self-identity begins to occur generally after high school, and more finally during or after the college and occupational transitions.* (Kich 1992:314–315)

Kich also stresses the importance of finding a community of biracial and bicultural people as part of the development and maintenance of a positive, stable identity as a biracial, bicultural person:

> *Many [biracial people] actively seek out the involvement of other biracial and bicultural people, as well as those of other ethnic and racial groups. They want contact that is not inhibited and that does not require a "full explanation" of their heritages. During the stage of self-acceptance, biracial people generally have come to value their identity as something constructed out of the relationship between personal experience and social meanings of ethnicity, race, and group membership. The simple assertion of being who they are, of being biracial, is the developmental achievement of this ongoing and unfinished process.* (1992:316)

Biracial and Bicultural Identity Development in Children

Jacobs argues that "it is possible to describe a developmental course for the formation of racial identity in biracial children" (1992:199–200). Central to Jacobs' formulation is the child's perception of skin color. Jacobs notes that skin color "is used in different ways by different biracial children, as well as by the same child at different times." He suggests that "preadolescent biracial children go through three qualitatively different stages of identity development" all involving their perception of their skin color.

Stages in the Development of Biracial Identity in Children

Stage I: *pre-color constancy:* During this stage children "experiment freely with color, as they have not yet classified people into socially defined racial categories and do not yet understand that skin color is invariant."

Stage II: *post-color constancy:* At this stage children have internalized a biracial label and have attained the concept of color constancy. This realization of color constancy forms the foundation for racial ambivalence, Jacobs believes. This ambivalence is "a consequence of a racial prejudice in society" and "experiencing and working through racial ambivalence is seen as a necessary task for people of color, including biracial children."

Stage III: *biracial identity:* At this stage ambivalence is diminished or absent. Jacobs believes it is at this point that "The child discovers that racial group membership is correlated with but not determined by skin color. Rather, racial group membership is determined by parentage" (Jacobs 1992:203–206).

Parenting Biracial Children

Parents can help children develop a positive biracial or multiracial identity by providing "their children the structure and the words that help them make sense of their experiences as they develop their self-concept and self-esteem. . . . Providing open communication about race and an interracial label validates and fosters the child's rudimentary interracial self-concept" ". . . In valuing each of the child's racial and ethnic heritages, parents structure emotional safety and confidence through a positive interracial label and through modeling an ability to discuss racial and ethnic differences openly" (Kich 1992:308).

A Strengths-Based Approach

Parents of biracial children need special understanding of several important factors to help their child build a positive biracial self-concept:

1. *Fostering ego strength:* early ego-enhancing treatment of the child in the family including building "secure attachments, the support of individuation, the fostering of social and physical competencies, and encouragement of self-assertion."

2. *Biracial labeling:* presentation of a biracial label to the child by the parents assists in developing a biracial identity. This is not always necessary but is helpful often since the child "must assimilate a racial and ethnic label that is more complex and less readily available outside of his or her family than the labels of Black, White, Asian, Chicano, and so on."

3. *Ambivalence and racial material:* Parents need to realize that "their children's racial ambivalence is a developmental attainment that allows the continued exploration of racial identity."

4. *Multiracial environment for parents and children:* A multiethnic community and social environment seems basic to positive biracial identity development. This is probably even more important for a biracial child than for either an African American or white child (Jacobs 1992:204–205).

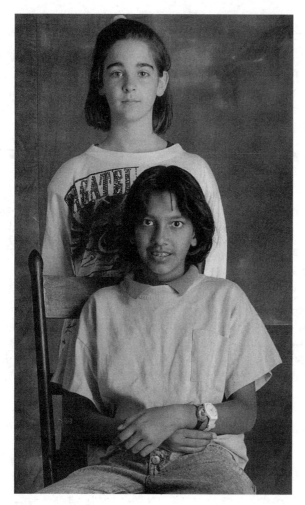

Assuming the young person seated in this photo is biracial and has white adoptive parents, what are some examples of ways those parents can foster ego strength, support biracial labeling, address racial ambivalence, and provide a multiracial environment to support positive identity development?

FOCUS: WHITENESS/WHITE IDENTITY

As we learned from exploring the notion of paradigms and in our discussion of Whiteness in Chapters 1 and 2, the dominant group tends to measure and value worth in terms of standards of whiteness. However, the concept of whiteness itself is such a "taken for granted" dimension of the traditional paradigm that as a racial construct it is largely unexamined.

Janet Helms (in Parks et al. 1996:626), a scholar who has done extensive research on the development of identity, especially racial identity, "suggested that, as the socially powerful race in this country, Whites undergo a process of racial identity development that is very different from that of nondominant groups." Parks et al.

suggest "for instance, as members of the dominant group, Whites are to some extent free simply to disengage from the development process through a change of job or locale, which eliminate their need to interact with members of other racial groups" (1996:626). In addition to being able to disengage from the white identity development process, Helms suggests that whites often deny "that a White *racial* group exists that benefits from White privilege" (1994:305).

Carter and Jones suggest a rationale for White racial identity theory in that it "allows for an understanding of various psychological expressions or resolutions regarding a person's own racial group membership and provides insight into how a person's own view of a racial self influences in turn views of other racial groups" (1996:4). They also stress that "Understanding a person's racial worldview from the perspective of racial identity theory also reveals how a person participates in and understands individual, institutional and cultural racism" (see discussion of racism, Chapter 2). Carter and Jones argue that

> *Every white person in the United States is socialized with implicit and explicit racial messages about him- or herself and members of visible racial/ ethnic groups (i.e., American Indians and Hispanic, Asian, and black Americans). Accepting these messages results in racism becoming an integral component of each white person's ego or personality. Evolving a nonracist white identity begins with individuals accepting their "whiteness" and recognizing the ways in which they participate in and benefit from individual, institutional, and cultural racism.* (1996:4)

White Identity Development Ego Statuses

Helms describes racial identity as "ego statuses that mature in a sequential manner" (in Carter and Jones 1996:4). There are a total of six ego statuses and while they may all be present in a person's ego structure at the same time, one status tends to dominate a white person's worldview at any given point. The statuses are as follows. Contact which is characterized by a naive denial that racism exists, acceptance of White values as "normal," and claims to be "color-blind." Disintegration is the stirring of internal conflict because of a recognition that racism exists; response to this status is often an overidentification or patronizing attitude toward African Americans. Reintegration is a reaction to disintegration and involves a withdrawal into white culture, denigration of African Americans, and belief in white superiority. Pseudoindependence is an intellectual, but not an emotional acceptance of African Americans, and often involves discomfort with close personal interaction with African Americans. Immersion-emersion is a search to recognize and rid oneself of personal racism and to define a nonracist white identity. Autonomy is the successful internal definition of a nonracist white identity characterized by openness to and interests in other cultures and the capacity for close personal relationships with African Americans, other people of color, and whites (Carter and Jones 1996:5–9; Parks et al. 1996:625; Helms 1994:304).

The statuses are summarized in the table below.

Summary of White Racial Identity Ego Statuses

Ego Status	Characteristics
Contact	Naiveté concerning people of color; lack of awareness of whiteness; claims to be "color blind"; racist without knowing it"
Disintegration	Awareness that whites receive preferential treatment over people of color; confusion, guilt or shame about this differential treatment based on color
Reintegration	Attempts to reduce confusion by strongly identifying with whites as superior to people of color; in denial of white racial advantage; likely to hold more prejudicial attitudes about people of color
Pseudo-Independence	Period of questioning assumptions about the inferiority of people of color; have not come to terms with racism; intellectually recognized racism, but internally/emotionally not able to deal with it; period of distancing—"only 'bad' whites are racist"
Immersion-Emersion	Person begins to fully come to terms with racism both intellectually and emotionally; begins to seek out and question other whites about recognizing and reducing racism; begins personally to do something about the reality of racism; attempts to define a personal nonracist white identity
Autonomy	Nonracist white identity is achieved and integrated into thinking, feeling and behaving; race becomes an accepted part of white identity; person is open to new information about races and is much more capable of cross-racial relationships and interactions; values diversity.

Source: Adapted from Carter and Jones 1996; Parks et al. 1996; Helms 1994.

FOCUS: WOMEN

As in the case of accounting for the developmental experiences of people of color, traditional approaches to research on human development have too often neglected or inaccurately portrayed women. However, a growing body of research on the developmental experiences and themes of women is emerging as a result of the work of a number of individuals and groups from a variety of disciplines and perspectives. The work of Sandra Harding, Evelyn Fox Keller, and others in the natural sciences (Harding 1986; Keller 1985); Nancy Chodorow in psychiatry and psychoanalysis (1978); Jean Baker Miller and her colleagues at the Stone Center for Developmental Services and

Studies at Wellesley College in development and psychology (Miller 1986; Jordan et al. 1991); Mary Belenky and her coresearchers with The Education for Women's Development Project in education (1986); Carol Gilligan's work to increase our understanding of women's developmental experiences (1982); Patricia Hill Collins's work in the area of African American feminist thought (1990); and many others have created tremendously helpful resources to begin to include and understand the alternative perspectives of women. The work of these researchers and many others is unfolding and very much in process. We will look at a number of these efforts in the sections that follow. In addition, Illustrative Reading 5.1 at the end of the chapter presents a summary of Miller's work on "The Development of Women's Sense of Self."

Women and Development: A Different Voice

In current discussions of women's development, perhaps most often referred to and most commonly used by social workers is the work of Carol Gilligan (1982). It is important to recognize as we explore the work of Gilligan and other researchers working in the area of women's development that there is a great deal of mutual influence and integration of one another's work among many of the scholars working in the area of women's development. This cooperation, interconnectedness, and interrelatedness is consistent with the alternative paradigm generally. It also reflects a recurring theme or pattern in women's development itself. Through her own research and the integration of research of others, such as Jean Baker Miller and Nancy Chodorow, for example, Gilligan offers an alternative perspective on human development that seeks to focus on and include women's developmental issues to a much greater extent than the traditional developmental approaches of Freud, Erikson, Piaget, Kohlberg, and Levinson.

As a result of her research and that of others, Gilligan suggests the need for a paradigmatic shift that includes rather than excludes the perspectives, experiences, and views of the world of women. In her work she extends developmental paradigms to include and reflect the unique experiences of women. The importance of this extension of developmental paradigms to include women is underscored by the reality that women constitute between 52 and 53 percent of the population. As we have noted before, women are hardly a minority, although they have minority status in the United States and most other societies due to their unequal power and access to resources.

Gilligan's work to include and better understand women's development resulted in her discovery of a "different voice" that she found was characterized not necessarily by gender but by theme. She found this theme originally as a result of her efforts to understand the development of moral decision making among women. The voice, Gilligan asserts, is not necessarily exclusively male or female but reflects two different modes of thought. One mode focuses on individualization and rights, the other on connectedness and responsibility. In other words, one mode reflects the dimension of separateness and impersonality consistent with traditional paradigm thinking. The other mode reflects the dimension of interrelatedness and the value of personal experiences and relationships characteristic of alternative paradigm thinking. Although these themes are not necessarily tied to gender, according to Gilligan, they do seem to reflect the different developmental experiences of males and females. The theme of relatedness and connection has also been found by a number of other researchers working in the area of women's development. The work of Jean Baker Miller (and her colleagues), published in 1976, reported that "women's sense of self becomes very much organized around being able to make and then maintain affiliation and relationships" (1976:83). Miller and her colleagues at the Stone Center for Developmental Services and Studies at Wellesley College came to refer to this significant and recurring theme in the developmental experiences of women as "self-in-relation theory" (Jordan et al. 1991:vi).

Gilligan's work and the work of others takes us beyond traditional paradigms of development by presenting evidence that "normal" development may very well be different for females than for males for a variety of reasons. Gilligan suggests that traditional models and scales of human development based almost exclusively on the study of males do not readily or necessarily apply to the development of females. She suggests that these differences in developmental experiences and patterns between males and females often result in depictions of females in traditional developmental models as developing "less normally" than males. Rather than women developing less normally, this alternative approach posits that "the failure of women to fit existing models of human growth may point to a problem in the representation, a limitation in the conception of human condition, an omission of certain truths about life" (Gilligan 1982:2). In other words, the problem is one of model not femaleness.

Women and Identity Formation

Gilligan's work focuses on women's identity formation and moral development. Her research focuses on adolescence and adulthood. However, she extends her approach to include assumptions about development during infancy and childhood as well. Gilligan's work is especially helpful in expanding understanding of the concepts of identity formation and moral development. These are central concepts in the traditional developmental models of Erikson and Kohlberg. As we will see, a shift in perspective, in this case from male to female, can result in dramatic shifts in the meanings attached to such apparently universal developmental issues as identity formation and moral development.

Gilligan reminds us that traditional models for explaining human development are often put forth as resulting directly from scientific, objective, and value-neutral processes. When we find that many of these models are based exclusively on the experiences of males, although their assertions about development are applied equally to females, the assumptions of objectivity and neutrality must be questioned. We are reminded of our earlier assertions about paradigms as human constructions subject to the limitations of the perspectives held by the humans creating them. This is essentially the case Gilligan makes about seeing life, specifically identity formation and moral development, through men's eyes only. As is the case with virtually all researchers concerned with individual development—both traditional and alternative—a primary concern of Gilligan's is that of identity formation. How do we come to see ourselves as we see ourselves? How we see ourselves has countless implications for how we behave.

Gilligan incorporated in her approach to understanding *identity formation* the alternative developmental perspective of Nancy Chodorow (1974, 1978). Chodorow tried to account for male/female personality and role differences by focusing on "the fact that women, universally, are largely responsible for early child care." Chodorow suggested that this early social environmental difference results in basic differences in personality development of girls and boys. She posited that personality formation is almost entirely set by three years of age, and that for both girls and boys the caretaker during the first three years is almost universally female. This early environment results in female identity formation taking place in a context of ongoing relationship, since "mothers tend to experience their daughters as more like and continuous with, themselves." Girls in turn see themselves as more "like their mother, thus fusing the experience of attachment with the process of identity formation" (in Gilligan 1982:7–8). This early environment also results in boys being experienced by their mother as male opposite. Boys "in defining themselves as masculine separate their mothers from themselves." By doing this, relatedness, connectedness, and empathy is less central in their early identity formation and definition of self. Individuation and separation is instead more central in males' identity formation (in Gilligan 1982:8).

Contrary to Freud's traditional notion of ego weakness in girls, Chodorow suggests that "girls emerge from this period [the first three years] with a basis for 'empathy' built into their primary definition of self in a way that boys do not." At the end of this early developmental process, "girls come to experience themselves as less differentiated than boys, as more continuous with and related to the external object-world, and as differently oriented to their inner object-world as well" (in Gilligan 1982:8).

Chodorow concludes that these different early experiences have significant consequences for the developmental experiences of both males and females throughout their lives. Attachment continues to be more important for female identity formation and separation and individuation remains more important for the development of masculinity in boys. Male identity tends to be threatened by intimacy, female identity, by separation. Males tend to have difficulty with relationships while females tend to have problems with individuation (in Gilligan 1982).

These different developmental paths are not necessarily problematic in themselves. They become problematic only when they are valued differently. For example, when the biases in the traditional literature of development defines "normalcy" as the "ability to separate." Empathy and connectedness then become "abnormal." When differences in development are valued differently *and* tied to gender, we see over half of the human family devalued because of different developmental experiences.

Sex differences in psychological research are neither new nor necessarily surprising. However, a problem emerges when "different" becomes defined as "better or worse than." When women do not conform to a standard based on men's interpretation of research data, the conclusion all too often is that there is something wrong with women, not with the standard (Gilligan 1982:14). In the case here of individuation and relatedness, the perspective of the observer has a good deal to do with the value accorded developmental experiences and behaviors of the observed. From Freud's and Erikson's male-centered perspective, identity constructed around attachment is ultimately a source of developmental weakness; from Chodorow's female-centered perspective, it is a source of developmental strength.

Women and Moral Development

Another core concern of researchers attempting to understand human behavior both from traditional and alternative perspectives is that of *moral development*. How do we come to define what is right and wrong and how do we come to base our decisions and actions on our definitions of what is right and what is wrong? Gilligan's approach to moral development emerged from looking at women's lives. Her alternative model is marked not by age-based developmental stages as are most traditional models—Kohlberg's for example—but by themes or principles. Her model integrates the following principles or themes:

1. Moral problems arise out of conflicting responsibilities rather than competing rights.

2. Moral problems require resolution through thinking that is contextual and narrative rather than formal and abstract.

3. Morality centers on the activity of care; it centers around responsibilities and relationships in the same way that morality as fairness centers on understanding rights and rules.

This framework's emphasis on context, relationship, and interrelatedness has much in common with several of the dimensions of alternative paradigm thinking that we explored earlier (Chapter 2).

In contrast, Kohlberg's is a morality focused on a reflective understanding of human rights. A morality of rights differs from a morality of responsibility in that it emphasizes separation rather than connection and sees the individual rather than the relationship as primary. Gilligan believes that a perspective on morality that emphasizes responsibility and relationship does not mutually exclude a sense of individuality or autonomy. She suggests, as Loevinger does, that we see autonomy in the context of relationship. Loevinger urges us away from traditional either/or dichotomous thinking about morality and suggests we replace this thinking with "a feeling for the complexity and multifaceted character of real people in real situations" (Loevinger in Gilligan 1982:21).

The responsibility conception of morality focuses on the limitations of any particular resolution and is concerned with the conflicts that remain. This conception does not focus on single solutions to single moral problems but focuses instead on the connectedness of any solution to an interdependent network of other problems and other solutions. In other words, it is an integrative, holistic, contextual approach consistent with one of the basic dimensions of our alternative paradigms and with social work purposes and values.

The gender implications of the two very different views of moral development are significant, Gilligan believes. Women's moral judgments show difference between the sexes but also give an alternate conception of maturity. Women bring to the life cycle a different and valuable point of view and a different and valuable ordering of priorities. For Gilligan (1982:23) "the elusive mystery of women's development lies in its recognition of the continuing importance of attachment in the human life cycle." Certainly such a perspective is an important one for social workers.

Gilligan cautions, though, that these different themes of moral development are not "gendered" in any absolute sense and should not result in generalizations about women's or men's development. Indeed, some women's sense of morality may be rights-focused and some men's may be responsibility-focused. However, given the differing findings of her work with female subjects and Kohlberg's work with male subjects, it is understandable that these differing notions of morality would be sources of uncertainty, confusion, and fear for any person whose sense of determining what is correct and "right" behavior comes from the other perspective. She suggests, for example, that it is understandable that a morality of rights and noninterference may appear unsettling to women in its potential justification of indifference and unconcern. It is also clearly understandable that from a male perspective, a morality of responsibility appears inconclusive and diffuse, given its insistent contextual relativism (Gilligan 1982: 23 and 123ff).

Another significant perspective that emerges from Gilligan's research is her notion of an *ethic of care,* more clearly delineated within women's identities and sense of morality. This ethic of care emphasizing relationship and responsibility for others is interconnected with the concept of "integrity" discussed by traditional paradigm researchers such as Erikson. *Integrity,* a focus of much adult developmental thinking, has a different (and richer, more complex) meaning for women, "because women's sense of integrity appears to be entwined with an ethic of care . . . to see themselves as women is to see themselves in a relationship of connection . . . the ethic or responsibility can become a self-chosen anchor of personal integrity and strength" (Gilligan 1982:171).

Gilligan believes that an "ethic of care" has significant implications for such societal concerns as aggression and hierarchy or inequality. She suggests that "women's development delineates the path not only to a less violent life but also to a maturity realized through interdependence and taking care." She points out that "just as the language of responsibilities provides a weblike imagery of relationships to replace a hierarchical ordering that dissolves with the coming of equality, so the language of rights underlines the importance of including in the network of care not only the other but also the self." She believes that "in the different voice of women lies the truth of an ethic of care, the tie between relationship and responsibility, and the origins of aggression in the failure of connection" (1982:172–173). Such a perspective on care, relationship, and responsibility has much in common with the historical mission and values of social work, with their emphases on inherent human worth and dignity and with social change to achieve social and economic justice and maximize individual and collective human potential.

The "ethic of care" is also consistent with our alternative paradigm's concern for integration and interrelatedness. The commonality is perhaps most evident in Gilligan's suggestion that it is essential to begin to integrate the two disparate voices reflected in traditional models and in her alternate model of human development. She believes the two voices are not mutually exclusive: "While an ethic of justice proceeds from the premise of equality—that everyone should be treated the same—an ethic of care rests on the premise of nonviolence—that no one should be hurt. In the representation of maturity, both perspectives converge in the realization that just as inequality adversely affects both parties in an unequal relationship, so too violence is destructive for everyone involved" (1982:174).

Criticism

Critics of Gilligan's approach and other researchers investigating interconnections among race, class, and gender in developmental experiences suggest that the experiences of the males and females in Gilligan's research can be assumed to reflect the experiences of persons who are white and relatively well-off financially (middle-class). These scholars are critical of Gilligan's work for not adequately addressing the diversity of characteristics, experiences, and environmental contexts among women. These criticisms have often focused also on the necessity of recognizing the interlocking nature of oppressions resulting from gender, class, and race in the United States and Western society.

Stack (1986:322), for example, finds that "the caste and economic system within rural southern communities creates a setting in which Black women and men have a very similar experience of class, that is, a similar relationship to production, employment, and material and economic rewards." Her suggestion is that in many cases women and men of color may have more in common with each other than do many white and black women because of the overriding impact of race and class. She suggests that for many African Americans "under conditions of economic deprivation there is a convergence between women and men in their construction of themselves in relationship to others, and that these conditions produce a convergence seen in women's and men's vocabulary of rights, morality, and the social good" (Stack 1986:322–323). However, Stack does not suggest that such work as Gilligan's should be discounted because of its lack of incorporation of factors of race and class along with gender. She suggests that future research should build upon this current work by adding dimensions such as race and class (1986:324).

Models of Women's Identity Development

In addition to the work of Carol Gilligan, Jean Baker Miller, and others concerned with understanding more fully the development and identity formation of women are models of women and development proposed by Helms and Conarton and Kreger-Silverman. The model developed by Helms was influenced by her work on racial identity development and is presented in Figure 5.5. The model developed by Conarton and Kreger-Silverman was influenced by the work of Carol Gilligan as well as Jung and Dabrowski (Wastell 1996) and is presented in Figure 5.6.

FIGURE 5.5   Womanist Identity

Pre-encounter (Womanist I)	Acceptance of traditional sex roles; denial of societal bias.
Encounter (Womanist II)	Questioning and confusion about gender roles. Tentative exploration of solutions to role conflicts.
Immersion-Emersion (Womanist III)	Externally based feminist stance. Hostility toward men; idealization of women. Intense relationships with other women.
Internalization (Womanist IV)	Internally defined and integrated female identity without undue reliance on either traditional roles or feminist viewpoint.

Adapted from: Parks, E. E., Carter, R. T., and Gushue, G. V. (1996, July/August). "At the crossroads: Racial and womanist identity development in Black and White women." *Journal of Counseling and Development, 74,* p. 625. Copyright American Counseling Association. Reprinted with permission.

FIGURE 5.6 Conarton and Kreger-Silverman's Development Theory

Phase	Feature
1. Bonding	Interdependence with mother as unique and central relationship. This connectedness enables female children to enter early into nurturing roles.
2. Orientation to Others	Caring and connectedness to others with thin ego boundaries. May lead to difficulty in recognizing that some relationships are unbalanced.
3. Cultural Adaptation	It is during this phase that many women become "pseudomen" to adapt to Western cultural demands. This is when girls lose their "voice" (Gilligan 1991).
4. Awakening and Separation	During this phase, women begin to assert themselves in ways that are threatening to men (e.g., rejection of traditional views on women's roles in child rearing, putting themselves before others).
5. Development of the Feminine	Deeper exploration of needs. This involves the examination of the self and mobilizing the necessary will to implement the necessary changes.
6. Empowerment	This is not to have power over others but to have power to prevent themselves from being disempowered by others. Women use methods of "cooperation, consensus and mediation" (Conarton & Kreger-Silverman, 1988:58).
7. Spiritual Development	This phase involves the intuitive process of self-examination in which the younger naive self is put to rest. Power is again the focus but in the context of innermost sources, which can often frighten people around them.
8. Integration	The task is for women to be "teachers and healers" to undo the damage of unaware societies and groups. In this phase, women become oriented outward and inward at the same time. This means allowing their families to tend to themselves.

Source: Wastell, C. A. (1996). "Feminist developmental theory: Implications for counseling." *Journal of Counseling and Development, 74,* p. 578. © ACA. Reprinted with permission.

Adult Women and Developmental Experiences

As with traditional studies of women's development, studies of women's midlife experiences have been relatively few and have been too often generalized from studies of men at midlife done by men. McQuaide suggests that earlier studies of women's midlife experiences are also limited because women's experiences have changed radically as a result of the women's movement, feminism, greater reproductive choices, and more women entering the workforce. In addition, McQuaide argues that studies of women have been "problem-based" rather than "strengths-based." McQuaide's study of midlife, white women living in the New York area found that "midlife, for white, middle-class and upper middle-class women, at least, is not a time of torment" (McQuaide 1998:21–29). The reader should note that McQuaide clearly identifies the narrow scope of the population she used in her research. What are the limitations of this sample in terms of race and geographic representation? McQuaide also found that well-being for the women she studied was increased by having a "confidante or a group of women friends, as well as having positive role models" (1998:29). She also found that for the women she studied, having a positive and strong self-concept in the face of a society marked by the social devaluation of mid-life women was important (McQuaide 1998:30).

Hunter and Sundel (1994) also argue for a more realistic and balanced appraisal of the realities of life for middle-aged women than has previously been presented in the literature and media. They do this by outlining current realities facing these women, both in terms of "Midlife Worries for Women" and in terms of "Midlife Advantages for Women."

MidLife Worries/Problems/Realities

"The middle years for women are often described as the worst—as a time of adolescent children, crises, suicides, the departure of husbands, empty nests, fading charms, melancholia, responsibilities for aging parents, and pressures to prepare for financial security in their final years. In addition, there are all sorts of physical reminders that one is not as young as one used to be" (Hunter and Sundel 1994:114).

- *Depression:* Depression increases for both men and women with age, but incidence is greater for women throughout their lives and twice as high as for men in midlife.
- *Physical health:* Most women are healthy in midlife, but health risks do increase.
- *Coronary heart disease:* Biggest killer of women in the United States of any disease. One in two women will die from it; African American women are 60 percent more likely than white women to die from coronary heart disease.
- *Breast cancer:* Responsible for 32 percent of cancers in women; leading cause of death in women aged 40–44; almost 80 percent of women with breast cancer are over 80.
- *Lung cancer:* In 1987, for the first time more women died from lung cancer than from breast cancer; it is now the leading cause of cancer death in women (Hunter and Sundel 1994:114–116).
- *Poverty:* 60 percent chance of a woman being poor in old age; much higher chance for African American and Hispanic women.
- *Caretakers of aging parents:* Caring for elderly parents is a major stressor for midlife women.

- *Daughter as caregivers to elderly parents:* While both spouses are living the wife is most likely to be caregiver for the ill elderly husband; but women and daughters are most likely to provide the care for most elderly.
- *Working daughters and caregiving:* Even though over half of all women 45–64 years old work outside the home, daughters are still the most likely to provide care for elderly relatives (Hunter and Sundel 1994:114–118).

Midlife Strengths/Realities

In addition to stressors and difficulties one must consider opportunities for midlife women.

- *Crisis is not likely:* No evidence to support midlife as necessarily a time of crisis for men or for women; most persons at midlife do not experience major crises, though questioning of goals may occur; midlife is not a time of increased divorce, neuroticism, suicide, or drastic career change.
- *Empty nest or menopause is unlikely to be a major trauma for midlife women:* On the contrary "for many women, midlife is a time of greater self-esteem and self-acceptance."
- *Prime Time: The 50s:* Mitchell and Helson (in Hunter and Sundel 1994: 119) suggested "that the middle or early post-parental period is the best time, or prime of life, for women because of changes in roles and freed-up energies." They found women in their 50s to rate their quality of life the highest of any period. Sources of this high quality of life include:
  - *Economic status:* Income for many women and their families tends to peak in the pre-retirement 50s.
  - *Empty nest:* Rather than a source of trauma, "the children's departure is usually viewed with anticipation, and the available time and space are not seen as 'empty'." Women are likely to have a greater sense of control and time to focus on their own development.
  - *Menopause:* "Major myth of menopause is that it causes emotional disturbance or a nervous breakdown and severe physical symptoms." There is significant evidence to suggest these claims are highly exaggerated and countered by positive elements of menopause: "few women at 50 see inability to have children as problem. There is also evidence that when controlling for income and employment status, mothers and women who never had children are no different in terms of happiness or satisfaction with life." Some researchers suggest changing the traditional decriptors of menopause, for example, changing the "symptoms" of menopause to the "signs" of menopause might help reduce the disease imagery.
  - *Sexual capacity and interest:* "whereas men's orgasmic capacity gradually decreases during the adult years, women's capacity does not decrease until about age 60."
  - *Intimate links with partners and friends:* intimacy and communication with partner and network of friends may very well increase (Excerpts from: Hunter and Sundel 1994:118–123).

Biology and Reductionism

We explored the notion of reductionism and traditional developmental theories in Chapter 4. Hunter and Sundel (1994:123–124) suggest that much research on women's development has been reductionist in its overemphasis on biological factors and neglect of other critical factors. They posit that much of the imbalance and one-dimensional biological approach to stereotypes of midlife for women, results from sexism because such empowering and independent portrayals do not support male dominance. To counter this imbalance, Gergen suggested that "theoretical frameworks for studying women should emphasize other aspects of women's lives, such as the political, economic, moral, aesthetic" in order to "liberate women from 'biology'" (in Hunter and Sundel 1994:123–124).

FOCUS: SEXUAL ORIENTATION

Next we turn our attention to alternate models for understanding the special developmental issues and tasks faced by gay men, lesbians and bisexual persons. Several different models of identity development are offered from a variety of perspectives for helping us develop a more holistic perspective on the development of gay men and lesbians.

Current estimates place the gay male and lesbian population at approximately ten percent of the general population. The percentage represents some twenty-five million people in the United States alone. The number of persons who identify themselves as bisexual is less certain. In addition to the significant number of gay men, lesbians, and bisexual persons in the population, the significance of increasing our understanding of the developmental and environmental experiences of gay men and lesbians is underscored by the intensity of controversy surrounding many issues related to sexual orientation. Central to these controversies is the question of whether gay men and lesbians should have the same rights and protections as heterosexuals in all spheres of personal and social life. The rights in question include such basic ones as parenthood, the right to form and have legal recognition of gay- and lesbian-headed families, the right to serve in the military and other social institutions, the right to have access to housing without discrimination, and the right to have partners and family members covered by health insurance and other job-related benefits taken for granted by heterosexual workers and their families.

Sexual Orientation and Biology

In addition, many questions remain about the origins and causes of homosexuality itself and about whether homosexuality is an orientation beyond the control of the individual or whether being gay or lesbian is a preference or a choice one makes. There is significant new evidence emerging from research in the natural sciences suggesting that biological factors operate in the determination of sexual orientation. These findings suggest that being a gay or lesbian person is no more chosen than being left-handed or brown-eyed is chosen. This is one of the reasons that the term *sexual orientation* is now preferred over the term *sexual preference*. *Preference* suggests one can choose to be or not be gay or lesbian. While one may choose not to openly acknowledge to self or to others one's homosexual identity, one's sexual *orientation* does not appear to be so clearly a matter of choice. This is perhaps best explained as the difference between acceptance of one's homosexuality and the choice not to accept or act on one's sexual feelings. The process of acknowledging gay or lesbian feelings and identity to self and/or others is often referred to as **coming out.**

In one study of gay men with twin and adopted brothers, substantial genetic influences in male sexual orientation were suggested. In this study homosexuality occurred among both brothers 52 percent of the time for identical twins who share their genes and 22 percent of the time among fraternal twins who share half the same genes. Among brothers with different biological parents but adopted into and raised in the same home, only 6 percent of the time did both brothers have a homosexual orientation (*Science News* 1992:6). In another study, significant differences in the hypothalamus of the brain were found between gay men and nongay men, again suggesting a biological link in sexual orientation, but this time through a study using physiological evidence rather than the more sociological evidence in the study of twins and brothers (*Science* 1991:956–957). These studies are, of course, not proof in any final sense, but they do raise important questions about biology and sexual orientation. Since both of these studies included only gay men and excluded lesbians, the biological origins of lesbian orientation are even less certain. Even given the uncertainties about the biological origins of gay or lesbian orientation, there are a number of theoretical models available that can help us understand the developmental experiences and environments of gay men and lesbians. We explore some of these models next.

Human Development Perspective On Lesbian, Gay Male, and Bisexual Development

According to D'Augelli, in the last twenty years (1974–1994) in terms of perspectives on lesbian, gay male, and bisexual persons, "the changes have been dramatic—from mental illness to alternative life-style to sexual variation to diverse minority" (1994:328). D'Augelli suggests a human development model for understanding the development of gay men, lesbians, and bisexual persons. The phases of this model are outlined below.

1. *Exiting Heterosexual Identity:* "This set of concerns involves personal and social recognition that one's sexual orientation is not heterosexual. . . . Exiting from heterosexuality also means telling *others* that one is lesbian, gay, or bisexual. This 'coming out' begins with the very first person to whom an individual discloses and continues throughout life, decreasing only to the extent that the person is consistently and publicly identified with a non-heterosexual label."

2. *Developing a Personal Lesbian-Gay-Bisexual Identity Status:* "An individual must develop a sense of personal socioaffective stability that effectively summarizes thoughts, feelings, and desires. . . . such an initial status may be subject to revision as more experience is accumulated. . . . To a large degree, they cannot confirm their sexual-orientation status without contact with others."

3. *Developing a Lesbian-Gay-Bisexual Social Identity:* "This involves creating a large and varied set of people who know of the person's sexual orientation and are available to provide social support. This, too, is a lifelong process that has a profound effect on personal development."

4. *Becoming a Lesbian-Gay-Bisexual Offspring:* "Parental relationships are often temporarily disrupted with the disclosure of sexual orientation. . . . Generally, families show patterns of adaptation, with parents, siblings, and members of the extended family coming to overlapping, but not identical approaches."

5. *Developing a Lesbian-Gay-Bisexual Intimacy Status:* "The psychological complexities of same-sex dyadic relationships are made much more problematic by the invisibility of lesbian and gay couples in our cultural imagery. . . . The lack of cultural scripts directly applicable to lesbian, gay, and bisexual people leads to ambiguity and uncertainty, but it also forces the emergence of personal, couple-specific, and community norms, which should be more personally adaptive."

6. *Entering a Lesbian-Gay-Bisexual Community:* "This set of identity processes involves the development of commitment to political and social action. For some who believe their sexual orientation to be a purely private matter, this never happens. . . . To be lesbian, gay, or bisexual in the fullest sense—to have a meaningful identity— leads to a consciousness of the history of one's own oppression. It also, generally, leads to an appreciation of how the oppression continues, and commitment to resisting it" (1994:324–328).

Multiple Meanings of Lesbianism

Rothblum (1994:630) asks the question: "What is a lesbian?" She notes that "Burch has differentiated between 'primary lesbians,' who have never had sexual relations with men, and 'bisexual lesbians,' who self-identified as heterosexual and had sexual relations with men before they had sexual relations with women. Very few women have had exclusively same-gender sexual experiences" (Rothblum 1994:630). Rothblum suggests that "Once women come out as lesbians, the lesbian community presumes that this will be permanent; in fact some lesbians subsequently become sexual with men" (1994:630). Rothblum also asks the important and often controversial question: "Is sexual orientation a choice or is it predetermined (e.g., genetic, hormonal)?" She indicates the varied perspectives on the answer to this question even between lesbians and gay men by noting that "generally, lesbians view sexual orientation as a choice (e.g., they state they became lesbians because it was more congruent with radical feminism), whereas gay men are more likely to view it as predetermined" (Rothblum 1994:630).

According to Rothblum, traditional definitions "of sexual activity, both the heterosexual and the lesbian/bisexual versions, focus on genital activity and thus ignore other, nongenital sexual experiences that women may have had" (1994:633). She specifically points out that

> We have no terminology for the early sexual crushes that some girls develop on
> other people, usually a female friend or female teacher. We have no language for
> the sexual feelings that arise between adult friends, even when both friends are
> in sexual relationships with other people. In contrast, if the friends engage in
> genital sexual activity with each other, we immediately have language; they are

having an affair. . . . In the lesbian communities, ex-lovers often remain friends and friends often become lovers . . . closeted lesbians may introduce their lovers to their family or co-workers as their friends. . . . Lack of language for sexuality that is not focused on genital contact means that such experiences are forgotten or cannot clearly be articulated. (Rothblum 1994:633)

What Is a Lesbian Relationship?

Rothblum points out that "the sex-focused definition of what constitutes a lesbian relationship" is extremely limited because it "ignores the reality of women's ways of relating" (1994:634). According to Rothblum, "for centuries, women have felt strong love, affection, and intimacy for other women, even when both women were married to men. When two unmarried women lived together as spinsters, they were considered to be in a **'Boston marriage,'** [emphasis added] a term that reflected the presumed asexual nature of the relationship (the word Boston usually referred to Puritan values)" (1994:635). Lillian Faderman (in Rothblum 1994:335) has described the passion and love between women in the 19th century:

It became clear that women's love relationships have seldom been limited to that one area of expression, that love between women has been primarily a sexual phenomenon only in male fantasy literature. "Lesbian" describes a relationship in which two women's strongest emotions and affections are directed toward each other. Sexual contact may be a part of the relationship to a greater or lesser degree, or it may be entirely absent.

Lewis's Model of Lesbian Development

An important addition to the literature on sexual orientation and development is the work of Lewis (1984). Her work is especially helpful because it focuses on the developmental experiences of lesbians, while the preponderance of research on sexual orientation uses male subjects and, like traditional or dominant perspectives, generalizes the gay experience to lesbians. Lewis's approach is also important in our efforts here because it operates from a strengths perspective. Lewis describes several developmental phases a woman may go through to form a healthy self-concept as a lesbian. These developmental phases are described below.

1. Awareness of being different may start as early as age four or five. Some young girls are able to verbalize this feeling and some are able to do so only later. For some this feeling of differentness stays below the level of awareness until adolescence or adulthood. Because of social stigma and lack of a vocabulary for same-sex attractiveness other than negative words like "queer" or "homo" the feeling may be denied or sublimated to try to conform to social roles consistent with heterosexuality. Childhood and particularly adolescence may be times of isolation and withdrawal with a sense of "what's wrong with me?"

2. Dissonance. Conflict occurs between socialization processes that tell her to marry and have children and her feelings of emotional and erotic attraction to other women. This usually occurs during adolescence and young adulthood. It often involves feelings of denial, shame, anxiety, and ambivalence. Such feelings may be heightened because, unlike members of visible minority groups whose parents may teach them coping skills for survival in a hostile environment, the young lesbian learns no coping skills and is likely to not be supported by her family.

As noted earlier, same sex attractions, experiences, and behaviors exist on a continuum from exclusively heterosexual to exclusively homosexual. Women in the middle of this range may not feel as much dissonance as those on the exclusively homosexual end. These women may have lived as heterosexuals earlier, but may later in life acknowledge identities as lesbians.

3. Relationships. Movement from internal feelings and verbal processes of same-sex identity to acting on these feelings and processes. Owing to the developmental importance for women of acting in the context of relationship, sexual exploration and experimentation is likely to occur in the context of a relationship in contrast to sexual exploration and experimentation for men. Because lesbians, like gay men, are unlikely to have access to role models or same-sex courtship experiences, during adolescence these relationships may be stormy and of relatively short duration. This process of relationship building and experimentation involves a "search for community" in which to build, nurture, and sustain relationships supported by a community network.

This period is likely to involve "coming out" in various degrees and contexts. Such coming out may result in definition of one's identity as a "separatist" and attempts to minimize contact with men and even with nonlesbian women. This separatism can be a healthy and functional period during which the woman can explore her own strengths, attitudes, and relationships. A woman may choose not to be separatist and may as a result experience some isolation from elements of the lesbian community for her maintenance of connection to the heterosexual world, while also feeling a lack of fit in the heterosexual world.

Family may present a formidable challenge to coming out. Coming out to family is frightening and difficult for many lesbians, but for many it is also an important part of claiming or reclaiming a positive self-concept and identity.

4. Stable Lesbian Identity. Emergence of a stable identity as a lesbian is accompanied for many by a sense of settling down. The woman becomes more self-accepting and resolves much of the earlier dissonance, fear, and anger. Development of a community of friends with similar values akin to a "fictive family" (this concept is defined in Chapter 6) offers additional support. This is a period often marked by formation of an ongoing committed relationship and establishment of a life-style around that relationship.

5. Integration. Involves an acceptance and comfortableness with her sexual identity that includes a positive self-concept. Her lesbianism becomes an accepted and established part of her overall identity. She may during this period decide to become more open about her identity, though remaining aware of the pain of doing so that results from an oppressive culture (Lewis 1984:464–468).

It is important to recognize that the processes discussed here, though presented as linear, do not necessarily occur linearly. Some parts of the process may be experienced more than once and not necessarily in the order presented. Changes in environments and relationships may result in renegotiating various elements of the process of building and rebuilding stable identity. Identity development may, for some persons, also be much more serendipitous. A sexual encounter or relationship with another woman may just "happen" without a great deal of forethought and the phases of sense of difference and dissonance and search for community may not have occurred. If after the encounter a woman chooses to integrate her same-sex feelings into her overall sense of identity the other phases may then occur (Lewis 1984:468).

Bisexualities

Many of the issues about sexuality as a continuum and as expressed in multiple ways (see earlier section on sexuality) can be applied to thinking about bisexuality. For example, bisexual identity and bisexual behavior are not necessarily the same thing. The box below provides some answers to common questions about bisexuality.

SOME COMMON QUESTIONS AND ANSWERS ABOUT BISEXUALITY

What do you mean by "bisexual" anyway?

Bisexuality means sexual or romantic attraction or behavior directed towards some members of more than one sex.

What is "a bisexual"?

A strict definition of a bisexual would be someone who has romantic and/or sexual relations with other people of more than one sex (though not necessarily at the same time). However, since not everyone has necessarily had the opportunity to act on their sexual/romantic attractions, some people prefer a looser definition; for instance, that a bisexual is a person who—in their own estimation—feels potentially able to have such attraction. This could be anyone who has erotic, affectionate, or romantic feelings for, fantasies of, and/or experiences with both men and women. A bisexual may be more attracted to one sex than the other, attracted equally to both, or find people's sex unimportant. The strength of their attractions to men and women may vary over time.

Source: *Bisexuality.* World Wide Web. Available: http://www.biresource.org/bisexuality.html

Bisexual Myths and Stereotypes

Eliason (1996) points out a number of myths and stereotypes about bisexual persons. These myths and stereotypes reflect the complexities of a non-binary notion of sexual orientation. While there are few models and relatively little research on strengths-based approaches to understanding sexual orientation in relation to gay men and lesbians, there are even fewer resources available to assist us in understanding the complexities of bisexuality both individually across the lifespan and socially in terms of group and community attitudes and perspectives concerning bisexual persons. According to Eliason "Most people appear to have even more negativity and bewilderment about bisexuals than gay men or lesbians" (1996:131).

Stereotypes

- Bisexuals are just confused—they cannot decide whether to be homosexual or heterosexual.
- Bisexuals are promiscuous and must always have a partner of each gender.
- Bisexuals are afraid to admit that they are really lesbian or gay.
- Bisexuals are incapable of sustaining a long-term relationship and will always leave one person for someone of the other gender. (Eliason 1996:131)

According to Eliason (1996:131), traditional myths and stereotypes about bisexual persons have more recently been exacerbated by misconceptions about the interrelationship of bisexuality and AIDS:

> There is also a strong feeling among some people that bisexuals are responsible for bringing AIDS into the heterosexual community. Centers for Disease Control researchers found that risk behaviors, not risk groups, are the important variable. The lesbian, gay, and bisexual communities are among the most knowledgeable about HIV transmission and safer sex techniques. The greatest risk appears to be the large number of men who identify themselves as heterosexual but regularly engage in sex with men and do not inform their female lovers or do not engage in safer sex practices.

Bisexual Research

Contrary to the misunderstandings and myths described above, there is some research that does help inform our understanding of the variation and complexity of bisexuality. Eliason (1994:131) points out, for example, that

> Weinberg, Williams, and Pryor found that there were many different ways to experience bisexuality. Some were more attracted to women than to men (i.e., rarely is there a 50–50 distribution of sexual attractions); a few were simultaneous bisexuals (at any given time, having a lover of each gender), but most were serial bisexuals with one lover at a time. Bisexuals were no more confused about their identities than were lesbians or gay men, and even heterosexuals often experienced some confusion (70% of bisexuals, 65% of lesbians and gay men, and 28% of heterosexuals were confused about their sexual identity at some time in their lives).

Bisexuality may be much more common than most people think. Research carried out at the Harvard School of Public Health in 1994 found that 20.8 percent of the men and 17.8 percent of the women studied admitted to same-sex sexual attraction/behavior at some time in their lives (Harley 1996:www).

Cass's Model of Homosexual Identity Formation

Cass (1984:143) presents a model of homosexual identity formation that focuses "on the homosexual situation as experienced and perceived by homosexuals themselves." Themes common in a variety of models of homosexual identity development include change and growth as central to identity development. This is true of Cass's model as well. Her model differs from some others in that it takes a strengths perspective and does not operate from the assumption "that people perceive the acquisition of a homosexual identity in a negative light." It also differs from some other models in that it applies to identity formation for both gay men and lesbians.

Cass perceives identity development for homosexuals to proceed through six stages according to a variety of cognitive, behavioral, and affective dimensions (1984: 147). At each stage, however, the decision not to proceed any further in the development of a homosexual identity may occur. Identity formation at any stage may take either a negative path away from acceptance and integration of a positive identity or a positive path toward acceptance and integration of a positive homosexual identity as part of one's total self-image. *Identity foreclosure* is the choice by an individual at any stage of homosexual identity development not to proceed any further. However, choosing identity foreclosure does not mean that homosexuality itself can be simply chosen or rejected. It simply means choices are made not to act upon feelings or continue to explore those feelings. Cass's stages of homosexual identity formation are:

Stage 1: *Identity Confusion.* Persons at this stage face considerable confusion. Their previous identities in terms of sexual orientation are questioned as they perceive that their behaviors "(actions, feelings, thoughts) may be defined as homosexual."

Stage 2: *Identity Comparison.* The person accepts the possibility of a homosexual identity. He or she faces feelings of alienation with the recognition of clear differences between one's self and nonhomosexual others. If identity foreclosure does not occur, the individual may choose to make contacts with other homosexuals as a way of lessening feelings of alienation.

Stage 3: *Identity Tolerance.* Tolerance rather than acceptance of a homosexual self-image is characteristic of this stage. Increasing commitment to homosexual identity results in seeking out companionship of other homosexuals. Disclosure of one's homosexuality to heterosexuals or "coming out" is rare during this stage. The tendency is to maintain two identities, a public identity shared with heterosexuals and a private identity shared with homosexuals.

Stage 4: *Identity Acceptance.* "Increased contact with the homosexual subculture encourages a more positive view of homosexuality and the gradual development of a network of homosexual friends." One attempts to both fit into society and retain a homosexual life-style. "Passing" or pretending heterosexuality is practiced in some contexts while there is also likely to be some selective disclosure to heterosexual others, especially friends and relatives.

Stage 5: *Identity Pride.* Feelings of pride in one's homosexuality, strong "loyalty to homosexuals as a group," and devaluing heterosexuality is characteristic of this stage. This stage also often includes intense anger about society's stigmatization of homosexuals. This anger is often turned to disclosure to and confrontation with heterosexuals in attempts to gain validity and equality for homosexuals.

Stage 6: *Identity Synthesis.* Positive contacts with non-homosexuals helps create a sense of not being able to simply divide the world into good homosexuals and bad heterosexuals. With this comes a sense of "people having many sides to their character, only one part of which is related to homosexuality." One develops a way of life in which homosexuality is no longer hidden and public and private selves are integrated into a positive identity (1984:147–153).

In contrast to Cass's model, the following model by Kimmel focuses on developmental issues related to adulthood and aging. It is perhaps helpful to think comparatively about this model, the traditional model of adult development by Levinson considered in Chapter 4, and the extension of Levinson's model to the experiences of African American men by Herbert earlier in this chapter.

Kimmel's Perspective on Adult Development and Aging

Kimmel (1978) presents an alternative perspective on adult development and aging of gay persons. While adulthood and aging is his focus, he also suggests some important implications for gay (or lesbian) sexual orientation during childhood and adolescence. Kimmel uses Levinson's model of adult development as a departure point. Like Herbert's research described earlier concerning African-American men, Kimmel finds a number of similarities and significant differences in the adult developmental experiences of gay men when Levinson's model is applied to a sample of gay men. Kimmel used data gathered from "14 gay men over the age of 55 in New York City" (1978:115). His data are somewhat limited in their representation of the diversity among gay persons because the study involved only white men who were almost exclusively well educated and middle-class and because the sample was quite small (1978:115).

Kimmel does address, though, the interlocking oppressions of gayness and aging in his study. He is primarily concerned with the experiences of gay men as they reach later adulthood, but his study revealed important information about the developmental experiences of gay men throughout their developmental journeys.

Kimmel notes the developmental difficulties faced by young gay persons due to the lack of role models. Because of the stigma toward gay persons and the prejudicial attitudes in the larger society, traditional developmental models assume that all persons are heterosexual. Kimmel notes, for example, that without access to "gay parent or grandparent figures to serve as role models" the gay young person is unable to know what to expect as aging occurs. Lack of information on what to expect as gay adult development and aging takes place prevents the formation of a positive identity early on in life and allows "the stigma of homosexuality to intertwine with the stereotypes about aging in our society" (1978:114).

Kimmel stresses that neglect of gay adult development has a negative impact on heterosexuals as well as gay and lesbian persons. He suggests a strengths perspective from which knowledge of gay community and interpersonal support (e.g., strong mutual support networks) and challenges (e.g., maintaining positive self-esteem and identity in the face of oppression) can inform in positive ways perspectives on adult development and aging much more generally.

Consistent with our concerns in this book that "truth" or knowledge is not an "either/or" or "binary" concept, Kimmel reminds us that sexual orientation is much more complex "than a dichotomy between exclusive heterosexuality and exclusive homosexuality" (1978:115). For many persons sexual orientation is much more ambiguous, ranging from persons who are predominantly heterosexual who engage in homosexual activities to a predominantly homosexual person who marries and has children.

Homosexuality results in important developmental differences throughout the life cycle. Little is known about the developmental issues, consequences, and experiences faced by gay and lesbian persons during childhood. However, there are significant indications not only from Kimmel's research, but from research in the natural/biological sciences as was suggested above, that strongly suggests very early and very likely genetic factors in the determination of one's sexual orientation. Such research carries a strong implication that while perhaps not recognized or acted upon in a direct sense, many developmental issues faced by children are quite likely to be influenced by sexual orientation. With sexual maturation and identity development during early adolescence usually comes recognition and beginning efforts to integrate into their psychosocial being/identity on the part of gay and lesbian persons their "sense of differentness" (1978:116).

Kimmel believes that late adolescence and early adulthood may have particular significance for lesbians and gay males. Their sense of "differentness" in sexual orientation may result in significant conflict between their sexual and affectional attraction to members of the same sex in a heterosexually focused world. In addition to the traditional uncertainties that come with awakening sexuality, for gay and lesbian young persons there are likely to be additional and more intense "guilt, anxiety or conflicts" (1978:117). This intense crisis as adulthood begins and that may involve family disruption and sometimes alienation, Kimmel believes, may actually result in a major strength for coping with a heterosexually oriented world through the remainder of adult life. Once weathered, "it may provide a perspective on major life crises and a sense of crisis competence that buffers the person against later crises." This and the ongoing experience of gay oppression may also, though, "leave a residue of anger and a sense of vulnerability not uncommon among minority group members" related to stigma and **homophobia** (*irrational fear of homosexuals*) in the larger social environment (1978:117). Many young persons struggling with sexual identity in combination with the other struggles of adolescence may not even survive to adulthood. Estimates of the number of adolescent suicides by gay or lesbian young people are as high as one out of three.

Kimmel strongly urges recognition of the diversity of gay and lesbian experiences at the same time that one must recognize developmental experiences shared by virtue of sexual orientation. In addition to great variations among gay males and lesbians in race, socioeconomic standing, occupation, religion, and politics, Kimmel describes six "social-sexual patterns" at various times during adulthood:

1. *"heterosexual marriage with or without periodic homosexual relations following or followed by a gay lifestyle;"*
2. *"celibacy with homosexual affectional orientation;"*
3. *"raising children, including adopted children;"*
4. *"long-term gay friend/lover relationship(s);"*
5. *"gay lifestyle with no long-term sexual relationships;"*
6. *"bisexual lifestyle without marriage."* (1978:118)

Aging, according to Kimmel, may be less traumatic for gay men and lesbians than for heterosexuals, given that for gay and lesbian persons the major developmental crisis is likely to have happened earlier in life when the persons are faced with coming to terms with their sexual orientation. Often this earlier crisis leads to some isolation from original families, and some researchers (Francher and Henkin in Kimmel 1978) suggest "leads to the homosexual community functioning as a quasi-family." This experience may provide supports to aging gay men and lesbians that are unavailable to traditional heterosexual persons in a more self-selected network of close friendships.

Kimmel's research pointed to significant developmental challenges as well as advantages as aging occurs for gay men. Challenges include hostility from the social environment; the importance of youthful attractiveness; loneliness around traditional family-centered holidays; some isolation from young persons resulting from the tendency to withdraw into a close circle of friends that may not include younger persons; and dealing with the death of a longtime lover, especially without social sanctions and supports. The reader should note that Kimmel's model was published prior to recognition of the AIDS epidemic and with this epidemic the process of coming to grips with the death of friends and partners now carries a heightened intensity for many gay persons both young and old.

Among the advantages/strengths Kimmel counted in his assessment of developmental issues faced by gay and lesbian persons were "a continuity of life, conscious preparation for self-reliance during the later years, experience in all of the relevant skills for maintaining oneself and one's home, and the importance of a self-created friendship network and social supports" (1978:120).

Kimmel uses Levinson's periods of adulthood to frame the postadolescent developmental experiences of gay men and lesbians. Levinson's *Early Adult Transition* (ages seventeen to twenty-two) marks the boundary between adolescence and adulthood. This is a time of formation of initial adult identity. For the respondents in a study of gay and lesbian psychologists by Riddle and Morin, this was a period during which, for lesbians, one's first same-sex sexual experience took place (for gay men this tended to occur during adolescence at approximately age fifteen). For gay men the early adult transition was a time when a gay man began considering himself homosexual (for lesbians this tended to happen at age twenty-three). The reader is cautioned to remember the hazards of forgetting that individual developmental differences result in significant ranges in chronological ages during which a specific developmental task happens.

Levinson's period, *Entering the Adult World* (ages twenty-two to twenty-eight), includes initial choices about occupations, love and peer relationships, values, and lifestyles. The psychologists referred to above reported having their first homosexual relationships during this period. Levinson's *Age 30 Transition* (ages twenty-eight to thirty-three) for the gay psychologists involved acquiring a positive gay identity and "coming out" or disclosing their gay identity to friends and parents (Kimmel 1978: 121–122).

For the gay men studied by Kimmel, Levinson's development events and stages varied considerably (1978:123). Kimmel stressed in his research, more so than did

Levinson, the important influence on developmental experiences of the historical context in which an individual lives. For example, a common assumption today is that gay bars serve as essential contexts for meeting others and establishing relationships and networks. Kimmel reminds us that if one lived during Prohibition this context did not even exist (at least not publicly) (1978:125).

Kimmel articulates two important research needs for more completely understanding gay adult development. These needs are consistent with our concerns throughout this book. First is the need for developmental studies focusing on women. Second is the need for "studies of persons who are not well-educated, economically successful, and white" (1978:125).

Kimmel points out some concerns especially important to gay persons. These include a concern for meeting the needs of the more vulnerable members of the gay community including adolescents, elderly, infirm, or disabled persons, gay parents, minority gays, and gay persons in poverty. Nearly all the respondents in Kimmel's study (and these respondents were among the most economically and educationally privileged) experienced overt or subtle oppression throughout their lives (1978:127).

Oppression against gay persons takes many forms and varies somewhat with the historical period in which one lives. For older gay men in Kimmel's study this included loss of ill lovers to relatives unable to accept the other partner; inability to ask for time off from work to care for a partner, due to fear of disclosing gayness; legal and inheritance problems; exclusion from intensive care units because partner is not defined legally as family; attitudes of institutional staff (physicians, nursing home staff, etc.). Kimmel stresses the strengths of the gay elderly he studied and concluded that "the stereotypes of the lonely, depressed, sexually frustrated aging gay man are not valid for the majority of the relatively elite male respondents studied to date" (1978:129).

FOCUS: PERSONS WITH DISABILITIES

Pati and Bailey note that "The U.S. Department of Labor's study, *Opportunity 2000,* asserts that one out of six Americans has a disability. And, as we age, each of us has a one-in-four chance of joining the ranks of persons with disabilities. Two out of three individuals with disabilities can work—and want to. Ironically, roughly 66 percent of this group are unemployed"(1995:56).

The Americans with Disabilities Act (ADA)

The Americans with Disabilities Act (ADA) is a significant piece of legislation and has multiple implications for social workers whether we are working at the individual, family, group, organizational, or community level. Orlin describes the significance of the act in that "ADA establishes that the nation's goals regarding individuals with disabilities are to ensure equality of opportunity, full participation, independent living, and economic self-sufficiency" (1995:234). The purpose of the act, then, is very consistent with the social work purpose of working to achieve social and economic justice.

What Does the ADA Cover?

- lodging
- facilities for public gathering:
  - exhibitions
  - entertainment
  - recreations
  - exercise
  - education
- stations used for public transportation
- service and social services establishments
- establishments serving food or drink (as long as they have contact with general public (Orlin 1995:234)

ADA: Definition of Disability

According to the Americans with Disabilities Act (ADA), **disability** means "with respect to an individual, a physical or mental impairment that substantially limits one or more of the major life activities of such individuals, a record of such an impairment, or being regarded as having such an impairment" (Orlin 1995:234–235).

To appreciate the full meaning of this definition of disability we need to understand what is meant, according to the Act, by such terms as "major life activities," "record of" impairment, or "regarded as" having an impairment, "reasonable accommodation," and "undue hardship." **Major life activities** as defined by the ADA are listed in the box below.

MAJOR LIFE ACTIVITIES

caring for oneself
performing manual tasks
walking
seeing
hearing
speaking
breathing
learning
working

Source: Orlin M. The Americans with Disabilities Act: Implications for social services. Copyright 1995, National Association of Social Workers, Inc., Social Work. Adapted by permission.

The term **record of** is a "provision [in the ADA] to protect people with a history of impairment such as persons with histories of mental illness or cancer and those who have been misclassified as having mental retardation or mental illness, for example." The term **regarded as** is intended in the ADA "to protect against discrimination based on the perceptions of others." For example, people with severe burns may not regard themselves as impaired, but encounter discrimination because others "regard" them as having a disability (Orlin 1995:235). Orlin distinguishes the ADA from other civil rights law by pointing out that "one concept that differs between public policy approaches to disability and race or gender discrimination is the concept of '**reasonable accommodation**'" (1995:236). This concept means the employer must make individualized accommodation "based on the specific needs of a qualified individual with a disability to enable that person to perform the essential functions of a job, unless such accommodation would be an 'undue hardship.'" **Undue hardship** is defined as "an action requiring 'significant difficulty or expense'" (ADA 1990). Any accommodation that would be unduly costly, extensive, substantial, or disruptive or that would fundamentally alter the nature or operation of the business or organization would be an undue hardship. Assessment of undue hardship existence varies from situation to situation depending on such factors as the resources of the organization available to make accommodation, for example, a small agency versus a large academic medical center (Orlin 1995:236). Often accommodations can be inexpensive and reasonably simple. (See Chapter 8 for examples of how some organizations have made "reasonable accommodations" for workers with disabilities.)

ADA Protections for Family, Volunteers, and Social Workers

Family members or people otherwise associated with people with disabilities are also protected by ADA, "because discrimination against a person with an association or relationship with a person with a disability is also prohibited" (Orlin 1995:238). Examples are:

- A person who does volunteer work with people with AIDS is protected from discrimination by his/her employer because of the association.
- A person with a spouse with a disability cannot be refused a job by an employer concerned that the spouse's impairment will cause the person to miss too much work.
- A child with a sibling who has AIDS cannot be denied admission to a day care center. (Orlin 1995:238)

The protection provided in ADA in the above areas is especially important to social workers and other professionals who provide services to persons with disabilities. It is intended to prevent discrimination against these professionals in the course of carrying out their professional responsibilities.

Persons with Disabilities and Social and Economic Justice

Kopels points out that in its research prior to passage of the ADA "Congress found that the 43 million Americans who have one or more physical or mental disabilities, are, as a group, severely disadvantaged due to discrimination in the critical areas of employment, housing, public accommodations, education, transportation, communication, recreation, institutionalization, health services, voting, and access to public services" (1995:338). Kopels also reminds us that "People with disabilities are statistically the poorest, least educated, and largest minority population in America (U.S. House of Representatives 1990). . . . In 1984, 50% of all disabled adults had incomes of $15,000 or less, as compared to only 25% of non-disabled adults (U.S. House of Representatives 1990)" (1995:337–338). This extreme poverty results from both the types of jobs traditionally available and the lack of access to training and education: "Individuals with disabilities, however, have traditionally been employed in low-status, low-paying jobs. They have not had equal access to educational and training opportunities that could have prepared them for more gainful employment" (Kopels 1995:338).

ADA and Advocating for Social and Economic Justice

Orlin suggests that "Because the primary objective of the ADA is full participation of people with disabilities in the mainstream of American society, agencies should review the extent to which individuals with disabilities participate in their programs. A Louis Harris and Associate nationwide poll of people with disabilities conducted in 1986 found a high correlation of disability with poverty; joblessness; lack of education; and failure to participate in social life, shopping and recreation" (1995:238).

Kopels urges social work students to ask questions about the physical and policy environments in their field placement agencies. You might also adapt these questions to the colleges and universities you attend as well.

Physical:

- Does agency have stairs, ramps, doorways, water fountains, restrooms, telephones, and other amenities that are accessible to clients with differing levels of abilities?
- What environmental modifications should be made?
- If the student became disabled while in field placement, would he or she be able to continue to work at the agency, or would "reasonable accommodations" need to be made?

Policy:

- Does the agency provide sign language interpreters, if necessary, during counseling sessions?
- Can clients with visual impairments read their records?
- Is there a uniform policy for maintaining the confidentiality of client records, or do records of certain clients, like those with HIV/AIDS, illegally contain special, identifying notations? (1995:343).

FOCUS: MEN

Kimmel and Messner (1995:xiv–xv) point out that just as "white people rarely think of themselves as 'raced' people [and] rarely think of race as a central element in their experience. . . . men often think of themselves as genderless, as if gender did not matter in the daily experiences of our lives." They note though, that researchers have been studying masculinity for many years. These studies traditionally have focused on three models:

1. Biological models have focused on the ways in which innate biological differences between males and females programmed different social behaviors.

2. Anthropological models have examined masculinity cross-culturally, stressing the variations in the behaviors and attributes associated with being a man.

3. Sociological models have [until recently] stressed how socialization of boys and girls included accommodation to a "sex role" specific to one's biological sex. (Kimmel and Messner 1995:xv).

Men, Masculinity, and Identity

Kimmel and Messner (1995:xix–xx) argue that the traditional models for studying masculinity have increasingly come into question for assuming the definition of masculinity is universal across cultures; for omitting historical realities; and for failing to account for issues of power that are central to getting a fuller understanding of male identity development. Research on masculinity has undergone significant change in the last twenty years and has become more inclusive of elements and realities of masculinity omitted from earlier traditional perspectives. Newer alternative models have been heavily influenced by feminist research directed toward understanding the relationship between males and females. Most significant among the results of newer alternative approaches to studying masculinity was the realization that "power dynamics are an essential element in both the definition and enactment of gender." Traditional sex role research had ignored both the reality of power relations and of the reality that men held the dominant position within the power relations between genders. In addition, alternative models "looked at 'gender relations' and understood how the definition of either masculinity or femininity was relational, that is, how the definition of one gender depended, in part, on the understanding of the definition of the other" (Kimmel and Messner 1995:xix).

Kimmel and Messner believe:

> *the research on masculinity is entering a new stage in which the variations among men are seen as central to the understanding of men's lives. The unexamined assumption in earlier studies had been that one version of masculinity—white, middle-age, middle-class, heterosexual—was the sex role into which all men were struggling to fit in our society. Thus, working-class men, men of color, gay men, and younger and older men were all observed as departing in significant ways from the traditional definitions of masculinity.* (1995:xix)

Masculinities

Newer alternative approaches see masculinity as multiple and present the newer notion of **masculinities** "the ways in which different men construct different versions of masculinity" (Kimmel and Messner 1995:xx). Kimmel and Messner suggest that more complete understandings of maleness and masculinity can be found through **social constructionist** approaches which seek to understand that one's identity as man "is developed through a complex process of interaction with the culture in which" one learns "the gender scripts appropriate to our culture, and attempt[s] to modify those scripts to make them more palatable"; through approaches that recognize "the experience of masculinity is not uniform and universally generalizable to all men in our society"; and through **life course** approaches which "chart the construction of these various masculinities in men's lives, and . . . examine pivotal developmental moments or institutional locations during a man's life in which the meanings of masculinity are articulated" (Kimmel and Messner 1995:xx–xxi).

NOMAS: An Alternative Vision of Maleness

An alternative perspective on masculinity and maleness is presented in the principles of the organization called NOMAS (National Organization of Men Against Sexism). NOMAS is an organization dedicated to enhancing men's lives and recognizes that

> *The traditional male role has steered many men into patterns such as isolation from children, lack of close relationships, denying of feelings, competitiveness, aggressiveness, preoccupation with work and success. NOMAS believes that men can live happier and more fulfilled lives by challenging, and un-learning, many of the old lessons of traditional masculinity. We are concerned with the full range of men's problems, and the difficult issues in men's lives.* (1996:www)

NOMAS: STATEMENT OF PRINCIPLES

NOMAS is an activist organization supporting positive changes for men. NOMAS advocates a perspective that is pro-feminist, gay and bi-affirmative, anti-racist and committed to justice on a broad range of social issues including class, age, religion, and physical ability. We affirm that working to make this nation's ideals of equality substantive is the finest expression of what it means to be a man. We believe that the new opportunities becoming available to women and men will benefit both. Men can live as happier and more fulfilled human beings by challenging the outdated rule of masculinity that embodies the assumptions of male superiority. Traditional masculinity includes many positive characteristics in which we take pride and find strength, but it also contains qualities that have been limited and harmed us. We are deeply supportive of men who are struggling with the issues of traditional masculinity. As an organization

Continued

NOMAS: STATEMENT OF PRINCIPLES   *Continued*

for changing men, we care about men and are especially concerned with men's problems, as well as the difficult issues in most men's lives. As an organization for changing men, we strongly support the continuing struggle for women for full equality. We applaud and support the insights and positive social changes that feminism has stimulated for both women and men. We oppose such injustices to women as economic and legal discrimination, rape, domestic violence, sexual harassment, and many others. Women and men can, and do, work together as allies to change the injustices that have so often made them see one another as enemies. Some of the strongest and deepest anxieties of most American men is their fear of homosexuality. This homophobia contributes directly to the many injustices experienced by gay men, lesbians, and bisexual persons, and it is a debilitating restriction for heterosexual men. We call for an end to all forms of discrimination based on sexual-affectional orientation, and for the creation of a gay-affirmative society. The enduring injustice of racism, which like sexism has long divided humankind into unequal and isolated groups, is of particular concern to us. Racism touches all of us and remains a primary source of inequality and oppression in our society. NOMAS is committed to examining and challenging racism in ourselves, our organization, and our communities. We also acknowledge that many people are oppressed today because of their class, age, religion, or physical condition. We believe that such injustices are vitally connected to sexism, with the fundamental promise of unequal distribution of power. Our goal is to change not just ourselves and other men, but also the institutions that create inequality. (NOMAS 1996:www)

Men and Violence

A key area of concern for understanding and changing traditional notions of masculinity is that of violence. We will examine violence in the context of families in Chapter 6. Here we will explore violence as a key issue and problem with which men must struggle, be accountable for, and address.

Violence against Women

Stout suggests a model for appreciating the degree and extent of male controls and violence against women through the presentation of a continuum of male control and violence. Stout notes "that acts of violence against women are not isolated and social work professionals must examine the context and culture in which violence prevails when working with victims, survivors, and perpetrators" (Stout 1991:307).

In Stout's (1991:307) continuum model "control over women moves from subtle to overt forms of violence." The continuum proceeds in the following way:

1. Language, research bias, and differential treatment
2. Street hassling
3. Economic discrimination

4. Sexist advertising
5. Pornography
6. Sexual harassment
7. Battering
8. Sexual abuse and rape
9. Femicide (Stout 1991:307)

Rothblum stresses that

> *Sex and violence against women are strongly associated in our society. . . . Most women, consciously or unconsciously, engage in a number of activities in order to avoid being raped by men (e.g., not listing their first name in the telephone directory, using a male voice on their telephone answering machine, not going out or driving or walking alone at night, taking self-defense courses, etc.). . . . Sex and fear of violence are so intertwined for most women that it is difficult to conceive of living a life free from that fear.* (1994:628–629)

Levy suggests the need to reconceptualize violence from a pathology-based perspective to one that recognizes violence is virtually normative in U.S. society. She suggests that

> *If violence against women is a mainstream experience affecting a majority of women, then 21st-century social work strategies to deal with it must address this violence as a normative cultural phenomenon rather than as idiosyncratic pathology. . . . Rather than labeling battering as pathology or a family systems failure, [feminists] have challenged mental health practitioners to assume that violence against women, like that directed toward children, is behavior approved of and sanctioned in many parts of the culture.* (1995:317–318)

Levy urges that

> *Society must redefine what normal masculinity is so that violent behavior toward women is seen as pathological and unacceptable. This change does not require categorization of violent behavior as a medically diagnosable pattern or disease but as behavior for which the perpetrator is held responsible. For example, young men in high school are generally ignored when they are seen pushing or hitting their girlfriends and are often surprised when accused of date rape. Their concepts of normal masculinity are shaken when confronted with the criminality of their behavior.* (1995:320)

Levy calls upon "Social work intervention in the 21st century [to] be guided by a definition of rape and battering as hate crimes against women, rather than seeing them exclusively as acts by 'a sick person.'" Further, she suggests that "Feminist social work practice that aims to eliminate violence against women must address the problem as a violation of human rights" (1995:321).

Violence and Perpetrators

Levy (1995:323) offers suggestions for intervention in and prevention of violence in the 21st century. She suggests, for example, using models already available for teaching children and youth skills for building healthy relationships as a means of **preventing violence.** Skills include the following:

Skills for Teaching Anti-violence Behavior
- Communication
- Problem solving
- Managing anger
- Assertiveness
- Mutual respect
- Flexibility
- Non-stereotyping of gender roles
- Empathy
- Stress management
- Conflict resolution
- Acceptance of variation of human sexuality
- Responsible and respectful sexuality (Levy 1995:323)

In addition, social workers can help prevent violence against women by

- *Encouraging partnership rather than dominance and subordination in relationships*
- *Redefining masculinity and femininity*
- *Recognizing power dynamics and violence against women as a socially sanctioned abuse of power*
- *Recognizing victims' strengths rather than pathologizing their responses to violence*
- *Valuing the diversity of women's experiences*
- *Seeking solutions through community and social change as well as through individual change* (Levy 1995:325)

Intervention for perpetrators of violence should include psychoeducational groups for rapists and batterers that emphasize the following:

1. *The perpetrator's responsibility for and ability to control violent behavior*
2. *Awareness of the seriousness, danger, and consequences of violent behavior*
3. *Awareness of one's motivation (and sense of entitlement) to dominate and control women as socially sanctioned, and sometimes as an outgrowth of feelings of powerlessness displaced onto women*
4. *Anger management techniques*
5. *Empathy with women*

6. *Relationship skills, such as communication, assertiveness, and problem solving*

7. *Stress-reduction skills*

8. *Development of social support*

9. *Dealing with substance abuse.* (Levy 1995:323)

SUMMARY/COMMONALITIES

Myers et al. (1991) suggest that there are a number of important commonalities in developmental frameworks and models that address the experiences of members of diverse groups such as persons of color; women; gay men, lesbians, and bisexual persons, and persons with disabilities. Common developmental processes include:

a) a denial, devaluation, or lack of awareness of their oppressed identity;

b) a questioning of their oppressed identity;

c) an immersion in the oppressed subculture;

d) a realization of the limitations of a devalued sense of self; and

e) an integration of the oppressed part of self into their whole self-identity (1991:54–55).

It is important to note also as we conclude this chapter that developmental issues and alternative perspectives on other diverse persons and groups and the interrelationships of multiple diversities will continue to be dealt with as we proceed through the other chapters. This will be especially the case in relation to family as a major context of individual development, but diversities will continue to be a thread as well in regard to groups, organizations, and communities as contexts in which individual developmental issues and tasks are played out.

Internet Search Guide

If you want to learn more about some of the topics discussed in this chapter by exploring the Internet, you can search the Net for the terms listed below. Remember that as you are "surfing" the Net, any of the search terms listed below can take you in many different directions. If you would like to visit specific Web sites related to this chapter, go to the Allyn and Bacon Web site at **http://www.abacon.com** and follow the links to Schriver or *Human Behavior and the Social Environment: Shifting Paradigms in Essential Knowledge for Social Work Practice.* There you will find a selection of sites related to content in this chapter.

1. commonality

2. diversity

3. African American

4. Alaskan Native

5. Native American	17. women & development
6. Asian Pacific American	18. aging
7. Hispanic	19. multiple intelligences
8. Ecological Perspective	20. bisexuality
9. Ecological Model	21. NOMAS
10. ethnicity	22. disability
11. bicultural	23. poverty
12. minority group	24. hunger
13. social class	25. malnutrition
14. stereotypes	26. U.N. Principles of Human Rights
15. racism	27. World Health Organization
16. sexual orientation	28. co-intelligences

REFERENCES

AmeriStat. (2000a). *Families in poverty: Racial and ethnic differences.* [Web site]. AmeriStat Population Reference Bureau and Social Science Data Analysis Network. Available: http://www.ameristat.org/incpov/family.htm [2000, 4/4/00].

AmeriStat. (2000b). *Key concepts.* [Web site]. AmeriStat Population Reference Bureau and Social Science Data Analysis Network. Available: http://www.ameristat.org/concepts.htm#death [2000, 4/4/00].

AmeriStat. (2000c). *Minority representation in Congress.* [Web site]. AmeriStat Population Reference Bureau and Social Science Data Analysis Network. Available: http://ameristat.org/racethnic/congress.htm [2000, 4/4/00].

AmeriStat. (2000d). *Mortality risk for select causes of death.* [Web site]. AmeriStat Population Reference Bureau and Social Science Data Analysis Network. Available: http://www.ameristat.org/racethnic/mortality.htm [2000, 4/4/00].

Andrews, A., and Ben-Arieh, A. (1999). "Measuring and monitoring children's well-being across the world." *Social Work, 44*(2): 105–115.

Balenky, Mary F., Clinchy, Blythe M., Goldberger, Nancy R., and Tarule, Jill M. (1986). *Women's ways of knowing: The development of self, voice, and mind.* New York. Basic Books, Inc.

Bureau of the Census. (1995). *Current population reports, series P23–189, population profile of the United States: 1995* (Current Population Reports: Special Studies Series P23–189). Washington, DC: U.S. Government Printing Office.

Carter, R. T., and Jones, J. M. (1996). "Racism and white racial identity." In Bowser, B. P., and Hunt, R. G. (Eds.). *Impact of racism on White Americans.* (2nd Ed.). Thousand Oaks, CA: Sage.

Cass, Vivienne C. (1984). "Homosexual identity formation: Testing a theoretical model." *Journal of Sex Research, 20*(2): 143–167.

Chodorow, Nancy. (1974). "Family structure and feminine personality." In Michelle Zimbalist Rosaldo and Louise Lamphere. (Eds.). *Women, culture and society.* Stanford: Stanford University Press.

Chodorow, Nancy. (1978). *The reproduction of mothering: Psychoanalysis and the sociology of gender.* Berkeley: University of California Press.

Collins, Patricia Hill. (1990). *Black feminist thought: Knowledge, consciousness, and the politics of empowerment.* Cambridge: Unwin Hyman, Inc.

Cross, W. E. (1971). "The Negro to Black experience: Towards a psychology of Black liberation." *Black World, 20*(9): 13–27.

D'Augelli, A. R. (1994). "Identity development and sexual orientation: Toward a model of lesbian, gay, and bisexual development." In Trickett, E. J., Watts, R. J., and Birman, D. (Eds.). *Human diversity: Perspectives on people in context.* San Francisco: Jossey-Bass.

Demo, D. H., and Allen, K. R. (1996). "Diversity within lesbian and gay families: Challenges and implications for family theory and research." *Journal of Social and Personal Relationships, 13*(3): 415–434.

Eliason, M. J. (1996). "Working with lesbian, gay, and bisexual people: Reducing negative stereotypes via inservice education." *Journal of Nursing Staff Development, 12*(3): 127–132.

Fong, R., Spickard, P. R., and Ewalt, P. L. (1996). "A multiracial reality: Issues for social work." In Ewalt, P. L., Freeman, E. M., Kirk, S. A., and Poole, D. L. (Eds.). *Multicultural issues in social work.* Washington, DC: NASW.

Food Research and Action Council, (2000). *Hunger in the U.S.* [Web site]. Food Research and Action Council. Available: http://www.frac.org/html/hunger_in_the_us/hunger_index.html [2000, 4/5/00].

Gardner, H. (1983). *Frames of mind: The theory of multiple intelligences.* New York: Basic Books.

Gardner, H. (1993). *Multiple intelligences: The theory in practice.* New York: Basic Books.

Gemmill, Gary, and Oakley, J. (1992). "Leadership: An alienating social myth?" *Human Relations, 45*(2): 113–129.

"Gene influence tied to sexual orientation." (1992). *Science News, 141*(1): 6.

Gibbs, Jewelle Taylor, and Huang, Larke Nahme, and collaborators. (1989). *Children of color: Psychological interventions with minority youth.* San Francisco: Jossey-Bass Publishers.

Gilligan, Carol. (1982). *In a different voice: Psychological theory and women's development.* Cambridge: Harvard University Press.

Gomes, Paula, and Mabry, C. Aldrena. (1991). "Negotiating the world: The developmental journey of African American children," in Everett, J., Chipungu, S., and Leashore, B. (Eds.). *Child welfare: An Africentric perspective.* New Brunswick, NJ: Rutgers University Press.

Gundry, L. K., Kickul, J. R., and Prather, C. W. (1994). "Building the creative organization." *Organizational Dynamics, 22*(4): 22–37.

Harding, Sandra. (1986). *The science question in feminism.* Ithaca, NY: Cornell University Press.

Harley, J. (1996). A19. *What is the Kinsey scale.* Available: http://www.gbnet.net/~jon/soc.bi/faq/a.html#A19.

Harley, J. (1996). A1. *What do you mean by 'bisexual' anyway?* Available: http://www.gbnet.net/~jon/soc.bi/faq/a.html#A1.

Harrison, Algea O., Wilson, Melvin N., Pine, Charles J., Chan, Samuel Q., and Buriel, Raymond. (1990). "Family ecologies of ethnic minority children." *Child Development, 61:* 347–362.

Helms, J. E. (1994). "The conceptualization of racial identity and other 'racial' constructs." In Trickett, E. J., Watts, R. J., and Birman, D. (Eds.). *Human diversity: Perspectives on people in context.* San Francisco: Jossey-Bass.

Herbert, James I. (1990). "Integrating race and adult psychosocial development." *Journal of Organizational Behavior, 11:* 433–446.

Hunter, S., and Sundel, M. (1994). "Midlife for women: A new perspective." *Affilia, 9*(2).

"Is homosexuality biological?" (1991). *Science: 253,* 956–957.

Jacobs, James. (1992). "Identity development in biracial children." In Root, Maria P. P. (Ed.). *Racially mixed people in America*. Newbury Park, CA: Sage.

Joint Center for Poverty Research. (2000). *Poverty Information*. [Web site]. Joint Center for Poverty Research. Available: http://jcpr.org/faq/faq_populations_frames.html [2000, 4/4/00].

Jordan, Judith, Kaplan, Alexandra, Miller, Jean Baker, Stiver, Irene, and Surrey, Janet. (1991). *Women's growth in connection: Writings of the Stone Center*. New York: Guilford Press.

Keller, Evelyn Fox (1985). *Reflections on gender and science*. New Haven: Yale University Press.

Kich, George Kitahara. (1992). "The developmental process of asserting a biracial, bicultural identity." In Root, Maria P. P. (Ed.). *Racially mixed people in America*. Newbury Park, CA: Sage.

Kimmel, Douglas C. (1978). "Adult development and aging: A gay perspective." *Journal of Social Issues, 34*(3): 113–130.

Kimmel, M. S., and Messner, M. A. (Eds.). (1995). *Men's lives*. (3rd ed.). Boston: Allyn and Bacon.

Kopels, S. (Fall 1995). "The Americans with Disabilities Act: A tool to combat poverty." *Journal of Social Work Education, 31*(3): 337–346.

Levy, B. (1995). "Violence against women." In *Feminist practice for the 21st century*. Van Den Bergh, N. (Ed.). Washington, DC: NASW.

Lewis, Lou Ann. (1984). "The coming-out process for lesbians: Integrating a stable identity." *Social Work, 29*(5): 464–469.

McQuaide, S. (1998). "Women at midlife." *Social Work, 43*(1): 21–31.

Miller, Jean Baker. (1976). *Toward a new psychology of women*. Boston: Beacon Press.

Miller, Jean Baker. (1986). *Toward a new psychology of women*. (2nd ed.). Boston: Beacon Press.

Miller, R. L. (1992). "The human ecology of multiracial identity." In Root, Maria P. P. (Ed.). *Racially mixed people in America*. Newbury Park, CA: Sage.

Myers, Linda J., Speight, Suzette, Highlen, Pamela, Cox, Chikako, Reynolds, Amy, Adams, Eve, and Hanley, C. Patricia. (1991). "Identity development and worldview: Toward an optimal conceptualization." *Journal of Counseling and Development, 70:* 54–63.

NOMAS. (1996). Available: http://www.spacestar.com/users/abtnomas/history.html

Ogbu, John U. (1978). "Caste and education and how they function in the United States." In *Minority education and caste: The American system in cross-cultural perspective*. New York: Academic Press.

Orlin, M. (1995). "The Americans with Disabilities Act: Implications for social services." *Social Work, 40*(2): 233–234. Reprinted with permission.

Parham, Thomas A. (1989). "Cycles of psychological nigrescence." *The Counseling Psychologist, 17*(2): 187–226.

Parks, E. E., Carter, R. T., and Gushue, G. V. (1996, July/August). "At the crossroads: Racial and womanist identity development in Black and White women." *Journal of Counseling and Development, (74):* 624–631.

Pati, G. C., and Bailey, E. K. (Winter 1995). "Empowering people with disabilties: Strategy and human resource issues in implementing the ADA." *Organizational Dynamics 23*(3): 52–69.

Rank, M., and Hirschl, T. (1999). "The likelihood of poverty across the American adult life span." *Social Work, 44*(3): 201–216.

Rothblum, E. D. (1994). "Transforming lesbian sexuality." *Psychology of Women Quarterly, 18*.

Seipel, M. (1999). "Social consequences of malnutrition." *Social Work, 44* (5): 416–425.

Smith, Elsie M. J. (1989). "Black racial identity development: Issues and concerns." *The Counseling Psychologist, 17*(2): 277–288.

Smith, Elsie J. (1991). "Ethnic identity development: Toward the development of a theory within the context of majority/minority status." *Journal of Counseling and Development, 70:* 181–188.

Spencer, Margaret Beale, and Markstrom-Adams, Carol. (1990). "Identity processes among racial and ethnic minority children in America." *Child Development, 61:* 290–310.

Spickard, P. R. (1992). "The illogic of American racial categories." In Root, Maria P. P. (Ed.). *Racially mixed people in America*. Newbury Park, CA: Sage.

Stack, Carol B. (1986). "The culture of gender: Women and men of color." *Signs, 11*(2): 321–24.

Stout, K. D. (1991). "A continuum of male controls and violence against women: A teaching model." *Journal of Social Work Education, 27*(3): 305–319.

Wastell, C. A. (1996). "Feminist developmental theory: Implications for counseling." *Journal of Counseling and Development, 74*, 575–581.

Weick, Ann. (1992). "Building a strengths perspective for social work." In Dennis Saleebey, *The strengths perspective in social work practice*. White Plains: Longman.

ILLUSTRATIVE READING 5.1

The following Illustrative Reading by Jean Baker Miller (1991) offers another perspective on women's development. This reading is a summary of Miller's work on "The Development of Women's Sense of Self." As noted earlier, the work of Gilligan, with its emphasis on the importance of relationship and interdependence in the development of women, was significantly influenced by the work of Miller. This reading by Miller also offers an additional perspective on the omission of important developmental realities of women from traditional theory such as that of Erikson. It is especially effective in presenting practical implications of women's developmental differences from men across the life span.

The Development of Women's Sense of Self

Jean Baker Miller

The concept of the self has been prominent in psychological theory, perhaps because it has been one of the central ideas in Western thought. While various writers use different definitions, the essential idea of a "self" seems to underlie the historical development of many Western notions about such vast issues as the "good life," justice, and freedom. Indeed, it seems entwined in the roots of several delineations of fundamental human motives or the highest form of existence, as in Maslow's self-actualizing character.

As we have inherited it, the notion of a "self" does not appear to fit women's experience. Several recent writers have spoken to this point, for example, literary critic Carolyn Heilbrun (1979) and psychologist Carol Gilligan (1982). A question then arises: Do only men, and not women, have a self? In working with women the question is quite puzzling, but an examination of the very puzzle itself may cast new light on certain long-standing assumptions. Modern American theorists of early psychological development and, indeed, of the entire life span, from Erik Erikson (1950) to

Reprinted with permission of Guilford Publications, Inc. from Judith Jordan, Alexandra Kaplan, Jean Baker Miller, Irene Stiver, and Janet Surrey (1991). *Women's Growth in Connection: Writings from the Stone Center.* New York: Guilford Press. An earlier version of this chapter was presented at The Stone Center Dedication.

Daniel Levinson (1978), tend to see all of development as a process of separating oneself out from the matrix of others—"becoming one's own man," in Levinson's words. Development of the self presumably is attained via a series of painful crises by which the individual accomplishes a sequence of allegedly essential separations from others, thereby achieving an inner sense of separated individuation. Few men ever attain such self-sufficiency, as every woman knows. They are usually supported by wives, mistresses, mothers, daughters, secretaries, nurses, and other women (as well as other men who are lower than they in the socioeconomic hierarchy). Thus, there is reason to question whether this model accurately reflects men's lives. Its goals, however, are held out for all, and are seen as the preconditions for mental health.

Almost every modern theorist who has tried to fit women into the prevalent models has had much more obvious difficulty, beginning with Freud and extending through Erikson and others. Some have not even tried. In Erikson's scheme, for example, after the first stage, in which the aim is the development of basic trust, the aim of every other stage, until young adulthood, is some form of increased separation or self-development. I am not referring at this point to the process by which each aim is attained (although that is an intimately related point that will be discussed below), but to the aim itself, the goal. It is important to note that the aim is not something like development of greater capacity for emotional connection to others; or for contributing to an interchange between people; or for playing a part in the growth of others as well as one's self. When the individual arrives at the stage called "intimacy," he is supposed to be able to be intimate with another person—having spent all of his prior development striving for something very different.

Much recent writing deploring men's inability to engage in intimacy has come from the women's movement. But men, too, have been making the same point. Almost all of modern literature, philosophy, and commentary in other forms portrays men's lack of a sense of community—indeed, it denies even the possibility of communicating with others.

Thus, the prevailing models may not describe well what occurs in men; in addition, there is a question about the value of these models even if it were possible to fulfill their requirements. These two questions are related, as I will try to suggest. It is very important to note, however, that the prevalent models are powerful because they have become prescriptions about what *should* happen. They affect men; they determine the actions of mental health professionals. They have affected women adversely in one way in the past. They are affecting women in another way now, if women seek "equal access" to them. Therefore, we need to examine them carefully. It is important not to embrace them because they are the only models available.

THE BEGINNINGS

What are some of the questions that arise when we try to bring women's experience into the picture? We can take Erikson's theories as a starting point, not to attempt a thorough examination of them, but to use them as a framework for consideration of a few of the many features in women's development.

In the first stage of life, according to Erikson, the central goal is the infant's development of a sense of basic trust. Another important dimension, however, is also involved. Even at that early stage in all infants, but encouraged much more in girls, the young child begins to be like and act like the main caretaker, who, up until now, has usually been a woman—not to "identify" with that person as some static figure described only by gender, but with what that person *actually* is doing. I think that the infant begins to develop an internal representation of itself as a kind of being that, for the moment, I will call by a hyphenated term—a "being-in-relationship." This is the beginning of a sense of "self" that reflects what is happening *between* people. The infant picks up the feelings of the other person, that is, it has an early sense that "I feel what is going on in the other as well as what is going on in myself." It is more complex because it involves "knowing"—feeling—what is going on in that emotional field between us. The child experiences a sense of comfort only as the other is also comfortable, or, more precisely, only as they are both engaged in an emotional relationship that is moving toward greater well-being, rather than toward the opposite— that is, only as the interactions in the emotional field between the infant and the adult are moving toward a "better" progression of events.* In this sense, the infant, actively exerting an effect on the relationship, begins to develop an internal sense of itself as one who changes the emotional interplay for both participants—for good or ill.

The beginnings of a mental construction of self are much more complicated than those suggested by such commonly used terms as *fusion* or *merger* for the mental constructions of the first stages of infancy, as drawn from Mahler (1975), object relations theorists, and others. New research on infant-caretaker interactions also indicates the inappropriateness of those terms (see, for example, Stern, 1980; Stechler and Kaplan, 1980; Klein, 1976). This research suggests that these constructs are not likely to describe adequately the complex internal representations of the self and the "other," or, rather, the internal self–other relational patterns that the infant is likely to create even from the earliest age.

When we talk about a sense of self in this field, we have been referring to a "man-made" construct meant to describe an internal mental representation. The suggestion here is that from the moment of birth this internal representation is of a self that is in active interchange with other selves. Moreover, this interaction has one central characteristic, and that is that people are attending to the infant—most importantly, attending to the infant's core of being, which means the infant's emotions—and the infant is responding in the same way, that is, to the other person's emotions. The earliest mental representation of the self, then, is of a self whose core—which is emotional—is attended to by the other(s) and in turn, begins to attend to the emotions of the other(s). Part of this internal image of oneself includes feeling the other's emotions and *acting on* them as they are in interplay with one's own emotions. This means that the beginnings of the concept of self are not those of a static and lone self being ministered to by another (incidentally, this construct has a strong male flavor), but rather of a self inseparable from dynamic interaction. And the central character of that interaction involves attending to each other's mental states and emotions.

This early "interacting sense of self" is present for infants of both sexes, but the culturally induced beliefs of the caretakers about girls and boys play a role from the

---

*This point has been made in various ways by many theorists, such as M. Klein, H. S. Sullivan, and several others. The features that they emphasize, however, are different.

moment of birth. These beliefs are, of course, internalized even in the woman care-taker, although more so in fathers, according to suggestions from some studies (e.g., Rubin et al., 1974; Block, 1978). Girls are encouraged to augment their abilities to "feel as the other feels" and to practice "learning about" the other(s). Boys are sys-tematically diverted from it—to their deprivation and detriment, in my opinion. (In my opinion, this redounds, too, to the detriment of the whole construction of our societal structure and of our models of thinking.)

Out of this interplay of experience one certainly develops a sense of one's self, that is, an internal or mental representation of one's self. Moreover, one develops a sense of one's self as a person who attends to and responds to what is going on in the relationships between two or more people.

Much of the literature tends to suggest that because she is the same sex as the caretaker, the girl cannot develop an internal sense of self; that is, that boys develop a sense of self because they separate themselves from the female caretaker. This is truly an incredible notion. First, it ignores all of the complexity of the interaction between caretaker and infant. It is as if there were no interaction because mother and child are both of the same sex—an amazing negation of the very ideas of girls and women.

Second, the literature has generally ignored the extraordinarily important char-acter of the interaction—that of attending to and responding to the other. This is the essential feature of what comes to be called "caretaking." It is also the basis of all con-tinuing psychological growth; that is, all growth occurs within emotional connec-tions, not separate from them. Current theories ignore, too, the likelihood that the early self is built on the model of this very process—as opposed to the very different kinds of interaction that exist in the current world. The very notion of true caretak-ing precludes anything that would lead the infant to feel submerged, fused, or merged with the other. These words may describe some of the phenomena observed after *dis-tortions* in caretaking have occurred, but they are unlikely to characterize the infant's prototypic sense of self.

Third, current notions tend to ignore the likelihood that the only possibility of having any sense of self at all is built on the core process I have described. As sug-gested above, it begins to be discouraged early on in boys. For girls, it is encouraged, but complications are added at this and at each succeeding phase of development.

Surrey has suggested that this early mental representation of the self in girls can be described as a more *encompassing* sense of self, in contrast with the more bound-aried, or limited, self that is encouraged in boys from a very young age. She suggests, too, the term "oscillating" sense of self as compared to the current, more linear model, with the "oscillation" following from the ongoing growth of empathy in the child as well as in the mother (see Surrey, Chapter 3, this volume; Jordan, Surrey, & Kaplan, Chapter 2, this volume). Many implications follow. To begin with, certain events in later life that other models see as detracting from the self are instead seen as satisfying, motivating and empowering. For example, to feel "more related to an-other person" means to feel one's self enhanced, not threatened. It does not feel like a loss of part of one's self; instead it becomes a step toward more pleasure and effectiveness—because it is the way the girl and woman feel "things should be," the way she wants them to be. Being in relationship, picking up the feelings of the other and attending to the "interaction between" becomes an accepted, "natural-seeming" way of being and acting. It is learned and assumed; not alien or threatening. Most important, it is desired; it is a *goal*, not a detraction or a means to some other end, such as one's own self-development. Thus, it forms a *motivation*.

We have come to think of this whole experience as so "foreign," I believe, because our cultural tradition has emphasized such a different direction. In the dominant and official culture, attending to the experience of others and to the relationships between people is not seen as a *requirement* of all of life. It has been relegated to the alien and mysterious world of mothers and infancy—and misunderstood. Sometimes, when I have tried to talk about this, psychiatrists have said, "Oh, I see what you mean. All right, I agree that women are more altruistic." That is not what I mean. That is attempting to slot this description into the old categories. It suggests a "sacrifice" of parts of a kind of self that has developed in a different fashion. To engage in the kind of interaction I am discussing is not a sacrifice; it is, in fact, a source of feeling better and more gratified, as well as more knowledgeable—about what is really happening. I believe it is closer to the elementary human necessities from which our dominant culture has become unnecessarily removed.

Another implication relates to self-esteem, or the sense of self-worth. The girl's sense of self-esteem is based in feeling that she is a part of relationships and is taking care of those relationships. This is very different from the components of self-esteem as usually described and, incidentally, as measured by most available scales. Another ramification involves the issue of competence or effectiveness. The girl and woman often feel a sense of effectiveness as arising out of emotional connections and as bound up with and feeding back into them. This is very different from a sense of effectiveness (or power) based in lone action and in acting against or over others. This sense of effectiveness can develop further in the next and all subsequent ages, but it grows upon this base.

AGENCY WITHIN COMMUNITY

To move quickly through the next ages of life, I will sketch a few suggestions about each of them, leading only as far as adolescence. Erikson speaks about the second stage of childhood as one in which the goal is autonomy; others have spoken about separation and individuation. I would suggest, instead, that we could think of this as a period when the child has more abilities, more possibilities "to do," and more physical and mental resources to use. The child also has an enlarged "point of view" on all events, as it were, that is, a more developed sense of how she or he sees things. There is not, however, nor need there be, any increased separation. Instead, there are new configurations and new "understandings" *in the relationship*. Maintaining the relationship(s) with the main people in her or his life is still *the* most important thing.

We might think of this as something like a phase called "agency-in-community." These words are borrowed from Bakan (1966) but not used with his definitions. Instead, by "agency" I am searching for a word again, a word that means being active, using all of one's resources, but without the connotations of aggression—another large topic, but one that cannot be developed here (see Miller, Chapter 10, this volume). Here, again, the "doing" is different from what has been described in the past. Often for little girls, it means doing *for* following the model of what the mother is doing (see Jordan, Surrey, & Kaplan, Chapter 2, this volume; Surrey, Chapter 3, this volume). What the mother is still doing with little children is attending to their feelings and "*doing for*" them, although not totally. So the action, again, has a different character—it is doing for other(s) within a relationship, with the little girls using increased powers, an increased number of "opinions" about how and what she wants "to do," and an increased assertion of what she can do.

In her internal representation of herself, I suggest, the girl is developing not a sense of separation, but a more developed sense of her own capacities and her greater ability to put her "views" into effect. That is, she has a sense of a larger scope of action—but still with an inner representation of a self that is doing this in relation to other selves. A larger scope of action is not equivalent to separation; it requires a *change* in her internal configuration of her sense of self and other, but not a separation.

The child can move on to a larger, but a more articulated sense of herself *only because of* her actions and feelings *in* the relationship. These actions and feelings are inevitably different from the other person's. They are obviously not identical. The point is that she is attuned to the feelings of the other person; and just as her feelings are influenced by other's feelings, so too, do they influence the other's feelings. She has a wide range of feelings and actions, and they vary at different times, with one or another in ascendancy, but they occur within the relational context.

Of course, the character of the relationship differs from that of infancy; new qualities come in. But this does not lead to a "separate" sense of self. It leads to a more complex sense of self in more complex relationships to other selves.

The whole notion of describing human interaction in geographic or spatial terms, along a scale of close or distant (i.e., separated), seems questionable. Surely it is the *quality* of the interaction that is the question—the interplay of "conceptualized feelings" (i.e., feelings *cum* concepts), the doing of good or bad to the other—in relation to the nature of each's needs. A growing child has the potential to do more than he or she could do before. The caretaker who recognizes and supports this enlarged ability does not become more distant. The caretaker becomes *more caring* in one more way—that is, *more related*—and the child does, too.

CHILDHOOD

When we move to the next stage, which is based on the oedipal stage, we may ask whether one reason that people, beginning with Freud, have had such trouble delineating this stage in girls is that it may not exist. There is no major crisis of "cutting off" anything, and especially relationships. And there is no need to fulfill the goal of "identifying with an aggressor," that is, the threatening and dominant male figure. (Several theorists believe that all of society, culture, and thought is built on this oedipal moment of identification with the aggressive father. It is interesting to think about the possibility that society need not be built on this base.) However, there is a message that may come in to play more forcefully at this time (though it begins earlier and it continues later)—that the girl should now focus all her energies on the well-being, growth, and development of men. Nonetheless, the relationship to the mother and to other women continues. A pronounced turning away from the mother and toward the father may occur because of particular conditions in particular families, especially when the mother herself encourages and models this way of being. Western culture has dictated that mothers should uphold the superior importance and power of the man. These forces begin to affect deeply the girl's sense of herself and her relationship to her mother and to complicate the relationship in many ways. However, the relationship to the mother and to other women continues, although it may be less obvious and it may be made to seem less important. There are ethnic, class, and historical variations in the degree of influence of the mother or father within the family, but, in general, the greater importance, value, and power of the father—and the devaluation of the mother—seems to come through psychologically.

In latency, or the period that, according to Erikson, has "industry" as its goal, there is increasing evidence that girls are not very latent. What girls may do is learn to hide more, if we are talking about sexuality, as Freud was when he initiated the use of the term. But if we are talking about relationships, this is certainly the time when the girls are very intensely involved in all of their relationships, especially with other girls. Many girls are very interested in men and boys, too, but the boys are often either not interested or actively deprecating and destructive to girls. The boys are out learning "industry," which others have talked about as "learning the rules of the game and how to play it" (Gilligan, 1982). Most of these rules, incidentally, seem directly traceable to war games. In a study of this period, Luria (1981) describes the events in a grade school playground. She talks about the boys' learning not only how to be "warlike" and to win out over others, but how to cheat and get away with it. When she asked the girls what they were doing, they often said, "Nothing." The girls are hanging around the edges of the playground "just talking." What are they talking about? They are talking about the issues in their families and how to solve them. In discussing their families, the girls are, of course, very involved in an emotional interaction with one another. Surrey (Chapter 3, this volume) has pointed out that the vast amount of psychological development that occurs within the relationships between girls at this time has been one of the major neglected areas in psychological study.

ADOLESCENCE

Adolescence has been seen as a time when the individual has greatly increased capacities. Traditionally, psychologists have *divided* them in several ways: for example, sexual capacities; aggressive capacities—which I will call, for the moment, agentic (the ability to act); and cognitive capacities, with the development of formal thought that greatly expands the universe. However, many studies still indicate that this is a time when girls begin to "contract" rather than expand. Clara Thompson (1942) noted this long ago. She said that for boys, adolescence is seen as a period of opening up, but for girls it is a time for shutting down. In different terms, Freud said this, too. Freud believed that girls now had to learn that they were not actively to use all of themselves and all of their life forces from a base centered in their own bodies and in their own psychological constructions. For Freud, this meant, of course, the derivatives of their sexual drive. Instead, these forces are now to be turned to the use of others—men, in the first instance, and to the service of the next generation, via childbearing. That is, girls had to resolve their psychological issues by becoming passive and masochistic—to accomplish the necessary submission to the man and to "sacrifice" themselves for children.

Freud's observations may have reflected much of what happened—and still happens. That is, in regard to sexuality, most girls still learn that their own sexual perceptions, sensations, and impulses are not supposed to arise from themselves, but are to be brought forth by and for men. Thus girls still tend to experience their physical and sexual stirrings as wrong, bad, evil, dirty, and the like. This is to say that part of what has been going on in the girl's earlier internal representations of herself has included several problematic parts. One of these involves bodily and sexual experience. This situation can lead to an attempt to deal with this experience by turning to passivity and submission. The girl picks up the strong message that her own perceptions about her bodily and sexual feelings are not acceptable. They acquire connotations of badness and evil. They become parts of her self that are shameful and wrong. She has sought to bring these parts of herself into relationships with others all along, but has had difficulty in doing so. She still seeks to act on these desires within relationships with others. But she meets opposition. In the face of this, the solution of "doing it for others" can seem to offer a ready answer. The problem is that this solution is one that attempts to leave her—and her sense of herself, with all of her own psychological constructions—out of the relationship.

In heterosexual relationships, if the girl or young woman tries to have her own perceptions, to follow her own desires, and to bring them into sexual experience with boys, she still is destined for conflict. Despite all of the recent talk, the girl's attempt to act on the basis of her own sexuality still leads to conflict with her potential male partners. It will also lead to internal conflict with certain components of her sense of self. One is the part that says she should—and that she wants to—be attuned to others, which leads to a conflict if the other is behaving in ways that are excluding her perceptions and desires from the relationship. Another is the part that has made sexuality an unacceptable aspect of her internal sense of self and therefore prevents her from bringing a large part of herself into the relationship.

A similar dynamic exists in regard to "agency," that is, the girl's capacity to perceive and to use her powers in all ways. Women are not supposed to do this, and they have incorporated the idea that to do so is wrong and shameful. The girl has learned and done many things, until now, within a relationship. However, because of societal influences, she has also incorporated a sense—again, to varying degrees—that she is not fully and freely to use all of her powers. During adolescence, however, she receives this as a much stronger message.

Thus her sense of self as an active agent—in the context of acting within a relationship and for the relationship—has been altered to some degree all along by a sense of a self who must defer to others' needs or desires. However, at adolescence she experiences a much more intense pressure to do so. Her sense of self as developed so far now faces a more serious conflict with the external forces she confronts.

The question is how she will deal with this conflict. As with sexuality, I believe that the major tendency is for the girl to opt for the relationship both in her overt actions and in an alteration of her internal sense of self. She will tend to want most to retain the self that wants to be a "being-in-relationship" but she will begin to lose touch with the definition of herself as a more active "being-within-relationship." If one part has to go, and until now it did, most girls lose more of the sense that they can bring their agency and sexuality, as they experience it, into the relationship.

To restate some of these points, at adolescence the girl is seeking fulfillment of two very important needs: to use all of her capacities, including her sexual capacity, but seeking to do so within a context that will fulfill her great desire to be a "being-in-relationship." This wish to do so has developed all through earlier ages. She wishes that the other person will be able to enter into a relationship in this fashion. I believe that the boy really has the same needs, at bottom. However, he has been much more preoccupied with trying to develop "himself" and a sense of his independent identity. The culture has made the very heavy demand that he be so preoccupied. It has been doing so all along, but it does so at adolescence in an even more forceful way. He has also picked up the idea that the girl should adapt to him, and he has not been encouraged to continue the development of the sense that he is primarily a boy-in-relationship with a primary responsibility for others and a desire to concentrate on the relationship between himself and others.

Thus girls are not seeking the *kind* of identity that has been prescribed for boys, but a different kind, one in which one is a "being-in-relation," which means developing all of one's self in increasingly complex ways, in increasingly complex relationships.

The model of a "being-in-relationship" that women are seeking is not easy to attain in present conditions. As I have tried to suggest, it is a very valuable model and, I believe, a model more related to reality—the reality of the human condition. In the current situation, however, it still tends to mean for women the old kind of relationship, with the suppression of the full participation of the woman's way of seeing and acting. This has been the historical pattern, certainly. For most women it is still the case. Even so, the woman's struggle continues into later life; but many more factors now complicate it.

PRACTICAL IMPLICATIONS

The practical implications are many. To suggest just a few, women probably do talk about relationships more often, and this is often misinterpreted as dependency. It is very important to listen carefully to what women are saying. Often it is not about wanting or needing to be dependent *or* independent, but about wanting to be in relationship with others and, again, to really comprehend the other; wanting to understand the other's feelings; wanting to contribute to the other; wanting the *nature* of the relationship to be one in which the other person(s) is engaged in this way (see Stiver, Chapter 8, this volume; Surrey, Chapter 3, this volume; Jordan, Surrey, & Kaplan, Chapter 2, this volume). Thus, very often I have heard described as dependent women who are taking care of (and still developing psychologically from taking care of) about six other people. Sometimes they were doing so within a framework that contained many factors of realistic dependency, such as economic dependency or social dependency. Sometimes they had to adopt the psychological framework of the other because that is what their partners expected or demanded. But that is better described as the condition of a subordinate (Miller, 1976), which is still the social condition. This distinction is important.

It is not because of relationships per se that women are suppressed or oppressed. The issue is the *nature* of the relationships. In fact, without the recognition of the importance of relationships to women, we do not help women to find a path that leads them to growth and development. Some psychologists fall into a tendency to encourage "independence" or "separation," which is not what many women want. In the past, mental health professionals encouraged dependency with submission. The point is that the construction of concepts on that axis is inappropriate and misleading.

Perhaps I can illustrate these points by referring briefly to parts of the therapeutic work with one young woman, Ms. D. Ms. D., a 23-year-old woman, had been depressed and had felt worthless in an extreme way since about the age of 13. She was clearly very intelligent and also had a profound quality of thought. She was exceptionally physically attractive.

She did not know where all of the troubles were coming from and could not connect their onset with any specific events. She saw her father as a sort of nice guy; he was light, humorous, and the parent she liked. By contrast, she perceived her mother as a difficult, agitated, "screaming" person, someone no one would want to be like or even to be around. This is one description of parents that therapists hear frequently.

There was one thing that seemed related to the trouble beginning at age 13, although Ms. D. did not make this connection initially. The main part of her relationship with her father appeared to center around her tagging along with him in what seemed his major interest, football. From the time she was about 12 or 13, he did not let her tag along anymore, nor did he let her play with him, her brothers, and the other neighborhood boys. This also is one fairly common occurrence.

She had two brothers, 2 and 4 years younger, to whom she felt very devoted. From young childhood, she had always been very sympathetic to them, felt she understood them, and did a great many things for them.

Something else began around age 13: Many boys began to pursue her. Some were clearly making a straightforward dash for sex; others seemed to seek her ability to hear their needs, to understand them, to be responsive, to be sympathetic, to help them—all of which she did. In neither case, however, were the boys interested in her feelings and concerns if she tried to bring these into the relationship. By the time of therapy, she had lost much of her ability to do so.

I will highlight in abbreviated fashion some of the features that emerged in therapy. Ms. D. came to see that she had developed in many ways, even with all that was bad and lacking in her life. She had related to others in a way that fostered their development. She did this and did it with pleasure and willingness, but she herself was not given much sense of self-worth and self-validation for doing so. No one recognized it fully, or gave her much affirmation for it. Thus, for one thing, she lacked a huge portion of the basis for self-esteem that she could and should have had. Second, almost no one reciprocated, that is, wanted to know and to respond to her needs and desires as she perceived and felt them.

Only after some time in therapy did she see that she had worked at bolstering her father (which she felt was her task) and her brothers; most important, she connected some of this to the "life's work" that had preoccupied her mother all along. She could see, for instance, that a great part of her mother's "ranting and raving," as she called it, resulted from the attempt to "shore up" her father and help her more valued brothers. Her father always had been shaky in his work, and there was a lot to do in the effort to help him "succeed." Her mother had been trying to do that. A large part of her mother's behavior was, however, both a cry for help at her felt obligation to accomplish an impossibility and a "protest" against having to accomplish that impossibility. Late in therapy, Ms. D. could begin to feel a sense of connection to her mother in the recognition that they both had been engaged in that task. Both had gained little sense of value from it. Simultaneously, her mother had not been able to value her daughter, as she had not been able to value herself.

After this recognition, Ms. D. was able to alter some of her resentment toward her mother, although acknowledging the ways that her mother had failed her. Later, too, she came to see her father as someone who had never been prepared or able to hear her concerns or to be responsive to her. She was able to perceive this only after she had finally become able even to *think* of seeking this kind of interaction with him. When she tried to bring her own needs into discussions with him, she perceived his inability to relate to her in this way. It was not like football.

Ms. D. had to confront her anger. She had a large amount of anger at both her father and her mother, for different reasons. It took a long time, but she became more able to allow herself her anger, as she also became able to see how much she had really contributed to others' development. That is, she had first to feel some sense of value before she could tolerate a view of herself as a person with anger (see Miller, Chapter 10, this volume). Then, the understanding and redirection of her anger further relieved her sense of worthlessness. Very importantly, she came to see that she would not have had a large amount of anger if she had not had her own set of perceptions, expectations, wishes, desires, and judgments, that is, the sense of self that she had thought she never had. She was angry because of the violation of the self she really had. She, like many people, particularly women, had said originally that she had no sense of self at all; she was able to discover one and then to go on to build on it.

Her biggest problem in a way remains: how to be the kind of self she wants to be, a being-in-relationship, now able to value the very valuable parts of herself, along with her own perceptions and desires—and to find others who will be with her in that way. She still encounters situations, particularly but not only with men, in which she feels annihilated as a person. I think she is experiencing situations that are common to all of us.

RICHER MODELS

To generalize from this example, then, the model of self-development as it has been defined so far does not help us to understand or to help women as well. Many women perceive the prospects held out by this model as threatening, for good reason. I think their perception reflects at bottom a fear of forfeiting relationships. By contrast, men's fears occur in different forms. Indeed, most men see the prospect of self-development not only as a desirable but also as a basic definition of what they must do in life. Moreover, seeking to understand women opens paths to enlargement of a model of a "self" to one that encompasses more fully the range of human necessities and possibilities.

For Ms. D. there had been problems in relationships, especially in having directed a large portion of her life to relationships that primarily benefited others. However, to have overlooked their value, and her value in them, would have robbed Ms. D. of the major source of her strength and her potential for greater strengths.

The features I have suggested are present even in many highly accomplished women and women who do not care for families in the concrete sense. There is a small group of women today who seek a sense of self similar to that which has been advocated for men. But even many of these women express many of the same themes. They are often the relatively advantaged women who feel very pressured to advance in careers. They often find that their desire to live and to work in a context of mutually enhancing relationships conflicts with male norms. There is pressure to believe that the latter are better and to devalue the relational desires in themselves.

Important evidence is emerging from other parts of the psychological field. Notably, Gilligan's (1982) work in developmental psychology suggests that women's sense of self and of morality revolves around issues of responsibility for, care of, and inclusion of other people. It is embedded in a compelling appreciation of context and an insistent unwillingness to construct abstractions that violate their grasp of the complexities of the connections between people. Women were previously seen as deficient or at a low level of development as a consequence of their encompassing these realms of context and of psychological connection. These features are found even in as accomplished a group as current women Harvard students. In other studies, McClelland (1979) finds that women tend to define power as having the strength to care for and give to others, which is very different from the way men have defined power.

As always, the artists have said it long ago. It is interesting to note that in much of literature the man has been in search of his self, as in *David Copperfield, Portrait of the Artist as a Young Man,* and many other novels. Women express desires, but they have tended to cast them in the overarching terms of wanting to make deep connection with another (others) and usually to enhance another, as in George Eliot's *Middlemarch* or Charlotte Bronte's *Villette.*

Overall, then, the concept of a "self" as it has come down to us has encouraged a complex series of processes leading to a sense of psychological separation from others. From this there would follow a quest for power over others and power over natural forces, including one's own body. This would seem to be inevitable if one cannot be grounded in *faith* in the kind of interconnections I have tried to suggest. Have such definitions of a separated self become conceivable *only* because half of the species has been assigned to the realms of life that involve such necessities as attending to the complex particularities of building the day-to-day emotional connections with others? This means, in effect, giving primary attention to participating in and fostering the development of other people—and even direct concentration on sustaining of the sheer physical life of others. Simultaneously, these realms delegated to women have been granted inferior value. They have not been incorporated into our perceptions as sources of growth, satisfaction, and empowerment. It then becomes difficult to conceive of them as the wellsprings of true inner motivation and development. But they are.

Another way to put this is to say that women's actual practice in the real world and the complex processes that those practices entail have not been drawn upon, nor elaborated on, as a basis of culture, knowledge, theory, or public policy. They then come to sound almost unreal or idealistic, but they are real; they are going on every day. If they were not, none of us would have lived and developed at all. But they have been split off from official definitions of reality.

An underlying question may be: Has our tradition made it difficult to conceive of the possibility that freedom and maximum use of our resources—our initiative, our intellect, our powers—can occur within a context that requires simultaneous responsibility for the care and growth of others and of the natural world? We cannot hope that such a sense of responsibility will develop *after* the person develops first as a separated "self," as currently defined. I believe that the search for the more appropriate study of women in women's own terms can not only lead to understanding women, certainly a valid goal in itself, but can also provide clues to a deeper grasp of the *necessities* for all human development and, simultaneously, to a greater realization of the realities of the vast, untapped human capacities. This is not an easy thing to do, because our whole system of thought, our categories, the eyes with which we see and the ears with which we hear have been trained in a system removed from this activity.

We have all been laboring under only one implicit model of the nature of human nature and of human development. Much richer models are possible. Glimpses of them have always been struggling to emerge, through the artists and the poets, and in some of the hopes and dreams of all of us. Now, perhaps, we can work at learning about them in this field.

6  *Perspectives on Familiness*

FAMILINESS

You may be wondering about the term *familiness* used in the title of this chapter. Why not "Perspectives on Family" or "Perspectives on *the* Family"? In this chapter, as throughout this book, our goal is to develop the most inclusive and varied set of perspectives from which to think about family that we can. To accomplish this we need to accept at the outset that *family* comes in many different shapes and sizes and accomplishes many different things for many different people. In order to respect this rich diversity, it is helpful to think not of *family* in the sense that there is one universal "best" or "most appropriate" family structure or set of family functions. Instead we want to begin with an expanded notion of *family* as multiple and diverse in both its forms and its functions.

The concept of *familiness* allows us to broaden what is often (traditionally) a quite limited notion of family. This concept reminds us as individuals and as members of particular families to think always about possible alternate structures and sets of functions that constitute *family* for others. The notion of familiness allows us to continue to respect the central role that family plays in virtually all our lives, but it also allows us room to accept that the family tasks fulfilled, the family needs met, the family structures (forms) used, and the environmental contexts in which family exists for us and for others are all subject to great variability and difference.

Our goal here is twofold. We want to develop more flexible, fluid, and multi-faceted perspectives from which to learn about alternate family forms and structures and their attendant issues. We also want to more fully understand traditional family structures and functions. Perhaps the most important implication of this somewhat unconventional term, *familiness,* is its use as a reminder to us that *family* as a social institution and *families* as the intimate and individualized arenas in which we carry out so much of our lives can and do change.

Familiness includes the traditional functions and responsibilities assigned by societies to families, such as childbearing, child rearing, intimacy, and security. It also recognizes the great diversity in structures, values, and contexts that define family for different people. In addition to traditional concerns when thinking about family, such as structure and function, *familiness* includes consideration of culture, gender, sexual orientation, age, disabling conditions, income, and spirituality.

We begin this chapter with assumptions similar to those with which we began Chapters 4 and 5 about the interrelatedness of the chapters of this book with each other. This part of our journey toward understanding human behavior in the social environment within the context of familiness is not separate from, but is quite interconnected with, the concerns, issues, and perspectives we have explored in the previous chapters. The content of this chapter will be interwoven with the perspectives and information we explore in the chapters to come. We noted in Chapters 4 and 5 that families, groups, organizations, and communities provide the environments or contexts in which individual behavior and development takes place. Familiness, our focus in this chapter, is a major context and has far-reaching influences on the developmental experiences and challenges of individuals. Individual members of families simultaneously have far-reaching and intense influences on the structure and functioning of the families of which they are a part. Families and family issues simultaneously influence and are influenced by the groups, organizations, and communities with which they interact and of which they are a part. This perspective is consistent with the systems thinking we explored in Chapter 3.

It is contended here, in fact, that familiness is a kind of intersection in our journey to more comprehensive understanding of HBSE. At this intersection our individual lives and experiences meet and are influenced by other individuals and other systems around us. Familiness has significant consequences for the choices we make about the travels we take later in life and for the quality of our experiences on those journeys. At the same time the issues related to familiness become major elements in our continuing developmental journeys. Indeed, as we shall see here and in the chapters to come, familiness has much in common with group, organizational, and community contexts of HBSE.

In many ways, especially when we include alternative notions of *family* in our thinking, the boundaries between systems are really quite blurred. It is often difficult to tell where family stops and group, organization, and community begin. *Family* is sometimes considered a specific type of small group, for example. This interweaving should not be seen as troublesome, however. It is yet another example of the ambiguity that threads its way along our journey to understanding HBSE. We will attempt to use this ambiguity to appreciate the interdependence of these system levels and as a means of further developing a sense of strength in the ambiguous and interdependent nature of family and the other system levels with which we are concerned.

We will find, as we explore the various models of and approaches to family in this chapter, that many of those approaches operate from similar assumptions to those of the approaches to understanding individual behavior and development we explored in Chapters 4 and 5. Many perspectives on family, for example, assume a stage-based, chronological, often linear progression of development. For example, in some cases we will find notions of family development to be strikingly similar to and consistent with Erikson's stage-based model for individual development. This is especially true of traditional perspectives on family. It is true to some extent also for some alternative approaches to family. As in the case of alternative models of individual development, we will find that alternative notions about family often begin with traditional models as departure points from which to then alter, expand upon, or offer contrasting perspectives on family functions and structures. Before exploring traditional and alternate perspectives on family we will consider some of the implications for social workers of how *family* is defined and some current issues and realities facing families today.

SOCIAL WORK AND FAMILIES

Social Work Implications

Hartman and Laird stress the importance to social workers of how *family* is defined. They note that the definitions of *family* that we use have a direct impact on the nature of the practice models we use for working with families. The definition of *family* also directly influences the kind of policies we have at local, state, and national levels regarding families. For example, as we noted in an earlier chapter, if the definition of *family* does not include gay and lesbian families or other persons living together as families but who are not legally recognized, the members of these families will not be eligible for benefits and rights typically available to family members. This can include such wide-ranging benefits and rights as coverage by health and life insurance policies or family visitation policies in hospitals. Hartman and Laird also stress how our personal definitions of *family* and our own experiences in families can be strong influences on how we deal with family issues in our practice of social work (1983:26).

Current Influences on Families

Perhaps the most significant reality facing families today is that of change. What this means for increasing numbers of families is that the so-called normal **nuclear family**—the husband as breadwinner, wife as homemaker, and their offspring all living in a residence apart from their other relatives—does not apply. In fact, according to Hartman and Laird, this kind of household applies to only 13 percent of all U.S. households (1983:39).

Some of the forces propelling this climate of change include the feminist movement, economic insecurity pressing more families to have multiple breadwinners, rising rates of divorce, single-parent households, remarriage, and cohabitation (Walsh 1993: 14). According to Walsh, today both parents work in paid employment in two-thirds of two-parent households. More than 70 percent of mothers with school-age children and 60 percent of mothers with preschool children work outside the home. Divorce ends 50 percent of all marriages. Over one-third of all children can expect to live in a single-parent household at some point, and by the year 2000, remarried families are expected to be the most common form of family. The number of adoptive families continues to increase among couples and single parents. Increasing numbers of gay and lesbian families are demanding rights and recognition for their families of choice (1993:15).

There is growing concern about many other changes as well. Walsh points out that one out of four babies is born to an unwed mother and one in four teenage girls gets pregnant. Over half of births to teenage girls overall and over 90 percent of births to African American teenage girls are nonmarital. The results of these "children having children" is that they are at a very high risk of long-term poverty, poor-quality parenting, and many other health and psychosocial problems of concern to social workers (1993:15). However, there are recent indications that rates of teen pregnancy are beginning to decline.

SEHB: The Social Environment and Family

Family as a Policy Instrument for Social Workers

The family (household) is one of the primary units of analysis used for policy development in the United States. For example, the family or household is a key level of data collection and analysis of the U.S. Bureau of the Census. Census data are, in turn, used to define and set policy in such fundamental areas as the definition of poverty and the determination of eligibility for many human service programs. Family or household is the unit of study and analysis used by many researchers trying to understand a wide variety of conditions and patterns that influence quality of life or well-being at a number of system levels in addition to families, including individuals, communities, and society at large.

Family and Poverty

For example, the National Survey of America's Families (NSAF) conducted by the Urban Institute collected and analyzed data on a number of areas related to individual and family well-being by surveying 44,000 households representing 100,000 people in 13 different states (Staveteig and Wigton 2000). The NSAF findings included information that 25 percent of nonelderly persons "lived in a family experiencing food problems in the previous year." In addition, NSAF revealed that "13 percent of all nonelderly persons lived in families that reported housing hardship during that year" (Staveteig and Wigton 2000). These food and housing hardships were quite unevenly divided among families depending on the race/ethnicity of the family (see Figure 6.1) (Staveteig and Wigton 2000).

While family poverty cuts across race and ethnicity, "whites are less likely than other groups to be poor. African American and Hispanic heritage families are about three times more likely to live in poverty than white families" (see Figure 6.2) (AmeriStat 2000). Just as family poverty is unevenly distributed depending on race or ethnicity, family income and affluence are unevenly distributed as well. Figure 6.3 illustrates that Asian/Pacific Islander and white families' median incomes are significantly higher than those of Native American, Hispanic, or African American families.

Another way of examining income inequality among families or households is to "compare the share of total household income going to households in each fifth of the income distribution. In 1970, households in the top 20 percent of the income distribution received about 44 percent of all income. By 1998, this number approached 50

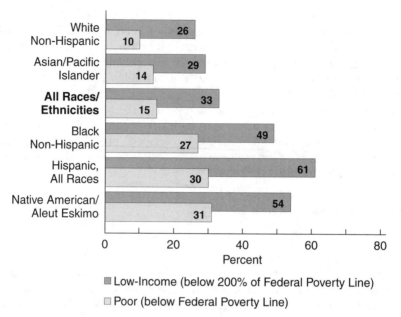

FIGURE 6.1   Nonelderly Who Are Low-Income and/or Poor, by Race
and Ethnicity, 1996

Source: Urban Institute calculations from the 1997 National Survey of America's Families.

percent" (AmeriStat 1999). Figure 6.4, which compares median household income and aggregate household income, shows that high-income families became more affluent between 1970 and 1998, and low- and moderate-income families received increasingly smaller portions of the income pie during the same period.

The Digital Divide: Technology and Families

Assessing the distribution of and access to technology as an important factor in economic and social well-being is another example of the family or household as an important unit of analysis. As technology becomes increasingly important in economic and social well-being, more attention is being given to the distribution of and access to technology across different groups within the population. Much of this attention is directed toward assessing the ability of families and households to acquire and use technology.

Kennedy and Agron point out that "equal opportunity has been a cornerstone of this nation for more than two centuries. But society has not always measured up to that ideal, and you don't have to go far to see the disparity between the exclusive suburban neighborhoods of the affluent and the decrepit slums of America's inner cities or the ramshackle homes of the rural poor" (1999). They also note the optimism among many educators and leaders that "the rapidly accelerating power of technology and the massive amounts of information available on the Internet. . . .could

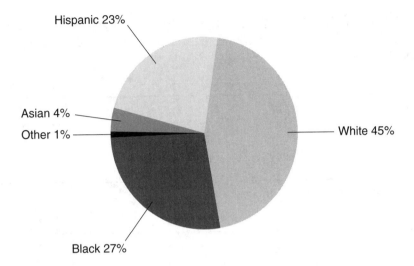

Note: White, black, Asian, and "other" categories exclude Hispanics, who may be of any race. The Asian category includes American Indians, Eskimos, Aleuts, and Pacific Islanders.

FIGURE 6.2   Distribution of Families in Poverty by Race/Ethnicity, 1998

Source: Population Reference Bureau: http://www.ameristat.org/incpov/3bg.gif

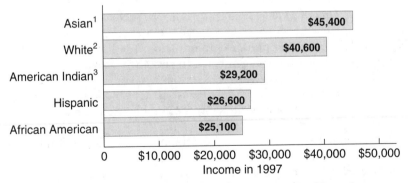

[1]Includes Pacific Islanders and excludes Hispanics.
[2]Excludes Hispanics.
[3]Includes Eskimos and Aleuts and excludes Hispanics.

FIGURE 6.3   Median Household Income by Race and Ethnicity, 1997

Source: Population Reference Bureau analysis of the March 1998 Current Population Survey. www.ameristat.org

FIGURE 6.4   Mean Household Income and Share of Aggregate Household Income (1998 Dollars) by Quintile, 1970 and 1998

Mean Houshold Income

	1970	1998
Lowest fifth	8,008	9,223
Second fifth	21,293	23,288
Third fifth	34,289	38,967
Fourth fifth	48,336	60,266
Highest fifth	85,581	127,529

Share of Aggregate Household Income

	1970	1998
Lowest fifth	4.1	3.6
Second fifth	10.8	9.0
Third fifth	17.4	15.0
Fourth fifth	24.5	23.2
Highest fifth	43.3	49.2

Source: http://www.ameristat.org/incpov/hshlds.htm

close the chasm between the haves and the have-nots" (Kennedy and Agron 1999). Kennedy and Agron caution, however, that "technology won't be able to close the digital divide if the divide itself is preventing the have-nots from gaining access to the technology" (1999).

According to a report by the U.S. government called *Falling Through the Net: Defining the Digital Divide,* "information tools, such as the personal computer and the Internet, are increasingly critical to economic success and personal advancement" (National Telecommunications and Information Administration 1999). At the same time the **digital divide**—the gap between those who have access to these informa-tion tools and those who do not—is a serious and complex concern. Who has access to technology and who is equipped to use that technology are increasingly deter-mining social and economic well-being, a central concern for social workers.

The digital divide is an example of the complex and multilayered impact of poverty on individuals, families, and communities. The complex inter-relatedness of poverty and technology is a particularly dramatic example of how multiple factors must be assessed, understood, and addressed in order to reduce poverty. In the case of the digital divide, some of the most influential factors that must be understood are income, race/ethnicity, geographic location, and education.

While the digital divide may seem primarily a matter of newer information tech-nology such as computers and the Internet, it is also very much about access to such basic technology as the telephone, because the primary means of accessing the Inter-net from homes is through telephone lines and modem connections. A **modem** is a "device used to connect the computer to a telephone line, often for the purpose of connecting to on-line services. A modem can either be located internally in the [personal computer], or can be an external device" (National Telecommunications and Information Administration 1999). While most homes have telephones today, there are still many homes without telephone service. The patterns associated with not having telephone service are closely linked to other factors associated with unequal access to information technology and to higher poverty rates such as race/ethnicity, education, income, and geographic location. According to the report, almost 95 percent of all white households have telephone service regardless of where they live. However, people of color living in a rural area are much less likely to have a phone. For example, of rural-dwelling American Indians/Eskimos/Aleuts, 76.4 percent have phones. For rural Hispanics, the percentage is 84.6, and for rural African Americans, the percentage is 85.4 (National Telecommunications and Information Administration 1999). Level of education also significantly affects the likelihood of having a telephone. While over 97 percent of college graduates have telephones, only 85 percent of persons with some high school education have phone service. Income also has a dramatic impact on the likelihood of having telephone access. Less than 79 percent of the lowest income households (less than $5,000 a year) have phones, while almost 99 percent of central city and urban households with incomes over $75,000 a year have phones. According to the U.S. Commerce Department, "if you are low-income, a minority, less-educated, a single parent with children, a young head of household, or live in the South, then you are less likely to have a telephone at home" (National Telecommunications and Information Administration 1999). Figures 6.5 (page 324), 6.6 (page 325), and 6.7 (page 326) illustrate the differences in telephone service by race/origin, education, income, and geographic location.

Rates of telephone access have remained relatively stable. However, significant changes in access to other electronic services have occurred among the population in the United States in recent years. Rates of computer ownership and Internet access have gone up dramatically. Computer ownership increased to 42.1 percent of the population in 1998. Only four years earlier, in 1994, the computer ownership rate was only 24.1 percent. Significant increases in both computer ownership and Internet access occurred among all groups in all locations in the United States. However, the digital divide is still prominent. Figures 6.8 (page 327), 6.9 (page 328), and 6.10 (page 329) illustrate the discrepancies in computer ownership by geographic location and by income, race/ origin, and education. Figures 6.11 and 6.12 show the extent of the digital divide in Internet access by geographic location and by education and race/origin. The digital divide is perhaps clearest in relation to whites and African Americans or persons of Hispanic heritage when other factors such as household type and income level remain the same. For example, "a White, two-parent household earning less than $35,000 is nearly *three times* as likely to have Internet access as a comparable Black household and nearly *four times* as likely . . . as Hispanic households in the same income category" (National Telecommunications and Information Administration 1999). It is interesting to note that the exception is Asian/Pacific Islanders, who exceed all other groups of color and whites in both computer ownership and Internet access.

Given the rapid rates of change in access to computers and Internet access, we need to ask the question: "Is the digital divide increasing or decreasing?" According to the U.S. Department of Commerce, the digital divide is becoming a "racial ravine" (with the exception of Asian/Pacific Islanders). The "gap between information 'haves' and 'have nots' is growing over time." According to the *Falling through the*

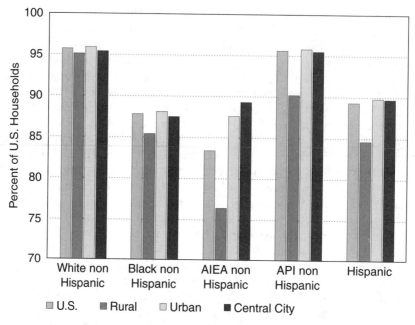

	U.S.	Rural	Urban	Central City
White non Hispanic	95.7	95.1	95.9	95.4
Black non Hispanic	87.8	85.4	88.1	87.5
AIEA non Hispanic	83.4	76.4	87.6	89.3
API non Hispanic	95.6	90.2	95.8	95.5
Hispanic	89.3	84.6	89.8	89.7

FIGURE 6.5   Percent of U.S. Households with a Telephone by Race/Origin (Total United States, Rural, Urban, and Central City Areas), 1998

Source: http://www.ntia.doc.gov/ntiahome/fttn99/FTTN_I/Chart-I-4.html

Net report, "with regards to computers, the gap between White and Black households *grew* 39.2 percent (from a 16.8 percentage point difference to a 23.4 percentage point difference) between 1994 and 1998. For White versus Hispanic households, the gap similarly *rose* by 42.6 percent." The gap is even wider in relation to Internet access. In only one year, between 1997 and 1998, the "gap between White and Black households *increased by 37.7 percent* (from a 13.5 percentage point difference to a 18.6 percentage point difference, and *by 37.6 percent* (from a 12.5 percentage point difference) between White and Hispanic households" (National Telecommunications and Information Administration 1999).

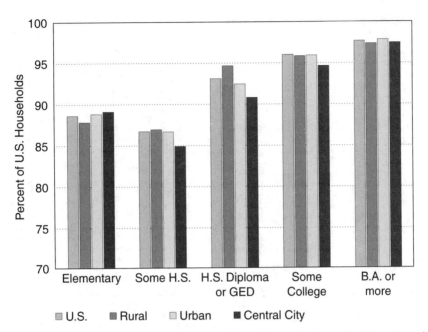

FIGURE 6.6 **Percent of U.S. Households with a Telephone by Education (Total United States, Rural, Urban, and Central City Areas), 1998**

Source: http://www.ntia.doc.gov/ntiahome/fttn99/FTTN_I/Chart-I-7.html

Family and Global Issues: Immigration

Immigration to the United States is considered in this chapter concerning families because the majority of people who immigrate do so in the context of families. According to the American Immigration Lawyers Association (AILA), "most legal immigrants, about 8 out of 11, come to join close family members." According to AILA, "family-sponsored immigrants enter as either immediate relatives—spouses, unmarried minor children, parents of U.S. citizens, or through the *family preference system,* for relatives of permanent residents and siblings of U.S. citizens." The AILA notes that "it is easy to see that family reunification is the cornerstone of our legal immigration policy. It is truly one of the most visible areas in government policy in which we support and strengthen family values. We acknowledge that family unification translates into strong families who build strong communities." The second priority is to allow in a relatively small number of immigrants with skills needed by businesses and industries when citizens with those skills are not available. The third priority of immigration policy is to allow oppressed persons fleeing religious and political persecution a haven. The intent is to offer protection to persons facing "ethnic cleansing, religious oppression, torture, and even death" because of their beliefs or practices (American Immigration Lawyers Association 1999). Given the intent to address oppression through immigration policy, it is unfortunate that immigrants may actually face discrimination and oppression in this country because of their immigrant status.

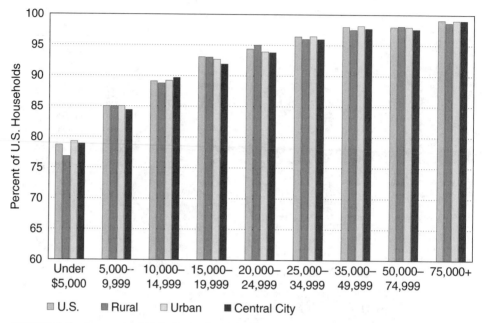

FIGURE 6.7   Percent of U.S. Households with a Telephone by Income (Total United States, Rural, Urban, and Central City Areas), 1998

Source: http://www.ntia.doc.gov/ntiahome/fttn99/FTTN_I/Chart-I-3.html

Immigrants and Oppression/Discrimination

Immigration has become a divisive issue among many individuals and groups in the United States. Even though the United States is in many ways a nation of immigrants, many people tend to be fearful and suspicious of immigrants. As is the case so often with prejudice and discrimination, many of the assumptions about immigrants are based on little fact. For example, some people argue that immigration should be reduced or ended because immigrants are a drain on the economy and public services. In fact, "immigrants pay more in taxes than they receive in public services, and are less likely to be on public assistance than U.S. born residents" (Hernandez and McGoldrick 1999:169). According to Hernandez and McGoldrick, "legal and undocumented immigrant families pay an estimated $70 billion a year in taxes while receiving $43 billion in services" (1999:169). In addition, many immigrants tend to be better educated than U.S.-born citizens and "education is the best predictor of a person's earnings." For example, "among the recent arrivals, 30 percent of the foreign-born adults over age 24 had an undergraduate, professional, or graduate degree in 1997, compared with 24 percent of U.S.-born Americans of the same age" (Population Reference Bureau 1999).

Others believe the majority of immigrants are in the United States illegally. AILA reports that "undocumented immigrants constitute only 1 percent of the total U.S. population and, contrary to popular belief, most of these immigrants do not enter the United States illegally by crossing our border with Canada or Mexico. . . .

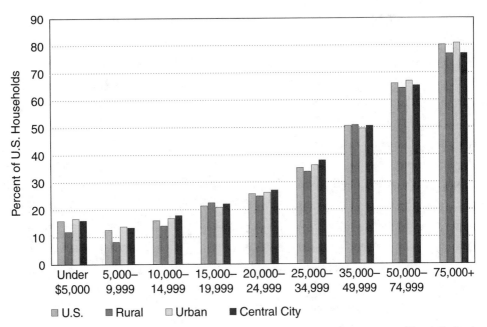

FIGURE 6.8   Percent of U.S. Households with a Computer by Income (Total United States, Rural, Urban, and Central City Areas), 1998

Source: http://www.ntia.doc.gov/ntiahome/fttn99/FTTN_I/Chart-I-2.html

[Of those] here illegally, 6 out of 10 enter the U.S. legally with a student, tourist, or business visa and become illegal when they stay in the United States after their visas expire" (Hernandez and McGoldrick 1999).

Impact of Immigration on Families

The process of immigration is stressful for all immigrant families and, depending on the circumstances that led to immigration, may be a challenge to the very survival of family members. Hernandez and McGoldrick point out that

> *People immigrate for many reasons: for work, study, political and economic survival, or increased life options. Families may migrate to escape oppression, famine, or life without a future. Although migration has become the norm for many people worldwide, it is still a stressful and long-lasting transition and one that is generally not recognized by our society as a whole.* (1999:170)

The stresses that accompany immigration vary according to the family member and the point in the life course of family members. For example, "acculturation processes can threaten the family's structural composition by reversing hierarchies and family roles." Young children may acculturate more quickly than older family members.

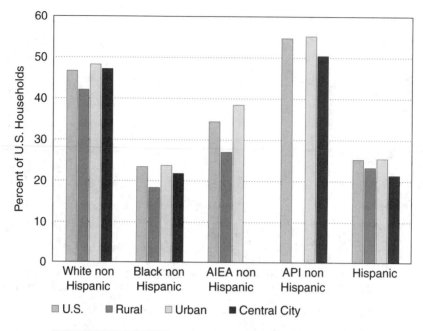

	U.S.	Rural	Urban	Central City
White non Hispanic	46.6	42.0	48.5	47.4
Black non Hispanic	23.2	17.9	23.8	21.8
AIEA non Hispanic	34.3	26.8	38.7	35.6
API non Hispanic	55.0	40.6	55.6	50.5
Hispanic	25.5	23.2	25.7	21.4

FIGURE 6.9 Percent of U.S. Households with a Computer by Race/Origin (Total United States, Rural, Urban, and Central City Areas), 1998

Source: http://www.ntia.doc.gov/ntiahome/fttn99/FTTN_I/Chart-I-13.html

As children move out of the family into school and community, they may move away from both their parents and their original culture. In addition, as children move into the new culture more quickly than their parents do, they may "take on the task of interpreting the new culture for the parents," and parental leadership may be threatened (Hernandez and McGoldrick 1999). Given both the complexities and the potential for oppression as immigrant families make the transition to the United States, it is important for social workers to recognize and understand the impact of this social environmental context on the human behavior of family members.

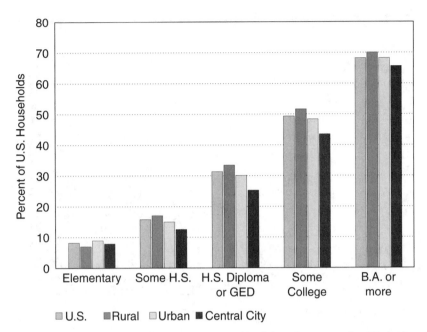

FIGURE 6.10   Percent of U.S. Households with a Computer by Education (Total United States, Rural, Urban, and Central City Areas), 1998

Source: http://www.ntia.doc.gov/ntiahome/fttn99/FTTN_I/Chart-I-17.html

APPROACHES TO UNDERSTANDING FAMILINESS

Before proceeding to explore traditional and alternative perspectives on familiness, we will examine two approaches to understanding family complexity. First we will explore life course theory which can help us understand the many levels of individual development and interactions with the social environment that operate in families. Then we will explore a family-centered approach to working with families. Family-centered social work practice is an emerging perspective that has much in common with strengths-based social work, with appreciation for diversities and with a number of other dimensions of alternative paradigm thinking.

Life Course Theory and Familiness

In Chapter 3 we defined and briefly described life course theory as a middle-range theory (reflecting elements of both traditional and alternative paradigm thinking) for helping us understand human behavior and the social environment. Life course theory has most often been considered an approach to understanding more fully family development and the intersections for family development with the developmental patterns of the individuals that make up the family. We explore the family-focused notion of life course theory here. We consider terms and concepts that make

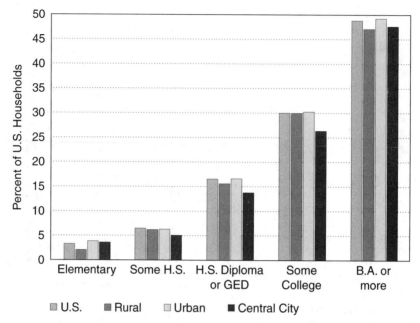

FIGURE 6.11   Percent of U.S. Households Using the Internet by Education (Total United States, Rural, Urban, and Central City Areas), 1998

Source: http://www.ntia.doc.gov/ntiahome/fttn99/FTTN_I/Chart-I-25.html

up the theory in four contexts: temporal, socio-structural, process and change, and family diversity.

Temporal Context

The **temporal context** is used to describe the multiple timeclocks that affect family life. Life course theory itself reflects a timeclock that is **sociogenic** in that it is concerned with the entire lifetime of individuals and families as they develop in the context of the larger society. Another sense of timeclocks within family development is referred to as ontogenetic time and ontogenetic events. The term **ontogenetic** describes the developmental levels of individuals as they grow, change, and age from birth to death and is indexed most simply but quite inexactly by chronological years. As we have noted elsewhere, some psychologists (Piaget, Kohlberg, Erikson, and Valliant) use age period or level or stages which describe that the behavior of individuals in families is in part a function of the individual's ontogenetic development level and of other family members' ontogenetic levels. **Ontogenetic time** and **ontogenetic events** are ways of describing that the behavior of individuals in families is in part a function of the individual's ontogenetic development level and of other family member ontogenetic levels (Bengston and Allen 1993:470–472; 480–481).

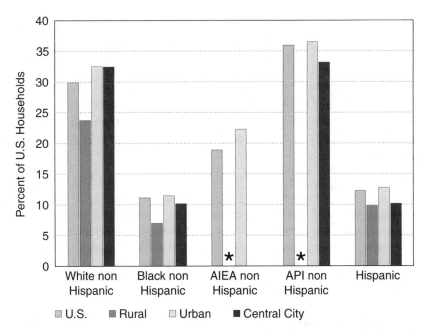

FIGURE 6.12   Percent of U.S. Households Using the Internet by Race/Origin (Total United States, Rural, Urban, and Central City Areas), 1998

Source: http://www.ntia.doc.gov/ntiahome/fttn99/FTTN_I/Chart-I-22.html

Another temporal or time-related concept that is important in understanding life course theory is that of generation. **Generation** refers to the position of individuals in the ranked descent within a biosocial family of procreation and succession. Related concepts are **generational time** and **generational events** which are a way of depicting that the behavior of individuals in families is also a function of generational placement with attendant roles and expectation.Generational time is also called family time. **Generational** or **family time** is indexed not only by biogenetic statuses within families (grandparent, parent, child), but also by the roles, expectations, and identities related to those statuses (Bengston and Allen 1993:471; 481).

Still another temporal context helpful in understanding life course theory is historical time and historical events. The concepts of **historical time** and **historical events** reflect that the behavior of individuals and families and of families as units, is also a function of secular or period events, especially geopolitical or economic events. This temporal context is usually indicated in terms of events, periods, or eras dominated by watershed geopolitical or economic events: the Civil War Period, the Depression, the Vietnam era (Bengston and Allen 1993:481–482). We should note, though, that some alternative theorists would argue that "real" historical impact is best understood in terms of the impact of these watershed events on the individual and family. In other words the local or personal consequences of these events on day to day life must be considered central.

Sociostructural Context

The **sociocultural context** is a way of understanding the social ecology of families in terms of several dimensions. Sociostructural context includes the concept of **social structural location** or the location of families in the broader social structure. This location of the family within the larger society influences the events they experience as the family and its members develop and interact over time. The sociostructural context also includes the **social construction of meaning** in that families and their members attach meaning to events that occur and interact at multiple levels: individual life span, generational, and historical events are interpreted through meanings adapted from social structure location and developed through family interaction (Bengston and Allen 1993:482–483).

Examples of the social construction of meaning might include: norms about the right time to marry, give birth, become a grandparent, and retire. The meanings attached to events also are influenced within families by their **cultural context.** Shared meanings reflected in cultural values both create and interpret life span, generation, and historical events as they impinge on families. Cultural values give meaning to change in families and those meanings may be quite different from one cultural context to another (Bengston and Allen 1993:483).

Continuity and Change

Life course theorists see families influenced significantly by both stability and change which are often referred to as homeostasis and adaptability or the dialectics of continuity and change. Families and members respond over time to individual developmental, generational, and historical events and their responses to this range of events reflect both change (adaptability) and continuity (homeostasis), or innovation and transmission. The concept of **diachronic analysis of families** is a process of analyses of processes over time—focusing on dynamic, as contrasted with static, elements of phenomena. Family processes are examined in addition to family structure. The notion of simultaneously attending to both continuity and change also implies that we cannot understand or explain development from just one point in time. Interactions among age, period, and cohort phenomena influence behaviors of families and individual members over time. Life course theorists stress the dynamic, nonlinear notion of change and its impact. For example individual, generational, and historical changes combined with the social context of those changes mutually effect members, families and the larger community, or social context (Bengston and Allen 1993:483–484).

Heterogeneity and Diversity among Families

Life course advocates also emphasize diversity among families and note that there is considerable diversity in the ways families react to and give meaning to individual developmental, generational, and historical events. These theorists also suggest that heterogeneity or diversity in families increases over time. They note that, for example, a family kinship network is increasingly diverse over time, adding and changing members through birth and marriage. In addition, life course theory recognizes there is considerable variation in family structure as a result of differences in location within the social structure: gender, race/ethnicity, or socioeconomic status (Bengston and Allen 1993:484).

Family-Centered Practice

An alternative approach to thinking about and working with families is referred to as a **family-centered approach**. Rounds et al. point out that "In a family-centered approach, family members, not professionals, determine who constitutes the family" (1994:7). In addition, they explain that "A family-centered approach stresses family-professional collaboration, which requires a high degree of trust, mutual respect, and participation by both parties" (Rounds et al. 1994:9). Often associated with a family-centered approach to practice is a family preservation perspective.

Family Preservation

Ronnau and Sallee (in Ronnau and Marlow 1993:540–541) describe the values that underlie a family preservation approach:

- People of all ages can best develop and their lives be enhanced, with few exceptions, by remaining with their family or relying on their family as an important resource.
- The family members' ethnic, cultural, and religious background, as well as values, and community ties are important resources to be used in the helping process.
- The definition of "family" is varied, and each family should be approached as a unique system.
- Policies at the local, state, and national levels should be formulated to strengthen, empower, and support families.
- The family members themselves are crucial partners in the helping process.
- Family members should be recognized as being in charge in order to resolve their own problems and avoid dependence upon the social service system.
- The dignity and right to privacy of all family members should be respected.
- Families have the potential to change, and most troubled families want to do so.

We will continue, as we proceed on our journey to understanding both traditional and alternative notions of family, to consider the social work practice implications of these changes occurring in families. For these and other reasons family provides the context for much social work practice. Families can be both barriers to and resources for reaching our potential as humans.

TRADITIONAL MODELS

The notion of family development as a series of predictable stages through which families pass is perhaps the oldest and most common framework for organizing traditional models for understanding family behavior and development. Duvall (1971:113–114) notes that some early stage models were quite simple. One early model consisted only of two stages:

1. the expanding family stage, taking the family from its formation to the time its children are grown; and

2. the contracting family stage, during which children leave the home and only the parents remain.

Duvall also describes a 1931 four-stage model. This model consisted of

1. married couples just starting out;

2. couples with one or more children;

3. couples with one or more adult self-supporting children; and

4. couples growing old.

Another four-stage model she described focused on the formal education system as a major determiner of family developmental stages. This model consisted of

1. preschool family;

2. grade school family;

3. high school family; and

4. all-adult family (Kirkpatrick et al. in Duvall 1971:114).

Some later stage-centered models of family life cycle included as many as twenty-four stages (Duvall 1971:114–115).

As noted above, many models of family development bear a striking resemblance to stage-based, chronological models of individual development, such as Erikson's model of individual psychosocial development. This similarity is not coincidental. Traditional approaches to family development are child focused or **child centered.** The developmental stages that an individual child passes through, according to many traditional models, in effect drive the development of the family. The family is pressed to change or react as a result of changes in the individual developmental stages of the child, usually the eldest child (Devore and Schlesinger 1991:274). For example, the birth of a child—the onset of the first stage of individual development—results in a shift from one developmental stage to another for the family. As we explore models of family development keyed to developmental stages of children, we will question the assumptions and inclusiveness of such models. For example, if all conceptualizations of family are premised on the bearing and rearing of children, are childless individuals or couples by definition excluded from having family (familiness)? We shall further explore this issue later in this chapter.

Traditional Definitions

Before exploring in more detail some models of family that are consistent with traditional paradigm thinking, it is perhaps helpful to define what is meant by *traditional family*.

Traditional definitions of family have generally focused either on structure or function. Structural definitions focus on relationship among members that are based on marriage, blood, or adoption. Functional definitions focus on tasks performed by family for its members or for society, such as child rearing, meeting affectional needs of adults, and transmitting the values of the larger society (Hartman and Laird 1983: 27–28).

Some traditional definitions have focused on both structure and function, such as Duvall's (1971) definition and list of family functions below. Here a family is defined as:

> *a unity of interacting persons related by ties of marriage, birth, or adoption, whose central purpose is to create and maintain a common culture which promotes the physical, mental, emotional, and social development of each of its members.* (1971:5)

She suggests that "modern" families implement this definition through six functions:

1. *affection between husband and wife, parents, and children, and among the generations;*
2. *personal security and acceptance of each family member for the unique individual he [she] is and for the potential he [she] represents;*
3. *satisfaction and a sense of purpose;*
4. *continuity of companionship and association;*
5. *social placement and socialization;*
6. *controls and sense of what is right.* (Duvall 1971:5)

Duvall suggests that this is a "modern" definition and outline of functions in contrast to "older" notions of the family. She suggests that it is modern because it replaces older notions of family in which "women 'slave over a hot stove,' preparing meals from foodstuffs they have grown and processed"; family members wear "homemade" garments; health and medical care is primarily provided by family members; education of children is done primarily by parents; children's play is supervised by parents rather than by day-care service staff; family protection is "dependent upon a rifle over the fireplace," instead of being provided by formal fire and police agencies (1971:3–4).

Such a "modern" definition suggests a great deal of historical change in notions of family arrangements and functions. Nevertheless both Duvall's notions of the "older" and the "modern" family reflect quite traditional perspectives on family. These notions suggest, for example, that a child-centered, two-parent, heterosexual white family with sufficient access to the resources necessary to carry out required family functions is the norm for family form and function. They suggest a definition of family with much in common with the "norm of rightness" we explored earlier (see Chapter 2) central to the "privilege" dimension of the traditional and dominant paradigm.

Neither the "older" nor the "modern" notion of family communicates a significant degree of potential for flexible alternatives in structure and function to include diverse family forms. Such family structures as extended families of multiple generations or "fictive kin" systems that include non-blood-related members of many African American families are not likely to be included. (We will explore the concept of fictive kin in more detail later in this chapter.) Functional definitions also present problems because of the lack of agreement in society about what functions family must or should fulfill. The controversies over who should be responsible for sex education, discipline, and care of children, and care of aged persons, persons with disabilities, and sick persons are examples of the uncertainties about what functions are included in functional definitions of the family (Hartman and Laird 1983:26–28). Recognizing the difficulties with traditional structural or functional definitions of family, we will next consider some traditional models of family and familiness. These models are based on relatively narrow structural and/or functional perspectives.

Duvall and Hill: National Conference on Family Life Model

Evelyn Duvall and Reuben Hill (in Kennedy 1978) cochaired a committee for the National Conference on Family Life in 1948 out of which emerged a model consisting of a sequence of eight stages. This model is child-centered and has been widely used and adapted since its creation. A major assumption of this model is that parenting children is the central activity of adult family life (Kennedy 1978:70).

This model of a family life cycle incorporated three criteria into eight stages. The three criteria included 1) a major change in family size; 2) the developmental age of the oldest child; and 3) a change in the work status of "father." The eight stages of the original model (Kennedy 1978:70) are as follows:

Stage 1: Establishment (newly married, childless)

Stage 2: New Parents (infant–3 years)

Stage 3: Preschool family (child 3–6 years and possible younger siblings)

Stage 4: School-age family (oldest child 6–12 years, possible younger siblings)

Stage 5: Family with adolescent (oldest child 13–19, possible younger siblings)

Stage 6: Family with young adult (oldest 20, until first child leaves home)

Stage 7: Family as launching center (from departure of first to last child)

Stage 8: Post-parental family, the middle years (after children have left home until father retires).

This model was adapted slightly by Hill in an article appearing in 1986. The passage of almost forty years resulted in virtually no substantive changes in the model itself (Hill 1986:21), although, as we shall see, significant changes were occurring in the form and function of family for many members of society. The most substantive change between the two models is perhaps the recognition in the final or eighth stage of the 1986 adaptation of the model that the producer of family income (breadwinner) is not necessarily the father as was the implication in the earlier model.

Family Developmental Tasks

The family life cycle approach, of which the Duvall and Hill model above is perhaps the most used example, was also influenced a great deal by the concept of developmental tasks. The notion of developmental tasks, if you recall from our earlier discussion of individual models of development, was a fundamental element used by Erikson and others to describe the activities individuals engaged in and struggled with as they moved through their various developmental stages. This concept was also a central organizing element used by family developmentalists to describe the activities and struggles faced by whole families as they moved along their developmental journeys. Eleanor Godfrey as early as 1950 defined family developmental tasks as "those that must be accomplished by a family in a way that will satisfy (a) biological requirements, (b) cultural imperatives, and (c) personal aspirations and values, if a family is to continue to grow as a unit" (in Duvall 1988:131). Duvall describes these basic family tasks as:

1. *providing physical care;*
2. *allocating resources;*
3. *determining who does what;*
4. *assuring members' socialization;*
5. *establishing interaction patterns;*
6. *incorporating and releasing members;*
7. *relating to society through its institutions; and*
8. *maintaining morale and motivation.* (Duvall 1988:131)

These basic tasks, according to family developmentalists, are addressed by every family at every stage of its life cycle. However, each family accomplishes these tasks in its own ways. If it does not, society steps in in the form of some agent of social control (including social workers) to try to ensure the accomplishment of the necessary tasks (Duvall 1988:131).

Changes in Traditional Family Life Cycle Models

Carter and McGoldrick (1980) offer another traditional model of family development from a life cycle perspective. Their model is directed toward use by family therapists in interventions with families. Carter and McGoldrick originally published their model as *The Family Life Cycle* in 1980. They published an adaptation of their original model in 1989 as *The Changing Family Life Cycle*.

The more recent adaptation of their model is only slightly different from the original. It remains focused on the "family life cycle stages of American middle-class families" (1989:13). The more recent version also continues their "view that the central underlying process to be negotiated is the expansion, contraction and realignment of the relationship system to support the entry, exit, and development of family members in a functional way" (Carter and McGoldrick 1989:13). In this respect the model remains very traditional and it has many similarities to the much earlier models described and presented (see Duvall and Hill model above). This model is presented in Table 6.1.

In their 1989 discussion of the family life cycle, Carter and McGoldrick recognized that many changes had occurred in the family in the recent past and more and more families, even American middle-class families, were not fitting the traditional

TABLE 6.1   The Stages of the Family Life Cycle

Family Life Cycle Stage	Emotional Process of Transition: Key Principles	Second-Order Changes in Family Status Required to Proceed Developmentally
1. Leaving home: Single young adults	Accepting emotional and financial responsibility for self	a. Differentiation of self in relation to family of origin b. Development of intimate peer relationships c. Establishment of self re: work and financial independence
2. The joining of families through marriage: The new couple	Commitment to new system	a. Formation of marital system b. Realignment of relationships with extended families and friends to include spouse
3. Families with young children	Accepting new members into the system	a. Adjusting marital system to make space for child(ren) b. Joining in childrearing, financial, and household tasks c. Realignment of relationships with extended family to include parenting and grandparenting roles
4. Families and adolescents	Increasing flexibility of family boundaries to include children's independence and grandparents' frailties	a. Shifting of parent child relationships to permit adolescent to move in and out of system b. Refocus on midlife marital and career issues c. Beginning shift toward joint caring for older generation
5. Launching children and moving on	Accepting a multitude of exits from and entries into the family system	a. Renegotiation of marital system as a dyad b. Development of adult to adult relationships between grown children and their parents c. Realignment of relationships to include in-laws and grandchildren d. Dealing with disabilities and death of persons (grandparents)
6. Families in later life	Accepting the shifting of generational roles	a. Maintaining own and/or couple functioning and interests in face of physiological decline: exploration of new familial and social role options b. Support for a more central role of middle generation c. Making room in the system for the wisdom and experience of the elderly, supporting the older generation without overfunctioning for them d. Dealing with loss of spouse, siblings, and other peers and preparation for own death. Life review and integration.

From Betty Carter and Monica McGoldrick, *The Changing Family Life Cycle*. Copyright © 1989 by Allyn and Bacon. Reprinted by permission.

model. Among the influences resulting in changes in the family life cycle were a lower birthrate, longer life expectancy, the changing role of women, and increasing rates of divorce and remarriage (1989:10–11). In addition to these influences, Carter and McGoldrick asserted that while in earlier periods "child rearing occupied adults for their entire active life span, it now occupies less than half the time span of adult life prior to old age. The meaning of the family is changing drastically, since it is no longer organized primarily around this activity" (1989:11). This recognition of movement away from a solely child-centered focus on family life is especially significant in light of our observations about this as a central feature of virtually all traditional models of family.

Divorce, Remarriage, and Stepfamilies

One especially significant change noted by Carter and McGoldrick was the rapidly growing rates of divorce and remarriage. Divorce and remarriage had in fact become so common in American families, they observed, that "divorce in the American family is close to the point at which it will occur in the majority of families and will thus be thought of more and more as a normative event" (1989:21).

Given the extent of divorce and remarriage occurring in U.S. society, the family forms that come about as a result of divorce are treated here as traditional family configurations. It is important to note, though, that for the family members going through divorce and remarriage, these transitions represent dramatic alternative family configurations. In recognition of the increasing frequency of divorce and remarriage, Carter and McGoldrick offer models for both the family in the process of divorcing and for the processes occurring in a family as a result of remarriage. These models are presented as Tables 6.2 and 6.3.

Because divorce touches the lives of so many family members today, efforts to understand the dynamics and impact of divorce have flourished. Most traditional studies of divorce, for example, have emphasized the difficulties and problems created for members of divorcing families, especially for the children in those families. More recent studies, however, note that there can be a wide range of responses to divorce on the part of family members. This range still includes the possibility of severe problems for some family members, but it also includes recognition of the potential for divorce and remarriage to bring quite positive results as well. For example, divorce may result in relief from intense conflict and life-threatening abuse for some people. Remarriage for many may present opportunities for forming satisfying and harmonious new relationships. Even when choosing to remain single, for many persons divorce provides an opportunity for personal growth and development (Hetherington, Law, and O'Connor 1993:208–209).

As divorce rates have climbed, remarriage rates and the number of persons living in stepfamilies have risen dramatically as well. A **stepfamily** is broadly defined as "a household containing a child who is biologically related to only one of the adults." In 1987 it was estimated that 35 percent of all adults were in step situations as "stepparents, parents who had remarried, or adult stepchildren." In addition, 20 percent of all children under nineteen years of age were stepchildren or half-siblings. Overall, this meant that in 1987, 33 percent of the entire population of the United States was in a step situation. Year 2000 statistics, when gathered, are likely to report that more people live in stepfamily situations than in any other type of family in the United States (Visher and Visher 1993:235).

TABLE 6.2   An Additional Stage of the Family Life Cycle for Divorcing Families

Phase		Emotional Process of Transition *Prerequisite* Attitude	Developmental Issues
Divorce	The decision to divorce	Acceptance of inability to resolve marital tensions sufficiently to continue relationship	Acceptance of one's own part in the failure of the marriage
	Planning the breakup of the system	Supporting viable arrangements for all parts of the system	a. Working cooperatively on problems of custody, visitation, and finances b. Dealing with extended family about the divorce
	Separation	a. Willingness to continue co-operative coparental relationship and joint financial support of children b. Work on resolution of attachment to spouse	a. Mourning loss of intact family b. Restructuring marital and parent-child relationships and finances; adaptation to living apart c. Realignment of relationships with extended family; staying connected with spouse's extended family
	The divorce	More work on emotional divorce: Overcoming hurt, anger, guilt, etc.	a. Mourning loss of intact family: giving up fantasies of reunion b. Retrieval of hopes, dreams, expectations from the marriage c. Staying connected with extended families
Post-divorce family	Single-parent (custodial household or primary residence)	Willingness to maintain financial responsibilities, continue parental contact with ex-spouse, and support contact of children with ex-spouse and his or her family	a. Making flexible visitation arrangements with ex-spouse and his [her] family b. Rebuilding own financial resources c. Rebuilding own social network
	Single-parent (noncustodial)	Willingness to maintain parental contact with ex-spouse and support custodial parent's relationship with children	a. Finding ways to continue effective parenting relationship with children b. Maintaining financial responsibilities to ex-spouse and children c. Rebuilding own social network

From Carter, B., and McGoldrick, M., *The Expanded Family Lifecycle.* Copyright © 1999 by Allyn & Bacon. Reprinted/adapted by permission.

Even given the numbers of persons living in step situations, to be in such a situation is still to live with a variety of negative stereotypes. The term *stepchild* is still used to indicate poor treatment or second-class status in many situations. Fairy tales

TABLE 6.3   Remarried Family Formation: A Developmental Outline*

Steps	Prerequisite Attitude	Developmental Issues
1. Entering the new relationship	Recovery from loss of first marriage (adequate "emotional divorce")	Recommitment to marriage and to forming a family with readiness to deal with the complexity and ambiguity
2. Conceptualizing and planning new marriage and family	Accepting one's own fears and those of new spouse and children about remarriage and forming a stepfamily Accepting need for time and patience for adjustment to complexity and ambiguity of: 1. Multiple new roles 2. Boundaries: space, time, membership, and authority 3. Affective Issues: guilt, loyalty conflicts, desire for mutuality, unresolvable past hurts	a. Work on openness in the new relationships to avoid pseudo-mutality. b. Plan for maintenance of cooperative financial and coparental relationships with ex-spouses. c. Plan to help children deal with fears, loyalty conflicts, and membership in two systems. d. Realignment of relationships with extended family to include new spouse and children. e. Plan maintenance of connections for children with extended family of ex-spouse(s).
3. Remarriage and reconstitution of family	Final resolution of attachment to previous spouse and ideal of "intact" family; Acceptance of a different model of family with permeable boundaries	a. Restructuring family boundaries to allow for inclusion of new spouse-stepparent. b. Realignment of relationships and financial arrangements throughout subsystems to permit interweaving of several systems. c. Making room for relationships of all children with biological (noncustodial) parents, grandparents, and other extended family. d. Sharing memories and histories to enhance stepfamily integration.

*Variation on a developmental scheme presented by Ransom et al. (1979)

From Carter, B., and McGoldrick, M., *The Expanded Family Lifecycle.* Copyright © 1999 by Allyn & Bacon. Reprinted/adapted by permission.

often perpetuate the notion of the "wicked stepmother" or the "mistreated stepchild," for example (Visher and Visher 1993:244).

Visher and Visher stress that for many individuals and families the transition through remarriage to stepfamily life is a challenging but satisfying journey. They note, though, that only recently has remarriage and stepfamily research moved away from a "deficit" or problem-focused approach. They suggest that there are several characteristics of successful stepfamilies. Among these characteristics are the following:

1. Expectations are realistic.   They recognize that instant love and adjustment is a myth and that emotional bonding takes time. They allow each member to come to accept the new relationship at his or her own pace; recognizing, for example, that young children are likely to develop close relationships with stepparents more easily than teenagers, who may be struggling with their identities and moving toward independence from the family.

2. Losses can be mourned. They allow recognition and grieving of relationships lost through divorce. Adults in the stepfamily realize the sadness resulting from this loss that may be displayed by children who have no control over the changes that have occurred in their lives.

3. There is a strong couple relationship. The couple works as a team and understands the importance of providing an atmosphere of stability for children. The couple relationship can also serve as a model for children as they move toward adulthood.

4. Satisfactory step relationships have formed. The stepparent has taken the time necessary to take on the parenting role. The couple works together as a team and the parent initially takes the more active parenting role but supports the development of a parent role by the stepparent. (It is possible that stepparents and stepchildren will not form a close interpersonal relationship, but the relationship will be one of tolerance and respect nevertheless.)

5. Satisfying rituals are established. The family will accept that there is no right or wrong way for family rituals, which may be different for each member. For example, members will develop a flexible and compromising approach to such things as the proper procedures for doing laundry, or celebrating a birthday, or cooking the holiday meal.

6. The separate households cooperate. Satisfactory arrangements will be worked out between the children's households. A "parenting coalition" on the part of all involved parents will be developed for the benefit of the children (Visher and Visher in Walsh 1993:244–250).

In addition to changes in families as a result of divorce, remarriage, and step-family arrangements, Carter and McGoldrick recognized several other "variations" that would have an impact on the family life cycle. These variations included differences from the American middle-class norm due to poverty and due to cultural differences (1989:20–25). They also recognized the potential for significant variations in the family life cycle as a result of differences such as sexual orientation (1989:60–61). That these variations were recognized in the context of a traditional perspective on the family is significant. These differences were still seen, however, only as variations on the "normal" or traditional model.

Grandparents as Parents

An illustration of a current variation in many families is the increasing role played by grandparents as parents. Jendrek (1994) points out that for many children in the United States the traditional divisions between parents and grandparents have blurred considerably, even disappearing for some. There has been a 44 percent increase in the number of children living with grandparents in the United States since 1980. This figure is for grandparents who maintain the home, and does not include homes maintained by children's parents in which grandparents provide care (1994:206). Ac-

PERCENTAGES OF CHILDREN LIVING WITH GRANDPARENTS

- African American = 15%
- White = 3.9%
- Hispanic = 5.7%

Source: Rothenberg, 1997: www

cording to the National Center for Health Statistics, 3.75 million children under the age of 18 (5.4 percent) live in the homes of their grandparents (Rothenberg 1997).

Grandparents provide regular care for grandchildren or assume other parental roles either formally through court orders or decisions or informally where the grandchild lives with or spends a regular portion of his/her day with a grandparent (Jendrek 1996:206). The grandparent-as-parent role is a form of kinship care (see discussion of kinship care later in this chapter).

Parental Roles

The role of parent from a legal perspective includes both legal and physical custody:

- Legal custody is "the right or authority of a parent, or parents, to make decisions concerning the child's upbringing" (Schulman and Pitt in Jendrek 1994:207). Ex. Decisions about medical care, education, discipline.
- Physical custody is "the right to physical possession of the child, i.e., to have the child live with the . . . parent" (Schulman and Pitt in Jendrek 1994: 207).

Combining the traditional parent roles regarding legal and physical custody results in three possible categories of "**grandparents-as-parent**" roles:

1. Custodial grandparents: "A legal relationship with the grandchild (adoption, full custody, temporary custody, or guardianship). . . . These grandparents assume the functions typically linked to parenthood in our society; they become the grandchild's physical and legal custodians." Grandparents typically assume custodial care of grandchildren because of severe problems in the grandchild's nuclear family including financial, emotional or mental health, and substance abuse problems (Jendrek 1994:207).

2. Day-care grandparents: These grandparents "are not casual baby-sitters; they provide grandchildren with daily care for extended periods. Day-care grandparents assume responsibility for the physical care of their grandchildren but assume no legal responsibility" (Jendrek 1994: 207).

3. Living-with grandparents: These grandparents "assume a parenting role that falls between that of the custodial and day-care grandparent. Living-with grandparents do not have legal custody but provide some, if not all,

of the daily physical care for the grandchild." Two categories of living-with grandparents:

- those who have one or more of the grandchild's parents living with them
- those who have neither parent in their household (Jendrek 1994: 207–208).

As Laird (in Walsh 1993:286) points out, "most studies of 'minorities' . . . start from a majority perspective (usually white, middle-class, male), comparing and searching for 'difference,' measuring the population of interest against some accepted norm and describing how it is different, exotic, or deviant." In the remainder of this chapter we will explore differences in familiness as alternatives to, as well as variations on, traditional models of family. Whenever possible we will present alternative notions on familiness from the perspective of the persons who represent those alternatives. In some cases, even presentation of alternative perspectives by persons representing an alternative perspective is limited because there is no language in traditional definitions and conceptualizations of family to describe alternative elements. For example, in describing gay and lesbian families, one finds no socially agreed-on terms to define the same-sex couple relationship or to name the role of the coparent (Laird in Walsh 1993:315).

THE ALTERNATIVE/POSSIBLE

As indicated earlier in this chapter, many alternative approaches to understanding familiness are extensions or adaptations of traditional models or perspectives. Other alternative approaches include perspectives that offer striking contrasts to traditional approaches. The alternative approaches to understanding familiness that we are about to explore will provide us with a number of concepts important for understanding human behavior in the social environment more generally, in addition to their usefulness in helping us to expand our understanding of familiness.

The alternative approaches we are about to explore tend to be more flexible and more pluralistic than are traditional approaches to thinking about families and familiness. They tend to accept that changes occurring in the environment often require changes in the structures and functions of families. They do not assume that all families do or should look and behave the same or that the same family will or should look and behave the same way at different times. These approaches tend to place greater emphasis on the environmental and social forces that influence family structures and functions. A number of the models also stress the interdependence of families with other related systems—individuals, groups, organizations, and communities.

Alternative Definitions

We are often presented with images that suggest that the only viable definition of family is one consistent with the traditional two-parent, child-centered, nuclear, white heterosexual, stage-based portrayals we visited in the preceding sections. While this perspective on family is an accurate portrayal of many families (though, as we noted earlier, the number of families fitting this definition is rapidly decreasing), there are many, many families not reflected in this portrayal.

Other, more flexible and pluralistic ways of defining family are needed to represent the great diversity of current family forms. These ways of defining family and familiness are more likely to include or reflect dimensions of alternative paradigm thinking that we have been exploring throughout this book, such as recognition of a diversity of family forms.

If multiple or diverse definitions of family forms are not available, great numbers of very real functioning families can be rendered invisible. Scanzoni and Marsiglio (1991), for example, remind us that Stack (1974) could not find any families in her research work in an urban African American community "until she redefined family as 'the smallest organized, durable network of kin and non-kin [i.e., friends] who interact daily, providing the domestic needs of children and assuring their survival.'"

Seligman suggests a basic and quite flexible alternate definition of families (in Scanzoni and Marsiglio 1991:117) based on the findings from his national survey in which 75 percent of the respondents, when asked to define "the family," defined it as "a group of people who love and care for each other." The central place of the quality of the relationships that constitute family is also stressed in a court ruling regarding the definition of family in a case supporting gay rights. In this case the judge concluded: "It is the totality of the relationship, as evidenced by the dedication, caring, and self-sacrifice of the parties which should, in the final analysis, control the definition of family" (Stacey in Walsh 1993:17). Another quite flexible definition of family is that of D'Antonio (in Scanzoni and Marsiglio 1991:117): "A unit comprising two or more persons who live together for an extended period of time, and who share in one or more of the following: Work (for wages and house), sex, care and feeding of children, and intellectual, spiritual, and recreational activities."

Toward an Integrative Approach

Hartman and Laird urge not only a flexible definition for family, but they remind us that most of us are really members of multiple families simultaneously. Their approach to defining family integrates traditional notions of family and alternate perspectives on family. They suggest that there are two categories of family: One is biologically based; the other is based on relationship. The first type they define as **family of origin.** By family of origin they mean:

> *that family of blood ties, both vertical (multigenerational) and horizontal (kinship), living or dead, geographically close or distant, known or unknown, accessible or inaccessible, but always in some way psychologically relevant. Also included in the family of origin are adopted members and fictive kin, people who, although not related by blood, are considered and have functioned as part of a family.*

The second type of family they refer to is **family as intimate environment.** This second type of family, they say, is:

> *that current family constellation in which people have chosen to live. Such a family group in our context consists of two or more people who have made a commitment to share living space, have developed close emotional ties, and share a variety of family roles and functions.* (Hartman and Laird 1983: 29–30)

Examples of this second type of family include "a middle-aged married couple whose children are reared; two elderly sisters, one a widow and the other a spinster, who share an apartment in a retirement community; a group of biologically related and unrelated adults and children who have formed a group or communal family in which a range of commitments exists." Hartman and Laird suggest that "a family becomes a family when two or more individuals have decided they are a family" by creating an environment in which they share emotional needs for closeness, living space, and the roles and tasks necessary for meeting the biological, social, and psychological needs of the members. They do not limit the definition of family only to those recognized by courts of law (1983:30–31).

Family Structure and Diversity

In addition to the two types of family relationships described by Hartman and Laird, the types of family structures within which we live reflect a great deal of diversity. The National Survey of American Families (NSAF) reported information on family structure by race and ethnicity. The findings indicated that while most white (71 percent) and Asian American (77 percent) children lived in two-parent families, "slightly more than half of Hispanic children and half of Native American children lived in two-parent families. In contrast, only about one-third of [African American] children lived with two parents" (Staveteig and Wigton 2000). Figure 6.13 provides details and definitions of differences in family structures by race and ethnicity. The diversity of family structures combined with variations in structure according to the race/ethnicity of families is another clear example of "diversity within diversity" (see discussion of diversity with diversity and multiple diversities in Chapter 2).

As we continue our journey toward more comprehensive ways to understand familiness, we will keep in mind these multiple and flexible notions of family. The following exploration of alternative notions of familiness is organized according to several "Focus" areas. This arrangement is similar to that used in Chapter 5 for alternative perspectives on individual development. The cautions suggested in that chapter concerning false divisions and oversimplification of multidimensional and interacting factors apply here as well.

FOCUS: PEOPLE OF COLOR

Harrison et al. use an ecological framework as a departure point for developing an alternative approach to familiness. This approach emphasizes the interaction of individuals with the social environment. Harrison et al. focus on the ecological challenges faced by the families of people of color in their interactions with social systems and institutions in the larger environment (1990:347). Others have stressed the importance of using a strengths-based approach to dealing with families of color as well (Boyd-Franklin in Walsh 1993:368–371; Attneave in McGoldrick, Pearce, & Giordano 1982:81–82). A strengths-based perspective for understanding families of color is consistent with the principles of the strengths-based perspective on social work described in Chapter 3. Central to a strengths-based approach to families of color is the notion of adaptive strategies.

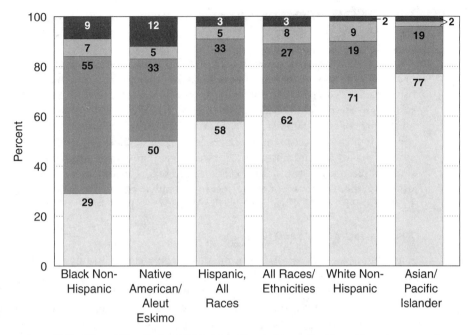

■ No-Parent Family (a child living with relatives other than his or her parents,
with unrelated adults, or as an emancipated minor)

▢ Blended Family (a biological or adoptive parent married to a spouse who
has not adopted child)

▨ One-Parent Family (an unmarried biological or adoptive parent who may or
may not be living with other adults)

▢ Two-Parent Family (two biological or adoptive parents)

FIGURE 6.13   Family Structure of Children, by Race and Ethnicity, 1997

Source: Urban Institute calculations from the 1997 National Survey of America's Families.

Adaptive Strategies

Families of color develop a variety of adaptive strategies to overcome environmental
barriers to their (and their members') well-being and development (Ho 1987). Harrison et al. describe **adaptive strategies** as observable social behavioral "cultural patterns that promote the survival and well-being of the community, families, and
individual members of the group" (1990:350). Adaptive strategies recognize the interdependence of community, individual, and family systems. This interdependence
offers an example of family as the intersection at which a variety of systems come together and interact with one another.

A strengths-based adaptive-strategies approach to studying and understanding families of color and their children offers an alternative to traditional deficit- or

pathology-focused approaches. The specific groups with which we are concerned include African Americans, American Indians/Alaskan Natives, Asian/Pacific Americans, and Latino Americans (Harrison et al. 1990:348).

An adaptive-strategies approach highlights the interconnectedness of the status of families of color, adaptive strategies, socialization goals, and child outcomes (Harrison et al. 1990:348). Through this approach we can delineate a number of contextual or environmental issues that interact to result in the need for adaptive strategies on the part of these families and their members. Specific issues addressed through this approach include racism and oppression, extendedness of families, role flexibility within families, biculturalism, and spirituality and ancestral worldview. While there are some differences in the nature of these strategies from one group to another, the strategies themselves seem to be strikingly similar across the groups (Harrison et al. 1990:350; Ho 1987; Boyd-Franklin in Walsh 1993).

Response to Racism and Oppression

A number of statuses or conditions interact in the social environments of families of color and result in the need to create adaptive strategies to respond effectively to those conditions. Basic among these is the status of minority group itself. As you may recall, minority group status is not necessarily determined by size of group, but by subordinate status ascribed to members of the group by majority or dominant groups in society. Harrison et al. remind us that a crucial variable "in majority-minority relations is the differential power of one group relative to another" (Yetman in Harrison et al. 1990:348).

In addition to the variable of differential power, ethnocentrism and competition for resources to meet human needs combine to form systems of ethnic stratification (Harrison et al. 1990:348). **Ethnocentrism** is defined by Logan (1990:18) as an individual's view that "their own culture [is] the most important way of life in the world and therefore [is] the context for measuring all other significant experiences and acts." The concept of ethnocentrism was discussed earlier in our more general discussions about traditional and alternate paradigms.

Another important concept is ethnic stratification. **Ethnic stratification** is "a system or arrangement where some relatively fixed group membership (e.g., race, religion, or nationality) is used as one of the standards of judgment for assigning social position with its attendant differential rewards" (Noel in Harrison et al. 1990:348). In other words, ethnic stratification is a system of differential treatment based on minority or majority group status.

Caste or castelike status is a specific form of ethnic stratification. You might recall that we explored this notion in the context of individual development in Chapter 5. As suggested by our discussions of social class in Chapter 5, caste and class are often compared and contrasted in discussion of social status. Caste and class are similar in that they both represent social positions held by persons or groups in a society. They differ, however, in that social class implies a position or status from which one can move as various conditions change. For example, increasing a family's educational level, income, or moving from one neighborhood to another may result in movement from a lower social class to a middle-class status. Caste status, however, is not nearly as amenable to such movement. You might recall again from our discussion in Chapter 5 that castelike status, especially in U.S. society, is much more ascribed. An **ascribed status** is permanent and based on characteristics or conditions not subject to the control of the individual, such as skin color, or, as Ogbu notes, historic conditions of slavery, conquest, or colonization.

For Ogbu, castelike groups in the United States may differ in many ways, but all have in common the element of being treated as exploitable resources. Examples of this treatment for specific groups include:

a) *the enslavement of Africans and, after emancipation, their segregation and perceived inferior status based on race;*

b) *military conflicts over land and territory between American Indians and European Americans, and the forced removal and transfer of Indians to reservations;*

c) *Asian Americans whose recent immigrants from Indochina sometimes suffer from the same subordination and exploitation endured by earlier immigrants from China, Philippines, and Japan (the latter were incarcerated during World War II); and*

d) *Hispanics who were incorporated through conquest and displacement.* (in Harrison et al. 1990:348)

Again, we see that while specific experiences vary considerably among different groups in this society, many conditions that result from these experiences are often shared by the members of different groups. Underlying these conditions is a theme of racism and oppression.

Effective adaptive strategies for families of color include recognition of the realities of racism and oppression for members in a society in which the traditional/dominant paradigm prevails in the existing social hierarchy (Harrison et al. 1990: 347–348; Boyd-Franklin in Walsh 1993). Harrison et al. stress, for example, that "historically, ethnic minority children were not included in samples of subjects studied for establishing normative trends or investigating theoretical questions. Most often data on ethnic minority children came from comparative studies with a controversial deficit explanation" (1990:348). Such findings offer dramatic examples of the invisibility or "abnormality (pathology)" accorded diverse persons (non-European descended) in much traditional paradigm research we explored in Chapter 2. Boyd-Franklin stresses that dealing with racism and oppression is central to family life for African Americans. For African American parents "normal family development" is a complex process that involves educating their children to recognize and deal with racism, discrimination, and negative messages from society about African Americans. African American parents must simultaneously help their children not to internalize the negative messages from society, but to be proud of who they are and believe that they can achieve in spite of racism and discrimination (in Walsh 1993:363).

The challenges faced by ethnic minority families result from long and shared histories of oppression and discrimination. The impact of these conditions on social and economic well-being of ethnic minority families has very real consequences in poverty, high unemployment, substandard or no housing, and poor health. All of these are of intense concern to social workers, for they present major barriers to families and their members reaching their fullest human potential. These obstacles, however, do not prevent ethnic minority families from pursuing goals of "educational achievement, economic development in the community, political power, affordable housing, and maintaining cultural and religious traditions" (Harrison et al. 1990: 349). One significant source of strength and support for pursuing these goals is the extended family.

Extended and Augmented or "Fictive" Family Networks

The specific nature or makeup of extended families differs considerably among ethnic minority groups. This family type is, however, found as an adaptive strategy and a strength across all the ethnic minority groups discussed here. The concept of extended family refers to multiple dimensions of familiness. **Extended family** as we use the term refers to more than traditional definitions of extended family as the nuclear family plus grandparents, aunts, uncles, and other kin related by blood or marriage. Included as members are not only parents and their children, but other relatives related by blood or marriage as well as non-blood or non-marriage-related persons who are considered by other family members, and consider themselves, family. Extended family for many families of color is really an "extensive kinship network." This network helps family members survive "by providing support, encouragement, and 'reciprocity' in terms of sharing goods, money, and services" (Stack in Boyd-Franklin in Walsh 1993:368).

For many African American families this network "might include older relatives such as great-grandparents, grandmothers, grandfathers, aunts, uncles, cousins, older brothers and sisters, all of whom may participate in childrearing, and 'non-blood relatives' such as godparents, babysitters, neighbors, friends, church family members, ministers, ministers' wives, and so forth" (Boyd-Franklin 1993:368). African American extended familiness expand family into community relationships through fictive kinship. **Fictive kinship** is "the caregiving and mutual-aid relationship among non-related blacks that exists because of their common ancestry, history, and social plight" (Martin and Martin 1985:5). Andrew Billingsley (1968) referred to this extended family form as **augmented family.** Billingsley (1992) more recently referred to this arrangement as **"relationships of appropriation."**

For many Native American families, extended family consists of a "collective, cooperative social network that extends from the mother and father union to the extended family and ultimately to the community and tribe" (Harrison et al. 1990:351). In many traditional Native American families, parenting is shared by several adults. In these traditional extended families "uncles and aunts often had particular disciplinary responsibilities toward their nieces and nephews, freeing biological parents for a much looser, more pleasure-oriented association with offspring" (Attneave in McGoldrick, Pearce, and Giordano 1982:72–73).

"The traditional Asian/Pacific-American family is characterized by well-defined, unilaterally organized, and highly interdependent roles within a cohesive patriarchal vertical structure" in which "prescribed roles and relationships emphasize subordination and interdependence . . . and esteem for . . . the virtue of filial piety" (Harrison et al. 1990:351). **Filial piety** is an intense sense of respect for and obligation to one's parents and ancestors.

Latino family extendedness emphasizes "strong feelings of identification, loyalty, and solidarity with the parents and the extended family" and involves "frequent contact and reciprocity among members of the same family." It has some similarities with the African American family "in that it is bilaterally organized and includes non-relative members (e.g., *compadres*)" (Harrison et al. 1990:351–352).

All of these forms of extended family offer a variety of sources of strength and support in addition to that offered by one's most immediate or nuclear family. It is crucial to recognize that there is great variation within groups (diversity-in-diversity) in the importance placed on extended family. These variations might be related to the number of generations a family has lived in the United States or whether or not one has access to extended family members. Some Native Americans who have moved to urban areas from their reservation communities to find employment, for example, may have great difficulty gaining access to their extended family support networks. Many first-generation or recent Asian and Latino immigrants may have had to leave their extended family in their country of origin.

Kinship Care

Closely associated with the adaptive strategy of extended family networks described above is the concept of **kinship care.** Scannapieco and Jackson describe the history of the concept. They note that the concept of kinship care has emerged from the research of a number of African American scholars (Stack 1974; Billingsley 1992) who "documented the importance of extended kinship networks in the African American community. As we noted earlier, the term 'kin' often includes any relative by blood or marriage or any person with close nonfamily ties to another" (1996:191). Billingsley referred to "augmented family" (1968) and "relationships of appropriation" (1992:31) to describe "unions without blood ties or marital ties. People become part of a family unit or, indeed, form a family unit simply by deciding to live and act toward each other as family." The history of kinship care is connected to the strong history of extended kinship in African and African American history: "The primary family unit in West Africa at the time of slavery in the United States was the extended family, which incorporated the entire community. Children belonged to, and were the responsibility of, the collective community" (Scannapieco and Jackson 1996:191). In West Africa, according to Yusane, " 'kinship relations were the foundation of social organization' and the 'extended family system is based on interdependent functions' that also serve as protection from calamities. African children were valued and viewed as an investment in the future" (in Scannapieco and Jackson 1996:191).

Scannapieco and Jackson also note that "Africans saw children as part of their immortality, and there were no 'illegitimate' children. All children were the shared concern of the community, and children were expected to care for their parents when the parent got old (respect for elders in the family and community continues as an African tradition" (1996:191).

Definition of Kinship Care. African American families continue to face extreme challenges to their well-being and existence in the late 1990s. African American children placed in out-of-home care have increased dramatically for a variety of reasons:

drug and alcohol abuse, teenage parenting, crime, and violence (Scannapieco and Jackson 1996; Edelman 1987).

The African American community is responding in a resilient manner through the adaptive response of informal and formal "kinship care." Grandparents are often the extended family members who assume responsibility for kinship care (see discussion of grandparents as parents earlier in this chapter). *Kinship care* has been defined as "the full-time nurturing and protection of children who must be separated from their parent by relatives, members of their tribes or clans, godparents, step-parents, or other adults who have a kinship bond with a child" (Child Welfare League of America in Wilhelmus 1998:118). This adaptive response is consistent with the strong history of African American extended family and community responsibility to the well-being of children (Scannapieco and Jackson 1996:190–192). Kinship care is sometimes referred to in two ways:

1. *Private Kinship Care:* Custody remains with the family member. Relative caregivers are not eligible for child-care payments, although other assistance might be available. Private kinship arrangements take various forms:

- The [relative] is caretaker, but the parent retains legal custody and can make any decisions regarding the kids.

- The [relative] has temporary legal custody, which public housing and some school districts require of caregivers. Legal custodians make decisions concerning daily care of the child, but parents are still involved in major decisions.

- The [relative] adopts the child, and rights of the birth parent are terminated. Few grandparents choose this option because it can end a relationship with their own child.

2. *Foster Kinship Care:* Relatives become the foster parents, but the state retains custody. (Gebeke 1996)

Today there are more African American children in kinship care than in traditional foster care. Social workers must recognize and support this important form of resilience (see Chapter 3) in the African American family and community. Central to effective practice in this area is learning to work with the " 'kinship triad,' made up of the children, the biological parents, and the caregiver relatives. . . . The social worker must keep in mind that the caregiver relative does not consider himself or herself a foster parent in the traditional sense. The caregiver relative is responding to the needs of the family, not the needs of the child welfare system. His or her decision is preserving the African American family" (Scannapieco and Jackson 1996:193–194).

Social Role Flexibility/Fluidity of Roles

This concept applied to ethnic minority families means that "familial social roles can be regarded as flexible in definition, responsibility, and performance. Parenting of younger siblings by older siblings, sharing of the breadwinner role among adults, and alternative family arrangements" are examples of this role flexibility (Harrison et al.

How does this image reflect the discussion of "social role flexibility" and "fluidity of roles" in the narrative?

1990:352). Freeman (in Logan et al. 1990:57ff) refers to this flexibility as **fluidity of roles** and suggests that it has historically been a significant source of strength for African American families as they faced survival in a hostile environment that often required family members to shift from one family role to another.

Pinderhughes points out that the flexibility of roles, although a source of strength and survival for many African American families, has often been viewed as a deficit "because it was different from the White middle-class nuclear family model" of very specific role expectations for males and females (in McGoldrick, Pearce, and Giordano 1982:112–113). Hines and Boyd-Franklin suggest that role flexibility results in a greater sense of equality for African American couples. They suggest that the emphasis put on equality between men and women by the women's movement has long been a reality for many African American women. Having a working mate is much less threatening for many African American men than for many white men because of this history of role flexibility (in McGoldrick, Pearce, and Giordano 1982:89–90).

Biculturalism

We explored this concept briefly in Chapter 5 as it related to individual development. This important concept carries even more significance in the context of family. **Biculturalism** is "the ability to function in two worlds" (Pinderhughes in McGoldrick, Pearce, and Giordano 1982:114). However, Harrison et al. stress the complexity of this process for people of color because of the devaluing of their original cultures by the majority group in U.S. society. People of color and their families are put in the position of accommodating or changing behaviors or beliefs to make them consistent with those of the majority culture, and simultaneously engaging in a complex process of keeping and giving up parts of the culture of origin. The result is a person who learns to "function optimally in more than one cultural context and to switch repertoires of behaviors appropriately and adaptively as called for by the situation" (Laosa 1977 in Harrison et al. 1990:352). Freeman refers to the virtual requirement of biculturality on the part of African American families as the "dual perspective." She notes that African American parents have the double responsibilities of socializing their children "to adapt to and function well in a larger society that often views their racial and cultural background in a derogatory manner. . . .[and] to retain a positive racial identity and meet expectations of their racial group that may be in conflict with expectations of the society" (in Logan et al. 1990:61).

Socialization is central to the process of becoming bicultural. We have discussed the concept of socialization in a variety of contexts so far in this book. We discussed socialization as a core concept in social systems thinking. We discussed the importance of socialization in many models of individual development. **Socialization** "refers to the processes by which individuals become distinctive and actively functioning members of the society in which they live" (Harrison et al. 1990:354). Thus socialization is a central and ongoing part of our individual development. Family is the context in which a great deal of socialization takes place.

A family's ethnicity and the socialization of its members are intricately interconnected. Ethnicity is an important factor in such general aspects of socialization as "values, social customs, perceptions, behavioral roles, language usage, and rules of social interactions that group members share" (Harrison et al. 1990:354).

In addition to the importance of socialization in the process of becoming bicultural, Harrison et al. present the notion of "socialization for interdependence" as an important socialization goal of the ethnic minority groups they studied. Ethnic minority children are socialized in the context of their family to develop a cooperative view of life in which cooperation, obligation, sharing, and reciprocity are central elements of their beliefs and behaviors (1990:355). This focus on interdependence and cooperation is in sharp contrast to the traditional or dominant paradigm's primacy on competition and independence.

An additional strength of biculturalism, most notably found in studies of bilingualism, is cognitive flexibility. The greater cognitive flexibility of bilingual children is reflected in their enhanced abilities "to detect multiple meanings of words and alternative orientations of objects" and "to attend to language as an object of thought rather than just for the content or idea" (Harrison et al. 1990:356).

Given the benefits of biculturality and the virtual necessity of ethnic minority families socializing their children to be bicultural in order to survive, what of biculturality and white people? James Leigh suggests that it is necessary for all people in the United States to become bicultural, not only members of ethnic minority groups. A major step in this direction is an acceptance and expectation of bilingualism. Leigh suggests that we all need to recognize that Black English, Spanish, and Native American languages are not "foreign languages." They are multiple languages reflecting the multicultural realities of U.S. society. In addition to incorporating multiple languages, Leigh suggests that we must also incorporate diverse "histories" into our understanding of the complex society in which we live. We must tell the history of America from the perspectives of its native peoples as well as from the perspective of Columbus and subsequent newcomers (1989:17–19).

Biculturality is not an option for social workers, it is a necessity. To be able to enter into the culture of another person is an essential skill for social workers living in a multicultural pluralistic society. Biculturality is very similar at the cultural level to empathy at the interpersonal level. Empathy at the cultural and at the interpersonal level should not be considered separate skills but two components of the same essential skill necessary for competent practice on the part of any social worker.

Spirituality and Ancestral Worldviews

As we learned in Chapter 1, worldviews are extremely influential in the way we see ourselves, others, and the world around us. Our worldviews are also strong influences on our families. We discovered, in our earlier exploration of worldviews, that the dominant worldview or paradigm was characterized by an emphasis on individualism and separateness in which every person is separate from every other person and is solely responsible for her or his own well-being. This Eurocentric individualistic worldview is contrary to the ancestral worldviews of many ethnic minority groups. For many minority groups a worldview emphasizing the interrelatedness of the self or the individual with other systems in the person's environment such as families, households, communities, and the ethnic group as a whole is held (Harrison et al. 1990:353, English 1991:20–24, Martin and Martin 1985).

Ancestral worldviews are reflected throughout the institutions responsible for imparting the beliefs and values of the group. In addition to and in conjunction with the family, religious and spiritual institutions hold and pass along the philosophical standpoints or worldviews of the people. Many African Americans hold a worldview with roots in an African philosophical position that stresses collectivism rather than individualism. The worldviews of many Native Americans perceive all aspects of life as interrelated and of religious significance although there is no single dominant religion among the many Native American cultures. Asian/Pacific American families stress a belief system in which harmony is a core value. Latino religious beliefs reinforce a belief system in which familism is a central tenet (Harrison et al. 1990:354). Such worldviews as these suggest much more in common with the core concerns of social work; with the principles of social systems and ecological thinking and with the growing emphasis in social work on the roles of spirituality and religion in understanding the lives of the people with whom we work.

The church often plays an important and supportive role for families of color. Church provides a sense of community and interrelatedness for many families. Family and church are so interrelated for some African Americans, for example, that church members may refer to other members as their "church family." One's church family may provide such important supports as role models for young family members and assistance with child rearing. For families trying to survive in what is likely a hostile environment, "churches often provide an alternative network for friends, junior choir, after school and summer activities, babysitting, and male and female adult role models." These role models are likely to include "the minister, minister's wife, deacons, deaconesses, elders, and trustee boards" (Boyd-Franklin 1993:369). Social workers need to be aware that such sources of strength and support as the "church family" may be available to assist African American families. Boyd-Franklin (1993:369–370) suggests that social workers need to become "acquainted with the ministers in African-American communities as these individuals have a great deal of power and influence" and can often provide a wide range of support for families.

Even for African American families that do not belong to a formal church, spirituality may play a significant role. This spirituality can be quite distinct from a "religious orientation." Consistent with an Afrocentric worldview that sees reality as both spiritual and material at the same time, spirituality is a part of every person (Myers 1985:34–35). This spirituality "is often a strength and a survival mechanism for African-American families that can be tapped, particularly in times of death and dying, illness, loss, and bereavement" (Boyd-Franklin 1993:370).

Familiness and Multiracial Realities

As we discovered in Chapter 5, as U.S. society becomes more diverse the boundaries between and among diversities are becoming more and more blurred. One example of this is the growing population of biracial and multiracial people. The issue of multiracial identity and heritage has special implications for families, both in the area of adoption/foster care and in the area of special challenges for parenting multiracial children (see Chapter 5 for a discussion of parenting challenges for multiracial children).

Multiracial Adoption and Foster Care

Same Race Adoption. Fong et al. note that the existence of substantial numbers of racially mixed people "suggests that social workers may have to recast the dialogue about what have been regarded as 'transracial' adoptions" (1996:22). *Transracial adoptions* are also referred to as "interracial," "interethnic," or "transethnic" adoptions (Hollingsworth 1998:104). They point out that the position taken by social work since the 1970s has been that children should be placed for adoption with parents of like ancestry. This policy was advocated initially and most strongly by the National Association of Black Social Workers [NABSW]. The formal position, put forth in 1974 by NABSW was: "Only a black family can transmit the emotional and sensitive subtleties of perception and reaction essential for a black child's survival in a racist society" (Smith in Fong et al. 1996:22). "Similar arguments can be made for placement of American Indian, Mexican American, and Asian American children" (Fong et al. 1996:22). The Indian Child Welfare Act of 1978 recognized the importance of maintaining cultural and community relationships as well as family relationship decisions about the welfare of Native American children. It gave "tribal courts exclusive jurisdiction over American Indian child custody proceedings" (Hollingsworth 1998:105).

Policy and practice in the area of multiethnic and multiracial adoption and foster care have remained unsettled. Since passage of the Multiethnic Placement Act of 1994, social workers and others concerned with child welfare have continued to struggle with fundamental issues about how to achieve what is best for children of color who may need out-of-home placement either temporarily (foster care) or permanently (adoption). Hollingsworth found five themes that have emerged from the ongoing struggle among organizations concerned with child welfare and transracial adoption:

1. That ethnic heritage is important;

2. That children be raised preferably by their biological parents or, when not possible, by other biological relatives;

3. That economic need alone is not an acceptable reason for children to be deprived of their biological parents;

4. That efforts should be made to ensure that adoptive parents of the same race as the child are available and systemic barriers should not interfere; and

5. That placement with parents of a different race is acceptable and even preferable when the alternative means a child is deprived of a permanent home and family. (Hollingsworth 1998:113)

Clearly the issue of multiethnic adoption is complex and must be considered from multiple perspectives. Hollingsworth argues that "seeking to solve the problems associated with the overrepresentation of children of color in the child welfare system by protecting transracial adoption is simplistic and fails to protect those who are most vulnerable in this society—the children dependent on that society." She suggests that "a more responsible approach is to understand and eliminate the circumstances that constitute the cause of the situation" (Hollingsworth 1998:114). One of the most significant circumstances that cause out-of-home placements is poverty.

Family Poverty, Diversity, and Out-of-Home Placement.   As indicated earlier in this chapter (and in other chapters), poverty is closely related to many other conditions that impede individual and family well-being. In addition, families of color (especially African American, Hispanic, and Native American families) are much more likely to experience poverty than white families. Hollingsworth argues that "living in poverty" is one of the reasons large numbers of children of color are in out-of-home placements. She notes that "over 46 percent of all African American children lived in poverty in 1993, as did 41 percent of all Latino children; only 14 percent of white children lived in poverty" (Children's Defense Fund in Hollingsworth 1998). In addition, "56 percent of children living with their mothers only were poor, compared to 12 percent of those living with married parents, and children of color were more likely than white children to live in mother-only households" (Hollingsworth 1998:111).

Poverty is closely associated with "circumstances that result in out-of-home placements." For example, the National Incidence Study of Child Abuse and Neglect found that

> *Children from families with annual incomes below $15,000 were 22 times more likely to experience maltreatment than children from families whose*

incomes exceeded $30,000. They were 18 times more likely to be sexually abused, almost 56 times more likely to be educationally neglected, and over 22 times more likely to be seriously injured. Children of single parents had an 87 percent greater risk of being harmed by physical neglect and an 80 percent greater risk of suffering serious injury or harm from abuse and neglect. (Hollingsworth 1998:113–14)

Multiracial Adoption and Foster Care.   Fong et al. (1996:22) suggest that for the many racially mixed children and people today, this policy, which assumed that everyone was a member of only one race, may be insufficient. They describe the Multiethnic Placement Act of 1994 as one example from the policy arena of dealing with this complex issue.

The Multiethnic Placement Act of 1994 (P.L. 103-382) challenges the traditional practice of using race and ethnicity as the deciding factor in adoption. The act bans discrimination in placement decisions based solely on race, color, or national origin. . . . It allows agencies to consider the cultural, ethnic, or racial background of children and the capacity of the prospective foster or adoptive parents to meet the needs of the children based upon their background; and stipulates that agencies engage in active recruitment of potential foster or adoptive parents who reflect the racial and ethnic diversity of the children needing placement.   (Smith in Fong et al. 1996:23)

The issue of the best family arrangement for mixed race children is complex and emotional for many reasons (see Chapter 5, Competing Individual and Communal values), Fong et al. do not take a side in the debate about adoption of children who are clearly of one race by parents of that race. However, they argue "that a child who is mixed Mexican and Chinese probably belongs as much with a Chinese family as with a Mexican family" (1996:23). They note, though, that others might legitimately argue "that children of African American heritage, for example, should be reared by black families because only those families can sufficiently nurture children's positive black identities" (Fong et al. 1996:23). Fong et al. add that this position is not universally accepted by African American scholars and human service professionals. They point to the position of African American psychologist, Prentice Baptiste:

Biologically, these [biracial] children are neither Black nor White, but equally a part of both races. But the Jim Crow traditions and laws will attempt to define all of them as Black regardless of their phenotypic appearance. Parents of interracial children must counter this attempt by teaching them that they are and culturally can be members of both races. Positive models of both races must be very apparent to these children during early years of development.   (in Fong et al. 1996:23)

Fong et al. stress that "this is an issue that policymakers and practitioners in adoptions and foster care will continue to ponder and debate" (1996:23).

FOCUS: WOMEN

Feminist Perspectives on Families and Familiness

Rather than offering a single perspective or model for thinking about and under-standing the interrelatedness of women and familiness, Ferree (1990) offers a syn-thesis of feminist issues and perspectives related to the family that she refers to as a **gender model.** Hers is perhaps an appropriate approach to take when exploring women and familiness. The family arena has traditionally created and enforced very different and often confining, oppressive, and exploitative roles and expectations for women members at the same time that women are central figures in virtually all tra-ditional (and most alternate) notions of family.

Demo and Allen remind us that "Feminists have exposed the sexist and hetero-sexist underpinnings of any definition of family that takes as given that there is one type of family that can stand in for all other types and that the identities and behaviors of family members can be described by using the concept of 'gender role'" (1996:427). They assert that

> *Reducing gender to a role ignores the structural features of gender and its in-terconnectedness to other dominant ways in which groups are differentially provided opportunities and oppressed.... A role ... reduces gender to the more narrow and depoliticized realm of interpersonal relationships.... So-ciologists do not describe class or race inequality as "class role" or "race role," recognizing that such descriptions hide the power relations of social stratifi-cation beyond individual experience or interpersonal interaction* (Demo and Allen 1996:427).

> *Ferree states that "a feminist perspective redefines families as arenas of gen-der and generational struggles, crucibles of caring and conflict, where claims for an identity are rooted, and separateness and solidarity are continually created and contested"* (Demo and Allen 1996:427; Ferree in Demo and Allen 1996:428).

Consistent with our attempts to explore alternatives to traditional approaches to thinking about familiness and its implications for understanding HBSE, the alternatives we explore here reflect efforts to recognize the often complex and oppressive forces emerging from traditional family arrangements. This part of our journey represents an-other point at which we can rethink or revision familiness in ways that empower all members of families, in this case specifically women members, to reach their full human potential. This, of course, has important implications for social workers' concerns about and responsibilities for assisting all humans in reaching their fullest human potential.

Ferree's synthesis of feminist thinking about the family sphere reflects several dimensions of alternate paradigm thinking in addition to the feminist dimension. It critically examines a number of the dimensions of traditional paradigm thinking. Her synthesis addresses issues of separateness versus interrelatedness; diversity; oppression; privilege; and masculinity/patriarchy.

Ferree describes a number of common themes of feminist premises in thinking about women and familiness. She notes that "male dominance within families is part of a wider system of male power." This patriarchal family arrangement is damaging to women and "is neither natural nor inevitable" (1990:866). Feminist analyses of family question the notion of family as separate from other social institutions such as political and economic institutions. They question notions of family as a "separate sphere" that is a safe and private haven unconnected to the public or outside world. On the other hand, feminist analyses remind us that violence and inequality characteristic of the public world also permeate in significant ways the family sphere. Feminist perspectives suggest that there are very different and often conflicting interests inside families that are associated with gender. Feminist critiques of traditional perspectives on the family suggest "a new approach that (a) defines families as fully integrated into wider systems of economic and political power and (b) recognizes the diverging and sometimes conflicting interests of each member" (1990:867). With this perspective in mind we will explore a number of issues and concepts important for understanding familiness and that have significant consequences for women in the context of family. These issues and concepts will include family violence, gender or sex roles, family work, and dual wage earner families.

Women, Families, and Violence

Feminist analyses of family have been particularly important in documenting and analyzing the widespread violence that occurs in the family context. Many of these analyses have described the connections between violence against women and the inequalities that characterize traditional families. Miller (1986) notes that violence against women in families has implications for everyone, not just for women.

Miller offers disturbing information on the extent and types of violence against women. She notes, for example, that based on current information available, estimates are "that rape occurs to one out of four women in the United States, that one third of female children and adolescents under the age of eighteen experience significant sexual abuse, and that violence occurs in one third to one half of U.S. families" (Miller 1986:xxi–xxii). Even women who have not directly experienced such forms of violence must live each day "with the pervasive threat of violence" (Miller 1986:xxiii).

Miller suggests that study of this context of inequality and violence or the threat of violence has resulted in important information about strengths of women who must survive in this context. She stresses that the increasing attention to and knowledge about violence in families has come about in large part as a result of the strength of survivors of violence against women and of the efforts of women directly involved in action to reduce family violence. The incredible strengths of women who live with violence or the threat of violence are perhaps most dramatically reflected in their continuing efforts "to create growth-fostering interactions within the family." Miller concludes that "women, as a group, struggle to create life-giving and life-enhancing relationships within a context of violence and life-destroying forces" (Miller 1986: xxiii). This complex and often contradictory family context in which goals of safety, peace, and security are sought in an environment often characterized by inequality and violence must be recognized in our attempts to more fully understand family. (See Chapter 5 for an additional discussion of violence.)

Gender or Sex Role?

Traditional notions of sex roles in families emerge out of and along with traditional notions of family and of the "proper" roles of family members, especially the roles of males and females. The traditional notion of family was based largely on the observations by social scientists of "white, middle-class suburban families of the 1950s." As we discovered earlier, what emerged was the nuclear family structure portrayed as the ideal or the norm. Within this structure men were to play the instrumental/breadwinner/leader role and women were to play the socioemotional/homemaker/supportive role (Walsh 1993:19).

Subsequently, we have begun to realize that this model of family caused significant problems for families and their individual members. Wives and mothers were overburdened with responsibilities for the well-being of husbands and fathers, as well as children, at the same time that society undervalued (and in monetary terms attached no value to) their contributions. Fathers and husbands, on the other hand, were seen as head of the household but were in fact on the margins of the family as a result of the demands of their breadwinner role. This placed even more responsibility for the family on wives and mothers. What appeared functional from the perspective of the masculine-focused dominant perspective "proved quite dysfunctional for women in families. . . . The disproportionate responsibility for maintaining the household and the well-being of husband, children, and elders, while sacrificing their own needs and identities, proved detrimental" to women's physical and mental health (Walsh 1993:20).

The traditional perspective on sex roles as equal and complementary made invisible the very real power differentials inherent in the perspective. The failure to recognize power differentials built into traditional notions of sex roles—men as strong and women as weak, for example—supported the continuing oppression of women within the structure of family. The analysis of power inequalities within traditional definitions of family has helped to recognize and bring into the open the abuses and inequalities of power and conflict that result in wife battering, marital rape, and incest (Walsh 1993:380). Not only do narrow, inflexible, and inequitable sex role definitions result in threats to the health of many women, but we know from the all-too-familiar cases of sexual and physical assault within the context of families that the result for many women can be fatal.

We have noted at a number of points in our journey that issues related to power and inequality are essential to understanding more comprehensively the complexities of HBSE. A gender model is helpful in this regard because it focuses on issues of domination, categorization, and stratification—all fundamental and necessary concepts for understanding power.

Ferree summarizes the problems with use of the traditional concept of "sex roles" for explaining family members' statuses, behaviors, and traits:

> *The role approach . . . obscures the dimension of power and the ongoing processes of conflict associated with change. Feminist explorations of family relationships are therefore increasingly cast in a fundamentally different theoretical context, that of gender.* (1990:868)

Ferree notes the fundamental difference between sex role explanations and gender explanations of human behaviors: "While the sex role model *assumes* a certain packaging of structures, behaviors and attitudes, the gender model analyzes the *construction* of such packages" (1990:868).

Family Work

The issue of work is another central element in a gender model for understanding familiness. Gender is intricately interconnected with determining the division of labor or work (both paid and unpaid) in families and households. A gender model calls upon us to recognize the interconnections of work and family. It suggests that both men and women must be considered simultaneously workers and family members. A gender model also requires that a historical perspective be introduced into any efforts to understand the place and nature of work and gender in the family.

The term *family work* is a helpful concept for thinking about work in the context of family. **Family work** refers to "the household chores and childcare tasks that must be performed by families to maintain the household and its members" (Piotrkowski and Hughes 1993:191). Traditional views of family see men as the only paid workers in the family and therefore men are seen as the "providers" for the other dependent family members—women and children. Women, on the other hand, are responsible for family work. A gender model suggests that such a version is not only inaccurate today but has historically not been an accurate portrayal (Ferree 1990:871).

How might the experiences of the woman in this photo reflect the concept of "second shift" described in the narrative? Might this woman need a "wife" in the sense described by Ferree in the discussion of "dual-wage-earner" families?

The gender perspective points out historical inaccuracies as a source of the "male provider myth." "It recognizes that women have always contributed significantly to the household economy, including through paid employment in and out of the home." Despite the male provider myth, women's "economic contributions have been substantial. . . . The social association of masculinity with the role of sole provider is new, not 'traditional.' " The construct of the "self-made man" emerged only in the nineteenth century. Ferree suggests that the self-made man was not self-made at all but was the result of "a gendered process in which mothers and wives have clearly prescribed, supporting roles" (1990:871–873). The picture of a household in which the ideal arrangement is a single (male) wage-earner with a support system (women and children) at home freeing him of responsibilities other than wage earning has important implications for women in current economic conditions requiring two wage earners rather than one in order to make ends meet.

Dual-Wage-Earner Families

For many women, entering the work force has resulted in what some writers have referred to as a "second shift." As more and more women have entered the full-time work force to share breadwinning responsibilites, there has not been a corresponding sharing of family work responsibilities by their husbands. Several studies have found that working women in two-wage-earner households continue to carry up to 80 percent of household and child-care responsibilities (Walsh 1993:20). The amount of family work done by husbands varies by ethnic group. Some data suggest that African American men do more of the family work than white men. This is an example of the greater role flexibility in African American families than in white families (Piotrkowski and Hughes 1993:192).

Ferree suggests that "women who enter conventionally male defined careers . . . need a wife . . . because the expectations built into the structure of the job and the workplace take such a full-time support system for granted." A two-"husband" family, in which both wage earners focus on career and have little time or energy left over to invest in family life, needs in effect to hire a wife. There are at least two possible responses to this need. One has implications for race and class because the "wife" hired is "typically a woman of color and/or a new immigrant" (1990:873). As indicated above, a second, and more likely response is for the wife who becomes a wage earner to simply add this role to her other responsibilities for the well-being of the family—often to the point of exhaustion. Some single mothers suggest that losing a husband actually *decreases* time pressures in housework (1990:874–875).

Yet another and seldom discussed response is the role of children in performing unpaid labor when both mothers and fathers work for pay outside the household. Several scholars suggest that children may do more housework than their fathers when their mothers work outside the home. The division of labor among children in the household is also gendered in that "daughters are still more likely to be given housework than sons, and among sons and daughters who do housework, daughters do more hours of work" (Ferree 1990:874–875).

The gender perspective also suggests that income coming into a household from wage earners is subject to gendering processes. It is not safe to assume that money coming to the household all goes into a common pot that is equitably divided based on family and individual needs. For example, women's earnings may be earmarked specifically for child care, while men's "bonuses" may be considered the man's alone. Still other evidence, especially evidence generated from studies of battered wives who have left their husbands, suggests that even in households generating substantial earnings, some members may in fact be living below poverty level owing to lack of access to the income generated by a husband unwilling to share that income fairly with his wife and children. Such gender inequities inside households are rarely accounted for in official data-gathering efforts:

> *Social policy continues to be driven by the implausible assumptions that all family members are equally well-off, that above-poverty-line household incomes imply no below-poverty-line individuals within them, and that increasing total family income has the same effect if it derives from a rise in male or female income.* (Ferree 1990:878)

The gender perspective suggests that both micro and macro transformation is needed in the "work-family" system. For us as social workers, this perspective helps us appreciate the implications for women and families in the areas of HBSE, practice, research, and policy. Such transformations need to include:

> *changes in transportation systems, home design, normal work schedules, recruitment and promotion structures, and national job creation policies [as well as more] traditional demands for affordable child care, more flexible work opportunities, and enforcement of equal opportunity policies for women. Because men's jobs and career paths are gendered and built upon a structure of family support that is also gendered, changes for women necessarily also imply changes for men, and men's reactions to change should be understood in these terms.* (Ferree 1990:874)

Summary

The gender perspective to increasing our understanding of alternate approaches to thinking about family is helpful in two ways that are especially important for us as social workers. It suggests that family systems are intricately interconnected with the other environmental systems that form the context in which individuals live and develop. It also suggests that family as a social construction is neither all good nor all bad; it is a complex arena with the potential for both supporting and putting up significant barriers to the well-being of its members.

As Ferree suggests, "both family and household are ever more firmly situated in their specific historical context, in which they take on diverse forms and significance. Race and class are understood as significant structural features underlying the diversity of family forms." She also urges that "rather than insisting on a dichotomous view of families as either solidary or oppressive, the gender model suggests that family relationships may be altruistic, or self-seeking, or carry an inseparable mix of motivations; that they may be simultaneously supportive and oppressive for women in relation to diverse others; that there is not one dimension of family power, but many" (1990:879).

FOCUS: SEXUAL ORIENTATION

Familiness from a Lesbian/Gay Perspective

Traditional approaches to family not only assume a nuclear, two-parent, white, child-centered family form, they also assume a heterosexual pairing/partnership as the foundation upon which family is built. Slater and Mencher (1991) and other scholars point out that such assumptions neglect a significant portion of the population and deny legitimacy to the family forms and functions that exist among gay and lesbian families. Like a number of other diverse family types, gay and lesbian families have for the most part been treated as if they were either deviant and dysfunctional or as if they did not exist at all. Our notion of familiness, along with our search for inclusiveness consistent with our notions of alternate paradigm, recognizes the need to understand family issues related to gay and lesbian families.

Slater and Mencher describe the neglect in traditional approaches to family of lesbian and gay male families in the areas of family life cycle models, predictable stresses of family life, and societally sanctioned rituals recognizing a family's successful negotiation of stressors and tasks presented at various stages of its life cycle. They note also the reinforcement of heterosexual family life cycle transitions and common tasks through cultural media such as "television, movies, magazines, greeting cards, literature, theater, and children's games." In all of these validations of heterosexual familiness, lesbian and gay families are excluded. Slater and Mencher remind us, for example, that "lesbians are legally barred from marriage, so that engagements, weddings and their anniversaries, joint last names, and joint legal status are withheld." They point out also that when family therapists have looked at differences between lesbians and heterosexuals, they have focused on "dysfunction and conflict" (1991:373–375).

To begin to remedy these problems, Laird suggests that gay and lesbian families must be included in efforts to understand familiness. She suggests further that lesbian and gay families can "teach us important things about other families, about gender relationships, about parenting, about adaptation to tensions in this society, and especially about strengths and resilience" (1993:284). Gay and lesbian families are both similar and different in many ways from heterosexual families.

To more completely understand gay and lesbian families, as in the case of heterosexual families, they must be viewed *intergenerationally:* "Each partner, child, and other family member is influenced by and must come to terms with the specific history and culture of his or her own family of origin and its sociocultural context" (Laird 1993:285). Also like heterosexual families, gay and lesbian families are not a monolithic group. They display a wide range of diversities. As Laird points out, gay men and lesbians vary in terms of race, class, sex, age, religion, political affiliation, and all the other differences displayed among any group of individuals. As a result, gay and lesbian families reflect this wide array of individual differences as well (Laird 1993:286). However, the general movement for gay liberation has been criticized by many of its diverse members for its lack of diversity and inclusiveness. Carrier, for example, suggests that gay liberation in the United States has been primarily a white, middle-class movement (in Laird 1993:291). Given this lack of diversity, very little is known about the family experiences of nonwhite, nonmiddle-class gay men and lesbians.

Slater and Mencher (1991) note several specific problems for lesbian (and less directly for gay) families when we are limited to traditional heterosexually based models of family. Traditional models provide a life cycle process and context that is multigenerational and begins with the launching of a young adult who then couples, raises her or his children, and launches them as young adults. This model is not applicable to the young lesbian woman. Her experiences in her family of origin with its heterosexual focus provide no image from which she can launch her own family. Traditional models also take for granted a system of social supports to assist families as they move through their life cycles. For lesbians there are no socially accepted rituals to support and recognize these passages. Because there are few studies of gay familiness or parenthood we are left to assume that similar dynamics operate for gay men as well.

Traditional models of family are also child-centered (see earlier discussion of traditional models). Slater and Mencher note that while some lesbians have and wish to have children, lesbian life is not as child-centered as traditional models of family life. They remind us that childless heterosexual couples also experience this lack of a place in traditional models. Childless couples and lesbian and gay couples do nevertheless "establish and maintain a family unit which passes through discrete stages with their attendant stresses, transitions, and accomplishments" (1991:376).

Lesbian families certainly share many of the common stresses and patterns of heterosexual families. This may be in large part because the heterosexual family is the only role model for familiness available to most lesbians. There are, however, significant differences in the family-related issues, experiences, and realities faced by lesbians. Slater and Mencher stress that many of the issues facing lesbian families are not stage-based, as is the case with traditional models, but are contextual and consist of recurrent themes regardless of stage. Prominent among these contextual issues is the reality of creating and sustaining family in a continually hostile environment that refuses any legitimacy for your form of family. Lesbian families must continually face issues related to their very viability as a family. Larger society portrays lesbian families as "unconnected individuals" rather than related family members. Lesbian couples are most often treated as "roommates" or "friends living together" (1991:376). Again, we are left to assume that similar issues arise concerning gay men and their families.

Verification and validation of lesbian (or gay) familiness are dependent almost totally on the couple themselves, for they receive no validation from the larger society as is the case for heterosexual families. In fact to seek public recognition for lesbian (or gay) familiness through social exposure is often to risk the members' jobs, families of origin, housing, safety, or child custody (Slater and Mencher 1990:376–377).

Traditional Family Development Theories: Implications for Gay and Lesbian Families

In Chapter 3 we explored a number of traditional theories for understanding and explaining human behavior and social environment. These theories included structural functional, psychoanalytic, social learning, social exchange, and human development theories. Demo and Allen (1996)* examined these same theories specifically for their

*Much of the following critical discussion of applications of traditional theories and concepts concerning family development to gay and lesbian persons and families relies heavily on the work of David Demo and Katherine Allen, in their article, "Diversity within lesbian and gay families: Challenges and implications for family theory and research." *Journal of Social and Personal Relationships* 13(3): 415–434. The author is most appreciative of their permission to quote their work extensively.

implications for gay and lesbian families. Their objective was not to dismiss any other theories or to claim one grand theory. Their purpose was

  1. To demonstrate that heterosexuality is a foundation for many theories of human and family development

  2. To argue that a multiplicity of theories is necessary to understand ever-increasing family diversity (Demo and Allen 1996:423).

Demo and Allen "argue that traditional family theories, rooted in positivist assumptions of objectivity and neutrality, are insufficient in and of themselves and that *in addition* to mainstream approaches we need theories that posit the social construction of reality and recognize the inevitability of differences and the instability of concepts" (1996:423).

Structural Functional Theory

According to structural functional theory

> *the nuclear family is defined by the "socially sanctioned cohabitation of a man and woman who have preferential or exclusive enjoyment of economic and sexual rights over one another and are committed to raise the children brought to life by the woman"* [Pits in Demo and Allen 1996:423]. . . . *In this family, for both biological and cultural reasons, the husband is assigned "instrumental" activities and responsibilities, while his wife is assigned "expressive" activities. . . . Functionalists view conformity to this role structure as essential for family stability, shared values and norms and social order.* (Demo and Allen 1996:423)

Implications for lesbian and gay families are reflected in the absence of gender-based division of labor. For functionalists such "non-gender-based divisions of labor evoke new, ambiguous and contradictory role expectations, challenge existing values, undermine family stability and threaten social equilibrium" (Demo and Allen 1996:424). This theory also suggests single-parent families and same-sex only parents are problematic.

Psychoanalytic and Social Learning Theories

Both psychoanalytic and social learning theories emphasize the importance of same-sex parent identification. Psychoanalytic theory sees this identification as necessary to resolve the Oedipus complex, which allows them to develop proper gender role identification and "acquire other socially acceptable traits." Social learning suggests the importance of same-sex parent as an important source of modeling and vicarious learning through imitation and observation for the child to learn appropriate behaviors. "Theories emphasizing the influence of same-sex or other-sex parents suggest . . . adjustment problems for children reared by gay or lesbian parents" (Demo and Allen 1996:424–425). However, these theories leave a variety of important assumptions unexamined:

  1. "The very real possibility that most children learn by observing two parents" whether they live with both or whether both parents are of the same sex or not. And they learn by observing many other family members, friends, and other adults and children.

2. "These theories are often *interpreted* to suggest that certain behaviors—such as heterosexuality, masculinity among males and femininity among females—are indicators of 'normal' development and adjustment." However, Freud suggested such behaviors and traits are overlapping continua and traits "that coexist in every individual" (Demo and Allen 1996:424–425).

Social Exchange Theory

"This theory directs attention to the bargaining process and balancing of power in families and, unlike many conventional family theories, it recognizes that the quality of marital interaction is more important than marriage per se in predicting adult well-being." Implications are that "This model could benefit substantially by being extended to— and tested on—lesbian and gay partnerships." A limitation is that social exchange theory "assumes rational actors making rational choices and ignores the timing and sequencing of events within personal and family careers" (Demo and Allen 1996:425).

Developmental Approach

Basically the developmental approach is structural-functionalist, but it adds to thinking about families the "notions of timing, sequencing and duration of events and life stages." The concepts of timing, sequencing, and duration of events and stages are valuable for studying gay and lesbian families. Some limitations of developmental theory are that it tends to be static and "reifies and glorifies gender roles and emphasizes stages rather than family processes, dialectics and change" (Demo and Allen 1996:425).

A Need for Multiple Approaches

Traditional family theories tend to stress clarity of stages and linear progression through them, clarity of roles, and clarity of family boundaries. They tend to see ambiguity in these areas as inherently problematic. They have neglected, however, to consider that the gay and lesbian families who struggle with ambiguities in these areas may result in creating "new ways of relating that are positive for postmodern family functioning" (Demo and Allen 1996:426). Demo and Allen suggest the need for multiple perspectives "to incorporate new insights and thus revise knowledge about families by including what was formerly invisible or excluded. In our view, a promising direction is to use the insights and applications of both positivist and post-positivist approaches" (1996:428).

Defining Gay and Lesbian Families

While gay and lesbian families have much in common with heterosexual families, they are also difficult to define because of their differences from traditional notions of family. Laird (1993:294) suggests that gay and lesbian families might be best referred to as **families of choice** *because they combine blood relatedness with love and choice*. Gay and lesbian families are "formed from lovers, friends, biological and adopted children, blood relatives, stepchildren, and even ex-lovers, families that do not necessarily share a common household. In fact, in some lesbian communities, the boundaries between family, kinship, and community become quite diffuse." A basic definition of **lesbian or gay family** is the "intimate, enduring interaction of two or more people who share a same-sex orientation

How might the partners in this couple and their families reflect diversity and "diversity within diversity" in some of the ways discussed in the text section "Defining Gay and Lesbian Families?"

(e.g., a couple) or by the enduring involvement of at least one lesbian or gay adult in rearing a child. . . . Many lesbian and gay adults simultaneously live in two worlds—their heterosexual family of origin and the lesbian or gay family they maintain as adults—creating an extended family environment that may be termed a 'mixed gay/straight' or 'dual-orientation family' " (Demo and Allen 1996:416). Given all these variations we must recognize that there is no "uniform or normative definition for 'gay family' any more than there is for 'American' family" (Laird 1993: 294). However, this lack of a single or clear definition of gay and lesbian family may suggest some significant strengths from which heterosexual family studies and social workers working with families might benefit:

> *With their relatively fluid boundaries and varied memberships, their patterns of nonhierarchical decision making, their innovative divisions of labor, and the relative weight given to friendship as well as blood relatedness, such families offer further challenge to dominant notions of family structure and function and present an opportunity for mental health professionals to assess the limitations in current definitions of family and kinship.* (Laird 1993:296)

Lesbian and Gay Families: Diversity within Diversity

Lesbian and gay family diversity is of interest to scholars because:

1. *These families have been stereotyped as a monolithic group, so their heterogeneity reveals diversity within diversity.*

2. *Their diversity helps to illustrate and elaborate our understanding of how diverse all families are.*

3. *Lesbian and gay families pose serious challenges and exciting opportunities for testing, revising and constructing family theories.* (Demo and Allen 1996:415–416)

There is little research on this configuration of "multiple minorities." Most research on gay or lesbian persons and families or children raised by lesbian or gay parents use study samples that are overwhelmingly either "white, well-educated, middle-class male[s]" or "white, middle- to upper-middle-class, formerly married lesbians." This tendency "obscures multiple layers of diversity within lesbian and gay families and restricts our ability to document the special problems as well as the special strengths of lesbian and gay families" (Demo and Allen 1996:420).

Differences among Lesbian and Gay Families. Demo and Allen (1996:416) outline a number of areas in which lesbian and gay families differ in order to illustrate that gay and lesbian families are clearly not a monolithic whole but are highly diverse. They list and describe differences in composition and structure, family processes, social stratification, interfamily diversity, and gender among gay and lesbian families. It is important to note that families with bisexual members, though very little research has been conducted on them, are likely to exhibit even higher degrees of variability in a number of these areas. It is also important to note the areas of diversity among gay and lesbian families that are also evident among heterosexual families. The degree of commonality between many gay and lesbian families and heterosexual families is significant. Demo and Allen (1996:416–417) list a variety of differences among gay and lesbian families:

- *"Composition and structure of lesbian and gay families differ according to* number, gender, and sexual orientation of adult(s) heading the household, length of couple relationship, household size, the presence and number of children, and sibling structure."

- *Family processes differ among families in nature of members'* interactions with one another in terms of the "nature and degree of involvement, support, nurturance, communication, conflict, tensions, and stresses."

- *Family differences in terms of social stratification and diversity* include "gender, sexual orientation, generation, age, race, and ethnicity."

- *Interfamily diversity* Regardless of number and degree of sexual orientation variation, it is important to recognize that "changes in sexual orientation over time and over stages in the life course add further complexity to the task of understanding how family relationships are influenced by sexual orientation and how diverse family structures evolve."

Family Roles

The issue of negotiation of roles within the lesbian family both represents a source of stress and demonstrates creativity and strength on the part of lesbian family members.

Heterosexual family members have been socialized since birth to the appropriate family roles expected of them. These roles almost exclusively emerge according to one's gender. Contrary to popular myths about lesbian and gay couples, most couples do not simply adopt traditional heterosexual versions of family roles. Lesbians' family roles tend to demonstrate greater role flexibility and divide tasks and responsibilities more according to individual preferences, abilities, and needs than is the case with prescribed gender-based traditional roles. This flexibility often requires repeated renegotiation as situations change and time passes, which is more complex than in traditional heterosexual families. However, this continuous renegotiation and evaluation may very well be outweighed by the increased liberation from rigid, confining traditional roles (Slater and Mencher 1991; Laird 1993).

Lesbian and Gay Couples and Relationships

Faced with recurring stressors in an often inhospitable social environment, lesbian families create innovative responses to meet their needs for familiness. These responses emerge both from the couple relationship and from the lesbian community. This loose community network not only offers a source of support and legitimation for lesbian families, it also in many ways functions as an extension of lesbians' families.

Lacking supports from the larger society, lesbian couples often adopt a particular sense of closeness not experienced by heterosexual couples. This intense connectedness is often described in heterosexual family therapy literature as "fusion" and usually carries a negative or pathological connotation. Even though this intense closeness is sometimes the source of some difficulties in maintaining separateness of individual identities for lesbian couples, it is more often found to be functional in its nurturance of a high degree of intimacy and interconnectedness when the larger environment provides little or no validation of individual couple identity (Slater and Mencher 1991:379; Laird 1993).

While lesbian couples have been stereotyped as forming relationships that are too close, gay men are often stereotyped as unable to form lasting couple relationships at all. As Laird points out, "the gay couple is tainted by social images that portray gay males as promiscuous, flamboyant, bar-hopping clones, with coupleness itself an anomaly" (1993:312). A number of researchers have attempted to move beyond these stereotypes to look more closely at the relationships and sexual behaviors of gay couples. The results have varied. Some research indicates that "openness" or extracouple relationships seem to enhance couple longevity. Some research indicates that closed couples were more "happy." Other research indicates that there are no differences "between open and closed couples together 3 years or longer, in intimacy, satisfaction, security, or commitment" (Laird 1993:312). We should note that what is important is the meaning of sexual relationships outside the couple for the couple themselves. "For some couples, an extra couple sexual encounter or affair may feel like the ultimate betrayal; for others it may be interpreted as an experience that has little to do with and does not contaminate the couple relationship" (Laird 1993:313).

Blumstein and Schwartz, in extensive research on the sexual behaviors of heterosexuals and homosexuals, found that regardless of the type of relationship, men tend to have more outside partners than women (in Laird 1993:313). This suggests that monogamy (relationships with no outside sexual partners) may "be more related to gender socialization than to sexual orientation." In gay relationships, it seems that "outside sex in the gay male couple is not related to gay men's overall happiness or commitment to the relationship." Laird reminds us that although gay men (like heterosexual men) are more likely to have sex outside of a couple relationship than are lesbians (or heterosexual women), "AIDS has and is shaping a trend toward more sexual exclusivity and more stability in gay male couple relationships" (1993:313).

Family and Community

As noted earlier, the lesbian community has created many innovative and positive responses to the general hostility and lack of support for lesbian familiness in the society at large. The lesbian community may often "offer the lesbian family its only source of positive public and social identity" (Slater and Mencher 1990:380). The lesbian and gay community allows members to discover and to communicate with each other and among families what is normal and typical for lesbian or gay families and individuals. The community allows members to begin to identify common experiences in meeting challenges and accomplishing family developmental tasks. Lesbian and gay communities are also a source of family rituals specific to the experiences and needs of lesbian and gay families. The community may, for example, offer a context for carrying out rituals borrowed from heterosexual culture, such as exchanging rings or anniversary cards. The lesbian community has also created its own unique validation rituals in recognition of the contextual issues faced by lesbian individuals and families. These include rituals to recognize "coming out" and lesbian commitment ceremonies.

Gay and lesbian communities are as diverse as heterosexual communities. Laird cautions that "we not assume, from experiences with one community, that we understand gay or lesbian 'culture' or 'norms' for all such communities." In addition, she stresses that we must also recognize that different members of the same community relate to the community differently and have very different perspectives on that community (1993:293).

Children of Lesbian and Gay Parents

Increasing research attention is being focused on the children of lesbian and gay parents. This new emphasis can be accounted for by several factors:

1. *The need on the part of gays and lesbians considering parenthood to understand the issues and challenges they may face;*

2. *The concerns of social scientists with how such families and their children cope with oppression;*

3. *The impact of this nontraditional family form on psychosocial development; and*

4. *The provision of more accurate information to a legal system that has operated largely on prejudice and mythology in custody situations and in addressing questions concerning the rights of gay and lesbian parents and their children.* (Laird 1993:313–314)

The findings of this research suggest that the children of gay and lesbian parents face special difficulties, such as social discrimination, ridicule, and even isolation. Adolescent children are especially vulnerable to peer pressure and harassment as they struggle with the development of their own identities. However, in spite of difficulties such as these "the peer and other social relationships of children of lesbian and gay parents do not differ significantly from those of any other children" (Laird 1993:313–315).

Perhaps the most often raised concern or myth about children of gay or lesbian parents is whether the children are more likely than the children of heterosexual parents to grow up gay or lesbian. "A number of researchers (Bozett 1981, 1987, 1989; Golombok et al. 1983; Hoeffer 1981; Huggins 1989; Kirkpatrick et al. 1981; Miller 1979; Paul 1986; and Rees 1979) have concluded that the sexual orientations/preferences of children of gay or lesbian parents do not differ from those whose parents are heterosexual" (in Laird 1993:315). Laird suggests that "this makes sense since it is equally clear that most homosexual adults were themselves reared in heterosexual families" (1993:316).

Children of gay and lesbian parents seem to grow and develop quite well in spite of the prejudice and discrimination they face. Some research on children of lesbian parents even indicates that they may benefit. They tend to be more flexible and tolerant than other children. One might also ask if there are not benefits to be gained by children of lesbian parents who are not raised in the traditional patriarchal family structure.

SUMMARY

In this chapter we explored some significant current influences on families. We have considered some social work implications of familiness. Traditional perspectives on family were examined, including definitions, historical perspectives on the family, family developmental tasks, life cycle notions of family, and some changes that have occurred in traditional perspectives on family. Divorce, remarriage, and stepfamilies were explored as traditional because of the number of individuals and families struggling with divorce and remarriage. It was recognized, though, that for the individuals struggling with the challenges of divorce, remarriage, and the formation of stepfamilies, these family constellations are in all likelihood considered alternative.

In this chapter we also explored alternative perspectives on familiness. We surveyed some alternative definitions of *family* or *familiness* and examined multifaceted definitions of *familiness* that attempt to integrate both traditional and alternative aspects. We explored a number of issues related to families and people of color. We employed an ecological approach to better understanding families of color. This approach included investigation of adaptive strategies employed by people of color to deal with the consequences of racism and oppression. Among the adaptive strategies explored were family extendedness, social role flexibility, biculturalism, and spirituality and ancestral worldviews.

This chapter addressed issues and concerns related to women in families. This included a feminist perspective on family and familiness. Within the feminist perspective we explored gender and sex roles, the concept of family work, family violence, and issues of concern in dual-wage-earner families.

Finally, in this chapter we explored the issues of familiness from the perspectives of gay and lesbian families. We struggled with definitions of gay and lesbian families. We looked at family roles, gay and lesbian couples and relationships, and the place of gay and lesbian community in considerations of familiness. We also examined some of the findings of research on the status of children of gay and lesbian parents.

The next chapter will focus on traditional and alternative notions about small groups. We will also consider the social work implications of a variety of approaches to understanding small-group structures and dynamics.

Internet Search Guide

If you want to learn more about some of the topics discussed in this chapter by exploring the Internet, you can search the Net for the terms listed below. Remember that as you are "surfing" the Net, any of the search terms listed below can take you in many different directions. If you would like to visit specific Web sites related to this chapter, go to the Allyn and Bacon Web site at **http://www.abacon.com** and follow the links to Schriver or *Human Behavior and the Social Environment: Shifting Paradigms in Essential Knowledge for Social Work Practice*. There you will find a selection of sites related to content in this chapter.

1. nuclear family
2. child-centered
3. divorce
4. remarriage
5. stepfamilies
6. sex roles
7. sexual orientation
8. families of choice
9. kinship care

REFERENCES

Ainslie, Julie and Feltey, Kathryn. (1991). "Definitions and dynamics of motherhood and family in lesbian communities." In *Wider Families*. Binghamton, NY: Haworth Press.

American Immigration Lawyers Association. (1999). *American is immigration*. [Web site]. American Immigration Lawyers Association. Available: http://www.aila.org/aboutimmigration.html [2000, 3/20/00].

AmeriStat. (1999). *The rich, the poor, and the in between*. [Web site]. AmeriStat Population Reference Bureau and Social Science Data Analysis Network. Available: http://www.amerstat.org/incpov/hshlds.htm [2000, 4/4/00].

AmeriStat. (2000). *Families in poverty: Racial and ethnic differences*. [Web site]. AmeriStat Population Reference Bureau and Social Science Data Analysis Network. Available: http://www.ameristat.org/incpov/family.htm [2000, 4/4/00].

Attneave, Carolyn. (1982). "American Indians and Alaska Native families: Emigrants in their own homeland." In *Ethnicity and family therapy*, McGoldrick, Monica, Pearce, John, and Giordano, Joseph. (Eds.). New York: Guilford.

Bengston, V. L., and Allen, K. R. (1993). "The life course perspective applied to families over time." In P. G. Boss, Doherty, W. J., LaRossa, R., Schuman, W. R., and Steinmetz, S. K. (Eds.). *Sourcebook of family theories and methods: A contextual approach.* New York: Plenum Press.

Billingsley, A. (1992). *Climbing Jacob's ladder: The enduring legacy of African-American families.* New York: Simon and Schuster.

Billingsley, Andrew. (1968). *Black families in white America.* Englewood Cliffs, NJ: Prentice Hall.

Boss, P. G., et al. (1993). *Sourcebook of family theories and methods: A contextual approach.* New York: Plenum Press.

Boyd-Franklin, Nancy. (1993). "Race, class and poverty." In *Normal family processes,* Walsh, Froma. (Ed.). New York: Guilford

Carter, Elizabeth, and McGoldrick, Monica. (1980). *The family life cycle: A framework for family therapy.* New York: Gardner Press.

Carter, Betty, and McGoldrick, Monica. (1989). *The changing family life cycle: A framework for family therapy* (2nd ed.). Boston: Allyn and Bacon.

Demo, D. H., and Allen, K. R. (1996). "Diversity within lesbian and gay families: Challenges and implications for family theory and research." *Journal of Social and Personal Relationships,* 13 (3):415–434.

Devore, Wynetta, and Schlesinger, Elfriede G. (1991). *Ethnic-sensitive social work practice* (3rd ed.). New York: Macmillan Publishing Company.

Duvall, Evelyn M. (1971). *Family development* (4th ed.). Philadelphia: J. B. Lippincott Company.

Duvall, Evelyn M. (1978). In Kennedy, Carroll E., *Human development: The adult years and aging.* New York: MacMillan Publishing Company.

Duvall, Evelyn M. (1988). "Family development's first forty years." *Family Relations,* 37: 127–134.

Edelman, Marian Wright. (1987). *Families in Peril.* Cambridge, MA: Harvard University Press.

English, Richard. (1991). "Diversity of worldviews among African American families." In Everett, Joyce, Chipungu, Sandra, and Leashore, Bogart, eds. *Child welfare: An Africentric perspective.* New Brunswick, NJ: Rutgers University Press.

Ferree, Myra M. (1990). "Beyond separate spheres: Feminism and family research." *Journal of Marriage and the Family,* 52:866–884.

Fong, R., Spickard, P. R., and Ewalt, P. L. (1996). "A multiracial reality: Issues for social work." In Ewalt, P. L., Freeman, E. M., Kirk, S. A., and Poole, D. L. *Multicultural issues in social work.* Washington, DC: NASW.

Freeman, Edith M. (1990). "Life cycle: Operationalizing a strengths perspective." In Logan, Sadye, Freeman, Edith & McCroy, Ruth. *Social work practice with black families: A culturally specific perspective.* New York: Longman.

Gebeke, D. (1996). *Grandparenting and stepgrandparenting: When grandparents become parents to their grandchildren.* [Web site]. North Dakota State University Extension Service. Available: http://www.ext.nodak.edu/extpubs/yf/famsci/fs561w.htm [2000, 3/20/00].

Harrison, Algea, Wilson, Melvin, Pine, Charles, Chan, Samuel, and Buriel, Raymond. (1990). "Family ecologies of ethnic minority children." *Child Development,* 61:347–362.

Hernandez, M., and McGoldrick, M. (1999). "Migration and the life cycle." In B. Carter and M. McGoldrick. (Eds.). *The expanded family life cycle: Individual, family, and social perspectives* (3rd ed., p. 541). Boston: Allyn and Bacon.

Hartman, Ann, and Laird, Joan. (1983). *Family-centered social work practice.* New York: Free Press.

Hetherington, E. Mavis, Law, Tracy, and O'Connor, Thomas. (1993) "Divorce, changes, and new chances." In *Normal family processes.* Walsh, Froma. (Ed.). New York: Guilford.

Hill, Reuben. (1986). "Life cycle stages for types of single parent families: Of family development theory." *Family Relations,* 35:19–29.

Hines, Paulette Moore, and Boyd-Franklin, Nancy. (1982). "Black families." In *Ethnicity and family therapy.* McGoldrick, Monica, Pearce, John, and Giordano, Joseph. (Eds.). New York: Guilford.

Ho, Man Kueng. (Ed.). (1987). *Family therapy with ethnic minorities.* Newbury Park, CA: Sage Publications.

Hollingsworth, L. (1998). "Promoting same-race adoption for children of color." *Social Work, 43*(2): 104–116.

Jendrek, M. P. (1994). "Grandparents who parent their grandchildren: Circumstances and decisions." *The Gerontologist, 34* (2):206–216.

Kennedy, Carroll E. (1978): *Human development: The adult years and aging.* New York: Macmillan Publishing Co., Inc.

Kennedy, M., and Agron, L. (1999). "Bridging the digital divide." *American School and University, 72*(2), 16–18.

Laird, Joan. (1993). "Lesbian and gay families." In *Normal family processes.* Walsh, Froma. (Ed.). New York: Guilford.

Leigh, James. (1989). "Black Americans: Emerging identity issues and social policy." *The Annual Ellen Winston Lecture.* Raleigh: North Carolina State University.

Logan, Sadye. (1990). "Black families: Race, ethnicity, culture, social class, and gender issues." In *Social work practice with black families: A culturally specific perspective.* Logan, Sadye, Freeman, Edith, and McRoy, Ruth. (Eds.). New York: Longman.

Logan, Sadye, Freeman, Edith, and McRoy, Ruth. (Eds.). (1990). *Social work practice with Black families: A culturally specific perspective.* New York: Longman.

Martin, Joanne, and Martin, Elmer P. (1985). *The helping tradition in the black family and community.* Silver Spring, MD: NASW.

McGoldrick, Monica, Pearce, John, and Giordano, Joseph. (Eds.). (1982). *Ethnicity and family therapy.* New York: Guilford Press.

Miller, Jean Baker. (1986). *Toward a new psychology of women.* (2nd ed.) Boston: Beacon.

Myers, Linda. (1985). "Transpersonal psychology: The role of the Afrocentric paradigm," *The Journal of Black Psychology.* 12(1):31–42.

National Telecommunications and Information Administration. (1999). *Falling through the Net: Defining the digital divide.* [Web site]. U.S. Department of Commerce. Available: http://www.ntia.doc.gov [2000, 4/8/00].

Pinderhughes, Elaine. (1982). "Afro-American families and the victim system." In McGoldrick, M., Pearce, J., and Giordano, J. (Eds.). (1982). *Ethnicity and family therapy.* New York: Guilford Press.

Piotrkowski, Chaya, and Hughes, Diane. (1993). "Dual-earner families in context." In *Normal family processes.* Walsh, Froma, ed. New York: Guilford.

Population Reference Bureau. (1999). *Immigration to the US—Part III.* [Web site]. Population Reference Bureau. Available: http://www.prb.org/pubs/bulletin/bu54-2/part3.htm#econ [2000, 4/4/00].

Ronnau, J. P.. and Marlow, C. R. (November 1993). "Family preservation, poverty and the value of diversity." *Families in Society: The Journal of Contemporary Human Services.* 74:538–544.

Rothenberg, D. (1997, 8/1/97). *Grandparents as parents: A primer for schools.* [Web site]. ERIC Clearinghouse on Elementary and Early Childhood Education. Available: wysiwyg://770/http://www.kidsource . . . ource/content2/grandparents.3.html [2000, 3/20/00].

Rounds, K. A., Weil, M., and Bishop, K. K. (January 1994). "Practice with culturally diverse families of young children with disabilities." *Families in Society: The Journal of Contemporary Human Services.* 75(1):3–14.

Scannapieco, M., and Jackson, S. (1996). "Kinship care: The African American response to family preservation." *Social Work, 41* (2):190–196.

Scanzoni, John, and Marsiglio, William. (1991). "Wider families as primary relationships." *Wider families.* Binghamton, NY: The Haworth Press.

Slater, Suzanne, and Mencher, Julie. (1991). "The lesbian family life cycle: A contextual approach." *American Journal of Orthopsychiatry, 61*(3):372–382.

Stack, C. (1974). *Allowrkin: Strategies for survival in a Black community.* New York: Harper and Row.

Staveteig, S., and Wigton, A. (2000). *Racial and ethnic disparities: Key findings from the national survey of america's families.* [Web site]. Urban Institute. Available: http://newfederalism.urban.org/html/series_b/b5/b5.html [2000, 4/8/00].

Visher, Emily, and Visher, John. (1993). "Remarriage families and stepparenting." In *Normal family processes.* Walsh, Froma. (Ed.). New York: Guilford.

Walsh, Froma. (1993). *Normal family processes.* (2nd ed.) New York: Guilford.

Wilhelmus, M. (1998). "Mediation in kinship care: Another step in the provision of culturally relevant child welfare services." *Social Work, 43*(2): 117–126.

ILLUSTRATIVE READING 6.1

The illustrative reading by Hurd, Moore, and Rogers provides us with a strengths perspective on African American parents and families. The research conducted from a strengths perspective by the authors of this reading reinforces the existence of a number of the adaptive strategies and realities of families of color addressed in this chapter. Their findings, for example, reflect higher levels of involvement of African American men in the lives of their children than is often reflected in both popular and scholarly media. Hurd, Moore, and Rogers also found themes related to strong extended family networks, strong beliefs in the value of education, and the importance of spirituality in the lives of African American families that are consistent with the discussion of these issues in this chapter.

Quiet Success: Parenting Strengths among African Americans

Elisabeth Porter Hurd, Carolyn Moore, and Randy Rogers

Abstract: Building on a model of family competence, the authors examined strengths among African American parents. Fifty-three parents described the values and behaviors that they imparted to their children. Support from external caregivers, which reinforced family competence, was studied. The study found substantial parental involvement, considerable support from other adults, and a high frequency of positive role modeling by African American men.

African American families in the United States currently number 7,854,800 (U.S. Census Bureau, 1992). Millions of these families raise children who become productive members of society. Although these families enrich the diversity of American parenting,

Elisabeth Porter Hurd is Assistant Professor and Carolyn Moore is Lecturer/Field Director, Department of Social Work, University of North Carolina, Greensboro. Randy Rogers is Family Development Specialist, Uplift, Inc., Greensboro, North Carolina. This article is based on work funded by the Lois and Samuel Silberman Fund. Reprinted by permission of Manticope Publishers, publisher of *Families in Society* (September 1995).

little has been written about the strengths of African American parents (Hale-Benson, 1986; McAdoo, 1988). Consequently, it has been difficult to refine social work practice to fit the experiences of this racial minority (Lum, 1992).

The present study explored the values, attitudes, and activities of African American parents by describing what they believed they were doing right. The parents were afforded the opportunity to define for themselves what they considered to be their strengths. This approach was considered a key factor in understanding the dynamics of parenting, despite the fact that other research has not used this approach to empower African American parents. In addition, a concerted effort was made to include African American fathers, because they are rarely used as direct participants in research on African American parenting (McAdoo, 1988). Finally, the communal nature of African American parenting was recognized by asking parents about the child-rearing support they received from others (Boyd-Franklin & Franklin, 1985; Manns, 1988). The findings of this exploratory study provide social workers and other human service professionals with new information with which to modify both the assessment and intervention processes when working with African American families.

REVIEW OF THE LITERATURE

A modest body of literature describes the strengths of African American families in fulfilling their socially appointed roles and functions (Billingsley, 1968; Billingsley, 1992; Hale-Benson, 1986; Hill, 1972; Lum, 1992; McAdoo, 1988; Royse & Turner, 1980; Smith, 1992; Washington & LaPoint, 1988). These strengths seem to belong to all African American families, regardless of their class and individual differences, having been developed in response to a need to survive in a racist society.

By 1903, scholars such as W. E. B. DuBois (1982) already had begun to describe the talents and abilities of their fellow African Americans. However, it was not until after the activism of the civil-rights movement that a new wave of scholars, among them Billingsley (1968) and Hill (1972), returned to the chronicling of strengths rather than deficits of African American families. Hill (1972) noted five major competencies: strong kinship bonds, strong work orientation, adaptability of family roles, high achievement orientation, and religious orientation. Hill's work was expanded by Royse and Turner (1980), who presented African American subjects with Hill's list of family attributes; the subjects believed that this list accurately described them.

Subsequent researchers have substantiated Hill's work. Peters (1988) found that African American parents placed a high priority on developing the self-esteem of their children; instilled the values of love, respect, personal uniqueness, and desire for educational achievement; and prepared their children to survive in a racist society. Washington and LaPointe (1988) included work and persistence, ethnic pride, religion, caring, and regard for achievement in children as African American values. Finally, Billingsley (1992), expanding his ground-breaking work (1968), categorized traditional values currently held by African Americans as a love of learning, a deep-rooted spirituality, a desire for self-governance, and committment to serving others.

None of these scholars would argue that all these characteristics are exclusive to African Americans or deny that individuals possess differing degrees of these traits.

These experts simply desire that family strengths be explored to counteract the general bias in social science research toward defining the African American family as deficient or pathological (Hale-Benson, 1986; Hill, 1972; McAdoo, 1988; Nobles, 1988; Royse & Turner, 1980; Smith, 1992).

COMPETENCE MODEL OF FAMILY FUNCTIONING

The competence model of family functioning (Waters & Lawrence, 1993) was used as the theoretical framework for examining family strengths. This model presumes that all individuals are motivated to behave as they do by an overriding desire to achieve competence, that is, they have an "inborn striving for mastery and growth, [a] need to make their world work, to grow and change and to strive for mastery both in the external world and in their internal development" (Waters & Lawrence, 1993, p. 7). Individuals carry this striving into their interactions with other family members.

That individuals seek to be competent within their environments is certainly not a new concept in social work practice theory. Social work scholars have long identified client strengths as an essential ingredient in motivating change (Hollis & Woods, 1981; Perlman, 1957; Reid & Epstein, 1972; Solomon, 1976). The competence model focuses on family strength as the *primary* factor to be assessed and utilized by the practitioner. The basic approach of the model is to discover all possible strengths within the family system and then redefine the presenting problems as manifestations of the drive for mastery of the environment gone awry rather than as personal or familial dysfunction.

Thus, the basic assumptions underlying this research were that parents try to raise their children competently, that they will be successful at some aspect of child care, and that parents who have problems with their environments nevertheless have strengths that can be used to improve their situations. Given the extended nature of traditional African American families, one further assumption was made: that adults who were not parents as defined in this study but who were emotionally connected to the family would strive to assist parents in their child-rearing efforts.

METHODOLOGY

Research Questions

This assumption of competence, that parents desire to raise children effectively and that others within the African American community desire to assist them in achieving mastery, led to the development of four research questions:

- What did African American parents perceive as their parenting competencies?
- What positive involvement did parents have with their children?
- Who else supported them in their quest to raise their children in the best way they could?
- How did African American men contribute positively to the care of children?

Participants

Participants were selected randomly from the membership of the Greensboro, North Carolina, affiliate of the National Black Child Development Institute (BCDI). Potential participants were asked if they were African American and if they were parents. *Parent* was defined as an adult who currently had primary responsibility for the care and development of one or more children and with whom the child or children resided. *Family* was defined as all individuals whom the parent considered to be members of the family system. All participants lived in the Piedmont Triad area of North Carolina—a metropolitan area of more than one million people.

Fifty-three parents from 50 families participated in the study. A few parents were hesitant about being interviewed and inquired about the use of the information to be collected. However, none of families contacted refused to be interviewed.

Procedures

Fifty face-to-face interviews were conducted over a three-month period in 1993. In 47 interviews, one parent was interviewed; in three interviews, married couples were interviewed together. The interviews were held either in the homes of the participants or at the BCDI office. The interviews lasted on average 35 minutes. Each interview was audiotaped and then transcribed by one of the researchers. The parents were interviewed either by one of the researchers (an African American woman) or the research assistant (an African American man); both researchers interviewed the parents of both sexes.

Parents were asked 19 questions adapted from previous studies (Hill, 1972; Manns, 1988; Peters, 1988; Smith, 1992) in consultation with an African American educator who has worked extensively with African American parents and children. Parents were asked to describe their child-rearing activities and philosophies and to discuss individuals who shared caregiving responsibilities. Demographic information was also requested.

Data Analysis

The design for analyzing the interviews was borrowed from the method of thematic analysis developed by Olson and Haynes (1993) in their interviews with single parents. The interviews were read five times by the two researchers. Each researcher independently identified parenting themes and patterns. When both researchers agreed on a theme based on the comments of participants, each interview was checked to determine the presence of the theme.

The executive director of Greensboro's BCDI affiliate, a professional with many years of experience in teaching and advocacy, reviewed 20% of the interviews selected at random. She concurred with the presence of the trends and themes identified by the researchers.

Three focus groups were then held at the BCDI office and the Guilford County Schools Family Resource Center. The purpose of these groups was twofold: to present the themes and accompanying information to five or more African American parents to test their validity and to gain suggestions for translating the research findings into services. These groups were made up of individuals drawn from the Greensboro community and did not include the original participants. One focus group consisted exclusively of African American fathers. All focus group members found the identified themes to be consistent with their experiences.

FINDINGS AND DISCUSSION

The purpose of this research was to allow African American parents to describe their family environments while focusing on their self-identified strengths. The 53 parents who were interviewed provided new insights into working with African American families, painting a picture of strong, vibrant, loving family systems having to cope with sometimes harsh environments.

Participant Characteristics

Thirty-eight (72%) of the 53 respondents were mothers and 10 (19%) were fathers. Elders—three grandmothers, one grandfather, and one great-aunt—were also participants. The largest group of participants (55%) were single parents; 40% of the participants were married. The remaining 5% were unmarried mothers living with their extended families. The income levels of the participants were neatly divided, with annual family incomes ranging from less than $10,000 to $100,000 per year. Equal percentages (19%) of parents earned the following three incomes: less than $10,000, $10,000–19,999, and $30,000–50,000. Seventeen percent earned $20,000–29,999, and 15% earned $50,001–100,000. Thus a well-balanced mixture of family economic situations—low, middle, and high income—was obtained.

Trends and Themes

Combining the statements of all respondents, three trends and eight themes of African American parenting emerged (see Table 1). The findings of both the trends and themes answered the first question of this study. *Trends* are parenting patterns based on quantifiable data; they speak to the second, third, and fourth research questions. *Themes* summarize narrative comments regarding self-perceived family values and behaviors; they flesh out the bare bones of the trend results.

 Trend one: *Substantial parental involvement in the lives of their children.* The 53 respondents selected activities that they did on a regular basis from a 32-item checklist of activities defined as promoting the welfare of children and offering potential opportunities to bond with or educate children. (For example, cooking together can include lessons on math or nutrition or can entail handing down family recipes.) In the joint interviews, the mothers and fathers completed separate checklists.

 All the parents interviewed had some degree of positive involvement in activities contributing to the well-being of their children; all but 12 reported a high degree of involvement, carrying out 16 or more activities regularly. The number of activities in which parents indicated that they were involved routinely with their children ranged

TABLE 1   Parent reports of African American family trends and themes

	n
Trend	
Substantial parental involvement	41
Plentiful support from external caregivers	36
Considerable male involvement	49
Theme	
Connection with family	43
Emphasis on achievement	42
Respect for others	38
Spirituality	37
Foster self-reliance	37
Importance of education	35
Teach coping skills	35
Self-respect and racial pride	30

N = 50

from 3 to 31. More than 50% of the parents engaged in 28 out of 32 activities on a regular basis (see Table 2).

Despite other responsibilities cited by parents, such as employment, education, church, and community projects, they still placed a high priority on activities conducted with their children. These activities were used as opportunities to teach values or behaviors, to communicate, and to bond with their children.

Trend two: *Plentiful support for parenting from external caregivers.* When participants were asked with whom, other than current spouses, they shared responsibility for parenting, 36 (68%) of 53 indicated that individuals who did not live with the children assisted in their rearing (see Table 3). Child care was furnished for various reasons: to care for children while parents were at work, to provide respite for parents, and to permit other adults to share leisure activities with children.

Trend three: *Considerable male involvement in the lives of African American children.* Children in all but one family (98%) had male relatives or friends who at least periodically participated in activities with them. Fathers, whether living in the home or not, were the most common male influence in the lives of their children. Other male relatives were the next most common group that spent time with children. Even children who did not have male relatives available interacted regularly with male role models; such men included church members, school personnel, and others, including a bus driver, karate instructor, choir director, and babysitter (see Table 4).

Parents believed that the interactions between these men and their children were unformally positive, with the men teaching constructive values and giving sound advice. Although much of their time together was spent in recreational activities, such as playing sports, fishing, or watching videos, these men also routinely helped children with their homework and taught them occupational skills. The most important aspect of the interactions, in fact, was reported to be the communication between the

TABLE 2   Types of parental involvement

Activity	n	%
Watching TV together	50	94
Shopping together	49	93
Visiting relatives	48	91
Eating meals together	47	89
Talking with child	45	85
Going to church	44	83
Visiting friends	43	81
Listening to music	43	81
Reading together	42	79
Telling stories/jokes	42	79
Helping with homework	41	77
Driving in the car	40	76
Teaching problem solving	38	72
Singing together	37	70
Teaching decision making	36	68
Cooking together	35	66
Teaching conflict resolution	35	66
Doing chores together	35	66
Playing games/cards	33	62
Going to the movies	33	62
Putting child to bed	33	62
Attending sports events	31	59
Playing sports	31	59
Getting child dressed	31	59
Giving bath	28	53
Going to concerts/theater	27	51
Preparing for church programs	27	51
Doing hobbies/crafts	27	51
Riding on the bus	18	34
Bowling	14	26
Fishing/hunting	12	23
Camping	5	9

N = 53

men and the children; trust was established in these relationships and children felt comfortable approaching their male mentors to discuss problems. For example, Mr. W, a father with two adolescents and a preteen, described his relationship with his children as follows:

> *I think I have a very good relationship with my children because we talk a lot. I always asked them what was on your mind. Whatever it is, you can talk to me any time. [It's] always important for African American fathers to stay as close to kids as possible. A father should be there to talk and let them know he cares, understands their feelings.*

TABLE 3   External caregivers sharing parenting

Relationship	n	%
Grandmother[a]	23	46
Grandfather[a]	13	26
Aunt[a]	10	20
Uncle[a]	9	18
Male friend	9	18
Father	5	10
Great-grandmother[a]	5	10
Female friend	4	8
Great-grandfather[a]	2	4
Godparent[a]	2	4
Great-uncle	1	2
Great-aunt	1	2

N = 50
[a]Category may contain more than one individual with the same relationship to the child.

Theme one: *Connection with family.* The theme most commonly developed in the interviews echoed the trends established. Families reported drawing strength from regular interactions with relatives. This phenomenon occurred in two ways not previously mentioned: (1) relatives were used as role models for parenting and (2) visits to relatives provided affection and support.

When asked who served as their role model for their own parenting, most parents (80%) named a relative, most commonly their own mothers. Two mothers who were raising young sons reflected on their mothers. One said, "My mother was a very strong woman who lived through a lot of trials and tribulations; I look up to her"; the other stated: she "taught me how to love, how to treat people, how to live in this world."

Fathers, grandparents, siblings, and uncles and aunts of the parents interviewed also served as role models. One father remarked that this father instilled values in him that he wants to pass along. He added, "I hope that my son becomes a friend and a brother like I have become of my father."

Many parents lived close enough to relatives to visit them regularly. As one mother put it, "We have spent real time knowing our relatives, being around them." Stories about relatives, living and dead, often were passed on to children during these visits as well.

Theme two: *Emphasis on achievement and effort.* Despite their experience that achieving occupational success was generally more difficult for African Americans, parents still encouraged their children to work hard and strive for satisfying careers. Parents were content, however, to allow their children to decide for themselves what career would be satisfying rather than to try to influence their choice. Almost three-

TABLE 4   Male involvement in child rearing

Relationship	n	%
Father	37	74
Uncle[a]	28	56
Grandfather[a]	17	34
Great-uncle[a]	10	20
Male cousin[a]	10	20
Family friend (male)[a]	9	18
Minister/church member[a]	9	18
Mother's boyfriend	8	16
Teacher/principal (male)	6	12
Boy Scouts/YMCA staff	5	10
Big Brother	4	8
Great-grandfather[a]	4	8
Older brother[a]	3	6
Godfather	2	4
Coach	2	4
Other men	6	12

N = 50

[a]Category may contain more than one individual with the same relationship to the child.

quarters (74%) said that their notion of success for their children had to do with self-actualization: to "grow up to be somebody," "grow up and be what you want to be," "be the best *you* you can be."

Participants believed that effort was the route to achievement: "Hard work can get you places." Children were admonished to "keep trying to better yourself" even if "they have to do ten times better [than whites] to succeed."

Theme three: *Recognition of the importance of respect for others.* Parents in this sample were committed to teaching children to respect others, especially their elders. Ways of conveying respect were thought to be showing compassion, helping others, and being moral and honest—"be straight up with people." One mother spoke for many when she said, "My values are that you treat people like you want to be treated."

Theme four: *Cultivation of spirituality.* The need to nourish the spiritual dimensions of their children was appreciated by many parents. Parents wanted their children "to put God first" in their lives and have "respect for that which is greater than we are." These parents derived considerable comfort and guidance from participating in religious activities such as attending church, joining in church-related activities, reading the Bible, and praying; they wished that their children would share in the benefits of religious faith. Church members also were considered part of some parents' families and assisted in child rearing.

Theme five: *Ability to foster self-reliance.* When asked to define the "survival skills" with which they prepared their children, parents listed various competencies.

These skills would enable children to be self-sufficient in the future. As one father said, "Whatever happens to me, they can face any obstacle in life." Teaching self-reliance, according to the participants, included tutoring in problem solving, conflict resolution, and planning for future goals as well as house-keeping, money management, sex education, safety at home and outside, and self-defense. One mother, a social worker, summed up her teaching on self-reliance by saying, "If I can teach them how to think, they can survive out there."

Beyond the basic life skills, however, many parents recognized the need to prepare their children to survive in a racist society. Children were taught to cope with discrimination, sometimes through assertiveness and sometimes through superior effort. One mother of two school-age daughters told her children, "Being a black child, you have to work extra hard."

Theme six: *Recognition of the importance of education.* The parents who were interviewed were generally adamant that their children should receive the best possible education. They both realized the importance of attaining "a good education" to ensure upward mobility and financial security for their children and encouraged learning for its own sake—"education is the number-one key to freedom." One mother told her sons, "Education is always important—you can learn whatever you want to learn because no one can take it away from you once you have it in your head." Another believed that her grandchildren would "feel good about getting something up there between their ears."

Theme seven: *Acceptance of life's pain and instruction in coping skills.* The consensus among the parents interviewed was that pain and tragedy in life are to be expected: "Life is a testing ground." Children should be equipped to cope effectively—"to endure what you have to endure"—rather than to be protected from reality. One young father was saving words of wisdom for his one-year-old son: "I'll tell him that it's going to hurt. It's all right to cry, but life goes on." A mother, the wife of a high-ranking army officer, told her two sons that "black males are targeted not to do well . . . but your father used his talents and skills to overcome barriers." The message is that success lies not in avoiding pain but in conquering it: "not giving up even when it's hard." Coping also included maintaining a positive attitude toward life. As one father of three expressed it, "Your attitude carries you in life."

Theme eight: *Recognition of the importance of self-respect and racial pride.* That their children respect themselves and acquire high self-esteem was a paramount concern to parents. Self-respect was inculcated in two ways: by demonstrating love and by informing children about their racial heritage and culture.

Parents promoted self-respect by respecting their children. Children should "feel the love in the house," said one mother. Other parents indicated that they made a practice of teaching their children that "they're special," that their children are "worthy of life, worthy of seeking the best"; one tells a daughter that "she is important, wonderful, God's gift"; another says of a son that "we try to make him believe that he is somebody and he can always be somebody."

At the same time, parents tried to instill their children with pride in being African American: "To get a good grip on race, they know they can be proud of their race." Some parents had participated in the civil-rights movement or were currently political activists and thus able to relate their experiences to their children. Others re-lied on family history to demonstrate how ancestors survived and triumphed over racism. An educational administrator followed the example of numerous parents by surrounding her four children at home with African American literature and encour-aging them to take black studies courses in school. Parents saw pride in self as inex-orably bound with pride in culture and heritage.

IMPLICATIONS FOR SOCIAL WORK AND FAMILY PRACTICE

This research reported on a sampling of African Americans' perceptions of their own parenting strengths. It took family competency as its theoretical framework, which as-sumes that all families strive for mastery of the parenting process and are likely to ex-hibit some success in that endeavor. Indeed, the parents interviewed proved to be nurturing, insightful, and active in meeting their parenting responsibilities. They also clearly were able to draw upon the support of other adults to supplement their efforts to raise healthy children despite environmental barriers.

Foremost among the obstacles faced by African American families are racism and poverty. It is critical to assert here that the results of this study do not in any way imply that the recognition of family strengths permits society to decrease efforts to assist families affected negatively by the social environment. Families who are poor, 31% of all African American families (U.S. Census Bureau, 1992), or who live in con-ditions of "ill health, inadequate education, and high unemployment," as do an ever increasing number of African American children (Edelman, 1985, p. 80), are forced to dissipate their strengths in the struggle to survive. The parenting successes that these families achieve beyond survival are extraordinary and deserving of future study. Given adequate resources and support, all parents might taste a measure of success in child rearing; social workers and family practitioners must continue to advocate for that goal.

Notwithstanding, the information furnished by these parents can promote cul-turally competent social work and family practice by increasing awareness of several factors:

- It is likely that most African American parents are heavily involved in ac-tivities that promote the well-being of their children.
- It is likely that parents are being supported in their child-rearing efforts by external caregivers.
- It is likely that African American children have positive male role models.
- It is likely that parents are attempting to transmit honorable values and teach responsible behaviors to their children.

By recognizing these patterns, professionals will not overlook people or re-sources in their interventions with African American families. By knowing what is val-ued in African American families, social workers and others will be better able to empower them. By focusing on the drive for parental competence, they will remem-ber to reward efforts as well as achievements in child rearing.

These findings further demonstrate the need for assessments of families to include members, especially fathers, who may not live in the household but are important elements of the family system. These external caregivers can play a vital role in family counseling, provide respite for at-risk parents, and supply psychologically comfortable placements for children who must be removed from the home. Practitioners need to advocate so that proper recognition by the educational, legal, and medical systems is accorded to these caregivers. Policymakers similarly should take into account the expanded structure of African American families, including the role played by out-of-the-home fathers, when developing programs for families.

When assessing families, it is essential to be cognizant of the competencies and the values and behaviors related to raising children that African American parents ascribe to themselves. It is useful to ask parents, if they do not volunteer information about their strengths, whether they share these same attributes. Practitioners can promote self-esteem in parents by sharing their assessment of perceived parental competencies.

In fact, as was predicted by the model of family competency, the participating parents not only strove to be good parents, but apparently were having some success. The strengths that parents recognized in their own families are the same as family traits correlated with producing stable, high-achieving, resilient children—for example, good communication skills, spirituality, affection, and positive family traditions (Clark, 1983; Garmezy, 1987; Olson & Haynes, 1993; Rutter, 1987).

That is not to say that these parents did not experience problems with their child rearing; they were not chosen as parental paragons. Rather, the competency model suggests that parents who do exhibit parenting problems possess strengths, even if these strengths are not being used effectively. Interventions with parents, in fact, can be tailored to draw upon the inherent desire for successful child rearing. First, this desire can serve as a powerful motivation for change in parental behaviors and thinking (Waters & Lawrence, 1993). Second, it can reveal the specific values and hopes of parents for themselves and their children and therefore offer personalized goals for change. Third, it can illuminate the barriers that keep parents from mastering the parenting process.

Family practitioners can design interventions or programs that build upon and improve existing interactions between parents or secondary caregivers and children. Naturally occurring patient-child interactions are an obvious starting place for necessary work to improve parenting skills; productive techniques already used by parents can be reinforced. If bonding is an issue, parents may be helped to use the activities they engage in regularly to communicate more effectively and to share affection with their children. Bonding may be especially applicable to men, who are more often out of the home than are women. If parental stress places children at risk of abuse, parents can be taught how to make their child-rearing activities less burdensome. If children's performance at school is below par, activities in which parents are already involved can be made more educational.

Continuing in their teaching role, social workers and other practitioners can educate policymakers and the public about the strengths of African American families. As with all races, a segment of these families is deeply troubled and in need of extensive social services. However, most African American families are in good shape

(Billingsley, 1992). These families would benefit from services designed to enhance family strengths rather than focusing on severe psychosocial problems. Further, practitioners can transfer African American parenting skills, such as the ability to teach children how to survive in harsh environments and to face the inevitable pain and tragedy that is part of life, to parents of other races who wish to expand their own child-rearing repertoires.

Finally, future research can contribute to increased understanding of parental and family strengths. More research needs to be conducted on positive interactions between African American parents and their children and between secondary caregivers and children so that social services can achieve a better fit with the needs of these families. Another fruitful topic to examine is the description of family strengths by parents who are not African American; a comparison of similarities and differences among ethnic groups would be useful. Research into successful parenting by individuals living in poverty could identify ways in which social services might break down barriers to effective parenting for clients in poverty.

It is essential to honor successful African American parents by adapting social work practice to recognize self-identified family strengths. Doing so may result in untold benefits; as one mother told her child, "Shoot for the moon—you may land on a star!"

REFERENCES

Billingsley, A. (1968). *Black families in white America*. Englewood Cliffs, NJ: Prentice-Hall.

Billingsley, A. (1992). *Climbing Jacob's ladder: The enduring legacy of African-American families*. New York: Simon & Schuster.

Boyd-Franklin, A., & Franklin, N. (1985). A psychoeducational perspective on black parenting. In J. McAdoo & H. McAdoo (Eds.), *Black children*. Beverly Hills CA: Sage Publications.

Clark, R. (1983). *Family life and school achievement: Why poor black children succeed or fail*. Chicago: University of Chicago Press.

Dubois, W. E. B. (1982). *The souls of black folks*. New York: New American Library.

Edelman, M. (1985). The sea is so wide and my boat is so small: Problems facing black children today. In J. McAdoo & H. McAdoo (Eds.), *Black children*. Beverly Hills, CA: Sage Publications.

Garmezy, N. (1987). Stress, competence, and development: The search for stress-resistant children. *American Journal of Orthopsychiatry, 57*, 159-174.

Hale-Benson, J. (1986). *Black children*. Baltimore, MD: Johns Hopkins University Press.

Hill, R. (1972). *The strengths of black families*. New York: National Urban League.

Hollis, F., & Woods, M. (1981). *Casework: A psychosocial therapy*. New York: Random House.

Lum, D. (1992). *Social work practice and people of color*. Pacific Grove, CA: Brooks/Cole.

Manns, W. (1988). Supportive roles of significant others in black families. In H. McAdoo (Ed.), *Black families*. Newbury Park, CA: Sage Publications.

McAdoo, J. (1988). The roles of black fathers in the socialization of black children. In H. McAdoo (Ed.), *Black families*. Newbury Park, CA: Sage publications.

Nobles, W. (1988). African American family life. In H. McAdoo (Ed.), *Black families*. Newbury Park, CA: Sage Publications.

Olson, M., & Haynes, J. (1993). Successful single parents. *Families in Society, 74*, 259-267.

Perlman, H. (1957). *Social casework: A problem-solving process*. Chicago: University of Chicago Press.

Peters, M. (1988). Parenting in black families with young children. In H. McAdoo (Ed.), *Black families*. Newbury Park, CA: Sage Publications.

Reid, W., & Epstein, L. (1972). *Task-centered casework*. New York: Columbia University Press.

Royse, D., & Turner, G. (1980). Strengths of black families: A black community's perspective. *Social Work, 25,* 407-409.

Rutter, M. (1987). Psychosocial resilience and protective mechanisms. *American Journal of Orthopsychiatry, 57,* 316-331.

Smith, D. (1992, September 25). *The psychology of blackness.* Paper presented at the North Carolina chapter, National Association of Black Social Workers Annual Conferences, Kernersville, NC.

Solomon, B. (1976). *Black empowerment: Effective social work in oppressed communities.* New York: Columbia University Press.

U.S. Census Bureau. (1992). *Current population reports.* Washington, DC: U.S. Government Printing Office.

Washington, V., & LaPoint, V. (1988). *Black children and American institutions.* New York: Garland Publishing.

Waters, D., & Lawrence, E. (1993). *Competence, courage, and change: An approach to family therapy.* New York: W. W. Norton.

7 ✦ Perspectives on Groups

$\mathcal{K}$nowledge about small groups is essential for social workers. Much of social work practice takes place in the context of small groups. Whether your practice is directed primarily toward individuals, families, organizations, or communities, much of what you do on a day-to-day basis will be done in the context of small groups. Addressing the needs of individuals and families will almost certainly require work in the context of some type of team. Medical social workers working with individuals and families, for example, are often members of multidisciplinary care teams made up of physicians, nurses, dietitians, physical therapists, and others. These teams are small groups and require understanding of the dynamics of small groups. Social workers practicing in an administrative or management context carry out much of their day-to-day practice through such small groups as work groups and committees. If your practice setting is at the community level, you are almost certain to be involved in task forces and citizen groups.

Certainly if you practice as a generalist social worker, you will be involved in small group efforts at many levels, including any combination of those described above. Practice in a public social services setting, for example, may require you to be involved in interdisciplinary teams, staff work groups, support groups for clients, community task forces, and any number of other types of groups. Our involvement as social workers in such a variety of group settings as those described above will require sufficient knowledge about small groups to be effective as both a member and a facilitator or leader of small groups.

DEFINITIONS

A very basic definition of a **group** is "a small, face-to-face collection of persons who interact to accomplish some purpose" (Brown 1991:3). Another definition suggests that a group is "two or more individuals in face-to-face interaction, each aware of his or her membership in the group, each aware of the others who belong to the group, and each aware of their positive interdependence as they strive to achieve mutual goals" (Johnson and Johnson 1991:14). Both of these definitions' concern for shared purpose and common interaction clearly differentiate a group from what is often referred to as an aggregate or a mere collection of individuals with no common purpose and little or no mutual interaction. An example of an aggregate or mere collection of people is the people with whom you might ride an elevator. These definitions also suggest a compatibility with the core purposes and values of social work and the assumptions we make about ourselves, others, and social work in this book.

HISTORICAL PERSPECTIVE

The small group as an important context for understanding and influencing human behavior has a multidisciplinary history. It has roots in the disciplines of education, psychology, sociology, and social work. Concern for understanding the influences of groups on individual and collective behavior is primarily a product of the twentieth century, although through much of modern history important questions about the place of groups in our individual and collective lives have been raised.

History of Group Theory and Practice

Twentieth-century researchers' concerns have been multifocused, including the role of groups in democracy, leadership, decision making, work, leisure, education, and problem solving. Social workers have focused their interests in small-group behavior in a range of areas from social reform to the role of groups in education, leisure, therapy, and citizenship.

An early institution through which the influences of groups on individual and community life were studied and used for problem solving was the settlement house movement of the early twentieth century. Later on social workers turned their interests in groups to the therapeutic or treatment potential of groups for dealing with mental illness and other problems in living. More recently, social workers have extended their interests in and work with groups to their use as a means of self-help and support for the persons with whom we work. Self-help and support groups are used to address a great variety of issues, from increasing political awareness, as in consciousness-raising groups in the women's and civil rights movements, to groups for dealing with addictions, physical or sexual abuse, and other personal difficulties that can benefit from the assistance of others with similar experiences (Brown 1991; Worchel, Wood, and Simpson 1992; Johnson and Johnson 1991).

History of a Group

Just as it is important to have some sense of the emergence in history of concern for small groups as a unit of study and as an important environment within which human behavior occurs, it is important to recognize the impact of historical factors on the development of any particular small group. Every small group with which we deal or to which we belong is heavily influenced by the past experiences of the members of the group. Group members do not enter group situations from a vacuum. We come to groups having had past experiences in groups—both positive and negative. We come to groups with perspectives on other people based on our past experiences with others. Depending on the quality of our past individual and group experiences, it is possible that two different people can join the same group at the same time and have diametrically opposed perceptions about what their shared experience in the new group will be like. Andrea can enter a group for the first time and see in the faces of the other group members rich and exciting possibilities for new friendships, new ideas, and new solutions to her problems. Mitchell can look at the same faces and see a terrifying collection of strangers and potential enemies waiting to create many more problems for him than they could ever solve. It is out of this diversity of perceptions, based on radically different pasts, that the challenge of groupness emerges. As social workers, we are often charged with guiding these very different people to share their differences in an attempt to confirm the hopes of Andrea and to allay the anxiety and the fears of Mitchell so both can benefit from each other's experiences and come closer to fulfilling both their potentials as humans.

We cannot hope to do this unless we are aware of the history and experiences we bring to the group ourselves. What, then, is this mysterious entity called the small group?

Before we explore specific approaches and concepts for understanding small groups, it may be helpful to recognize some similarities among models and concepts used for understanding human behavior in group environments and approaches to understanding human behavior at other levels with which we are concerned in this book. Models for understanding small-group development, for example, share a number of things with models for understanding individual and family development. Perhaps the most apparent similarity is that of stage-based models of group development. Many approaches to understanding the development of any particular group include some framework based on developmental stages. Many of the concepts for explaining small-group structures and functions also can be applied to organizational and community levels of human behavior. Such concepts as leadership, roles, norms, and socialization are examples of concepts used for understanding small groups that we will see again as we explore organizations and communities.

TRADITIONAL AND ALTERNATIVE PERSPECTIVES

We will examine a number of basic dimensions and concepts commonly used to explain small-group structures and dynamics, whether discussing traditional or alternative perspectives on groups. As we explore these basic dimensions and concepts we will examine the different emphasis placed on the concepts in traditional and alternative paradigm thinking.

Process and Product Dimensions

One way of thinking about a group is to consider whether the group is product or process focused. Some students of groups have emphasized the product or outcome dimension, while others have been primarily concerned with internal group processes that occur during the life of a group. The dimensions of outcome and process are also sometimes referred to as **task** and **maintenance**, or **instrumental** and **expressive** (Worchel, Wood, and Simpson 1992; Anderson and Carter 1990; Napier and Gershenfeld 1985). All these terms suggest that groups operate simultaneously on two levels. **Task level** is concerned with the accomplishment of the concrete goals of the group—a task force must complete a grant application to begin a service to people with AIDS or who are HIV positive, for example. The **process dimension** is concerned with the socioemotional needs of the task force members—task force members must develop effective processes for relating to one another and for addressing their individual feelings related to AIDS and HIV in the group context in order to effectively complete the task. The members must be able to work together.

Goals and Purposes

Most researchers and practitioners agree that all groups must have elements of both outcome and process. There is a good deal of disagreement, however, on which element of this dimension should be of primary concern. The amount of attention to task or process is influenced by the goals or purposes of the group. A **group goal** is most simply defined as a place the group would like to be (Napier and Gershenfeld 1985:181–225).

Traditional perspectives would suggest that a task-oriented group such as the one discussed above might give precedence to accomplishing its goal of completing the grant application over concerns for how well the group members were able to "get along" with each other. Alternative perspectives would suggest, however, that the group is not driven so exclusively by its stated goal or purpose at all times. The group cannot be successful in accomplishing its stated task if its members disagree about or are too anxious about their own feelings about the controversial issue of AIDS/HIV to focus on that task. The group cannot accomplish its task unless members can get along with each other well enough to unite in their efforts to accomplish the task and unless they are comfortable enough as individuals with the group's goal to invest their individual energies in pursuit of that group goal. These are process and socioemotional dimensions that cannot be separated from the product or task dimensions.

Some groups have purposes or goals that are more process or socioemotionally oriented than task or outcome oriented: a men's consciousness-raising group formed to address members' concerns for developing ways of relating to and behaving toward each other and to women in ways that are nonsexist, for example. Such a group is concerned primarily with changing members' ways of thinking, relating, and behaving. Its focus is process oriented. However, it also requires that the group accomplish concrete tasks as well. Members will need to determine tasks they will undertake to operate the group—when, where, and how often they will meet, for example. However, the task dimension is clearly secondary to the process concerns of the group for focusing on socioemotional and relationship dimensions.

Goals and purposes of groups, whether process or product focused, may be determined externally or internally. The task force goal to develop a grant application for AIDS/HIV services may have resulted from an agency board of directors' decision to develop services in this area and the board's direction to the staff to form a task force to implement its directive. It might have emerged as a result of external concerns raised by persons in the community who were HIV positive, who had AIDS, or who provided care for persons with AIDS. It might also have emerged from discussions among the persons who were members of the task force about the needs for such services and about the possible mechanisms for funding services. The men's consciousness-raising group's goals or purposes may also have been determined externally or internally. The group might have been created by agency management as a result of complaints by women coworkers, for example, of sexist behavior and sexual harassment by their male colleagues. The group might also have emerged out of its members' own recognition of their difficulties in relating to and behaving toward the women in their lives in nonsexist ways.

Whether groups' goals and purposes come about as a result of external or internal forces has important consequences for the ways groups will operate. As social workers who are likely to find ourselves in the position of facilitating or being a member of groups with externally imposed as well as internally determined goals and purposes, we must appreciate the influence of these factors on ourselves and other group members.

Membership

The examples of external and internal determination of goals for a group also suggest that members of groups come to be members in different ways. The different sources of goal setting for the AIDS/HIV task force and the men's group illustrate that membership might be voluntary or involuntary. The task force members called upon by the board of directors of their agency and the men required to be members of the consciousness-raising group because of their coworkers' complaints probably felt very different about being a part of their respective groups than did the task force members and the men's group members who decided among themselves that they wanted to become members of their group.

Membership describes the quality of the relationship between an individual and a group. Group members, whether they are in the group voluntarily or involuntarily, know they are members of the group. How we come to be a group member and how we feel about our membership in a group influences the level of membership we will have in the group. It influences how much of ourselves we will invest in the group.

Group membership can be differentiated by levels. **Formal or full psychological membership** suggests that we have invested ourselves significantly in the group and its goals; we feel a high degree of commitment to the group's goals and to the other group members. The other members of the group likewise see and accept us as full members of the group. When we are voluntarily a member of a group, and when we participate directly in determining the group's goals, we are more likely to experience full psychological membership.

We do not have this degree of membership in all groups to which we belong. We might be a marginal member of some groups. **Marginal members** are not willing to invest themselves fully in the group. They may do what is necessary to remain a member of the group, but only what is minimally necessary. Marginal members do make contributions to groups, but to a much lesser degree than full psychological members. There are a number of factors that result in marginal membership. We may be in the group involuntarily. We may not feel that we were a part of the process of forming the goals of the group. If the goals of the group were determined externally, for example, we may feel less ownership in its goals and therefore be more marginal as a member. We may also be a marginal member if we simply do not have time to become a full member but wish to support the goals of the group and contribute what we can in support of the group goals.

Another level of membership in groups that is worthy of note is aspiring membership. An **aspiring member** is one who is not formally a member of a group but wishes to be a member. As an aspiring member we might identify strongly with the goals of the group, but we may not be able to become a formal member of the group for a variety of reasons. The group may not have room for us or we may not meet membership criteria for the group (Napier and Gershenfeld 1985:74–111).

As group facilitators and members, social workers need to be particularly aware of this level of membership. Aspiring members offer a rich potential source of new group members who are likely to invest a great deal of energy in helping the group to achieve its goals. As social workers, we should also be concerned that aspiring members are not being excluded from membership in a group because of barriers that deny them access. If an aspiring member has a disability that makes it impossible for her or him to get to the group meetings and therefore does not apply for formal membership, we must act to move that aspiring member to full membership. If a member aspires to be a part of a group but finds or believes that her or his gender, sexual orientation, income, or other difference prevents him or her from being a full member, we must act to remove such barriers to membership.

Leadership, Followership, and Decision-Making

Bass (in Gastil 1994:954–955) provides a **general definition of leadership** as "an interaction between two or more members of a group that often involves a structuring or restructuring of the situation and the perceptions and expectation of the members. . . . Leadership occurs when one group member modifies the motivation or competencies of others in the group. Any member of the group can exhibit some amount of leadership." Gastil argues that leadership is "only *constructive* behaviors aimed at pursuing group goals" (1994:955). One traditional approach to leadership put forth by Lewin suggests three styles of leadership:

1. **Democratic leadership** focuses on group decision making, active member involvement, honest praise and criticism, and comradeship. (We will examine in more detail democratic leadership later in this section);

2. **Autocratic leadership** characterized by domineering and hierarchical leader behavior; and

3. **Laissez-faire** leadership characterized by an uninvolved, non-directive approach to leading (in Gastil 1994:955).

Other traditional notions of leadership tend to frame this element of group life as a set of inborn traits, as the product of the situation or environment, or as emerging from the position of leadership held by the person. The **trait** notion suggests that leaders are born. It implies that leadership is possible only for people who have the traits of leadership and that these people (leaders) are somehow destined for greatness or influence well above the rest of us. **Situational leadership** suggests that leaders emerge out of the requirements of a particular situation. If a person has the necessary expertise required to solve a particular problem, the requirements of the situation create the leader. **Positional leadership** suggests that leaders are created by the positions they hold. The position of chair or president will evoke from its holder the qualities necessary to lead. The authority or influence necessary for leadership comes out of the position or title. Trait, situational, and positional notions of leadership are incomplete or either/or perspectives. Either you have the magical traits of leadership or you do not; either you find yourself in a situation requiring your expertise or you do not; either you end up in a leadership position or you do not. These traditional notions are incomplete and leave out some important considerations. They suggest that leaders and followers are mutually exclusive roles (Napier and Gershenfeld 1985:227–296).

ALTERNATIVE

Functional Leadership

An alternative perspective on leadership suggests that leaders and followers are not so dichotomous or separate from each other. A **functional definition** of leadership suggests that leadership is simply behavior that assists a group to achieve its goals. Such a definition recognizes the potential for anyone in the group to be a leader. Leadership is demonstrated simply by doing what is necessary to help the group reach its goals, whether they be process or product related. Such a definition recognizes that sometimes people have the necessary characteristics or traits to lead in a particular context. One member's temperament may allow him or her to more readily lead the group in efforts to resolve conflict than others in the group, for example. A functional definition also suggests that a person with a leadership position such as chair or president may more readily lead the group in some formal activities—convening or adjourning the group, for example. A functional perspective also suggests that there are times when the environment or situation may call upon the expertise of a particular member to lead the group, such as a group facing a financial crisis calling upon a member with accounting skills to lead it through the crisis. Functional leadership offers an alternative notion of leadership that recognizes leadership within a group as mobile and flexible. A functional definition makes it difficult to distinguish leaders from followers, because everyone is viewed as having the potential for leadership. Functional leadership might be effectively practiced through a rotating rather than a fixed structure of leadership in groups. Rotating leaders also reduces tendencies toward hierarchical and positional group structures. Alcoholics Anonymous groups are examples of group efforts in which functional and nonhierarchical forms of leadership are emphasized.

The potential for leadership on the part of all group members, however, may not necessarily be realized. Unless group members recognize the existence of this potential in each other and unless they allow each other to act on their potential, it will not be realized. In effect, this alternative notion of leadership suggests that, contrary to traditional notions, leaders are not simply born or created by positions or situations; leaders are created by followers. Other members of the group allow leaders to lead by accepting the leadership behavior of the member who leads (Napier and Gershenfeld 1985:227–296).

Some researchers suggest that the concept of leadership as traditionally understood, especially trait or "great person" notions, is alienating. Gemmill and Oakley (1992: 120) suggest that by accepting the necessity of a leader or of a hierarchy with leaders at the top, we "de-skill" everyone else in the group. We relinquish our potential for developing our own "critical thinking, visions, inspirations and emotions" when we define leadership as a special quality or set of qualities held only by some special person (or select group of persons) other than ourselves. By turning over decision making and power to someone else through traditional ways of defining leaders we *are* able, however, to remove much of the uncertainty and ambiguity we are likely to experience in small groups with functional, rotating, or nonhierarchical leadership approaches. In doing so we—the followers—are relieved of making risky, sometimes frightening decisions. In turning ourselves over to a leader, we are, unfortunately, also relieved of the opportunity to participate equally in addressing issues that directly affect us (Gemmill and Oakley 1992:117–123).

This notion of leadership is compatible with the dimensions of alternate paradigm thinking. It replaces hierarchy with equality. It incorporates a feminist perspective in redefining power from "power over" to "power as the ability to influence people to act in their own interests, rather than induce them to act according to goals and desires of leaders" (Gemmill and Oakley 1992:124). It "re-visions" or reconceptualizes leadership as supportive and cooperative behaviors rather than imperrsonal and competitive behaviors. It redefines leadership as "people taking the initiative, carrying things through, having ideas and the imagination to get something started, and exhibiting particular skills in different areas" (Bunch and Fisher 1976 in Gemmill and Oakely 1992:124–125).

Democratic Groups *ALTERNATIVE*

As has been the case with other alternate or "new" perspectives, this alternative view of leadership has a great deal in common with what we historically have defined—although we have rarely practiced it—as democracy or democratic decision making. This reconceptualization also is more compatible with the core concerns of social work. It emphasizes several elements of what has been defined as **unitary democracy**—cooperation, common ground, relationship, and consensus (Gastil 1992:282).

Gastil (1992:278–301) defines small-group democracy and the decision-making processes that must take place in democratic groups. According to Gastil, **democratic groups** have power and they distribute that power among members equally. They are inclusive and their members are fully committed to democratic process. They are based on relationships among members that acknowledge their individuality while also recognizing mutual responsibilities as group members. Democratic groups operate through processes that ensure each member equal and adequate opportunities to speak and participate. These opportunities are coupled with a willingness on the part of members to listen to what others have to say. The element of listening is perhaps harder to ensure than that of guaranteeing the opportunity to speak. One is meaningless, however, unless the other is present. This decision-making process also protects a member's right to speak and be heard in dissent from a position taken by the group as well (Gastil 1992). Illustrative Reading 7.1 demonstrates the interplay of diversity, democracy, and the importance of dissent in democratic groups and processes.

Democratic Leadership/Followership

A definition of **democratic leadership** is "behavior that influences people in a manner consistent with and/or conducive to basic democratic principles and processes, such as self-determination, inclusiveness, equal participation, and deliberation" (Gastil 1994:956). Gastil specifies that "leadership is behavior, not position" (1994: 957). A democratic group is called a *demos*.

Three primary functions of democratic leadership behavior:

1. *Distributing responsibility:*
   - "Seeks to evoke maximum involvement and the participation of every member in the group activities and in the determination of objectives"
   - "Seeks to spread responsibility rather than to concentrate it" (Krech et al. in Gastil 1994:958)

2. *Empowerment:*
- Requires a politically competent membership skilled at speaking, thinking, organizing, and many more tasks
- Democratic leaders avoid behaviors associated with a "great man" [*sic*] model of leadership
- Democratic leaders show genuine care and concern for members without being paternalistic
- Democratic leaders seek to make members into leaders; seek to make themselves replaceable

3. *Aiding deliberation:*
- Through constructive participation, facilitation, and maintenance of healthy relationships and a positive emotional setting
- Through careful listening and respectful acknowledgment of others' views (Gastil 1994:958–961).

Facilitation.   Gastil (1994:961) differentiates the concept of facilitation from participation. **Facilitation**, according to Gastil, is a form of **metacommunication**, which is communication *about* the group's deliberation. Facilitation involves:

1. Keeping deliberation focused and on track

2. Encouraging free discussion and broad participation, sometimes needing to discourage verbosity and draw out shy or marginalized voices (at the community level this may mean outreach to isolated or marginalized groups who have not, but should have a voice in public debate)

3. Encouraging "members to observe the norms and laws that the demos has adopted"

4. Maintaining a healthy emotional setting, positive member relationships, and a "spirit of congeniality" (Gastil 1994: 961)

Distribution of Leadership.   Gastil stresses that democratic leadership should be distributed widely among the group members. He believes that diffusing leadership does not make a group "leaderless," instead it makes the group "leaderful." This "leaderful" or diffused leadership is reflected in the suggestions below:

- In the ideal demos, more than one person serves every leadership function, no individual does an inordinate amount of the leading, and every group member performs leadership functions some of the time
- In most cases it is possible to rotate leadership functions among the membership so that individual members become capable of serving a variety of leadership functions (Gastil 1994:962).

Follower Responsibilities.   The wide distribution of democratic leadership behaviors among all members requires significant follower responsibilities. **Followers:**

1. Must take responsibility for the well-being of the demos
2. Must be accountable for their actions and decisions
3. Are ultimately responsible for maintaining their autonomy (independence)
4. Recognize ways they can function as leaders
5. Must be willing to work with those leading (Gastil 1994:963-964).

When Is Democratic Leadership Not Appropriate?

This alternative approach to democratic leadership is not appropriate for all group settings. **Democratic leadership is not appropriate**

- When the problem is clearly defined and has an obvious technical solution, e.g., setting a broken bone
- When an "executive" or "judge" is needed to interpret a decision of the demos, but judge/executive must remain accountable to demos
- If group is indifferent to a problem
- When the problem is not within the jurisdiction of the group (Gastil 1994: 964–965).

Why Do People Reject Democratic Leadership?

- Because the democratic structure threatens their undemocratic authority. To move toward democracy would cost status, power, money.
- Some people have authoritarian values and have a strong belief in "the justness and efficiency of powerful, directive authorities."
- "Most people have, to some degree, an unconscious and conscious desire for a hero, a charismatic figure capable of solving our problems and sweeping away confusion."
- Some people reject the very notion of leadership and do not believe in the necessity of leaders (anarchic) (Gastil 1994:970).

This decision-making process is very different from traditional autocratic approaches to decision making based on hierarchical structures in which leaders have sufficient power and authority to impose their position and will on members. It is also quite different from traditional notions of democratic leadership styles of decision making in which only majority rule is emphasized. This model's emphasis on high degrees of participation and efforts to achieve consensus seeks decisions that respect the concerns and standpoints of all members. It does not suggest that every member will agree equally with every decision made by the group, but that every member will feel sufficiently heard to abide by the decision of the group. Such decision-making processes take considerably more time than traditional autocratic or simple majority rule processes, but both process and product are beneficiaries of the responsible participation and resources of all members rather than of a few in leadership positions (Gastil 1992).

Implementing alternative models of leadership, followership, and decision making is quite challenging and demands a great deal from group members. These models require a high degree of self-awareness on the part of all members. Members must be aware, for example, of limits on the group's time. Members must be as careful to ensure that others have time to speak and be heard as they are concerned with their own opportunities to speak and to be heard. Members are challenged through these processes to be as concerned with the collective good as they are with their individual well-being. These cooperative, collective, and highly participative processes are often very difficult to learn and to implement. This is especially the case for many of us who have been socialized into competitive, individualistic, and hierarchical structures and processes for group decision making.

While cooperative, collective, and participative leadership and decision-making processes seem at odds with the competitive, individualistic, and hierarchical leadership and decision-making approaches consistent with the dominant paradigm, alternative approaches have a long history of use by many Native American tribes in North America. Attneave reminds us that for many of these tribes:

> *Tribal histories never suggested the impatient solution of majority vote so revered by "democracies." If a sizable portion of the band, tribe, or village dissented, discussion continued until some compromise could be reached. Except when asked specifically to do so, no one spoke for anyone else, and each was expected to participate. Discussions could last for hours, even days, until all were heard and a group decision was reached.* (Attneave in McGoldrick, Pearce, and Giordano 1982:66–67)

Attneave (1982:67) notes that even today the influence of the old alternative approaches can be seen and that "tribal meetings still last for hours, and tensions can be high as one faction seeks consensus while another pushes for a majority vote." This is an indication of the challenges to be faced when alternative perspectives and traditional ones meet.

Roles and Norms

Other basic concepts that help us to understand human behavior in the context of groups include roles and norms. **Roles** are expectations about what is appropriate behavior for persons in particular positions. Roles may be formally assigned, such as president or recorder, or they may be informal and based on the interests and skills of individuals such as harmonizer (someone the group looks to to keep the peace) or summarizer (someone skilled in restating the key elements from a discussion).

As members of groups we play multiple roles, depending on the current needs and demands of the group. Sometimes our multiple roles tend to contradict each other. When we find ourselves in this situation we are experiencing role conflict. **Role conflict** "refers to the disparity which an individual experiences among competing roles" (Brown 1991:75). We are likely to experience role conflict, for example, if we are assigned by our agency administrator to facilitate a group and we attempt to play roles to facilitate a functional, democratic, and consensus-oriented leadership style, but we are given a very short time to accomplish the goal set for the group by the administrator. We experience a conflict between the demand of the alternate roles required to be a consensus builder and the traditional and more time-saving leadership roles based on majority rule or even autocratic leadership.

Such conflicts are often not easily resolved. In most instances resolution requires a compromise between what we would prefer ideally and what is possible practically. For example, if there is insufficient time to reach complete consensus, we can still emphasize the need for everyone to participate in discussions and decision making to the maximum extent possible. We can also look to the other group members for ways to make the process as participative as possible, given the time constraints, rather than shifting entirely to an autocratic approach.

Norms are the "group's common beliefs regarding appropriate behavior for members." Norms guide group members' behaviors in their interactions with each other (Johnson and Johnson 1991:16–17). They help members know what to expect of others and what is expected of them. Roles and norms are important concepts for understanding both traditional and alternate perspectives on groups. The specific nature of the roles and norms that structure a group may serve either to maintain power inequality and restrict diversity or they may serve to guide groups to ensure that power is shared equally and that diversity is sought and respected. Norms for a specific group emerge over time and must be learned by new members entering the group. This process of learning the norms of the group is referred to as socialization. We have discussed socialization processes previously in the context of individual development and as a process through which families transmit to their children the values and rules of behavior of the family and the society in which the family lives.

Conformity and Deviance in Groups

Two factors related to roles and norms important to consider in groups, both as a leader or facilitator and as a group member, are the concepts of conformity and deviance in groups. **Conformity** refers to "bringing one's behavior into alignment with a group's expectations" (Sabini 1995:A3). **Deviance** is defined as violation of "norms or rules of behavior" (Curran and Renzetti 1996:10). We will explore these concepts by looking more at the related concepts of idiosyncrasy credit, groupthink, and risky shift.

Idiosyncrasy Credit

Hollander defines **idiosyncrasy credit** as "the potential for individuals to behaviorally deviate from group norms without being sanctioned," and also as the " 'positively disposed impressions' a person acquires as a member of a group" (in Estrada et al. 1995: 57). Idiosyncrasy credit or the ability to deviate from group norms without negative sanction from other group members can be gained in a number of ways. It can be gained by importing it from external sources (you secure outside funding for your group to reach its goals); by being assigned a high-status role within the group (your status as group chair); by displaying competence (your negotiating skills allowed you to settle a troubling conflict within the group); by conforming to group norms (you almost always adhere to group norms, so you are occasionally allowed to

1 - You use outside sources to further the group's goals
2 - You are promoted w/in the group
3 - By displaying competence
4 - You usually conform to group norms → they trust you'll do it again
5 - The group trusts your deviance will be good for the group

violate a norm, with the group trusting that based on your history you will return to adhering to the norms); or by being group-oriented in your motivation (the group trusts that your deviance will be good for the group because you have in the past worked for the good of the group). Hollander noted that there are limits to the extent and use of idiosyncrasy credits that group members will allow. Hollander posited that "members will only allow them to act differently in a manner that is consistent with their high-status roles" (in Estrada et al. 1995:58–59).

Groupthink

The concept of idiosyncrasy credit is an example of groups allowing members to deviate from their norms or rules. Group researchers have also noted the power of groups to press members to conform to group decisions, even when the group's decision may not be the best possible decision. Neck and Manz note that "excessive emphasis on group cohesiveness and conformity can interfere with effective thinking processes" (1994: 933). Janus (1982) called this phenomenon *groupthink*. **Groupthink** is "a mode of thinking that people engage in when they are deeply involved in a cohesive in-group, when the members' striving for unanimity override their motivation to realistically appraise alternative courses of action . . . a deterioration of mental efficiency, reality testing, and moral judgment that results from in-group pressures" (Janus 1982:9).

Neck and Manz note that "groups exert enormous pressures on their members to conform to the norms established by the group social system." They suggest that these pressures can be either negative or positive depending on the nature of conformity being pressured (1994:944). Groupthink is a term used to indicate when the outcome of pressure to conform resulted in a decision by the group that had a negative outcome. A number of researchers have explored the conditions that lead to groupthink as well as ways to prevent groupthink. Symptoms of groupthink include:

1. Direct social pressure placed on a member who argues against the group's shared beliefs

2. Members' self-censorship of their own thoughts or concerns that deviate from the group consensus

3. An illusion of the groups' invulnerability to failure

4. A shared illusion of unanimity

5. The emergence of self-appointed mind guards that screen out adverse information from outside the group

6. Collective efforts to rationalize

7. Stereotyped views of enemy leaders as weak or incompetent

8. An unquestioned belief in the group's inherent morality (Neck and Manz 1994:932–933).

Neck and Manz (1994:933) also point out that groupthink can result from faulty decision-making processes within the group. *Decision-making defects* include:

1. Incomplete survey of alternatives
2. Incomplete survey of objectives
3. Failure to examine the risks of the preferred choice
4. Failure to reappraise initially rejected alternatives
5. Poor information search
6. Selective bias in processing information at hand
7. Failure to work out contingency plans

Some tendencies toward groupthink also come about as a result of what Neck and Moorhead (1995:550) refer to as a **closed leader style.** *Closed leader style:*

1. Does not encourage member participation
2. Does state his/her opinions at the beginning of the meeting
3. Does not encourage divergent opinions from all group members
4. Does not emphasize the importance of reaching a wise decision

Teamthink and Avoiding Groupthink. If we are aware of the symptoms and the faulty decision-making processes that lead to groupthink, we can work to avoid it in our work in groups. Neck and Manz (1994:940) suggest the concept of **teamthink** as an alternative to groupthink and as a way to prevent groupthink from occurring. *Teamthink* includes:

1. Encouragement of divergent views
2. Open expression of concerns/ideas
3. Awareness of limitations/threats
4. Recognition of member's uniqueness
5. Discussion of collective doubts.

Other mechanisms for avoiding groupthink included using **methodical decision-making procedures** to "ensure that the group adheres to a highly structured and systematic decision-making process . . . [and make groupthink less likely] by promoting constructive criticism, nonconformity, and open-mindedness within the decision-making group" (Neck and Moorhead 1995:549). Miranda suggests that the effective use and management of **conflict** in a group can help prevent groupthink: "Productive conflict leads to group satisfaction with outcomes and a perception that the conflict has been useful. Productive conflict also leads to an improved group climate and greater group cohesion and is likely to enhance the quality of the group's decision" (1994:124).

Janus (1982:262–271) makes a number of suggestions for avoiding groupthink. They include:

1. Assignment of role of critical evaluator to each member
2. Leader impartiality in setting goals and directions for group

3. Setting up of several independent policy-planning and evaluation groups to work on the same problem

4. Periodic division into separate outside groups and reconvening to work out differences

5. Member discussion and deliberations outside the group with trusted colleagues and reporting back of their findings (This suggestion does not apply to groups with a norm of confidentiality within the group.)

6. Invitation of one or more outside experts (non-core group members) to each meeting

7. Assignment of one member to the role of devil's advocate at each meeting

8. Spending time attending to interrelationships among group members

9. After consensus is reached, holding a "second chance" meeting to express doubts and rethink as necessary.

While groups are usually expected to render decisions more conservative than those that might be made by individuals, some researchers (Stoner 1961; Brown 1965, 1974 in Sabini 1995:34–36) have noted the concept of the risky shift. The concept of **risky shift** refers to group decisions that shift toward higher risk as a result of risk-taking being valued by a culture. While the phenomenon of risky shift does occur, conservative shifts are also possible depending on the make-up of the group and the nature of the discussion in the group leading up to a decision.

Individual and Group Dimensions

Traditionally, some researchers have directed their interest toward the individuals who constitute groups, while others have concentrated on the group as an entity in itself, separate in many ways from the individuals who make it up (Johnson and Johnson 1991:15; Worchel, Wood, and Simpson 1992:2). Alternative perspectives on groups suggest that we must recognize the importance of groups both for the individuals who make them up and the group as a whole entity.

Process and outcome, goals and purposes, and levels of membership may all look very different, depending on whether one is looking at the dimension from the perspective of the individual group member or from that of the group as whole. Much of what must happen in a group involves striking a balance between what is best for the individuals who make up the group and what is best for the group as a whole. At all levels groups must struggle to achieve an optimum balance between meeting the individual needs of the members and the needs of the group as an entity.

As social workers who will be responsible for facilitating and practicing in groups, we must recognize the need to help blend the goals of individual members with the purposes of the group in such a way that one does not constrain the other but actually complements the other. All the concepts and dimensions of groups we have explored thus far must be considered in our efforts to help individual members and the group as a whole to accomplish their goals. We must recognize that whether a group's goals are set internally or externally and whether its membership is voluntary or invol-

untary will influence whether the individuals who constitute the group can come together as a group and operate as a unit. A group in order to be a group must create a
bond among its members, often referred to as cohesiveness. This is a complex and difficult task that cannot be accomplished without the support of group members.

As we discussed in our examination of membership, individuals come to groups
with a range of levels of commitment and investment in the group. Individuals come
to groups with their own goals for being there. For involuntary members, the goal
may be simply to put up with and put into the group enough to survive until they
can leave. For voluntary, full psychological members the individual goal may be to do
whatever is necessary to see the group's purposes fulfilled. Their individual goal may
be virtually the same as the group's goal. This is of course more likely if the members
feel they have been a part of fashioning the group's goal and if they can therefore see
themselves and their individual goals reflected in the group's goal. Alternative perspectives on groups that place a premium on process and participation, cooperation,
consensus decision making, shared or functional leadership tend to be more able to
blend individual and group interests and needs.

Agendas

Achieving a balance between the needs of the individual and those of group, however,
cannot be achieved effectively unless members feel able to state and make known to
other members their own goals, interests, and reasons for participating in the group.
This process is sometimes referred to as agenda setting in groups. If individuals are able
to voice their individual agendas for the group, the members can then work to effectively blend members' individual agendas with the purposes or goals of the group to
create more integrated **surface agendas**. When agendas are not brought to the surface in this manner they are referred to as **hidden agendas.** You have probably heard
this term in reference to groups with which you have been associated. One member
may suggest to another (usually outside the context of the group meeting) that one of
the other members has a hidden agenda. What they really mean is that that member
has individual goals he or she wishes to achieve through the group that have not been
brought to the surface and shared with the other members of the group. A hidden
agenda is not necessarily damaging to the group, but hidden agendas often create difficulties for groups. They are often sources of confusion and interfere with group
progress in setting and moving toward shared group goals. On the other hand, if a
member has an unspoken individual goal that he or she wishes to achieve through the
group that is not contrary to the goals of the group, it need not be problematic. For
example, in the men's group we discussed earlier, if a member has as an individual and
unspoken goal, improving his ability to use what he learns in the group to help him
socialize his young son to behave in nonsexist ways, this hidden agenda will not likely
interfere with the group's overall goal of reducing its members' sexist behaviors.

Just as individual and group goals must be blended and can become problematic
if they conflict, roles played by members in groups may serve to advance the interests
and needs of the group or they may serve to further individual interests and needs and
conflict with the well-being of the group. Napier and Gershenfeld (1985:238–244)
discuss individual and group roles in their discussion of leadership behavior in groups.

They suggest that any member may exercise leadership by assuming roles conducive to the group's accomplishment of its tasks. They differentiate between group task (or product) and group maintenance (or process) focused roles. They also suggest that roles that serve the individual's interests over those of the group tend to create problems in the group's functioning.

Napier and Gershenfeld list a number of task- or product-oriented roles that serve to help the group select and move toward common outcomes. The **initiator** gets the ball rolling by proposing tasks or goals to the group. The **information** or **opinion seeker** requests facts and seeks relevant information about a group concern. The **information** or **opinion giver** offers information about group concerns. The **clarifier** or **elaborator** interprets and reflects back to the group ideas and suggestions to clear up confusion and offer alternatives. The **summarizer** pulls together related ideas and restates the suggestion after the group has discussed them and offers a decision or conclusion for the group to accept or reject. The **consensus tester** checks with the group periodically to see how much agreement there is to find out how close the group is to reaching a consensus. The product-oriented roles can be found to differing degrees in different groups. Not all groups are characterized by all of these roles (1985:238–244).

Group-Focused Roles

Group maintenance, process, or socioemotional roles that help the group move forward as a group are also suggested by Napier and Gershenfeld (1985). The **encourager** demonstrates warmth, friendliness, and responsiveness to others and gives recognition and opportunities for others to contribute to group efforts. The **expressor of group feelings** attempts to feed back to the group his or her sense of the mood or affective climate of the group. The **harmonizer** attempts to reconcile differences and reduce tensions by helping group members to explore their differences. The **compromiser** is willing to try to reconcile their differences. The **gatekeeper** attempts to keep channels of communication open by helping to bring all members into participation to help the group solve its problems. The **standard setter** suggests standards for the group to use and tests group efforts against the standards of the group. It is important to restate here that these different roles do not necessarily represent separate members of groups (Napier and Gershenfeld 1985:239–244, 279–280). Our functional definition of leadership implies that different members of the group demonstrate or play these roles at different times depending on the needs of the group and its individual members. As in the case with product-oriented roles, not all groups display all of these process-oriented roles.

Individual-Focused Roles

Individual roles represent sets of behaviors that serve the needs of individuals, often at the expense of the well-being of the group. Individuals playing these roles are concerned with meeting their own needs and interests. Napier and Gershenfeld (1985: 241–242) suggest several individual roles that interfere with a group's ability to reach its goals. The **aggressor** tends to attack and belittle the positions and contributions of others, often sarcastically. The **blocker** suggests why a suggestion will not work and why his or her position is the only one worthy of attention. The **self-confessor** uses the other group members to ventilate about personal problems and to seek sympathy. The **recognition seeker** offers his or her personal response to a problem as exemplary of what should be done in the current group situation. The **dominator** attempts to take over the proceedings of the group by interrupting others, by flattering other members, or by asserting his or her superior status. The **cynic-humorist** uses double-edged humor to remind the group of the pointless nature of its efforts. The **special interest pleader** attempts to sway the group to his or her individual preference by suggesting that his or her position is representative of an entire group of similarly minded people outside the confines of the group.

It is important to recognize that some of the behaviors associated with individual roles described above are not inherently harmful to the group's efforts. Certainly at times confrontation, conflict, discussion of personal problems, comparing a current group predicament to similar past individual experiences, humor, and reminding group members of the interests of persons outside the immediate group can be quite helpful to groups. These roles and their associated behaviors become harmful only when they are played at the expense of the good of the group and serve to help individuals gain power over the group for their individual interests and needs.

Stage Theories and Models

Johnson and Johnson (1991:19) note that there are many different approaches that incorporate the notions of stages or phases through which groups pass. These approaches, they suggest, can be divided into two types. "*Sequential-stage theories* specify the 'typical' order of the phases of group development" and "*recurring-phase theories* specify the issues that dominate group interaction which reoccur again and again" (Johnson and Johnson 1991:19). Sequential theories are more prescribed and less flexible approaches to the study of groups. They are more consistent with traditional paradigm thinking. Recurring-phase theories are more emergent and fluid and are more compatible with alternative notions of groups.

Hare (1994:441) addresses the diversity of opinions about groups evolving through a series of predictable phases or stages. "Even when phases can be identified, group members may need to recycle through the initial phases several times before they are ready to deal with the task at hand" (Hare 1994:441).

Sequential-Stage Theories

Traditional notions of group life have much in common with traditional notions of individual development. This is especially the case in their conceptualization of groups as a relatively fixed sequence of stages, each of which the group must pass through in a fixed order as it develops and pursues its purposes or goals. There are a number of different models of groups based on sequential-stage theories.

A common sequential-stage model of groups is that of Tuckman and Jensen (1977 in Napier and Gershenfeld 1985:467; Johnson and Johnson 1991:395). They based their model on an extensive review of the literature on group development. This model includes five stages referred to as forming, storming, norming, performing, and adjourning.

1. *Forming* is a stage of uncertainty and some discomfort as new group members come together for the first time in a new situation.

2. *Storming* occurs as group members raise questions and display resistance to the demands of the group. This is a period of conflict and rebellion.

3. *Norming* is the group's establishment of mechanisms for resolving conflict, working together as a group, and accomplishing the group purpose. Order is established.

4. *Performing* is the actual carrying out on the part of the group and its members of the tasks necessary to accomplish its purpose.

5. *Adjourning* is the termination phase of the group. It occurs as the task is completed and the group members make preparations to end their work together.

Another sequential stage model posits seven stages through which groups pass during their development (Johnson and Johnson 1991:395):

1. *defining and structuring procedures and becoming oriented;*
2. *conforming to procedures and getting acquainted;*
3. *recognizing mutuality and building trust;*
4. *rebelling and differentiating;*
5. *committing to and taking ownership for the goals, procedures, and other members;*
6. *functioning maturely and productively; and*
7. *terminating.*

Brown (1991:69–74) synthesizes the work of a number of researchers on small groups, including a number of social work researchers (Garland, Jones, and Kolodny 1973; Hartford 1971; Sarri and Galinsky 1985 in Brown 1991). His model also incorporates some aspects of the Tuckman and Jensen model outlined above. Brown's synthesis is summarized below:

1. *Origin Stage:* This is also referred to by some as a pregroup stage. This stage occurs as an idea for a group, and the sharing of that idea with others is transformed into the decision to create a group.

2. *Formation:* This phase includes people's feeling of uncertainty upon entering a group situation. This phase recognizes that people bring to a new group their past experiences—both positive and negative—with groups.

3. *Power and control:* Differences and conflicts emerge during this stage as people struggle to maintain their personal interests and values at the same time that they are asked to submit to the needs and purposes of the group. An informal structure begins to form, with members taking a variety of task and maintenance or socioemotional roles.

4. *Intimacy:* This stage occurs when the socioemotional climate of the group is able to incorporate the differences in personality and experiences of the members. Norms or accepted patterns of behavior begin to take shape. Also, an informal status hierarchy may emerge as people demonstrate leadership behavior that assists the group in achieving its purposes.

5. *Maturation:* Not all groups progress to this stage because of their inability to negotiate the differences necessary to problem-solve or because of insufficient time within which to accomplish the necessary tasks. Groups that reach this stage experience a balance of socioemotional and task activities. They are able to effectively attend both to the product and process dimensions of the group in order to get the work of the group done. People feel able to express their differences and have them respected. At this stage conflict is likely to occur, but it is not counterproductive to the group's continuance as it was in the power and control phase. There is a high degree of cohesiveness or feelings of connectedness to each other on the parts of group members.

6. *Separation:* This is the termination or ending phase. This phase may not be experienced by all groups or it may not be experienced by all group members at the same time in any final sense. Separation occurs most noticeably in time-limited groups that meet for a specified purpose or purposes and then disband. In groups that are not time limited, but are ongoing, members come and go in a more fluid way. Separation may be occurring for some members at the same time that other members are newly joining the group in such open-ended groups. Ambivalence characterizes the group or members undergoing termination.

Recurring-Stage Alternatives

Many alternative notions of groups accept that groups tend to develop in stages. However, alternative perspectives place much more emphasis on circular or looping patterns within the overall framework of stages or phases. Alternative perspectives are less linear than traditional notions and they are more multidimensional. They accept and even expect that developmental stages are subject to recurrence throughout the life of a group.

Recurring-stage perspectives accept that change and movement are ongoing and necessary in groups. These alternative approaches, however, accept that often for groups to progress they must return to previous stages and revisit past issues. Going forward often means going backward. Conflict may recur periodically in the group's development, for example. Changes in the larger environment may cause the group to change its goals or its membership. These external changes may in turn cause the group to return to internal issues of origin, or conflict. External changes may also cause the group to jump ahead to consider termination or separation issues.

Both external and internal changes make it necessary for a group to revisit previous phases or to jump ahead nonsequentially to new stages. These many uncertainties are part of the reality of change that groups must face and they raise important questions about the reliability of a traditional, linear, fixed-stage perspective on groups. They suggest that an alternate recurring-phase perspective might be more appropriate.

Social Systems/Ecological Perspectives

Social systems or ecological perspectives on groups offer another often used alternative approach to groups. As we discussed in Chapter 3, social workers have found social systems or ecological perspectives helpful frameworks for incorporating some of the important social and environmental influences on human behavior. A systems framework is helpful in our attempts to understand group behavior more completely for this same reason. It recognizes the dynamic nature of groups and the interrelatedness of the larger environment, the group itself, and the members of the group.

Small groups can be viewed as social systems (Anderson and Carter 1990; Brown 1991). In doing so we are able to take advantage of the emphasis in social systems thinking on recognizing the interrelatedness and mutual influence of one entity, in this case the small group, with entities or systems in the larger environment. Systems thinking also allows us to look inside the system of concern or focal system, the small group in this context, to see the interrelatedness and mutual influences of the component parts or subsystems on one another. This is especially helpful in thinking about small groups because it provides us a framework within which to place a number of things we have been learning during this part of our journey toward more comprehensive understanding of HBSE.

For example, a social systems framework allows us to fit the personal and historical experiences gained by group members in their interactions with the larger environment prior to joining a group with the impact of these experiences on the person's perceptions and behaviors inside the group. The impact of racism or sexism that a member experiences outside the group is very likely to influence the behavior of the member inside the group. A systems approach also recognizes the influence of events that occur in the larger environment or suprasystem during the life of a group on the behavior of the group. If cutbacks in agency funding cause the layoff of one or more members of the task force seeking funds to create services for people who are HIV positive and people with AIDS, that small group will be forced to respond in some way. Reducing the scope of its goals, reorganizing responsibilities or tasks within the group, spending time processing the confusion and disruption caused by the change in membership, or perhaps even terminating for lack of sufficient human resources to continue its work are all possible responses within the group to the change occurring in the environment external to the group. This environmental change in turn has a major impact on the subsystems or component parts of the task force. Some individuals not only must leave the group, but they are now out of work entirely. Other members are faced with additional work and attendant stress as a result of the loss of other members.

Other concepts from systems thinking can also help us to understand small groups. The concept of *holon* (Anderson and Carter 1990) appropriately applies to small groups. It defines a critical characteristic of systems as being both a whole and a part at the same time. Certainly our task force on AIDS/HIV and our men's group can be seen as simultaneously whole entities and parts of other systems—agencies, communities, professions. Energy and linkage (Anderson and Carter 1990) are other helpful concepts in thinking about small groups. Energy, defined as the "capacity for action," (Anderson and Carter 1990) aptly describes the potential for groups to act and move to solve problems and to develop. Linkage or the ability to connect with other systems to exchange or transfer energy is another helpful way of understanding how small groups do their work. The subsystems, the individual members, of small groups connect with each other and exchange energy as they attempt to define issues, acquire resources, and bring about desired changes. At the same time small groups link with systems in the larger environment to exchange energy. The very goal of the AIDS/HIV task force was to link with other systems external to it in order to acquire funding. The purpose of the men's group was to allow group members to more effectively link or interact with women in the larger environment in nonsexist and nonexploitative ways.

Anderson and Carter (1990) also describe organization as an essential characteristic of social systems. *Organization* is the ability of a system to put its parts together into a working whole. Certainly the characteristics of leadership, followership, membership, and roles and norms all reflect the efforts of small groups to organize or structure themselves to achieve their goals.

Traditional perspectives on small groups and alternate approaches when considered together offer us a great deal of information from which to choose as we attempt to facilitate and be members of groups. In addition to these perspectives, it is essential that issues of diversity and oppression be considered in conjunction with any perspective or framework for understanding human behavior in a group environment.

Diversity, Oppression, and Groups

Groups: Oppression and Social and Economic Justice

Understanding group behavior in the social environment requires serious attention to issues of diversity. Successful group membership or group facilitation requires knowledge of and respect for the differences that we and other group members bring to the group. Groups also can be effective contexts for addressing oppression.

Garvin (in Sundel, Glasser, Sarri, and Vinter 1985:461ff) suggests a number of group formats that might be helpful in efforts to empower oppressed people. Groups can be appropriate for addressing needs of members of such diverse groups as gay men and lesbians, elderly persons, persons with disabilities including persons with mental illnesses, and persons living in poverty. The history of social work with groups has its origins in social reform and the settlement house movement (see historical perspective section above). This history reflects the potential for social work in group contexts to address the needs of oppressed persons.

Garvin describes a number of group formats for use in working with oppressed persons. These formats illustrate more generally the kinds of groups social workers use in their work. We have mentioned some of these group types previously. They include:

1. *Consciousness-raising groups.* Time limited groups that help members share their experiences and explore their feelings about their oppressed status. These groups also help members explore possible avenues to empowerment.

2. *Treatment groups.* Groups that attempt to modify dysfunctional behaviors, thinking, and feelings. For example, a treatment group for gay men might assist the members to deal with feelings of depression and low self-esteem that can result from harassment and other forms of discrimination. It is essential that the group facilitator have a positive perspective on gay and lesbian sexual orientation. This reinforces again the need for social workers to be self-aware and to address our own tendencies toward homophobia (fear of homosexuality).

3. *Social action groups.* Groups directed to bringing changes in the larger environment in order to reduce oppression. Such groups can also teach members valuable skills in working with others and can help members increase their self-esteem.

How might the groups in this photo reflect some of the issues and concerns discussed in the text section "Groups and People of Color?" Which of the 5 types of group formats useful for working with oppressed persons (described by Garvin) might be represented in this photo?

4. *Network and support groups.* These groups can assist members in reducing feelings of social isolation and in recognizing their strengths by helping members to connect with others in similar situations to provide mutual support and to seek resources.

5. *Skill groups.* These groups have as goals development of members' empowerment skills. Empowerment skills learned and practiced in these groups might include group leadership, social change, communication, and networking (Garvin in Sundel, Glasser, Sarri, and Vinter 1985:466–467).

Groups and People of Color

Davis (1985) outlines a number of important considerations both for persons of color and white persons as group members and as facilitators. Davis (1985:325) stresses that issues of color affect all group contexts and perspectives. He urges that "those practitioners who believe their particular group work orientation transcends race and culture would perhaps do best by minorities to refrain from working with them" because race and culture are such powerful forces in this society.

Davis outlines a number of areas related to group dynamics in which race or color plays an important part. These areas include:

1. *Group composition.* Should groups be racially homogeneous or heterogeneous? The purpose of the group should be considered carefully in answering this question. Traditionally, groups purposefully composed of racially similar persons have been formed to enhance ethnic identity. Groups composed of people of different racial and ethnic backgrounds have often been formed to reduce racial prejudice. Davis suggests that a more complex question of racial composition is raised when race is unrelated to the group's purpose. Preferences of group members vary markedly by color. African Americans have been found to prefer group composition to be approximately half white and half nonwhite. Whites appear to prefer African Americans to compose no more than 20 percent of the members. These findings suggest that for African Americans it is important to feel, in the context of the small group, that they are not in the minority. Whites, on the other hand, appear to be threatened when they are not in the majority. Davis (1985:328–332) suggests that because neither minority persons of color nor majority whites prefer to be in a minority, workers should attempt racial balance in group composition.

Racial balance will also help avoid tokenism in group composition. **Tokenism** is the practice of giving the appearance of representation and access to resources or decision making without actually doing so. For example, one low-income-neighborhood person is placed on a task force to decide whether a potentially lucrative convention center project should be allowed to displace residents of the low-income neighborhood. All the other task force members are wealthy business executives and land developers who are likely to benefit financially from the project. While the task force composition might give the appearance that the neighborhood is represented, it is highly unlikely that the neighborhood person will be able to counter the interests of the other members. The low-income-neighborhood resident is a token (Davis 1985:328–332).

2. *Culture and communication.* It is important to recognize that cultural communication styles are important influences in any group. Davis illustrates the contrast between the high value placed on restraint and humility by Asian culture and the value placed on confrontation as a means of testing the validity of one's point of views by many African Americans. Davis suggests that such differences do not mean that different cultures should avoid being mixed in small groups, but that these differences must be taken into account in group process (1985:332).

3. *Trust.* Issues of trust among members and between members and facilitators must receive special attention when dealing with groups composed of whites and persons of color. Experiences brought to the group from the external environment often result in persons of color hesitating to disclose information about themselves to whites out of feelings of distrust based on discriminatory treatment by whites in the larger society. Persons of color also assume, often justifiably so, that white persons know so little about them because of segregation in society that whites have little of value to offer in understanding or solving their problems. On the other hand, whites often are unwilling to accept or trust that minority persons of color, even when in the position of expert, have anything of value to offer (Davis 1985:332–334).

4. *Status and roles.* Groups composed of persons of color and of whites must attend carefully to issues of status and roles in the group. There is often a tendency to attach statuses and roles within groups according to the patterns of minority/majority relations in the larger society. This is especially problematic when white group members are unaware of changes in status in the larger society of many persons of color who have overcome obstacles and barriers to attain statuses and roles equal to those of whites (Davis 1985:334).

Diversity and Creativity in Groups

[handwritten margin note: POSITIVES & NEGATIVES TO DIVERSITY IN GROUPS]

Concerns are often raised about the difficulties and problems that flow from diverse groups, especially racially mixed groups. McLeod et al. remind us, to the contrary, that the theme of "'value-in-diversity,' rests on a hypothesis that ethnic diversity, at least when properly managed, produces tangible, positive effects on organizational outcomes" (1996:249). In the corporate context for example, scholars "suggest that ethnic diversity may be related to increased organizational creativity and flexibility . . . [and] that the insights and sensitivities brought by people from varying ethnic backgrounds may help companies to reach a wider variety of markets" (McLeod et al. 1996:249).

A key argument underlying the notion of diversity as a positive factor in small groups "is that the variety of perspectives and experiences represented on heterogeneous teams contributes to the production of high-quality ideas. Moreover, the variety in perspectives can stimulate further idea production by group members" (McLeod et al. 1996:250). In other words, diversity in perspectives and thought processes results in increased creativity in problem solving in groups. McLeod et al. note that Kanter refers to this as **kaleidoscope thinking,** "twisting reality into new patterns and rearranging the pieces to create a new reality. . . . Having contact with people from a variety of perspectives is one condition necessary for kaleidoscope thinking" (1996:250).

The conflict that may emerge in groups as a result of member diversity may also be an asset. Nemeth, for example, suggests that "minority dissent appears to stimulate exactly what theorists have recommended for improved performance and decision making, that is, a consideration of the issue from multiple perspectives" (in McLeod et al. 1996:250).

However, there is relatively little empirical research testing this "value-in-diversity" hypothesis and some research suggests advantages of homogeneous groups. For example, Watson, Kumar, Michaelsen found that "during the early stages of group development, ethnically homogeneous groups perform better than heterogeneous groups" (in McLeod et al. 1996:249). McLeod et al. conducted research using ethnically diverse groups of graduate and undergraduate students from a large midwestern university. [Note: Using your skills at paradigm analysis, deconstruction, and critical thinking, what might be the limitations of this research?] McLeod et al.'s hypothesis was: "Ethnically diverse groups will produce higher quality ideas than will all-Anglo groups." Their "preliminary analyses showed that the ideas produced by the groups with four ethnic groups represented were judged significantly more feasible than the ideas produced by the groups with three ethnic groups represented and by the all-Anglo groups. . . . The ideas produced by the heterogeneous groups were judged as significantly more feasible . . . and more effective . . . than the ideas produced by the homogeneous groups." However, "the members of homogeneous groups reported marginally significantly higher levels of interpersonal attraction than did members of heterogeneous groups" (1996:252–258).

McLeod et al. concluded that their findings supported the hypothesis "that diverse groups will have a performance advantage over homogeneous groups on a creativity task requiring knowledge of different cultures. On the other hand, . . . [they] also found evidence suggesting that members of heterogeneous groups may have had more negative affective reactions to their groups than did members of homogeneous groups" (1996:257).

The researchers in this study suggest therefore that diversity in groups is complex and that both increased numbers (quantity) of diverse members and quality of the interaction among members or "proper management of diversity" are equally important in reaping the potential benefits of an increasingly diverse workforce (McLeod et al. 1996:260–261).

Practice Implications of Diversity in Groups

Davis et al. stress that "race is such an emotionally charged area of practice that leaders may fail to identify and deal with racial issues because they wish to avoid racial confrontations, are anxious, or perhaps are unsure about how to proceed" (1996:77). Davis et al. stress that the "color blind" approach that says race is transcended when different people come together in a group for a common purpose denies the significance of race (1996:78). These scholars point out, instead, that "whenever people of different races come together in groups, leaders can assume that race is an issue, but not necessarily a problem" (Davis et al. 1996:77). However, due to the history of race relations, individuals' perceptions of racial difference, and issues in the larger environment race can be a significant source of tension in these groups. Both leaders and members need to be prepared to understand and address racial tensions in racially mixed groups.

Davis et al. (1996:83) suggest there are three basic sources of racial tension within racially mixed groups of people of color and white people. These sources of tension are from:

1. Within individual group members
2. The nature of the group itself
3. The environment of the group

In order to deal with racial tensions, Davis et al. (1996:83–84) suggest the leader needs "trifocal" vision. This trifocal vision requires leaders to:

1. *Consider issues related to individuals such as:*
   - Have general knowledge of how different populations tend to view power, authority, status, interpersonal boundaries, typical cultural and family expectations, but must be careful not to overgeneralize in these areas
   - Be sensitive to the specific racial makeup of the group and the number of persons from each group: unequal numbers can lead to subgrouping and domination by members of one group; equal numbers may not be perceived as balanced on the part of group members used to being a majority (e.g., whites).

2. *Consider issues related to the group itself such as:*
- Group purpose and goals, especially if different members from different races have different expectations of focus or purpose
- Norms that promote recognition and respect for differences, member equality, and open discussion of racial issues can help prevent members from being cautious, mistrustful, and guarded.

3. *Consider issues related to the larger environment such as:*
- Climate of society
- Events in the members' neighborhoods
- The sponsoring organization's reputation for responsiveness to racial concerns
- The way member's significant others view the group.

Within racially mixed groups, according to Davis et al. (1996:85), problems concerning racial issues can occur at three levels:

1. *Between members and leaders:* If the leader is the only representative of a particular race, he/she can feel isolated; leaders can be insensitive; members can doubt the leader's ability due to race; leaders who are people of color may find their competence challenged by whites and members of other races.

2. *Between members:* Racist behaviors/comments leading to verbal or physical attacks; subgroup formation by race to dominate; members who avoid discussing sensitive topics; members don't participate because they feel isolated or under attack because of their race.

3. *Between member and environment:* Institutional racism in community and society; member's reluctance to attend meetings in unfamiliar territory; sponsoring organizations perceived as unresponsive.

Groups and Gender

Just as the patterns of interaction and treatment in larger society impact on small-group dynamics around issues of race and color, group behavior is influenced powerfully by issues related to gender. Social workers must respect and understand the impact of gender on group dynamics. Rosabeth Moss Kanter has studied the interactions of males and females in small group and organizational contexts extensively.

Kanter has found evidence that "the presence of both men and women in the same group heightens tension and may put women at a disadvantage" (1977:372). She also suggests that power and status differentials between men and women in society tend to be replicated in small mixed-gender groups. Since "males have generally higher status and power in American society than females . . . when men and women are ostensible peers, the male's external status may give him an advantage inside the group. . . . In mixed groups of 'peers' men and women may not, in fact, be equal, especially if their external statuses are discrepant" (1977:373).

Kanter also describes differential impacts of gender in leadership of work groups. Kanter (1977:374) suggests that "even if women have formal authority, they may not necessarily be able to exercise it over reluctant subordinates." She cites the example of a case in which a woman "had formal leadership of a group of men, but the men did not accept this, reporting informally to her male superior."

Kanter suggests a number of strategies for reducing the inequalities and difficulties faced by women in mixed-gender work groups. She suggests that the most important means of addressing this problem is to "change the sex ratio in the power structure of organizations, to put more women in positions of visible leadership" (1977:381). She notes that even if this "simple" solution were possible, real change is a more complex matter. She describes the norms of human relations training, a small-group approach often used to improve the ability of people to work together in small groups.

> *Human relations training (for example, running sensitivity workshops) is not an effective strategy by itself. The norms of human relations workshops are particularly suited for helping men develop new behavioral repertoires and self-insights counterbalancing the stereotypical tendencies of the male role. Where the male role stresses instrumental leadership, a task and power orientation, a humanistic approach emphasizes learning the expression of feelings; where the male role stresses analytic and intellectual reasoning, human relations emphasize learning to pay attention to emotions; where the male role stresses an identity based on achievement with respect to tasks, human relations norms emphasize learning to receive and be influenced by feedback from others; where the male role stresses aggression and competition, human relations norms emphasize learning to behave cooperatively.* (1977:381)

These norms are already a stereotypical part of the female role, Kanter suggests. While they may be helpful to men, she calls also for training to assist women in understanding and dealing with such stereotypical male characteristics as "the experience of power, task orientation, intellectualizing, behaving 'impersonally' and addressing large groups, invulnerability to feedback and new experiences in interpersonal behavior for many women." (1977:383) What Kanter is suggesting is that in order to survive in a work world ruled by traditional and dominant worldviews, women must have access to information about the patterns of behavior underlying these worldviews.

She suggests, more importantly, and similar to Davis's observation about the racial composition of groups, that

> *the relative proportion of men and women in work groups and training groups should . . . be taken into account in designing programs. Whenever possible, a 'critical mass' of females should be included in every working group—more than two or three, and a large enough percentage that they can reduce stereotyping, change the culture of the group, and offer support without being a competitive threat to one another. If there are only a few women in the sales force, for example, this analysis suggests that they should be clustered rather than spread widely.* (1977:383)

Only if we attend carefully to issues of diversity in the groups we create, those we facilitate, and those to which we belong will our efforts result in effective groups.

Relationship of Feminist Perspectives and Social Work with Groups. Lewis notes that principles of social work with groups have a number of commonalities with principles of feminism (1992:273):

1. A *common consciousness* of the embedded details of victimization

2. The systematic *deconstruction* of negative and disadvantaging definitions of reality

3. The process of *naming*, of identifying the consequences of established structures and patterns

4. Trust in the *processes within the group* to reconstruct a new reality and to provide the context within which to test and practice new language, behaviors, expectations, and aspirations

5. A belief in the *power of the group*, united to bring about desired changes in the context, however small these may be

6. A *sense of community* through the experience of reaching out and discovering allies and "same-thinkers and doers" in the wider social context

Groups and Persons with Disabilities

As we noted in Chapter 3, there are 43 million persons with disabilities in the United States. Given the number of persons with disabilities in the population and given the special needs of this group, it is very likely that social workers will work with persons with disabilities in virtually all kinds of small group situations. As a result it is important to be sensitive to the needs, feelings, and strengths of persons with disabilities. Brown (1995) outlines a specific set of rights of people with disabilities in groupwork. This "Bill of Rights" can help us make sure we are respectful and inclusive of persons with disabilities in our work in groups. The first two sections of the table reflect ADA standards. "The third section on ethics and accommodation [is] . . . based on 'due care' in standards of practice and the accommodation process" (Brown 1995:73).

Helpful suggestions for insuring that persons with disabilities are able to exercise their full rights within group contexts are included in what Patterson et al. (1995:79) refer to as:

Disability Etiquette for Groups

1. It is appropriate to acknowledge that a disability exists, but asking personal questions is inappropriate unless one has a close relationship with the person with the disability.

2. It is important to speak directly to the person with a disability, even when a third party (e.g., attendant, relative, interpreter) is present.

3. It is appropriate to use common words such as *look* or *see*, for individuals with visual impairments, as well as *running* or *walking* with people who use wheelchairs.

4. It is appropriate to offer assistance to a person with a disability, but one should wait until it is accepted before providing the assistance. Clarification should

Rights of People with Disabilities in Group Work

Places of Public Accommodation and Telecommunication	• The right to access and full utilization of all public accommodations • The right to access and full utilization of telecommunication • The right to access and full utilization of public ground transportation
Inclusion and Accommodation	• The right not to be discriminated against on the basis of disability when being referred or requesting participation in group work • The right not to be discriminated against on the basis of being regarded as a person with a disability • The right of the individuals to be judged for inclusion in the group on their own merits • The right to be tested fairly • The right to request and to be provided with reasonable accommodation that is not an undue hardship • The right not to be disqualified from group membership based on the inability to perform nonessential role functions • The right not to be limited, segregated, or classified as a person with a disability • The right not to be discriminated against as a direct threat to the safety or the health of others, unless certain standards are met • The right of individuals not to be retaliated against because they made a charge, testified, assisted, or participated in any manner in an investigation, proceeding, or hearing to enforce any provision of ADA or other legislation that was developed to protect their rights • The right not to be discriminated against because of an association with people with disabilities • The right not to be discriminated against by a third party contract
Ethics and Accommodation	• The right and responsibility to initiate discussion with the facilitator about any accommodation needs • The right to reveal a disabling condition to the group leader and to members without begin discriminated against • The right to expect the development of group norms that recognize the value of diversity within the group, the distribution of group roles based on abilities, and the value of accommodation to maximize use of resources • The right to receive feedback about what can be changed, rather than feedback about what is personally degrading because of a disability • The right not to be the target of scapegoating because of disability as the group negotiates power and communication distribution within the group

Adapted from Brown 1995 *The Journal for Specialists in Group Work*, v. 20 (2), 73–75. Copyright American Counseling Association. Reprinted with permission.

be sought from the individual with the disability if the group leader is unsure of how or what type of assistance is needed.

In addition, Patterson et al. provide a listing of suggestions for use by group leaders in groups where some members have disabilities including blindness, mobility impairment, deafness, or speech impairment.

Specific Suggestions for Four Common Disabilities a Group Leader Might Encounter

Blindness	• If the person seems to need assistance, identify yourself and let the person know you are there by a light touch on the arm. • Let the person take your arm and follow the motion of your body. • When seating the person, place his or her hand on the side or back of the chair. • Use verbal cues and specificity in giving directions (e.g., left, right, three steps down). • Early in the group have each member identify him- or herself upon speaking until the person with blindness has learned to recognize members' voices.
Mobility Impairment	• When conversing for any length of time with someone who uses a wheelchair, sit down to have the dialogue at eye level. • Leaning or hanging on the individual's wheelchair should be avoided because this is part of the person's body space. • If a group member uses a manual wheelchair, it is appropriate to offer assistance if any distance is involved or when carpeting makes propelling the wheelchair more difficult.
Deafness	• The group members and leader should be positioned in such a way that the individual with the disability has a clear view of the speaker's mouth. • Speak clearly, without exaggerating, and use a regular speed and tone of voice. • When an interpreter is used, both eye contact and speech should be directed toward the individual with deafness and not the interpreter (e.g., "John, I look forward to having you in our group" vs. "Tell John I look forward to having him in our group"). • The interpreter's ethical code includes confidentiality.
Speech Impairment	• Maintain eye contact and be patient. • Do not interrupt or finish sentences for the group member. • Do seek clarification if you do not understand the individual's speech.

Note: Adapted from Patterson et al. 1995 *The Journal for Specialists in Group Work*, v. 20 (2), 79. Copyright American Counseling Association. Reprinted with permission.

Effective Groups

Groups can be said to be effective if they accomplish three things: 1) goal achievement; 2) maintenance of good working relationship among members; and 3) adaptation to changing environmental conditions that allow effectiveness to be maintained. Johnson and Johnson offer a model of effective groups that includes nine dimensions:

1. *Group goals must be clearly understood, be relevant to the needs of group members, highlight the positive interdependence of members, and evoke from every member a high level of commitment to their accomplishment.*

2. *Group members must communicate their ideas and feelings accurately and clearly.*

3. *Participation and leadership must be distributed among members.*

4. *Appropriate decision-making procedures must be used flexibly to match them with the needs of the situation.*

5. *Conflicts should be encouraged and managed constructively. . . . Controversies (conflicts among opposing ideas and conclusions) promote in-*

*volvement in the group's work, quality and creativity in decision mak-
ing, and commitment to implementing the group's decisions. Minority
opinions should be accepted and used.*

6. *Power and influence need to be approximately equal throughout the
group. Power should be based on expertise, ability, and access to information, not on authority.*

7. *Group cohesion needs to be high. . . .Cohesion is based on members liking
each other, desiring to continue as part of the group, and being satisfied
with their group membership.*

8. *Problem-solving adequacy should be high.*

9. *The interpersonal effectiveness of members needs to be high. Interpersonal
effectiveness is a measure of how well the consequences of your behavior
match your intentions.* (1991:21–24)

SUMMARY

All of the perspectives, concepts, and dimensions we have considered in this chapter
are important to help us understand groups. Currently as students and teachers and
as social workers and future social work practitioners, we do and will continue to conduct much of our work in the context of small groups. We create groups, we facilitate groups, and we can expect on almost a daily basis to spend time as a member of
some small-group effort.

In this chapter we have explored groups as contexts in which both process and
product are inextricable concerns. We have examined a number of issues involved in
the formation and achievement of group purposes and goals. The interrelated and interdependent nature of membership, leadership, followership, and decision making
was considered. A variety of roles and norms played by group members and their significance for the individuals playing them and for the group as a whole have been investigated. We have outlined a number of stage-based models of group development,
recognizing that while stages are a part of group development they do not occur only
in linear or fixed sequences. Social systems or ecological frameworks for explaining
many aspects of groups have been sketched, along with recognition of some of the
limitations of this common approach used by social workers to understand groups.
We have stressed the absolute necessity of considering issues of oppression and of diversity in our work with and in groups. We noted that regardless of purpose or goal,
serious attention must be given to issues concerning persons of color, persons with
disabilities, and gender in all the groups with which we are associated.

Only by attending to the multiple, complex, interdependent, and interrelated
dimensions of groups can we be effective in our group work. By doing so we can gain
a much more complete and holistic picture of groups than we can from concentrat-
ing on any one perspective. This multiple-perspective approach is consistent also with
our attempts in this book to develop a worldview that is inclusive and that incorporates a "both/and" rather than an "either/or" approach to understanding HBSE.

As throughout this book, the knowledge we explored here about groups is interdependent and interconnected with the things we have learned about individuals

and familiness on our voyage toward understanding human behavior and the social environment. The information we gathered during this part of our journey is related to and interconnected with our explorations in the chapters on organizations and communities that follow.

Internet Search Guide

If you want to learn more about some of the topics discussed in this chapter by exploring the Internet, you can search the Net for the terms listed below. Remember that as you are "surfing" the Net, any of the search terms listed below can take you in many different directions. If you would like to visit specific Web sites related to this chapter, go to the Allyn and Bacon Web site at **http://www.abacon.com** and follow the links to Schriver or *Human Behavior and the Social Environment: Shifting Paradigms in Essential Knowledge for Social Work Practice*. There you will find a selection of sites related to content in this chapter.

1. groupthink
2. leadership
3. democratic groups
4. diversity and groups
5. groups and gender
6. groups and disabilities

REFERENCES

Anderson, Ralph, and Carter, Irl. (1990). *Human behavior in the social environment: A social systems approach* (4th ed.) New York: Aldine de Gruyter.

Attneave, Carolyn. (1982). "American Indians and Alaska Native families: Emigrants in their own homeland." In McGoldrick, Monica, Pearce, John, and Giordano, Joseph. (Eds.). *Ethnicity and family therapy.* New York: Guilford.

Brown, Beverly M. (1995). "The process of inclusion and accommodation: A bill of rights for people with disabilities in group work." *The Journal for Specialists in Group Work, 20*(2):71–75.

Brown, Leonard N. (1991). *Groups for growth and change.* New York: Longman.

Curran, D. J., and Renzetti, C. (1996). *Social Problems: Society in Crisis.* (4th ed.). Boston: Allyn and Bacon

Davis, L. E., Galinsky, M. J., and Schopler, J. H. (1996). "RAP: A framework for leadership of multiracial groups." In *Multicultural issues in social work.* Ewalt, P. L., Freeman, E., M., Kirk, S. A., and Poole, D. L. (Eds.). Washington, DC: NASW Press.

Davis, Larry. (1985). "Group work practice with ethnic minorities of color." In Sundal, Martin et al. (Eds.). *Individual change through small groups.* (2nd ed.) New York: The Free Press.

Davis, Larry, E. Galinsky, Maeda J., and Schopler, Janice H. (1995). "RAP: A framework for leadership in multiracial groups," *Social Work, 40*(2):155–167, appearing in Ewalt, P., et al. (1996). *Multicultural Issues in Social Work.* Washington, DC: NASW Press. Reprinted with permission.

Estrada, M., Brown, J., and Lee, F. (1995). "Who gets the credit? Perceptions of idiosyncrasy credit in work groups." *Small Group Research, 26*(1):56–76.

Garvin, Charles. (1985). "Work with disadvantaged and oppressed groups." In Sundel, Martin et al. (Eds.), *Individual change through small groups.* (2nd ed.). New York: The Free Press.

Gastil, John. (1992). "A definition of small group democracy." *Small Group Research,* 23(3):278–301.

———. (1994). "A definition and illustration of democratic leadership." *Human Relations,* 47(8):953–975.

Gemmill, Gary, and Oakley, Judith. (1992). "Leadership: An alienating social myth?" *Human Relations, 45*(2):113–139.

Hare, A. P. (1994). "Types of roles in small groups: A bit of history and a current perspective." *Small Group Research, 25*(3):433–448.

Janus, I. L. (1982). *Groupthink.* (2nd ed.). Boston: Houghton Mifflin.

Johnson, David, and Johnson, Frank. (1991). *Joining together: Group theory and group skills* (4th ed.). Englewood Cliffs, NJ: Prentice Hall.

Kanter, Rosabeth Moss. (1977). "Women in organizations: Sex roles, group dynamics and change strategies." In Alice Sargeant, *Beyond sex roles.* St. Paul: West.

Lewis, E. (1992). "Regaining promise: Feminist perspectives for social group work practice." *Social Work with Groups, 13*(4):271–284.

McLeod, P. L., Lobel, S. A., and Cox, T. H. (1996). "Ethnic diversity and creativity in small groups." *Small Group Research.* vl 27 (2):248–264.

Miranda, S. M. (1994). "Avoidance of groupthink: Meeting management using group support systems." *Small Group Research, 25*(1):105–136.

Napier, Rodney, and Gershenfeld, Matti K. (1985). *Groups, theory and experience* (3rd ed.). Boston: Houghton Mifflin Company.

Neck, C. P., and Manz, C. C. (1994). "From groupthink to teamthink: Toward the creation of constructive thought patterns in self-managing work teams." *Human Relations,* 47(8):929–952.

Neck, C. P., and Moorhead, G. (1995). "Groupthink remodeled: The importance of leadership, time pressure, and methodical decision-making procedures." *Human Relations,* 48(5):537–557.

Patterson, J. B., McKenzie, and Jenkins, J. (1995). "Creating accessible groups for individuals with disabilities." *The Journal for Specialists in Group Work, 20*(2):76–82.

Sabini, J. (1995). *Social psychology.* (2nd Ed.). New York: W. W. Norton.

Sundell, Martin; Glasser, Paul; Sarri, Rosemary; and Vinter, Robert, Eds. (1985). *Individual change through small groups* (2nd Ed.). New York: The Free Press.

Worchel, Stephen; Wood, Wendy; and Simpson, Jeffry A. (Eds.). (1992). *Group process and productivity.* Newbury Park, CA: SAGE Publications.

ILLUSTRATIVE READING 7.1

The illustrative reading by Chang addresses several fundamental concepts crucial to social workers and to our approaches to understanding and working with groups. Chang reinforces the importance of democratic approaches to interacting with other groups and within groups in an increasingly diverse society. In this reading Chang explores the fundamental importance of approaching diversity as a source of strength and innovation rather than as source of divisiveness with the potential to damage progress and democracy. This reading is especially significant because the author integrates the concepts of democracy and diversity with the concept of social capital. The concept of social capital will be explored in more detail in later chapters, but Chang's article offers an excellent beginning definition of this concept so central to understand the social environment as both context of and strong influence on human behavior, particularly related to group and intergroup dynamics. In the article the author illustrates the relevance of the concept of social capital across system sizes from its influence on individual development to its importance at the family, group, organization, and community levels. Chang concludes the article with a summary of what she considers are qualities necessary for success in working in and with diverse groups.

Democracy, Diversity, and Social Capital

Hedy Nai-Lin Chang

What we seek—at every level—is pluralism that achieves some kind of coherence, wholeness incorporating diversity. . . . To prevent the wholeness from smothering the diversity, there must be a philosophy of pluralism, and an open climate for dissent and opportunity for sub-communities to retain their identity and share in the setting of larger group goals. To prevent diversity from destroying the wholeness, there must be institutional arrangements for diminishing polarization, for teaching diverse groups to know one another, for coalition-building, dispute resolution, negotiation and mediation.

—John Gardner

A mosaic of people from different racial, cultural, and linguistic backgrounds, the United States is one of the most ethnically diverse societies in the world. While this diversity has occurred more rapidly in some states and urban areas, we are, as a country, undergoing a profound demographic transformation. As we move into a century during which there will be no majority ethnic group, our nation is grappling with critical questions about how we function as a society. Will we invest in the well-being of all groups living within our borders and find ways to draw strength from our diversity? Or will we allow our nation to become a society of haves and have-nots, with the demarcations falling primarily along racial lines? Will people of all backgrounds have the opportunity to exercise their rights and responsibilities as members of a democracy? Or will authority and power be consolidated into the hands of a few? Will we become a society torn apart by divisions of race, language, and class, or will we find the common ground that can enable us to remain a cohesive whole?

How we understand and respond to our diversity is essential to any discussion of social policy in this country, especially how we design strategies to strengthen and foster the existence of social capital. According to Robert Putnam, social capital comprises the features of social life—the network, norms, and trust that enable participants to act together more effectively to pursue shared objectives. Social capital is critical to the well-being of any community because its presence increases people's ability to work together to solve problems that cannot be addressed by individuals working in isolation.

While social capital alone cannot ensure a thriving multiracial democracy, it is essential. In the United States, social capital is needed to ensure cooperation and mutual support *among* and *across* people from different racial, cultural, and linguistic

Hedy Nai-Lin Chang is codirector of California Tomorrow, a nonprofit organization committed to building a strong and equitable multiracial, multicultural, and multilingual society. From the *National Civic Review*, vol. 86, no. 2, Summer 1997. Copyright © 1997 Jossey-Bass Publishers. Reprinted by permission of Jossey-Bass, Inc., a subsidiary of John Wiley and Sons, Inc.

SOCIAL CAPITAL → BEING WILLING TO WORK W/ PEOPLE TOWARD A COMMON GOAL ?

Perspectives on Groups | *427*

groups. Social capital is integral to groups' ability to develop and retain their individual identities and histories, as well as to find the common ground that can bind them together. What we, as a country, must discover is how to nurture social capital in a rapidly changing, increasingly diverse society. This article will explore this challenge by first examining the origins of social capital and then suggesting possible approaches to sustaining and generating it.

ORIGINS OF SOCIAL CAPITAL IN A DIVERSE SOCIETY

The development of social capital begins with what people learn from their families, neighbors, community institutions, and schools. Some of these concepts are taught directly. Many beliefs and norms are acquired as people hear and observe the words, the actions, the successes, and the challenges encountered by other members of their community.

Social capital is inextricably linked to what happens to people when they are children. How young people are treated has an enormous impact on whether they feel proud of themselves and their community and whether they develop a sense of self-confidence and efficacy. Feeling that you have something to contribute is often a prerequisite for being willing to work with others toward a common goal. Relationships with families and neighbors play a crucial role in shaping whether our youth grow into adults who feel a sense of connection to people from the same and different cultural, linguistic, or racial backgrounds and whether or not they have the skills and language to be able to communicate and interact with others.

Childhood is also a critical time for learning basic values such as respect for elders, commitment to family, and neighborliness. Values lay the foundation for being concerned about more than one's own welfare. Values play a critical role in determining whether networks, norms, and trust advance the health of a community, as opposed to contributing to its decline. A group like the Ku Klux Klan is, for example, a network tied together by strong norms and trusting relationships, but its purposes work against the creation of a strong multiethnic democracy. What is needed in a diverse society is a value system that cultivates respect and caring for people from different racial, cultural, and linguistic backgrounds as well as members of one's own ethnic group or groups.

Social capital is also strengthened when adults have opportunities to reflect upon their values, develop trusting relationships with people who are from the same and different backgrounds, and recognize the assets and strengths they can contribute to their communities. What happens to people as they get older can reinforce their beliefs, or it can force them to question what they learned as children. In some cases, adults find that they must reexamine and even change their beliefs and norms because what they learned earlier is no longer appropriate, given the changes that have occurred in this society

NURTURING SOCIAL CAPITAL IN A DIVERSE SOCIETY

The challenge for the United States is to design strategies that will foster social capital within and across the diverse groups living within its borders. An underlying assumption of this article is that both types of social capital are necessary to the well-being of our society as a whole. If a particular group or community has difficulty providing its children and adults with a sense of self-worth and human connection, then society as a whole suffers. At the same time, however, the existence of strong and vibrant subcommunities do not by themselves guarantee a sense of unity across groups.

Described next are several suggestions for nurturing social capital in a diverse society. The illustrations of these concepts are based upon my experience working to promote the welfare of children, youth, and families in California, where the demographic changes affecting this nation have been most dramatic. Far from being an exhaustive list, these ideas are intended to stimulate thought and dialogue about what is possible as our country enters the uncharted territory of creating a multicultural democracy.

First, we should *recognize and support different ways of generating social capital.* While the overall process may be similar, the exact way social capital develops can differ significantly across different groups. In some situations, for example, the entity that plays a major role in affirming values and establishing networks may be a religious institution, whereas, in other places, the workplace or the corner Laundromat may be pivotal. For some groups, mothers or fathers may be primarily responsible for basic socialization and child rearing, while, in others, this role is shared with grandparents or other relatives. Understanding how to nurture social capital in a multiplicity of settings requires being aware of the fact that where, when, and how social capital forms reflects a wide range of factors including economic conditions, racial experience, linguistic background, and cultural practices and beliefs.

Being open to the experiences of people from different ethnic backgrounds is important to understanding how social capital can be sustained. Without this sensitivity and insight, it is all too easy to unwittingly develop public policies that have an adverse impact on the formation of social capital of certain groups. Racial, cultural, and linguistic minorities are in an especially risky position because their norms and practices are often different from the dominant Anglo European norms that generally shape the nature and content of governmental policies and practices.

Consider, for example, the increasingly prevalent view that children should be taught English at earlier and earlier ages and that bilingual education should be eliminated. The problem with such a view is that it promotes policies and programs that emphasize only English and may regard the use of children's home language as an obstacle to their development. There is evidence that bilingual education can facilitate the understanding of concepts at an early age and make the child more proficient—even in English—later on. Policies that emphasize English to the exclusion of the home language contribute to and reinforce the likelihood that children will lose their home language. In the United States, English is clearly the language of power and success. It pervades the media, business, and schools. People who speak languages other than English are often ridiculed or treated as having a lower intelligence. The message that English is the most important language is easily and quickly internalized. Children and youth frequently refuse to speak their home languages out of embarrassment or shame, even with their families.

The loss of the home language can have a devastating impact on the development of social capital. Retention of one's home language is often critical to maintaining strong emotional and social ties to family members and other community members as a child, and even into adulthood. First, speaking the home language is essential to family cohesiveness, especially if parents or grandparents do not speak English. Unlike their children, adults are much less likely to have opportunities to learn English, even when they are highly motivated to do so. When children cease to speak their home language, grandparents and parents are in many ways robbed of their capacity to offer guidance, discipline, comfort, and support. Second, language serves as a vehicle for transmitting ideas, beliefs, and customs. Languages often contain words that are impossible to accurately translate. When people cease to speak the language of their family and community, they begin to miss the subtle, but often crucial, nuances of their heritage. Loss of home and community languages significantly reduces the capacity of groups to convey their hopes, values, and traditions to a future generation.

Ironically, many of the people seeking to promote English and eliminate bilingual programs probably perceive themselves as working to increase the levels of social capital across groups by ensuring the existence of a common language. What this example illustrates, however, is that public policies based solely upon the experience of one ethnic group rarely have the intended impact.

Second, we should *identify common values that can bind us together.* This country often seems to be caught between two myths. The first myth is that everyone is alike and therefore requires the same treatment. The problem with this belief is that it leads to policies like the one described earlier, which have an adverse impact because they overlook crucial differences in the ways groups and communities develop. The second myth is that people today are so different that they have nothing in common. This myth perpetuates current fears that society is being torn into separate ethnic enclaves. The challenge before us is to learn to recognize those common values that can bind us together and, at the same time, promote respect and appreciation for our differences.

Establishing some universal values that encompass our differences is necessary for our individual as well as collective success. Such universal values are important because they serve as shared goals that offer groups the opportunity to work together. The process of working together provides people with the opportunity to identify each other's strengths and approaches, as well as to gain a deeper understanding of each other's challenges and issues.

Sometimes the problem is not a lack of common values but a failure to articulate the beliefs we hold in common. One value, for instance, which should and must be reasserted is the right of children to a free and quality public education. This is a fundamental right because education in America is key to success. The right to a public education lies at the heart of the American dream of equal opportunity. It is crucial for individual well-being as well as collective health. A democracy depends on a well-educated populace, yet this right is being challenged today on many fronts. It has been challenged by California's Proposition 187, a successful 1995 ballot initiative that barred undocumented immigrants from receiving publicly funded social services or attending public schools. In other settings, this right has been threatened by the unthinkably high suspension rates of African American and Latino male students, who are then left with no educational alternative. Another form of attack has been the failure to ensure that all schools, including those operating in low-income communities, have books, materials, and qualified teachers.

Unfortunately, however, the people and groups struggling to retain their individual or group's right to quality education too often fail to recognize that they in fact share a common goal. Rather than working together to fight for this common right, groups fall into the trap of fighting against each other. In California, a number of African American and legal immigrants living in low-income communities supported Proposition 187 because they felt that allowing undocumented students to go to schools simply takes resources away from their children. But supporting initiatives like Proposition 187 is not what will increase resources to their children. It doesn't, for example change the fact that schools are suffering from an eroding local tax base of inner cities, or ensure that teachers are equipped to educate an increasingly diverse population. It simply excludes those with the least political power and allows the larger society to avoid facing questions of how to support and develop a viable system of public education. Allowing the right to public education to be eroded for one group may in fact place the children of another group in greater danger. It sets a precedent where we, as a nation, are allowed to discard some children because they are deemed unnecessary for our future.

Rather than waiting to see who will be deemed irrelevant next, people need to join together to reestablish quality education as a basic right rather than a privilege available only to a select few. This right must be upheld by people of all backgrounds, not merely those groups who find the future of their children in danger. Shared values and goals offer this society the chance to reap the benefits of its collective wisdom and foster the potential of all its members.

Third, we should *increase awareness of our interdependency across differences in race, language, and culture*. Promoting social capital requires helping people to understand that their individual welfare is dependent upon the well-being of a larger society. In a diverse society, this means helping people to see themselves as members of a larger, multiethnic community, not just as being tied to those with whom they share a racial, cultural, or linguistic background. For example, one challenge facing the state of California is that more than 50 percent of its children are persons of color, while the voting population is still 80 percent white. Ensuring that resources are available to support the development of strong community institutions, whether they are schools or recreational programs, involves convincing this 80 percent white voting population that their welfare depends upon investing in the well-being of children who may not look like them.

The need for members of different ethnic groups to recognize their interdependence is especially obvious at the local level. Throughout the nation, communities traditionally made up of members from a particular ethnic group, whether white, black, Latino, or Asian, now find that they also include at least some people of another ethnic group. The future of these neighborhoods depends upon different groups learning to collaborate with one another.

Two years ago, some colleagues and I spent several days providing technical assistance to a school in a low-income community that was shifting rapidly from being predominantly African American to becoming significantly Latino. During the course of our visit, we met with both African American and Latino parents and soon discovered that many Latino parents were concerned about going to school meetings because they were being robbed when they did. In addition, they blamed the African Americans parents for stealing from them because they thought that the African American parents knew the times of the school functions. In fact, the African American parents weren't the thieves. Rather they were experiencing the same problems, but their solution was to stay home.

Divided by the competition over scarce resources, a history of mistrust and the inability to communicate with each other, the Latino and African American parents in this community were not able to recognize their common challenges or work together to find solutions. Yet their ability to find ways to communicate, build trust, and work together is critical to the health of their neighborhood. The housing complex in which they live is integrated with Latino and African American families living next door to each other. In order, for example, to form a neighborhood watch, families would need to be able to count on their neighbors, regardless of whether they were African American or Latino, to watch over their homes. Tackling even larger issues such as the lack of jobs, poor transportation, or the absence of youth development programs requires more clout than either group possesses by itself.

Fourth, we must *invest in leadership development*. Building social capital involves cultivating people who have the skills and capacity to promote and support the implementation of the three strategies discussed earlier. While it is important to recognize and appreciate a wide range of leadership styles and approaches, my experience also suggests that people who are effective in diverse settings tend to share a number of similar qualities including:

- A solid grounding in their individual and group identity, including an understanding of how their background may positively and negatively shape their world view and behavior.

- An understanding of the impact of racial. linguistic, cultural, and class oppression on communities, families, and individuals.

- The ability to assess a situation through multiple lenses and to recognize when another person's perception may be different because of their racial, cultural, socioeconomic, or linguistic experience and history.

- The capacity to appreciate and value different cultures, traditions, and beliefs.

- A commitment to engaging in and modeling power sharing across groups.

- The ability to recognize and affirm common values, goals, and challenges across differences in race, language, and culture.

The responsibility for cultivating these skills and knowledge is a shared one. It is a challenge that must be met by the variety of organizations and people who play a significant role in nurturing the development of young people as well as adults.

8  *Perspectives on Organizations*

Topics Addressed in this Chapter:

➤ **HISTORICAL PERSPECTIVE ON ORGANIZATIONS**
➤ **BASIC CONCEPTS/DEFINITIONS**
  Types of Organizations
➤ **TECHNOLOGY, ORGANIZATIONS, AND SOCIAL POLICY**
  The Digital Divide and Organizations: Technology, Poverty, and Inequality
     Policy and Organizational Responses to the Digital Divide
➤ **TRADITIONAL PARADIGMS**
  Scientific Management or Classical Theory
  Bureaucracy
  Human Relations
     The Hawthorne Studies
  Theory X and Theory Y
  Systems Perspectives
  Contingency Theory

➤ **STRENGTHS/WEAKNESSES/CRITICISM**
➤ **ALTERNATIVE PARADIGMS**
  Organizational Culture
  Organizational Climate
  The "Iron Law of Oligarchy"
  A Critical Perspective
  Consensus Organizations
     Comparison of Consensus and Bureaucratic Organizations
     Limits of Consensus Organizations
  Modified Consensus Organizations
  Feminist Approaches to Organizations
  Chaos/Complexity Theory and Organizations
  Theory Z
     Japanese Management Techniques Applicable to Social Work
        Management Practices Used in Japanese Social Welfare Agencies
  Total Quality Management
  Learning Organizations
     Learning Culture

➤ **CONCLUSION**

*O*rganizations form the contexts in which much of our daily lives are carried out. They form the environments in which a vast array of human behaviors take place. For many of us, virtually all aspects of our lives are intertwined with and influenced by organizations. To give us some idea of how much of our own and others' lives are touched by organizations from the time we are born until the time we die, let us consider some examples of organizations. We very likely were born in or with the assistance of an organization—a hospital, public health agency, prepared childbirth program. We are likely to be socialized or educated in the context of organizations—day care, preschool/Headstart, grade and high schools, higher education institutions, vocational/technical schools. We very likely play in the context of organizations—organized sports, girls'/boys' clubs, Scouts, Jack and Jill, health/exercise clubs, fraternities/sororities. We may pray in and mark major life events with rituals in the context of formal religious organizations—church, synagogue, temple, mosque. We probably do or will work in an organizational context—human service agencies, corporations, health and mental health organizations. We get many of our basic subsistence needs met through organizations—grocery, clothing, drug and department stores, food banks, housing authorities, banks, restaurants. We probably will grow old in the context of organizations—senior centers, home health or chore services, nursing homes. We may very well die in an organizational context—hospital, hospice. While this sampling is not intended to be an exhaustive list of the organizations that influence us throughout life, it does give us a place to start in considering the far-reaching impact of organizations on our individual and collective lives (Etzioni 1964).

If you reflect on the examples of organizational contexts above, it is not difficult to recognize that many of the organizations through which human needs are met are also contexts in which social workers work. Whether we are working to meet our own needs or those of other individuals, families, groups, or communities, we are very likely to be acting in or through an organizational environment. We are concerned here, of course, with what organizations do to help us meet human needs. We are also concerned here with how organizations can and do present barriers to or may even prevent us from meeting our needs and reaching our full potential as humans. We are concerned, especially, with the role of organizations in helping or hindering diverse persons as they proceed through the life course. And we are concerned with the roles that diverse persons have in constructing the organizations that impact so directly and comprehensively on their lives.

Organizations reflect and are reflected in the paradigms or worldviews of the persons who construct and operate them. Since organizations have such a high degree of influence on our day-to-day lives throughout our lives, it is imperative that we all share in creating and operating them. Only in this way will organizations be responsive to the needs of diverse persons.

As we begin to investigate what we mean when we talk about organizations, we need to recognize that much of the information on small groups from the previous chapter will apply to organizations as well. Much of the activity that organizations are engaged in happens through a variety of small groups. If you think about an organization in which are involved, you can probably recognize that much of your involvement in relation to the organization is carried out through different small groups. You are likely, for example, to be a member of a committee or work group within the organization. You are also likely to have membership in informal groups within the organization—a group of organization members you eat lunch with on a regular basis, for instance. So much of an organization's activity is carried out in small groups that it begins to look as if the organization is really a collection of small groups. Because of this it is important that we use what we know about small groups to help us better understand organizations.

In this chapter we will visit a number of perspectives on formal organizations. We will explore the notion of organizational culture. We will look to history for some perspective on how we came to be a society so reliant on the structures and processes of formal organizations to accomplish so many of our individual, family, group, and community tasks. We will look to traditional notions of organizations for understanding about the nature of the existing organizations with which we and the people with whom we work must deal every day. We will explore some alternative notions of how organizations might/can be changed or structured to meet human needs and accomplish the core concerns of social work. We hope to use the understanding we gain about organizations in order to make them more responsive to our needs and to the needs of others. We seek avenues in this part of our journey to create and re-create organizations that are inclusive of the visions and voices of all the peoples with whom social workers are concerned.

HISTORICAL PERSPECTIVE ON ORGANIZATIONS

We may think of a society characterized by so many different kinds and sizes of organizations directed toward a dizzying range of purposes and goals as a modern phenomenon. However, organizations have long been a basic context within which a wide range of human behavior and interaction takes place. It is true that the number and variety of organizations has increased greatly in the twentieth century. However, organizations and the study of organizations have been with us for a long, long time. Etzioni reminds us that the pharaohs employed organizations in the creation of the pyramids. Chinese emperors over a thousand years ago made use of organizations to build irrigation systems. The first popes created the universal church as an organization to manage a world religion (Etzioni 1964:1). Iannello (1992:3) notes that the philosophers of ancient Greece were interested in the study of organizations as a means of achieving specific goals and purposes.

Shafritz and Ott (1987:1) suggest it is safe to say that humankind has been creating organizations ever since we began hunting, making war, and creating families.

Organizational study as a deliberate and focused field of exploration, especially in terms of managing large organizations, is largely a product of the twentieth century, however. Much of the study of organizations during the twentieth century has been done focusing on business or profit-making organizations. There is, though, a growing body of information that focuses on not-for-profit or public service organizations. Most students of organizations agree that the rise of industrial (and more recently the emergence of postindustrial) society in the twentieth century has resulted in great increases in the quantity, size, and type of formal organizations in almost every area of life. This proliferation of formal organizations directed toward achieving a multitude of goals has greatly increased our interest in understanding formal organizations.

As we have learned about paradigms in general, our beliefs about what organizations are, what they do, and how they do it have not come about in a vacuum. They have been greatly influenced by the people, times, and cultures associated with their development. Shafritz and Ott (1987:2) suggest that "the advent of the factory system, World War II, the 'flowerchild'/anti-establishment/self-development era of the 1960s, and the computer/information society of the 1970s all substantially influenced the evolution of organization theory." We can add to this list important recent and currently unfolding influences, such as the reorganization of Eastern Europe, the growing recognition that we are all citizens of one global and interdependent society, current concerns about the impact of modern organizations on the environment of our planet, and the emergence from such important movements as the women's movement and other human rights movements of concerns about participation and inclusion of all humans in determining the nature of our organizational lives. As we explore traditional and alternate perspectives on organizations, we will travel a route that parallels many of the historic influences of the early, middle, and late twentieth century. We will also visit some organizational paradigms likely to emerge in the early twenty-first century. To begin to understand organizations we need some basic concepts and definitions.

BASIC CONCEPTS/DEFINITIONS

Whether exploring traditional or alternative notions about organizations, it is helpful to have at least a very general definition from which to explore differences in perspectives on organizations. Etzioni (1964:3) uses Talcott Parsons's basic definition of **organizations** as "social units (or human groupings) deliberately constructed and reconstructed to seek specific goals." Another common definition says that "an organization is a collection of people engaged in specialized and interdependent activity to accomplish a goal or mission" (Gortner, Mahler, Nicholson 1987:2). Iannello (1992:8) suggests that one might simply define organizations "as systems of continuous, purposive, goal-oriented activity involving two or more people." All three of these basic definitions differ slightly, but they share some essential and basic common ground. All three recognize organizations as collectivities of people working together to accomplish a goal (or goals).

Within this common ground, however, there is a wide range of possibilities for differences in perspectives. The characteristics of the people involved in the organization, how those people are arranged in relation to one another, the nature of the goal (or goals), and the specific parts different organizational members play in accomplishing the goal (or goals) are just some of the sources of different perspectives among students of organizations.

An organizational **goal** can be defined simply as the desired or intended ends or results to be achieved by an organization (Neugeboren 1985:27) or as a "desired state of affairs which the organization attempts to realize" (Etzioni 1964:6). The nature of goals varies greatly from organization to organization and may even vary within the same organization over time. Different human service organizations may share a basic mission or purpose of improving the quality of life for people in the communities they serve. Human service organizations may vary greatly, however, in the specific goals they pursue in order to improve the quality of life.

Neugeboren (1985:5–17) suggests that there are three kinds of goals pursued by human service organizations. **Social care** goals are those directed toward changing the environment in order for people to improve the quality of their lives and reach their maximum potential. **Social control** goals are those directed toward controlling the behavior of people who are deemed to be deviant and who interfere with the ability of others to maximize their potential and improve the quality of their lives. **Rehabilitation** goals are those directed toward changing individuals so they will have improved quality of life and better opportunity to reach their fullest potential. Organizations may have multiple goals. Human service agencies such as state departments of social or human services may encompass social care (day-care licensing to ensure high-quality environments for young children, provision of concrete services such as food stamps), social control (legal consequences for parents when child-abuse allegations are substantiated), and rehabilitation (parenting classes for abusive parents to assist in changing parenting behaviors that led to child abuse).

Goal displacement is characteristic of an organization that is pursuing goals contrary to the goals it originally and officially proclaimed. An example of organizational goal displacement is an adolescent group home originally begun to rehabilitate troubled teens that becomes a social control institution to incarcerate adolescents. Organizations may also be characterized by **goal succession.** This is the replacement of one goal by another goal when the original goal has been accomplished or it has declared itself unable to accomplish its original goal. The March of Dimes was an organizational effort originally directed to obtaining resources necessary to find a cure for polio. Upon the virtual elimination of the threat of polio—in no small way a result of the efforts of the March of Dimes—the organization adopted a new goal that included combating birth defects. Goal succession is likely to be a functional change in goals; goal displacement is likely to be dysfunctional (Etzioni 1964:10ff).

Organizations with multiple goals may experience conflict over the amount of organizational resources or energy to devote to their various goals. Such conflict may be especially pronounced if an organization is undergoing goal displacement in a situation in which the organization's stated goals are different from and may compete with its actual goals. Think about the potential for conflict within the adolescent group home in the example above. If some staff want the home to rehabilitate troubled teens so they can return to their families and the community, while other staff see the goal as removal from the community and incarceration, the potential for significant conflict in the organization is very great.

Types of Organizations

There are three types of organizations or organizational sectors with which social workers are most likely to work and need to understand. One type, **private-for-profit** organizations, sometimes referred to as **market sector organizations,** include businesses and corporations organized with the primary goal of making an economic profit. A second type of organization is the **governmental** organization. Governmental organizations comprise the **public sector** and include local, state, and national governmental organizations. Public health, education, and human service organizations are some of the most common public sector organizations. A third type of organization is the **private-not-for-profit** organization. These organizations are also referred to as **non-governmental organizations** or **NGOs.** (NGO is a term more often used to describe this type of organization outside the United States.) Nongovernmental organizations comprise what is often referred to as the **voluntary or civil sector.** They include a wide range of organizations that provide civic and human services (Urban League, Lions Clubs, League of Women Voters, for example) which are funded by private citizens (donations), fund-raising organizations (United Way, for example), or privately funded foundations (Ford or Kellogg Foundations, for example). Historically social workers have been more involved in public sector and voluntary or not-for-profit sector organizations. However, increasingly social workers are both working in or in partnership with market sector organizations in order to achieve human well-being and reduction of poverty and oppression (Rifkin 1998).

Differing perspectives on organizational concepts and types result in very different notions about what organizations are like, what they should be like, and what they might be like. These differences have significant implications and consequences also for the organizations' ability to respond positively to the core concerns of social work we are addressing in this book. As in the chapters dealing with each level of human behavior we explore in this book, we will address notions about organizations from both traditional and alternative paradigmatic perspectives.

There are several traditional models of or approaches to organizations that have had major influences on the way the organizations we deal with every day are structured and operated. These perspectives did not emerge in a vacuum. They emerged from and along with the larger historical context of the twentieth century. As we learned about paradigms generally, the different traditional paradigms often emerged as reactions to or extensions of prior notions of what organizations should be and do.

TECHNOLOGY, ORGANIZATIONS, AND SOCIAL POLICY

As in so many areas, technology is having a profound impact on the nature of organizations and organizational life. Technology may be seen as blurring the boundaries between organizational and community life in some ways. However, it might be more accurate to say that technology is providing organizations with alternative avenues for influencing community life and achieving organizational goals within communities. For example, the Internet can offer voluntary or civic sector organizations a very direct mechanism for communicating and achieving their purposes within communities.

An example of a civic organization using the Internet of fulfill its goals within the community is the League of Women Voters' online effort in collaboration with the Center for Governmental Studies called DemocracyNet (DNet). The League is "a nonpartisan political organization [that] encourages the informed and active participation of citizens in government, works to increase understanding of major public policy issues, and influences public policy through education advocacy" (League of Women Voters 2000).

Common concerns about the U.S. political process include decreasing voter turnout and increasing costs of campaigning, which make political office unattainable for many moderate- and low-income citizens. Both of these trends are particularly important to social workers, because political participation is a primary means of influencing social policy to improve the well-being of the populations we serve. Technology may offer help in increasing citizen involvement in the political process and making campaigning more affordable. Westen points out that "a 1996 AT&T poll reported that two-thirds of all Americans would use the Internet to find out more about political candidates if the information were available, and nearly half would rather vote by computer than from a polling booth" (Westen 1998).

DNet is an interesting example of how the Internet plays an increasingly important role in shaping public policy and in the basic democratic process as well. The goal of DNet "is to increase voter understanding of important public policy problems, allow candidates to debate their positions in an 'electronic town hall' before online audiences, reduce the pressure on candidates to raise campaign funds, foster greater civic participation and interaction between voters and candidates, and create new online political communities" (DNet 2000). Since it began, DNet has grown from providing information on local elections in California to providing up-to-date information on issues and elections in all 50 states and for the year 2000 presidential campaign.

The Democracy Network offers candidates and voters free access to a wide range of features and options. Perhaps the most creative is the Issue Grid. The DNet Issue Grid

> *Allows electoral candidates, using a password and unique ID number, to access a private section of the network's Issue Grid, pick an issue from a preexisting menu or create their own issue, submit a statement of up to one thousand words . . . on that issue, and then sign off. A large red check mark automatically appears in the public portion of the Issue Grid, indicating that the candidate has submitted a position on that issue. At the same time, the words "No Comment" appear under names of the candidate's opponents, and those opponents are notified of the posting of the new issue by e-mail or fax.* (Westen 1998)

However, as Westen notes, technology cannot determine the future and health of our democracy because "in the end, that outcome is determined by the spirit and skills of the people themselves. But technology can provide the electorate with the ability to make improved decisions" (Westen 1998). The reader is encouraged to visit DNet online at www.dnet.org.

Next we discuss the impact of technology on schools and education by exploring the digital divide. By examining the impact of technology on schools as organizations, we are able to observe that in the area of technology, schools can be both part of the problem and part of the solution. Schools can prevent students, families, and communities from accessing and using technology to improve well-being. However, schools can also, often with the assistance of governmental organizations, play a significant role in creating access to technology.

The Digital Divide and Organizations: Technology, Poverty, and Inequality

The disparities in access to technology at the individual and household levels for many low-income, rural, and central-city dwellers and for many persons of color, known as the digital divide (see discussion of "Digital Divide" in Chapter 6), are also evident at the organizational level. This is especially the case with access to technology in the schools. Schools are organizations with significant responsibility within communities to socialize students to become contributing members of their communities and the society. Education of students to teach them to use technology is an important part of the larger socialization process today. While education for technology is growing rapidly in schools, that growth is not equitable among all schools.

For example, "the National Center for Education Statistics reports that 89 percent of the nation's public schools had access to the Internet in 1998, compared with 35 percent in 1994." However, "schools with the highest proportion of minority or poor students lag behind in terms of classroom Internet access." Kennedy and Agron point out that "schools with 50 percent or more minority students have only 37 percent of their classrooms hooked to the Internet, and schools with more than 70 percent of their students eligible for free- and reduced-price lunch have only 39 percent of their rooms connected online. In comparison, 62 percent of classrooms in low-poverty schools are connected to the Internet" (1999). Getting schools connected to the Internet today is also hampered by a history of neglect of the schools in many poor communities and communities of color. Kennedy and Agron stress that "many buildings are old and need costly rewiring and upgraded electrical capacity for modern computers. Older schools are more likely to have to remove asbestos to rewire their buildings, adding even more to the expense. The heat generated by computers may require the expense of additional cooling capacity" (Kennedy and Agron 1999). In addition, even if schools are able to make the changes necessary in buildings and to purchase the necessary technological equipment, they may "find themselves with inadequate funding for upgrading or replacement, software and content, hardware and software maintenance, professional development for teachers, and the hiring and retention of necessary technical-support personnel" (Kennedy and Agron 1999).

Policy and Organizational Responses to the Digital Divide

Given the disparities in access to information tools by significant segments of the population, it is important to recognize the extent and nature of the digital divide. However, this is not enough. We must also respond in ways that support the closing of the divide. One means of improving access for individuals and households is through community access centers (CACs). CACs include "schools, libraries, and other public access points." A Department of Commerce report on the digital divide suggests that CACs are improving access for many persons among those groups families discussed above and in

Chapter 6 who currently lack access at home. According to the report, providing public access can play an important role in poverty reduction that will in turn reduce the digital divide. The report suggests that groups with lack of home access such as those "with lower incomes and education levels, certain minorities, and the unemployed" are using CACs and the "Internet at higher rates to search for jobs or take courses. Providing public access to the Internet will help these groups advance economically, as well as provide them the technical skills to compete professionally in today's digital economy" (National Telecommunications and Information Administration 1999).

Kennedy and Agron stress the role of schools both as public access centers and as critical sources of education about technology. They note that society has often turned to schools to help address social problems such as hungry children through school lunch and breakfast programs. Now, they suggest that "when children are coming to school without knowledge about computers or access to technology, schools are expected to step in" (1999).

However, poor schools need support from the larger environment in order to assist their students and their communities in overcoming the digital divide. One federal policy response to inequality in school access to technology is referred to as **"the E-rate."** The E-rate, authorized by Congress as part of the Telecommunications Act of 1996, "provides discounts on telecommunications and Internet technologies to schools and public libraries. The discounts range from 20 to 90 percent, and the poorest schools and libraries receive the largest discounts" (Kennedy and Agron 1999). This is one approach that can help schools meet the needs of their communities by serving as CACs. Specific ways schools can help meet the technological needs of students and families include:

- Holding a lab night for students and parents to work together at computers.
- Having loaner equipment, such as computers, instructional videos, and calculators, for families to borrow.
- Allowing families to borrow software.
- Looking into a telecommunications hookup between homes and school.
- Keeping labs open before and after school, in the evenings and during the summer.
- Seeking funds to serve groups with limited economic means.
- Partnering with the public library to make your equipment available to students in the summer.
- Offering programming classes as part of a latchkey program. (Kennedy and Agron 1999)

TRADITIONAL PARADIGMS

There are several broad categories of traditional perspectives on organizations. These broad areas are sometimes referred to as schools of thought. They include classical approaches (scientific management or machine theory and bureaucracy), human relations, systems, and contingency theory. Within these broad categories there are a number of basic concepts that can help us to understand the nature of the organizations with which we deal on a day-to-day basis. These theories and concepts also will help us, as social workers, to better understand the organizational context within which we work and through which the people with whom we work seek services to improve the quality of their lives. The organizational context, then, has important implications for both the quality of our own lives—for we spend so much of our time in this context—and the quality of life of the people with whom we work—for the organizational context is pivotal in determining whether or not people will receive the basic resources necessary to improve the quality of their lives. Once again we see that our interests and those of the people with whom we work are interconnected.

Scientific Management or Classical Theory

Scientific management is a conceptual framework (or body of theory) for defining, structuring, and managing organizations that is consistent with the positivistic, scientific, objective, and quantitative dimension of the traditional paradigm. As its name implies, it is closely connected to and relies on the assumptions of science as the ideal approach to understanding organizations. Scientific management was put forward as a theory about organizations by Frederick Taylor in the very early part of the twentieth century. (He presented a paper outlining his approach to the American Society of Mechanical Engineers as early as 1895.) This school of thought has been tremendously influential in defining the structures and processes that make up much organizational life today. This is perhaps understandable, given the influence and power accorded scientific approaches to understanding human behavior generally during the twentieth century (Pugh, Hickson, and Hinings 1985).

Taylor's scientific management was directed toward maximizing efficiency in industry. Efficiency is an important basic concept related to organizations and is a major concern in virtually all organizational theories. **Efficiency** is defined as the production of the maximum amount of output for the least amount of input. It is, in other words, doing the most with the least possible amount of resources. Efficiency is often discussed in conjunction with another basic organizational concept, effectiveness. **Effectiveness** is defined simply as the degree to which the goals or purposes of an organization are accomplished. As we noted above, a primary concern of organizations is attainment or accomplishment of goals (Pugh, Hickson, and Hinings 1985).

According to Taylor, scientific management could achieve maximum effectiveness and efficiency in the attainment of organizational goals through four basic principles. Faithful adherence to these four principles would result in finding the "one best way" to perform a task, do a job, or manage an entire organization. The first principle involved creating a "science of work" for each worker's job or task. This was accomplished by taking what was typically known about each task and objectively or scientifically studying what was known and what needed to be done to accomplish the task. This new information was recorded, tabulated, and reduced to formal laws, rules, or even mathematical formulas that defined and standardized each task necessary to do a job. This process of studying, recording, and codifying work tasks is sometimes referred to as "time and motion studies." These studies sought to create a perfect match between the actions of workers and the activities carried out by machines. They sought to unite workers and machines into one smooth and efficient process for carrying out necessary tasks. While this principle applied in Taylor's model almost exclusively to production in factory settings, it was extended over the years to many other organizational settings as well. For example, studies of human service offices procedures to reduce unnecessary movement or effort in order to increase the number of clients seen is an example of this principle in a nonfactory environment. Task analysis, work load analysis, and time studies are all examples of efforts to scientifically analyze tasks and processes in social work agencies to make operations efficient (Taylor in Grusky and Miller 1981).

The second principle focused on the scientific selection and training of workers. The process of objectively studying each of the workers for their fitness for a particular task, then training them very deliberately to efficiently accomplish that task was quite different from traditional arrangements in which workers determined what they were suited for doing and then set about to train themselves as best they could to do the work for which they were hired. This was yet another means of making work scientific. This concern for careful selection and training of workers was adapted far beyond the factory system. In social work education and practice, the education and selection processes used to ensure that individuals are suited and prepared for the professional jobs they will carry out is an example of this concern. The specific requirements for education of social workers as reflected in the Council on Social Work Education (CSWE), accreditation requirements, the continuing education requirements of many social work agencies, and the requirements for specific amounts and kinds of continuing education activities for renewal of social work licenses in many states are all examples of how this principle has influenced social work education and practice. If you have been through or will go through an application or screening process to be fully admitted to the social work program or school in which you are taking this course, your experience is consistent with this principle of scientific management (Taylor in Grusky and Miller 1981).

Taylor's third principle focused on bringing together management and workers to ensure that the scientific principles resulting from the study of the tasks to be completed and the careful selection and training of workers to carry out those tasks were successfully implemented in the work setting. This principle involved management's taking responsibility for closely monitoring the workers to make sure they were performing their jobs in accordance with scientific principles. This principle also required that workers be rewarded appropriately for adhering to the standardized rules for carrying out specific tasks. Most often this reward took the form of economic benefits, specifically increases in pay. Taylor, though, suggested that there were other "plums" that could be offered, such as better or more kind treatment of workers and allowing workers greater say in what they preferred as rewards for adhering to scientific principles. There is some confusion about Taylorism—as scientific management is sometimes called—in respect to notions of reward. This theory is often described as seeing economic reward as the only motivator for workers. It is safe to say that economic rewards were considered the primary source of motivation, but as Taylor suggests above, workers might also consider better treatment by management a kind of reward as well. Regardless of the kind of reward, the purpose of "plums" was to ensure that workers performed in accordance with the scientific standards for their jobs. The notion of supervision and evaluation of social workers and the relationship of salary increases to evaluation results as determined by managers or supervisors in agencies are examples of how this principle applies in social work settings (Taylor in Grusky and Miller 1981).

The fourth principle of scientific management focused on expanding the role played by managers in the overall production process. Taylorism saw managers as having many responsibilities previously thought to be within the purview of the workers themselves. As can be seen from the preceding three principles, managers became responsible for studying, defining, standardizing, and monitoring the tasks carried out by workers. Managers in effect took over from workers planning, decision making, and judgments about what jobs were to be done and how those jobs were to be carried out. This change resulted in a redivision of labor in the work setting. In many ways a new class of managers was created within work organizations. These managers, while assuming new responsibilities previously held by workers themselves, simultaneously took away some of the freedoms workers had previously held. Examples of this new division of labor can readily be seen in social work settings today. Especially in large agency settings, the promulgation of regulations and procedures by managers about how tasks are to be carried out and the expectation that direct service workers will then implement those regulations and procedures is an example of this principle. The supervision, evaluation, and establishing of rewards in the form of salary increases by management are all examples of this new division of labor between workers and managers (Taylor in Grusky and Miller 1981; Taylor in Shafritz and Ott 1987; and Pugh, Hickson, and Hinings 1985).

 Organizations operating according to the principles of scientific management are characterized by several themes. These themes include: high degrees of specialization in jobs and the qualifications and training of personnel, a clear division of labor, a distinct hierarchy of authority, and assumptions that workers are motivated primarily by economic rewards.

Bureaucracy

Another classic model of organizations was put forth by Max Weber in his formulation of bureaucracy. Weber (1864–1920) formulated the structure and characteristics of bureaucracy during approximately the same time period that Taylor's scientific management was emerging. Bureaucracy, in one form or another, defined in one way or another, and often symbolizing the shortcomings of organizational life, is almost a synonym for organization today. Bureaucracy in a number of respects has similarities with the scientific management theory we explored earlier. Bureaucracy values highly two dimensions of the traditional or dominant paradigm. It puts a premium on many of the elements of the positivistic, scientific, objective, and quantitative dimension of the traditional paradigm and on rationality and impersonality (Shafritz and Ott 1987; Pugh, Hickson, and Hinings 1985).

Weber outlined a number of **characteristics of bureaucracy**. First is the notion of a stable and officially stated structure of authority. Areas of authority within a bureaucracy are explicitly spelled out by rules or administrative regulations. Second, there is a clear "pecking order" or hierarchy of authority. This hierarchy clearly delineates who is responsible to whom within the bureaucratic organization. It provides a graded system of supervision in which lower offices are responsible to higher offices. Third, the organization's management is based on extensive written records of transactions, regulations, and policies that are kept over time. It is these written records that provide standardization and stability to the management of the organization. However, many people believe this emphasis on written records of activities and transactions is often taken to such extremes that workers' ability to do their jobs effectively is hindered. This over-emphasis on paperwork is disparagingly referred to as **"red tape."** Fourth, the persons who fulfill management functions—those who run the organization—have specialized training and expertise that specifically prepares them for their jobs. Fifth, organizational responsibilities take precedence in the day-to-day life of personnel. In other words, one's official duties come first. Sixth, management of a bureaucracy follows a system of stable and comprehensive rules learned by managers through specialized education for their positions. Seventh, employment in a bureaucracy is seen as a "vocation" or career for which the person is specially trained and that the person sees as a duty to perform. Eighth, the persons who manage a bureaucratic organization should be separate from those who own the means of production. This prevents individual interests from interfering with decision making for the good of the organization and helps ensure rational decision making. To make sure this is the case, managers receive a fixed salary for their work rather than an hourly wage. Ninth, the resources of the organization must be free from outside control in order for managers to allocate and reallocate resources purely on the basis of the needs of the organization. This includes resources in the sense of personnel as well as financial resources. In other words, administrators must have the authority to hire, fire, and move personnel from one position to another within the organization (Shafritz and Ott 1987; Pugh, Hickson, and Hinings 1985).

Weber's framework for bureaucracy was conceptualized as an **"ideal type."** By this it is meant that this structure is one toward which organizations should strive. It is not assumed that this type necessarily exists in any complete or perfect way in any given organizational setting. However, it was assumed in this framework that the closer an organization can come to this ideal structure, the more efficient and effective it will be in accomplishing its goals. We know from systematic study of existing organizations, as well as from our individual personal experiences, that no single organization is likely to include all the characteristics of a bureaucracy. We also know from the many criticisms of bureaucratic organizational life that incorporating the ideal characteristics of bureaucracy does not necessarily guarantee that the organization will reach its goals, nor that it will do so with maximum efficiency (Shafritz and Ott 1987; Pugh, Hickson, and Hinings 1985; Grusky and Miller 1981).

There are a number of other considerations in addition to the characteristics of bureaucracies that are important to think about as we attempt to develop more comprehensive understanding of HBSE in organizational contexts. Many of these other characteristics take us in the direction of alternative paradigm thinking. They include consideration of nonrational factors in organizational life, consideration of the impact of linkages to the external environment on the internal life of the organization, and consideration of personal as well as impersonal factors on our organizational experiences. Recognition of these other considerations lead to some approaches significantly different from those of scientific management and bureaucracy with their central concerns for rationality and efficiency.

These different approaches include human relations, decision theory, and systems models. While these approaches differ markedly from the classic approaches we have explored thus far, they are nevertheless considered here under traditional paradigms because they have more in common with traditional and dominant paradigmatic assumptions than with the dimensions of alternative paradigms we have outlined in this book. We might best think about these models as middle-range perspectives along a continuum leading us toward newer alternative or possible views of organizations.

CHARACTERISTICS OF BUREAUCRACY

1. Stable and official structure of authority.
2. Clear hierarchy of authority ("pecking order").
3. Written records kept over time.
4. Specialized training and expertise.
5. Official duties come first.
6. Stable and comprehensive system of rules.
7. Career employment.
8. Managers separate from "owners" of organization.
9. Managers free to allocate and reallocate resources.

Human Relations

What has come to be known as the human relations theory of organizational behavior emerged from and in many ways became a reaction to the focuses on rationality, machinelike precision, planning, and formality of classical scientific management and bureaucratic theory. Human relations thinking, however, did not discount entirely the traditional concerns of organizational life such as efficiency, effectiveness, and goal centeredness. Nor did it suggest that scientific management approaches be done away with entirely. It suggested instead that these concerns were insufficient to understand the complexities of modern organizational life (Etzioni 1964).

The Hawthorne Studies

Human relations thinking emerged directly from classical scientific approaches. Elton Mayo (1880–1949) is considered by many to be the founder of the human relations school. It was in the process of seeking to extend understanding of the necessary factors for truly efficient and productive organizations that human relations emerged somewhat unexpectedly. In the process of carrying out a series of studies that have come to be referred to as the Hawthorne Studies, Elton Mayo and his colleagues happened upon the basic concepts of human relations approaches. Two of the studies within the Hawthorne series illustrate some of the fundamental "surprises" that became the human relations school. One study involved exploring the effect of lighting or illumination in the work area on worker productivity. In this study, illumination was manipulated according to the hypothesis that optimum illumination would result in improved worker output. Contrary to this hypothesis, the researchers found that whether illumination was increased, decreased, or left alone, worker output increased. This led to the finding that the attention given the workers in the experiment and their interpretation of this attention as symbolic of the organization's interest in and concern for their perspectives was a crucial factor in their productivity. This has come to be known as the **Hawthorne effect.** In other words, workers were motivated to produce by other than purely economic rewards. They were also motivated by informal factors such as individual attention and concern for their input in the operation of the organization (Etzioni 1964; Pugh, Hickson, and Hinings 1985).

A second experiment in the Hawthorne series resulted in an equally "surprising" finding. This study is referred to as the Bank Wiring Room study because it involved observing and manipulating factors in a work setting in which telephone switchboards (called "banks") were being wired. This study resulted in the finding that not only informal factors such as individual attention affected worker productivity, but that groups of workers developed informal systems of managing output quite separate from the direction provided by management. The effect of this **informal group structure** was to set production norms or expectations about what were appropriate levels of production. On the one hand the group was concerned with not overproducing in the belief that overproduction would lead to layoffs of workers. On the other hand the group was concerned that production be "fair" in the sense that management and owners were not taken advantage of by unfairly low levels of production (Etzioni 1964; Pugh, Hickson, and Hinings 1985).

A number of the **basic concepts of human relations thinking** emerged from these studies and many others carried out since the original Hawthorne studies. First, the importance of individual attention and positive social interaction as well as economic rewards in worker productivity and satisfaction uncovered a virtually unexplored level of organizational life that centered on informal, nonrational, emotional, and unplanned interactions. Second, the pivotal role of informal social groups in efficiency and productivity was discovered. These groups functioned according to informal and internal norms, leadership structures, communication patterns, and levels of participation that had not been considered at all important to the scientific management proponents (Etzioni 1964; Gortner, Mahler, and Nicholson 1987; Pugh, Hickson, and Hining 1985; Grusky and Miller 1981).

It is helpful to note here that these early studies of organizational life out of which the human relations school emerged significantly increased interest in understanding the role and behavior of small groups in our day-to-day lives. Many basic concepts such as small-group norms, leadership, decision making, roles, communication, and goals, which are explored in Chapter 7 focusing on perspectives on small groups, have direct linkages to efforts to understand organizational life. This is consistent with our perspective in this book that sees human behavior and the social environment as an interlocking and overlapping network of mutually interdependent processes and contexts.

The tendency here may be to see only the differences between scientific management and human relations perspectives. We need to keep in mind, though, that neither of these schools of thought questioned in any fundamental ways the traditional and dominant forms of organizational life. Both schools saw maximum efficiency and productivity as the consuming purpose of organizations. Both schools accepted hierarchies of power and control (whether they be formal or informal) as givens in organizational life. Neither of these schools saw significant conflict among the interests of the various groups within organizations. It was assumed in these traditional approaches that what was good for the organization's owners and managers at the top of the hierarchy was good for its line of lower-level workers at the bottom of the organizational hierarchy. In short, neither of these schools provided fundamentally new or alternative models within which to carry out our organizational lives.

Theory X and Theory Y

As researchers continued to seek ways to maximize organizational efficiency, productivity, and goal achievement, the concerns of behavioral scientists began to influence organizational studies. Douglas McGregor (1906–1964), a social psychologist, became interested in the influence of managers' underlying assumptions about human behavior on their management practices. McGregor was specifically interested in managers' basic assumptions about what motivated people to behave as they do. His work led him to formulate two sets of assumptions about human motivation. One set he called **Theory X**. It reflects a belief on the part of managers that their role was to direct and control the activities of workers. The second set of assumptions he referred to as **Theory Y**. These assumptions reflected the beliefs of managers that their role was one of creating supportive relationships in which organizational members could exercise their inherent tendencies to grow, develop, and learn for their own benefit and that of the organization. McGregor's **Theory X assumptions are**:

1. *The average human being has an inherent dislike for work and will avoid it if he[she] can.*

2. *Because of this human characteristic of dislike for work, most people must be coerced, controlled, directed, or threatened with punishment to get them to put forth adequate effort toward the achievement of organizational objectives.*

3. *The average human being prefers to be directed, wishes to avoid responsibility, has relatively little ambition, wants security above all.* (Pugh, Hickson and Hinings 1985:167)

McGregor's Theory Y posits a very different perspective on what motivates us. Theory Y assumptions follow:

1. *The expenditure of physical and mental effort in work is as natural as play or rest. The ordinary person does not inherently dislike work.*

2. *[Humans] will exercise self-direction and self-control in the service of objectives to which [they] are committed.*

3. *The most significant reward that can be offered in order to obtain commitment is the satisfaction of the individual's self-actualizing needs. This can be a direct product of effort directed towards organizational objectives.*

4. *The average human being learns, under proper conditions, not only to accept but to seek responsibility.*

5. *Many more people are able to contribute creatively to the solution of organizational problems than do so.*

6. *At present the potentialities of the average person are not being fully used.* (Pugh, Hickson, and Hinings 1985:167–168)

Theory X is more consistent with the assumptions of scientific management and traditional paradigm thinking. Theory Y assumptions about human motivation are much more in line with the core concerns of social work. In addition, Theory Y assumptions are philosophically more consistent with the dimensions of alternative paradigms we have outlined in this book than are those of Theory X.

Systems Perspectives

Systems theories or perspectives on organizational behavior have much in common with general social systems structures and processes we discussed earlier in this book (Chapter 3). As in the case of our earlier discussion of social systems approaches, systems approaches to organizations represent a kind of middle ground between traditional and alternative paradigms. Systems perspectives on organizations, for example, have a significant reliance on scientific and quantitative tools consistent with traditional paradigm thinking used to analyze organizational systems. However, systems approaches also present integrated holistic perspectives on organizations and their environments consistent with alternative paradigm thinking. (This is especially true of open-system perspectives on organizations and the related contingency perspective on organizations. See below.)

Systems approaches to organizational analysis represent attempts to synthesize the classic or scientific management schools (emphasis on detailed scientific, empirical, quantitative study of organizations) and the human relations school (recognition of the reality of unplanned events and informal structures). Organizational systems thinkers differentiate between closed- and open-systems perspectives. A **closed-system** perspective views organizations as total units in and of themselves with occurrences in the environment surrounding the organizations having little impact on the organization itself. It is often suggested that Weber's machinelike bureaucratic structure with its completely rational planning and decision making separate from environmental influences represents a closed-system approach. **Open-systems** perspectives see organizations as units very much influenced by the larger environment in which they exist (Katz and Kahn in Shafritz & Ott 1987:252–254).

The systems school views an organization as a complex and interconnected set of elements interacting in dynamic processes influencing both internal elements and the environment surrounding the organizations. Organizations as systems must change or adapt as the environment in which they exist changes. Katz and Kahn (in Shafritz and Ott 1987:254–259) outline nine characteristics of open systems that they believe apply to organizations as open systems:

1. *Importation of energy:* Organizations must bring in energy from the external environment in the form of material and human resources. Organizations are neither self-sufficient nor self-contained.

2. *Through-put:* Organizations use the energy they import to produce products, train people, or provide services.

3. *Out-put:* Organizations send products into the external environment.

4. *Systems as cycles of events:* The pattern of energy exchange which results in out-put is cyclical. An organization takes in raw materials (energy), uses that energy to produce a product or service (through-put), returns that product or service to the environment (out-put) in exchange for money to purchase additional raw materials with which to begin repetition of the cycle.

5. *Negative Entropy:* A process necessary for organizations to fight off entropy (tendency for a system to lose energy or decay) and to build up energy reserves. (Anderson and Carter (1990) use the term synergy in a very similar way. Synergy, the use of energy through increased interaction of the system's parts to create additional energy, may be a more "manageable" concept.) In an organization, a for-profit organization in particular, this is the process of making a profit on out-put.

6. *Information Input, Negative Feedback, and the Coding Process:* Set of processes through which organizations develop mechanisms to receive information on their performance in order to correct problems. Organizations develop selective processes through which they code information input to filter out unnecessary or extraneous information.

7. *The Steady State and Dynamic Homeostasis:* A movable balance established by organizations taking in energy and information, using it, then exporting it in return for needed resources in a functional way. It is a movable balance in the sense that it represents a continuous but dynamic state of change rather than a static state.

8. *Differentiation:* Tendency of organizations to develop toward greater complexity and greater specialization of functions. (In organizations, this concept is consistent with the notion of division of labor we explored in our discussion of bureaucracy.)

9. *Equifinality:* The possibility of a system to attain its goals through a variety of different processes or paths.

You have very likely by now noticed a great deal of commonalty between the open-systems concepts used in relation to organizations above and the more general social systems concepts we explored earlier in this book. This is an example of the widespread influence that systems thinking has had in the natural, social, and behavioral sciences.

Contingency Theory

Before we leave systems perspectives on organizations, we should visit briefly a close "relative" of organizational systems thinking. This is contingency theory. **Contingency theory** suggests that the effectiveness of any organizational action—a decision, for example—is determined in the context of all the other elements and conditions in the organization at the time the action is taken. Contingency theory posits that everything is situational and that there are no absolutes or universals. Contingency theorists assert that organizations always act in a context of relative uncertainty. In other words, they make decisions at any given point based on incomplete information. Given the incompleteness of the information, organizations must make the best decision they can with the information they do have.

Both systems and contingency theorists have as a major concern the processes of and variables influencing decision making in organizations. A significant component of systems and contingency theories is decision making. Shafritz and Ott (1987:234–238) suggest that use of complex quantitative tools and techniques to assist in gathering and processing the most information possible in order to make the best decision possible in an uncertain environment is a central theme of systems and contingency theorists. Such decision-making processes based on the assumption of incomplete information and uncertainty has been referred to as "satisficing" (March and Simon 1958 in Gortner, Mahler, and Nicholson 1987:258).

STRENGTHS, WEAKNESSES, CRITICISM

Before considering alternative paradigmatic perspectives on organizations, it is helpful first to consider some things that the traditional and dominant perspectives do and do not tell us about the realities of human behavior in organizational environments. The traditional perspectives on organizations we have explored so far tell us much about this level of human behavior that will be helpful in our social work practice and in our personal lives. These traditional notions, however, leave much untold or unclear about this important arena as well.

Classical traditional perspectives such as scientific management and bureaucratic theory (also referred to as rationalistic or mechanistic perspectives because of their concern with rational goal setting and decision making aimed at achieving machine-like efficiency in organizations) told us much about the formal structure of organizations. Human relations thinking, with its concern for the nonrational and social elements of organizations, revealed much about the informal aspects of organizations. Systems and contingency theories presented us with perspectives that recognize both the formal and the informal aspects of organizations in addition to stressing the influences of the larger social environment on organizations.

These traditional perspectives, however, leave much unsaid about other important dimensions of organizational life. Classical perspectives (scientific management and bureaucracy) as well as human relations perspectives all assume, for example, that hierarchy is a necessary prerequisite for efficient and effective goal achievement in organizations. Systems approaches also assume some degree of hierarchy, although its specific characteristics may change in response to environmental conditions. Some alternative perspectives question the essential nature of hierarchy in organizations (Iannello 1992).

Flowing from the assumption of hierarchy of traditional perspectives—classical, human relations, and systems—is the assumption that power must be divided unequally among the members of the organization. Power here is defined as the ability to influence movement toward accomplishment of goals. Whether this is according to formal and rational structures in bureaucracy, informal and nonrational networks in human relations approaches, or flexible and changeable arrangements based on environmental conditions in systems thinking, all of these traditional approaches include an inherent power differential among members.

In addition, these traditional perspectives see inequality or unequal distribution of power as basically functional for organizational members. In scientific management, lower-level workers benefit from power differences by having their basic economic needs met even though management and owners benefit materially to a greater extent in proportion to their greater power. In human relations thinking, not only are formal differences in power recognized, but the informal social networks reflect differences in power among network members as well. These formal and informal power inequities serve different, though overall functional, purposes. They support the realization of the organization's formal goals and they support the informal (social or personal) goals of members.

System's approaches see power differences as necessary and of mutual benefit in service to overall system goals and the goals of subsystems. Systems approaches do recognize the necessity for power (authority) distribution to be rearranged periodically in response to changes in the environment. It is interesting to note that traditional organizational paradigms rarely use the term *power*. *Power* is instead referred to as authority over persons and resources within the organization that is necessary to maintain itself and to reach goals. Some alternative perspectives explicitly address issues of power and power inequities in organizations and seek ways to make power distribution within organizations more apparent so that it can be redistributed more equitably. Alternative perspectives also tend to approach power differences among organizational members as problematic rather than functional.

Another area in which alternative and traditional perspectives differ is that of conflict. Scientific-management approaches see truly rational and formal organizations as basically nonconflictual. Human relations approaches when optimally implemented see informal structures as reducing the need for conflict to the point that these organizations have sometimes been referred to as "big happy families." Systems approaches go a bit further in recognizing that organizational conflict exists but they suggest that effective organizational systems will be "self-righting" in that they will make whatever adjustments are required to address and reduce conflict in order to return to a positive and mutually beneficial balanced state. Systems approaches, while recognizing the existence of conflict, see it as an exception, not a norm. (Buckley has addressed issues of conflict—he calls it "tension"—as a more "normal" part of systems behavior than most other systems thinkers.) Most systems approaches, nevertheless, operate from assumptions of cooperation and harmony (Barnard and Simon in Abrahamsson 1977:151).

What is needed are alternative organizational perspectives that recognize the reality of differences or conflicts among members and that create mechanisms for using conflict resolution processes as an ongoing avenue for strengthening the organization (Abrahamsson 1977; Iannello 1992).

ALTERNATIVE PARADIGMS

As we begin to explore alternative paradigms we emphasize that we do not want to exclude information provided by traditional perspectives. We want to extend that information in order to gain more comprehensive, inclusive perspectives on organizations. We are reminded here that alternative paradigms, while often critical of traditional perspectives, also often use traditional thinking as a departure point. In this respect it is helpful to recall the importance of historical perspective and the notion of continuum in our thinking about HBSE. Our goal, as we proceed on our journey to explore alternative perspectives on organizations, is to fill in some of the gaps in our knowledge and to clarify some of the areas left unclear by traditional organizational thinking, as we noted above. We are especially concerned with finding perspectives that are consistent with the core concerns of social work. Alternative perspectives are more "in process" than many traditional perspectives. Because many of the alternative perspectives are only now emerging, there are fewer examples of them around us. These alternative perspectives are also less "finished" in that their potential for improving the quality of our organizational lives can only be guessed in many respects. We begin our exploration of alternative perspectives with the notion of organizational culture as an approach to thinking about organizations in more holistic ways.

Organizational Culture

Regardless of whether an organization's goals, practices, or philosophical perspectives bring it more in line with traditional paradigm or alternative paradigm thinking, it can be thought of as having an organizational culture that reflects and supports its prevailing view of the world. Earlier in this book we defined *culture* as the accumulation of customs, values, and artifacts that are shared by a group of people.

Schein (1992:7–15) suggests that organizations have many of the characteristics commonly associated with culture. He especially emphasizes that organizations are cultures by virtue of the shared experiences that organizational members hold in common. These shared experiences merge into a whole pattern of beliefs, values, and rituals that become the "essence" of the **organization's culture** and help provide stability. Organizational members adhere to these patterns, but they are not likely to be conscious of them in their day-to-day activities. This invisible or "taken for granted" aspect accounts for some of the difficulty outsiders have in fully understanding a given organization. It also accounts for some of the confusion and discomfort that new organizational members are likely to experience when they first enter the organization. This taken-for-granted aspect also helps explain why longtime members of an organization have difficulty explaining to new members or to outsiders exactly how the organization operates.

What does this image portray about the "organizational culture" and "organizational climate" in which these men work?

Schein (1992:11–12) stresses that all organizations do not develop smoothly integrated cultures shared equally by all organization members. When this integration is lacking the results are likely to be ambiguity and conflict. Lack of an integrated culture can come about because of turnover in organizational membership or because of the different experiences from outside the organization that its members bring with them. As a result, such organizations may be continuously trying to create an integrated whole from the shared and unshared experiences of members. Some organization members, leaders for example, are likely to play a larger role than others in the processes of creating or changing the culture.

This perspective on organizational culture can help us understand both stability and change in social work and human service organizations. This notion of culture combined with our perspective on traditional and alternative paradigms can help us to understand some of the problems within organizations and between organizations and the people they attempt to serve. For example, how can an organization with a culture characterized by patriarchal, white, quantitative, competitive, and privileged perspectives respond effectively to consumers and new organizational members whose worldviews are characterized by feminist, multicultural, qualitative, or cooperative perspectives? The concept of organizational culture can help us understand the difficulty faced by women or people of color when they enter organizations (and they typically enter as lower-ranking members, rather than as members in formal leadership positions) that have historically been made up only of privileged white males with a traditional paradigm perspective. It can also help us appreciate how important it is that the organizational culture of social work organizations reflect and respect the larger culture of the communities and people they serve.

Organizational Climate

In addition to the somewhat invisible but highly influential concept of organizational culture is the concept of organizational climate. These two concepts are highly interrelated. They both communicate the "feel" of an organization. *Organizational culture* includes such basic components as the fundamental beliefs and values of the organization. **Organizational climate,** on the other hand, reflects how organization members communicate organizational culture in more visible or observable ways. For example, how members interpret or communicate to others the organization's policies, practices, and procedures (Schneider et al. 1996:7–9). It is important to assess the climate of an organization in order to determine the nature of the culture communicated to consumers, other organizations, and the larger community of which the organization is a part. Schneider et al. identify **four key climate dimensions:**

1. The nature of interpersonal relationships. *Is there mutual sharing and trust or conflict and mistrust? Are relationships between . . . units cooperative or competitive? Does the organization support socialization of newcomers or a sink-or-swim approach? Do people feel that their personal welfare is important to those around them and to top management?*

2. The nature of the hierarchy. *Are decisions affecting work and the workplace made only by top management or are they made with participation*

from those affected by the decision? Is the organization characterized by a team approach to work or strictly an individualistic competitive approach? Does management have special perquisites that separate them from their subordinates, such as special parking or dining facilities?

3. The nature of work. *Is the work challenging or boring? Are jobs adaptable by the people performing them, or are they rigidly defined so that everyone must do them the same way? Does the organization provide workers with the necessary resources (tools, supplies, information) to get the work done?*

4. The focus of support and rewards. *Are the goals of work and the standards of excellence widely known and shared? What gets supported: being warm and friendly to [consumers] or being fast? Is getting the work done (quantity) or getting the work right (quality) rewarded? On what basis are people hired? To what goals and standards are they trained? What facets of performance are appraised and rewarded?* (1996:10–11)

The "Iron Law of Oligarchy"

An alternative to traditional approaches to organizational behavior emerged at virtually the same time that Taylor's perspectives (discussed earlier) on scientific management and rationality in organizations were gaining prominence. This alternative appeared also at about the same time that Weber's notions about bureaucratic structure were being introduced. This alternative perspective preceded the more recent notions of organizational culture and climate. However, as you read this section, keep in mind the concepts of organizational climate and culture which can help you understand the kind and feel of the organization Michels described. Robert Michels published his work describing the "Iron Law of Oligarchy" in its original German in 1911. Scientific management and the theory of bureaucracy gained prominence roughly during the period from the turn of the century to 1930. Michels's work, however, took a decidedly contrary and pessimistic approach to the kinds of organizations Taylor and Weber were heralding as the answer to the organizational needs of the time.

Michels suggested that rather than organizations striving to meet the rationally specified needs of the organization as a whole, they instead serve the needs only of an elite few who gain control of the organization. He became convinced that formal organizations made democracy (participation and decision making by a majority of organizational members) impossible and inevitably resulted in **oligarchy**—government or control by the few.

As organizations grew in scale their original goals would always end up being displaced by the goal of maintaining the organization in service to the interests of a small group of controlling elites. As an organization grew and became more bureaucratic it would employ a "ruling class" of managers or leaders. Their self-interests in maintaining the prestige and influence that accompanied their leadership positions resulted in a growing gap between the top and the bottom of the organizational hierarchy. Leaders no longer represented the interests of followers (Michels in Grusky and Miller 1981; Pugh, Hickson, and Hinings 1985; Iannello 1992).

Michels originally based his theory on his studies of revolutionary democratic political parties that grew into conservative political bureaucracies far removed from their original democratic goals. He came to believe that the development of oligarchy would happen to any organization regardless of its original purpose because oligarchy was a function of growing size or scale and the accompanying emergence of specialization and hierarchy. He was convinced that bureaucracy and democracy were inherently in opposition with one another (Michels in Grusky and Miller 1981; Pugh, Hickson, and Hinings 1985).

As the self-interests of the organizational ruling class began to take precedence over original, more democratic goals of organizational members, Michels suggested that the leaders of the organization would stress the need for internal unity. The harmony of ideas and views, along with the need to avoid or suppress tension and conflict, would become paramount. He also suggested that the ruling elite would put forth notions about dangers and hostility in the environment surrounding the organization, underscoring the need to hide internal differences from those outside the organization in order to maintain the status quo of the organization (Pugh, Hickson, and Hinings 1985:207–210).

Michels's view of the difficulty (the virtual impossibility, he came to believe) of large organizations' goals remaining consistent with democratic ideals was indeed a pessimistic one. Whether it was entirely justified is perhaps open to some argument. However, his alternative perspective does suggest that traditional models of organization are far from ideal and entail significant problems and risks in terms of ethics and values of which social workers need to be aware.

The tendency toward serving a select few powerful and prestigious leaders rather than the needs of all organizational members (and consumers of organizational services, as well, we might add) is certainly inconsistent with a number of core concerns of social workers. This tendency is contrary to concerns about maximum participation, self-determination, rights to resources, social and economic justice, and respect for diversity. As social workers and members of organizations (both as leaders and as followers), we need to recognize and act to prevent tendencies toward organizational oligarchy.

A Critical Perspective

Kathleen Iannello (1992) presents a contemporary alternative perspective on organizations that follows in part from her belief that Michels's iron law of oligarchy, while criticized by a number of students of organizations, certainly has not been refuted. Indeed, she suggests that it is out of the hierarchical nature of traditional organizations that Michels's oligarchy grows (Iannello 1992:3–25). If you recall, from our earlier exploration of traditional perspectives, hierarchy is considered a necessary component of modern organizational structures. This is especially so in a bureaucracy, perhaps the most common modern organization form (Iannello 1992:3–7, 12).

Iannello's critical perspective suggests that alternatives to hierarchy are possible. However, to create alternatives we must first recognize that hierarchy is embedded throughout the values, norms, and ideologies of the larger society. We must not accept the traditional organizational assumption that hierarchy is inherent in organizations, but not necessarily connected to hierarchical norms, values, and ideologies in the larger society.

This critical perspective expands on traditional open-systems theory (explored earlier) in its emphasis on the interrelatedness of organizational structure and the values, norms, and ideologies of the surrounding environment. Iannello (1992:7–10) suggests that this critical perspective goes beyond traditional open-systems theory in its recognition of the entire *society* as the environment having an "important and pervasive" influence on the nature of the organization. This perspective is in contrast to open-systems notions of an environment consisting only of those systems having a direct impact or influence on the organization, for example, other competing organizations in the immediate environment of the focal organization.

The critical perspective goes beyond open systems and much other traditional organizational thinking in another respect. It incorporates historical perspective as an additional pivotal consideration necessary for developing alternative models of organizations (Iannello 1992:10). This perspective suggests, for example, that much is to be learned by asking "why," in a historical sense, an organization is structured as it is. How did it come to be the way it is? This questioning can engage us in paradigm analysis at the organizational level. For example, we might ask who founded the organization? What was their worldview? What were their values? Did they recognize the importance of difference? Did they see the organization's purpose as preserving or restoring human dignity and assisting members to reach their maximum potential? How was power distributed within the organization?

The critical perspective questions the necessity and inherent nature of hierarchy in organizations. It offers a different perspective on the meaning of hierarchy, and from this alternative perspective it calls attention to some of the problems created by hierarchy. Through its alternative analysis of hierarchy, the critical perspective raises a number of issues related to the dimensions of traditional and alternative paradigms with which we are concerned here. Specifically, it addresses such issues as power, domination, and privilege. It offers a definition of **hierarchy** as "any system in which the distribution of power, privilege and authority are both systematic and unequal" (Iannello 1992:15).

This perspective's critique of hierarchy includes the concept of alienation of lower-level workers resulting from their lack of access to and participation in decision-making processes. The critique also questions the social control directed toward lower-level members of the hierarchy by those at the top in order to maintain their positions of power.

By looking beyond traditional narrow or closed-system organizational perspectives to include societal values and historical influences, the critical perspective reflects several dimensions of alternative paradigm thinking. This critical view allows the incorporation of a feminist perspective. It allows us to question the influence of patriarchal and masculinist societal values on organizational structures such as hierarchy.

Its historical perspective allows inclusion of broader interpretive, personal, experiential standpoints in addition to traditional "great person" accounts for thinking about the past and present structures of organizations. It allows serious consideration, for example, of power relations in organizations based on the experiences of all organization members rather than only the experiences of "key" administrators or decision makers (Iannello 1992:3–13). In this respect it more readily allows for the inclusion of women's perspectives in thinking about organizations. For it is at lower levels in organizational hierarchies—clerical and administrative assistant positions, for example—that women have historically been concentrated.

Consensus Organizations

Iannello develops a model of nonhierarchical organizations she refers to as consensus. These organizations operate "primarily through a consensus decision-making process." We visited traditional notions of decision theory in conjunction with our discussion of traditional-systems approaches earlier. The decision-making process followed in consensus organizations operates in a much more participative way in contrast to the centralized and alienating decision making by managers and leaders at the top levels of the hierarchy in traditional organizations. **Consensus decision making** occurs only after an issue has been widely discussed, with participation of a broad base (ideally all) of the organization members. After this discussion takes place, "one or more members of the assembly sum up prevailing sentiment, and if no objections are voiced, this becomes agreed-on policy" (Iannello 1992; Mansbridge in Iannello 1992:27).

Iannello notes that consensus organizations are also referred to by some as cooperative or collective organizations. She defines **consensus organization** as "any enterprise in which control rests ultimately and overwhelmingly with the members-employees-owners, regardless of the particular legal framework through which it is achieved" (Iannello 1992; Rothschild and Whitt in Iannello 1992:27). Consensus organizations attempt to "humanize the workplace, to put meaning and values back into jobs in order to reconnect the worker with society." To accomplish this goal these organizations focus on maximizing the level of commitment on the part of all workers to this primary goal. The means used to increase commitment and reduce alienation in consensus organizations is reducing hierarchy.

Examples of existing models of consensus organizations include the Israeli kibbutzim and a number of historical Native American tribal organizations. However, we should be careful not to over-generalize. We need to recognize that different kibbutzim and current Native American tribal government organizations operationalize consensus principles to different degrees. Ideally, a kibbutz operates on consensus assumptions and principles. These include shared and egalitarian decision making in all aspects of organizational life. This principle is implemented through weekly meetings of the entire organizational membership and a complex system of committees. This allows face-to-face decision making. Leadership positions within the organization are elected and rotated among members to discourage hierarchy. Leadership positions offer no individual rewards for the individuals who hold them. Rewards within the organization are linked to achievement of collective rather than individual goals (Iannello 1992:32).

As noted in the earlier discussion of consensus-based decision making in small groups, Attneave stresses the central role played by consensus in many Native American tribal government organizations. While the earlier discussion focuses on a preference for consensus in small-group decision making, Attneave stressed that this form of decision making operated whether the group was "the tribe, the band, the family or any other coherent cluster of people." Attneave noted that "tribal histories never suggested the impatient solution of majority vote so revered by 'democracies' " (Attneave 1982:66–67).

Comparison of Consensus and Bureaucratic Organizations

How do consensus and bureaucratic organizations compare in terms of some of the basic issues and concerns of organizations generally? Rothschild and Whitt studied a number of consensus organizations, and Iannello used their findings to compare consensus and hierarchical bureaucratic organizations along several dimensions. A summary of this work follows:

1. **Authority:** *In contrast to the ideal bureaucratic structure, in which authority is vested in the individual according to position or rank within the organizations, authority in the consensual organization rests with the collectivity.*

2. **Rules:** *In the consensual organization, rules are minimal and based on the "substantive ethics" of the situation. In the traditional organizations, rules are fixed, and emphasis is placed on conformity to the rules.*

3. **Social control:** *For the consensual organization, social control is based on something akin to peer pressure. Social control rarely becomes problematic, because of the homogeneity of the group....Within a bureaucracy, social control is achieved through hierarchy and supervision of subordinates by their superiors, according to the formal and informal sanctions of the organizations.*

4. **Social relations:** *For the collective, social relations stem from the community ideal. "Relations are to be holistic, personal, of value in themselves." In the traditional model, the emphasis is placed on impersonality, which is linked to a sense of professionalism. "Relations are to be role based, segmental, and instrumental."*

5. **Recruitment and advancement:** *In the consensual organization, recruitment is based on friendship networks, "informally assessed knowledge and skills," and compatibility with organizations' values. The concept of advancement is generally not valued, since there is no hierarchy of positions and related rewards. Within the bureaucratic model recruitment is based on formal qualifications and specialized training. The concept of advancement is very meaningful for an individual's career and is based on formal assessment of performance according to prescribed rules and paths of promotion.*

6. **Incentive structure:** *For the consensual organization, "normative and solidarity incentives are primary; material incentives are secondary." For bureaucracy, "remunerative incentives are primary."*

7. **Social stratification:** *The consensual organization strives to be egalitarian. Any type of stratification is carefully created and monitored by the collectivity. In the bureaucracy, there are "differential rewards" of prestige, privilege, or inequality, each justified by hierarchy.*

8. **Differentiation:** *In the consensual structure, division of labor is minimized, particularly with regard to intellectual versus manual work. Jobs and functions are generalized, with the goal of "demystification of*

expertise." Bureaucracy maximizes division of labor to the extent that there is a "dichotomy between intellectual work and manual work and between administrative tasks and performance tasks." Technical expertise is highly valued and specialization of jobs is maximized. (Iannello 1992:28–29)

Limits of Consensus Organizations

There are a number of factors that limit the ability of organizations to successfully implement nonhierarchical structures. Some of these are summarized below:

1. **Time:** *Consensus-style decision making takes more time than bureaucratic decision making, in which an administrator simply hands down a decision....The idea of consensus, in which every member of an organization must agree to a decision, conjures up the picture of long, drawn-out sessions in which members may never agree. However, real-world experience has demonstrated that the endless rules and regulations of bureaucracies can also lead to protracted disputes....It is important to recognize that both bureaucracies and consensual organizations are capable of making decisions quickly or slowly, depending on the nature of the issue.*

2. **Emotional intensity:** *There is more emotional intensity in the consensual setting. Consensual organizations provide face-to-face communication and consideration of the total needs of the individual. As a result, conflict within the organization may exact a much higher personal cost; individuals are held more accountable for their actions. In the bureaucratic organization, impersonality and formality make conflict less personal and therefore easier to handle. But bureaucratic procedure also alienates people and is less satisfying personally....[The] degree of emotional intensity has positive and negative aspects for members of both organization types.*

3. **Non-democratic habits and values:** *As members of a hierarchical society, most of us are not well prepared to participate in consensual styles of organization. Our earliest contact with organizational life in educational and other settings is bureaucratic.*

4. **Environmental constraints:** *Environmental constraints—economic, political, or social pressures from the outside—are more intense in consensual organizations because such groups often form around issues that run counter to the mainstream of society....Consensual organizations can also at times benefit because they provide a service or offer an avenue of participation that is not available through other organizations. This has been true, for example, of organizations providing alternative health care or food co-ops providing natural or organically grown foods.*

5. **Individual differences:** *While bureaucracies are able to capitalize on differences in the attitudes, skills, and personalities of individual members, such differences may pose a problem for organizations based on consensual process. For consensual organizations such diversity may lead to conflict. Yet while this point has merit, it paints a somewhat false picture of both*

> *bureaucratic and consensual organization. . . . Some argue that bureaucracy breeds sameness, encourages lack of creativity, and provides little in the way of reward for anyone attempting to break out of set patterns. When such rewards exist they are reserved primarily for those at the top of the organization. Yet others have pointed out that bureaucracies, or at least public bureaucracies, have the most diverse membership of any institutions. Thus, it is unsurprising that members of consensual organizations, which are frequently homogeneous, are likely to agree on issues that face the organization.* (Rothschild and Whitt, Iannello in Iannello 1992:29–31)

An alternate perspective would suggest that it is possible for similarity and difference to coexist. For example, it would seem that there can be homogeneity in terms of shared philosophy and values simultaneous with diversity in ethnicity, gender, and sexual orientation. However, the above limitations do leave the issue of conflict as a potential source of growth and strength somewhat unaddressed.

Modified Consensus Organizations

Based on the assumptions and principles of consensus organizations, their comparison with hierarchical/bureaucratic organizations, and the limitations of both models, along with her study of three different consensus organizations, Iannello develops an organizational type she refers to as "modified consensus." The elements of this model have a good deal of consistency with core concerns of social work. Modified consensus organizations are characterized by alternative structures and processes from those of traditional models. These differences include the areas of decision making, non-hierarchical structures and processes, empowerment, and clarity of goals.

Modified consensus organizations assure broad-based participation in decision making, but are also conscious of the need to make timely decisions for the sake of operational efficiency. This is accomplished by differentiating between critical and routine decisions. Critical decisions are those that involve overall policy and have the potential for change in the fundamental direction of the organization. Critical decisions are made by the entire membership; in hierarchical organizations, only those at the top make critical policy decisions. In modified consensus organizations, routine decisions are those that are important in the day-to-day operation of the organization. Routine decisions are delegated horizontally within the organization according to the skills and interests of organizational members.

A second area of difference between modified consensus and traditional organizations is in concern for process. Process issues include concern for consensus, emerging leadership, and empowerment. Central to process is trust. This essential trust is fostered by maintaining consensus through the participation and agreement of all organization members in the critical decisions faced by the organization. The trust built through consensus on critical decisions in turn engenders sufficient trust among members to allow routine decisions to be delegated. Without mutual trust among members, the domination of some by others in the organization, characteristic of traditional hierarchical organizations, would be difficult to avoid.

Leadership is essential in both traditional and alternative organizations. The nature of leaders and the processes for development of leadership varies significantly between traditional and modified consensus organizations, however. Modified consensus organizations look within their membership and recognize its variety of abilities and expertise as the source of leadership. Efforts are made to maximize the skills of members. Members with specific skills provide ongoing education and training of other members who want to learn these skills. Central to this process is rotation of members through various positions of leadership within the organization. The assumption is that all members have the potential for leadership in a wide range of areas. This perspective is very different from traditional notions of leadership that hold leadership to be characteristic only of the specialized experts at the top of the hierarchy. (See discussion of traditional and alternative notions of leadership in Chapter 7 for a detailed discussion of different perspectives on leadership.)

Modified consensus organizations also seek to minimize power and maximize empowerment. Iannello (1992:44–45) describes power as "the notion of controlling others, while empowerment is associated with the notion of controlling oneself." Therefore, within organizations based on empowerment, members monitor themselves. In organizations based on power, there must be an administrative oversight function. This perspective is consistent with our earlier discussions of empowerment as power to accomplish one's goals or reach one's potential rather than "power over" others.

In the organizations she studied, power "is a relational concept that has a win/lose element to it" (1992:120). The members of the women's organizations she studied and found most consistent with modified consensus structure and operation rejected the idea of voting on major decisions for this reason. To vote meant there would always be some members who perceived themselves to have "lost" (unless voting was unanimous). "With consensus decision making, based on the concept of empowerment, it is perceived that everyone 'wins' because all members agree to the final decision" (Iannello 1992:120).

Feminist Approaches to Organizations

As indicated in the discussion of consensus-based organizations, feminist theory offers an important alternative perspective on organizational behavior. This theoretical perspective is increasingly being applied to thinking about organizational life. For example, Gilligan's theory that women's development (see Chapter 5) is based on an ethic of care and the centrality of relationships has been applied to organizational life and business enterprises. Liedtka notes that "Gilligan's metaphor of the web to represent feminine thinking, has been juxtaposed against the use of hierarchy to represent masculine thinking" (1996). Burton also suggests that "in one sense it might be said that traditional, economics-based approaches to management have concentrated on the legalistic, contractual, masculine side of human existence" (1996). These alternative organizations based on relationships and caring "are not bureaucracies. . . . The rules in a bureaucracy become, over time, the ends rather than the means. Thus, caring, even for the customer or client, is subordinated to perpetuation of the organization in its current state" (Liedtka 1996).

Core concepts from Gilligan's theory are associated with other new management theories such as stakeholder theory and the notion of learning organizations (see discussion of learning organizations in this chapter). "Stakeholder theory, like the ethic of care, is built upon a recognition of interdependence." Stakeholder theorists suggest that "the corporation is constituted by the network of relationships which it is involved in with employees, customers, suppliers, communities, businesses and other groups who interact with and give meaning and definition to the corporation" (Liedtka 1996).

According to Burton, newer approaches such as "stakeholder theory might then be said to be the feminine counterpart to traditional management" theories (1996). Stakeholder theory

> *seems to promote a more cooperative, caring type of relationship. Firms should seek to make decisions that satisfy stakeholders, leading to situations where all parties involved in a relationship gain. The inherent relatedness of the firm under stakeholder theory forces firms to examine the effect of their decisions on others, just as the inherent relatedness of humans in feminist theory forces us to examine the effect of our decisions on others.* (Burton and Dunn 1996)

The concept of the learning organization, another alternative approach to organizational management, also reflects elements of feminist theory, especially the ethic of care. The learning organization also appreciates the importance of relationship and interconnectedness characteristic of much alternative paradigm thinking, including feminist perspectives. For example, the learning organization is closely linked with "communities that share a sense of purpose that connects each member to each other, and to the community at large. Learning organizations are characterized by an ability to maintain an open dialogue among members, that seeks first to understand, rather than evaluate, the perspectives of each. . . . Care-based organizations would seem ideally suited for such processes" (Burton and Dunn 1996).

Caring organizations recognize the importance of employees and frontline workers as the primary providers of services to consumers: "It is the employees who deal directly with these customers who ultimately determine the firm's success or failure. The rest of the organization, including senior management, exists to support and respond to, rather than control and monitor, these frontline workers" (Liedtka 1996). Such organizations will be characterized by listening to the needs of their consumers and by willingness to experiment to meet the changing needs of consumers. As Liedtka points, out, "they will need to listen, to inquire, and to experiment. They will be collaborative enterprises. . . which value the diversity of their workforce, and who work in partnership with their suppliers and in the communities in which they reside" (Liedtka 1996).

Chaos/Complexity Theory and Organizations

In Chapter 3 we explored alternative theories that were extensions of social systems thinking. Included in these discussions were chaos and complexity theories. Students of organizations have begun to explore the application of these two theoretical perspectives to organizational behavior. These perspectives are increasingly presented as alternatives to traditional bureaucratic approaches to organizations. One of the most significant differences in the newer approaches of chaos and complexity is their focus on the importance of recognizing the positive aspects of change and flexibility, while traditional bureaucratic approaches seek stability and standardization. Evans points out, for example, that "traditional systems theorists have held that equilibrium or stability is the desirable state for an organization," but chaos theorists contend "that a condition of loosely bounded instability appears necessary to enable existing structures and patterns of interaction to respond to environmental demands." New paradigm managers focus more on developing "organizational processes and systems that support the agency's capacity, self-renewal, and self-organization" (1996). Wheatley suggests that consistent with newer extensions of systems thinking, organizations can be described as "living systems." She posits that

> *As living systems, organizations possess all of the creative, self-organizing capacities of other forms of life. The people within all organizations are capable of change, growth, and adaptation—they do not require outside engineering or detailed design. People are capable of creating structures and responses that work, then moving into new ones when required. We possess natural capacities to work with change in a creative and effective way.* (Wheatley and Kellner-Rogers 1996)

For social workers, a particularly helpful aspect of newer organizational thinking is its focus on the benefits and need for diversity in organizations. Evans stresses that "one excellent source of creative disorder is work force diversity. Organizational culture traditionally works to smooth out, if not eliminate, difference, but public managers can endeavor to counter this tendency by flexible job assignments, creating diverse work groups, and recognizing the unique contributions of individual women and men" (Evans 1996).

Another element of new-paradigm organizational thinking is its emphasis on understanding the multiple layers and complexity of organizational life. Zhu discusses the complementary nature of Eastern philosophical recognition of complexity and interconnectedness within organizations. Zhu points out that complex "systems involve multiple dimensions which are at once differentiated and interconnected." From this "Oriental systems approach" the organizational environment is closely connected to the larger social environment in "a dynamic web of multiple relations: relations within the complexity of 'the world,' relations between the human mind and that world, and relations among human beings" (Zhu 1999).

These newer approaches also incorporate a more spiritual approach to organizational management. They shift the focus "from structural and functional aspects of organization to the spiritual characteristics and qualities of organizational life." Overman suggests these managers focus "on energy, not matter; on becoming, not being; on coincidence, not causes; on constructivism, not determinism; and on new states of awareness and consciousness" (Overman 1996).

Alternative approaches to management stress the importance of relationships, social networks, and small groups. One approach is referred to as "the **network organization,** in which individuals or small groups use networks of personal contacts and contractual relationships to bring together the resources needed for each venture" (Hendry 1999).

Theory Z

We included in traditional approaches to understanding organizations a discussion of Theory X and Theory Y. These were organizational theories based on sets of assumptions about people held by managers. Douglas McGregor proposed Theory X as an approach to management based on the assumption that people were basically lazy and irresponsible. Theory X held that because people would naturally seek to avoid work and responsibility, a major part of the manager's responsibility was to constantly watch workers to make sure they were working and fulfilling their responsibilities. Theory Y, on the other hand, held that people "are fundamentally hardworking, responsible, and need only to be supported and encouraged" (Ouchi 1981:58–59).

William Ouchi (1981) developed an alternative theory of organizational management that he termed Theory Z. Like Theories X and Y, Theory Z was an approach to management premised on assumptions about humans. However, Theory Z had its basis not in traditional Western assumptions about humans, but in assumptions about humans based on Japanese culture and reflected in many Japanese organizations and approaches to management. While not all Japanese firms displayed all Theory Z characteristics to the same degrees, Ouchi found a significant number of Japanese firms that reflected a Theory Z perspective. Ouchi compared U. S. corporations with these Japanese firms and found fundamental differences in the assumptions underlying the business enterprises in the two countries. He contrasted the elements of the two approaches as follows:*

Japanese Organization	U.S. Organization
Lifetime employment	Short-term employment
Slow evaluation and promotion	Rapid evaluation and promotion
Non-specialized career paths	Specialized career paths
Implicit control mechanisms	Explicit control mechanisms
Collective decision making	Individual decision making
Collective responsibility	Individual responsibility
Holistic concern	Segmented concern

The Theory Z emphasis on job security, collective decision making, and collective responsibility for decisions, along with a holistic perspective, has a good deal of similarity with the consensus and modified consensus models described above. Unlike consensus and modified consensus notions, Theory Z has been applied to very large profit-making organizations, including major U.S. and multinational business corporations.

Ouchi suggests that participative or consensus decision making is perhaps the best-known feature of Japanese organizations. A consensus approach has also been widely researched and experimented with in the United States and Europe.

A group or team approach is a central mechanism for implementing consensus-based decision making in Theory Z organizations. A **team** approach, sometimes referred to as **quality circle** or **quality control circle**, is a cohesive work group with the ability

*From: *Theory Z: How American Business Can Meet the Japanese Challenge,* by William G. Ouchi. Copyright © 1981. Reprinted by permission of Perseus Books Publishers, a member of Perseus Books.

to operate with a significant degree of autonomy in the areas for which it is responsible. While teams are often formal and official work groups, many times these teams are not officially created but simply form from among organization members to address a problem or issue that arises. Ouchi describes the function of quality control circles:

> *What they do is share with management the responsibility for locating and solving problems of coordination and productivity. The circles, in other words, notice all the little things that go wrong in an organization—and then put up the flag.* (1981:223)

A team approach is central to Theory Z-type organizations in both the United States and Japan. In the United States, the Theory Z organization's focus on consensus decision making is usually implemented at the small-group level within the large organization. Ouchi describes the typical participative decision-making structure and process as it has been adapted in the West:

> *Typically, a small group of not more than eight or ten people will gather around a table, discuss the problem and suggest alternative solutions. . . .The group can be said to have achieved a consensus when it finally agrees upon a single alternative and each member of the group can honestly say to each other member three things:*
>
> 1. *I believe that you understand my point of view.*
> 2. *I believe that I understand your point of view.*
> 3. *Whether or not I prefer this decision, I will support it, because it was arrived at in an open and fair manner.* (Ouchi 1981:36–37)

In Japan consensus decision making operates on a much larger scale through the interaction and interconnections of many groups, large and small, within the organization. This more extensive use of group decision making is possible because people are much more likely to operate from a framework of shared philosophy, values, and beliefs than are people in U.S. organizations. Included in this shared framework in Japan is a strong sense of collective values, an assumption that employment is for life, a sense of trust, and an assumption of close personal relationships among people in the workplace. Given this underlying cultural belief that collective interests take precedence over individual interests, along with an assumption that one's employment in a Japanese company will be for life, it is crucial that everyone who will be touched by a decision will have a say in that decision. In effect, everyone must agree with decisions because everyone may very well have to live with the decision for the rest of their working lives. A basic trust among all parties in the workplace is also supportive of collective decision making. Emphasis on collective decision making and collective responsibility for those decisions, along with a high level of interpersonal trust among members, results in much less explicit hierarchies in Japanese organizations. Conflict and disagreement, however, must be kept to a minimum in these organizations.

There is some indication that, because of economic problems facing Japanese corporations, some re-thinking of employment for life is taking place. However, given the strong cultural basis of lifetime employment in Japan, the potential for change at the corporate level is unclear.

Our earlier discussion of organizational culture suggested that there is less ambiguity and conflict when there is an integrated and homogeneous organizational culture. In addition, it suggested that there is less organizational conflict when the external cultural experiences of organization members are similar to and compatible with the culture of the organization. The Japanese cultural value of collective decision making and collective responsibility is reflected in and quite compatible with Japanese organizational culture based on long-term employment, trust, and close personal relationships.

A significant limitation of Theory Z organizations both in Japan and in the United States is their inability to deal with cultural diversity. They tend to depend on a homogeneous internal organizational culture. This in turn makes it unlikely that people will be brought into the organization if they come from external cultures that are diverse. The consensus and modified consensus approaches discussed earlier also depended on or assumed a high degree of homogeneity among organizational members, at least in terms of organizational goals, philosophy, and values. While consensus, modified consensus, and Theory Z organizations reflect many values consistent with alternative paradigm perspectives and with the core concerns of social work, their inability to incorporate, much less to celebrate, diversity is a major limitation. Fortunately, there is an alternative organizational approach that recognizes and incorporates diversity. This approach is called "managing diversity" and we will explore it in a later section.

Japanese Quality Management Techniques Applicable to Social Work

Keys (1995) explored Japanese social welfare organizations and their management processes, especially in the area of total quality management. Keys focused on elements of Japanese quality management that can be applied to social work and human service organizations. What follows are several basic Japanese processes Keys found useful. In addition, a list of specific management practices used in Japanese social welfare agencies is provided. These quality management approaches are quite consistent with general principles of **Total Quality Management** (TQM). Compare the practices used in Japanese social welfare agencies with the basic principles of TQM described later.

Management Practices Used in Japanese Social Welfare Agencies:

1. *Flexible job descriptions:*   Flexibility allows adaptability in job duties and responsibilities as well as quick responses to client service needs. According to Keys, flexibility avoids the 'not in my job description' syndrome often heard in U.S. human services agencies (1995:165).

2. *Use of NEMAWASHI information decision-making processes:*   "Cultivating the roots." Consists of informal discussion and compromises that precede formal meetings and pave the way for a consensus that everyone in the agency can actively support. (Not everyone is consulted in advance, but the groundwork is laid by securing support from key people.) This differs from typical U.S. management which is strict, top-down, and authoritarian.

GENERALLY USEFUL JAPANESE PROCESSES INCLUDE:

- Traditional and formal participatory management practices
- Lifelong training
- Participation by service workers in most agency decisions

(Keys 1995:164–165)

3. *The RINGI decision-making process:* Circulation of a *ringi-sho,* a written memo, "which serves as a communications device and as evidence of prior discussion and distribution of a decision. . . . Members . . . affected by the decision read and place their personal seal (*Hanko,* a small rubber signature stamp) on the *ringi* document." This gives top management evidence of staff consensus to decisions.

4. *Promotion of the WA:* WA means and reflects Japanese management concerns for unity, morale and harmony. Many Japanese devices in social welfare organizations promote WA. For example, various comprehensive, lifelong, training strategies are part of promoting WA. Emphasis is on not just imparting knowledge, but on allowing employees to get to know each other on a personal level and imparting the values and the philosophy of the organization to the employee. This helps avoid workplace conflicts, fosters teamwork, and creates an informal support system for employees.

5. *Job reassignment and rotation:* "Any employee may be retrained to do any job. . . . Systematic training policies familiarize employees with one another's jobs. . . . *Jinji-ido* describes the process of planned and routine rotation and reassignment of employees to various jobs. . . . *Amakudari* is the process by which a manager is retired from a social welfare-related government agency . . . to take a major management position in a public or nongovernmental social agency." *Shukko* employees rotate to an affiliated organization. Job rotations such as these may be signs of eventual promotion.

6. *Extensive training:* Employment is usually considered to be for life/retirement. Training often takes the form of retreats for new employees and annual social excursions/events, often overnight with a morning pep talk about the values and principles of the organization. There may also be discussion among employees.

7. *Total quality control (TQC) or TQM:* The Japanese concentrate on continuous quality improvement or business process improvement. **Quality Circles** (QC) are groups or team processes designed to improve work procedures and reduce problems. Periodic staff meetings involve examining and suggesting work improvement to their superiors. Line workers rather than supervisors or managers usually chair these meetings. Management is committed to taking these meetings seriously (Adapted from Keys 1995).

Total Quality Management (TQM)

Total Quality Management (TQM) "is a management approach to long-term success through customer satisfaction. TQM is based on the participation of all members of an organization in improving processes, products, services, and the culture they work in" (Bennett et al. in Colon 1995:105). *TQM principles* include:

1. A focus on the consumer of the organization's services

2. Involvement of everyone in the organization in the pursuit of quality

3. A heavy emphasis on teamwork

4. Encouragement of all employees to think about and pursue quality within the organization

5. Mistakes are not to be covered up but are to be used as learning experiences/ opportunities

6. Workers are encouraged to work out problems solvable at their level and not to pass them along to the next level

7. Everyone is on the quality team and everyone is responsible for and encouraged to pursue quality (Ginsberg 1995:20).

Learning Organizations

The concept of a learning organization is an attempt to go beyond the notions of total quality management, especially the notion of adapting to changes as they occur. According to Hodgetts et al. **learning organizations** "not only *adapt* to change, but they *learn and stay ahead of* change" (1994:12). A learning organization is characterized by:

1. An intense desire to learn about itself

2. A strong commitment to generating and transferring new knowledge and technology

3. Openness to the external environment

4. Values that emphasize shared vision and systems thinking

5. Focus on interrelationships among factors and long-term rather than short-term approaches to problems (Hodgetts, et al. 1994:12–13).

Learning Culture

Barrett (1995:40) provides a helpful list of competencies characteristic of organizational cultures that support and nurture a learning environment. These competencies include:

1. *Affirmative Competence.* The organization draws on the human capacity to appreciate positive possibilities by selectively focusing on current and past strengths, successes, and potentials.

2. *Expansive Competence.* The organization challenges habits and conventional practices, provoking members to experiment on the margins, makes expansive promises

that challenge them to stretch in new directions, and evokes a set of higher values and ideals that inspire them to passionate engagement.

3. *Generative Competence.* The organization constructs integrative systems that allow members to see the consequences of their actions, to recognize that they are making a meaningful contribution, and to experience a sense of progress.

4. *Collaborative Competence.* The organization creates forums in which members engage in ongoing dialogue and exchange diverse perspectives.

These levels of competence are quite compatible with alternative paradigm thinking generally and alternative thinking about organizational life more specifically. For example, they focus on strengths-based thinking and collaborative approaches. These competencies also reflect a postmodern or deconstructive tone in their call to focus on the margins of organizational discourse in order to be more inclusive of diverse perspectives and as a source of creative solutions beyond the status quo.

Global Issues

In addition to changing realities about organizational and work life in the United States, we must begin to recognize and respond to the global nature of our everyday lives. We are more than ever citizens of the planet Earth, in addition to being inhabitants of the United States. One approach to thinking globally within the corporate world which seems applicable to social workers seeking excellence in the organizations we work for and administer is that of the world-class organization.

World-Class Organizations

A number of researchers and futurists interested in the rapidly changing and increasingly international and global nature of organizational environments are advocating the concept of world-class organization. Hodgetts et al. defines a **world-class organization** as "the best in its class or better than its competitors around the world, at least in several strategically important areas" (1994:14). Thus, these writers believe that "any organization, regardless of size or type, can be world-class." World-class organizations include the characteristics of both total quality organizations and learning organizations (see discussions of TQM and the learning and intelligent organization). According to Hodgetts et al. (1994:14–18). World-class organizations, however, can be distinguished by additional characteristics or additional emphasis on characteristics of both total quality and learning organizations. Such organizations have:

- A customer-based focus, similar to a TQM organization, but also include:
  - Shared vision for customer service
  - Shared ownership of the customer service tasks and solutions
  - Organizational structure, processes, and jobs designed to serve the customer
  - Empowered teams for generating new ideas and approaches to improve customer service

- Information systems designed to monitor and predict the changing needs of the customer
- Management systems that ensure prompt translation of the customers' requirements to organizational actions
- Compensation systems designed to reward employees for excellent service to customers
- Continuous improvement on a global scale
  - Emphasize global nature of learning
  - Utilize global networking, partnerships, alliances, and information sharing
- Fluid, flexible or "virtual" organization
  - Respond quickly, decisively, and wisely to changes in the environment
  - Depend on outside partnerships and temporary alliances
  - Develop a fluid, flexible, and multiple-skilled workforce
- Creative human resource management
  - Effectively energize employee's creativity in decision making and problem solving
  - Constant training ("goof around and learn")
  - Effective reward systems: positive recognition for success; recognition is open and publicized throughout the organization; recognition carefully tailored to the needs of the employee; rewards are given soon after they are earned; relationship between performance and reward is understood by everyone in the organization
- Egalitarian climate
  - Value and respect for everyone: employees, consumers, owners, suppliers, community, and environment
  - Shared vision/information
  - Holistic view of employees
  - Open communication
  - Business ethics, community citizenship
  - Environment-friendly systems
  - Mentoring, coaching, buddy system
  - Employee involvement participation
  - Sponsor of community, wellness, and family programs
- Technological support
  - Computer-aided design (CAD) and manufacturing
  - Telecommunications networks
  - Database systems
  - Interorganizational communication systems
  - Multimedia systems
  - Continuous technical training (adapted from Hodgetts et al. 1994: 14–18).

The Intelligent Organization

Colon (1995:103–105) suggests several strategies for developing an intelligent solution/organization:

1. Systems Thinking. *Managers look for interrelationships and processes of change rather than cause-effect chains and snapshots.*

2. Environmentally sensitive: *Necessary but not sufficient, must also be internally sensitive.*

3. Maximize potential Individual contributions. *Have internal set of structures and functions that maximize the potential contributions of the individuals*

4. Recognize non-economic motivators. *Major motivating factor among workers besides pay are mainly psychological*

   - *Respectful treatment,*
   - *Interesting work,*
   - *Recognition for a job well done,*
   - *Opportunity for skill development,*
   - *Provision of the opportunity to express ideas about how to do things better, and*
   - *Knowledge about what is happening in the organization*

Increasing intimacy may increase interpersonal conflicts. However, conflict is not necessarily negative. Through conflict, organizations can grow and develop. Conflict necessitates problem solving and generates the application and growth of intelligence (Colon 1995:104–105).

Managing Diversity

R. Roosevelt Thomas, Jr., president of the American Institute for Managing Diversity, has done extensive research and consultation related to the realities of diversity in American corporations. Based on this research and experience he has developed an approach to organizations and management called "managing diversity" (MD). He defines this approach as a " 'way of thinking' toward the objective of creating an environment that will enable all employees to reach their full potential in pursuit of organizational objectives" (Thomas 1991:19). Other proponents of MD suggest that it means recognizing that individuals are different and that this diversity can be a strength rather than a weakness for organizations. Advocates of MD also stress that managing diversity is necessary to deal with current labor force and workplace realities.

Thomas (1991) suggests that managing diversity goes beyond affirmative action approaches and recognizes the growing tendencies among employees to celebrate their differences. He suggests that while affirmative action was and continues to be necessary, it can only help get minorities and women into an organization. It cannot ensure that once in an organization they will be able to reach their full potential. The goal of managing diversity is "to develop our capacity to accept, incorporate, and empower the diverse human talents of the most diverse nation on earth" (Thomas 1990:17). MD is an approach that can pick up where affirmative action leaves off.

Thomas offers a number of guidelines that are intended to help managers of business organizations to manage diversity. A number of these guidelines can readily be adapted to the kinds of organizations social workers work in and with. To implement an MD approach a manager or organization needs to do the following:

- Clarify your motivation for managing diversity and realize that a diverse work force is not something that an organization "ought" to have, but it is a current work force reality or will soon be reality;
- Clarify your vision to one in which the image is one of fully tapping the human resource potential of every member of the work force;
- Expand your focus to one in which the basic objective is not simply to assimilate minorities and women into a dominant white male culture but to create a dominant heterogeneous (diverse) culture;
- Audit your organizational culture so you can understand the "taken for granted" assumptions that may operate to prevent minorities and women from reaching their full potential;
- Based on your organizational audit, modify any assumptions about what the organization is or should be like that can prevent minorities and women from reaching their full potential. For example, to assume that an organization should be like a "family" is likely to carry with it such dominant and traditional patriarchal assumptions as "father knows best" or "sons will inherit the business";
- Modify your systems. Recognize that formal and informal systems such as mentoring must be available to minorities and women in the same way they offer assistance to white men;
- Help your people "pioneer." Learning to manage diversity is a change process with no tried and tested "solution" and no fixed "right way" to manage it. To effectively manage diversity people must be change agents. Allow people to try new solutions and encourage them to learn from their mistakes, rather than punishing them.
- Continue affirmative action. While affirmative action is not *the* answer, you cannot manage diversity in a work force that is not diverse. Affirmative action helps ensure that a diverse work force exists to be managed (Thomas 1990: 112–117).

Other concrete approaches to assist in managing diversity have met with success in a number of settings. These approaches include sensitivity or awareness training to help organization members become and remain aware of the behaviors and attitudes that support diversity in the work force and multicultural participation councils to help oversee diversity management (Thomas 1990; Dominguez 1991).

The Pluralistic Workplace

Nixon and Spearmon (1991:155) provide some extremely significant facts about the nature of the U.S. workforce by the end of the 1990s and the beginning of the 21st century:

- The average age of the workforce will be 39, and the supply of young entrants to the labor force will dwindle.
- Only 15 percent of the new entrants to the work force will be native white men.
- Women will constitute 64 percent of the new entrants to the labor force.

- People of color will make up 29 percent of the new entrants to the work force, double their present share of the labor market.
- Immigrants will represent 22 percent of the labor force.
- Some 600,000 legal and illegal immigrants will enter the United States annually throughout the remainder of this century (Johnston and Packer in Nixon and Spearmon 1991).*

Nixon and Spearmon urge that in this environment of rapid change, organizations, including social work and human service organizations, must be prepared to change along with the changing nature of the workforce.

Principles of Pluralistic Management

Using the work of Crable, Kunisawa, Copeland, and Thomas, Nixon and Spearmon outline a number of principles of pluralistic management. They define **pluralistic management** as "leadership that aggressively pursues the creation of a workplace in which the values, interests, and contributions of diverse cultural groups are an integral part of the organization's mission, culture, policies, and procedures and in which these groups share power at every level" (1991:156–157). Principles of pluralistic management include the following:

- Achieving a pluralistic work force is not only a moral imperative but a strategic one.
- Top management must make a commitment to create a pluralistic work force before fundamental structural and systemic changes can occur in the organizations.
- A genuinely pluralistic workplace means changing the rules to accommodate cultural differences in style, perspectives, and world views.
- The contemporary definition of diversity embraces groups of individuals by race; ethnicity; gender; age; physical characteristics; and similar values, experiences, and preferences.
- Cultural awareness and appreciation at the individual or group level are necessary but not sufficient conditions to transform an organization into a pluralistic workplace. Fundamental changes must take place in the institution's culture, policies, and administrative arrangements.
- Pluralistic managers value their own cultural heritage and those of others in the workplace.
- Pluralistic managers understand the value of diversity and seize the benefits that differences in the workplace offer.
- Pluralistic managers work to overcome barriers that hinder successful and authentic relationships among peers and subordinates who are culturally different from the mainstream stereotype.
- The empowerment of employees through career development, team building, mentoring, and participatory leadership is a cornerstone of the pluralistic workplace.

*Nixon, R., and Spearman, M. *Building a Pluralistic Workplace*. Copyright 1991, National Association of Social Workers, Inc. "Skills for Effective Human Services Management." Adapted by permission.

- Pluralistic management incorporates issues of diversity in organization-wide policies and practices and is not restricted to equal employment opportunity (EEO) policies and procedures.
- Skill in pluralistic management is an integral component of managerial competence.
- The ultimate goal of pluralistic management is to develop an organization that fully taps the human-resources potential of all its employees.

Nixon and Spearmon note that these principles "resonate with two central values of the social work profession: respect for the dignity and uniqueness of the individual and self determination" (1991:157).

A Typology of Organizational Progression to Pluralism

Nixon and Spearmon (1991:157–158) offer a helpful four-level typology to assess an organization's level of progress toward being a truly pluralistic workplace.

Level 1: Token EEO organization. Hires people of color and women at the bottom of the hierarchy; has a few token (see definition of token in Chapters 7 and 9) managers who hold their positions only as long as they do not question organization policies, practices, mission, and so on.

Level 2: Affirmative Action Organization. Aggressively recruits and supports the professional development of women and people of color and encourages non-racist, non-sexist behaviors; to climb the corporate ladder, women and people of color must still reflect and fit in with policies, practices, and norms established by dominant white men.

Level 3: Self-renewing Organization. Actively moving away from being sexist and racist toward being pluralistic; examines its mission, culture, values, operations, and managerial styles to assess their impact on the well-being of all employees; seeks to redefine the organization to incorporate multiple cultural perspectives.

Level 4: Pluralistic Organization. Reflects the contributions and interests of diverse cultural and social groups in its mission, operations, and service delivery; seeks to eliminate all forms of oppression within the organization; workforce at all levels (top to bottom) reflects diversity; diversity in leadership is reflected in policymaking and governance structures; is sensitive to the larger community in which it exists and is socially responsible as a member of the community (Nixon and Spearmon 1991:157–158).

Organizations and People with Disabilities

We have addressed a number of issues throughout this book related to social work and persons with disabilities (see Chapters 5 and 7, for example). We have especially explored the content and implications of the Americans with Disabilities Act. The following table provides an illustration of some accommodations made by organizations to take advantage of the potential and expertise of persons with disabilities. Issues related to community and disability are discussed further in Chapter 9.

Sample Accommodation Problems and Solutions

Problem: A plant worker with a hearing impairment had difficulty using the telephone.
Solution: A telephone amplifier that worked in conjunction with his hearing aids was purchased for $48.

Problem: A clerk lost some use of her hands and was unable to reach across the desk to her files.
Solution: A lazy susan file holder was provided at a cost of $85.

Problem: An insurance salesperson with cerebral palsy had difficulty taking notes while talking on the telephone.
Solution: Her employer purchased a headset phone for $50.

Problem: A person with one hand who was applying for a job as a cook could perform all required tasks except opening cans.
Solution: The employer called the Job Accommodation Network and was given a list of one-handed can openers, bought one for $35, and hired the applicant.

Problem: An employee's wheelchair could not fit in the restroom.
Solution: The facilities were enlarged and a handrail installed for $70.

Problem: A company wanted to hire a clerk even though she could not access the vertical filing cabinets from her wheelchair.
Solution: The firm moved the files into a lateral file at a cost of $450.

Problem: An employee's condition mandated two-hour rest periods.
Solution: The company adapted her schedule, and she worked with the same total hours. No cost to the company.

Adapted from Pati, G. C, and Bailey, E. K. (1995). *Organizational Dynamics* v. 23(5) (Winter 1995). © 1995 with permission of Elsevier Science.

CONCLUSION

Finding and implementing alternate organizational approaches consistent with core social work concerns and with alternative paradigm perspectives presents a significant and continuing challenge. While we have explored a number of alternative perspectives, no one perspective seems completely consistent with social work core concerns and alternate paradigm principles. An organizational culture perspective helps us appreciate the importance and power of subtle and taken-for-granted elements of organizational life. The "iron law of oligarchy" alerts us to the dangers of elitism and hierarchy in organizations. Consensus, modified consensus, and Theory Z organizations offer much in the area of shared decision making and mutual respect among members. However, they tend to be unable to accept and welcome high degrees of diversity among members. A managing diversity approach focuses on the strength of diversity and the importance of integrating diverse members for the good of the entire organization. This approach does not, however, address issues of consensus. None of the alternatives emphasize the need to address and constructively manage conflict within organizations.

We noted, when we began the discussion of alternative perspectives on organizations, that there were fewer and less complete models for these organizations than for more traditional organizational models. Perhaps this incompleteness can be a source of growth and hope for creating alternative organizations that incorporate more dimensions of alternative paradigm thinking. If we recognize that the search for alternative models is still in process, we can begin to recognize ourselves as "pioneers" in much the way Thomas (1990) suggested. As pioneers we are faced with the challenge of incorporating and adapting existing alternative organizational approaches (and traditional approaches as well) in order to create new alternatives. These new alternatives, we hope, will allow us to maximize participative or shared decision making, support mutual respect for all organization members, recognize the connection between the quality of our personal lives and that of our organizational lives, welcome diversity as a source of strength and creativity, and accept that out of diversity will come conflict that can be managed for the benefit of all organizational members. The real challenge is to fashion alternatives that accomplish all of the above elements in one integrative and humane whole.

SUMMARY

In this chapter we explored definitions and historical perspectives on organizations generally, in addition to discussing a number of specific traditional and alternative perspectives on organizations. In considering traditional perspectives, scientific management, bureaucracy, human relations, and Theory X and Theory Y were discussed. Theory Y, systems, and contingency theory perspectives were discussed as somewhat mid-range perspectives having some characteristics or qualities of both traditional and alternative paradigms.

We addressed alternative organizational approaches within the framework of organizational culture. Using organizational culture as a backdrop, Michel's "Iron Law of Oligarchy," Iannello's critical perspective, consensus, and modified consensus organizational approaches were addressed. Theory Z, teams or quality circles, and managing diversity perspectives were also presented as alternative perspectives on organizations.

We concluded this chapter with the recognition that no single alternative perspective was entirely consistent with alternative paradigm principles or social work core concerns. The challenge we were left at the end of this chapter was to continue to search for newer alternatives that incorporate the separate strengths of alternative and traditional models while avoiding their shortcomings.

Internet Search Guide

If you want to learn more about some of the topics discussed in this chapter by exploring the Internet, you can search the Net for the terms listed below. Remember that as you are "surfing" the Net, any of the search terms listed below can take you in many different directions. If you would like to visit specific Web sites related to this chapter, go to the Allyn and Bacon Web site at **http://www.abacon.com** and follow the links to Schriver or *Human Behavior and the Social Environment: Shifting Para-*

digms in Essential Knowledge for Social Work Practice. There you will find a selection of sites related to content in this chapter.

1. human service organizations
2. scientific management
3. Hawthorne Effect
4. Douglas & McGregor (Theory X & Theory Y)
5. Systems Perspective and organizations
6. contingency theory
7. organizational culture
8. managing diversity
9. Total Quality Management
10. Japanese management
11. Urban League
12. League of Women Voters
13. digital divide

REFERENCES

Abrahamsson, Bengt. (1977). *Bureaucracy or participation: The logic of organization.* Beverly Hills: SAGE Publications.

Anderson, Ralph, and Carter, Irl. (1990). *Human behavior in the social environment: A social systems approach* (4th ed.). New York: Aldine de Gruyter.

Attneave, Carolyn. (1982). "American Indians and Alaska Native families: Emigrants in their own homeland," in McGoldrick, Monica, Pearce, John, and Giordano, Joseph. (Eds.). *Ethnicity and family therapy.* New York: Guilford.

Barrett, F. (1995). "Creating appreciative learning cultures." *Organizational Dynamics, 24*(2):36–49.

Burton, B., and Dunn, C. (1996). "Feminist ethics as moral grounding for stakeholder theory." *Business Ethics Quarterly, 6:* 133–147.

Colon, E. (1995). "Creating an Intelligent Organization." In Ginsberg, L. and Keys, P. (Eds.). *New management in the human services.* (2nd ed.). Washington, DC: NASW.

Dominguez, Cari M. "The challenge of workforce 2000." *THE BUREAUCRAT: The Journal for Public Managers.* Winter 1991–92:15–18.

DNet. (2000). *The Democracy Network: About CGS.* [Web site]. League of Women Voters Education Fund and the Center for Governmental Studies. Available: http://www.dnet.org/About_CGS.htm [2000, 4/10/2000].

Etzioni, Amitai. (1964). *Modern organizations.* Englewood Cliffs, NJ: Prentice Hall.

Evans, K. G. (1996). "Chaos as opportunity: grounding a positive vision of management and society in the new physics." *Public Administration Review, 56:* 491–494.

Ginsberg, L. (1995). "Concepts of new management." In Ginsberg, L. and Keys, P. (Eds.). *New management in the human services.* (2nd ed.). Washington, DC: NASW.

Gortner, Harold F.; Mahler, Julianne; and Nicholson, Jeanne. (1987). *Organization theory: A public perspective.* Chicago: The Dorsey Press.

Grusky, Oscar and Miller, George (Eds.). (1981). *The sociology of organizations: Basic studies* (2nd ed.). New York: The Free Press.

Hendry, J. (1999). "Cultural theory and contemporary management." *Human Relations, 52*(5): 557–577.

Hodgetts, R. M., Luthans, F. and Lee, S. M. (1994). "New paradigm organizations: From Total Quality to Learning to World Class." *Organizational Dynamics, 22*(3):5–19.

Iannello, Kathleen P. (1992). *Decisions without hierarchy: Feminist interventions in organization theory and practice.* New York: Routledge.

Kennedy, M. and Agron, J. (1999). "Bridging the digital divide." *American School and University, 72*(2): 16–18.

Keys, P. R. (1995). "Japanese quality management techniques." In Ginsberg, L. and Keys, P. (Eds.). *New management in the human services.* (2nd ed.). Washington, DC: NASW.

Lambrinos, Jorge J. (1991). "Tomorrow's workforce: Challenge for today." *THE BUREAU-CRAT: The Journal for Public Managers.* Winter 1991–92:27–29

League of Women Voters. (2000). *The democracy network: About the LWV.* [Web site]. The League of Women Voters Education Fund. Available: http://www.dnet.org/About_LWV.htm [2000, 4/10/00].

Liedtka, J. (1996). "Feminist morality and competitive reality: a role for an ethic of care?" *Business Ethics Quarterly, 6:* 179–200.

National Telecommunications and Information Administration. (1999). *Falling through the net: Defining the digital divide.* [Web site]. U.S. Department of Commerce. Available: http://www.ntia.doc.gov [2000, 4/8/00].

Neugeboren, Bernard. (1985). *Organizational policy and practice in the human services.* New York: Longman.

Nixon, R., and Spearmon, M. (1991). "Building a pluralistic workplace." In Edwards, R. and Yankey, J. (Eds.). *Skills for effective human services management.* Washington, DC: NASW Press. Reprinted by permission.

Ouchi, William G. (1981). *Theory Z.* New York: Avon Books.

Overman, E. S. (1996). "The new science of administration: chaos and quantum theory." *Public Administration Review, 56:* 487–491.

Pati, G. C., and Bailey, E. K. (1995). "Empowering people with disabilities: Strategy and human resource issues in implementing the ADA." *Organizational Dynamics, 23*(3):52–69.

Pugh, D. S.; Hickson, D. J.; and Hinings, C. R. (Eds.). (1985) *Writers on organizations.* Beverly Hills: SAGE Publications.

Rifkin, J. (1998). "A civil education for the twenty-first century: preparing students for a three-sector society." *National Civic Review, 87:* 177–181.

Schein, Edgar. (1992). *Organizational culture and leadership.* (2nd ed.) San Francisco: Jossey-Bass.

Schneider, B., Brief, A. P., and Guzzo, R. A. (1996). "Creating a climate and culture for sustainable organizational change." *Organizational Dynamics, 24*(4):7–19.

Shafritz, Jay M., and Ott, J. Steven. (1987). *Classics of organization theory* (2nd ed.). Chicago: The Dorsey Press.

Taylor, Frederick W. (1981). "Scientific management." In Grusky, Oscar, and Miller, George A., eds. *The sociology of organizations: Basic studies* (2nd ed.). New York: The Free Press.

Thomas, R. Roosevelt, Jr. (1990). "From affirmative action to affirming diversity." *Harvard Business Review,* March–April 1990:107–117.

Thomas, R. Roosevelt, Jr. (1991) "The concept of managing diversity." *THE BUREAU-CRAT: The Journal for Public Managers.* Winter 1991–1992:19–22.

Westen, T. (1998). "Can technology save democracy?" *National Civic Review, 87:* 47–56.

Wheatley, M., and Kellner-Rogers, M. (1996). "Breathing life into organizations." *Public Management, 78:* 10–14.

Zhu, Z. (1999). "The practice of multimodal approaches, the challenge of cross-cultural communication, and the search for responses." *Human Relations, 52*(5): 579–607.

ILLUSTRATIVE READING 8.1

The Illustrative Reading by Fishley, "I Am John," provides a historical perspective on the nature of the organizational environments and treatments to which people with developmental disabilities have been subjected in the United States and their behavioral responses to these environments and treatment. Table 1 in the reading provides a helpful summary of labels applied to, the attitudes about, and the living situations of people with developmental disabilities through the years. It is interesting to note that people with developmental disabilities were not believed to have the potential for learning and development until relatively recently. This reading reveals the powerful influence of the social environment, especially the organizational, institutional, and community environment, on persons with disabilities. This reading reflects the powerful influences of these social environments either as a detriment to or a significant asset for the developmental experiences of persons with developmental disabilities.

Persons with Disabilities—I Am John

Pat Fishley

"John's" story details the history of services provided to people with mental retardation in the United States from the 1720s to the present. Although "John" is fictitious, the facts relating to mental retardation, service, and treatment through the years are accurate. There are no social workers in John's life story mainly because mental retardation has not been a part of schools of social work curriculum. John's life might have been different if there had been social workers advocating for him.

When an individual is kept in a situation of inferiority, the fact is that he does become inferior.
—Simone de Beauvoir

My name is John. I was born in Mentor, Ohio. I'm six feet tall and have brown hair and brown eyes. I work hard Monday through Friday. I bowl on Saturdays and swim on Sundays. I like to watch baseball and football on TV. In the summer, I play on a softball team. I like rock and roll music and pizza. I also have mental retardation. Because of this condition, people treat me differently; some feel sorry for me, some are afraid of me, and some laugh at me. Usually, people think I'm like everyone else who has mental retardation. I don't know why; people don't say my grandmother acts like everyone else who has arthritis. I do have trouble learning new things and some things I may never learn (kind of like my brother with algebra).

1720s—HOUSE OF CORRECTION

Through history, people have tried to help me the best way they knew how (see Table 1). In 1722, I was sent to a house of correction. This was a place for anyone thought to be a menace or threat to society. They called me a "misfit" or "deviant." The house of correction was a scary place. I lived with criminals, vagabonds, beggars, insane people, drunks, musicians, blind people, and crippled people. People told me that it was for my own good because I didn't "fit" into society. Living there made me wonder what society was like because I sure didn't feel like I "fit in" at the house of correction. There, people stole from each other and hit and hurt each other; one man talked to someone no one else could see. I tried to leave this place once because I was scared that I'd be hurt if I stayed. But when they brought me back, I was hurt by the people

Pat Fishley, "I Am John." *Health and Social Work*. Reprinted by permission. Copyright © 1992. National Association of Social Workers, Inc., Health & Social Work.

TABLE 1   History of Labels for, Attitudes about, and Living Situations of People with Developmental Disabilities

Year	Label	Attitude[a]	Living Situation
1722	Misfit, deviant	Menace, threat to society—incarceration	House of correction
1850	Idiot, imbecile, feeble minded	"Make the deviant less deviant through education"—segregation	Boarding school/asylum
1881	Idiot, imbecile, feeble minded	Society's degenerates—negative reinforcement	Farm colony
1890s	Idiot, imbecile, feeble minded	Burden of charity—separation	"Asylum for unteachable idiots," "asylum for feeble-minded women"
1920s to 1960s	Retardate, moron, mildly retarded, moderately retarded, severely retarded, profoundly retarded	Holy innocent, eternal child—protection, confinement	State-run institution
Late 1960s to 1970s	Developmental disability	Deinstitutionalization, developmental model—least restrictive environment	Intermediate care facility, mental retardation comprehensive center
1980s	Individual with a developmental disability	Dignity of risk, individual growth and potential—active treatment	Alternative placement in group homes, apartments
1990s	Consumer, friend, neighbor, coworker	Community access, participation—empowerment	Community-based supported living, option of choice

[a]These labels and concomitant attitudes are listed as applied by "professionals" working with developmentally disabled individuals. Society's labels and attitudes have always lagged behind professional labels and attitudes, especially in the more progressive 1960s, 1970s, and 1980s.

I thought were supposed to take care of me. I never tried to leave again. I stayed at the house of correction until the early 1850s.

1850s—BOARDING SCHOOL

It was then that someone decided that the "deviant could be less deviant" through education (Wolfensberger, 1976, p. 48). We (people with mental retardation) still weren't sent to schools with our brothers and sisters. Boarding schools were built just for us. We were supposed to be at these schools only from age 7 to 14. We lived at these schools away from our families and away from the city. I liked being at the school better than at the house of correction because people treated me better, and it wasn't as scary. Sometimes, though, I thought I wasn't trying hard enough. I couldn't learn what they tried to teach me. I knew they were trying to help me, but I wasn't getting it. Sometimes, if what they were teaching was too hard, I'd say I was sick so I wouldn't have to go to school. When they found out I wasn't really sick (they called it "attention-getting behavior"), they would leave me alone (they called it "ignoring"). I couldn't understand why they left me alone when they knew I wanted attention.

These boarding schools were selective in who could attend. They would take only those they thought were "improvables." My friend couldn't go with me because he was a "cripple" and had epilepsy. These schools were going to teach us to "stand and walk normally, have some speech, eat in an orderly manner and engage in some kind of meaningful work" (Wolfensberger, 1976, p. 49). Some people at the school did learn these things and were sent to the city to work and live. They were called "curables." Those of us who didn't learn were called "imbeciles," "idiots," or "feeble minded." When I turned 14, I couldn't go to the city because I didn't learn enough. I had to stay at the boarding school until the 1880s.

1880s—FARM COLONIES

Once again people began to look at us differently. They believed that we chose not to learn, because although they tried to help us, we didn't get better. We were called "degenerates."

People believed that if we weren't going to learn, we would work on a farm. If we worked hard enough, we wouldn't be "deviant." If we could farm, we would be able to take care of ourselves and be "self-supporting."

In 1881 we were moved farther away from the city. We planted vegetables and took care of the animals. It was hard work and we did it all day every day. If we did something wrong or not fast enough, they yelled at us and called us "idiots." I tried to do everything right and fast; then they didn't say anything. I guess they were ignoring me again. I don't think it's enough to tell someone only what they're doing wrong. We never really learned what to do, only what not to do. We were also responsible for taking care of those who were blind or couldn't walk. At night, we slept in a large, one-room building on straw.

People called us a "burden on taxpayers." It was believed that having more people live and work on the farm would cost less because we would be able to grow enough food to be self-supporting. Some farms had 500 to 600 people. Because of the size, they were called "farm colonies." Some people called them "funny farms" or "happy farms."

1890s—ASYLUMS

In the late 1890s, people decided that we weren't producing enough to take care of ourselves, even though we worked very hard. We stopped farming but remained in the big buildings. The name of the buildings changed. We now lived in "custodial asylums for unreachable idiots" or "asylums for feeble-minded women." We didn't have anything to do. Sometimes, I would go outside for a walk. Sometimes I couldn't find my way back through the fields. Then the people who watched me had to come and find me. At first I was happy they found me, but they yelled at me and said I was being "manipulative." I don't know what that means, but I think they were saying that I was trying to make them do something they didn't want to do. We were called a "burden of charity." We were also called "holy innocents" and "eternal children." People treated us like we were children—it didn't matter how old we were.

In the late 1890s, people wanted to make it illegal for us to marry, have children, and live in the city.

> *The only hope seen was in the prevention of procreation of individuals likely to produce retarded persons. Three methods suggested themselves: forbidding the mating of retarded persons by law; preventing procreation of those retarded persons who might mate by sterilization; and preventing both mating and procreation by means of segregation. . . .A national marriage law to prohibit marriage to the feeble-minded and insane was proposed as early as 1897 . . . and was widely supported.* (Wolfensberger, 1976, p. 59)

These were called preventative laws. People believed that if we didn't marry, if we were sterilized, and if we didn't live in the city, mental retardation would be eliminated.

1920s—STATE-RUN INSTITUTIONS

In the 1920s, a man came to the asylum with a game for us to play, the Stanford-Binet Intelligence Scale. He asked me about things I didn't understand. He didn't ask me about planting crops, milking cows, or about anything that I did know. I guess I didn't do well because I stayed at the asylum. They changed the name of our building again. Now I lived in a state-run institution. We were called "morons" or "retardates." They kept us in big, unheated buildings—all of us together—with nothing to do. We didn't even have to get dressed. Some people didn't even have to get out of bed. Those of us who did get out of bed had only one place to go—a large room with nothing in it except a few benches. Sometimes I felt like the cattle we took care of on the farm—just waiting to be herded from one place to another.

The people who took care of us stayed in a locked room and watched us from behind a screened window. I guess they needed protection, too. They came out to give us food or pills. I don't think they liked being locked up, either, because none of them stayed very long. It was always someone new giving me food. If we ever got angry or frustrated—maybe because we didn't like being cold or bored or being together all the time, or if we were sick—they would give us pills to "control" us. I stopped letting them know how I felt because I didn't like the way the pills made me feel.

They kept bringing in more people to live there. I'm not sure where they all were coming from—we still weren't allowed to marry, to have kids, or to live in the city. I guess a lot of people were scoring 83 or less on the Stanford-Binet Intelligence Scale.

> *By the 1920s, standardized intelligence tests were developed and used to measure intelligence. In 1959, people who scored 83 or less on the Stanford-Binet Intelligence Scale and who showed impaired adaptive behavior were labeled*

as mentally retarded. However, in 1973, the American Association of Mental Deficiency [AAMD] lowered the score from 83 to 63 or below. This action removed the label of mental retardation from millions of people. By selecting and using various standards, society thus determines what people are to be considered mentally retarded. (Gardner & Chapman, 1985, p. 5)

1960s—DEINSTITUTIONALIZATION

In the 1960s things started to change for us. Everyone was talking about civil rights and social reforms. The president of the United States, John F. Kennedy, started a task force, the President's Committee on Mental Retardation, to look into how we lived. The president's brother Robert Kennedy said,

> *In state institutions for the mentally retarded . . . we have a situation that borders on a snake pit. . . . The children live in filth, many of our fellow citizens are suffering tremendously because of lack of attention, lack of imagination, lack of adequate manpower. [There is] very little future for . . . children who are in these institutions. . . . And I'm not saying that those who are the attendants or the ones who run the institutions are at fault. And I think it's long overdue that something be done about it.* (Wolfensberger, 1976, p. 114)

People said the way we lived was "deplorable." I'm not sure what that means, but if it has anything to do with 2,000 people living in a building to "hold" 600, or if it has anything to do with the building being 100 years old with bars on the windows and the doors always locked, no heat in the buildings, people living in their own human waste, no clothes to wear, and no privacy ever, then I guess it was "deplorable." The task force said some of us had to leave the institution. They called this "deinstitutionalization."

In 1967, Ohio Senate Bill 169 was passed. This law allowed many of us to go home. It provided services in our "county of origin." That meant that we would have services and a place to live close to our families. I wanted some of my friends to come with me, but they couldn't because they weren't born where I was. For years, we weren't allowed to be near our families, but now I could receive services only in the county I was born in.

1970s—PUBLIC LAWS

In 1970, the U.S. Congress passed the Developmental Disabilities Services and Facilities Construction Amendments. Developmental disabilities included mental retardation, cerebral palsy, autism, and epilepsy. Being identified as someone with a disability was better than being "feeble minded," an "imbecile," or a "moron." People started to talk about what we needed to learn in order to live as independently as possible. It was better than hearing about how much we couldn't do or would never be able to do.

Three other laws were passed between 1973 and 1978 that helped people with developmental disabilities. The Education for All Handicapped Children Act of 1975 allowed my friend who couldn't go to the boarding school in 1850 because he had epilepsy to receive an education. The Developmentally Disabled Assistance and Bill of Rights Act in 1975 said that we have the same civil rights as nonhandicapped people. It also said that the places we live (residential programs) can't receive money from the federal government if they don't have these programs (written plans of what we need to learn and how we're going to learn it) for us. Also, physical or chemical restraints (pills) can't be used in place of programs or to punish us. The Rehabilitation Act of 1973 stated that employers and schools can't discriminate against us because of our disabilities.

In 1973, the American Association on Mental Deficiency redefined "deficiency" as a score of 68 or less on the Stanford-Binet Intelligence Scale (Gardner & Chapman, 1985). They also talked about "adaptive behavior," things that I needed to learn so that I could do what other people my age do and so I could do more things on my own.

1970s—COUNTY OF ORIGIN, COMPREHENSIVE CENTERS

Because of these new laws, I moved to the Lake County Board of Mental Retardation/ Developmental Disabilities (Deepwood Center) in Mentor—that's the city I was born in, and it's where my family lives. Deepwood Center was built because of Ohio Senate Bill 169. It's a "comprehensive center" (sounds better than "asylum for feeble-minded"). Comprehensive means any services that I need are in one place. They have a school called Broadmoor. There's a workshop that has two names; some people call it sheltered industries, others call it vocational guidance center (VGC). Deepwood Center has two buildings for people to live in: a child developmental center (CDC) and an adult residential center (ARC). Recreation therapists taught us to swim and play baseball and took us to Special Olympics in Columbus. Speech therapists helped us talk. Physical therapists helped us walk. Occupational therapists helped us use our hands. Nurses were there all the time. We went in a station wagon to see doctors.

1973—ACTIVE TREATMENT

In 1973, I moved into the CDC. It was small—only 30 beds (in different rooms—not all together like some places I lived). I had one roommate and my own closet. We had a backyard with swings and a slide to play in. The people who took care of us didn't stay behind locked doors; they worked with us, showing us how to dress, bathe, brush our teeth, make our beds, and eat our meals. Once a staff person rented a movie. We watched the movie and ate popcorn. It was fun.

When I moved to CDC, my parents could pick me up on Sundays and holidays to spend the day with them. I even learned to dial the phone so I could talk to my family whenever I wanted.

In the morning, we rode a school bus to Broadmoor School. At school, we had teachers who helped us read, write, and count. We played in the gym and swam in the pool. Sometimes we went on picnics or to the zoo. We had physical, occupational, and speech therapists who worked with us. I was in a class that helped me learn work skills. I learned to fold towels so I could work in a laundry; I learned to clean and sweep the floors so I could be a housekeeper; I learned to run the dishwasher so I could work in a restaurant. At 22, I graduated from Broadmoor.

After gradation, I was sent to VGC to work. VGC was big, and there were lots of people. I worked in a group with 15 other workers and one supervisor. The supervisor helped us learn different jobs such as assembly work, piecework, and collating, which companies sent to VGC for us to do. The supervisor also helped me make sure I was doing a job correctly and helped me count all the work I'd done so that I would get paid for every piece. My first paycheck was $15.75 for two weeks' work. I was so excited! I went to the bank at the mall with one of the staff to cash my check and to buy a new record and a new shirt that I wanted. The rest of the money I took back to the bank and put in my own savings account.

At the same time I went to work at VGC, I also moved up to the ARC to live. ARC was bigger than CDC. It had 68 beds in different rooms. People said I was high functioning (that means only mild or moderately retarded) so I lived on the second floor. My case manager said I had to learn to do things that were age appropriate (that I should do things that other people my age do). At my individual habilitation plan meeting—when all the staff who worked with me got together with me and my parents to plan what things I should learn next year—we talked about my liking baseball, swimming, and rock and roll music. These things were called a "leisure program." The speech therapist also wanted me to be in a "socialization group" so I could go to restaurants and plays with five or six friends. People were always asking me what I wanted to do or where I wanted to go. We didn't always do what I wanted, but I like that people asked. I also got to go to the mall to shop and picked out my own clothes. Staff said that they would teach me how to walk to the mall so I could shop by myself or with a friend, but first I needed to learn about money in the "budget program."

1983—DIGNITY OF RISK

In 1983, Residential Alternatives in Supportive Environments (RAISE) opened apartments for people with developmental disabilities. I was asked if I would like to live in an apartment (just like my brother's). The staff at ARC and RAISE and my family and I made plans for me to move with only one roommate. Staff come to the apartment to teach us to cook, shop, and budget our money. Staff let me make my own decisions, even if I decide something they know is not good. Staff say that's how you learn. During the week, I took a bus to VGC to work in the kitchen.

In 1986, I started to work in a Creative Learning and Employment Opportunities program. I got a job at a restaurant. I get picked up at my apartment in a van to go to work. At the restaurant, I work in the dish room. I work with four to five people. We stack all the dishes and put them in the dishwasher. When the dishes are clean we stack them on a counter so the cook can use them again. We also clean the kitchen and mop the floors. I get paid more money (minimum wage) than I did at VGC. I don't get to keep all the money, though; some of it goes to pay taxes and some of it is for when I retire.

1990—SUPPORTED LIVING

In 1990, Supported Living began. Supported living means that the state gives money to the county board of mental retardation/developmental disabilities to help people with mental retardation live in the community. In supported living, people with mental retardation choose where and with whom they want to live, and then staff comes in to help. They have an individual service plan that finds out what I need to be able to live in the community. I need someone to help me budget my money and to help me get to work, doctor appointments, and activities such as dances and baseball games. Some people need help with cooking, laundry, and buying furniture and others with bathing, dressing, or buying a special wheelchair with a motor. These services are put in place right in our homes or apartments. In supported living, they don't take us away from the city to teach us to live in the city; we learn right where we live.

1990s—INDIVIDUAL GROWTH AND POTENTIAL

I like living in the city. I'm learning new things and making my own decisions. Staff say I'm learning because of the "dignity of risk"—because I'm allowed to try new things. Yet, somehow, I think I've always learned what people have taught me. When people were angry with me because I didn't "fit in," I learned to fight. When people laughed at me or were afraid of me, I learned to be quiet and withdrawn. I learned to be helpless when I was protected from and by society. I learned to be "deviant" when I was deprived and isolated. I learned to be a "degenerate" when I was segregated. I acted like a child when I was viewed as an "eternal child." But when I was given some support, encouragement, and dignity, I learned to work for a living, pay the rent, and join a softball team. I'm becoming a person, an individual. I do things independently—on my own.

I live in an apartment. I'm six feet tall and have brown hair and brown eyes. I work hard in a restaurant. I bowl on Saturdays and swim on Sundays. In the summer, I play on a softball team. I like rock and roll music and pizza. I vote. I pay taxes. I have a girlfriend. We go to rock concerts and dances. I also have mental retardation. I am John.

ABOUT THE AUTHOR

Pat Fishley, LSW, ACBSW, is Case Manager, Deepwood Center, Case Management Services, 9083 Mentor Avenue, Mentor, OH 44060.

REFERENCES

Developmental Disabilities Services and Facilities Construction Amendments of 1970, P.L. 91-517, 84 Stat. 1316.

Developmentally Disabled Assistance and Bill of Rights Act, P.L. 94-103, 89 Stat. 486 (1975).

Education for All Handicapped Children Act of 1975, P.L. 94-142, 89 Stat. 773.

Gardner, J. F., & Chapman, M. S. (1985). *Staff development in mental retardation service: A practical manual.* Baltimore: Paul H. Brookes.

Rehabilitation Act of 1973, P.L. 93-112, 87 Stat. 355.

Wolfensberger, W. (1976). The origin and nature of our institutional models. In *Changing patterns in residential services for the mentally retarded* (pp. 35–82). Washington, DC: President's Committee on Mental Retardation.

ILLUSTRATIVE READING 8.2

The illustrative reading by Delgado explores a type of organization often neglected by social work education—the small business. Delgado integrates the importance of a particular type of small business—Latina-owned beauty parlors—with social workers' concerns for poverty reduction, diversity, and community revitalization and well-being. The author examines the disproportionate extent of poverty in communities of color, but adopts a strengths perspective for addressing poverty by demonstrating the positive and complex roles played by Latina-owned beauty parlors in community well-being. The reader is encouraged to compare the content of Illustrative Reading 7.1 by Chang with this reading, and to apply the concept of social capital to the beauty parlors studied by Delgado. The reading by Delgado also illustrates the important linkages among individuals, families, groups, organizations, and the larger community in his examination of the important and diverse contributions to individual and community well-being provided by small businesses owned and operated by members of diverse communities. In this respect, this reading is also helpful to keep in mind as we explore community systems in the following chapter.

Role of Latina-Owned Beauty Parlors in a Latino Community

Melvin Delgado

Communities of color in large urban areas of the United States have been the focus of a national debate about persistent poverty and its associated social problems. Unfortunately, the debate has taken a deficit perspective and largely has ignored community assets in the development of policies and services. Neighborhood revitalization efforts must build on community assets to achieve success. This article examines the multifaceted role small businesses—particularly Latina-owned beauty parlors—can play in Latino communities and raises implications for social work interaction with these businesses.

Key words: *community revitalization; Latinas; small businesses; strengths perspective*

The United States is currently struggling with how to best address persistent poverty and the high rates of social problems associated with its existence in urban centers (Hoechstetter, 1996; Jennings, 1994). Moore and Pinderhughes (1993) characterized the debate on the underclass as "who is responsible for the condition of the poor—the individual or society? Is persistent poverty caused by behavioral pathology or the economic structure?" (p. xii). The answers to these questions have profound implications

Melvin Delgado, PhD, is professor of social work and chair of the macro practice sequence, School of Social Work, Boston University, 264 Bay State Road, Boston, MA 02215. Funding for the research reported in this article was made available by grants from the Center for Substance Abuse Prevention (5H86SP02208) and the Carlisle Foundation, Framingham, MA.

for the development of strategies to eliminate persistent poverty. Unfortunately, the debate has taken a deficit perspective toward communities (Saleebey, 1992, 1996) and has ignored community assets in the search for revitalization strategies (Kretzmann & McKnight, 1993; McKnight & Kretzmann, 1991).

A focus on community social problems has a long historical record in the United States (Halpern, 1995):

> The neighborhood has long been an important locus for efforts to address the causes and consequences of poverty in American society. Over the course of the past century neighborhood-based initiatives have been called on to reduce class conflict, counter feelings of anger and alienation, localize control of institutions, create jobs and reverse neighborhood decline, and address a variety of specific poverty-related problems. (p. 1)

Thus, the revitalization of neighborhoods presents many challenges for social work and other professions in helping to promote policies and services that address the needs of communities in a manner that meaningfully involves their populations in the decision-making process.

Much attention has been paid to the high-risk environment of inner-city children and their families (Kozol, 1995) and the need for government (local, state, and federal) and the private sector to collaborate to create positive change at the community level (Perez & Martinez, 1993). Any efforts to revitalize these communities must enhance local assets. This article examines the nature and extent of persistent poverty among one population of color—the Latino population. A case study of Latina-owned beauty parlors in a large New England city illustrates the multifaceted role Latino businesses can play in the social-economic network of the community. Implications for social work practice in Latino communities are presented.

LITERATURE REVIEW

Poverty

There are an estimated 22 million Latinos in the United States (Castex, 1994). The median income for Latino families is $23,884, compared to $39,239 for non-Latino white families (Institute for Puerto Rican Policy, 1993). All Latino groups have incomes below the national median (Holmes, 1996); Puerto Rican families have the lowest income of any group ($20,654), followed by Mexican families ($23,018). Cuban families have the highest median income of any Latino group ($30,095). Puerto Rican families have the highest percentage of people living below the poverty rate (39.4 percent), followed by Mexican families (29.5 percent), Central or South American families (24.6 percent), other Latino families (20.6 percent), and Cuban families (18.0 percent). These rates are in sharp contrast with the poverty rate of 9.4 percent for non-Latino white families (Institute for Puerto Rican Policy, 1993).

However, despite the high concentration of poverty among most Latino subgroups, they have not received sufficient national attention. Enchautegui (1994) identified five reasons for this inattention: (1) misperceived identity, (2) lack of widespread attention to the working-poor population, (3) geographical concentration,

(4) lack of political participation, and (5) differences among Latino subgroups. The interplay among these factors has resulted in Latinos being considered "invisible" in national policy.

The literature on Latino poverty can be categorized into three schools of thought (Borges-Mendez, 1993; Enchautegui, 1994; Hurtado, 1995; Institute for Puerto Rican Policy, 1996; Melendez, 1993; Moore & Pinderhughes, 1993; Morales & Bonilla, 1993; Perez & Cruz, 1994; Perez & Martinez, 1993; Segura, 1992; Torres, 1995): (1) Poverty is the result of an interplay between immigrant status and rapid demographic changes (high rates of female-headed households and fertility); (2) Latinos are an "underclass" (low formal educational achievement and lack of or inconsistent employment history); and (3) a lack of market-attractive skills exclude Latinos from high-wage jobs. Morales and Bonilla (1993), in their analysis of the economic forces of the 1980s, raised serious concerns about the limited economic opportunities for Latinos and other people of color:

> *White family incomes and net worth rose, even as these indicators fell among African Americans and Latinos. . . . The resources available to individuals narrowly defined their ability to improve and invest in communities, thereby reinforcing spatial demarcations in the spread of economic social inequality. . . . Members [Latinos] of this large and expanding segment of society are having to come to terms with the possibility that they may never reach parity with the average American without concerted efforts to change their circumstances that must involve the nation as a whole.* (pp. 1–2)

Their summary of results from a series of studies on the economic status of Latinos noted "economic structuring has been critical in increasing poverty in Latino communities. But the emphasis is on the complexity of economic restructuring rather than on the construction of the manufacturing sector alone. . . . New Latino immigrants [can] help to revitalize and stabilize impoverished Latino communities" (p. xxxvii).

Melendez (1993) focused on the local level:

> *Notwithstanding the difficulties involved in dissecting the causes of poverty for Latinos in Massachusetts, it is of foremost importance that . . . from a policy perspective, we need to know whether human-capital strategies or industrial policies are more likely to have a positive impact on the labor-market standing for Latinos, and whether social policies targeting support services for families will have a stronger impact than economic development or labor-market interventions.* (p. 25)

Osterman's (1989) profile of the poor population in Boston noted,

> *Who is poor in Boston? . . . The short answer is that Boston poverty has decreased since 1980; and that the substantial poverty which remains in 1989 is a phenomenon of women, single parents, families, minorities, and the disabled. . . . Further, by adding any of these factors together, poverty rates*

(percentage of a group that is poor) grow even higher. For instance, if you consider the group with the highest poverty rate in Boston—Hispanics—and the family structure with the highest poverty—single parents—you get a startling result: eight out of ten Hispanic single parents are poor. And nearly three-quarters of Hispanic children are growing up in poverty. (p. 9)

Ethnic Small Businesses

The social work profession has largely ignored the presence and role of small businesses in the life of communities of color. This lack of attention may be the result of an interplay among several factors: a general lack of attention given to ethnic businesses in professional education; a pervasive feeling that ethnic businesses, like their white counterparts, are capitalistic in nature, and thus should be avoided; and a lack of knowledge of how these establishments can work with social workers to reach underserved groups. However, despite these views, ethnic businesses can play critical roles in the life of a community (Halter, 1995). Delgado (1996), in a study of Puerto Rican grocery stores and restaurants, identified eight key roles these institutions can play in the life of the community that extend beyond the selling of food: (1) providing credit; (2) cashing checks (many Latino communities do not have automatic teller machines); (3) providing community-related news and information; (4) providing information from the homeland; (5) counseling customers in distress; (6) providing information about and referral to social services agencies; (7) assisting in filling out or interpreting government forms; and (8) providing cultural connectedness to the homeland through the selling of videotapes, publications, and so forth.

The development of ethnic businesses necessitates the allocation of resources beyond obtaining start-up capital. According to Waldinger, Aldrich, and Ward (1990), owners of ethnic businesses confront at least seven major challenges in establishing a business: (1) obtaining the information about establishing a business, (2) acquiring start-up and operational capital, (3) obtaining the skills and knowledge to operate a business, (4) recruiting and supervising employees, (5) relating to customers and suppliers, (6) surviving business competition, and (7) withstanding political attacks. As a result, an ethnic business represents a barometer of the extent to which a community can or is willing to support "its own." Thus, any neighborhood revitalization strategy must actively promote the development and support of small businesses (Halpern, 1995; Levitt, 1993; Melendez, 1993).

Latino Small Businesses

Latino small businesses can play an influential role in the community that goes beyond that usually associated with a commercial establishment (Sarason & Koberg, 1994). According to Levitt (1995), owners of Latino commercial establishments are motivated by more than economic motives; they are also motivated by a sense of "social responsibility" that translates into providing culturally appropriate help for those customers in need, including financial assistance, counseling or advice, and information on formal and informal resources for help. Consequently, Latino businesses can take on the role of nontraditional social services centers.

Delgado and Humm-Delgado (1982) identified a number of Latino merchant establishments in their analysis of Latino natural support systems and noted that these establishments were attractive to Latinos because they were owned, operated, staffed, and controlled by those in the community. Owners often lived in the community and fulfilled leadership roles. The authors, however, did not mention gender-based natural supports such as beauty parlors. These institutions, with few exceptions, cater to women and are an excellent source for outreach to Latinas. Delgado (in press b) referred to these institutions as "nontraditional settings."

Nontraditional settings are an indigenous source of support and are a place where individuals can gather to purchase a product or service or congregate for social purposes. These settings can facilitate conversation and the exchange of concerns and advice, minimizing the stigma for those seeking assistance. Exchange of advice and assistance is mutual; these settings are generally staffed by individuals who share the same ethnic, socioeconomic, and other key factors such as gender and religion as the patrons (maximizing psychological, geographical, and cultural access) and have a primary role that incorporates being a "helper."

Latina Beauty Parlors

The professional literature has not examined beauty parlors as economic settings and sources of support for Latinas and other women of color (Delgado, in press a). The popular press has reported on a number of beauty parlors where concerted efforts have been made to reach women in distress, with or without support from social services agencies. However, a systematic study of the role of and services provided by these establishments, their motivation for helping, characteristics of owners, and experiences in helping women with personal problems has not been reported in the popular press or the literature.

METHOD

Questions

This study asked the following questions to guide social services organizations in their quest to better serve the Latino community in the United States: Who are Latina beauty parlor owners and their customers? What are the operational characteristics of typical beauty parlors? What prompted the Latina owners to help customers? What kinds of social services are provided?

Procedure

In spring 1996, a small-scale survey of Latina beauty parlors was conducted in the city of Lawrence, Massachusetts. Lawrence is located about 35 miles north of Boston and has the highest concentration of Latinos in the state. The total population is about 72,000, of which 29,000 are Latino (41.6 percent). The Latino community is almost equally divided between Dominicans and Puerto Ricans (Gaston Institute, 1992, 1994).

This study built on an earlier one conducted in Holyoke and Lawrence (Delgado, in press a). The initial study involved four beauty parlors (two in each city) and six botanical shops (five of which were located in Lawrence). In that study, geographical sections in each city were selected, and all Latino-owned establishments (for profit and not for profit) were identified and interviewed. The Lawrence study reported in this article was done in a different geographical area of the city selected because of its high concentration of Latino-oriented establishments. A local Latino community-based agency (Centro Panamericano) cosponsored the research. This agency was selected because of its reputation in the community and previous collaboration with the author.

The study involved a two-stage process. The initial stage required locating and listing all of the beauty parlors within a geographical area. The second phase involved an interviewer (Latina staff member) visiting the establishments and conducting an in-person interview with the owners. The interviews lasted about 50 minutes.

Survey Instrument

The survey instrument consisted of four sections and 32 open-ended questions. Data were obtained on the following topics: development of a business and customer profile, identification of social services provided, identification of customer needs, and owner willingness to collaborate with agencies in delivery of services. Unfortunately, the instrument obtained only minimal information about such topics as financing the start of a business, revenue, and expenditures. (All of the beauty parlor owners received financial support for business development from their families.)

FINDINGS

Latina-owned beauty parlors attracted a client base that was far broader that just adult Latinas (Table 1). Surprisingly, all of the beauty parlors served men, with two establishments serving an equal number of men and women. All of the beauty parlors served a wide range of ages, reaching children, adults, and elderly people.

TABLE 1 Characteristics of Clients of Latina-Owned Beauty Parlors

Beauty Parlor	Racial/Ethnic Composition (%)			Gender (%)		Age Range (Years)
	Latino	White	African American	Female	Male	
A	80	10	10	80	20	5–80
B	90	5	5	50	50	6–70
C	85	10	5	50	50	10–50
D	90	5	5	60	40	13–65
E	75	10	15	90	10	5–70
F	80	5	15	55	45	7–80
G	90	5	5	85	15	6–75

All but two of the beauty parlors had been in existence less than five years (Table 2). Hours of operation were fairly similar among the establishments. Days of operation only differed on whether or not the parlor was open on Mondays or Tuesdays, with most open six days per week.

The beauty parlors fulfilled a multifaceted role in the community (Table 3). The Latina owners expressed willingness to involve themselves in leadership roles on social agency boards, advisory committees, task forces, and so forth. None of the owners, however, had ever been approached by local social services agencies to engage in collaborative projects. All of the owners indicated a willingness to collaborate with local human services agencies in an effort to help the community in a variety of social services areas, most notably alcoholism and family violence. The women, with few exceptions, recognized the impact of social problems on the customers and their families. Some of the beauty parlors, however, were willing to collaborate only in particular activities; only two were willing to collaborate in all activities mentioned in the survey.

Lazzari, Ford, and Haughey's (1996) research of Latinas identified as being leaders in the community found that these women possessed a belief in themselves, were willing to accept the responsibility that goes with leadership, and viewed their work as a "duty" to the community: "Factors that supported and sustained the women in their extensive amount of community involvement included seeing the need, feeling personal satisfaction, receiving support from others, and having personal beliefs and characteristics" (p. 201). Quotes from this study's beauty parlor owners (translated from Spanish) touched on the factors identified by Lazzari et al.: "I cannot stand by and watch my community suffer," "A job well done entails not just making the customer more attractive physically but also emotionally," "Simply put, I

TABLE 2   Beauty Parlor Organizational Characteristics

Beauty Parlor	Year Opened	Hours of Operation	Days of Operation
A	1994	7 hours Tuesday through Thursday 10 hours Friday and Saturday	Tuesday through Saturday
B	1986	8 hours Tuesday through Thursday 10 hours Friday and Saturday	Tuesday through Saturday
C	1989	8 hours Monday 9 hours Tuesday through Thursday 10 hours Friday and Saturday	Monday through Saturday
D	1991	8 hours Tuesday through Thursday 10.5 hours Friday and Saturday	Monday through Saturday
E	1995	9 hours	Monday through Saturday
F	1994	8 hours Tuesday through Thursday 11 hours Friday and Saturday	Monday through Saturday
G	1996	9 hours	Monday through Saturday

TABLE 3 Activities Provided by Latina-Owned Beauty Parlors and Social Services Collaborative Possibilities

Beauty Parlor	Willingness to Participate in Leadership Role	Approached by Social Agency to Collaborate	Willingness to Collaborate	Distribute Pamphlets	Distribute Videotapes	Hold Lectures or Discussions	Provide Counseling or Advice	Provide Information or Referrals
A	Yes	No	Yes	Yes	No	Yes	Yes	No
B	Yes	No	Yes	Yes	No	No	No	No
C	Yes	No	Yes	Yes	No	Yes	Yes	Yes
D	Yes	No	Yes	Yes	No	No	Yes	No
E	Yes	No	Yes	Yes	Yes	Yes	Yes	Yes
F	Yes	No	Yes	Yes	No	No	No	No
G	Yes	No	Yes	Yes	Yes	Yes	Yes	Yes

could not have succeeded without the support of my family, friends, and customers," "Being a part of the community requires more than operating a business; it requires caring about what goes on beyond the walls of my beauty parlor."

DISCUSSION AND IMPLICATIONS FOR PRACTICE

This study highlights the important role Latina-owned beauty parlors can play in the community. The high number of beauty parlors established during a recession period in the state reflected a strong resiliency base within the community. These settings attracted a diverse client base, thus having the potential to reach a wide sector of the community. Community revitalization efforts, as a result, must incorporate these and other small businesses in their work.

Latino small businesses have a ready-built market that can be expected to continue to expand. This trend, in combination with increasing residential segregation, will increase the influence these institutions can wield in the community.

The results also highlight the need for policy development to encourage small business development. Waldinger, Aldrich, Bradford, et al. (1990) suggested that policies that encourage development of ethnic businesses must be twofold: "budding an infrastructure that fosters small business development in general and enacting and enforcing systemic policies of equal economic opportunity for ethnic and racial minorities" (p. 197). These suggestions can take the form of social services organizations sponsoring workshops for small business development, contracting with small businesses for goods and services whenever possible, and facilitating the provision of consultation for owners. Latino small businesses can be organized into coalitions to increase their visibility, advocacy, purchase of supplies, and so forth. In turn, owners are an excellent community resource to be tapped for agency boards, advisory committees, task forces, and commissions.

Latino small businesses can provide access to services for disempowered groups in their role as urban sanctuaries (residents can patronize a business without fear of being rejected because of their ethnic or racial background), as providers of culture-specific items and services, and as providers of information related to the homeland. Their accessibility to the community (geographical, psychological, cultural, and logistical) makes these institutions excellent settings for collaboration with social services organizations (Delgado, 1995a, 1995b). Beauty parlors and other small businesses can help distribute, public education information (in Spanish), make referrals, perform crisis intervention, interpret correspondence for non-English-speaking clients, and fulfill other important roles. However, these establishments should not be expected to engage in all possible collaborative activities.

Although many of these establishments are willing to collaborate if asked, unfortunately, few have been provided with this opportunity. Approaching these establishments should be viewed developmentally. Collaboration, will be labor intensive and require a great deal of patience and follow-through on the part of social services organizations (Delgado, 1994). Nevertheless, such efforts will prove rewarding for the profession, the initiating social service agency, and the Latino community (De La Rosa, 1988).

CONCLUSION

Neighborhood revitalization will be an elusive goal if indigenous assets are not a part of the strategy. Latinos, like other people of color, have endured tremendous hardships in the United States. Small businesses have historically played and continue to play an influential role within ethnic communities. This role extends far beyond the selling of a product or a service for profit.

Only now has the social work profession, probably more so than any other helping profession, taken a serious look at Latino businesses as a community resource. Latina-owned beauty parlors take on greater significance because they address the needs of an undervalued subgroup. The social needs of Latinas are addressed within a cultural context that both respects and appreciates their struggles in society. These settings have women providing services in an affirming and nonstigmatizing manner. However, for those business owners who are willing to help, endless possibilities exist for primary, secondary, and tertiary intervention projects.

REFERENCES

Borges-Mendez, R. (1993). The use of Latino immigrant labor in Massachusetts manufacturing: Evidence from Lowell, Lawrence, and Holyoke. In E. Melendez & M. Uriate (Eds.), *Latino poverty and economic development in Massachusetts* (pp. 104–124). Boston: University of Massachusetts, Mauricio Gaston Institute for Latino Community Development and Public Policy.

Castex, G. M. (1994). Providing services to Hispanic/Latino populations. *Social Work, 39,* 288–296.

De La Rosa, M. (1988). Natural support systems of Hispanic Americans: A key dimension of well-being. *Health & Social Work, 13,* 181–190.

Delgado, M. (1994). Hispanic natural support systems and the alcohol and drug abuse field: A developmental framework for collaboration. *Journal of Multicultural Social Work, 3,* 11–17.

Delgado, M. (1995a). Hispanic natural support systems and the AOD field: Issues and challenges. *Alcoholism Treatment Quarterly, 12,* 17–32.

Delgado, M. (1995b). Puerto Rican elders and natural support systems: Implications for human services. *Journal of Gerontological Social Work, 24,* 115–130.

Delgado, M. (1996). Puerto Rican food establishments as social service organizations: Results of an asset assessment. *Journal of Community Practice, 3,* 57–77.

Delgado, M. (in press a). Latina-owned businesses: Community resources for the prevention field. *Journal of Primary Prevention.*

Delgado, M. (in press b). *Social work practice in nontraditional urban settings.* New York: Oxford University Press.

Delgado, M., & Humm-Delgado, D. (1982). Natural support systems: Source of strength in Hispanic communities. *Social Work, 27,* 83–89.

Enchautegui, M. (1994). *Latino neighborhood and Latino neighborhood poverty.* Washington, DC: Urban Institute.

Gaston Institute. (1992). *Latinos in Lawrence.* Boston: University of Massachusetts.

Gaston Institute. (1994). *Latinos in Lawrence: Poverty, income, education, employment, and housing.* Boston: University of Massachusetts.

Halpern R. (1995). *Rebuilding the inner city: A history of neighborhood initiatives to address poverty in the United States.* New York: Columbia University Press.

Halter, M. (Ed.). (1995). *New migrants in the marketplace: Boston's ethnic entrepreneurs.* Boston: University of Massachusetts Press.

Hoechstetter, S. (1996). Taking new directions to improve public policy (Editorial]. *Social Work, 41,* 343–346.

Holmes, S. A. (1996, October 13). For Hispanic poor, no silver lining. *New York Times,* p. E5.

Hurtado, A. (1995). Variations, combinations, and evolutions: Latino families in the United States. In R. E. Zambrana (Ed.), *Understanding Latino families: Scholarship, policy, and practice* (pp. 40–81). Thousand Oaks, CA: Sage Publications.

Institute for Puerto Rican Policy. (1993). *Puerto Ricans and other Latinos in the United States: March 1992* (Datanote). New York: Author.

Institute for Puerto Rican Policy. (1996). *The status of Puerto Rican children in the U.S.* (Datanote). New York: Author.

Jennings, J. (1994). *Understanding the nature of poverty in urban America.* Philadelphia: Temple University Press.

Kozol, J. (1995). *Amazing grace: The lives of children and the conscience of a nation.* New York: Crown.

Kretzmann, J. P., & McKnight, J. L. (1993). *Building communities from the inside out.* Evanston, IL: Northwestern University, Center for Urban and Policy Research.

Lazzari, M. M., Ford, H. R., & Haughey, K. J. (1996). Making a difference: Women of action in the community. *Social Work, 41,* 197–205.

Levitt, P. (1993). The social aspects of small-business development: The case of Puerto Rican and Dominican entrepreneurs in Boston. In E. Melendez & M. Uriate (Eds.), *Latino poverty and economic development in Massachusetts* (pp. 143–158). Boston: University of Massachusetts, Mauricio Gaston Institute for Latino Community Development and Public Policy.

Levitt, P. (1995). A todos les llamo primo (I call everyone cousin): The social basis for Latino businesses. In M. Halter (Ed.), *New immigrants in the marketplace. Boston's ethnic entrepreneurs* (pp. 120–140). Boston: University of Massachusetts Press.

McKnight, J. L., & Kreztmann, J. P. (1991). *Mapping community capacity.* Evanston, IL: Northwestern University, Center for Urban and Policy Research.

Melendez, E. (1993). Latino poverty and economic development in Massachusetts. In E. Melendez & M. Uriate (Eds.), *Latino poverty and economic development in Massachusetts* (pp. 15–27). Boston: University of Massachusetts, Mauricio Gaston Institute for Latino Community Development and Public Policy.

Moore, J., & Pinderhughes, R. (1993). Introduction. In J. Moore & R. Pinderhughes (Eds.), *In the barrios: Latinos and the underclass debate* (pp. xi–xxxix). New York: Russell Sage Foundation.

Morales, R., & Bonilla, F. (1993). Restructuring and the new inequality. In R. Morales & F. Bonilla (Eds.), *Latinos in a changing U.S. economy: Comparative perspectives on growing inequality* (pp. 1–27). Newbury Park, CA: Sage Publications.

Osterman, P. (1989). *In the midst of plenty: A profile of Boston and its poor.* Boston: Boston Foundation, Persistent Poverty Project.

Perez, S. M., & Cruz, S. (1994). *Speaking out loud: Conversations with young Puerto Rican men.* Washington, DC: National Council of La Raza.

Perez, S. M., & Martinez, D. (1993). State of Hispanic America: Toward a Latino anti-poverty agenda. Washington, DC: National Council of La Raza.

Saleebey, D. S. (Ed.). (1992). *The strengths perspective in social work practice.* New York: Longman.

Saleebey, D. S. (1996). The strengths perspective in social work practice: Extensions and cautions. *Social Work, 41*, 296–305.

Sarason, Y., & Koberg, C. (1994). Hispanic women small business owners. *Hispanic Journal of Behavioral Sciences, 16*, 355–360.

Segura, D. (1992). Walking on eggshells: Chicanas in the labor force. In S. B. Knouse, P. Rosenfeld, & A. L. Cubertson (Eds.), *Hispanics in the work force* (pp. 173–193). Newbury Park, CA: Sage Publications.

Torres, A. (1995). *Between melting pot and mosaic: African Americans and Puerto Ricans in the New York political economy.* Philadelphia: Temple University Press.

Waldinger, R., Aldrich, H., Bradford, W. D., Boissevain, W. D., Chen, G., Korte, H., Ward, R., & Wilson, P. (1990). Conclusions and policy implications. In R. Waldinger, H. Aldrich, & R. Ward (Eds.), *Ethnic entrepreneurs: Immigrant business in industrial societies* (pp. 177–197). Newbury Park, CA: Sage Publications,

Waldinger, R., Aldrich, H., & Ward, R. (1990). Opportunities, group characteristics, and strategies. In R. Waldinger, H. Aldrich, & R. Ward (Eds.), *Ethnic entrepreneurs: Immigrant business in industrial societies* (pp. 13–48). Newbury Park, CA: Sage Publications.

9  *Perspectives on Community (ies)*

Topics Addressed in this Chapter:

➤ **HISTORICAL PERSPECTIVES ON COMMUNITY**
➤ **DEFINING COMMUNITY**
➤ **TRADITIONAL PERSPECTIVES**
   Community as Place
   Community as Functions
   Community as Middle Ground, Mediator, or Link
   Community as Ways of Relating
   Community as Social System
➤ **ALTERNATIVE PERSPECTIVES**
   Alternative Approaches to Community
   SEHB and Community: Poverty Reduction
        Strength/Assets
   Community Building/Community Renewal
   People- and Place-Based Strategies
   Community Building and Physical Environment
   Comprehensive Community Initiatives
        Community-Building Principles
        Community-Building Themes
   Economic Perspectives on Community: Capital
        Assets
   Types of Capital: Financial, Human, and Social
        Financial Capital
        Human Capital
        Social Capital
        Bridging Capital versus Localized Social Capital
   Civil Society, Civic Culture, and Civil Ethic
   Social Capital and Diversity
   Nonplace Community
        Community and Technology
        Community, Technology, and Social and Economic Justice
        Virtual Community
   Technology and Community
   Technology and Social Networks
   Community as Social Network
   Qualitative Aspects of Community
        African American Community Qualities

*E*ach stop along our journey toward understanding human behavior and the social environment, thus far, has been important. In some respects, though, this chapter on community may be the most important. Such an assertion is not intended to lessen the importance of understanding human behavior at individual, family, group, and organizational levels. Instead, the notions of community we explore here highlight the importance of these other levels by bringing them together into one arena.

In a sense we have been talking about community all through this book. Who we are as individuals is influenced greatly by the community contexts within which we live. Who we are as individuals significantly influences the nature of the communities in which we live. Families, groups, and organizations also carry out their lives and seek to fulfill their potential and goals in the context of community. All of these levels of human behavior are intricately intertwined in and with community. The core concerns of social work are interconnected with and define qualities of community to which social workers aspire. The dimensions of both traditional and alternate paradigms reflect ways of viewing community—albeit very different views. The very concept of paradigm or worldview reflects the elements that together form community (regardless of the nature of the specific elements). When Kuhn (1970) discussed paradigm shifts in the natural sciences (see Chapter 1), he did so using the language of community. The assumptions we made at the beginning of our journey about the relationships among ourselves, social work, and the people with whom we work are also essential relationships to consider in defining and giving meaning to community.

It is not an exaggeration to say that we cannot talk about social work in the spirit in which we have done so here without also talking about community. It is always within the construct of community that we practice social work. The individuals, families, groups, and organizations with which and through which we practice social work are fundamental building blocks of community. It is in response to the needs and demands of humans at these levels that we construct and reconstruct community.

Community is an inclusive but somewhat elusive concept for many of us today. Much has been written about the "loss of community" and about the "search for community." These notions suggest the significant changes occurring in people's views of community. They are also consistent with our attempts in this book to embark on a journey in "search" of more holistic ways of understanding HBSE. In this chapter we embark on a journey in search of community.

This chapter on community can be viewed as both closing and opening anew the circle that is human behavior and the social environment. Community is where the individual and the social environment come together. An inclusive perspective on community can help social workers answer the perennial question confronting our field: "Should the resources and interests of social workers best be directed toward individual or social change?" The answer, it seems, is a resounding yes! We must focus on both—and that focus must simultaneously be directed internally to us and externally to the world around us. We can do nothing else, for each is contained in the other. We must change ourselves in order to change the world. As the world changes, we change (Bricker-Jenkins and Hooyman 1986). Community represents that level of human behavior at which we as individuals connect with the social or collective world around us.

As we explore notions of community both from traditional and alternative perspectives, we will see that as has been the case with paradigms generally, the kinds and quality of communities are influenced more by the worldviews of some of us than others. It will be our quest here to explore notions of community that will allow all members of communities to participate, learn from one another, and be represented in this important sphere of life. For community provides important opportunities and challenges to expressing individual and collective human differences in all their richness and complexity.

HISTORICAL PERSPECTIVES ON COMMUNITY

How people have thought about community in the past was influenced by the dominant worldviews in place at the time. The ways in which we think about community presently are greatly influenced by the dominant paradigms of the historical periods in which we live, as are the ways we think about human behavior and the social environment generally.

The revolutionary changes in perspectives on the individual brought about by the Renaissance in Western Europe had a great impact also on perspectives on the individual's place in much of the larger collective world of community. Again, we are reminded that the individual and the social are indeed closely (even inseparably) interrelated. These revolutionary changes occurring in Western Europe had influence far beyond this relatively limited geographic region of the globe. The new paradigms of the Renaissance (you might recall from our discussion in Chapter 1) came to define and dominate the modern world. Central to this revolution was the belief in the centrality of the individual rather than of society or the collective.

Anthropologist David Maybury-Lewis (1992:68ff) believes this shift from the centrality of the collective to the individual had significant implications, positive and negative, for both family and community. He suggests that

> *the glorification of the individual, this focus on the dignity and rights of the individual, this severing of the obligation to kin and community that support and constrain the individual in traditional societies . . . was the sociological equivalent of splitting the atom. It unleashed the human energy and creativity that enabled people to make extraordinary technical advances and to accumulate undreamed of wealth.* (1992:68)

In addition to the implications of the Renaissance view of the supremacy of the individual, the emergence of modern science in the nineteenth century also had significant influence on the global environment of which human communities are a part. The emergent philosophy of science was based in large part on the assumption that the natural world existed to be mastered by and to serve humans. A belief in humans' right to exploit nature had religious roots as well. "Medieval Christianity also taught that human beings . . . were created in God's image to have dominion over this earth." These beliefs in the supremacy of humans over nature were in stark contrast to the worldviews of many tribal peoples, who saw strong interconnections and mutuality between humans and the other elements of the natural world and beyond (Maybury-Lewis 1992:73).

A worldview focusing on mutual interdependence of individuals, families, communities, and the larger world rather than one based on individuality and exploitation of nature results in significantly different perspectives on the place of community in the scheme of things. A worldview based on interdependence has much to teach us about how to live together with each other; how to create "a sense of community through intricate and time-tested webs of inclusion" (Utne 1992:2).

These alternative and historically older perspectives, from which we can learn much, have continued to exist, although they have been largely ignored in dominant worldviews. These alternatives represent, for the most part, roads not taken by the constructors of dominant paradigms as they defined what community is or should be. Examples of alternative perspectives continue to exist in the beliefs about and views of community held by many indigenous peoples in the United States and around the globe. Many of the alternate notions about community that we will explore here as "new" ways of thinking about community actually have their roots in ways of thinking about community that are much "older" than those views currently dominant. This is another way of recognizing that our journey to a more holistic understanding of community represents a completing of a circle through which we can begin anew to think about HBSE, rather than a linear notion of a journey that ends at a specific destination "at the end of the line" in the present.

DEFINING COMMUNITY

Community is a complex and multifaceted level of human behavior. It is made even more complex, and hence somewhat more difficult to define, because it is such an inclusive (and, as noted earlier, a somewhat elusive) concept. Definitions of community need to incorporate human behavior at the individual, family, group, and organizational levels. To do this we take the position here that there are multiple ways of defining community. Different definitions focus on different facets of or perspectives on communityness. Different definitions may also reflect varying degrees of consistency with the dimensions of traditional or alternative paradigms we discuss in this book.

As we explore traditional and alternative perspectives on community, we will encounter a number of basic elements used to think about community. These basic elements will include such notions as **community as a collective of people.** This *includes individuals, groups, organizations, and families; shared interests; regular interaction to fulfill shared interests through informal and formally organized means; and some degree of mutual identification among members as belonging to the collective.*

Anderson and Carter (1990:95–96) suggest that community is a perspectivistic notion. This notion of multiple "perspectives," rather than a "single definition of" community is perhaps appropriate here because it implies that community is different things to different people. This broad notion allows inclusion of traditional as well as alternative perspectives as individuals, families, groups, and organizations come together or separate in distinct communities. It allows us to incorporate the multiple perspectives we have explored on all the other levels of human behavior throughout this book into our thinking about communities. For example, when we discuss the important roles of individuals in community, we can now think about the important roles played by all individual members, including women and men; people of color and white people; people with disabilities and temporarily able-bodied people; poor people and people who are financially well-off; old and young people; gay men, lesbians, bisexual and heterosexual people. When we discuss the important roles played by families within the context of community, we can now think about alternative and diverse family forms, including gay and lesbian families and augmented or fictive families, as important elements of community in addition to traditional nuclear or simple extended family forms.

TRADITIONAL PERSPECTIVES

Community as Place

Perhaps the most traditional perspective on community is one that associates community first and foremost with a geographical location—a place, in which we carry out most of our day-to-day activities. Our hometown or our neighborhood, for example. Reiss offers a typical example of place-focused perspectives on community. He suggests that "a community arises through sharing a limited territorial space for residence and for sustenance and functions to meet common needs generated in sharing this space by establishing characteristic forms of social action" (1959:118).

Traditional perspectives on community as territory or space were used as a basis to describe both small rural communities and large urban cities. Dwight Sanderson (in Warren and Lyon 1988:258–260) described a rural community geographically as the rural area in which the people have a common center of interest (such as a village or town center) and a common sense of obligation and responsibility. Sanderson suggested a method developed by Galpin to locate the boundaries of rural communities. You locate the rural community by beginning at the village or town center and mark on a map the most distant farm home whose members do their business there (Sanderson in Warren and Lyon 1988:259).

Weber defined *city* as an economic marketplace or market settlement that was a specific geographic space. He defined **city** as a place where local inhabitants could satisfy an economically substantial part of their daily wants on a regular basis in the local marketplace. He saw city as a place in which both urban (city dwellers) and nonurban (people from the surrounding rural area) could satisfy their wants for articles of trade and commerce. These articles of trade were produced primarily in the local area surrounding the city or were acquired in other ways and then were brought to the city for sale (Weber in Warren and Lyon 1988:15–17). These notions of rural communities and cities as geographic locations (places) in which we carry out a variety of activities or functions to meet our needs are probably the most traditional ways we think of community.

Community as Functions

Warren extends the perspective on community as place by describing in more detail the nature of the functions that are carried out in the place or space that is community. He suggests that **community** is "*that combination of social units and systems that perform the major social functions having locality relevance.* In other words, by *community* we mean the organization of social activities to afford people daily local access to those broad areas of activity that are necessary in day-to-day living*" (1978:9).

Warren describes these activities or functions as five types:

1. *local participation in production-distribution-consumption of necessary goods and services by industry, business, professions, religious organizations, schools, or government agencies.*

2. *socialization or the transmission of knowledge, social values, and behavior patterns to members by families, schools, religious organizations, and other units.*

3. *social control to influence members' behaviors to conform to community norms through laws, the courts, police, family, schools, religious organizations, and social agencies.*

4. *social participation in activities with other members through religious organizations, family and kinship groups, friendship groups, business, government programs, and social agencies.*

5. *mutual support for community members in times of need through care for the sick, exchange of labor to help members in economic distress, and assistance for other needs by primary groups such as families and relatives, neighborhood groups, friendship groups, local religious groups, social service agencies, insurance companies, and other support units.* (Warren 1978:10–11)

Community as Middle Ground, Mediator, or Link

Community has often been viewed as a kind of "middle ground" or context in which individuals' "primary relationships" such as those in family and close friendship groups come together with their "secondary relationships," which are more specialized associations such as those in formal organizations (work, school, religion). This notion of community suggests that community is that place where the individual and the society meet.

Warren (1978:9) stresses the linkages between the people and institutions of a local community and the institutions and organizations of the larger society. Another aspect of this approach, especially when combined with the notion of community as that location in which all our daily needs are met, is that community is a microcosm of society. It is an entity in which we can find, on a smaller or local basis, all the structures and institutions that make up the larger society (Rubin in Warren and Lyon 1983:54–61). As we will see later when we explore alternative perspectives on community, significant questions have been raised about whether this is a realistic or necessary way of perceiving community.

Community as Ways of Relating

Another traditional approach to community shifts the central focus on community from the relatively concrete or instrumental notions of geographic place or a set of specific functions to a much more interactional or affective focus on community as ways people relate to each other. This is a much more affective- or "feeling"-focused way of defining community. As we will see, this perspective on community offers a number of avenues for expanding our notions of community to include alternative, more inclusive views of what community means.

This approach to community focusing on the ways members relate to one another emphasizes identification or feelings of membership by community members and feelings by others that a member is in fact a member. This notion also stresses sharedness. It emphasizes feelings of connectedness to one another on the part of community members. This perspective on community can be referred to as a sense of "we-ness" or a "sense of community" that is felt by members.

Ferdinand Tönnies (in Warren and Lyon 1988:7–17) formulated what has become a classic way of describing two contrasting ways people relate to each other as members of collectivities. His formulations have often been used in relation to discussion of different ways people relate to each other in different community contexts. Tönnies's conceptualization is helpful here because while it focuses on ways of relating, it also lends itself to thinking about the nature of relationships that predominate in large urban communities compared to those in small rural communities. In other words, it allows us to incorporate place as well as relationships in our feelings about community. In addition, Tönnies's approach suggests a historical perspective on changes in the ways people have tended to relate to one another within community over time.

Tönnies's formulation is based on two basic concepts. One he referred to as gemeinschaft, the other he termed gesellschaft. **Gemeinschaft relationships** are ways of relating based on shared traditions, culture, or way of life and on a sense mutual responsibility arising out of that shared tradition. He associated gemeinschaft relationships with the ways people related to each other in small stable rural communities where people knew each other well, shared many past experiences, and expected to continue long relationships with each other into the future. He suggested gemeinschaft relationships were based on what he called natural will. **Natural will** reflected a quality of relationship based on mutuality in which people did things for one another out of a sense of shared and personal responsibility for one another as members of a collective.

Gesellschaft relationships, on the other hand, were ways of relating to each other based on a contractlike exchange in which one member did something for another in order for that person to return the favor in the form of needed goods, money, or services. This way of relating was based in what Tönnies referred to as rational will. **Rational will** reflected impersonal ways of relating not based on shared culture, tradition, or personal relatedness over time. Gesellschaft relationships were founded on the rational reality that people needed things from each other to survive, and to get those things one had to exchange goods, services, or money for them. Gesellschaft relationships were more likely to characterize life in large urban cities where people were not likely to know one another well or share a past with the people with whom they had to interact to get their needs met (Tönnies in Warren and Lyon 1988:7–17).

Tönnies believed that gesellschaft and gemeinschaft relationships could and often did exist simultaneously. Some needs were met contractually based on rational will and some were met out of a sense of mutual responsibility based on natural will. One form tended to predominate, however, depending on whether the community context was traditional and rural (gemeinschaft) or impersonal and urban (gesellschaft). Tönnies saw the emergence of capitalist industrial urbanized societies to replace traditional societies dominated by agrarian rural communities as a historical movement from gemeinschaft relationships predominating in collective life to their replacement by gesellschaft relationships (Tönnies:7–17 and Warren:2–3 in Warren and Lyon 1988).

Community as Social System

Notions of community as a social system offer a somewhat more comprehensive or holistic view of community than many of the other traditional notions. Like notions of community as relationship, approaches to community as a social system offer some helpful avenues to pursue as we search for more comprehensive and inclusive alternatives to traditional notions of community.

The advantages of a systems view of community are similar to the advantages of a systems view of some of the other levels of human behavior we have explored. A systems view allows us to see the various components or subsystems of communities—the individuals, families, groups, and organizations that make up communities. A social systems view allows us to recognize the influence on communities of other systems and subsystems in the larger environment—the influence of state and national governments on the local community, for example. A systems approach also acknowledges that influences among systems components and between communities and the environment are reciprocal. A systems view suggests that a community influences the larger environment at the same time that the community is influenced by the larger environment. In recognizing these reciprocal influences, a systems view can help us to appreciate the reality of ongoing change in community life. Perhaps an illustration of these reciprocal influences will help.

Prior to the Civil Rights Act of 1964, it was common practice for various community subsystems—local restaurants, hotels, service stations, or bus companies, for example—to deny their services or to provide inadequate services to African Americans. This discrimination had a direct impact on the day-to-day lives of many individuals in local communities. In response to this discrimination, individual African Americans began to organize themselves within their local communities and across many different communities and they began to demand equal access to community services. As more and more people began to demand change, their collective influence began to be felt at state and national levels.

At the state level a number of individual states reacted to these demands by attempting to silence the calls of their citizens for equal rights. At best, many states responded by doing nothing and continuing their discriminatory practices. The civil rights movement continued to grow from the acts of individual people in individual communities to a national movement that would not accept the unwillingness of state and local systems to change and provide equal services to African Americans. Instead, participation in the civil rights movement demanded that the national government intervene and stop the continued discrimination at the state and local level.

After much conflict and much time passed, the national government responded by creating and beginning enforcement of the Civil Rights Act. This national legislation had a direct influence on states and localities by making it unlawful to discriminate against people of color in public accommodations and services. In turn, as the Act began to be enforced, its influence was felt by many individual citizens. Individuals who had practiced discrimination against people of color in the areas covered by the Civil Rights Act now had to suffer consequences if they were found breaking the law. Individuals who had been discriminated against now knew they had the support of federal law in their efforts to obtain equal services.

ALTERNATIVE PERSPECTIVES

Our efforts to travel to and explore alternative ways of knowing and viewing community will involve a number of the dimensions of alternative paradigms we outlined in Chapter 2. It will include interpretive, intuitive, qualitative, subjective approaches, feminist perspectives, diversity-focused visions, personal and integrative perspectives, and perspectives addressing oppression and discrimination in community. Our journey will use as points of departure a number of the elements of traditional perspectives on community as well. Some parts of our journey will involve looking in different ways at some of the traditional perspectives on community. In our search for alternatives, as was suggested earlier, we will return to some older visions of community held by indigenous peoples in various parts of the globe.

Alternative Approaches to Community

As the 1990s became the early 2000s, a number of exciting developments emerged in thinking about community and its role in the daily life of individuals and families and in the larger society of which community is a building block. This new thinking (or rethinking) about community presents some important possibilities for social workers as we work to assist communities and their members in using their assets to achieve both individual and collective well-being. This new thinking offers more holistic or comprehensive approaches to understanding many interrelated elements of community life than in the past. These approaches have far-reaching implications for virtually all the foundation areas that make up social work education and practice: not just human behavior and the social environment, but also social policy, research, practice, human diversity, social and economic justice, values and ethics, populations-at-risk, and field practicum. These new developments integrate theoretical approaches to understanding community (the knowledge base) with policy and practice approaches to bring about positive community changes that are consistent with social work values and ethics. In addition, these alternative approaches reinforce the interconnections among well-being at the individual, family, group, organization, and community levels. Among the concepts and approaches that make up this exciting new direction for understanding and intervening in and with communities are:

- Community building
- Community renewal
- Community assets and strengths
- Social capital
- Civil ethic and civil society

SEHB and Community: Poverty Reduction

One of the most promising themes that flows through these concepts and approaches is of fundamental concern to social workers: poverty reduction. As we have indicated in other chapters, the theme of poverty reduction is of critical importance to social work because it is at the core of so many of the other concerns that social workers attempt to address such as infant mortality, substance abuse, violence, racism and sexism, child abuse and neglect, hunger, homelessness, and teen pregnancy. Poverty reduction is also a theme that unites our efforts across all system levels—individual, family, group, organization, community, and society.

As is so often the case, many of these newer alternative approaches to community strengths and needs by addressing the overarching issue of poverty really take us back to social work history—a history that was first and foremost about addressing human needs resulting from lack of physical and social resources. However, these alternative approaches also integrate new developments in strengths-based and assets-based theory and practice that have emerged in the profession only recently. Next we will explore some of these alternative developments in thinking about community.

Community Building/Community Renewal

A new response to poverty reduction at the community level is "known as **community building;** its goal is overhauling the nation's antipoverty approach and creating communities that work for the low-income families who live there" (Walsh 1997). Community building is also referred to as **community renewal.** Walsh stresses that community building takes a more comprehensive approach to poverty in theory and practice because it goes beyond analyzing poverty only in terms of jobs or income "but [also] as a web of interwoven problems—poor schooling, bad health, family troubles, racism, crime, and unemployment—that can lock families out of opportunity, permanently." In addition, community-building initiatives work toward poverty reduction at multiple levels to address economic, social, and political marginalization that locks people and communities into poverty (1997).

Ewalt, a social worker, stresses that "it is clear that redeveloping impoverished communities requires a multifaceted approach that addresses the physical and economic conditions of neighborhoods as well as the social and cultural aspects" (1998b). Such strategies also acknowledge the "linkages and interconnectedness among the various strands of an individual's life and of the importance of family and neighborhood influences in determining individual level outcomes" (Connell et al. in Naparastek 1998:12). This recognition of the multilayered and ever-changing influences of the larger social environment on individual development is consistent with life-course theory discussed in Chapter 5.

Central to community building or community renewal is the idea "that the path toward individual, neighborhood, and corporate renewal is indivisible from or, at the very least, dependent on efforts to rebuild a sense of community. Ultimately, the culture of renewal represents the individual American's revived search for meaning—but within the context of community" (Louv 1997).

Strengths/Assets

The concept of community building also conveys an asset rather than a deficit approach to poverty reduction consistent with alternative paradigm thinking. For example, it uses a metaphor of "building"—a constructive concept—rather than earlier and traditional metaphors, such as that used in 1960s-era approaches to poverty reduction which often referred to as "the war on poverty." As Walsh points out, "war is about destruction, community building is about creation" (1997). Community building uses the existing assets of poor communities as the foundation for development. This approach focuses first "on the strong institutions, associations, and individuals that still exist in poor communities—from schools and churches to the corner grocer who employs teenagers and the stay-at-home mom who watches latchkey kids—rather than focusing solely on deficits like crime, unemployment, or school failure" (Walsh 1997).

People- and Place-Based Strategies

Another indication of the comprehensive or holistic approach taken by community builders is the attempt to reunite what Walsh refers to as the traditional split "between 'people' and 'place' strategies." Traditional antipoverty approaches tended to be divided into two parts: "human services—the 'people' people, [that] focused on the education, family support, and health care needs of the poor—and the 'place' strategists, the community development field that focuse[d] more on rebuilding neighborhoods—with housing, retail development, and attempts at job creation—than on human development" (Walsh 1997).

Naparastek points out the mutually reinforcing nature of an approach integrating both people- and place-based strategies: "A community-building approach looks at the whole picture, acknowledges the interconnectedness of people- and place-based strategies, and recommends a course of action in which solutions are tied together in such a way that they reinforce one another" (1998:11). Such approaches can help improve the effectiveness of community-based social work practice. "Linking place- and people-based strategies through community-building has significant implications for social work, because it means improving the delivery and quality of human services, strengthening community organization, stimulating economic development, and in every possible way improving the quality of life of residents while affecting physical improvements," according to Naparastek (1998:11).

Community Building and Physical Environment

A significant part of place-based community building involves the actual physical design of homes and neighborhoods. Community building strives for physical construction of homes and neighborhoods that support the creation of a "sense of community." This focus on physical design is referred to as an architecture of community renewal. Examples of these innovative design changes include:

- Placing the garage or carport around back, or hiding it on the side of the structure
- Building houses with front porches to increase interactions with neighbors and a sense of community
- Clustering housing and offices closer together so workers might be able to walk to their jobs
- Using mass transit rather than cars (Louv 1996)

Louv suggests that the design of schools today should support a sense of community but often do not: "Schools in the late 19th and early 20th centuries strove for stateliness and grandeur . . . . Looking at the typical suburban school, one wants to exhort it: 'Buck up! Show some pride! Remember that you're crucial to the community!' " Another innovative design approach is to "allow each single-family house to have a garage apartment or cottage at the rear of its lot. . . . [So grandparents] may be available for baby-sitting and other household assistance, but without the frictions of sharing their children's living quarters 24 hours a day. . . . These apartments also can be used by grown sons and daughters, especially after a divorce or a job layoff" (1996).

Comprehensive Community Initiatives

Holistic and integrative approaches to community building and renewal are often referred to as **comprehensive community initiatives (CCIs).** Ewalt cites the definition of comprehensive community initiatives (CCIs) by Kubisch, Weiss, Schoor, and Connell. According to this definition, CCIs

> *Contain several or all of the following elements and aim to achieve synergy among them: expansion and improvement of social services and supports, such as child care, youth development, and family support; health care, including mental health care; economic development; housing rehabilitation and/or construction; community planning and organizing; adult education; job training; school reform; and quality-of-life activities such as neighborhood security and recreation programs.* (Ewalt, 1998b:3)

To make these new comprehensive community-building approaches work and for social workers to become effective in helping them work, Naparastek and Dooley suggest the need for linking community building "to social work practice in a form that requires competence in the processes of place-based and people-based strategies . . . ; the need for social work practitioners who are familiar with community theory and community organizations, who understand the processes of physical and economic development, and who have core knowledge of social work values and commitment to grassroots participation" (Naparastek 1998:14).

Community-Building Principles

The National Community Building Network, formed in 1993 by a number of private foundations (Ford, Casey, and Rockefeller) and other community-building initiatives, developed a set of eight principles to guide community-building efforts:

1. Integrate community development and human service strategies. Traditional antipoverty efforts have separated "bricks and mortar" projects from those that help families and develop human capital; each approach needs the other to be successful.

2. Forge partnerships through collaboration. Building community requires work by all sectors—local residents, community-based organizations, businesses, schools, religious institutions, health and social service agencies—in an atmosphere of trust, cooperation, and respect.

3. Build on community strengths. Past efforts to improve urban life have too often addressed community deficits; our efforts build on local capacities and assets.

4. Start from local conditions. There is no cookie-cutter approach to building community; the best efforts flow from and adapt to local realities.

5. Foster broad community participation. Many urban programs have become professionalized and alienated from the people they serve; new programs and policies must be shaped by community residents.

6. Require racial equity. Racism remains a barrier to a fair distribution of resources and opportunities in our society; our work promotes equity for all groups.

7. Value cultural strengths. Our efforts promote the values and history of our many cultural traditions and ethnic groups.

8. Support families and children. Strong families are the cornerstone of strong communities; our efforts help families help themselves. (Walsh 1997)

These eight principles provide a framework for understanding some of the more specific developments in the arena of community development and revitalization. Next we will explore some of the more specific elements of a community-building approach.

Community-Building Themes

The Urban Institute has endorsed the above principles of community building, but also offers some community building themes that are more specific and provide guidance in translating the eight principles into practice. According to the Urban Institute, community building needs to be:

1. *Focused on specific improvement initiatives in a manner that reinforces values and builds social and human capital.* As neighborhood residents work together on community projects such as cleaning up a vacant lot, working on crime prevention, planning housing repair and rehabilitation, or improving neighborhood schools, they are "automatically building social capital—developing friendships and mutual trust, sharing and strengthening common values, learning how to work together as a team to get things accomplished, building confidence that they can achieve meaningful results, and strengthen their own institutions" (Kingsley et al. 1997:34–35). According to Kingsley et al., "building social capital is most importantly a means of building human capital—strengthening the capacities of individuals and families to overcome adversities and create and take advantage of opportunities" (Kingsley et al. 1997:35).

2. *Community driven with broad resident involvement.* Rather than simply "participating" in community development activities as was the case earlier federal programs such as Community Action Programs and Model Cities programs in the 1960s and 1970s, today's community-building initiatives emphasize that community-building efforts are *community driven*. In other words, community residents must be "truly in charge and accountable for results" (Kingsley et al. 1997:36). However, "community driven" does not imply that noncommunity entities such as private foundations and federal agencies are excluded from development activities. In fact, these newer approaches to community building stress the importance of partnerships with many different groups and organizations both inside and outside the community. This partnership is one in which government or fundors do not direct the effort; rather they participate in citizen initiatives that are directed by residents (Kingsley et al. 1997:36). In addition, this "community driven" approach does not exclude professionals such as social workers from involvement in community development projects. However, social workers and other professional are increasingly being seen as "facilitators" rather than "managers." This new role focuses on providing "good professional advice and support, while reinforcing community leadership instead of eroding it" (Kingsley et al. 1997:37).

3. *Comprehensive, strategic, and entrepreneurial.* Because poor communities face so many interrelated challenges, community-building efforts must be comprehensive and deal with a range of community issues such as economic opportunity (jobs and training), physical development and infrastructure (streets, garbage, water, utilities, etc.), safety (police), community institutions (schools, hospitals, libraries, recreation), and social capital (strong, supportive, and trusting relationships and networks among community members). While these efforts need to be comprehensive, not everything can occur at once, so communities need to be focused or strategic in their efforts. Residents need to prioritize what most needs to be accomplished first. One alternative means of developing priorities is to begin with an evaluation of assets rather than problems (see below). In addition, these efforts need to be entrepreneurial—they need to produce a concrete and useful outcome. In this way the community can demonstrate its ability to use its assets to really get things done (Kingsley et al. 1997:38–9).

4. *Asset-based.* Kretzman and McNight stress the importance of reinventing community development efforts by focusing first on assets that exist in the community. Regardless of the degree of poverty and other challenges faced by community members, all communities have significant assets. These assets need to be inventoried, recognized, and used. In this respect, these new community-building approaches are very much strengths-based and are very different from earlier approaches that focused first and foremost on what was wrong with a community rather than what was right with it. Kretzman and McKnight suggest that assets can be inventoried or mapped by looking at different levels and types of assets which they refer to as *tiers*. The first tier, referred to as *"primary building blocks,"* are "assets and capacities located inside the neighborhood and largely under neighborhood control." These include the assets of individuals such as skills, talents, experiences of residents. They note that these individual assets include the "gifts of labeled people"—mentally ill, disabled, and elderly community members. The first tier also includes the assets of community organizations such as business, religious or "faith-based" organizations, civic organizations, and communications organizations (newspapers, radio, TV). The second tier of assets includes *"assets within the community but largely controlled by outsiders"* such as private and non-profit organizations like colleges and universities, hospitals, and social service agencies as well as physical resources (vacant land, buildings, housing, energy and waste resources) and public institutions (schools, libraries, police, fire departments, parks). The third and final tier of assets includes *"resources originating outside the neighborhood and controlled by outsiders."* These include such assets as expenditures for welfare, capital improvement resources (improvements paid for by taxes from outside the community), and public information (public television and radio stations) (emphasis added, Kingsley et al. 1997:40).

Naparastek argues that "a neighborhood's assets must include not only its material resources (everything from schools and bank branches to vacant storefronts and welfare checks), but also its human assets—such as life experiences, skills, and readiness to commit time and energy to a sustained effort. Any serious attempt to help people regain control of their lives must provide opportunities to invest and build on such assets (1998:13)."

5. *Tailored to neighborhood scale and conditions.* Kingsley et al. suggest that community-building efforts need to be carried out at the neighborhood level because of size and diversity. The efforts need to be carried out in a context that is small enough for people to have a significant amount of face-to-face contact so neighbors can get to know each other as they work together to benefit the community. As noted above, the relationships that come from working together to solve mutual problems help build individual and community social capital. The optimal size of a neighborhood unit is approximately 5,000 to 6,000 residents, or roughly the number of people typically needed to support an elementary school. The second reason for the neighborhood focus is diversity of issues faced by different neighborhoods. All neighborhoods face problems or sets of problems that are unique to that neighborhood (Kingsley et al. 1997:41).

6. *Collaboratively linked to the broader society to strengthen community institutions and enhance outside opportunities for residents.* While poor neighborhoods have many assets and unique configurations of challenges facing them, they do not exist in a vacuum, and they need resources from the larger community and social environment to solve their local problems. So rather than attempting to separate from the larger environmental context, neighborhoods must create collaborations and partnerships with entities in the larger environment. For example, financial resources necessary to renew communities require a combination of internal and external resources, and educational and job opportunities necessary for residents to move out of poverty require linkages and partnerships with groups and organizations outside the immediate community, even though ideally the education acquired will be used to benefit the local community and the paycheck generated by jobs outside the immediate community will be spent buying products and services from local community business and organizations to the greatest extent possible.

7. *Consciously changing institutional barriers and racism.* Community building requires that institutions, such as banks and other lending institutions, that previously abandoned poor communities reinvest in the community in ways that benefit residents and allow the lending institution to make a reasonable return on its investment (for example, countering tendencies to "redline"—deny loans or mortgages on property in poor neighborhoods—see discussion of redlining in this chapter). One of the most critical needs of many poor communities is to address and redress both personal and institutional racism. As Kingsley et al. point out, "since a great deal of the isolation of minority communities is the product of racial discriminations, race matters in community building efforts" (1997:44). Because racism and discrimination are so integrally connected to poverty in communities with significant numbers of people of color, race and racism must be openly addressed and racist behaviors and institutional practices must be changed (Kingsley et al. 1997:44–45).

Economic Perspectives on Community: Capital

Assets

Driving these new approaches to community renewal is a growing recognition on the part of social workers and others that poverty reduction at the individual, family, and community level is to a very great extent about assessing, using, and growing assets. "Asset building is a new way of thinking about antipoverty strategies; its emphasis on resources rather than problems has much in common with the strengths perspective in social work practice and policy development" (Page-Adams and Sherraden 1997:432). Assets involve multiple types: human, physical, and fiscal. The concept of assets and asset development is closely related to the concepts of human, economic, and social capital discussed in sections that follow. A shift to an assets-based practice and policy framework would cause a paradigm shift in the profession that would result in social workers advocating for policies that "invest in people instead of programs" (Beverly 1997:23ff).

A number of years ago, "Sherraden (1988, 1990, 1991) suggested that households and communities develop not by income alone (the dominant theme of the welfare state), but also by savings and asset building. In this usage, the term 'assets' is restricted to the concept of wealth, including both property and financial holdings" (Page-Adams and Sherraden 1997:423). "Sherraden proposed a system of individual development accounts (IDAs)—matched savings for purposes such as education, home ownership, and small business development" (Page-Adams and Sherraden 1997:423–24). Based on evaluation of asset development programs, Yadama and Sherraden concluded that "it appears that assets lead to more positive attitudes and behaviors, and the same attitudes and behaviors lead to more assets" (in Ewalt, 1998a:68).

In addition to Individual Development Accounts (IDAs) to be used for home ownership, educational investments, or small business development, Sherraden also foresees other types of asset development accounts such as Individual Training Accounts (ITAs) to be used by individuals to invest in human capital development through education and training chosen by individuals to meet their education and training needs. Beverly and Sherraden note that the Council on Adult and Experiential Education and participating employers who set up ITAs for their employees "have found that workers make much better use of these training funds than of training that is offered *en masse* to all employees. Because the money is 'theirs' workers make careful choices about how to invest in themselves, and they are committed to the training" (1997:24).

Types of Capital: Financial, Human, and Social

Consistent with the community-building principle of combining or integrating both "people-" and "place-based" strategies is the increasing concern over the multiple types of capital necessary to comprehensively address poverty at the personal, family, and community levels. While there are numerous types of capital, perhaps the three most common and relevant for social workers are: financial (or economic), human, and social capital.

Financial Capital

Financial capital refers to money or property that is available for investment or "use in the production of more wealth" (Dictionary 1995). In other words, financial capital is resources available to use to create more resources. It is interesting that for a profession with a long history of concern for reducing poverty, we have been so hesitant to incorporate the concept of financial capital and capital or asset creation in the policies and programs we support. It would seem fundamental that many of the multitude of difficulties poor people face result from inadequate financial capital—they do not have access to the resources necessary to accumulate financial capital. A growing number of social workers are working to incorporate concepts such as capital and assets into social work programs and policies. For example, growing interest in social development in social work, both in the United States and internationally, reflects this increasing recognition of the importance of economic assets to individual and collective well-being. Midgley points out that "social development is characterized by the integration of social and economic processes and the promotion of the social welfare of all. At the same time, social development is 'particularly concerned with those who are neglected by economic growth or excluded from development' " (Midgley in Beverly and Sherraden 1997:3).

Human Capital

Human capital refers "to an individual's skills, knowledge, experience, creativity, motivation, health, and so forth. . . . Like other forms of 'capital,' human capital is expected to have future payoffs, frequently in the form of individual employment opportunities, earnings, and productivity in market and non-market sectors" (Beverly and Sherraden 1997:1–2). Beverly and Sherraden suggest that unlike financial capital, human capital can be used, but it cannot be used up because "individuals cannot be separated from their knowledge, skills, and other individual attributes" (Beverly and Sherraden 1997:2).

The concept of human capital is of significance to social workers interested in alternative approaches and policies concerned with poverty reduction because it "represents a broad social development strategy" and because it is strengths- and assets-based (Beverly and Sherarden 1997:3). Beverly and Sherraden argue that "because social workers have traditionally advocated for improvements in social welfare and have a particular concern for those who are marginalized, it is particularly appropriate to promote investments in human capital [and] . . . investments in human capital have the potential to integrate economic development with improvements in social welfare" (1997:25–26).

Human capital is also an important concept for social workers because there is a great deal of empirical evidence that building human capital has positive outcomes for people in areas such as improved employment opportunities, higher wages, and better fringe benefits (health insurance, retirement benefits, etc.). In addition, other assets accrue for individuals as a result of increases in human capital, including increased savings, improved health outcomes, and improved access to and use of social resources such as information and influence. Communities also benefit from increases in the human capital held by their members. For example, Beverly and Sherraden note that community members with higher levels of education are more likely to volunteer, make charitable donations, and participate in political activities in their communities. Communities with better-educated members also tend to be more economically viable. Finally, Beverly and Sherraden also note intergenerational benefits to increases in human capital holdings. Increased levels of human capital on the part of mothers has a positive impact on the health of their children. Children of parents with higher levels of education generally obtain more education for themselves than their peers with less well educated parents (Beverly and Sherraden 1997:3–10).

All these positive outcome suggest that social workers would do well to use human capital theory as a significant policy and practice framework. Beverly and Sherraden argue that the social work "profession should consider the formation of human capital as a central commitment and organizing theme. . . . Social work practice . . . should be viewed not merely as an endeavor to solve problems, but also as an opportunity to build human capital—in knowledge, skills, experience, credentials, position, health, physical ability, mental cap[a]city, and motivation—that can contribute to future well-being" (1997:16). These authors also suggest some quite specific and concrete areas in which social workers can help the people with whom we work build their human capital at both policy and practice levels. These areas include working to increase investments in early childhood development, including advocating for basic nutrition and health care for all preschool children because good nutrition in infancy and early childhood can offset some of the learning difficulties faced by many poor children. Advocating for increased financial support for college education, vocational education and training (including computer and information technology training), and lifelong learning is also important (Beverly and Sherraden 1997:17–23).

Social Capital

One of the most engaging concepts and a cornerstone of the new or alternative community theory is that of social capital. Understanding the meaning, significance, and use of this core concept can help us link social work principles and values to the new work on community building and renewal. It can also help us appreciate the mutually reinforcing and interrelated nature of human behavior at the individual, family, group, organizational, community, and societal levels.

"The term **social capital** has been used for about forty years to describe resources that are neither traditional capital (money or the things money buys) nor human capital (skills or know-how). . . . *Social capital refers, then, to resources stored in human relationships, whether casual or close*" (emphasis added, Briggs 1997). It "is the stuff we draw on all the time, through our connections to a system of human relationships, to accomplish things that matter to us and to solve everyday problems" (Briggs 1997). "Defined simply, it consists of networks and norms of civic engagement" (Wallis et al. 1998). Social capital means "the sum of our informal, associative networks, along with social trust—the degree to which we feel we can expect strangers to do right by us" (Lappé and DuBois 1997).

Social capital is closely related to both financial and human forms of capital. For example, "businesses have never thrived, nor have economies flourished, without social capital. Not that social capital is an adequate substitute for the other kinds of capital. . . . Rather, social capital makes the other kinds work well. It greases the gears of commerce, along with other areas of life" (Briggs 1997).

The concept of social capital is important in helping us understand both poverty and community development. It also has a significant role to play in empowerment approaches to reducing poverty and building strong families and communities (Wallis et al. 1998). According to Wallis et al., "in both the public and nonprofit sectors, there is growing belief that programs that empower communities strengthen the resources they can provide to individuals. From this perspective, community development and individual development are intertwined, and social capital suggests the substance that is both binding and created between them" (1998).

Robert Putnam, one of the early scholars to introduce the concept of social capital in the social sciences, stressed the connections between economic and social capital. Putnam concluded,

> *after studying the role of informal relationships in economic success in Italy, that the "norms and networks of civic engagement contribute to economic prosperity and are in turn reinforced by that prosperity. . . . Chief among these norms is reciprocity, the willingness of people to help one another with the expectation that they in turn can call for help." In addition, "Putnam uses the term social capital to describe reserves of mutual assistance created through norms and networks of civic engagement. Just as monetary capital accumulated through one set of activities can be invested elsewhere, social capital suggests the possibility of applying reserves of mutual assistance accumulated from one set of activities to others, thereby mobilizing collaborative action to further community well-being."* (Wallis et al. 1998)

Warner suggests that the concept of social capital evolved from an initial individual and family emphasis to a community focus: "Early work on social capital focused at the individual or family level in an effort to understand how stocks of social capital contribute to individual education or economic achievement." However, Warner notes that Putnam later explored the nature of social capital at the community level or "public" capital which resides in groups or networks of groups within communities. This public- or community-based form of social capital comes about in the community through "organized spaces for interaction, networks for information exchange, and leadership development" (1999:375).

According to Briggs, the concept of social capital is now used in connection with family, neighborhood, city, societal, and cultural system levels. Briggs gives some helpful examples of how social capital works at multiple levels:

> *It is used by individuals . . . to "get by" (for social support), that is, to cope with the everyday challenges that life presents, from flat tires to divorces. When we confide distress to a friend or listen as a confidante, social capital is at work, directly serving the person in distress but also renewing the relationship in ways that will, over time, be used by the speaker and the listener. When poor moms share caregiving tasks and rides to church along networks of relatives, friends, and acquaintances, they each draw on social capital. . . . These kinds of support often, but not always, come from people who are alike in race, class, and other terms. What is more, we are born into many of these supportive ties (to kin, for example). (Briggs 1997)*

Briggs suggests that a second use for social capital is to "get ahead:"

> *Social capital is used for social leverage, that is, to change or improve our life circumstances, or "opportunity set." When we ask a friend who is "connected" to put in a good word as part of a hiring or grantmaking decision, or when an inner-city kid, through a personal tie, gets a shot at a life-changing scholarship, this too is social capital. (Briggs 1997)*

A number of scholars and practitioners who study and use the concept of social capital in their work stress that while the concept itself is value-neutral, the uses and impacts of social capital may be either negative or positive: "as a resource or means, social capital has no right or wrong to it until some judgment is made about the ends to which we put it. We covet social capital for the reasons that many people covet money: not for what it is but for what we can do with it" (Briggs 1997).

Wallis, for example, points out that "although social capital helps facilitate actions, those actions may be either beneficial or harmful. Social capital that benefits a narrowly defined social group may not benefit a larger social group or society in general" (1998). Briggs stresses that "social capital that benefits me may not benefit my neighbors. That is, individuals may further their own aims through social capital without doing much for the community at large" (1997). Briggs illustrates "that profitable youth gangs and mafia rings depend on social capital. Sweetheart corporate deals, including those that cheat taxpayers, depend as much on off-the-books social capital as they do on mountains of legal paperwork. The now impolitic 'old boy network' functioned, and still functions in many places, through trusting ties among the 'boys' involved, to the detriment of those excluded" (1997). Just as social capital can be used for negative or positive purposes, it is also not equally distributed among individuals and communities: "not all groups have equal access to social capital. Reserves of social capital are unevenly distributed and differentially accessible depending on the social location of the groups and individual who attempt to appropriate it" (Schulman and Anderson 1999).

Warner helps us understand both the multiple levels and linkages of social capital across system levels and its unequal distribution by outlining three forms of social capital:

1. Horizontal social capital is found "in communities where horizontal ties within community are strong and norms of broad community participation exist and tend to produce more egalitarian and robust democratic structures."

2. Hierarchical social capital "is characterized by patron–client relations (and gangs) which can stifle development and skew governmental and economic structure to the interests of a particular group."

3. Absence of social capital "is found in communities with few networks among residents: wealthy 'gated communities,' which substitute economic capital for social networks, and poor and isolated communities characterized by insecurity, fear, and isolation." (1999:374–5)

If social capital is to be a useful concept for social work policy and practice, two questions need to be asked. *First, can social capital be consciously created? Second, given the unequal distribution of social capital among individuals and communities, can the creation of social capital be facilitated by external entities such as governments?* Warner points out that government certainly has played a role in decreasing community opportunities and resources for social capital development, such as its "abandonment of inner city public institutions" and in rural areas through school consolidation, which results in loss of the personal, family, and local community networks necessary for social capital construction (1999:379–80). This being the case, she argues that governments can and should be active in supporting social capital development for poor rural and urban communities.

She suggests that "at the individual level [social capital is] formed within the bounds of family, work, and school. . . . In communities where forums for interaction no longer emerge as natural extensions of work, school, or play, they can be intentionally created and designed to encourage development of social capital to enhance community problem solving." Warner provides examples of intentionally creating or supporting "public spaces" that act as places for citizens to engage in conversations and activity to enhance community effectiveness and democracy. She suggests "these spaces may be incidental (sidewalks), voluntary (clubs and associations), or quasi-official (planning board hearings), but they must be relatively participatory to enable the communication essential for public democratic discourse." Through these mechanisms "the citizen becomes a producer as well as a consumer of community" (Warner, 1999:376–379).

To facilitate the creation of social capital, governments must undergo a paradigm shift in the way they relate to communities: "Local government must shift from acting as controller, regulator, and provider to new roles as catalyst, convener, and facilitator. . . . Government programs are most effective in promoting community level social capital when they develop a facilitative, participatory structure and involve participant as partners, not clients, in program design." Warner illustrates the difference in traditional and alternative roles played by government entities by contrasting Head Start with its requirement that parents be involved in decision making through its policy councils with traditional hierarchical school decision making where most decisions are made by professionals rather than by parents (Warner 1999:384–9).

Warner also suggests the need for professionals, including social workers, to make fundamental changes in both their roles and their policies/programs. She suggests, for example, that programs which narrowly focus on individual social capital development such as parenting skills or job training "are unlikely to connect participants to broader community or extra-community resources." These kinds of "social services and community development programs are designed to address deficits rather than assets in communities. Highly professionalized services assume that the professional has the expertise while the client has the problem." Shifting to participatory, partnership-based management on the part of traditional social service agencies and schools will involve a significant paradigm shift. Warner notes that "participatory management represents a major organizational innovation for hierarchical, professionalized government structures" (Warner 1999:384–9).

The process of building social capital is similar to the concept of *synergy* in social systems thinking (see Chapter 3) in that "social capital is built up through repeated exchanges among people (or organizations) over time. It depends on regular borrowing and lending of advice, favors, information, and so on, and "depends on making regular deposits and withdrawals into a system of relationships, some of them quite casual, others very intimate" (Briggs 1997). The destruction or loss of social capital results from processes similar to those involved in entropic systems (see Chapter 3) in that "it breaks down through disuse as much as through the distrust that alienates" (Briggs 1997).

Bridging Capital versus Localized Social Capital

An important concept for understanding the dynamics of social capital creation and use for positive outcomes is **bridging capital.** In poor and "disenfranchised neighborhoods, there are often significant amounts of social capital. The problem is the lack of **bridging capital,** or *connections with people and institutions throughout the wider community*" (emphasis added, Wallis et al. 1998). Wallis notes that "Putnam distinguishes two types of social capital: **Localized social capital** 'accumulates in the course of informal social interactions that families and people living in communities engage in through their daily lives.' *Bridging capital* 'connects communities and organizations to others' (Wallis et al. 1998). Bridging capital also connects social capital with financial, physical (community buildings, businesses, schools, material goods, equipment, etc.), and human capital and serves to mobilize "these resources toward attaining larger social objectives" (Wallis et al. 1998).

Wallis stresses that "the distinction between [local and bridging capital] is important in explaining why a community rich in informal social interactions might still be poor in its capacity to provide economic opportunities. For example, people living in a poor inner-city neighborhood or rural village can participate in rich daily social interactions yet still be socially isolated from the larger city or region within which they reside" (1998).

Civil Society, Civic Culture, and Civil Ethic

The concept of social capital is often associated with the concept of *civil society*. Bradley suggests that "**civil society** . . . is the sphere of our most basic humanity—the personal, everyday realm that is governed by values such as responsibility, trust, fraternity, solidarity, and love" (emphasis added in Wallis et al. 1998). "The common element binding local and bridging capital is a norm of civic engagement (or civic ethic)" (Wallis et al. 1998).

The multiple layers that interact in the creation and use of social capital which result in and flow from civil society are sometimes referred to as a *"nested structure."* This nested structure comes about in the following way: "The civic ethic begins with personal affinities and relationships that build trust, and it then brings small groups of citizens together in common purpose. These private networks in turn form the basic building blocks of civic culture, creating a climate that supports the growth of cooperative problem solving" (Wallis et al. 1998).

Using the nested structure concept, "family, neighborhood, and community represent basic levels of social organization. Social interaction, social capital, civic infrastructure, and a civic culture are the elements critical to building a healthy civil society. Each of these four elements is present in some form at each of the levels of social organizations and links different levels of social organizations together" (Wallis et al. 1998).

Social Capital and Diversity

Social capital is a useful concept in understanding and addressing issues of diversity, discrimination, and oppression in communities. For example, people who work in community building suggest that social capital is "often created and expressed differently according to how it was influenced by race, class, and ethnicity" and stress that people who work in the area of community building in communities with diverse populations "need to have extensive familiarity with work in different cultural contexts to successfully identify and use social capital effectively" (Wallis et al. 1998).

In addition, to be effective in community building and renewal in poor and disenfranchised communities with populations of persons of color, efforts must include "addressing the impact of racism as part of their problem solving effort in community building" (Wallis et al. 1998). Racism and discrimination can "be tied in with the theme of social capital, especially in recognizing that some groups organize around racial prejudice and that this is a negative form of social capital" (Wallis et al. 1998). Individual and institutional racism are fundamental barriers to the creation of effective relationships among individuals, families, groups, organizations, and communities so essential to the creation and positive use of social capital. Illustrative Reading 9.1 by Sullivan speaks eloquently to the importance of recognizing diversity in assessing, analyzing, and building social capital and civic culture in communities of color.

Nonplace Community

A **nonplace community** is a community in which attachment to a specific place or geographic territory is absent and is not considered essential for community to exist.

Nonplace communities are sometimes referred to as "**communities of the mind,**" "**communities of interest,**" or "**identificational communities**" (Anderson and Carter 1990; Longres 1990). It is perhaps difficult to perceive of community as not primarily associated with a place because we are socialized from early on to think of community primarily as a place, e.g., our "hometown." Nonplace perspectives of community are also a bit more difficult to grasp because of our more general socialization to traditional paradigm thinking. If we cannot see, feel, hear, or observe objectively an entity through our senses (consistent with scientific thinking), we have difficulty accepting that that entity in fact exists.

On the other hand, this notion of community might be a bit easier to grasp if we recall that a number of aspects of traditional approaches to community have not been primarily place-based. When we talk about community in terms of relationships, or functions, or networks of linked subsystems, we are not talking primarily about place. However, we do usually assume that those relationships, functions, or networks exist in some more or less constant relationship to a place. Nonplace notions of community suggest that one need not associate these aspects of "communityness" with a specific or constant place. Community as social network is discussed as a special type of nonplace community later in this section.

The notion of nonplace communities as "identificational communities" can be a helpful one. It suggests that a central feature of a nonplace community is a feeling of commonalty or identification with the other members of the community. This perspective is a helpful way to conceptualize many diverse communities—the African American community, the gay or lesbian community, the Catholic community, the community of cancer survivors. Nonplace notions of community can help us to recognize that it is possible, indeed likely, that we are members of several communities simultaneously. **Identificational communities include** "groups such as ethnic/cultural/religious groups, patient groups, friendship groups, and workplace groups. While membership in these communities often overlaps with geographic communities, membership is not determined by place, but by interest or identification with the group" (Longres 1991; Germain 1991 in Fellin 1993:60)

Professions can also be thought of as nonplace communities or "communities of interest"—the social work community, for example. As social workers, we share common interests with other members of the profession. We identify with and are identified by others as members of the social work professional community. If we think about the basic elements of community we began this chapter with, we can compare the social work profession with these elements and assess whether social work reflects these community elements. Certainly social workers form a collective of people (primarily comprised of individuals and groups rather than entire families and organizations) with shared interests. Our shared interests are even codified in the Code of Ethics of the profession. As social workers we interact regularly on an informal basis with other social workers—with our colleagues in our agency or with colleagues we went to school with and with whom we continue to maintain contact, for example. We also have formally organized mechanisms for fulfilling our shared interests—the National Association of Social Workers (NASW) sponsors state and national conferences and meetings for its members to share their common professional interests, for example. The Council on Social Work Education holds an Annual Program Meeting each year that brings together members of the social work education community from around the country to share their interests. Such meetings as these not only provide opportunities to share professional interests, but they also serve to allow members of the community to maintain their personal relationships with other members of the social work community. They help reinforce our feelings of membership in the larger social work community. The purpose of NASW itself is focused on furthering the professional interests of social workers. We mutually identify ourselves as members of the social work community and others identify us as members of the social work community (both other social workers and members of other communities). In all these ways we nurture our sense of community.

Nonplace perspectives on community can help us maintain a sense of community and can give us reassurance and security even when we are separated from other community members or when we move from one geographic location to another. A Cambodian refugee can "reunite" with his or her community by connecting with other Cambodian people in the new location. Even if there are no other Cambodian people in the new location, one's sense of identity as a member of the Cambodian community can remain with the person and help the person have a sense of belonging although separated from other community members.

In this respect our nonplace communities can have a historical dimension. Some of what provides us with a sense of belonging, a sense of community, does not exist in the present. Past experiences of community upon which we build our current beliefs about community exist primarily as memories. These memories of the past are important avenues for determining the nature of community for us today. Stories of ancestors and friends who have died also help provide a sense of community or communalness— connectedness to other humans—that is an essential part of community.

Community and Technology

Another important consideration in nonplace notions of community is that of technology. Much of the ability to maintain a sense of community regardless of whether it is place-based or not is the ability to communicate with other members of the community. The communication technology available to many of us today enables us to maintain and access community relationships almost instantly. Telecommunications, fax, electronic mail, the Internet, computerized bulletin boards and other forms of computer-assisted communication, overnight mail almost anywhere, and other developing technologies all revolutionize our ability to create and maintain the relationships necessary for nonplace community to exist. Modern transportation systems allowing us to physically travel from one place to another quickly and temporarily (air travel, freeway systems, high-speed rail, etc.) enable us to maintain some face-to-face contact with the members of our nonplace communities over time.

Community, Technology, and Social and Economic Justice

It is important to recognize that such avenues to expanded visions of community are unequally available to different members of the human community. Much of the technology necessary to maintain nonplace community is expensive. Think about the concerns most of us have about the amounts of our long-distance telephone bills from month to month or of the cost of air travel or of owning and maintaining an automobile. Think about the reality that many of us do not have access to telephones at

What might the photo communicate about technology and social and economic justice? What might this photo communicate about the "digital divide?"

all and certainly cannot afford air travel or the cost of owning and maintaining a car. Consider that for some of us with disabling conditions the ability to create and maintain nonplace community may be essential to our survival, but unattainable without access to expensive technology or modes of transportation. If we are unable to move about freely in order to participate in place community to meet our daily needs, nonplace relationships and networks and the resources necessary to maintain them become extremely important means of establishing and maintaining a sense of belonging or any sense of community.

Virtual Community

One of the more recent notions of non-place community is that of the virtual community created through the world wide web of the Internet. **Virtual reality** is "a computer simulation of a real or imaginary system that enables a user to perform operations on the simulated system and show the effects in real time" (Websters 1995:1234). **Virtual communities** are defined by Howard Rheingold, author of *The Virtual Community: Homesteading on the Electronic Frontier*, as:

> the social aggregations that emerge from the Net when enough people carry on those public discussions long enough, with sufficient human feeling, to form webs of personal relationships in cyberspace. (in Lapachet 1996:www)

Lapachet notes that "one must add that participants interact via computer mediated communication." She notes further that

> *Virtual communities include, but are not limited to, such entities as LIST-SERVs, newsgroups, network chat forums (America Online), forums (CompuServe), some Internet Relay Chat sessions and Bulletin Boards (BBSs).* (1996:www)

Lapachet (1996:www) describes the requirements as well as the advantages and disadvantages of virtual communities. Some of the advantages and disadvantages relevant to social work concerns include:

Advantages
- The technology has the power to bring enormous leverage to ordinary people.
- It provides a forum for people to discuss topics of interest.
- It allows participation at the convenience of the participant.
- It allows participation by many different people from many different places.
- It hides race, gender, sexual orientation, disabilities, etc.
- It promotes interaction with others that can lead to physical meetings.
- It provides a sense of anonymity.
- It has no built-in opinion restraints.

Disadvantages
- It requires knowledge of reading, writing, and typing.
- Discrimination is different, but not absent.
- There are no built-in opinion restraints.
- It is easy for a few to dominate the discussion.
- Obtaining network access can be a problem.
- Participant must have a computer, or access to a computer.
- It takes time.
- There is the possibility of losing touch with reality.
- It is difficult to navigate and find items of interest.
- It provides a sense of anonymity.

Lapachet (1996:www) notes also that "The impact of virtual communities on individuals and physical communities can have positive and negative effects. Some of the effects could be considered both positive and negative" as is indicated in the lists above. Of particular interest to social workers concerned with strengthening communities are some specific advantages and disadvantages noted by Lapachet:

> *The biggest advantage is that the technology that makes virtual communities possible has the potential to bring enormous intellectual, social, and commercial leverage as well as, most importantly, political leverage to ordinary citizens at relatively little cost. Virtual communities give people the opportunity to discuss the issues of the day (or whatever) with each other and, if necessary or desirable, organize action. Computer mediated communication and virtual communities are a real way for people to have a say in the actions govern-*

ment and large corporations pursue. The relatively low cost of communicat-
ing information to a large number of people conveniently makes this possible.
(1996:www)

Lapachet notes also, though, that this advantage can be a disadvantage:

The medium must be used intelligently and deliberately by an informed pop-
ulation, however, because the same technology that can be used to organize
can also be used to spread misinformation. Government and large corpora-
tions could use the medium to feed trivial information in large doses to the
public, effectively numbing people into a state of information overload, thus
dismantling the usefulness of the medium by turning computer mediated
communication into a drug. *(1996:www)*

The concept of virtual community has special significance for rural and isolated persons and communities

For people in rural communities, virtual communities can provide a lifeline.
Some communities are so isolated, or small, that few special interest groups exist.
For these people, virtual communities can allow participants to enjoy their
hobby or interest, even though the nearest participant is hundreds of miles away.
(1996:www)

As noted earlier in the discussion of the potential impact of technology on community life, the inability to participate or gain membership in virtual communities can
result from lack of resources resulting from social and economic injustice, particularly
poverty. Lapachet notes the following barriers:

Literacy is only one barrier to virtual communities that exists. Access to the
networks can be a barrier to participation in virtual communities, also. In
order to be a virtual community participant, people must, first, have access
to modem-equipped computers. Currently, 6% of the adult population with
income of $10,000 per year or less own a home computer. 18% in this income
range use a computer at work. That figure moves up as family incomes in-
crease. 35% of adults, where the family income is $50,000 to $74,999 per year,
own a home computer, while 53% of those adults use one at work.... These
figures ... point out an already large disparity in access. With the price of
computers plummeting, the disparity could be growing larger.... Currently
there are few, if any, community-open computing facilities. Without access,
however, people cannot participate and again, large segments, with poten-
tially valuable and diverse points of view will be shut out. *(1996:www)*

It is important that social workers understand that virtual communities exist and
that for a growing number of people virtual communities can provide a significant opportunity for acquiring a meaningful "sense of community." It is equally important
that we recognize both the advantages and disadvantages that virtual communities
hold for individual and community life including those listed above. For social workers, it is especially important to recognize and continually evaluate the implications of

technology and technological advances for the core social work concern of social and economic justice.

Notions of nonplace community highlight that community involves many important qualitative elements. Community is not necessarily a place and a place is not necessarily a community. Such a multidimensional and qualitative perspective on community does not rely on place, although it may be created from and associated with any number of places. A nonplace perspective on community allows us to create individualized communities that have meaning for us personally. Such perspectives are subjective and interpretive, but very valuable ways to think about community.

Technology and Community

As the notion of "virtual community" has received increasing attention, concerns have arisen that as we become more reliant on computer-based communication, we will lose the benefits of face-to-face communication so critical to maintaining healthy communities. Others argue that computer-based communication can be a significant benefit in strengthening our community and social networks. Still others argue that the significance of electronic communication is not its potential for either destroying or replacing community, but simply as a tool to supplement community and social life. Calhoun, for example, suggests that "the reality, however, seems to be that the Internet matters much more as a supplement to face-to-face community organizational and movement activity than as a substitute for it" (1998:382). Fischer suggests that computer-mediated communication, like other communication technologies such as the telephone, is more about "technologies as tools people use to pursue their social ends than as forces that control people's actions" (Fischer 1997:115). Calhoun reminds us "that like other technologies, the Internet mainly makes it easier for us to do some things we were already doing and allows those with the resources to do some things they already wanted to do" (Calhoun 1998:383).

Others who have studied the impact of communication technology caution us to be realistic about the communities within which we live before being too pessimistic about virtual community: "When critics describe online communities as more isolated than 'real-life' groups, their comparison seems to be to an ideal of community rather than to face-to-face communities as they are actually lived. There is a great deal of loneliness in the lives of many city dwellers" (Kollock and Smith 1999:16).

Technology and Social Networks

One of the more helpful ways of understanding the idea of virtual community is that of community as a social network (see section on social networks below). We are reminded, as we learned earlier in this chapter, that long before the emergence of virtual community as an idea, the concept of community had evolved beyond the traditional notion of community as a physical space only. Wellman points out that "even before research on online groups had begun, researchers on community had gone through a very important shift. Community is now conceptualized not in terms of physical proximity but in terms of social networks. Telephones, automobiles, and airplanes have long meant that it was possible to establish and sustain important social relationships outside of one's immediate physical neighborhood" (in Kollock and Smith 1999:17).

Wellman argues that computer-mediated communication can help us deal with some of the isolation that is part of much of modern community life:

> *Community has moved indoors to private homes from its former semi-public, accessible milieus such as cafes, parks, and pubs. This dispersion and privatization mean that people must actively contact community members to remain in touch instead of visiting a cafe and waiting for acquaintances to drop by. By contrast, computerized conferences support connections with large numbers of people, providing possibilities for reversing the trend to less public contact. Because all members of newsgroups and discussion groups can read all messages—just as in a cafe conversation—groups of people can talk to each other casually and get to know the friends of their friends. "The keyboard is my cafe," William Mitchell enthuses. (1996)*

The ability of computer-mediated communication to help build social networks has received considerable attention in the literature. **Computer-supported social networks** (CSSNs) are described as follows:

> *When computer networks link people as well as machines, they become social networks, which we call computer-supported social networks (CSSNs). . . . Members of virtual community want to link globally with kindred souls for companionship, information, and social support from their homes and workstations. White-collar workers want computer-supported cooperative work (CSCW), unencumbered by spatial distance, while organizations see benefits in coordinating complex work structures and reducing managerial costs and travel time. Some workers want to telework from their homes, combining employment with domestic chores . . . ; management foresees reduced building and real estate costs, and higher productivity. (Streibel 1998)*

These CSSNs have actually existed for some time. Streibel points out that "CSSNs began in the 1960s when the U.S. Defense Department's Advanced Projects Research Agency developed ARPANET to link large university computers and some of their users." CSSNs moved into the sphere of our everyday lives beginning in the mid-1980s as

> *Personal computers have become increasingly connected (through modems, local networks, etc) to central communication hosts. These hosts have become linked with each other through the worldwide "Internet" and the "World Wide Web" (encompassing information access as well as communications). Together with other interconnecting computer networks, the overall network has become known simply as "The Net," a "network of networks" . . . that weaves host computers (using high capacity communication lines), each of which is at the center of its own local network. (Streibel 1998)*

Community as Social Network

Both CSSNs and the concept of social capital discussed earlier reflect alternative approaches to community as a social network. A social network approach is a nonplace perspective on community. The notion of social network represents somewhat of a middle ground between traditional and alternative paradigm thinking about community. Some suggest that it is not in itself a community, but that it is an important component of community for many people. Netting, Kettner, and McMurty (1993:103–104), in their discussion of the importance of social networks as community resources, use Balgopal's definition:

> *Social networks such as kin, friends, neighbors, and coworkers are supportive environmental resources that function as important instruments of help. . . . Social networks provide emotional resources and strength for meeting the need of human relatedness, recognition, and affirmation. They also serve as mutual aid systems for the exchange of resources such as money, emotional support, housing, and child care.*

Certainly this perspective suggests that social networks include many of the supports and resources commonly thought of as part of community whether it is a place or nonplace community.

Other researchers have attempted to trace or map social networks as a means of understanding community. This approach, referred to as network analysis, has included attempts to describe community by focusing on interpersonal relationships. This alternative was used by Wellman and Leighton (in Warren and Lyon 1988:57–72) to try to discover if large urban *gesellschaft*-like communities had completely done away with personal *gemeinschaft*-like ways in which community members might relate to one another. They were especially concerned with if and how these personal and primary relationships could exist in the large and relatively impersonal urban context. Based on their analysis, they determined that personal relationships remained strong and important to urban dwellers but these relationships often extended well beyond the geographic boundaries of neighborhoods or communities and included relatives and friends in distant places. Although the primary personal relationships were not necessarily territorially or place based, people were able to maintain them through modern communications technology and transportation systems. This approach to network analysis concluded that a more workable alternative perspective on community was one that included both place, in terms of neighborhood or geographically defined community, and nonplace community networks that functioned to meet primary mutual support and identification needs not met in the urbanized and mobile environment characteristic of much of modern society.

Qualitative Aspects of Community

McKnight (1987:54–58) posits an **ideal community vision** that is inclusive of all community members and offers a qualitatively different experience in living from that possible in organizational or institutional life. McKnight suggests a number of other ways that communities can be defined by considering their differences from formally constructed and explicitly goal-directed organizations or institutions (see discussion of organizational goals, Chapter 8). McKnight sees community and formal organizations as oppositional in many ways. He suggests that institutions operate to *control* people while the means of association through community is based on *consent*.

McKnight's vision is inclusive in that he finds a place even for those who have been excluded from community and labeled as in need of institutionalization either in the traditional sense of a mental (or other social control) institution or in the more contemporary sense of human service systems that he sees as the equivalent of institutions without walls. The themes of community, he suggests, include:

1. **Capacity.** *Recognition of the fullness of each member because it is the sum of their capacities that represents the power of the group. Communities are built upon recognizing the whole depth—weaknesses and capacities [strengths] of each member.*

2. **Collective Effort.** *The essence of community is people working together. One of the characteristics of this community work is shared responsibility that requires many talents. Thus, a person who has been labeled deficient can find . . . support in the collective capacities of a community that can shape itself to the unique character of each person.*

3. **Informality.** *Transactions of value take place without money, advertising, or hype. Authentic relationships are possible and care emerges in place of its packaged imitation: service.*

4. **Stories.** *In universities, people know through studies. In businesses and bureaucracies, people know by reports. In communities, people know by stories. These community stories allow people to reach back into their common history and their individual experience for knowledge about truth and direction for the future.*

5. **Celebration.** *Community groups constantly incorporate celebrations, parties, and social events in their activities. The line between work and play is blurred and the human nature of everyday life becomes part of the way of work. You will know you are in community if you often hear laughter and singing. You will know you are in an institution, corporation, or bureaucracy if you hear the silence of long halls and reasoned meetings.*

6. **Tragedy.** *The surest indication of the experience of community is the explicit common knowledge of tragedy, death, and suffering. (1987:57–58. Copyright © 1987 by Social Policy Corporation. Used with permission.)*

"To be in community is to be a part of ritual, lamentation, and celebration of our fallibility. Knowing community is not an abstract understanding. Rather it is what each of us knows about all of us. . . . It is only in community that we can find care" (McKnight 1987:58; McKnight 1992:90).

African American Community Qualities

Barbara Solomon's (1976:57) discussion of ways of defining African American community questions the appropriateness of traditional place-based and quantitative definitions. She suggests a way of defining African American communities that is much more qualitative in focus:

> *The physical proximity of peoples in some geographical location is not enough to define community. A degree of personal intimacy must also be present among the residents of the physical space. This aspect of community has generally been ignored by social scientists whose image of community has been colored by those characteristics amenable to quantitative analysis, e.g., income level, crime rate, or incidence of hospital admissions. Personal intimacy, however, is indicated through the existence of such relationships as friendship and marriage and such feelings as confidence, loyalty, and interpersonal trust.* (1976:57)

McKnight's and Solomon's community visions, with their recognition of the value of qualitative dimensions, including personal strengths and fallibilities; informality; collective efforts and responsibility; stories as avenues to knowing and understanding; accepting as real and legitimate both celebration and tragedy; and the importance of personal intimacy, relationships, confidence, loyalty, and trust have much in common with many of the dimensions of our alternative paradigm. Even though McKnight's vision is set in opposition to modern human service organizations, and Solomon's vision is offered in part as a critique of existing social science definitions of community (among which can be included those created and used by many social workers), they both include much that is consonant with the core concerns and purposes of social work.

Intentional Communities

Communes

Both McKnight's and Solomon's perspectives on community suggest that the boundary between community and family and small group often blurs. This is especially true when we consider intentionally formed communities, specifically communal perspectives on community. Communal living has often been studied as an alternative approach to traditional family forms. Communal living has also been studied as an intentional effort to construct new forms of community living. For our purposes this difference in perspective is not problematic. It helps us realize that the boundaries between different levels of human behavior are blurred and change according to the perspective of the observers and participants involved. It might be helpful to reconsider levels of human behavior as not mutually exclusive but existing on a continuum that is not linear but spiral. For example, as family forms change and expand from nuclear to extended or networks of fictive kin (see Chapter 6 on families) they spiral into forms that resemble community almost as much as (or perhaps more than) they resemble traditional family forms. So, while we consider communal living here as a form of alternative community, keep in mind that in many ways we might just as appropriately have included it in our chapter on families.

Whether viewed from the perspective of family or community, efforts in communal or communitarian living represent efforts to create alternatives to traditional arrangements for living together. Aidala and Zablocki (1991:89) define a commune as

> *any group of five or more adults (with or without children) most of whom are unrelated by blood or marriage, who live together without compulsion, pri-*

marily for the sake of some ideological goal for which a collective household is deemed essential.

Marguerite Bouvard (1975 in Warren 1977:561, n. 1) adapts a definition of the Federation of Intentional Communities and includes both family and community:

Communes are free as opposed to blood-related families. . . .[A commune] must include a minimum of three families and also common economic, spiritual, and cultural institutions.

Communitarian movements tend to come about during times of social and cultural transition. Such movements have occurred periodically throughout history and have included religious, political, economic, and alternative family foundations. The most recent and most studied flurry of activity in communal-living experiments occurred in the United States during the 1960s and 1970s.

Aidala (1989:311–338) suggests that communes allow conditions of social and cultural change in which old patterns of living are questioned and new patterns have not yet emerged. She suggests that they are "intense ideological communities [which] allow limited experimentation with alternatives in work, family, politics, religion, and their intersections." She believes that "communal experiments functioned for their participants, and one might argue, for the larger society as well, as part of the process of changing norms for family life" (1989:312). She notes that commune members "were concerned with working out norms, justifications, and habitual practices to support cohabitation, delayed childbearing or childlessness, assertive women, emotionally expressive men, working mothers, child-tending fathers, and relationships based upon discussion and negotiation rather than predefined, obligatory roles" (1989:334). It is interesting to compare these goals with the core concerns and values of social work, such as self-determination, rights for each person to reach their fullest human potential, social and economic justice, and equality. Aidala suggests also that the very existence of communal experiments, whether they ultimately failed or succeeded in achieving their purposes, were important voices questioning the status quo of traditional family forms and human relationships (1989:335).

Aidala and Zablocki also find evidence that significant numbers of commune members were not explicitly seeking new family forms but joined communal groups in search of "consensual community" in which "to live in close relationship with others with whom one agreed about important values and goals. Communes were attempts to intentionally expand networks of emotional support beyond conventional bonds of blood and marriage" (1991:88). Nevertheless, the boundaries of family and community often merged in communal life. "Forming a communal household had to do not only with common location but with a particular type of relationship among members characterized by holistic, affectional bonds, and equally important dimensions of *shared belief and conviction*" (1991:113). Note the elements of family, groups, and community in these descriptions of communes. Aidala (1989) and Aidala and Zablocki (1991) refer to these communal arrangements as "wider families." This is perhaps a helpful way to appreciate the intersection of the several levels of human behavior reflected in these experiments.

Rosabeth Moss Kanter (in Warren 1977:572–581) perhaps best summarized the core issues and concerns faced by communes or utopian communities. The central issue, she believed, was that of commitment. The basic concerns were how members arranged to do the work the community must have done to survive as a group, and how the group managed to involve and satisfy members over a long period of time.

The issue of commitment Kanter referred to reflects the important search for a fit between individual needs and interests and those of the community that is central to communal struggles. She suggested that "commitment . . . refers to the willingness of people to do what will help maintain the group because it provides what they need." When a person is committed, what that person wants to do is the same as what that person must do. The person gives to the group what it needs to maintain itself and receives in turn what the person needs to nourish her/his sense of self (1977:574).

Kanter listed several specific problems with which communes must deal in order to ensure both their survival and group and individual commitment. These problems are listed below.

1. *How to get work done without coercion.*
2. *How to ensure decisions are made, but to everyone's satisfaction.*
3. *How to build close, fulfilling relationships, but without exclusiveness.*
4. *How to choose and socialize new members.*
5. *How to include a degree of autonomy, individual uniqueness, and even deviance.*
6. *How to ensure agreement and shared perception around community functioning and values.* (Kanter in Warren 1977:572)

These perspectives on communes may run counter to many of the stereotypes we might hold about communes as rather normless contexts for excessive and irresponsible behaviors such as drug abuse and irresponsible sexual activity. While these excesses may have been a part of some communal experiences (as they are a part of noncommunal life), those who have studied communal life have found that these intentional communities are much more likely to be serious attempts to find workable alternatives to the historic needs of individuals, families, groups, and communities.

New Towns

Communes are almost exclusively efforts on the part of private individuals and groups to find new visions of community by creating intentional communities. There have been government-assisted experiments in the creation of intentional communities as well. Government efforts to create new communities or "new towns" began as an effort to respond to the "urban crisis" that erupted during the 1960s. This crisis of community came about in large part because of the history of oppression and exclusion of many community members, especially persons of color and low-income persons, from meaningful participation in the life of the community. These individuals and groups had been denied access to participation in the locality-relevant functions of community necessary to meet individual and family needs (see Warren, above).

New towns were an effort to build new communities that would not be characterized by the oppression and discrimination that had been so harmful to so many people and had culminated in the explosions that were the urban crisis of the 1960s. New towns were sanctioned by the federal government in the form of loan guarantees to private developers who would literally build new communities. The federal government loan guarantees came with the requirement that new towns provide plans for including a wide representation of people as potential community members—people of color, low-income people, older persons, persons with disabilities. The fundamental concern was for new communities to ensure optimum "quality of life" or "the well-being of people—primarily in groups but also as individuals—as well as the 'well being' of the environment in which these people live" (statement from 1972 Environmental Protection Agency conference quoted in Campbell 1976:10). Many people have pointed out that few if any new towns actually lived up to these high expectations.

The basic concept of new towns was not really new when it received renewed interest in the late 1960s. The "Garden City" concept had been in place in Britain since the turn of the century. In the United States new towns emerged after World War I, and government support for several so-called greenbelt towns began in 1929. The new towns of the 1960s were comprehensive efforts to build community with consideration for both physical and social environments. They were planned "to provide for a broad range of social, economic, and physical activities within a defined area of land and within a predetermined time period" (Campbell 1976:17). Socially they were to include a full range of educational services and health, recreation, civic, and religious organizations. Economically they were to include businesses, industry, and professional endeavors. Physically they were to include "infrastructure" of roads and utilities as well as housing for a wide range of income levels. This comprehensive range of services was to be carried out in economically viable, environmentally sound, and socially interactive ways. Citizens of new towns were to have meaningful participation in governance and decision making throughout the development process (Campbell 1976:17).

Government support for new town development decreased to virtually nothing by the end of the 1970s. As a result, this experiment in government-supported intentional community development probably was not in place long enough even to effectively evaluate its success or failure. Certainly, as noted earlier, there is little doubt that new towns failed to reach the lofty potential declared for them by their proponents. New towns, like other experimental intentional communities, held great promise for the quality of life they hoped to provide and might serve as helpful models of what community life might be like under varying conditions. Campbell suggests that the greatest challenge of new towns was

> to structure and maintain an environment . . . in which human potential is enhanced, and finally, one where people irrespective of age, sex, race, religion, or economic condition can positively interact with each other and nature. (1976:266)

Community: Social and Economic Justice and Oppression

The challenges faced by new towns reflect the need to undo existing patterns of oppression and unequal distribution of power in traditional communities. Our alternative paradigm requires us to recognize and work toward the reduction of existing oppression at all levels of human behavior. Community, because of its inclusiveness of other levels of human behavior, is a critical context for recognizing—with the goal of reducing—oppression and unequal distribution of power.

An essential first step to reducing oppression and unequal distribution of power is the recognition of their existence. One way to begin to recognize the existence of oppression and inequality in communities is to think about the physical structure of the traditional communities within which we live. How are they arranged? How segregated are community members from each other in terms of color and income or class? How does this segregation come to be? How is it maintained?

Community and Discrimination

Where we live is a powerful influence on much of what we experience in other spheres of our lives. Where we live is a powerful influence on whom we have as friends; on whom we have as role models and associates; on where and with whom we go to school; on the kinds of jobs and resources to which we have access; and on the quality of our housing. Segregation in housing results in different people having fundamentally different experiences in relation to the influences we listed above. In the United States segregation is most often based on color and/or income. While segregation based on color in many areas of life (schools, public accommodations, jobs, housing) has been made illegal through such legislation as the 1964 Civil Rights Act and the 1954 Supreme Court ruling (Brown versus Topeka Board of Education) we need only to look around us to become aware of the continuing reality of segregation in our communities.

Logan (in Warren and Lyon 1988:231ff) and Feagin and Feagin (1978:85ff) describe several types of institutionalized discrimination in communities that serve to create and maintain oppression and unequal distribution of power. These mechanisms of oppression include blockbusting, racial steering, and redlining.

Blockbusting is a practice followed by some real estate brokers in which the racial fears of whites about African American families are used to manipulate housing markets. Blockbusting can happen when a previously all-white neighborhood begins to become integrated. After a few African Americans move into the neighborhood, white home owners are manipulated into selling their property, often at lower than market value, out of fear. These same homes may then be sold at significantly inflated prices to new incoming African American persons. **Racial steering** is a process that perpetuates existing patterns of segregation. Racial steering involves realtors or rental-property management agents steering people to specific areas of communities in order to maintain racial or economic segregation. **Redlining** is a form of discrimination used by some banks and other lending institutions that declares certain areas or sections of communities as bad investment risks. These areas often coincide with poor neighborhoods or neighborhoods with larger populations of people of color. The term *redlining* came from the practice by some institutions of actually outlining in red on a map the areas in which they would not approve home loan or mortgage applications. This practice prevents low-income people or people of color from acquiring loans in order to become home owners rather than renters. It also negatively affects communities because it prevents community people from purchasing and rehabilitating deteriorating rental housing (Logan 1988:231–241; Feagin and Feagin 1978:85–115).

These practices provide examples of mechanisms for creating and maintaining segregation, discrimination, and oppression in communities. These processes are all directly related to housing. Housing is only one element of community life. However, because where we live influences so many of the other sectors of our lives, it seems fundamental that we recognize housing as a cornerstone of systems of oppression in communities. Housing segregation directly influences other patterns of segregation; perhaps most fundamental among these is school segregation. It can be argued that until we are willing to—indeed, until we insist on the opportunity and right to—live in truly integrated neighborhoods and communities we will most likely never be able to eliminate oppression and discrimination in this or the other sectors of life. All of us as humans must have the right to live in the communities and neighborhoods we choose.

By living close to others we come to know, respect, and understand the complexities of those persons different from ourselves. By living among people different from ourselves we can learn to compromise, to respect, and learn from difference, to celebrate and be strengthened by difference. The examples we have used here focus on low-income people and people of color. They can readily be applied also to people different from us in other ways—in sexual orientation, religious beliefs, disabling conditions, or age, for example.

Social Development Approach

One approach to community building and improvement with a global perspective is that of social development. **Social development** has been defined in multiple and interrelated ways. It has been described as

- *"the process of planned change designed to bring about a better fit between human needs and social policies and programs." (Hollister)*
- *"directed towards the release of human potential in order to eliminate social inequities and problems" (Meinert, Kohn, and Strickler)*
- *"an intersystemic and integrated approach designed to facilitate development of the capacity of people to work continuously for their own welfare and the development of society's institutions so that human needs are met at all levels especially the lowest" (Billups and Julia)*
- aiming *"to foster the emergence and implementation of a social structure in which all citizens are entitled to equal social, economic, and political rights and equal access to status, roles, prerogative and responsibilities, regardless of gender, race, age, sexual orientation, or disability" (Chandler).* (Sullivan 1994:101)

All of these definitions share a concern for gaining access to basic resources to fulfill human needs for community members. Sullivan argues, however, for an expanded notion of basic human needs from the traditional notion of needs for housing, food, clothing, etc. to include "the provision of opportunities, the ability to maximize individual and collective potential, assurance of equal rights and protection of the natural environment" (Sullivan 1994:107–108). This expanded notion of the goals of a social development approach are certainly consistent with social work values and ethics, respect for human diversity, and social and economic justice. The definitions of social development above and the more inclusive notion of basic human needs are also consistent with such approaches as strengths, feminist, and empowerment perspectives on bringing about the necessary changes at the community and individual levels to accomplish the goals and fulfill the requirements of the definitions (see Chapters 1, 2 and 3).

Diversity and Community

Recognizing and removing barriers to help create community environments in which the benefits of diversity can be realized are fundamental concerns for social work at the community level. The intentional communities we explored earlier, such as communes and new towns, reflect significant concerns for diversity in a number of respects. Certainly a central concern for us as social workers (or soon-to-be social workers) is the degree to which human diversity is respected and incorporated in community. Perspectives on communities consistent with the alternate paradigms we consider in this book will attempt to maximize and respect diversity among community members as a source of strength. At the same time, alternate perspectives must balance the importance of diversity in communities with the importance, especially for many members of oppressed groups, of living around and within communities of people with whom we have much in common and that can provide us with a sense of positive identity, security, and history.

Religion and Community

A significant element of community life for many people is that of religious institutions. Maton and Wells describe the potential for both positive and negative contributions of religion to community well-being. They define **religion** very broadly as "encompassing the spectrum of groups and activities whose focus extends beyond the material reality of everyday life (i.e., to a spiritual reality)" (1995:178). You might want to compare this definition of religion with our earlier definitions of religion and spirituality.

Religious Institutions and Community Development. Maton and Wells (1995) point out the role that many religious organizations have played in community development efforts. They note that

> *Religious organizations, especially those in urban areas, have a vested interest in revitalizing surrounding neighborhoods and communities. This form of environmental change may have a preventive effect by reducing stress related to urban infrastructure decay and enhancing supportive resources.* (Maton and Wells 1995:182)

Religious Institutions and Social Action. In addition to community development directed toward improving the physical structures and well-being of community members, religious organizations have often played significant roles in social action to bring about social and economic justice in communities. Church involvement in social action has an especially rich history and tradition in the African American community. Maton and Wells point out that

> *especially in the South, black churches functioned as the institutional centers and foundation of the [civil rights] movement. . . . Black churches provided*

> *the movement with the leadership of clergy independent financially from the white society and skilled at managing people and resources, an institutionalized financial base, and meeting place where strategies, tactics and civil rights organizations were developed. Furthermore, black churches supplied the movement with "a collective enthusiasm generated through a rich culture consisting of songs, testimonies, oratory and prayers that spoke directly to the needs of an oppressed group."* (Maton and Wells 1995:187–188)

Religious Institutions as a Negative Force in Community Life. We must be aware that while churches and other religious institutions have played very positive roles in community life, they have also historically contributed to individual and community problems in a variety of areas. Maton and Wells point out that

> *some religious principles and values can lead to inappropriate guilt and anxiety, or a limited view of the nature of emotional problems. . . . Organized religion's . . . considerable psychological and economic resources, can be used to subjugate and disempower rather than empower groups, such as women and racial minorities. . . . Religion's focus on helping the "less fortunate," while generating many volunteer and economic resources, can lead to a paternalistic, disempowering approach to those in need. Also, because mainstream religion is part of the current power structure in society, it often does not take part in empowerment activities that challenge the current structure.* (1995:189)

Social workers need to be aware of the significant potential for churches to assist communities and their members. At the same time we need to recognize their potential for exacerbating individual and community problems.

Community and People with Disabilities

Mackelprang and Salsgiver (1996:9ff) describe two alternative paradigms for achieving social and economic justice for people with disabilities: the Minority Model and the Independent Living Perspective. The **minority model** was the foundation for "the birth of disability consciousness" in the United States and arose out of the civil rights turbulence of the 1960s. Mackelprang and Salsgiver (1996) assert that this movement matured with the development of the independent living concept in the early 1970s.

Independent Living Perspective. Mackelprang and Salsgiver stress that "Independent living encourages people with disabilities to begin to assert their capabilities personally and in the political arena" (1996:10).

Some Principles and Examples of the Independent Living Model

1. Independent living proponents view people with disabilities not as patients or clients but as active and responsible consumers.

2. Independent living proponents reject traditional treatment approaches as offensive and disenfranchising and demand control over their own lives.

3. Independent living proponents retain their own personal responsibility to hire and fire people who provide attendant or personal care rather than allowing formal structures to provide and control the professional care givers.

4. Independent living proponents prefer attendants who are trained by the individuals with disabilities themselves instead of licensed providers like registered nurses.

5. Independent living proponents see empowerment as self-developed and not bestowed by someone else. For example, social workers are viewed only as consultants, not as prescribers of care or treatment plans.

6. Independent living proponents believe that the greatest constraints on people with disabilities are environmental and social.

7. Independent living proponents espouse a philosophy that advocates natural support systems under the direction of the consumer. (Mackelprang and Salsgiver 1996:10–12)

Independent Living: Strengths and Limitations.   Mackelprang and Salsgiver suggest that social work has much to learn from the independent living perspective and "can benefit greatly from a shift in focus from case management in which clients are labeled 'cases' to a consumer-driven model of practice that acknowledges self-developed empowerment and not empowerment bestowed from others" (1996: 12–13). They also note, however, that "the independent living approach can be criticized as viewing problems too much from an external perspective. Independent living may be too quick to assume that consumers already have knowledge and abilities rather than recognizing that they may need assistance to develop their strengths" (Mackelprang and Salsgiver 1996:12). They recommend a partnership between social work and independent living proponents in which social work can contribute its multi-systems and ecological approach and the disability movement "can help social work enhance approaches to clients, better empower oppressed and devalued groups, and understand the needs of people with disabilities" (1996:13).

Community and Sexual Orientation

Special issues exist for lesbians or gay men in the community context. Urban areas may offer more opportunity for persons to accommodate diversity within diversity than do small or rural communities. Some research suggests that "for most lesbians and gay men, partners and friends are more reliable and constant sources of social and emotional support than family of origin members. As a result, relations within the community assume a special significance for lesbian and gay individuals and their families" (Demo and Allen 1996:420). Homophobia both in the community and internalized homophobia have significant consequences for individual and community life for gay men and lesbians:

> *On a daily basis, lesbian and gay parents and stepparents must confront internalized and externalized homophobia when they come out to their children's teachers, the parents of their children's peers and other members of the community. Even routine tasks, such as filling out forms at a child's day-care center that ask for information about "mother" and "father" are daily re-*

minders that mainstream heterosexual society neither recognizes the child's family . . . nor accommodates lesbian or gay stepparents. (Crosbie-Burnett and Helmbrecth 1993 in Demo and Allen 1996:420)

Toward a Strengths Approach to Community

Perhaps an ideal community is one in which individual identity and identity as a member of the community are integrated. Myers (1985:34–35) finds such a holistic-perspective in an Afrocentric worldview. The African concept of "extended self" actually includes community. Self and community are not separate or distinct systems. She notes that "self in this instance includes all of the ancestors, the yet unborn, all of nature, and the entire community" (Myers 1985:35). Utne (1992:2) suggests the benefits and strengths of a non-Western, more inclusive perspective on community. He recommends that "perhaps we in the West will listen to what [indigenous] people have to teach us and start making different choices. Perhaps someday our children will know the experience of community conveyed by this common phrase of the Xhosa people of southern Africa: 'I am because we are.'"

Collins (1990) offers an important feminist perspective on community and diversity. Her perspective reflects the strength of African American women in creating and maintaining communities in which they and their families have historically been able to survive in the struggle against oppression in the surrounding environment. Her perspective reflects an Afrocentric worldview in which holism and unity are central. Collins's (1990:53) perspective also recognizes the critical influence on African American individuals, families, organizations, and communities of the slavery and oppression comprising so much of the history of African peoples in the United States. She suggests that these historical conditions resulted in significant differences between African American and white communities. She describes an alternative to traditional white communities in which family, extended family, and community merged and in which "Black communities as places of collective effort and will stood in contrast to the public, market-driven, exchange-based dominant political economy in which they were situated" (Bethel in Collins 1990:53).

Black women played significant roles in the creation and maintenance of this alternative community. Women provided the stability necessary for these communities, whose primary concern was day-to-day survival (Collins 1990:146). The empowering, but not overpowering, role played by African American women in their communities and families is portrayed in the following excerpt:

> *African American women worked to create Black female spheres of influence, authority, and power that produced a worldview markedly different from that advanced by the dominant group. Within African American communities Black women's activities as cultural workers is empowering. . . . The power of Black women was the power to make culture, to transmit folkways, norms, and customs, as well as to build shared ways of seeing the world that insured our survival. . . . This power . . . was neither economic nor political; nor did it translate into female dominance.* (Radford-Hill in Collins 1990:147)

Collins also summarizes the alternative meaning of community that emerges from an Afrocentric worldview as one that stresses "connections, caring and personal accountability." This historical worldview, combined with the realities of oppression in the United States, resulted in alternative communities that empowered their members. These communities were created not through theorizing, but instead they came about "through daily actions" of African American women. These alternative communities created

> *sanctuaries where individual Black women and men are nurtured in order to confront oppressive social institutions. Power from this perspective is a creative power used for the good of the community, whether that community is conceptualized as one's family, church community, or the next generation of the community's children.* (Collins 1990:223)

Resiliency and Community

We explored the concept of individual resiliency earlier. This concept is also relevant to understanding human behavior in the community environment, for individual resilience is heavily influenced by the quality of community life. Saleebey (1996:300) notes that community is more and more recognized as critical to individual resiliency. Communities can help or hinder resiliency and have been referred to in two ways as they relate to resiliency:

1. **Enabling niches:** *places where individuals become known for what they do, are supported in becoming more adept and knowledgeable, and can establish solid relationships within and outside the community.*
2. **Entrapping niches:** *individuals are stigmatized and isolated. Membership in the community is based on collective stigma and alienation.* (Saleebey 1996:300)

Specific characteristics of communities that "amplify individual resilience" include:

- *Awareness, recognition, and use of the assets of most members of the community*
- *Information networks of individuals, families, and groups*
- *Social networks of peers*
- *Intergenerational mentoring relationships that provide succor, instruction, support, and encouragement*
- *Many opportunities to participate and make significant contributions to the moral and civic life of the community and to take a role as a full-fledged citizen*
- *High expectations of members* (Saleebey 1996:300)

Community: Wellness and Resilience

All of the above characteristics are reciprocal for improving the well-being of the individual and the community. Saleebey also notes the relation of wellness and resilience to community: They both

> *suggest that individuals are best served, from a health and competence standpoint, by creating belief and thinking around possibility and values, around accomplishment and renewal, rather than centering exclusively on risk fac-*

> *tors and disease processes. . . . Both indicate that health and resilience are, in the end, community projects, an effect of social connection, the aggregation of collective vision, the provision of mentoring, and the reality of belonging to an organic whole.* (Saleebey 1996:301)

SUMMARY

In this chapter, within the larger context of traditional and alternative approaches to community, we explored a variety of different but often interrelated types of, and perspectives on, communities. Historical perspectives on community were reviewed. Issues related to defining community were discussed.

Within the arena of traditional perspectives on community, a number of ways of thinking about community were presented. Community as a specific place and community as a set of functions was explored. Community was discussed as a middle ground, mediator, or link between small systems such as individuals, families or groups, and larger societal systems. Community as ways of relating or as patterns of relationships and community as a social system were described.

Alternative perspectives on community included the notion of nonplace community. Community as a social network or web of relationships and resources through which members meet needs and face challenges in life was discussed as an alternative to more traditional notions. Qualitative aspects of community were explored, including discussion of some qualitative aspects of African American communities. Intentional communities, including communes and new towns, were presented.

Issues of oppression and power at the community level were included among alternative perspectives. The notion of heterogeneity or diversity and community life was presented. In this discussion a strengths approach to community was included.

Internet Search Guide

If you want to learn more about some of the topics discussed in this chapter by exploring the Internet, you can search the Net for the terms listed below. Remember that as you are "surfing" the Net, any of the search terms listed below can take you in many different directions. If you would like to visit specific Web sites related to this chapter, go to the Allyn and Bacon Web site at **http://www.abacon.com** and follow the links to Schriver or *Human Behavior and the Social Environment: Shifting Paradigms in Essential Knowledge for Social Work Practice*. There you will find a selection of sites related to content in this chapter.

1. nonplace community
2. intentional community
3. communes
4. blockbusting
5. virtual community
6. religion and community
7. Center for Social Development (Washington University)
8. National Committee on Civic Renewal
9. National Civic League
10. Institute for Civil Society
11. Urban Institute
12. Internet Communities
13. American Society on Aging
14. Alliance for Technology Access

REFERENCES

Aidala, Angela A. (1989). "Communes and changing family norms: Marriage and lifestyle choice among former members of communal groups." *Journal of Family Issues, 10*(3):311–338.

Aidala, Angela A., and Zablocki, Benjamin D. (1991). "The communes of the 1970s: Who joined and why?" *Marriage and Family Review, 17*(1–2):87–116.

Anderson, Ralph, and Carter, Irl. (1990). *Human behavior in the social environment.* (4th ed.). New York: Aldine De Gruyter.

Beverly, S., and Sherraden, M. (1997). *Human capital and social work* (97–2). St. Louis: Washington University George Warren Brown School of Social Work, Center for Social Development.

Briggs, X. N. de Soyza. (1997). "Social capital and the cities: advice to change agents." *National Civic Review, 86:* 111–117.

Bouvard, Marguerite. (1977). "The intentional community movement." In Roland L. Warren, ed., *New perspectives on the American community: A book of readings* (3rd ed.). Chicago: Rand McNally College Publishing Company.

Bricker-Jenkins, Mary, and Hooyman, Nancy R., (Eds.). (1986). *Not for women only: Social work practice for a feminist future.* Silver Spring, MD: National Association of Social Workers, Inc.

Calhoun, C. (1998). "Community without propinquity revisited: communications technology and the transformation of the urban public sphere." *Sociological Inquiry, 68*(3): 373–397.

Campbell, Carlos. (1976). *New towns: Another way to live.* Reston, VA: Reston Publishing, Inc.

Collins, Patricia Hill. (1990). *Black feminist thought: Knowledge, consciousness, and the politics of empowerment.* Cambridge: Unwin Hyman, Inc.

Demo, D. H., and Allen, K. R. (1996). "Diversity with lesbian and gay families: Challenges and implications for family theory and research." *Journal of Social and Personal Relationships, 13*(3):415–434.

Dictionary, Webster's II New Collegiate (1995). Boston: Houghton Miflin Company.

Ewalt, P., Freeman, Edith, and Poole, Dennis. (Eds.). (1998a). *Community building: Renewal, well-being, and shared responsibility.* Washington, D.C.: NASW Press.

Ewalt, P. (1998b). "The revitalization of impoverished communities." In P. Ewalt, E. Freeman, and D. Poole (Eds.). *Community building: Renewal, well-being, and shared responsibility* (pp. 3–5). Washington, DC: NASW Press.

Feagin, Joe R., and Feagin, Clairece Booher. (1978). *Discrimination American style: Institutional racism and sexism.* Englewood Cliffs, NJ: Prentice Hall.

Fellin, P. (1993). "Reformulation of the context of community based care." *Journal of Sociology and Social Welfare 20*(2):57–67.

Fischer, C. (1997). "Technology and community: Historical complexities." *Sociological Inquiry, 67*(1): 113–118.

Kanter, Rosabeth Moss. (1977). "Communes and commitment." In Warren, Roland L., *New perspectives on the American community: A book of readings.* Chicago: Rand McNally College Publishing Company.

Kingsley, G. M., and Gibson, J. (1997). *Community building: Coming of age:* The Urban Institute.

Kollock, P., and Smith, M. (1999). "Communities in cyberspace." In M. Smith and P. Kollock. (Eds.). *Communities in cyberspace* (pp. 323). London: Routledge.

Kuhn, Thomas S. (1970). *The structure of scientific revolutions* (2nd ed.). Chicago: The University of Chicago Press.

Lapachet, J. (1996). *Virtual communities: The 90's mind altering drug or facilitator of human interaction?* Available: http://bliss.berkeley.edu/impact/students/jaye/jaye_asis.html.

Lappé, F. M., and Du Bois, Paul M. (1997). "Building social capital without looking backward." *National Civic Review, 86:* 119–128.

Logan, John R. (1988). "Realities of black suburbanization." In Warren, Roland L., and Lyon, Larry. *New perspectives on the American community* (5th ed.). Chicago: The Dorsey Press.

Longres, John. (1990). *Human behavior in the social environment.* Itasca, IL: F. E. Peacock.

Louv, R. (1996). "The culture of renewal, part I: Characteristics of the community renewal movement." *National Civic Review, 85:* 52–61.

Louv, R. (1997). "The culture of renewal, part 2: Characteristics of the community renewal movement." *National Civic Review, 86:* 97–105.

Mackelprang, R. W., and Salsgiver, R. O. (1996). "People with disabilities and social work: Historical and contemporary issues." *Social Work, 41*(1):7–14.

Maton, K. I., and Wells, E. A. (1995). "Religion as a community resource for well-being: Prevention, healing and empowerment pathways." *Journal of Social Issues, 51*(2):177–193.

Maybury-Lewis, David. (1992). "Tribal wisdom." *Utne Reader, 52:*68–79.

McKnight, John L. (1987). "Regenerating community." *Social Policy, 17*(3):54–58.

McKnight, John L. (1992). "Are social service agencies the enemy of community?" *Utne Reader, 52:*88–90.

Myers, Linda J. (1985). "Transpersonal psychology: The role of the Afrocentric paradigm." *The Journal of Black Psychology, 12*(1):31–42.

Naparastek, A., and Dooley, D. (1998). "Countering urban disinvestment through community-building initiatives." In P. Ewalt, E. Freeman, and D. Poole. (Eds.). *Community building: Renewal, well-being, and shared responsibility* (pp. 6–16). Washington, DC: NASW Press.

Netting, Ellen; Kettner, Peter; and McMurty, Steven. (1993). *Social work macro practice.* New York: Longman.

Page-Adams, D., and Sherraden, M. (1997). "Asset building as a community revitalization strategy." *Social work, 42*(5): 423–434.

Reiss, Albert J., Jr. (1959). "The sociological study of communities." *Rural Sociology, 24:* 118–130.

Rubin, Israel. (1983). "Function and structure of community: Conceptual and theoretical analysis." In Warren, Roland L., and Lyon, Larry. *New perspectives on the American community.* Homewood, IL: The Dorsey Press.

Saleebey, D. (May 1996). "The strengths perspective in social work practice: Extensions and cautions." *Social Work, 41*(3): 296–305.

Sanderson, Dwight. (1988). In Warren, Roland L., and Lyon, Larry. *New Perspectives on the American community* (5th ed.). Chicago: The Dorsey Press.

Schulman, M. D., and Anderson, C. (1999). "The dark side of the force: a case study of restructuring and social capital." *Rural Sociology, 64*(3): 351–372.

Solomon, Barbara. (1976). *Black empowerment: Social work in oppressed communities.* New York: Columbia University Press.

Streibel, M. (1998). "Information technology and physicality in community, place, and presence." *Theory into Practice, 37*(1): 31–37.

Sullivan, W. P. (1994). "The tie that binds: A strengths/empowerment model for social development." *Social Development Issues, 16*(3):100–111.

Tönnies, Ferdinand. (1988). "Gemeinschaft and Gesellschaft." In Warren, Roland L., and Lyon, Larry. *New Perspectives on the American community* (5th ed.). Chicago: The Dorsey Press.

Utne, Eric. (1992). "I am because we are." *Utne Reader, 52:*2.

Wallis, A. D., Crocker, J. P., and Schecter, B. (1998). "Social capital and community building: part one." *National Civic Review, 87:* 253–271.

Walsh, J. (1997). "Community building in theory and practice: three case studies." *National Civic Review, 86:* 291–314.

Warner, M. (1999). "Social capital construction and the role of the local state." *Rural Sociology, 64*(3): 373–393.

Warren, Roland. (1977). *New perspectives on the American community: A book of readings* (3rd ed.). Chicago: Rand McNally College Publishing Company.

Warren, Roland L. (1978). *The community in America* (3rd ed.). Chicago: Rand McNally College Publishing Company.

Warren, Roland L. (1988a). Introduction. In Warren, Roland L., and Lyon, Larry. *New perspectives on the American community* (5th ed.). Chicago: The Dorsey Press.

Warren, Roland. (1988b). "The good community." In Warren, Roland L., and Lyon, Larry. *New perspectives on the American community* (5th ed.). Chicago: The Dorsey Press.

Warren, Roland and Lyon, Larry. (1983). *New perspectives on the American community*. Homewood, IL: The Dorsey Press.

Warren, Roland and Lyon, Larry. (1988). *New perspectives on the American community* (5th ed.). Chicago: The Dorsey Press.

Weber, Max. (1988). "The nature of the city." In Warren, Roland L., and Lyon, Larry. *New perspectives on the American community* (5th ed.). Chicago: The Dorsey Press.

Webster's II New College Dictionary. (1995). Boston: Houghton Mifflin Co.

Wellman, Barry, and Leighton, Barry. (1988). "Networks, neighborhoods, and communities: Approaches to the study of the community question." In Warren, Roland L., and Lyon, Larry. *New perspectives on the American community* (5th ed.). Chicago: The Dorsey Press.

Wellman, B., Salaff, J., and Dimitrova, D. (1996). "Computer networks as social networks: collaborative work, telework, and virtual community." *Annual Review of Sociology, 22:* 213–238.

ILLUSTRATIVE READING 9.1

The illustrative reading by Sullivan demonstrates the important and positive, though seldom recognized, role of social capital development among urban African American adolescents. Rather than the crisis in social capital suggested by some scholars, Sullivan finds a large and positive degree of social capital in poor communities and among youth. Her article offers a helpful integration of some of the alternative community concepts addressed in this chapter. In addition, Sullivan critically examines traditional perspectives on leadership within African American communities and offers a new paradigm of leadership. Her new paradigm seems much more consistent with the strengths- or assets-based and democratic approaches to groups, organizations, and communities we have explored in this book thus far. As the author indicates, movement to the new paradigm, like all paradigm shifts, will require a comprehensive rethinking about such fundamental social concerns as equality, inclusiveness, and partnership within and among communities.

A comparison of this illustrative reading with Illustrative Reading 8.2 by Delgado and Illustrative Reading 7.1 by Chang can give the reader a fuller appreciation of the significance of the concept of social capital, especially in the context of diverse communities, groups, and organizations.

Hip-Hop Nation: The Undeveloped Social Capital of Black Urban America

Lisa Y. Sullivan

Observers of public life and civil society agree that the civic health of a community is largely determined by the availability and abundance of its "social capital." Used in this context, social capital refers to both the informal and formal networks and asso-

Lisa Y. Sullivan is program consultant for the Rockefeller Foundation, where she facilitates a design team in development of a new and innovative fellowship program for the next generation of American leaders. She was previously director of the field division at the Children's Defense Fund. She has published articles on community service, social problems, and race relations. *National Civic Review*, vol. 86, no. 3. Fall 1997 © Jossey-Bass Publishers. Reprinted by permission of Jossey-Bass, Inc., a subsidiary of John Wiley and Sons, Inc.

ciations of ordinary citizens who have the capacity to facilitate, coordinate, and co-operate in efforts that benefit the entire community. Although academics like Harvard political scientist Robert Putnam have warned that our current civic crisis has much to do with a decline in formal associational life, my activism and organizing experience in central cities suggests that informal associational life is alive and well—especially among the poor and young.[1] While Putnam may have observed a general decrease in citizen participation in traditional social and civic associations, a significant number of citizens from the inner city are creating and participating in vibrant informal networks of twenty-first century associational life.

For the most part, the social capital of the future remains organized around the immediate needs of individuals seeking new, mutually supportive relationships. Often these new associations center on issues of care and support. In cities ravaged by alcohol, cocaine, heroin addiction, and the nexus of the HIV/AIDS pandemic, networks of care, support, and counseling are some of the strongest, most vibrant, and most visible civic infrastructures existing in poor communities and neighborhoods.

As in the past, others of these informal networks are organized around recreation and social entertainment. For example, between Atlanta and Boston, there is a thriving network of inner city women's basketball enthusiasts who convene regularly for holiday and weekend tournaments. In much the same manner that basketball has served as an informal convener of inner city males and females, tennis, golf, and skiing have become the catalyst of primarily black middle-class networks. These tournaments, ski trips, and racquet clubs are vibrant, thriving, and increasingly common examples of formal black associational life.[2] Likewise, the emergence of book clubs inspired by television talk show host Oprah Winfrey have taken on increased significance in the lives of young middle-class black professional women.

The existence of abundant social capital and vibrant informal networks is most evident among urban youth. in particular, urban youth culture—also known as hip-hop culture and more recently as popular culture—provides a unique and important space for the development and evolution of new styles, leaders, and networks. Within the subcultures of rap artists, musicians, poets, graffiti artists, filmmakers, fashion designers, graphic artists, and party promotors, intricate informal associations exist that are capable of massive mobilization and community cooperation.[3]

A recent public demonstration of this claim was the growth and evolution of the black college event formerly known as "Freaknic." What began in the early 1980s in the Atlanta University Center as a picnic in Piedmont Park sponsored by the DC Metro Club (a campus club for kids from the Washington, D.C., area) grew in a decade to become a major public event that by the spring of 1994 was attracting tens of thousands of college and noncollege young African Americans. Similar examples include the annual black Greek Picnic and Penn Relays in Philadelphia as well as the Myrtle Beach, South Carolina, annual end-of-the-year or commencement celebration. In addition, in urban and suburban retail and commercial space, the visibility of large groupings of young people suggests that the concept of mutual support and informal association is thriving among urban youth.

In an age of youth violence, increased concern about juvenile delinquency and irrational adult fear, coupled with the predisposition to scapegoat adolescents, it is hard for most to comprehend that the young are highly organized and that their social capital abounds. Although society may not approve, condone, or accept that youth gangs, posses, street organizations, or crews are meaningful and constructive forms of associational life, they exist as the primary networks for inner-city adolescent social development. I am not referring here to organized gangs involved in illicit or illegal business. Instead, I am talking about the neighborhood teenagers who "roll" twenty deep in a pack to the mall on Saturday, and who refer to themselves as crews, posses, or more recently as street organizations.

EVOLUTION OF INFORMAL SOCIAL CAPITAL AMONG URBAN YOUTH

Twenty years ago, I was a teenager in the nation's capital. I belonged to several crews. First and foremost, there was my loyalty to the street that nurtured and raised me until I left home at age eighteen for college. Back when neighborhood movie theaters existed in the District of Columbia, all the kids on our street would roll together to see the Saturday matinee. As the oldest child, I was responsible for my younger sister and her friends. At times, my peers teased me about having to babysit the little kids; but I later found out that most of them, too, could not roll unless I did because their parents perceived me as being the most mature child on the block. Back in 1977, I would never have claimed to be a crew leader.

At the movies, our block blended in with the other crews from our community. All of us collectively constituted my second crew: the geographic neighborhood. Now, the older neighborhood teens regularly "beefed" with the leaders of the crews from Riggs Park, Petworth, and Fort Stevens. We had boundaries that distinguished crew affiliation, and we frequently used the battle of go-go bands to determine neighborhood superiority.[4] We challenged neighborhood crews athletically and hosted good old-fashioned block party competitions judged by the best food, the most people, and the best band performance. A successful block party required a high level of community organization and networking of neighborhood associations. Important activities included (1) collecting petition signatures from local residents to close a street to traffic and agree to host the block party; (2) securing the requisite permits from the D.C. police department to hold the block party; (3) renting the stage and sound equipment from the D.C. parks and recreation department; (4) securing in-kind donations of food, paper products, and sodas from local merchants and grocery stores; (5) finding lots of parents willing to "cook out" for hundreds of neighborhood youth from noon until sundown; and (6) arranging for a popular neighborhood leader to serve as master of ceremonies and help coordinate the programmatic activities.

Beyond where I lived, I also belonged to crews that reflected my social independence and interests. There was my tennis court crew, my basketball and softball crew, my crew from high school, and the crew I rolled with to parties and other social activities. All of this associational life was in addition to the "organized" adult-supervised activities that my parents identified. As an average inner-city teenager, my associations and networks were largely organized around my informal crew life.

Crack cocaine, guns, escalating youth violence, increased social despair, misery, and marginalization have transformed the crew over the past twenty years.[5] Now, crossing neighborhood boundaries can be deadly, and guilt by association can lead to being locked up or shot. Nevertheless, the crew remains the locus of youth affiliation. Far too many adults have failed to understand the power and influence of these informal and formal crew associations and their inherent social capital. Sadly, the strength and evidence of the crew is too often visible, active, and effective only in the face of sickness, death, and tragedy. In too many inner-city neighborhoods, wakes and funerals have become massive gatherings for youth in search of refuge and healing from the violence and despair of poverty and neglect.

WHITHER BLACK YOUTH CIVIC ENGAGEMENT?

There is no dearth of associational life or social capital among the young, the black, or the poor. The October 1995 Million Man March was an extraordinary example of this fact. Regardless of the controversy surrounding Benjamin Chavis, Louis Far-rakhan, and the Nation of Islam, the strategy for mobilizing grassroots support for the march demonstrated the extent to which black nationalist leadership understands the networks and social capital that exist within urban black communities. By utiliz-ing the black press—both radio and print—to get out the message, while organizing at the street corner level, primarily through networks of barbershops, march orga-nizers ensured that the core community would know about (and formulate its own opinion about) the event before mainstream black or white leaders and institutions could challenge its legitimacy. In much the same manner that Harvard professor Henry Louis Gates, Jr., has identified the long-standing existence of a contemporary black theater movement organized around socially relevant themes that appeal to the black poor and working class,[6] the Million Man March effectively evoked the social capital and institutional infrastructure of the black community.

In an important and critical assessment of black civic and political life in the post-civil rights era, political scientist Robert Smith argues with passion and clarity that in the period since passage of the 1964 and 1965 civil rights legislation, black leaders have devoted themselves exclusively to the process of securing mainstream po-litical and economic incorporation, at the expense of an increasingly isolated and mar-ginalized core constituency.[7] Alienated from mainstream American politics and public life, the young and poor have also increasingly found themselves estranged from the black civil rights establishment. Disengaged from traditional black liberal organiza-tions, their social capital has gone underutilized, underdeveloped, and ignored in the late twentieth century.

Smith observes further that in the post-civil rights period, black civil rights or-ganizations have focused narrowly on lobbying congress or litigating in the courts. Neither strategy has required these organizations to broaden their base of political participation to include more or new people in the decision-making process. The critical shortcoming, then, is that this top-down, hierarchical, middle-class model of organization and strategy emphasizes elite interaction rather than constituent de-velopment and empowerment. Consequently, black civic and political life has been reduced to annual conventions, conferences and meetings, symbolic rallies and marches, and press conferences that habitually omit the participation and inclusion of black urban youth. Predictably, the political strategy of mainstream incorporation has isolated black civil rights leadership from its core constituency: the young and poor.[8]

Beyond this critique, students of black electoral participation have observed that the self-interest of elected officials, regardless of race, has also undermined the civic development of poor black communities.[9] Persistently low voter participation and turnout continue to plague black politics at the local, state, and national levels. Although this phenomenon reflects a larger crisis in American democracy, the nonparticipation of poor black youth in meaningful political discourse, political parties, and nonpartisan political organizations reveals the extent to which civic infrastructure in the black community suffers from atrophy. More than thirty years ago, the preeminent civil rights strategist Bayard Rustin observed that the future of the movement would require a strategic shift from protest to incorporation into mainstream electoral politics.[10] As we approach a new century, it now appears that the civil rights movement is experiencing a crisis of relevancy as the political incorporation strategy has proved unable to solve the major socioeconomic problems facing poor black communities. This profound crisis in black public life includes:

- A decline in organized grassroots community activism
- A decline in philanthropic, union, and nonprofit institutional support for targeted, nonpartisan minority, youth, and low-income voter registration and education initiatives
- Widespread disappointment among black youth with the performance of black elected and appointed officials, as well as traditional civil rights leaders and clergy
- Deconstruction of the institutions and mechanisms for implementation of civic education and political mobilization in low-income communities

Basically, low voter registration and turnout rates compounded by low civic participation and engagement have reinforced the indifference and unresponsiveness of local, state, and national policymakers toward young black people. The self-fulfilling prophecy of pragmatic electoral politics has come true in most inner-city communities. The least attention is now paid to those neighborhoods and communities that demonstrate a low level of interest and participation in the process that elects its leaders. This is a rule of thumb followed by politicians regardless of their race, ethnicity, or class. It is this reality that explains how and why black inner-city communities have watched the collapse and devastation of their public and civic infrastructure while black mayors, police chiefs, and school superintendents presided.

TOWARD A MORE EFFECTIVE USE OF BLACK URBAN SOCIAL CAPITAL

Renewing black public life is a necessary prerequisite for restoring both the health of this nation's urban communities and the civic engagement of black youth. It is a task that requires significant resources—intellectual, human, and financial. At the core of what must be done is what public philosopher Harry Boyte has described as popular civic education.[11] Through citizen education, America must renew civic discourse deeply grounded in the culture, traditions, and ways of life of the ordinary people who ultimately must rebuild their communities. The future of black public life is therefore dependent upon cornmunity-based citizenship initiatives that emphasize civic literacy, leadership development, community participation, and engagement.

Unfortunately, revival of popular civic education will not rehabilitate black public life on its own merit. Although it is a necessary condition, it is not sufficient for fundamental social change. Instead, a major paradigmatic shift must occur within black public life, coupled with a renewed focus on civic engagement at the neighborhood level. This fundamental shift is necessary for restoring the capacity of the post-civil rights, postindustrial urban black community to affect social change. Without a major transformation of the leadership paradigm that currently guides and dominates black political culture, black public life and its civic infrastructure will not recover from the late twentieth-century socioeconomic crisis.

Historically, public life in the black community has been dominated by loyal, race men. Traditionally, they have led community institutions like the church, schools, businesses, and social and civic organizations. This model of leadership has been predisposed to autocratic, antidemocratic, and egotistical tendencies. As a consequence, generations within the black community have experienced a monolithic leadership paradigm that often validated notions of elite, sexist, hierarchical, antidemocratic, command-and-control relationships with its core black constituency. Entrenched in black political culture and psychology, this model is frequently internalized and replicated by black women and youth.[12]

Few have challenged the presumptions of this model. Even fewer have been willing to acknowledge that the father of twentieth-century black liberalism and elitism, W. E. B. Du Bois, revised his theory of race leadership in 1948. In 1903, when Du Bois published his essay "The Talented Tenth," he defined the commitment to service that the educated few owed the rest of the black community. It was the duty of the enlightened race leaders—the black aristocracy—to lead the unsophisticated black masses. By midcentury, however, Du Bois advanced the idea that a group-centered leadership capable of empowering the masses was a more desired model of race leadership. Thus his reexamined, restated theory of the Talented Tenth evolved into the doctrine of the "Guiding Hundred."

To date, black liberal elites have failed to acknowledge Du Bois's revelation and have therefore failed to transcend his theory of the Talented Tenth. As activist-intellectual Joy James has observed, Du Bois revealed, in the restatement of his thesis on race leadership, a dynamic and evolving analysis that underscored the importance of class and the important social and political agency of ordinary black people.[13] It is therefore quite appropriate that black America's preeminent twentieth-century intellectual must now serve as the point of departure for transcending the promotion of an elite-driven black leadership strategy into the twenty-first century.

It would be a gross mistake to assume that black elitism is the sole source of the contemporary black leadership crisis and its inability to maximize existing social capital. On the contrary, autocratic, nondemocratic, sexist tendencies—particularly among grassroots nationalist organizations—is equally debilitating. The modern civil rights movement makes clear the dependence of black social progress on the leadership of young people and women. Martin Luther King's emerging leadership was inextricably linked to the social capital and civic infrastructure of the resourceful middle-class black women who organized the 1955 Montgomery bus boycott and the mass social action of poor domestic workers and day laborers who walked to work for a solid year in order to desegregate the public transportation system in their segregated city.

Unfortunately, the heroic mythology of Martin (and Malcolm) has in the post-civil rights era paralyzed the development of a new black leadership paradigm. Black America is stuck on the great messianic, charismatic male leadership paradigm, and this nostalgia has significantly warped the community's perception and understanding of its potential social capital.

Again, despite its emphasis on great men, the organizing lessons of the Million Man March demonstrate precisely who possesses the untapped social capital within the black community. In the months preceding the march, it was no accident that organizers chose to actively engage, pursue, and mobilize black women to support the effort. In communities across this nation, black women's social clubs, associations, and informal networks helped raise money and organized buses that delivered a million black men to the nation's capital. Likewise, the coordination and mobilization of young black men, from college campuses to street organizations, was most impressive. More than anything else, the success of the Million Man March mobilization was testimony to the underutilized social capital in black communities across the nation.

THE PROMISE OF A NEW LEADERSHIP PARADIGM

Restoring black public life, its civic infrastructure, and the promise of urban America requires new vision, new strategies, and a new leadership paradigm. As the nation approaches a new century, finding new ways of doing business around public issues in the black community becomes increasingly important. Doing public business in a new manner requires significant organizational transformation. A twenty-first-century black leadership paradigm will be forced to consider several important points:

- The value of democratic practice within the movement for social change
- The existence of ideological pluralism within the black community
- The need to systematically develop the leadership of black women and youth
- The need to view the leadership contributions of elites as equal and in partnership with ordinary citizens
- The need to replace the charismatic great leader with the collaborative leadership of ordinary citizens
- The need to restore citizenship, democracy, and the belief that ordinary people in local communities can solve their problems and build community capacity with the support of the independent sector, government, and private enterprise

Increasingly, public life and civic engagement require leaders to hear, understand, and consider the views of frustrated, marginalized citizens—especially black youth. It is through collaborative processes that ordinary citizens begin to catalyze, energize, and facilitate their neighbors in community problem solving. In the process, they create new associations, networks, organizations, aiiiances. partnerships, and forums.

By definition, collaborative leadership brings people to the table and engages them in a process of building trust and shared vision. Consequently, collaborative leaders must be active and involved in building relationships and a credible process that engages citizens in public life. As David Chrislip and Carl Larson have eloquently observed, getting extraordinary things done in the twenty-first century will require a new kind of leadership with a new set of skills.[14] Black public life and civic engagement is no exception to this rule. The traditional hierarchical model of leadership must now give way to more collaborative leadership, willing to include alienated and often marginalized poor black youth in the conversation about the future of their communities.

Sustained by their vision and deeply held belief that ordinary people have the capacity to create their own visions and solve their own problems, collaborative leaders with a commitment to participatory democracy will renew black public life and build a new kind of civic infrastructure that takes full advantage of the abundant social capital of urban America.

NOTES

1. See Putnam, R. D. "Bowling Alone: America's Declining Social Capital." *Journal of Democracy,* Jan. 1995, pp. 65–78.
2. For further discussion, see Sullivan, L. "Civil Society at the Margins." *Kettering Review,* Winter 1997, pp. 63–65.
3. For recent mainstream articulations of the importance of hip-hop culture and its impact on the global economy, see Romero, D. J. "Influence of Hip-Hop Resonates Worldwide." *Los Angeles Times,* Mar. 14, 1997, p. 1; and Levine, J. "Badass Sells." *Forbes,* Apr. 21, 1997, pp. 142–148.
4. In much the same manner that rap evolved in New York City, Go Go music is the popular musical expression of inner city youth in Washington, D.C. For further discussion and background, see Wartofsky, A. "Go-Go Goes On." *Washington Post,* Nov. 16, 1996, p. C1.
5. For an excellent discussion of the transformation of social norms among young people in urban communities, see Canada, G. *Fist, Stick, Knife, Gun: A Personal History of Violence in America.* Boston: Beacon Press, 1995; and Taylor, C. *Girls, Gangs, Women, and Drugs.* East Lansing: Michigan State University Press, 1993.
6. For a provocative discussion of social class and black popular culture, see Gates, H. L., Jr. "The Chitlin Circuit." *New Yorker,* Feb. 3, 1997, pp. 44–55.
7. For this important thesis on post-civil rights black politics, see Smith, R. C. *We Have No Leaders: African Americans in the Post-Civil Rights Era.* Albany: State University of New York Press, 1996.
8. For an excellent case study of Detroit's inner-city black community and its relationship to black politics, see Cohen, C., and Dawson, M. "Neighborhood Poverty and African American Politics." *American Political Science Review,* 1993, *87* (2), 286.
9. See Steele, J. "Knowledge Is Power: Enhancing Citizen Involvement and Political Participation in Targeted Central Brooklyn Communities." Unpublished paper, Breakthrough Political Consulting, Brooklyn, New York, 1996.
10. See Rustin, B. "From Protest to Politics: The Future of the Civil Rights Movement." In *Down the Line: The Collected Writings of Bayard Rustin.* Chicago: Quadrangle Books, 1971.
11. See Boyte, H. C., and Kari, N. N. *Building America: The Democratic Promise of Public Work.* Philadelphia: Temple University Press, 1996.
12. For a very important essay on black women's leadership development into the twenty-first century, see Noble. J. "Paradigm Shifts Facing Leaders of Black Women's Organizations." In *Voices of Vision: African American Women on the Issues.* National Council of Negro Women, 1996: and for an examination of similar tendencies among black college students, see Sullivan, L. "Beyond Nostalgia: Notes on Black Student Activism." *Socialist Review,* 1990, *4,* 21–28.
13. See James, J. *Transcending the Talented Tenth: Black Leaders and American Intellectuals.* New York: Routledge, 1997.
14. See Chrislip, D., and Larson, C. *Collaborative Leadership: How Citizens and Civic Leaders Can Make a Difference.* San Francisco: Jossey-Bass, 1994.

ILLUSTRATIVE READING 9.2

The following reading by Mokuau and Matsuoka illustrates the struggle to maintain community and culture in the context of loss of sovereignty by native peoples, in this case native Hawaiians. This reading links the devastating impact of historical oppression on entire communities and cultures to the very real problems faced by individuals and families such as infectious diseases, poverty, and loss of traditional governance structures and processes. The reading, in addition to its illustration of problems faced as a result of oppression, also provides a strengths-based approach to addressing the problems faced. These strengths are found in culturally sensitive and empowering approaches to rebuilding community and using culturally appropriate mechanisms for economic development. The article helps us understand appropriate supportive and advocacy roles that can be played by social workers to enhance the community building process and move to achievement of social and economic justice.

Turbulence among a Native People: Social Work Practice with Hawaiians

Noreen Mokuau and Jon Matsuoka

Indigenous peoples throughout the world are facing cultural deterioration, and many populations are even threatened by extinction (Linden, 1991). Aboriginal peoples generally share a history of colonization and are bereaved of the right to self-determination, their own land, and their own resources (International Work Group for Indigenous Affairs, 1992). In the United States, the cultural demise of native populations has been increasingly recognized in the human services literature. The social condition of American Indian populations is characterized by severe poverty and poor physical and mental health (Davenport & Davenport, 1987; Miller, 1982; Nofz, 1988). Information on Alaska Natives is scarce but reflects a high-risk health profile (Healthy People 2000, 1990).

Like other indigenous populations, Hawaiians experience an array of health, social, and economic problems (Alu Like, 1985; Blaisdell, 1989; Mokuau, 1990; Papa Ola Lokahi, 1992). Hawaiians have disproportionately high rates of heart disease (Aluli, 1991; Wegner, 1989), cancer (Le Marchand & Kolonel, 1989), and diabetes (Johnson, 1989). Also, Hawaiians live five to 10 years less than other populations in Hawaii (Gardner, cited in Johnson, 1989).

Socioeconomic indicators portray a population that has not fared well under a Western-based economic and educational system. Hawaiians tend to fall into the lowest income brackets (Papa Ola Lokahi, 1992) and to have the lowest levels of educational attainment in the state (Blaisdell, 1989). Finally, Hawaiians rank highest in the state in an array of social problem categories including cases of child abuse and neglect (State of Hawaii, Department of Human Services, 1988), placements in correctional

Noreen Mokuau, DSW, is professor, and Jon Matsuoka, PhD, is associate professor, School of Social Work, University of Hawaii, 2500 Campus Road, Honolulu, HI 96822. Copyright 1995, National Association of Social Workers, Inc. *Social Work 40*(4), 1995:465–472.

facilities (Kamehameha Schools/Bishop Estates, 1983), and teenage pregnancies (Papa Ola Lokahi, 1992).

Although it should be noted that multiple factors predispose Hawaiians and other indigenous populations to the complex social problems in society, the lack of self-governance is one such factor. The centennial of the illegal overthrow of the Hawaiian monarchy by American business people—the turning point for Hawaiian sovereignty and self-determination—was observed in 1993. This article discusses the unique plight of Hawaiians by analyzing historical and current social problems and describing culturally appropriate prescriptions for empowerment that focus on the development of native government and economies.

HISTORY OF OPPRESSION

The history of Hawaii after the first Western contact made by Captain James Cook in 1778 can be conceptualized as a series of events that dismantled a thriving indigenous society. These events, whether inadvertent or deliberate, provided Westerners with a great share of control over Hawaii's resources. Infectious disease and depopulation began in 1778, the influence of missionaries and loss of cultural values and traditions began in 1820, land rights were lost in 1848, and the monarchy was overthrown in 1893.

Infectious Disease and Depopulation

Hawaii's ecology developed over millennia in environmental isolation. Natural organisms existed in a closely interdependent network and developed little resistance to outside threats. As a result, the native people had no built-up immunities and were virtually defenseless to disease. The vast oceanic distances among the Pacific island groups had effectively prevented the spread of bacterial or viral illnesses anywhere in Polynesia.

Contact with Western sailors and merchants led to the introduction of infectious diseases and the massive decline of the Hawaiian population. In addition to syphilis and gonorrhea, epidemics of tuberculosis, cholera, smallpox, measles, influenza, and bubonic plague heightened the rate of Hawaiian depopulation (Fuchs, 1961). The earliest medical accounts in the postcontact era depict virtual genocide (Daws, 1974). In the 100 years following Western contact, the Hawaiian population dropped from an estimated 800,000 to 1,000,000 to 40,000, a reduction of at least 95 percent (Stannard, 1989).

Influence of Missionaries and Loss of Culture

Following the arrival of sailors and merchants came Christian missionaries from New England who intended to spread their beliefs and lifeways to the native peoples of the Pacific. Missionaries were effective in penetrating Hawaiian culture to introduce new standards and criteria for living. After their arrival in 1820, missionaries devoted their efforts to developing schools for Hawaiian children, and by 1831, 1,000 schools had been built. The indoctrination of Christian attitudes and beliefs at the early-school-age level of socialization ensured that subsequent generations would live according to Christian doctrines.

The missionaries' sphere of influence extended far beyond religion and education. They imposed an array of religious proscriptions that discontinued traditional sexual practices, various art forms including hula, and the native language. The Hawaiian worldview that permeated every aspect of daily life was replaced by a fundamentally different Christian perspective. The influence and domination of the missionaries continued into the 20th century. The descendants of the original missionary families eventually dropped their religious goals in favor of business pursuits. A conglomeration of corporations founded by missionary families were instrumental in the overthrow of the Hawaiian monarchy and dominated Hawaiian business and politics for most of this century.

Division of Land and Loss of Rights

Once they had successfully infiltrated Hawaiian society, missionaries and their descendants persuaded King Kamehameha III to modify the system of land control and ownership. The new land division system, the "Great Mahele," significantly altered traditional land use patterns and opened the way for foreign ownership. Under this new system, major reassignments of all royal lands were made by the king to ensure the land rights of Hawaiians in a period of increased foreign occupation and mounting pressures for "land reform." The Great Mahele divided lands into crown lands (retained for the king), government lands (given to the Hawaiian government), Konohiki lands (given to various chiefs), and Kuleana lands (given to native tenants) (Chinen, 1958).

Despite the king's good intentions, the move was catastrophic. Foreign people, primarily Americans, dominated the government council that instituted land ownership policies and procedures; many Hawaiians did not understand Western notions of the value of property (Fuchs, 1961); and cash-poor Hawaiians could not compete for land titles (Dudley & Agard, 1990). Thus, the majority of Hawaiians became dispossessed of land and resources while foreign land ownership quickly escalated (Dudley & Agard, 1990).

By the end of the 19th century, white men owned four acres of land for every one owned by a native (Daws, 1974) and developed the land into large-scale farms on which they grew sugarcane and pineapple. When faced with a labor shortage, the landowners imported thousands of indentured workers from Asia. The introduction of plantation agriculture to Hawaii along with waves of foreign laborers transformed the ecology and continued the process of social change in Hawaii.

Overthrow of the Monarchy and Loss of Power

After the Great Mahele and the expansion of foreign investments in land and business, Americans sought to gain greater political influence over the islands (Fuchs, 1961). In January 1893 a well-orchestrated movement involving American businessmen and a heavily armed U.S. military led to the dethronement and imprisonment of reigning monarch Queen Lili'uokalani.

A provisional government was established. Over the next few years this illegal government seized control over all the crown and Hawaiian government lands and began selling them. Government officials and their business associates bought thousands of acres of Hawaiian land. By the time the buying spree had ended, Americans owned 95 percent of all private lands in Hawaii.

The provisional government moved to annex Hawaii to the United States. A constitution was developed that contained a clause disallowing Hawaiians to vote on the issue of annexation. Hawaiians at the time strongly opposed annexation and hoped for a return to self-rule (Lili'uokalani, 1964; McPherson, 1991). Despite the protests of the native people, Hawaii became a territory of the United States in 1898.

Once Hawaii became a territory, the provisional government ceded all the unsold crown and government lands to the United States. The procurement of indigenous lands violated major national standards related to indigenous peoples: "A sound national policy does require that [indigenous peoples] within our states should exchange their territories upon equitable principles, or, eventually, consent to become amalgamated in our political communities" (Chief Justice John Marshall, cited in McPherson, 1991, p. 478). Neither an equitable exchange or an opportunity to consent was provided to Hawaiians during annexation (Blaisdell, 1989; McPherson, 1991).

CONTEMPORARY ISSUES AND DYNAMICS

Sociocultural and environmental changes spurred by outside forces continue to characterize Hawaii's evolutionary process. In the 35 years since statehood, Hawaii has undergone unprecedented rates of economic growth associated with tourism development. During this period, foreign competition, skyrocketing land values, and the prospects of greater profits in tourism have motivated major landowners to shift their interests from agribusiness to resorts.

Since 1960 the income generated from tourism has increased more than 2,000 percent, and the trajectory of growth is projected to steadily increase. During the 1980s Hawaii experienced 10 percent to 15 percent annual growth in the number of tourists. In 1990, 6.5 million tourists visited Hawaii. The Hawaii Visitors Bureau projected that by 2005, the number of tourists will surpass 11 million (Pai, 1984).

Steadily over the years, developers of premier hotels, golf courses, and luxury housing acquired rights to develop some of Hawaii's most scenic and pristine coastlines. These developments cumulatively deprived Hawaiians of access to the natural resources on which they relied for subsistence. In addition, the economy has become overly dependent on the tourism sector, leaving Hawaii vulnerable to external economic forces and with an economy increasingly characterized by low-paying service-sector jobs.

The general tolerance and openness of Hawaiians to foreign people became their Achilles' heel during their years of contact with Westerners. The newcomers saw opportunities for personal profit and managed to penetrate traditional establishments and advocate for further change. Westerners who established a foothold in Hawaiian society eventually wrested power from its leaders and imposed new, self-serving measures and standards. Hawaiians who refused to accept this new order were left out of a system that rewarded enterprising individuals.

Two explanations exist for the lack of economic mobility among Hawaiians. First, from the time that Polynesians first arrived in the Hawaiian Islands about 1,200 years before Captain Cook (Daws, 1974), Hawaiians developed a culture that was attuned to the elements of the Hawaiian ecosystem. Hawaiians understood and respected the intricate rhythms of the land and water and practiced an environmental conservation that closely regulated essential resources and allowed them to sustain a population of up to 1 million people. As a point of comparison, the present population of Hawaii is about 1 million, and natural fisheries and prime agricultural lands have sustained irreparable damage caused by pollution and overdevelopment. The bulk of Hawaii's food supply is now imported (Rohter, 1992).

For Hawaiians, the loss of power and rights in their homeland was analogous to losing their sense of purpose and identity. Hawaiian epistemology often lost relevance amid modernization and industrialization that spelled the end of a subsistence economy and associated lifeways. The experiences of Hawaiians were dramatically different from those of people who migrated to Hawaii from the continental United States or Asia.

Hawaiian values and beliefs conflict with the rules governing the economy in which they are required to participate. For example, success in a Western economic system generally requires aggressiveness, individualism, and materialism. These attributes are antithetical to primary Hawaiian cultural values that encourage deference, mutuality, and spiritualism.

Loss of power and value conflict at least partially explain the lack of economic mobility among many Hawaiians. Acknowledgment of these factors shifts the blame for Hawaiians' low socioeconomic status from personal attributes (for example, laziness, low intelligence) to the effects of oppression.

PRESCRIPTIONS FOR ENHANCING QUALITY OF LIFE

One strategy to improve the quality of life of Hawaiians is to identify and revitalize cultural features that are critical to their well-being. This strategy is based on the assumptions that Hawaiian health is indelibly linked to properties inherent in the culture and that many Hawaiians have a predilection for tradition and an aversion to Westernization, especially when it is imposed on them. As their ability to perpetuate traditions weakens because of the rapidly changing environment, Hawaiians are predisposed to social problems.

A "cultural repair" model that finds reliable alignments between the past and contemporary society offers a radical shift from a traditional ideology that defines "functional" according to a Western-oriented social context. Indigenous people may perceive the Western social context to be inherently pathological. The traditional approach to social work practice involves working with dysfunctional individuals to enhance their adaptive capabilities so that they become functioning members of society. This approach is built on the assumption that society is sane and that problematic individuals lack requisite skills or cognitive capabilities. From an indigenous perspective, deviance may be a predictable response to inappropriate options or a healthy response to an unhealthy situation.

In Hawaii, there are two primary indigenous movements under way that focus on cultural repair. Each movement strives to empower Hawaiians through some form of self-governance. The first aims to restore Hawaiian sovereignty by reclaiming ceded lands and creating an independent system of government. The second relates to developing community-based economies that are consonant with Hawaiian cultural values.

Sovereign Nation Movement

In the 1990s a primary effort of Hawaiian activism has centered on reclaiming an indigenous land base that would serve as a foundation for Hawaiian sovereignty (Ka Mana O Ka 'Aina, 1990). Much of the Hawaiian sovereign nation movement has been guided by the circumstances of American Indian nations. For the more than 300 American Indian nations in the United States, sovereignty has provided varying degrees of rights in regard to the establishment of native governments and the development of economies (MacKenzie, cited in Ramirez, 1993).

A multitude of Hawaiian organizations are striving to create a sovereign nation. Although these organizations are united by the common interest in sovereignty, some differences exist in philosophy and the definition of sovereignty (Akana, 1991). Dudley and Agard (1990) identified at least three positions or models of sovereignty ascribed to by these organizations. One model specifies recognition of the Hawaiian nation within the territorial United States—a "nation within a nation" concept. This model is similar to the sovereign status of many American Indian nations, which are distinct political entities operating within the system of American government. A second model specifies that the Hawaiian nation exist within the boundaries of the United States but assume a status that is separate and egalitarian in nature—a "nation to nation" relationship. This status is similar to that achieved by the Iroquois, who have been recognized by the United Nations as a separate entity from the United States. This latter model is viewed as an incremental step toward the ultimate goal of total separation. A third model calls for total separation from the United States and the restoration of the sovereign Hawaiian nation.

Common to all models advocating for sovereignty are the needs to educate Hawaiian communities about sovereignty and its implications and to effect changes at the federal level of government to achieve their goals. In line with this agenda, Hawaiian organizations solidified their political stance by forming a coalition called Hui Na'auao. Since its formation in 1991, the coalition has conducted island-wide workshops and organized assemblies on the cultural, spiritual, historical, legal, and equitable basis for sovereignty (Ward, 1991b).

A second course of action among advocates of sovereignty has involved efforts to stimulate interest and concern among those within the federal government. Through collaborative efforts initiated by Hawaiian leaders, government representatives have developed and are proposing legislation on Hawaiian sovereignty before federal decision-making bodies (for example, the U.S. Senate) (Ward, 1991a). These actions are based on a strategy to disseminate information beyond the shores of Hawaii to generate broader support and to promote solidarity among Hawaiians, American Indians, and their political allies.

Community-Based Economic Development

For many leaders in Hawaiian communities, economic development is considered the key to cultural survival, self-sufficiency, and self-determination. Community-based economic development (CBED) ventures are viewed as an antidote to one-dimensional economic development centered around tourism.

Until recently, arguments supporting the perpetuation of tourism development were based on the notion of a "trickle-down" economy that was thought to benefit everyone, including those at the bottom of the socioeconomic ladder. However, the persistence of poverty-level wages in the high-growth sectors of the economy indicate that prosperity is not being evenly distributed. At the same time, unabated tourism development is consuming the resources that are vital to the continuation of traditional Hawaiian practices. In the face of diminishing options, Hawaiians have sought jobs in tourism, and many have become part of a "working poor" class.

CBED promotes the collective and entrepreneurial interests of residents (Blakely, 1989) and reflects a unique set of social, economic, historical, and physical qualities. It offers a re-examination of traditional notions of quality of life that have been tied exclusively to the generation of jobs and tax revenues. In the case of CBED, quality of life is redefined to include community cohesion and stability, a sense of environmental kinship and spirituality, and an economic base that is consistent with cultural goals and values.

An underlying philosophy of CBED as it applies to Hawaiians is that work constitutes a form of therapy and is the basis for one's cultural identity. CBED projects in Hawaii center around traditional economic activities including fishing (for example, aquaculture and ocean harvesting) and farming (for example, cultivating taro). The procedures and techniques involved in these activities are a blend of traditional themes and high technology.

The various CBED projects in Hawaii are family-run operations or community development corporations (CDCs) that receive startup funds from public and private donors. Some CDCs have offered employment opportunities to "high-risk" youths and former convicted felons to reconnect individuals with the land and reshape their identity around being Hawaiian. This is done by connecting work activities to cultural themes and beliefs. For example, taro planting occurs ceremonially according to prayer and planetary cycles.

One exemplary CBED project on the island of Oahu is directed by an indigenous human services worker and is staffed by individuals who have formal and informal training in social work, law, farming, fishing, and aquaculture. This private, nonprofit fishing, farming, and cultural education project exists on funding from the state, the sale of its products, and miscellaneous public and private sources. The project, which is designed to resemble the traditional economic system of *ahupua'a* (segment of land that runs from the mountains to the sea) that allowed Hawaiian clans to exist on mountain-cultivated taro and marine resources, resocializes Hawaiian youths and adults with criminal or psychiatric histories and educates Hawaiian schoolchildren through special programs. Participants are taught Hawaiian history; exchange feelings and perspectives on being Hawaiian; and through work programs learn ancient technologies in cultivation, fishing, and food processing.

IMPLICATIONS FOR SOCIAL WORK

The lessons learned from the history and the current plight of Hawaiians suggest an important direction for the social work profession. Given the chronicity of social problems afflicting Hawaiians and other indigenous peoples in U.S. society, social workers must exert as much effort in community development as they have given to single client issues.

The proposed solutions to Hawaiian social problems generally lie outside the realm of traditional social work interventions. In relation to sovereignty, however, the social work profession has a long history of organizing communities, empowering socially oppressed people, and facilitating social change by working within the "establishment" (Rothman, 1970). This experience can lend itself to a Hawaiian or other indigenous peoples movement that seeks sovereignty and self-determination.

In social work practice, a social action approach is designed to alter an inequitable situation by preparing communities to use various strategies to attain an equitable share of resources and political power. Social workers trained in community organization can serve as consultants to indigenous leaders. Leaders may possess talents and attributes that enable them to garner the political and spiritual support of their constituents but may not be trained in more technical areas. The role of non-indigenous social workers, however, is dictated by their area of expertise, and services are generally not rendered unless solicited by the community.

For social workers serving in advisory or advocacy positions in these movements, a prerequisite to community acceptance and the success of social action is an understanding of the historical context of oppression. Knowledge of how these experiences have shaped a people's worldview and sociopolitical orientation is a significant aspect of cultural sensitivity (Rivera & Erlich, 1984). Knowledge of history provides clues for culturally appropriate intervention.

Community-based economic development efforts in Hawaii have been spearheaded for the most part by indigenous leaders who have no formal training in economics or social work. Social workers who have supported these efforts have applied their formal training in community organization to activities including advocacy and consensus building, community education, mediation of community and government or corporate disputes, grant writing, and research. Research has played a critical role in providing empirical, scientific support for community initiatives. In Hawaii, social work researchers have been instrumental in documenting public attitudes regarding proposed development projects and making projections about social changes, social problems, and increases in human services in communities. Social work researchers also have served as expert witnesses at hearings before government committees authorized to make decisions on controversial development projects.

CONCLUSION

A healthy community is one where residents are bonded to a stable economy that provides them with a sense of personal self worth, where they are able to freely cultivate and practice the cultural traditions of their forbears, and where they can express an environmental kinship that reinforces their well-being. Although the maintenance of these traditional features has been difficult if not impossible amid rapidly changing environments, the inherent will of Hawaiians has thus far prevailed over the forces of change. In cases where vital cultural features have been destroyed over time, communities are attempting to restore and reintegrate them into a contemporary Hawaiian community. One hundred years is a long time to live according to the strictures of another society and is a long time to forget about the past. The multitude of Hawaiian groups striving to work toward self-governance is a testament to their enduring cultural pride and heritage. Social work can play a role in the restoration of the rights and privileges of this indigenous population.

REFERENCES

Akana, R. (1991, October). OHA, sovereignty organization take up self-determination issue. *Ka Wai Ola O OHA, Office of Hawaiian Affairs*, p. 19.

Alu Like. (1985). *E Ola Mau: The native Hawaiian health needs study: Medical task force report*. Honolulu: Author.

Aluli, N. E. (1991). Prevalence of obesity in a native Hawaiian population. *American Journal of Clinical Nutrition, 53*, 1556S-1560S.

Blaisdell, K. (1989). Historical and cultural aspects of native Hawaiian health. *Social Process in Hawaii, 32*, 1–21.

Blakely, E. J. (1989). *Planning local economic development: Theory and practice*. Newbury Park, CA: Sage Publications.

Chinen, J. J. (1958). *The great Mahele*. Honolulu: University of Hawaii Press.

Davenport, J., & Davenport, J. III. (1987). Native American suicide: A Durkheimian analysis. *Social Casework, 68*, 533–539.

Daws, G. (1974). *Shoal of time: A history of the Hawaiian islands*. Honolulu: University Press of Hawaii.

Dudley, M. K., & Agard, K. K. (1990). *A call for Hawaiian sovereignty*. Honolulu: Na Kane O Ka Malo Press.

Fuchs, L. H. (1961). *Hawaii pono*. San Diego: Harcourt Brace Jovanovich.

Healthy People 2000. (1990). *Healthy People 2000: National health promotion and disease prevention objectives* (DHHS Publication No. PHS 91-50212). Washington, DC: U.S. Government Printing Office.

International Work Group for Indigenous Affairs. (1992). *International Work Group for Indigenous Affairs* [brochure]. Copenhagen, Denmark: Author.

Johnson, D. (1989). Diabetes: Epidemiology and disability. *Social Process in Hawaii, 32*, 104–112.

Ka Mana O Ka 'Aina. (1990). *What is sovereignty?* (Bulletin of the Pro-Hawaiian Sovereignty Working Group). Honolulu: Author.

Kamehameha Schools/Bishop Estates. (1983). *Native Hawaiian educational assessment project*. Honolulu: Author.

Le Marchand, L., & Kolonel, L. (1989). Cancer: Epidemiology and prevention. *Social Process in Hawaii, 32*, 134–148.

Lili'uokalani. (1964). *Hawaii's story: By Hawaii's queen*. Rutland, VT: Charles E. Tuttle.

Linden, E. (1991, September 23). Lost tribes, lost knowledge. *Time*, pp. 46–56.

McPherson, M. M. (1991). Trustees of Hawaiian affairs v. Yamasaki and the native Hawaiian claim: Too much of nothing. *Environmental Law, 21*, 453–497.

Mokuau, N. (1990). The impoverishment of native Hawaiians and the social work challenge. *Health & Social Work, 15*, 235–242.

Miller, N. (1982). Social work services to urban Indians. In J. Green (Ed.), *Cultural awareness in the human services* (pp. 157–183). Englewood Cliffs, NJ: Prentice Hall.

Nofz, M. (1988). Alcohol abuse and culturally marginal American Indians. *Social Casework, 69*, 67–73.

Pai, G. (1984). *Employment forecasting and social policy: The search for stability in an uncertain world*. Prepared for the Hawaii State Employment Plan Conference of the State Commission on Power and Full Employment, Honolulu.

Papa Ola Lokahi. (1992). *Native Hawaiian health data book*. Honolulu: Author.

Ramirez, R. (1993, January 13). Native Americans provide sovereign clues. *Honolulu Star Bulletin*, pp. A1, A3.

Rivera, F. G., & Erlich, J. L. (1984). An assessment framework for organizing in emerging minority communities. In F. Cox, J. Erlich, J. Rothman, & J. Tropman (Eds.), *Tactics and techniques of community practice* (pp. 98–108). Itasca, IL: F. E. Peacock.

Rohter, I. (1992). *A green Hawaii: Sourcebook for development alternatives.* Honolulu: Na Kane O Ka Malo Press.

Rothman, J. (1970). Three models of community organization practice. In F. Cox, J. Erlich, J. Rothman, & J. Tropman (Eds.), *Strategies of community organization* (pp. 20–36). Itasca, II,: F. E. Peacock.

Stannard, D. E. (1989). *Before the horror: The population of Hawaii on the eve of Western contact.* Honolulu: University of Hawaii, Social Science Research Institute.

State of Hawaii, Department of Human Services. (1988). *A statistical report on child abuse and neglect in Hawaii, 1988.* Honolulu: Program Development, Family and Adult Services Division and Planning Office.

Ward, D. (1991a, October). Draft bill launches sovereignty discussion. *Ka Wai Ola O OHA, Office of Hawaiian Affairs*, pp. 1, 15, 23.

Ward, D. (1991b, October). Hui seeks sovereignty grant for workshops. *Ka Wai Ola O OHA, Office of Hawaiian Affairs*, pp. 1, 5.

Wegner, E. L. (1989). Hypertension and heart disease. *Social Process in Hawaii, 32,* 113–133.

10 ✦ Putting It All Together:

Toward More Complete Views of Humans and Knowledge about Us

This chapter is intended to help us connect HBSE (or we might now say SEHB) content with content in the other required professional foundation areas of the social work curriculum. This chapter will link the content of HBSE and traditional and alternative paradigms for thinking about that content to required social work research, practice, and policy areas. It will offer some suggestions for ways all this content can be applied in the field. This chapter suggests that social workers can gain important perspectives from other disciplines. It also suggests that social workers have much to offer other disciplines through the unique values, skills, and knowledge that constitute social work.

ENDING IS BEGINNING

As has been the case throughout this book, this chapter is presented as another part of our journey toward understanding HBSE. However, contrary to what we might expect of the final chapter in a book that has been presented as a kind of journey, this chapter is not intended to bring us to the end of, or to some final destination in, our journey. This chapter is, instead, intended to be a beginning for journeys yet to come or for journeys (for some of us) already in progress.

In the spirit implied above, this chapter is offered as a kind of commencement. If you have ever been to a graduation ceremony, you may have heard the ceremony referred to as a commencement. If one thinks about the definition of commencement—it means beginning—this might seem a strange description for a graduation ceremony. After all, graduation is a ritual to mark the end of a long period of education—high school, grade school, college or even preschool in some cases—is it not? Well, as speakers at these ceremonies often point out, graduation or commencement ceremonies actually mark the beginning of the graduate's next phase of life rather than the end of their education. The graduate is expected to use the knowledge, values, and skills acquired during the period of education that they have concluded in order to go forward in life.

This analogy seems an appropriate way to think about the point to which we have come in our journey here to acquire more complete understanding of human behavior and the social environment. What we really must do now that we have become acquainted with a variety of both traditional and alternative perspectives on HBSE at individual, family, group, organizational, and community levels is use or apply this increased understanding as we go about completing the other requirements for our social work education. More important, as we go forward to do social work and to live the rest of our lives, we must continually seek means to apply the many different ways of viewing human behavior and the social environment that we have considered in our travels throughout this book.

The journeys we must take to use our increased understanding of HBSE are quite likely already in progress. We probably embarked on many of these journeys simultaneously with our journey to more fully understand HBSE. In fact, throughout our journeys in this book we were simultaneously travelling on other journeys required of those who seek to become social workers. For example, in addition to HBSE, all accredited social work programs require study and course work (or sequences of courses) in the areas of practice, research, policy, and field practicum, as well as foundation content in values and ethics, social and economic justice, diversity and populations-at-risk (CSWE:1992). It is quite likely that as you have read this book and carried out the work necessary to complete your HBSE course work, you were also engaged in work in one or more of these other required areas. As you continue your social work education, you will take courses and gain content in all of these areas.

One of our purposes in this chapter is to tie what you have learned about HBSE here to the other required sequences of study in social work education. To achieve this purpose, we will consider some of the ways the content of this book connects with required practice, research, policy, field practicum, values and ethics, social and economic justice, diversity, and populations-at-risk content to form the whole that is education for social work.

To make the necessary connections, it is perhaps best to end where we began. We can do this by recognizing the connections of traditional and alternative paradigm thinking with other areas of social work education in addition to the HBSE areas and concerns we have explored in this book. We began this book by recognizing that HBSE is knowledge for practice and that the nature of the paradigms we use to think about, to create, and to value this knowledge for practice influences greatly our own behaviors, our relationships with others, and our work as social workers. What we have explored throughout this book is quite directly related to the other areas of social work study—practice, research, policy, and field—and to the foundation areas of values and ethics, social and economic justice, diversity, and populations-at-risk.

INTERCONNECTIONS

Our knowledge of HBSE forms the foundation of knowledge for and guides our practice. That knowledge is created through research processes that reflect and are influenced by the paradigms or worldviews of researchers, research subjects, and research consumers. The perspectives or worldviews of the persons making social welfare policy are very much influenced by their perspectives (paradigms) and in turn very directly influence the nature of the social policy through which the programs social workers and the people with whom we work must operate. It is this context of multiple paradigms—traditional and alternative—in which knowledge (HBSE) is created (research) and applied (practice) and through which social programs are created and implemented (policy) that constitutes the arenas (field settings) in which we do our work. None of these areas or elements are separate from one another and all of them are intensely influenced by the paradigms or worldviews of the many and varied persons involved in this complex of activity we call social work practice.

Traditional or Alternative or Both?

As we have made our journey through this book, we have been faced with a series of opportunities for choices about the knowledges we create and use to do social work. These have been framed around our notions of traditional and alternative paradigms. Traditional paradigms have been presented as most often dominating knowledge creation and validation processes. Alternative paradigms have been presented as other, less dominant sources and sets of choices about knowledge creation and validation from which we might choose as we do social work. We have attempted, as we explored both traditional and alternative perspectives, to suggest that we are not faced simply with a series of sets of "either/or" propositions from which we merely select one or the other "correct" choice.

Through the use of historical perspective, we have recognized that often what is today considered quite traditional and dominant was in the past considered an alternative to previously existing and dominating perspectives. This historical perspective suggests a continually unfolding stream of knowledge about HBSE that is never complete or conclusive. It also suggests that this continuum does not unfold in necessarily even or just ways, but often results in or from one group or individual having more power than others in creating and enforcing a particular worldview. It is this realization that calls upon social workers to operate with a critical eye that views the world always through the lens of social work values. For it is this lens that allows us to select from among the many traditional and alternative choices available the knowledge we need and that is most appropriate to the specific situations in which and persons with whom we practice social work.

Alternative Paradigms and Social Work

Given that some paradigms have historically dominated (as we have consistently seen throughout this book), we are called upon to seek out alternative, though less obvious, perspectives. We are even called upon to create new knowledge consistent with the core values of social work in order to ensure that the people with whom we work have maximum opportunity to realize their fullest potential. This process of seeking alternatives to traditional perspectives requires us to listen to the voices and see the world through the eyes of the less powerful. It is through the very act of listening to and looking toward these persons that alternative paradigms can be discovered and the processes of empowerment can unfold.

These alternative voices and visions come disproportionately from the persons and groups with whom social workers work. This reality is both the primary challenge to and the richest opportunity for us as social workers to be forces for individual and social transformation.

But how are we to meet this challenge and take advantage of this opportunity to go beyond traditional paradigms? More specifically, how do we do this within the existing framework of social work education—HBSE, research, practice, policy, and field practicum? We have devoted ourselves throughout this book to discovering how to accomplish a fuller understanding of HBSE by beginning with traditional perspectives and then going beyond the traditional to alternative perspectives. We can use this framework to inform our approaches to research, practice, policy, and field as well. Remember, all of these essential areas are interconnected and all are interwoven with attention to social work values and ethics, social and economic justice, diversity and populations-at-risk.

Research and Knowledge for Practice (HBSE/SEHB)

Traditional perspectives on research have relied almost exclusively on those consistent with the traditional paradigm. These perspectives have been driven by positivistic, scientific, objective, and quantitative approaches. Such approaches are important and have helped us understand much about social work practice. There is much knowledge, however, that is not accessible through these approaches. Recognizing this, as we discovered earlier in this book, research paradigms are shifting toward alternatives that are more focused on interpretive, intuitive, subjective, and qualitative approaches.

Some alternative paradigm researchers suggest that access to new knowledge through *research in partnership with the persons we have historically identified as our clients may indeed be central to effective social work practice and to the creation of social welfare policies that support all persons in their struggles to reach their fullest potential as humans.* This new knowledge can be discovered only by going beyond traditional approaches to the creation and valuing of knowledge. We must look beyond (though we need not and should not abandon) strictly positivistic, scientific, objective, and quantitative "ways of knowing" and ways of evaluating what is "worth knowing."

Research, Practice, and Field Partnerships

One alternative approach through which we can extend social work knowledge, more closely adhere to social work values, work toward social and economic justice, and more closely connect practice and field settings is to engage in new research partnerships with the people with whom we work. This approach can allow us to include in our research persons often excluded from traditional and dominant research efforts. If we engage in research partnerships with the persons with whom social workers have historically practiced, this inclusion will happen. Remember, these persons include significant numbers of women, people of color, low-income persons, gay and lesbian persons, aged persons, and persons with disabilities. They are the persons excluded from traditional privilege as we have defined it in this book.

This partnership approach to research requires us to connect with the people with whom we work in new ways. Rather than focusing on separating ourselves from the subjects of our research and emphasizing detached and impersonal perspectives, we can come to see ourselves and the subjects of our research as mutual and equal partners in a process from which we can all gain. We can begin to look to the subjects of research not as impersonal, detached objects, as has traditionally been the case, but as teachers and equal partners with much to contribute to our understanding and to their well-being.

Reason (1988) describes an alternative approach to research that he and Rowan referred to as "co-operative experiential inquiry: research that was *with* and *for* people rather than *on* people." He offers this description of their approach:

> *It is a way of doing research in which all those involved contribute both to the creative thinking that goes into the enterprise—deciding on what is to be looked at, the methods of the inquiry, and making sense of what is found out—and also contribute to the action which is the subject of the research. Thus in its fullest form the distinction between research and subject disappears, and all who participate are both co-researchers and co-subjects. Co-operative inquiry is therefore also a form of education, personal development, and social action.* (1988:1)

Though Reason and Rowan are not speaking as social workers, in many respects the alternative research perspective they describe has much relevance for both social work research and practice, for it is a process through which both parties to the research more fully develop as humans. Much alternative paradigm research of the type Reason and Rowan report emerges out of disciplines including education, political science, and organizational or social psychology. This alternative perspective offers an excellent example of what we mean when we say social work is informed by other disciplines. Such alternative paradigm research also provides an important example of the potential for social work perspectives and values to inform research and practice in other disciplines in substantive ways. This alternative research/practice conceptualization (as do those of other new paradigm researchers such as Guba and Lincoln, 1981 and 1989, for example) also carries significant policy implications. As this research informs and alters the way practice is conducted, policies regarding processes and structures through which practice is conducted will need to be changed as well.

Practice and/as Policy

It seems impossible to separate alternative paradigms for understanding HBSE and alternative approaches to doing research from their connections to and consequences for social work practice and social policy. Alternative paradigm thinking respects the interrelatedness of research, knowledge, policy, and practice. Perspectives that respect this interconnectedness are also reflected in some of the frameworks for organizing social work knowledge discussed earlier in this book such as systems perspectives and strengths-based perspectives.

Feminist thinking certainly recognizes the interrelatedness of research, knowledge, and practice. Feminism, is also as much about policy and politics as it is about personal ideology. Feminist perspectives on social work directly link practice that is individual-focused (directed to bringing changes in the individual's perspectives and coping abilities) to policy-focused practice (practice directed to bringing macro-level social change or transformation).

The diversity and oppressions dimensions, with their focus on social and economic justice, of the alternative paradigm described in this book also carry important implications for social work practice and policy across system levels. The dimension of alternative paradigm thinking that stresses interrelatedness and integration suggests direct connections between knowledge for practice and policy development as well.

James Leigh (1989) provides an effective illustration of the interplay of all these dimensions across systems levels. He asserts that individual self-definition and self-determination is a key to collective empowerment for people of color. Leigh reminds us that *liberation for a people means individual self-definition and self-determination as well as community control and the achievement of power as a group.* The importance of identity formation and development to the well-being of diverse individuals and families has been a theme throughout much of our exploration of HBSE in this book.

Leigh emphasizes that "self-identity leads to a sense of group identity which permits one to join forces with others in affecting social issues that will impact on their lives. One can term group identity as political power" (1989:21). This is an excellent example of the complex interplay of individual and social change, along with their policy implications, across the system levels within which social workers traditionally practice—individual, group, organization, and community.

Re-visioning through Alternative Paradigms

Laura Brown (1989:445–458), in discussing the heterosexist assumptions underlying practice in psychology, presents an analysis quite relevant to social work practice and to our concerns in this book. She provides us a glimpse of the view of the world through the eyes of gay men and lesbians. In an article titled "New Voices, New Visions: Toward a Lesbian/Gay Paradigm for Psychology," Brown offers important perspectives on the power of traditional and dominant paradigms and on the potential benefits to be gained by all of us from alternative perspectives or worldviews. She asks the reader to try to view the world from a perspective in which gay/lesbian reality is central (1989:448). Such a world, she suggests, is not unitary but reflects multiple experiences among people resulting from differences in age, class, gender, and individual experiences in identity development. She suggests, though, that the persons living in such a world do share many important things in addition to their equally important differences. She suggests that from this perspective the world must be viewed biculturally by its inhabitants. Gay men and lesbians must survive and seek to thrive in a heterosexist world with little or no acceptance of alternative gay and lesbian realities, even in the context of one's family of origin. The gay man or lesbian must simultaneously seek to fulfill his or her identity as a gay or lesbian through social networks and intimate relationships (1989:447–450).

Were social work practitioners, whether gay/lesbian, bisexual or heterosexual, able to see the world through the lens that Brown suggests, new and beneficial alternatives for thinking about many aspects of human behavior could become available to us. Such a perspective offers examples of new ways of understanding the challenges and difficulties faced by persons outside traditional paradigmatic domains, as well as the strengths and potential for healthy reconceptualization of many aspects of human behavior offered by viewing the world through this alternative lens.

The issues that arise from the worldview Brown presents are important well beyond developing a greater understanding of the life situations of gay or lesbian persons. For example, such a perspective reveals the complexity of such processes as "passing." The concept of **passing** means behaving in ways that contradict one's individual and group identity in order to survive or gain benefits from dominant-group power holders. This concept is equally important for many persons of color as well as for gay and lesbian persons. Passing is a concept also applicable to many persons with disabilities that are less visible or that can be hidden from view (epilepsy, much mental illness, etc.) who feel they must hide or deny this part of themselves for fear of being denied employment opportunities or losing their current employment. Passing is an example of how some persons outside the traditional "norm of rightness" (see Chapter 2) feel they must deny who they are in order to be what is acceptable to the powerful enforcers of the dominant paradigm.

Seeing the world through the lens of the gay/lesbian paradigm Brown describes can teach social workers much about important strengths that many persons who fall outside the traditional or dominant paradigm avail themselves of in order to survive and thrive. Such a paradigm can teach us all much about the strengths to be found in such important areas of human behavior as management of difference (resulting in the biculturality discussed earlier), marginality, and normative creativity central to the lives of many gay and lesbian persons, but rarely addressed in traditional perspectives on human behavior.

She asserts that

> *the constant "management of difference" (deMonteflores 1986 [in Brown: 450]) can lead to a rich and distinctive perspective on reality if we are willing to embrace and value it, rather than stigmatize it as not conforming to the dominant group. The bicultural perspective of lesbians and gay men facilitates an understanding of the rules by which the mainstream culture operates, while simultaneously being able to envision new forms by which the same tasks might be accomplished.* (1989:450)

Marginality, or "the experience of existential otherness" (Adair and Adair 1978 in Brown 1989), is another element of Brown's gay and lesbian paradigm (also shared by many "others" including people of color and women) that can, as many feminists have argued, open doors to alternative realities and structures for living by depending on and valuing the very differences that create marginality and exclusion from the dominant paradigm. From such a position of marginality one can call into question the necessity of traditional patriarchal structures and perspectives that are so much a part of traditional male roles and behaviors and so influential in traditional family structures. Gay males, for example, by virtue of being so far outside many traditional expectations about male roles and behaviors can be freed to see alternative, less patriarchal possibilities for male existence (Grahn 1984 in Brown 1989:451). Such "other" ways of seeing and behaving can affirm alternative perspectives and challenge traditional patriarchal patterns. Gay men and lesbians, for example, have offered important models of families that are structured and function in nonpatriarchal, much more egalitarian ways to the benefit of both adult and child members (Brown 1989:451).

Brown proposes also that out of the "otherness" and differentness from the norms of traditional paradigms can come exciting creativity. Because there are no "road maps," clear rules, or roles to guide gay and lesbian human behavior in traditional paradigms, gay men and lesbians have had to make "up the rules as we go along" (1989:451). This necessity of "inventing" new rules and roles is both "terrifying and exhilarating," according to Brown. It holds great potential, however, for those who choose to see its positive creative potential. Brown suggests that

> *those who claim this as a positive and possibly unique aspect of our experience as lesbians and gay men begin to embrace the possibilities for actively decon-*

structing and re-enacting our visions of human behavior far beyond the field of gay and lesbian studies. (1989:452)

BEGINNINGS

Brown's illustration of some of the things to be learned by viewing the world through gay and lesbian eyes is intended as but one example of what we might learn if we "put it all together" and really attempt to see the world from the perspective of persons usually excluded from dominant worldviews. *In order to practice social work for the benefit of the people with whom we work (and, we would argue, in doing so benefiting ourselves), we must continually seek to learn from those persons different from ourselves.* We must seek constantly to understand how others construct, view, survive, and thrive in their worlds. We must learn from others about their worlds and we must be willing to teach others about our worlds. In doing so we are certain to discover exciting and beneficial differences and we are equally certain to discover unrealized and empowering commonalities. We must seek integration of these processes throughout all of our social work education. We must search our liberal arts and sciences requirements for ways to find, understand, and celebrate our differences and our similarities. These processes must flow through all the foundations that make up social work education—HBSE, research, practice, policy, field, values and ethics, diversity, social and economic justice, and populations-at-risk.

An approach in which we constantly seek and discover the constantly changing and emerging knowledge necessary for sensitive and effective social work practice should serve the people with whom we work and ourselves well. It should result in partnerships through which we become engaged with others in research, practice, and policy activities through which we transform ourselves as we transform the world. These ongoing and mutual transformations can move us toward the fulfillment of all our human potential and thereby we will fulfill our responsibilities as social workers and as humans.

REFERENCES

Brown, Laura S. (1989). "New voices, new visions: Toward a lesbian/gay paradigm for psychology." *Psychology of Women Quarterly, 13*:445–458.

Council on Social Work Education (CSWE). (1992). *Handbook of accreditation standards and procedures* (4th ed.). (CPS). Alexandria, VA: Author.

Guba, Egon G., and Lincoln, Yvonna S. (1981). *Effective evaluation: Improving the usefulness of evaluation results through responsive and naturalistic approaches.* San Francisco: Jossey-Bass Publishers.

Guba, Egon G., and Lincoln, Yvonna S. (1989). *Fourth generation evaluation.* Newbury Park, CA: SAGE Publications.

Leigh, James W. (1989). "Black Americans: Emerging identity issues and social policy." *The Annual Ellen Winston Lecture.* Raleigh: North Carolina State University.

Reason, Peter (Ed.). (1988). *Human inquiry in action: Developments in new paradigm research.* London: SAGE Publications.

Index

Etzioni, Amitai, 433–436, 445–446
Evans, K. G., 462–463
Everett, Joyce, 90, 92
Ewalt, Patricia, 50–59, 508, 509, 514
Exchange theory, 130, 368
Extended families, 350–351
External validity, 83

Facilitation, group, 400
Faderman, Lillian, 281
Families of choice, 368–369
Familiness, 315–377
    alternative and possible models of,
        344–373
    changes in traditional family life cycle,
        337–342
    concept of, 316–318
    family as intimate environment,
        345–346
    family of origin, 345
    family preservation and, 333
    gender perspective on, 359–364
    global perspective on, 325–329
    grandparents as parents, 342–344
    lesbian/gay perspective on, 365–366
    life course theory and, 329–344
    and multiracial realities, 356–358
    National Council on Family Life
        model, 336–337
    nuclear family, 318, 361–362, 366–367
    people of color and, 346–358
    sexual orientation and. See Gay and
        lesbian families
    social work and, 318–329
    technology and, 320–325
    traditional and dominant models of,
        333–344, 361–362, 366–367
    violence and, 295–296, 360
    women and, 359–364
Family-centered approach, 333
Family life cycle, 333–344
    changes in traditional life cycle models,
        337–342
    life course theory and, 329–344
    National Conference on Family Life
        model, 336–337
    stage models of family and, 333–334
Family Life Cycle, The (Carter & Mc-
    Goldrick), 337–342
Family preservation approach, 333
Family roles
    family work and, 362–364
    flexibility and fluidity of, 352–353
    in gay and lesbian families, 370–371
Family work, 362–364
Feagin, Clairece Booher, 534
Feagin, Joe R., 534
Feedback, 136
Fellin, P., 521
Feminism, 86–89
    definitions of, 86–87
    familiness and women, 359–364
    groups and, 420
    individual and social change, 121–122
    organizations and, 461–462
    postmodernism and, 89
    spirituality and, 87–88, 134–135
    standpoint theory, 89
Fenby, Barbara L., 74
Ferree, Myra M., 359–364
Fictive kin systems, 335–336, 350–351
Filial piety, 350
Financial capital, 514
Fischer, C., 526
Fishley, Pat, 479–486
Fluidity of roles, 352–353

Focal system, 135
Followers, 400–401
Fong, R., 262, 356, 358
Food insufficiency, 240
Formal membership, 396
Formal operations, 194
Foster care, 356–358
Foucault, Michel, 123
Fourth Force in psychology, 149
Fractals, 151
Free association, 188
Freire, Paulo, 98
Freud, Sigmund, 187–193, 196, 271
Freudian theory of development,
    187–193, 196, 271
Full psychological membership, 396
Functional leadership, 398–399
Functional theory, 130
Functions, community and, 503

Gaia theory, 152–154
Galileo Galilei, 14
Gardner, H., 126, 184, 244–246
Gastil, John, 397, 399–402
Gay and lesbian families, 342, 365–373.
    See also Sexual orientation
    children in, 366–367, 372–373
    defining, 368–373
    familiness in, 365–366
    problems of, 365–366
    psychoanalytic theory and, 367–368
    structural functional theory and, 367
    traditional approach and, 366–368
Gays. See Sexual orientation
Gebeke, D., 352
Gemeinschaft relationships, 504–505,
    528
Gemmill, Gary, 178, 398–399
Gender model, of the family, 359–364
Gender splitting, 206–207
General intelligence, 184–185
Generation, 331
Generational time/generational events,
    331
Generativity vs. stagnation, 199, 203
Genital stage, 191
Genotype, 23–24
Germain, Carel, 119, 133, 134
Gershenfeld, Matti K., 394–398,
    407–409
Gesellschaft relationships, 505, 528
Gibbs, Jewelle Taylor, 242, 250–253,
    254–256
Gibbs, L. G., 9
Gilligan, Carol, 192, 196, 198–199, 204,
    208–209, 269–274, 461
Ginsberg, L., 468
Giordano, Joseph, 346, 350, 353
Glasser, Paul, 413–414
Gleick, J., 151–152
Global perspective
    on family and immigration, 325–329
    on organizations, 469
    on poverty, 239–241
Goal displacement, 436
Goal succession, 436
Godfrey, Eleanor, 337
Goldstein, Howard, 16–17, 27–28, 121
Gomes, Paula G., 215–232
Good communities, 531–532, 536
Gortner, Harold F., 435, 446, 449–450
Gotthoffer, Doug, 2
Gould, Stephen Jay, 184–185
Grandparents, as parents, 342–344
Green, J., 147
Green, Michael, 188–192, 194

Group(s), 391–425
    conformity and deviance in, 403–406
    creativity in, 416–417
    decision making by, 397–402, 405–406
    defined, 392
    diversity in, 413–423
    effective, 422–423
    gender and, 418–420
    goals and purposes of, 394–395
    historical perspective on, 392–394
    individual and group dimensions,
        406–409
    leadership and decision-making,
        397–399, 405–406
    membership, 396–397, 407
    oppression and, 413–414
    people of color and, 414–416
    people with disabilities and, 420–422
    roles and norms, 402–403, 408–409,
        415–416
    stage theories and models, 409–411
    systems perspective in, 411–413
Groupthink, 404–406
Grusky, Oscar, 442–444, 446, 454, 455
Guba, Egon G., 6, 8, 15, 75, 80–82,
    85–86, 95, 566
Gundry, L. K., 246
Gushue, G. V., 257, 276
Gutierrez, L. M., 29, 144–147
Guzzo, R. A., 453–454

Handicaps. See People with disabilities
Harding, Sandra, 268
Hare, A. P., 409
Harley, J., 244, 284
Harrison, Algea O., 247, 346–355
Hartman, Ann, 83–84, 318, 335, 336,
    345–346
Hawthorne effect, 445–446
Healy, William, 188–192
Heineman Pieper, M., 62, 79–80
Helms, J. E., 21–25, 70–71, 209–210,
    257, 266–268
Hendry, J., 463
Henry, W., 207
Henslin, J. M., 130
Herbert, James I., 260–261
Hermeneutics, 73–74
Hernandez, M., 326–328
Herrnstein, R. J., 184–185
Hetherington, E. Mavis, 339
Heuristic research, 79–80
Hickson, D. J., 441, 443–448, 454–455
Hidden agendas, 407
Hierarchy, 136, 455–457
Hill, Reuben, 336
Hillman, James, 75
Hinings, C. R., 441, 443–448, 454, 455
Hirschl, T., 11, 239
Hispanics/Latinos. See also Ethnic minor-
    ity families
    demographic status of, 247, 248
    fictive kin systems and, 351
History
    community and, 500–501
    groups and, 392–394
    historical time/historical events, 331
    organizations and, 434–435
    paradigms and, 12–16
    of social work, 15, 16–17
HIV/AIDS, 288, 394–397, 412–413
Ho, Man Kueng, 347–348
Hodgetts, R. M., 468, 469–470
Hokenstad, T., 170–171
Hollingsworth, L., 356–358
Holoarchy, 150